EXAMKRACKERS MCAT®

101 PASSAGES:
BIOLOGY 1 MOLECULES:
BIOCHEMISTRY

Major Contributors:
Austin Mattox
Kaitlyn Barkley
Jennifer Birk-Goldschmidt, M.S.
Andrew Elson
Laura Neubauer
Christopher Stewart

Contributors:
Leena Asfour
Kristin Bater
Jacob Ball
Maher Bazzi
David Collins
Erik Davies
Erin Glennon
Jay Li
Ian Magruder
Christina Snider
Darren Sultan

Art Director:
Erin Daniel

Designer:
Dana Kelley

Published in the United States of America by Osote Publishing, New Jersey.

ISBN 10: 1-893858-91-X
ISBN 13: 978-1-893858-91-6

To purchase additional copies of this book or other books of the 101 Passage series, call 1-888-572-2536.

Examkrackers.com
Osote.com

Printed and bound in the United States of America.

PHOTOCOPYING & DISTRIBUTION POLICY

Read this First

Practice is essential to success on the MCAT®. MCAT® practice is the best way to develop the key skills you will need to get a high score.

The 101 passages and associated questions in this book were carefully designed to simulate exactly the content, length, style, tone, difficulty and format of real AAMC MCAT® passages, questions, and answer choices. Each chapter in this book has three tests. The first two are of exact MCAT® section length and the third is a half-length mini-MCAT® section for additional practice. Both passage-based questions and stand-alone questions are just like the questions you'll see on MCAT® day, and are included in a 3:1 ratio, just like the real MCAT®.

The Examkrackers 101 series covers every single topic and subtopic tested by the MCAT®. Topics that require more drilling and topics that are especially difficult are covered by multiple questions. Each chapter in *101 Passages: Biology 1 Molecules* tests the content covered by the corresponding chapter in Examkrackers *Biology 1 Molecules* manual. To maximize your MCAT® preparation, take the tests in each chapter following your review of that chapter in the manual. To stay in touch with how the science you review is tested on the MCAT®, coordinate your content review with simulated MCAT® practice, chapter by chapter.

The MCAT® is all about how flexible and adaptable you are with the basics. Real MCAT® passages and questions will always present you with new and unfamiliar situations. It is only through simulated MCAT® practice that you will learn to see what simple science is relevant and then recall and apply the basics with confidence. Through practice and focus on the questions you get wrong, you will develop essential skills that bring a high score on MCAT® day.

In this section you will find information on:

- Using the warm-up passage to assess your skills
- MCAT® Timing
- MCAT® Simulation
- How to use this book to increase your MCAT® score
- Scoring your practice tests
- Complete MCAT® preparation with Examkrackers

How to Begin: Assessing Your Skills

This book begins with one "warm-up" passage. Use it to familiarize yourself with the look, feel, and format of MCAT® biochemistry passages and questions. Give yourself about eight minutes to take the warm-up test. While working through the passage and the associated questions, observe yourself and notice your own approach. Immediately after taking the warm-up test, look at the following checklist of strategies and skills. Based on the passage and questions in the warm-up, evaluate which skills come naturally to you and which skills you will work to build as you continue through this book.

- Energy
- Focus
- Confidence
- Timing
- Narrating the passage
- Identifying and answering research questions
- Applying simple science in new situations
- Clear, simple, and connected organization of the content in your mind
- Simplifying the questions and answers
- Eliminating weak answer choices

Choose two or three skills to focus on throughout Test 1 and continue to build new skills as you proceed through the book. Return to this page and check off strategies and skills as you master them.

MCAT® Timing

Examkrackers 101 books are great tools with which to master MCAT® timing before MCAT® day. The tests can be taken untimed or timed. As you initially practice brand-new skills, go slowly in order to master them. Take timed tests to prepare for timing on MCAT® day. The practice tests in this book are exactly like the real MCAT®: 10 passages and 59 questions in 95 minutes. The mini-tests are precisely scaled to AAMC MCAT® timing: 5 passages and 31 questions in 50 minutes. Timing on MCAT® day is a skill that you will build through timed practice.

Take a 5 second break before reading each passage. Look at the clock only once, at the halfway point (the 29th question). If you are before the 47-minute mark, slow down. If you are after the 47-minute mark, speed up. Developing an intuitive sense for good MCAT® timing and pace is an essential skill. Eventually, you will come to know whether you are on pace as you go without looking at a clock. You will know when you are getting sandbagged in order to speed up and when you are rushing so that you can slow down.

After you take a test, assess your timing skills. If you did not finish the test before the allotted time, determine where you are spending time that you could save. If you finished with time to spare, determine how you could spend more time toward a higher score on your next practice test.

Plan a schedule in advance. Choose a distribution for these tests throughout your study period. For example, if you are studying over a ten-week period, take one test from this book every week on the same day. Do not save all the tests for the weeks immediately prior to the MCAT®, as MCAT® skills require time and practice to develop. It is important to stay in touch with the MCAT® and MCAT® practice throughout your study period. Between tests, give yourself adequate time to review the test you take each week. Consciously plan what you will do differently on the next test in order to increase your MCAT® score.

MCAT® SIMULATION

When you are ready to take your first simulated, full-length test, choose an environment that is not familiar or comfortable, e.g. a public library, not your couch at home. Ensure that you will maximize focus and minimize distraction for one sitting of at least 95 minutes. If needed, you may use disposable earplugs, just as on MCAT® day. During the test, do not look at or answer the telephone, do not sit and stare out the window, and do not get up for any reason, such as to get a drink or to go to the bathroom. Treat each practice test like the real thing.

It is always a good idea to mark up the multiple choice questions *on the test itself* as you go through them. If 'A' can't be correct, then mark it off and go to 'B'. If 'B' is *possible*, circle it, and go to 'C', and so on. That way you are eliminating and narrowing choices that are *not possible* or are *less likely*. Using the process of elimination is a very helpful technique on the MCAT®. The computer-based test allows the use of strikethrough and highlight functions right on the screen to help with narrowing down choices. It is not very practical or helpful to write your answers or considerations on a piece of notebook paper as this does not simulate MCAT® day.

How to Use This Book to Increase Your MCAT® Score:

REVIEW

Test and question review is the single most important thing you will do to change your MCAT® score.

Always leave time for review of each test. Your score will change through careful review of each practice test you take, not through repetitive practice.

Every question you get wrong is a gift, an opportunity to increase your score. Always think about how questions you get wrong are valuable – they are the pearls that will lead you directly to a high MCAT® score.

You will need ninety-five minutes to take the test and at least ninety minutes to review it.

Immediately after completing each test, take notes on what happened during the test.

Then, take a short break for an hour or less. Next sit down and check your answers. At the end of each test, you will be directed to the page in the back of the book where you can find the answers, and answer explanations, for that test. Every page of the tests has a tab and footer telling you what test you're working on. Every page of the answers and explanations has a tab and footer telling you which test is being covered. Always be sure these match when checking your answers. No need to flip through pages and pages of explanations looking for the right test.

Make a list of question numbers you marked and/or got wrong. Do not yet read the answer explanations.

Compare your score to the last practice test you took. Your raw score is the number you answered correctly out of 59. Did your raw score increase since the last test? If yes, what did you do differently? Make a note to keep doing what worked. If no, what was different today? Make a commitment to change strategies that did not work.

Make time to retake the questions you answered incorrectly before looking at the answer explanations. This allows you to build the most important MCAT® muscles of all: problem solving and independent thinking. Once you see the answer explanation, you lose the opportunity to learn how to solve the MCAT® question yourself. This may sometimes require multiple attempts or reinforcement of science, but the purpose of practice is for you to learn how to *solve* the questions. Reading the explanation of how to get to the right answer should come only after you have tried your hardest to find your own way there.

Once you have made a second attempt, read the answer explanation for each question you got wrong in order to learn to think in ways that will get you a high score. Examkrackers answer explanations are uniquely process-oriented, meaning that they reveal the way to think like the MCAT®. The answer explanations show you the reasoning process that leads to the elimination of each weak answer and the selection of the best answer. Our answer explanations will help you identify new strategies that work and will help you learn to think in ways that bring a high score.

It can also help to review those questions you got right in order to reinforce the skills, confidence and concepts that allowed you to solve those problems.

SMART PRACTICE

There are two kinds of practice: practice that is repetitive and practice that is smart. Practice that is repetitive, in which you do the same thing over and over again, will reinforce skills that you already have and will also reinforce any habits you may have that are not working.

1. Before each test, plan on what skills you want to add, build, reinforce or replace with this practice test. Use the list provided above as well as any skills you have added. Make specific "When… Then…" commitments (see below).
2. Be conscious or self-aware during each test, in order to evaluate what you are doing while you are doing it. Take notes during the test on what you are thinking or feeling, what skills you are struggling with, what is happening that you notice, etc.
3. Smart practice finally means evaluating immediately *after* each test how the commitments helped. If your score increased what did you do differently that accounts for the increase – commit to continuing with this new skill. If your score decreased, what in your approach or environment was different – commit to replacing what is not working.
4. Repeat this process throughout the study period.

MAKING COMMITMENTS

Immediately after each test, make specific commitments for what you plan next – what will you keep doing more of and what still needs to change?

Commitments work best if new, good habits are linked to old, bad habits. I can make a commitment not to speed on the highway tomorrow, but inevitably I will find myself speeding yet again. Change comes when I decide that

When I speed, **then** I will immediately slow down to 54 mph.
Similarly**:**
When I fall into negative thinking while taking the test,
Then I will take a five-second break and refocus on the question in front of me**.**
Or
When I have trouble understanding what I am reading,
Then I will take a five-second break and resume reading, narrating with the basics that I know

When you commit to avoiding the mistakes that led you to incorrect answers in one test, you will see improvement in your raw score on the next test.

Look toward the next date you will take a practice test. Document your commitments and keep them ready at hand to review before you begin your next practice test.

Scoring Your Practice Tests

The goal is to see your scores on Examkrackers practice materials improve over time.

The best way to utilize your raw score is to be sure it increases with each practice test you take, whether as skill-building or simulation. The best way to do this is to make specific commitments to replace what isn't working with effective MCAT® skills.

Note: Even if Examkrackers derived a scaled score from thousands of our students, it would not accurately predict your AAMC MCAT® score. Unlike the AAMC MCAT® which includes easy questions, Examkrackers practice questions simulating the MCAT® are largely of the medium and difficult level, in order to improve your MCAT® skills and to help you learn how to think like the MCAT®. Our students are at different stages of preparation for the MCAT® and do not represent the MCAT® day student population. Any scaled score other than that directly from the AAMC does not correlate to AAMC MCAT® scores. Only a scaled score from the AAMC can accurately predict your AAMC MCAT® score.

Your goal should be to get more items right and fewer wrong with each Examkrackers practice test you take. A higher score with each practice test reflects that you are using the questions you get wrong and those you get right to learn and practice new skills that will increase your score.

Complete Your MCAT® Preparation

Note: *101 Passages: Biology 1 Molecules* contains only biochemistry/molecular biology passages and questions to maximize your biochemistry practice. The AAMC MCAT® integrates biochemistry and biological systems. For integrated MCAT® simulation, use our full-length, online *EK-Tests*®. Visit www.examkrackers.com for details.

To complete your preparation for the Biological and Biochemical Foundations MCAT® section, use this book along with Examkrackers *Biology 1: Molecules*, *Biology 2: Systems*, and *Reasoning Skills* manuals, and look for *MCAT® 101 Passages Biology 2: Systems* . Together these tools provide in-depth instruction in the skills needed to get a high score on the "Biological and Biochemical Foundations" MCAT® section.

To prepare fully for the four sections of the MCAT®, Examkrackers *Complete Study Package* includes six manuals packed with content review, MCAT® strategy, and guided practice. The corresponding *MCAT® 101 Passages* series allows you to practice the methods and build the skills taught in Examkrackers study manuals. Or, take an Examkrackers Comprehensive MCAT® Course (information available at our website, below).

Examkrackers Live MCAT® Hotline is a service available ten hours per week so your questions can be addressed directly and interactively by expert, high scoring MCAT® instructors.

EK-Tests® are the best full length simulated MCAT® product available on the market. Each electronic test matches the MCAT® in sources, style, format, question types, length, skills and content tested. Tools to maximize review and score improvement are built-in.

Regularly visit the Examkrackers Forums where students' questions are answered and any errata are posted.

Go to www.examkrackers.com or call 1.888.KRACKEM to learn more about Examkrackers materials, support and live MCAT® preparation, both online and in-person.

Toward your success!

TABLE OF CONTENTS

Passage: 1

Time: 8 minutes

INSTRUCTIONS: Use these warm-up passages and questions to become familiar with the MCAT® Biological Sciences section and to assess your skills before beginning Practice Test 1A.

Most questions in the Biological and Biochemical Foundations of Living Systems test section are grouped with a descriptive passage. Select the best answer to each question using background knowledge and the given passage. A portion of this test section is comprised of discrete questions, which are independent of any passage and one another. Select the best answer for each discrete question. Indicate your selection by blackening the corresponding oval on your answer document. If you are unsure of the answer, rule out incorrect choices and select from the remaining options. You may access a periodic table found on the last page of this book at any point during this test section.

Passage 1 (Questions 1-5)

Inborn errors of metabolism (IEM) represent a large group of diseases resulting in congenital disorders of metabolism. There is a wide variety of disorders under this category which comprise about 15% of all single gene mutations. Errors can affect lipid metabolism (e.g. Tay-Sachs disease), sugar metabolism (e.g. Von Gierke's disease), and protein metabolism (e.g. Maple Syrup Urine Disease). Lesch-Nyhan Disease (LND) is the result of mutations in the X-linked gene encoding the purine metabolic enzyme, hypoxanthine guanine phosphoribosyl transferase (HPRT). LND gives rise to severe neurological anomalies, including mental retardation and a compulsive and aggressive tendency to self-injure. The association between the genotype and phenotype of this disease has been previously linked to synapsin (Syn), an important protein in dopaminergic cell maturation that requires phosphorylation by a cyclic AMP (cAMP) dependent kinase to be activated.

To examine the relationship between the neurological symptoms and purine metabolism with the goal of finding a treatment for this disorder, levels of synapsin were compared between affected and non-affected populations, as well as the different enzymes involved in its synthesis and activation. The results are displayed in Figure 1.

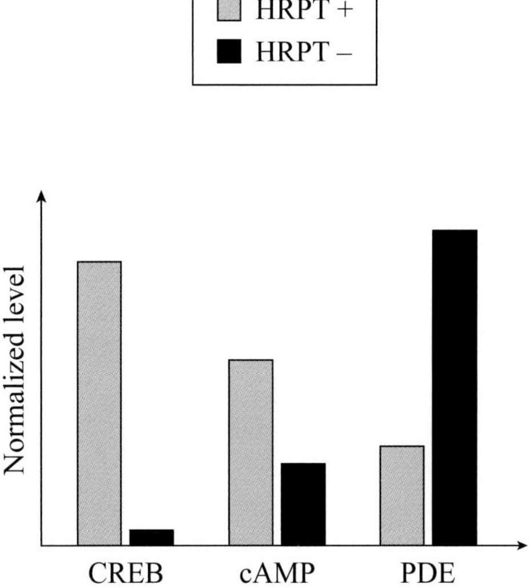

Figure 1 Levels of cAMP, CREB and PDE in HPRT+ and HPRT− cells: CREB is a cAMP response element-binding protein and a transcription factor believed to be responsible for the promotion of Syn gene expression; PDE is a phosphodiesterase, an enzyme responsible for hydrolyzing cyclic nucleotides

Based on these results, a second experiment was conducted in which researchers attempted to modulate levels of cAMP and study the effect on the levels of synapsin in the cell. Two drugs were investigated: forskolin, which is an adenylyl cyclase (AC) activator, and papaverine, which is a phosphodiesterase (PDE) inhibitor. The structures of these molecules are shown in Figure 2, and the results of the experiment are displayed in Figure 3.

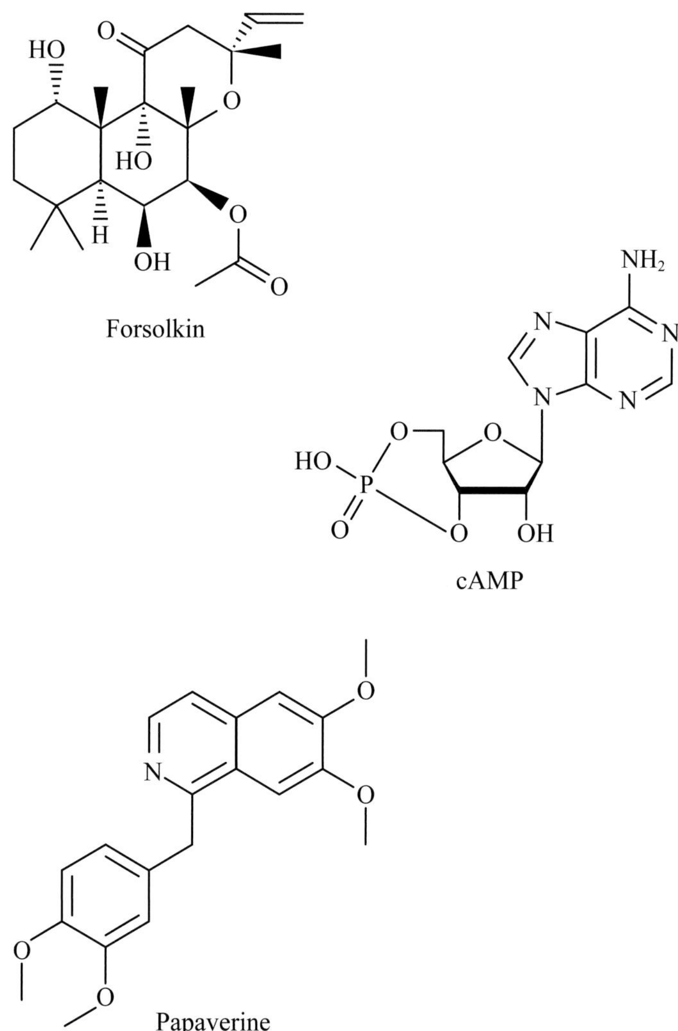

Figure 2 Structure of the three molecules: forskolin, cAMP and papaverine

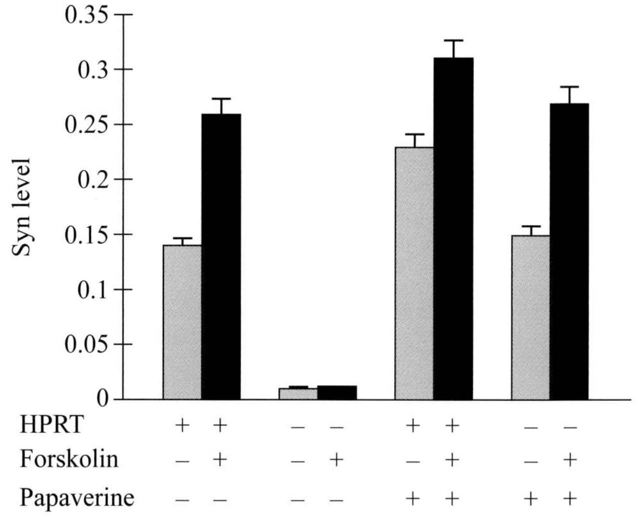

Figure 3 Effect of forskolin and papaverine on the level of Syn in wild type mice and HPRT− mice

This passage was adapted from "HPRT-Deficiency Dysregulates cAMP-PKA Signaling and Phosphodiesterase 10A Expression: Mechanistic Insight and Potential Target for Lesch-Nyhan Disease?" Guibinga G-H, Murray F, Barron N. *PLoS ONE*. 2013. 8(5): e63333. doi:10.1371/journal.pone.0063333 for use under the terms of the Creative Commons CC BY 3.0 license (http://creativecommons.org/licenses/by/3.0/legalcode)

Question 1

For which of the following processes does the passage provide the least evidence as the cause of decreased activity of synapsin in the development of LND?

- ○ **A.** Decreased gene expression
- ○ **B.** Decreased phosphorylation
- ○ **C.** Increased cAMP degradation
- ○ **D.** Increased CREB inhibition

Question 2

The Lineweaver-Burk (LB) plot is derived from the Michaelis-Menten equation, in which the x-intercept represents $-1/K_m$, and the y-intercept represent V_{max}. Which of the following plots best represents the effect of papaverine on the activity of PDE?

○ **A.** ○ **B.**

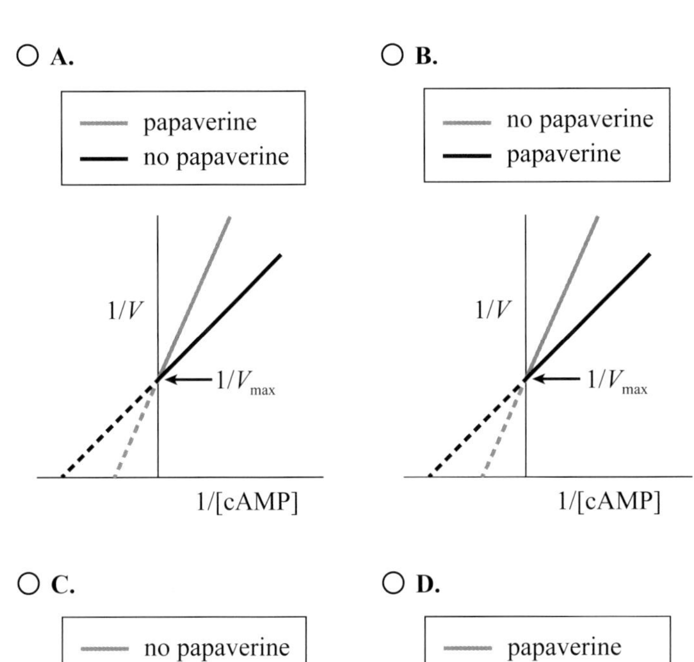

○ **C.**

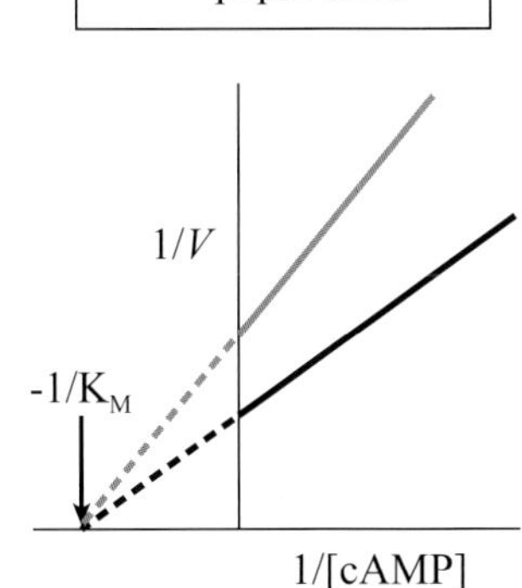

○ **D.**

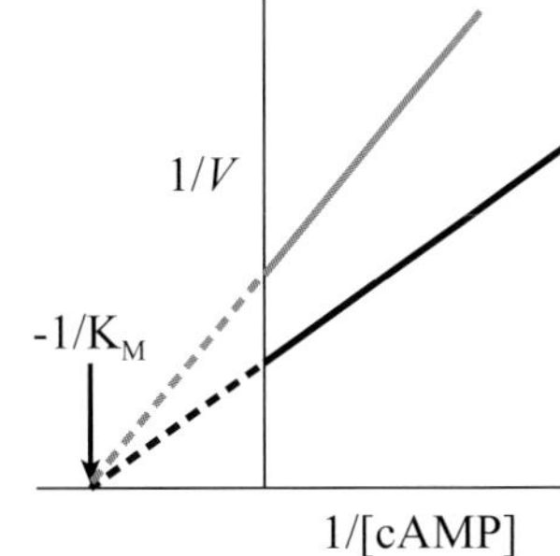

Question 3

According to Figure 3, which drug or combination of drugs can be used in LND to replenish the levels of synapsin to the physiologic levels of a wild type individual?

- ○ **A.** Forskolin alone
- ○ **B.** Papaverine alone
- ○ **C.** Papaverine and Forskolin together
- ○ **D.** Neither

Question 4

Synapsin is phosphorylated by Protein Kinase A (PKA), a cAMP-dependent enzyme. There are four spots on PKA where cAMP can attach to activate the protein. The more cAMP molecules are attached, the easier additional cAMP molecules can bind. Cyclic AMP exhibits:

I. allosteric interaction.
II. positive cooperativity.
III. positive feedback.

- ○ **A.** I only
- ○ **B.** I and III
- ○ **C.** I and II
- ○ **D.** I, II and III

Question 5

Knowing that PDE also catalyzes the degradation of cyclic GMP (cGMP) but not cyclic TMP or cyclic CMP, which of the following statements best describes the specificity of the enzyme?

- ○ **A.** PDE is specific to nucleotides that can form two hydrogen bonds in DNA.
- ○ **B.** PDE is specific to nucleotides that can form three hydrogen bonds in DNA.
- ○ **C.** PDE is specific to nucleotides that have a purine ring in its base structure.
- ○ **D.** PDE is specific to nucleotides that have a pyrimidine ring in its base structure.

STOP. If you finish before time is called, check your work. You may go back to any question in this test.

ANSWERS & EXPLANATIONS for the Warm-Up Passages can be found on p. 185.

Biological Molecules and Enzymes

TEST 1A

Time: 95 minutes
Questions 1–59

DIRECTIONS: Most questions in the Biological and Biochemical Foundations of Living Systems test section are grouped with a descriptive passage. Select the best answer to each question using background knowledge and the given passage. A portion of this test section is comprised of discrete questions, which are independent of any passage and one another. Select the best answer for each discrete question. Indicate your selection by blackening the corresponding oval on your answer document. If you are unsure of the answer, rule out incorrect choices and select from the remaining options. You may access a periodic table found on the last page of this book at any point during this test section.

Passage 1 (Questions 1-4)

Cholesterol is one of the main components of lipid rafts, which provide signaling platforms capable of activating various cellular signaling pathways. Cholesterol accumulation and dysregulated cholesterol metabolism is reported in various malignancies, including leukemia and freshly isolated blood cancer acute myeloid leukemia (AML) cells show high rates of cholesterol import and/or synthesis.

Cyclodextrins (CyDs) are cyclic oligosaccharides, which have hydrophilic external faces and hydrophobic internal environments. CyDs interact with cell membrane components, such as cholesterol and phospholipids, resulting in the induction of hemolysis at high concentrations. Additionally, 2-hydroxypropyl-β-cyclodextrin (HP-β-CyD) is used clinically as a pharmaceutical delivery vehicle for poorly water-soluble drugs (Figure 1).

Figure 1 Structure of 2-hydroxypropyl-β-cyclodextrin (HP-β-CyD)

HP-β-CyD has already been approved for the treatment of Niemann-Pick Type C disease (NPC), a lysosomal lipid storage disorder caused by the failure to metabolize cholesterol. Scientists suspected that HP-β-CyD could be used as a novel anticancer agent by directly modulating cholesterol homeostasis in cancer cells and investigated anticancer activities of HP-β-CyD using various leukemic cell lines in vitro.

Researchers plated 1×10^6 Pro-B Ba/F3 cancer cells that expressed wild-type fusion oncogene BCR-ABL (Ba/F3 BCR-ABLWT) and evaluated the effect of various millimolar (mM) concentrations of HP-β-CyD on leukemic cell viability. The results are shown in Figure 2.

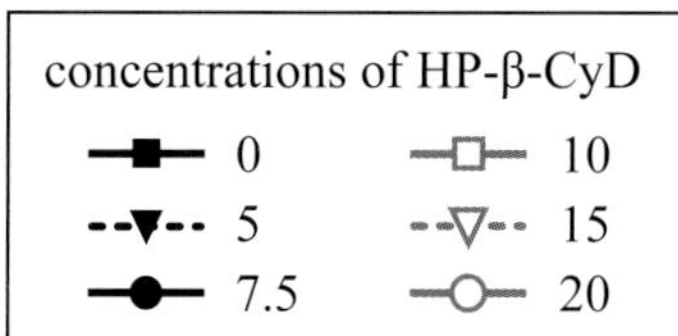

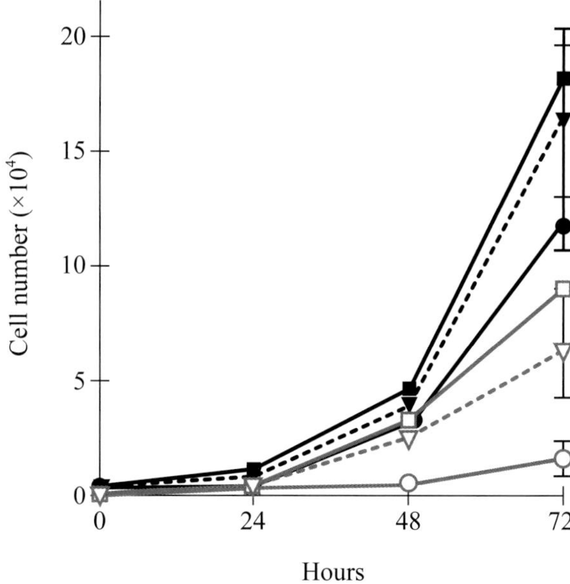

Figure 2 Effects of HP-β-CyD on leukemic cell growth

To clarify whether HP-β-CyD-induced apoptosis is also associated with cholesterol depletion, scientists evaluated the effect of CyDs on cholesterol concentration in Ba/F3 BCR-ABL WT leukemia cells treated with various concentrations of HP-β-CyD. The results are shown in Figure 3.

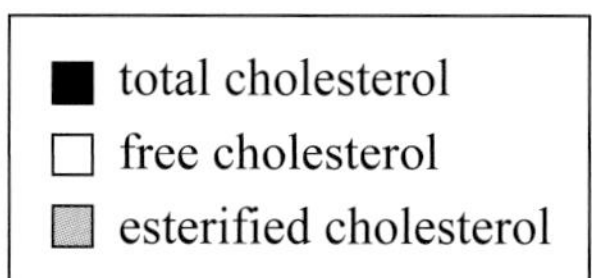

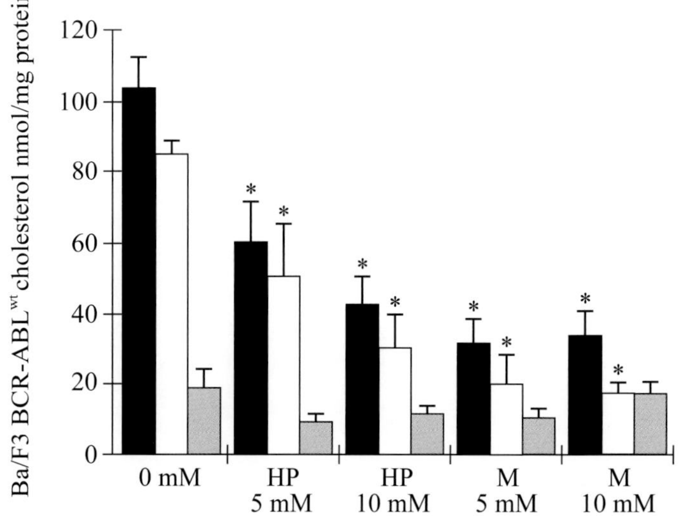

Figure 3 Disruption of cellular cholesterol homeostasis by β-CyDs.

Based on their studies, the scientists concluded that HP-β-CyD-mediated modulation of cellular cholesterol inhibits leukemic cell proliferation. Because rapidly proliferating cells may require cholesterol for new membrane synthesis, they predicted that HP-β-CyD may be a novel treatment for chemotherapy-resistant cancers.

Question 1

Treatment of persons with AML with HP-β-CyD is LEAST likely to affect:

- **A.** production of thyroid hormone T_3.
- **B.** efficient organization of the immunologic synapse.
- **C.** synthesis of bile salts.
- **D.** calcium absorption in the intestinal tract.

Question 2

Increasing concentrations of HP-β-CyD most likely lead to:

- **A.** decreased cell death due to increased mitochondrial membrane fluidity.
- **B.** decreased cell death due to impaired lipid raft formation.
- **C.** increased cell death due to increased permeability of small molecules across the plasma membrane.
- **D.** increased cell death due to increased plasma membrane fluidity.

Question 3

Which of the following curves best depicts the relationship between HP-β-CyD and mitochondrial membrane fluidity?

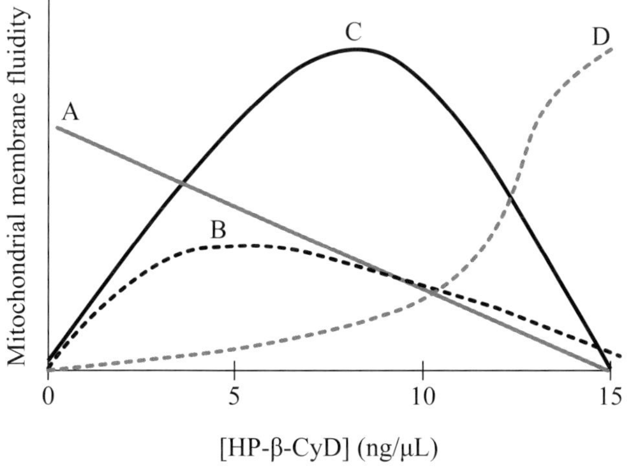

- **A.** A
- **B.** B
- **C.** C
- **D.** D

Question 4

In vivo treatment of mouse models of colorectal cancer with HP-β-CyD failed to show decreases in tumor mass over time. This experimental evidence:

- **A.** strengthens the authors' conclusions that cholesterol efflux mediates cancer cell death.
- **B.** weakens the authors' conclusions that cholesterol efflux increases cancer cell apoptosis.
- **C.** weakens the authors' conclusions that HP-β-CyD can effectively deliver lipophilic chemotherapeutic agents.
- **D.** neither strengthens nor weakens the authors' conclusions that HP-β-CyD induces cholesterol efflux from cancer cells.

TEST 1A

Passage 2 (Questions 5-9)

Colorectal carcinoma (CRC) is one of the most common cancers and a leading cause of death worldwide. Numerous studies have linked natural compounds with decreased risk of developing cancer, including compounds of the flavonoid family. Luteolin (30,40,5,7-tetrahydroxyflavone), which is present at high levels in fruits, is the most abundant member of the flavonoid family.

Ceramide is the key intermediate of sphingolipid metabolism. The effects of ceramide are antagonized by sphingosine-1-phosphate (S1P), a pro-mitogenic and survival factor, and the balance between S1P and ceramide is essential for cellular homeostasis. Additionally, sphingosine kinase (SphK1) and S1P lyase are up- and down-regulated, respectively, leading to S1P accumulation in CRC.

Scientists investigated the potential role of both ceramide and S1P in luteolin cytotoxicity in CRC. The basal level of ceramide was measured before and after 24 hour treatment with cytotoxic doses of luteolin in CRC cells and normal colon cells. The results are shown in Figure 1. Cell viability at various concentrations of ceramide were also measured (Figure 2).

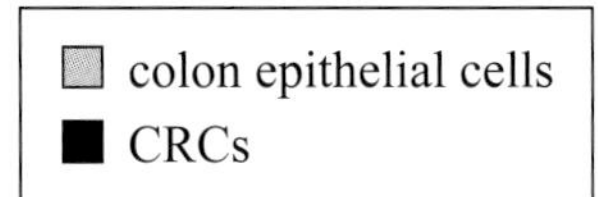

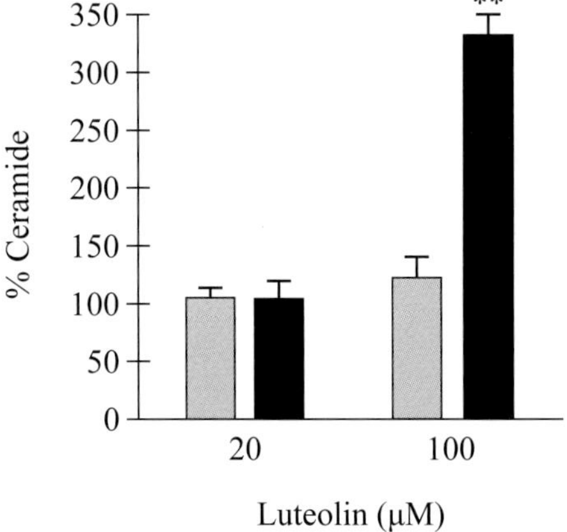

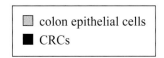

Figure 1 Effect of luteolin treatment on cellular ceramide levels

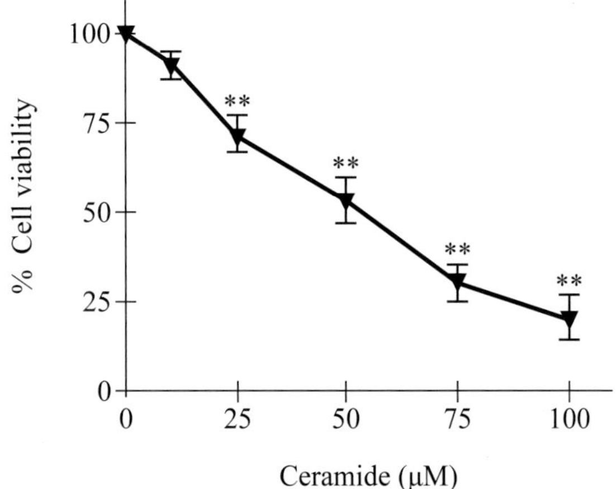

Figure 2 Effect of ceramide on cell viability of CRCs

Newly synthesized ceramide formed in the ER needs to reach the Golgi apparatus for the biosynthesis of complex sphingolipids. Neo-synthesized ceramide in the ER can move to Golgi through a vesicle-mediated route, and this transport is functional to both sphingomyelin and glycosphingolipid biosynthesis. To investigate the mechanism underlying the ceramide accumulation induced by luteolin, radiolabeled sphingosine was incorporated into growth medium of CRCs cultured in the presence and absence of 100 μM luteolin. The effect of luteolin on ceramide metabolism to sphingomyelin and complex glycosphingolipids is shown in Figure 3.

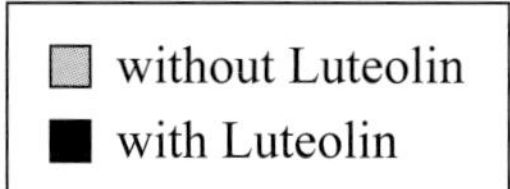

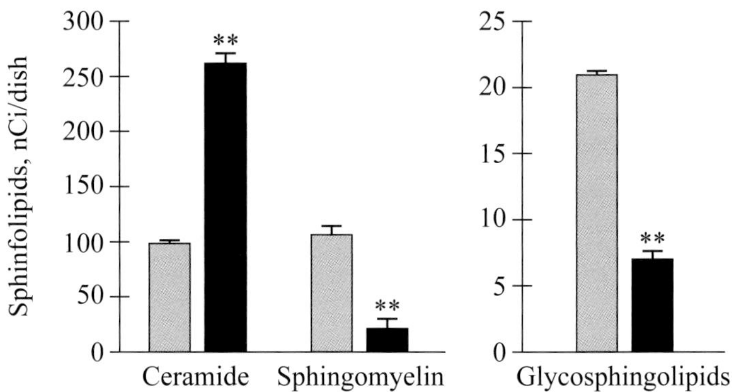

Figure 3 Effect of luteolin on ceramide metabolism to complex sphingolipids.

Question 5

SphK1 is likely to act by:

I. increasing the local concentration of ATP and sphingosine.

II. increasing the kinetic energy required to transfer a phosphate to sphingosine.

III. spatially reorienting ATP and sphingosine.

○ **A.** I only
○ **B.** I and II
○ **C.** I and III
○ **D.** II and III

Question 6

Which of the following amino acids is LEAST likely to facilitate the transfer of a phosphate from ATP to sphingosine in sphingosine kinase?

- O **A.** S
- O **B.** H
- O **C.** Y
- O **D.** I

Question 7

The phosphate on S1P may play a role in preventing the ribosome from synthesizing complex proteins through repulsive forces. Experimental evidence from which of the following experiments is LEAST likely to support the role of electrostatic forces in peptide formation?

- O **A.** Addition of phosphoric acid to an *in vitro* translation experiment hindered oligopeptide production.
- O **B.** Addition of bicarbonate to an *in vitro* translation experiment hindered oligopeptide production.
- O **C.** Decreased levels of magnesium in an *in vitro* translation experiment supplemented oligopeptide production.
- O **D.** Increased levels of zinc in an *in vitro* translation experiment supplemented oligopeptide production.

Question 8

Luteolin most likely mediates cell death by:

- O **A.** inhibiting the transport of sphingomyelin precursors to the Golgi.
- O **B.** inhibiting the synthesis of sphingomyelin in the smooth endoplasmic reticulum.
- O **C.** increasing the permeability of the mitochondrial membrane.
- O **D.** decreasing the concentration of cholesterol in the plasma membrane.

Question 9

In an additional experiment, scientists discovered that radiolabeled S1P was exocytosed out of the cell and could induce rapid proliferation of neighboring CRCs. S1P acts by:

- O **A.** binding a cell surface receptor.
- O **B.** binding a cytoplasmic receptor.
- O **C.** binding a nuclear receptor.
- O **D.** binding an ER membrane receptor.

Passage 3 (Questions 10-13)

Atherogenesis is the process of forming atheromas, collections of fat and inflammatory cells in the intima of blood vessels. Atheromas are a precursor for many conditions such as cardiovascular disease (CVD) resulting in stroke and heart attack. Atherogenesis has been highly associated with the metabolic syndrome (MetSyn), a condition diagnosed with the presence of any three of more of the following: central obesity, reduced high density lipoprotein (HDL), elevated plasma triglycerides (TG) or glucose, or high blood pressure. The prevalence of metabolic syndrome in the US remains high, affecting more than 20% of the adult population.

Apolipoproteins (apo) are structural components of lipoprotein particles that also direct particle metabolism. The level of apoB (found in low density lipoproteins; LDL) and apoA1 (in HDL), as well as their ratio can serve as markers of CVD risk. The functions of apo are likely to be affected by posttranslational modifications. ApoC3 and apoE are modified by glycosylation during transit through the Golgi apparatus, where carbohydrate chains are enzymatically attached to specific serine or threonine residues in these proteins. Sialic acids (amino sugars) are commonly found as terminal oligosaccharide residues on glycosylated lipoproteins including apoC3 and apoE.

A researcher hypothesized that not only are the levels of apolipoproteins different in patients with metabolic syndrome compared to healthy controls, but the level of glycosylation can also play an important role in the risk of developing CVD. In patients with metabolic syndrome, the researcher found that the total plasma level of apoA1 was lower, whereas apoB, apoC3, and apoE were higher. The most extensively glycosylated (di-sialylated) isoform of apoC3 was reduced in LDL and HDL fractions by 30% and 25%, respectively. Similarly, the glycosylated isoform of apoE was reduced in LDL and HDL fractions by 26% and 37%, respectively.

Question 10

HDL and LDL are colloquially referred to as "good" and "bad" cholesterol for their respective decreased and increased risk of CVD development. How can this reference be explained?

- O **A.** HDL carries cholesterol from the adipocytes to arteries, whereas LDL does the opposite.
- O **B.** HDL carries cholesterol from the arteries to adipocytes, whereas LDL does the opposite.
- O **C.** HDL carries cholesterol from the liver to the arteries, whereas LDL does the opposite.
- O **D.** HDL carries cholesterol from the arteries to the liver, whereas LDL does the opposite.

Question 11

NEU3 is a plasma sialidase. According to the passage, what would be the relationship between NEU3 activity and atherogenesis?

- O **A.** Increased activity corresponds to decreased glycosidation of apo, which is correlated with increased atherogenesis.
- O **B.** Increased activity corresponds to decreased glycosidation of apo, which is correlated with decreased atherogenesis.
- O **C.** Increased activity corresponds to increased glycosidation of apo, which is correlated with increased atherogenesis.
- O **D.** Increased activity corresponds to increased glycosidation of apo, which is correlated with decreased atherogenesis.

Question 12

The first step of atherogenesis is the attachment of lipoproteins to the endothelium of blood vessels. This is achieved by an interaction between the glycoproteins. Which of the following could be used in an experiment to decrease the rate of this first step in an attempt to decrease atherogenesis?

I. Inhibiting post-translational modifications in endothelial cells
II. Introducing antibodies against endothelial glycoproteins
III. Introducing antibodies against lipoprotein glycoproteins

- O **A.** I only
- O **B.** I and II
- O **C.** II and III
- O **D.** I, II and II

Question 13

By examining the carbohydrate chain of HDL, scientists noted that most sugars are made of 6-membered rings. Which of the following disaccharides can be hydrolyzed into 6-membered ring sugars?

- O **A.** Sucrose and maltose
- O **B.** Sucrose and lactose
- O **C.** Maltose and lactose
- O **D.** Amylose and amylopectin

Questions 14 through 17 do not refer to a passage and are independent of each other.

Question 14

Susan decides to go on the "grapefruit diet" in order to lose ten pounds before her sister's wedding. Two months into her low fat diet, her doctors informs her that she has a new vitamin deficiency. Her deficiency is most likely NOT:

- O **A.** Vitamin A.
- O **B.** Vitamin B.
- O **C.** Vitamin D.
- O **D.** Vitamin E.

Question 15

Which of the following molecules would be found in high concentrations in the plasma membranes of mammals living in cold environments?

- O **A.** Phosphatidylcholine
- O **B.** Sphingomyelin
- O **C.** Cholesterol
- O **D.** Phosphatidylinositol

Question 16

Which of the following monosaccharide moieties is NOT a hexose?

- O **A.** Glucose
- O **B.** Galactose
- O **C.** Ribose
- O **D.** Fructose

Question 17

Glycoproteins, synthesized in the endoplasmic reticulum, contain both carbohydrate and amino acid components. Glycoproteins are most likely to be found in which part of the cell?

- O **A.** Plasma membrane
- O **B.** Cytosol
- O **C.** Nucleus
- O **D.** Mitochondria

Passage 4 (Questions 18-22)

Infertility affects up to 10% of couples attempting to conceive every year. While maternal contributions to infertility have been better characterized, paternal influences through the fitness of spermatozoa remain unknown. The mitochondria of the spermatozoa control numerous functions and are considered to be hallmarks of sperm functionality. In addition to their role as an ATP source via oxidative phosphorylation (OXPHOS), other functions in regulating the lifespan of spermatozoa have attracted major research attention to these organelles.

Experiment 1

Alteration in the redox homeostasis of the cell leads to sperm senescence and death. The mitochondria of defective sperm are the major source of radical oxygen species (ROS) originating from electron leakage in the electron transport chain (ETC). To test the hypothesis that the disruption of complexes I and III leads to sperm malfunction due to oxidative stress, sperm samples were incubated in presence of rotenone and antimycin, inhibitors of complexes I and III, respectively. The levels of ATP were quantified and served as an inverse correlate of ROS generation. The results are shown in Figure 1.

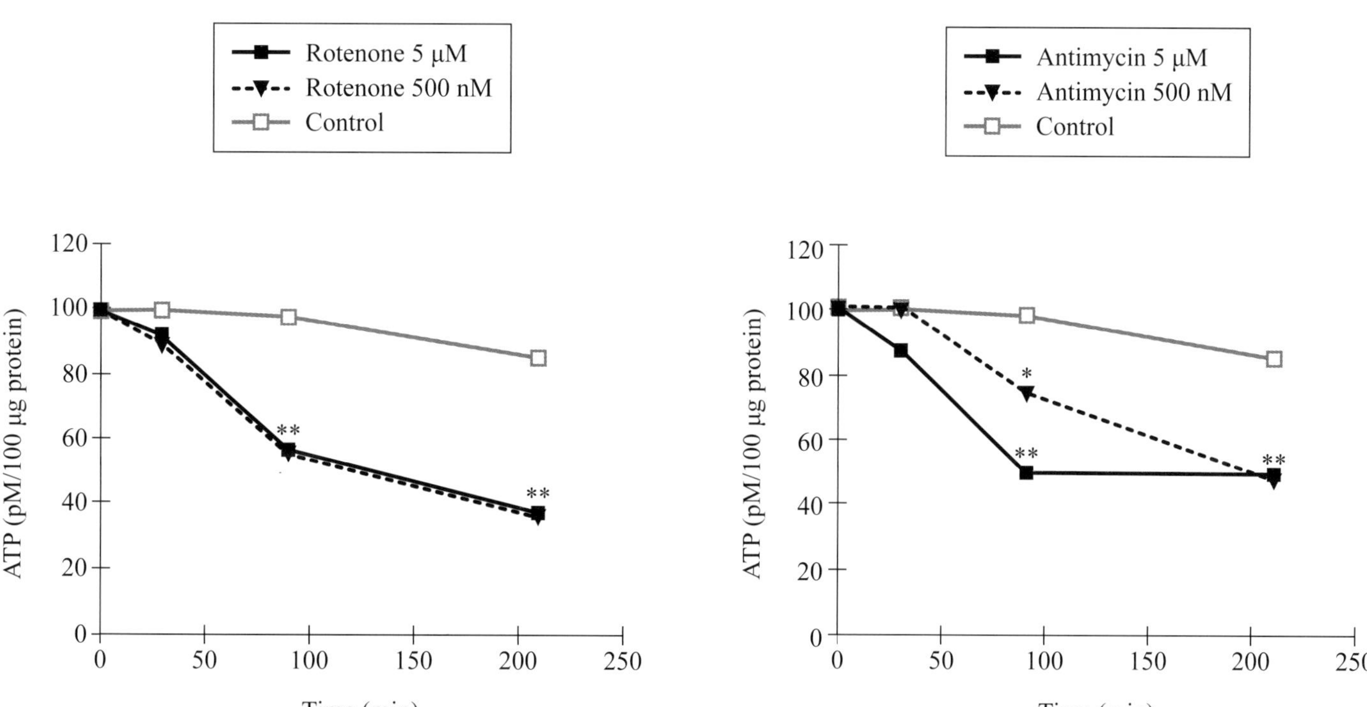

Figure 1 Effect of the inhibition of Complexes I and III of the electron transport chain on the ATP content of spermatozoa

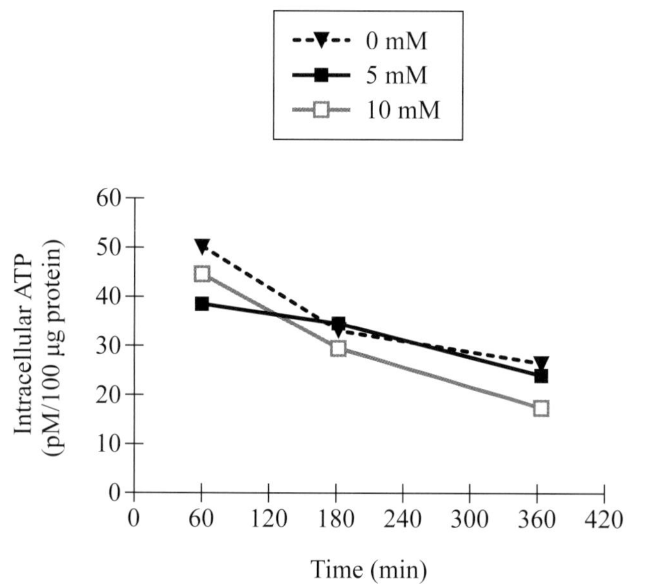

Figure 2 Effect of 2-Deoxy-D-Glucose on the ATP content of spermatozoa

Experiment 2

Because ATP production is not completely abolished, either membrane potential is not completely suppressed or other sources of ATP may be present. To understand the role of glycolysis in spermatozoa ATP production, sperm were incubated in presence of 0, 5, and 10 mM of 2-Deoxy-D-Glucose. This is a glucose analog that inhibits glycolysis via its actions on hexokinase, the rate limiting step of glycolysis. It is phosphorylated by hexokinase to 2-DG-P and cannot be further metabolized by phosphoglucose isomerase. This leads to the accumulation of 2-DG-P in the cell and the depletion in cellular ATP. The results are shown in Figure 2.

Question 18

Carbohydrates like fructose are the primary source of energy for spermatogonia. Which statement best describes the role of carbohydrates in the cell?

I. Carbohydrates store the most energy per dietary mole that can be oxidized to ATP.
II. Carbohydrates are easily stacked for space efficient storage.
III. Carbohydrates can be added to proteins and exported to the cell surface.

- A. I only
- B. I and II
- C. I and III
- D. II and III

Question 19

Spermatozoa rely heavily on fructose to power glycolysis and oxidative phosphorylation. Supplementation of the diet with which of the following molecules would be most likely to increase fructose concentrations in spermatozoa?

- A. Maltose – Maltose
- B. Lactose – Lactose
- C. Sucrose – Sucrose
- D. Galactose – Lactose

Question 20

Intracellular use of ATP following 10 mM administration of 2-Deoxy-D-Glucose most closely follows:

- A. 0th order kinetics.
- B. 1st order kinetics.
- C. 2nd order kinetics.
- D. 3rd order kinetics.

Question 21

Upon transport into the cytosol, glucose is phosphorylated to glucose-6-phosphate by hexokinase. Which of the following curves best represents the reaction mediated by hexokinase?

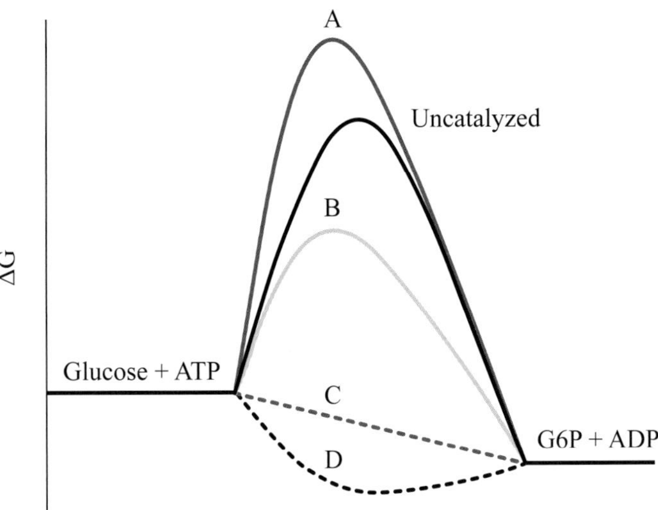

- A. A
- B. B
- C. C
- D. D

Question 22

Inhibition of hexokinase by 2-Deoxy-D-Glucose is LEAST likely to be:

- A. an example of competitive inhibition.
- B. overcome by the addition of D-Glucose.
- C. overcome by increasing the transcription of hexokinase.
- D. an example of allosteric inhibition.

Next ▶

Passage 5 (Questions 23-27)

The most common form of lactose intolerance (LI) results from either a genetic inability to produce lactase, an enzyme that breaks down lactose to glucose and galactose, or from an age-related down-regulation of lactase production. The breakdown of lactose reaction is shown in Figure 1. A central hypothesis in LI is that dairy avoidance leads to reduced intake of protein and calcium, which consequently results in poor growth, short stature and low bone mineral density.

Figure 1 Breakdown of lactose to galactose and glucose

A study was designed to address these two important questions and provide the needed data on height and vitamin D status of these children. Prepubertal children of ages 3-12 years with LI were compared to healthy, age- and gender-matched controls. Inclusion criteria included prepubertal status, diagnosis of LI by hydrogen breath test, and no history of calcium or vitamin D supplementation. Vitamin D deficiency was defined as 25-hydroxyvitamin D [25(OH)D] <50 nmol/L.

This study showed no significant difference in the serum concentration of 25(OH)D between children with LI and their normal controls. However, when adjusted for BMI, both the normal weight LI (Group 1) and overweight/obese LI patients (Group 2) had similar serum concentrations of 25(OH)D to the overweight/obese controls (Group 3), but significantly lower 25(OH)D levels than the normal weight controls (Group 4). The overall difference in height z-score between the LI children and controls was plotted. The normal weight LI patients had similar height as normal controls, while the overweight/obese LI group was taller than the normal weight controls, and of similar height as the overweight/obese controls.

This passage was adapted from "Lactose Intolerance: Lack of Evidence for Short Stature or Vitamin D Deficiency in Prepubertal Children." Setty-Shah N, Maranda L, Candela N, Fong J, Dahod I, et al. *PLoS ONE*. 2013. 8(10) e78653. doi:10.1371/journal.pone.0078653 for use under the terms of the Creative Commons CC BY 3.0 license (https://creativecommons.org/licenses/by/3.0/legalcode).

Question 23

Which of the following best describes the relationship between the breakdown products of galactose?

- **A.** They are anomers.
- **B.** They are epimers.
- **C.** They are stereoisomers.
- **D.** They are diastereomers.

Question 24

Based on what is known about lactose intolerance in prepubertal children, researchers could reasonably hypothesize that these individuals fail to:

- **A.** break α-1,4 linkages.
- **B.** break β-1,4 linkages.
- **C.** break α-1,2 linkages.
- **D.** break β-1,2 linkages.

Question 25

A detection molecule is designed that binds to glycosidic linkages and fluoresces as a signal in order to determine the density of these bonds within a sample. Which of the following groups from paragraph 3 likely has the highest signal in their digestive tracts?

- **A.** Group 1 after milk deprivation.
- **B.** Group 2 after a large glass of milk.
- **C.** Group 3 after milk deprivation.
- **D.** Group 4 after a large glass of milk.

Question 26

Lactose intolerance describes a condition in which the enzyme lactase fails to yield glucose and galactose from lactose. In a follow-up study, investigators discovered another enzyme that fails to yield the breakdown products glucose and glucose. What is this enzyme?

- **A.** Sucrase
- **B.** Fructase
- **C.** Maltase
- **D.** Aldolase

Question 27

Which of the following is true about human digestion of carbohydrates?

- **A.** They must be in the same absolute configuration as most amino acids.
- **B.** They must be in the opposite absolute configuration as most amino acids.
- **C.** It is a passive process that ultimately leads to absorption.
- **D.** They must be in the L-configuration.

TEST 1A

Questions 28 through 31 do not refer to a passage and are independent of each other.

Question 28

Which of the following is true of glycogen?

○ **A.** It is composed of alpha linkages of glucose and fructose.

○ **B.** It is primarily stored in adipose tissue.

○ **C.** It is synthesized in muscle and liver cells.

○ **D.** It is formed mainly in the fasting state.

Question 29

The Sanger method of DNA sequencing utilizes dideoxy-nucleotides (ddNTP) to interrupt DNA synthesis. Which carbons of the ddNTPs are missing hydroxyl groups?

○ **A.** 2′ and 5′

○ **B.** 3′ and 5′

○ **C.** 2′ and 4′

○ **D.** 2′ and 3′

Question 30

Zidovudine is a drug used in the treatment of HIV and is composed of a sugar bound to a six-membered heterocyclic ring that has two nitrogens and a methyl group. Which of the following is most similar to the drug?

○ **A.** Pyridoxine

○ **B.** Adenine

○ **C.** Guanine

○ **D.** Thymine

Question 31

The hydrophobic nature of nitrogenous bases makes it highly unfavorable for them to be exposed to the cytosol. How is it that DNA can exist in a stable conformation within the cell?

○ **A.** The nuclear envelope excludes cytosol and maintains a hydrophobic environment.

○ **B.** B. The sugar-phosphate backbone interacts with the cytosol and protects the bases.

○ **C.** C. Base-pairing balances out hydrophobic interactions and stabilizes the DNA.

○ **D.** D. Cells constantly regenerate DNA due to destabilizing hydrophobic interactions.

Passage 6 (Questions 32-35)

Growing evidence suggests that apoptosis induced by the Fas/CD95 death receptor is mediated by the formation of Fas/CD95 aggregates in lipid rafts, which are collections of phospholipids and cholesterol that assemble with certain clusters of proteins depending on information conveyed to the cell. Clustering of death receptor Fas/CD95 can be achieved not only by interaction with its natural ligand FasL/CD95L, but through non-physiological agents independently of its ligand, providing a new framework for novel therapeutic interventions. Edelfosine (EDLF) is the prototypical compound of a promising family of synthetic antitumor lipids, collectively named as synthetic alkyl-lysophospholipid analogues, which induce selective apoptosis in tumor cells while sparing normal cells. Stimulation of Fas/CD95 results in receptor aggregation and recruitment of the adapter protein Fas-associated death domain-containing protein (FADD), through interaction between its own death domain and the clustered receptor death domains. FADD, in turn, contains a death effector domain that binds to the zymogen form of procaspase-8, forming the death-inducing signaling complex (DISC), composed of Fas/CD95, FADD and procaspase- 8, which drives cells to apoptosis.

To investigate how EDLF impacts Fas/CD95, FADD, and procaspase-8 distribution in the plasma membrane, cells were exposed to a control compound or EDLF. The cells were then lysed, and the levels of protein were measured by Western Blot (Figure 1). In order to quantify apoptosis, terminal deoxynucleotidyl transferase-mediated dUTP nick-end labeling (TUNEL) was used. TUNEL detects the 3'-OH ends of DNA exposed during the internucleosomal cleavage that occurs during apoptosis. Additionally, endogenous expression of Fas/CD95 was modulated by RNA interference using short hairpin RNA (shRNA) to understand the effects of protein concentration on EDLF-induced apoptosis (Figure 2). shRNA binds complementary mRNA sequences in the cytosol, targeting the mRNA sequences for degradation. TUNEL results are shown in Figure 2.

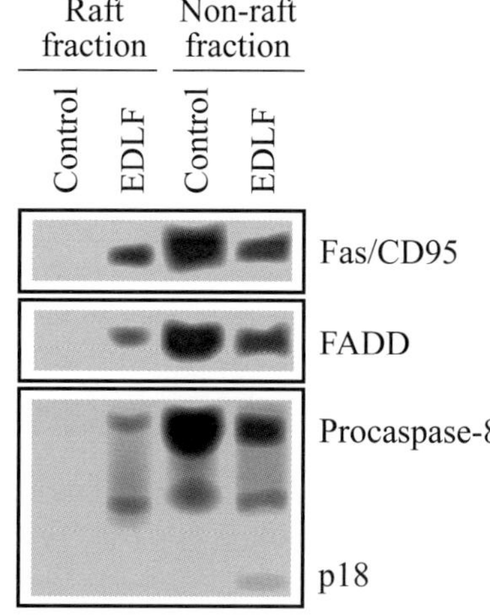

Figure 1 DISC formation in lipid rafts following exposure to edelfosine (EDLF)

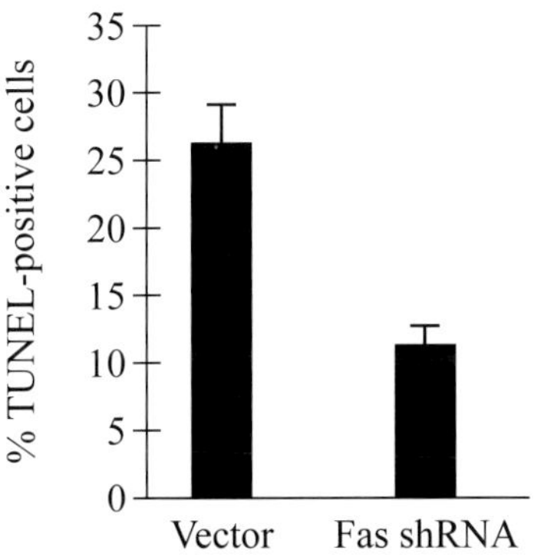

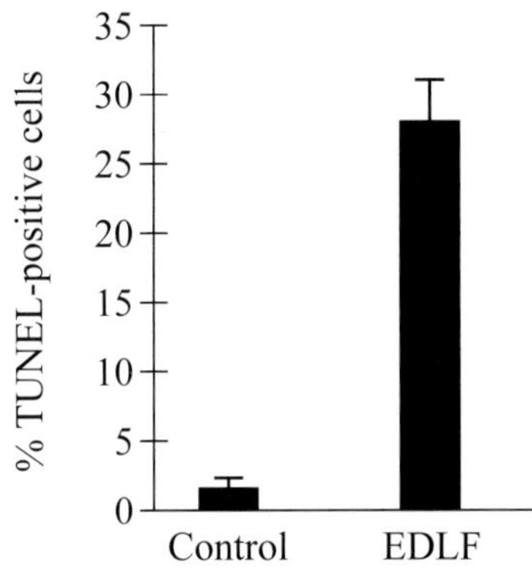

Figure 2 Involvement of DISC constituents in edelfosine-induced apoptosis as assessed by TUNEL assay

This passage was adapted from "Involvement of Raft Aggregates Enriched in Fas/CD95 Death-Inducing Signaling Complex in the Antileukemic Action of Edelfosine in Jurkat Cells." Gajate C, Gonzalez-Camacho F, Mollinedo F. *PLoS ONE*. 2009. 4(4) doi:10.1371/journal.pone.0005044 for use under the terms of the Creative Commons CC BY 3.0 license (http://creativecommons.org/licenses/by/3.0/legalcode).

Question 32

Upon stimulation of cells with edelfosine, how did the number of Fas/CD95 molecules present on the non-raft portion of the plasma membrane change ?

- O **A.** The number of Fas/CD95 molecules increased.
- O **B.** The number of Fas/CD95 molecules decreased.
- O **C.** The number of Fas/CD95 molecules remained the same.
- O **D.** The number of Fas/CD95 molecules present cannot be determined from the experiments.

Question 33

In the Western Blot presented in Figure 1, the anti-FADD antibody bound FADD utilizing a key alpha helix. What type of interaction allows alpha helices to maintain their helical shape?

- O **A.** Covalent bonding
- O **B.** Ionic bonding
- O **C.** Electrostatic interactions
- O **D.** Hydrogen bonding

Question 34

Fas/CD95 mRNA levels were decreased in the experiment profiled in Figure 2 by shRNA. Further experimental data concluded that the key nucleotide sequence the shRNA bound to in the mRNA was 5′-UGCAUGCA-3′. The most likely sequence of the shRNA was :

- O **A.** 5′-TGCATGCA-3′.
- O **B.** 5′-UGCAUGCA-3′.
- O **C.** 5′-ACGUACGU-3′.
- O **D.** 5′-ACGTACGT-3′.

Question 35

In order to conduct the TUNEL assay, researchers must heat cellular DNA to a high enough temperature to allow the terminal ends of DNA to unravel and bind the probe. Which of the following sequences, when paired with its reverse complement, would require the highest temperature to denature?

- O **A.** 5′-TTTTAAGCT-3′
- O **B.** 5’-AATAGGGC-3′
- O **C.** 5′-GCGGGCTA-3′
- O **D.** 5′-TTTTAAAAT-3′

TEST 1A

Passage 7 (Questions 36-39)

More than half of currently approved antiviral drugs are nucleoside-based analogs. Nucleoside analogs used in antiviral therapy are prodrugs which require activation by cellular enzymes to their active forms before reaching the intended target enzymes. Due to the similarity in chemical structure of natural nucleosides and nucleotides to the nucleoside analogs (NAs) used as drugs, there is a potential for cross-reactivity with enzymes along their metabolic pathways. For example, NAs could inhibit enzymes of nucleotide metabolism by binding within the active sites. Alternatively, they might bind to regulatory sites and thus serve as inhibitors or activators. An example of a nucleoside analog is shown in Figure 1.

NH_2 N N N N HO O HO OH

Figure 1 An example of a nucleoside analog

With the advent of highly active antiretroviral therapy (HAART), the incidence of HIV associated dementia (HAD) has drastically fallen, while the cumulative prevalence of HIV associated neurocognitive disorders (HAND) has risen. Nucleoside analogue reverse transcriptase inhibitors (NRTI), an integral component of HAART, are widely used to inhibit human immunodeficiency virus (HIV) replication. Since NRTIs cannot form 3′-phosphodiester bonds themselves, they are phosphorylated by host cell enzymes to active triphosphates, which inhibit HIV reverse transcriptase and/or act as chain terminators when incorporated into a viral DNA chain. HAART cannot eradicate HIV due to virus reservoir, drug resistance and other reasons, which leads to lifelong antiviral therapy in HIV infected patients. Long-term exposure to NRTIs can result in inhibition of DNA polymerase γ, which is responsible for mitochondria DNA (mtDNA) synthesis, resulting in oxidative stress and eventual mitochondrial dysfunction.

Question 36

The nucleoside analog in Figure 1 is most likely a derivative of which nucleotide?

- O **A.** Adenine
- O **B.** Uracil
- O **C.** Cytosine
- O **D.** Thymine

Question 37

Based on the information in the passage, the overall rise in HAND can be attributed to which of the following?

- O **A.** The decreased incidence of HAD
- O **B.** High sensitivity of neurons to mitochondrial dysfunction
- O **C.** The inhibition of reverse transcriptase
- O **D.** The failure of NRTI conversion from a prodrug

Question 38

NRTIs are considered prodrugs because :

- O **A.** they lack a phosphate group.
- O **B.** they lack a nitrogenous base.
- O **C.** they lack a pentose sugar.
- O **D.** they are meant to prevent elongation of the DNA chain.

Question 39

What combination of data would most likely lead the researchers to conclude that DNA polymerase γ is more susceptible to NRTIs than DNA polymerase III?

I. ATP depletion proceeding cell death of normal cells

II. Absence of cytoplasmic kinase mRNAs proceeding oxidative stress

III. The presence of abnormally large cells proceeding mitochondrial dysfunction

- O **A.** I only
- O **B.** I and II
- O **C.** III only
- O **D.** II and III

Passage 8 (Questions 40-44)

Salicylic acid (SA) and its derivatives, have been used for millennia to reduce pain, fever, and inflammation by inhibiting cyclooxygenase COX2. To investigate whether aspirin has additional targets in humans, besides the cyclooxygenases, that may be responsible for some of aspirin's multiple pharmacological activities, cultured human cells were screened with salicylic acid and another compound, glycyrrhizin, to identify many new potential targets of SA.

Among identified targets was Glyceraldehyde 3-Phosphate Dehydrogenase (GAPDH), a cytosolic homotetrameric enzyme that plays a central role in the production of energy, via glycolysis. In addition to this housekeeping role, other functions of this protein include its participation in DNA repair and transcription through its DNA binding activities.

Experiment 1

SA and glycyrrhizin were incubated with GAPDH and the levels of inhibition determined by measuring the disappearance of glyceraldehyde-3-phosphate, the substrate for GAPDH. The results of the inhibition assay with SA are shown in Figure 1.

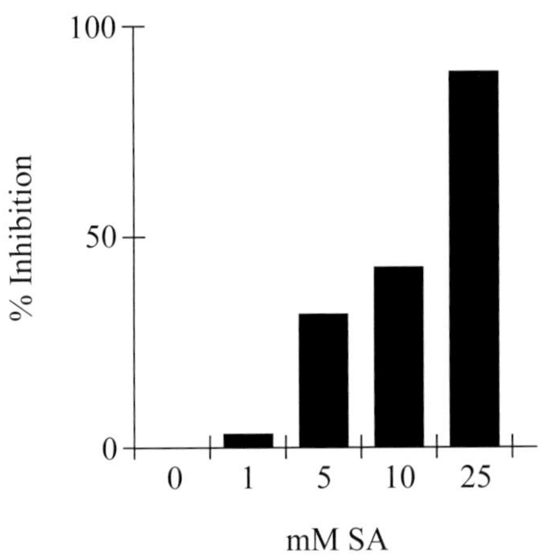

Figure 1 SA-binding activity of GAPDH

Experiment 2

Given the predicted involvement of GAPDH in modulating transcription, cells incubated with glycyrrhizin (Figure 2) were lysed and the nucleus isolated by ultracentrifugation in order to determine how glycyrrhizin affected nuclear translocation. MNNG is known to cause robust translocation of GAPDH and was used as a positive control. The results are shown in Figure 3.

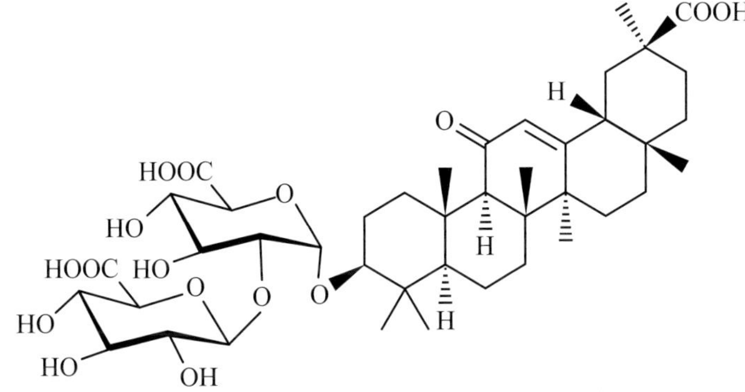

Figure 2 Structure of glycyrrhizin

	Glycyrrhizin					
	0 μM	0 μM	3 μM	10 μM	30 μM	100 μM
MNNG	–	+	+	+	+	+
Nuclear GAPDH						

Figure 3 Western blot showing the effects of glycyrrhizin on GAPDH nuclear translocation

Question 40

GAPDH binding to DNA is most likely stabilized by what type of forces within DNA?

- **A.** Hydrogen bonds
- **B.** Van der Waals interactions
- **C.** Disulfide bonds
- **D.** Electrostatic attractions

Question 41

GAPDH may play a role in mediating nucleotide excision repair that occurs when two T bases are cross-linked by UV radiation. DNA polymerase δ resynthesizes the missing nucleotides by catalyzing:

- **A.** the attack of the 5′ deoxyribose on the γ phosphate of the incoming nucleoside.
- **B.** the attack of the 3′ deoxyribose on the γ phosphate of the incoming nucleotide.
- **C.** the attack of the 5′ base on the β phosphate of the incoming nucleoside.
- **D.** the attack of the 3′ nucleotide on the α phosphate of the incoming nucleotide.

TEST 1A

Question 42

The structure of SA is shown below. Which of the following amino acids is LEAST likely to facilitate binding of SA to eukaryotic GAPDH?

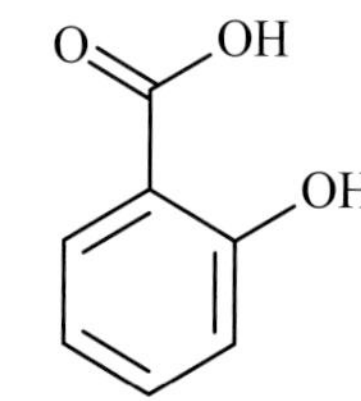

Salicyclic acid (SA)

I. D-Alanine
II. L-Threonine
III. D-Serine

- **A.** I only
- **B.** II only
- **C.** I and II
- **D.** I and III

Question 43

The nuclear localization sequence that allows GAPDH to translate to the nucleus is most likely composed of:

- **A.** nucleic acids.
- **B.** carbohydrates.
- **C.** fatty acids.
- **D.** amino acids.

Question 44

Treatment of human cells with increasing concentrations of glycyrrhizin is most likely to result in:

- **A.** increased translocation of GAPDH to the nucleus.
- **B.** increasing binding of GAPDH to DNA.
- **C.** decreased translocation of GAPDH to the nucleus.
- **D.** decreased binding of GAPDH to RNA.

Questions 45 through 48 do not refer to a passage and are independent of each other.

Question 45

Which of the following amino acids does NOT rotate plane polarized light?

- **A.** Ile
- **B.** Val
- **C.** Pro
- **D.** Gly

Question 46

Human insulin is composed of two polypeptide chains (A and B) connected by two disulfide bonds. The amino acid composition of the chains is as follow:

Chain	Nonpolar	Polar	Acidic	Basic
A	6	13	2	0
B	14	10	2	5

When insulin is run through gel electrophoresis under physiologic pH, it will:

- **A.** travel towards the negative pole.
- **B.** travel towards the positive pole.
- **C.** not migrate.
- **D.** split, with chains A and B traveling in opposite directions.

Question 47

The hemoglobin-oxygen saturation curve has a sigmoidal shape. The shape of the curve is characteristic of which of the following phenomenon?

- **A.** Cooperativity in the absence of an allosteric inhibitor
- **B.** The change in blood pH as hemoglobin circulates the body
- **C.** Multiple binding spots on an enzyme
- **D.** Various isoforms of hemoglobin

Question 48

Which of the following would be most likely to disrupt the bonding between the thiol groups of two cysteine amino acids?

- **A.** $HOCH_2CH_2SH$
- **B.** CH_2Cl_2
- **C.** $CO(NH_2)_2$
- **D.** CH_3COOH

Next ▶

Passage 9 (Questions 49-52)

Alzheimer's disease (AD), the most common cause of dementia in older people, is a progressive neurodegenerative disorder. The disease is associated with appearance of β-sheet plaques and tangles in brain tissue that gradually kills neurons in brain cortex, hippocampus, amygdala and certain other brain regions, causing the levels of acetylcholine (ACh) neurotransmitter produced by them to decline. This is known as cholinergic-deficit hypothesis for the AD.

Normally ACh is broken down as soon as it is produced, due to the activity of an enzyme known as acetylcholinesterase (AChE) present in neural synapse. There is no effective treatment available for AD, but inhibition of ACh breakdown by blocking the AChE has been proven to slow down disease progression. Researchers interested in discovering new AChE inhibitors used computational modeling to get more specific results for the human enzyme. Derivatives and heterodimers of chemicals isolated from traditional Chinese medicines (Figure 1) with potential anti-AChE activity were screened on the basis of steric fit.

Compounds A and B were dual binding site inhibitors that bound to the AChE active site, as well as its catalytic groove. Compounds C, D, and E bound to the AChE active site only. Docking studies identified that the presence of less than 5 hydrogen-bond donors and less than 10 hydrogen-bond acceptors predicted a low Km. *Hydrastis canadensis*, one of the plants included in the study, is a traditional Chinese homeopathic remedy and contains berberastine and berberine. Visual results for berberastine-5C-pyrimidine docking with the modeled AChE showed that the pyrimidine ring blocked the catalytic site and could be a candidate for AD treatment.

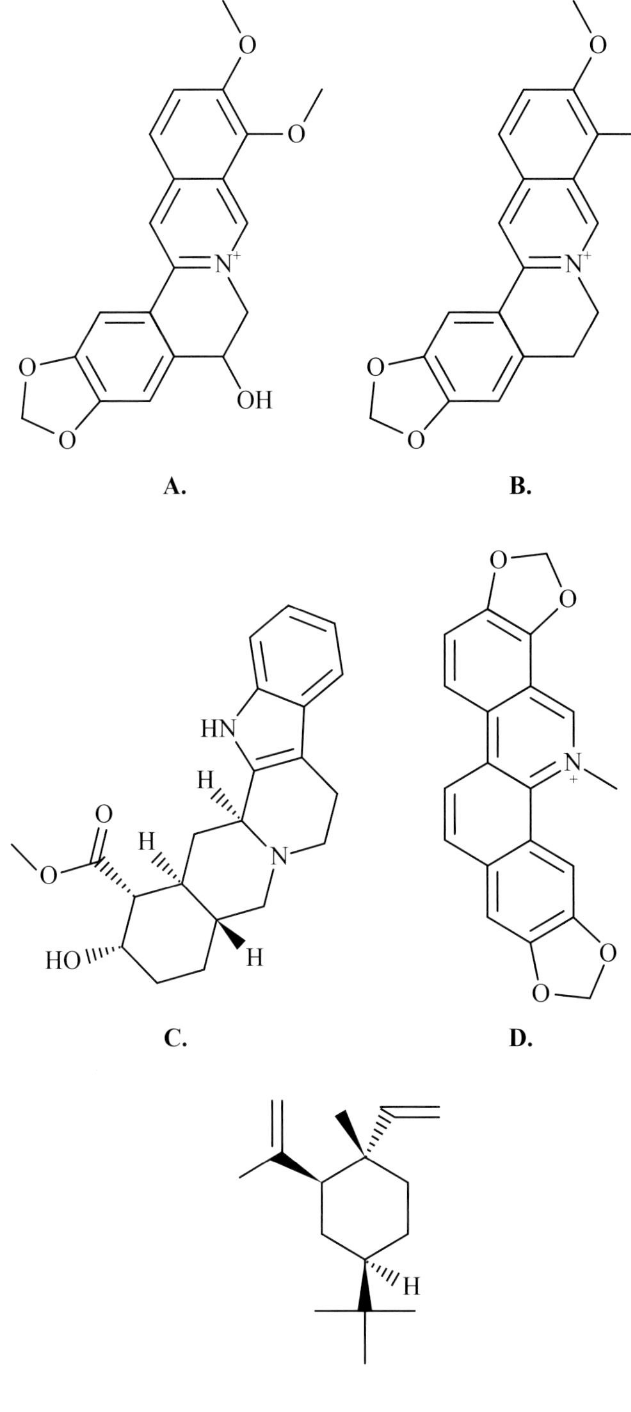

Figure 1 Two dimensional structures of top phytochemical leads used in study

Biological Molecules and Enzymes

TEST 1B

Time: 95 minutes
Questions 1–59

DIRECTIONS: Most questions in the Biological and Biochemical Foundations of Living Systems test section are grouped with a descriptive passage. Select the best answer to each question using background knowledge and the given passage. A portion of this test section is comprised of discrete questions, which are independent of any passage and one another. Select the best answer for each discrete question. Indicate your selection by blackening the corresponding oval on your answer document. If you are unsure of the answer, rule out incorrect choices and select from the remaining options. You may access a periodic table found on the last page of this book at any point during this test section.

Passage 1 (Questions 1-4)

The clinical success of immunotherapy for cancer relies on the selection of target antigens that are highly expressed in tumor cells but absent in normal tissues. Advances in the fields of tumor immunology, cancer genomics, and gene transfer technologies have permitted the development of therapies based on transfer of tumor-reactive T cells for the treatment of human malignancies.

Current efforts in identifying target antigens for immunotherapy are focused on the neo-antigens generated by somatic mutations present in tumors but absent in normal tissues. In order to expand the repertoire of antigens that can be targeted, which would expand the number of patients and tumor types that can be treated, scientists developed a T Cell Receptor (TCR) targeting the synovial sarcoma X breakpoint family, SSX2. The synovial sarcoma X breakpoint (SSX) genes are located on the X chromosome and play a role in promoting cancer. TCRs allow killer T cells to recognize cancer neo-antigens and kill the mutated cells via lysozyme and granzyme. cDNAs encoding for the TCR targeting SSX2 were transfected into human T cells and the transfected T cells were tested against a breast cancer cell line.

One of the cDNAs, TCR-5, promoted the greatest killing of breast cancer cells. The scientists next evaluated whether the codons for TCR-5 could further be optimized to enhance TCR-5 expression and/or biological activity. Three cDNAs encoding the same amino acid sequence as TCR-5 but with a nucleotide sequences optimized for codon usage in humans were compared in their ability to mediate lysis of breast cancer cells. One cDNA with low levels of DNA methylation provided the T cells with the greatest killing potential and may provide an additional therapeutic option to target malignant breast cancer.

Question 1

Recent research revealed that the protein SSX2 can be expressed on the surface of normal breast epithelial cells when an inflammatory reaction is occurring nearby. How would this affect the utility of targeting the SSX2 protein for immunotherapy by TCR binding?

- O **A.** It would decrease the utility of SSX2 in all circumstances.
- O **B.** It would decrease the utility of SSX2 only in instances of local inflammation.
- O **C.** It would increase the utility of SSX2 in all circumstances.
- O **D.** It would increase the utility of SSX2 only in instances of local inflammation.

Question 2

One of the alternative codons used to optimize TCR-5 expression generated a point mutation that substituted the amino acid arginine for threonine in the neo-antigen binding site of the TCR. What effect would this codon substitution have on the ability of T cells to cause breast cancer cell lysis?

- O **A.** It would increase the ability of T cells to lyse cancer cells.
- O **B.** It would decrease the ability of T cells to lyse cancer cells.
- O **C.** It would not affect the ability of T cells to lyse cancer cells.
- O **D.** No effect of the amino acid substitution can be predicted without additional information.

Question 3

The cDNA encoding the TCR responsible for activating release of lysozyme and granzyme differs from genomic DNA because:

- O **A.** it does not contain introns.
- O **B.** it contains additional enhancer elements.
- O **C.** it is single stranded.
- O **D.** it codes for multiple proteins .

Question 4

In a separate experiment, scientists discover that breast cancer cells can mitigate the lysogenic activity of lysozymes and granzymes released from T cells by maintaining a lower intracellular pH through increased glycolytic activity. Which of the following experimental conditions would lead to increased killing of breast cancer cells?

- O **A.** A high extracellular concentration of amino acids
- O **B.** A low extracellular concentration of carbohydrates
- O **C.** A high extracellular concentration of fatty acids
- O **D.** A low extracellular concentration of nucleic acids

Passage 2 (Questions 5-8)

HIV-1 infection is characterized by an ongoing replication leading to T-lymphocyte decline that is paralleled by the switch from CCR5 to CXCR4 co-receptor usage. Several computer algorithms have shown that third variable region (V3 loop) of the HIV-1 envelope glycoprotein (gp120) plays an important role in HIV-1 infection. The V3 loop is likely the primary determinant for binding to CCR5 or CXCR4. Both, CXCR4 and CCR5 are cell membrane associated G-protein-coupled receptors that trigger calcium signaling after binding their chemokine ligands.

Binding of gp120 to CD4, the receptor on T-lymphocytes, is thought to initiate the exposure of a protruding cluster of three V3 loops that orient towards the chemokine receptor. In this state the V3 loop consists of two structural elements, including a conserved antiparallel strand at the base of the loop that is joined by a bond between two Cysteine residues and an alpha helical turn-motif at the top of the loop. The anti-parallel strand and alpha helix are linked via a kinked linker chain. Occupation of the V3 positions by one of the amino acids lysine or arginine is an indicator for CXCR4 usage. Generally, CXCR4-viruses possess V3 sequences that have overall positive charge higher than the V3 sequences of CCR5-viruses.

Experiment 1

In order to better understand the role of K and R residues in the V3 loop, V3 loop mutants with all possible RRR-to-KKK triplets were constructed and analyzed for co-receptor usage and ability of HIV-1 to infect T cells. The results are shown in Figure 1. HIV-1 has the general potential to use CXCR4 and/or CCR5 but only the CCR5 pathway can be blocked by medical interventions, so it is important to monitor co-receptor tropism of the most frequent viruses in patients to adapt treatment procedures.

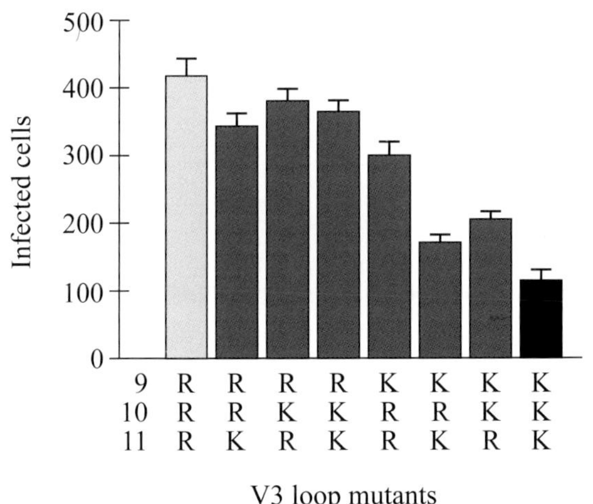

Figure 1 Infection rates of RRR-to-KKK V3 loop mutants

Question 5

The disulfide bond important to maintaining V3 loop stability is most likely to be disrupted by:

- **A.** urea.
- **B.** changing pH.
- **C.** mercaptoethanol.
- **D.** organic solvents.

Question 6

Which of the following amino acids is most important in linking the alpha helix and the anti-parallel sheet of the V3 loop?

- **A.** Lysine
- **B.** Aspartic Acid
- **C.** Proline
- **D.** Glutamic Acid

Question 7

A separate study on the structure of CCR5 found that a metal enzyme co-factor was required to allow for efficient folding of the protein. Which of the following co-factors is LEAST likely to be involved?

- **A.** Magnesium
- **B.** Tin
- **C.** Manganese
- **D.** Zinc

Question 8

A synonymous mutation in which arginine of the V3 loop (N Terminus – RRR – C Terminus) is most likely to decrease viral infectivity?

- **A.** A synonymous mutation in the arginine at the N terminus
- **B.** A synonymous mutation in the arginine at the C terminus
- **C.** A synonymous mutation in the middle arginine between the N and C termini
- **D.** A synonymous mutation in any of the residues has an equivalent effect

Passage 3 (Questions 9-12)

The protein Tau has been shown to participate in the microtubule stabilization and organization system which regulates cellular morphogenesis, cytoskeleton functionality and axonal transport. Alternative splicing gives rise to six isoforms expressed from the same gene in the central nervous system. Tau is a highly soluble protein devoid of any well-defined secondary or tertiary structure and contains a large number of serine and threonine phosphorylation sites.

The aggregation and hyperphosphorylation of Tau have been implicated to have a particular role in neurodegenerative processes. A precise knowledge of the particular molecular events involving Tau protein in Alzheimer's disease remains elusive. The interaction of Tau protein with DNA in neuronal and non-neuronal cells has been repeatedly reported. Although this protein is mainly found in the cytosol of neuronal cells, it has also been localized within the nucleus of neuronal and non-neuronal cells.

Tau-DNA interaction *in vitro* was studied by flowing Tau solutions on a DNA activated sensor surface assembled on a surface plasmon resonance instrument (Figure 1). This technique monitors macromolecular interactions taking place at the interface between a solid (usually gold) surface and a buffered solution. A monochromatic laser radiation (632.8 nm) from a He-Ne laser is then directed upon the interface, under total reflection conditions. Interaction between the immobilized molecules and those flowing through the cell produces changes in the interface refraction index, which, in turn, provokes changes in the light reflected intensity, therefore supplying a physical signal to follow the interaction in real time. The reflectance-increase observed after injecting the Tau solution denotes the doubled-stranded DNA-binding of the unphosphorylated form of Tau, purified from expression in *E.coli*.

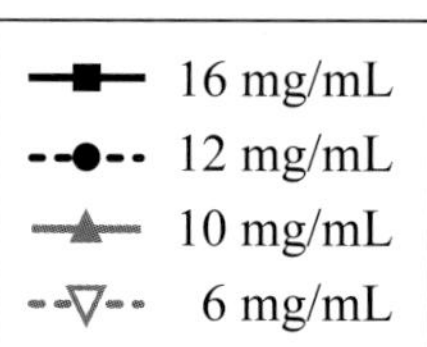

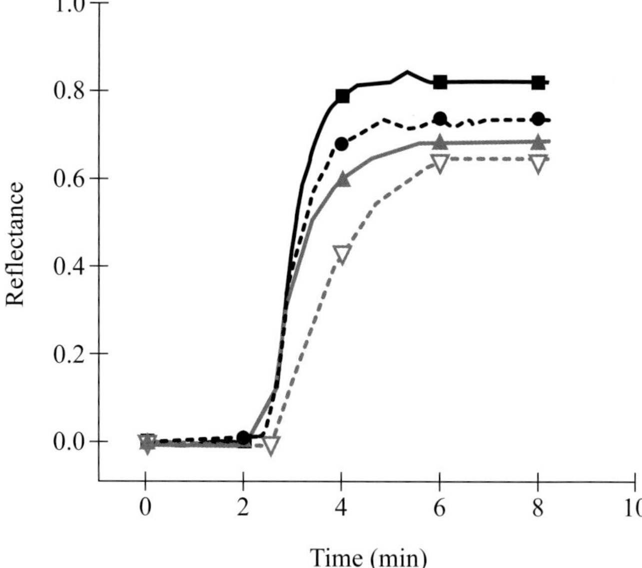

Figure 1 Reflectance time-course after flowing Tau protein solutions on DNA activated sensor surface at various concentrations

This passage was adapted from "Thermodynamics of the Interaction between Alzheimer's Disease Related Tau Protein and DNA." Camero S, Benitez M, Cuadros R, Hernandez F, Avila J, et al. *PLoS ONE*. 2014. 9(8) doi:10.1371/journal.pone.0104690 for use under the terms of the Creative Commons CC BY 4.0 license (https://creativecommons.org/licenses/by/4.0/legalcode).

Question 9

Aggregation of the protein Tau results in the formation of neurofibrillary tangles, a primary marker of Alzheimer's disease. The Tau proteins most likely aggregate as the result of:

- O **A.** protein misfolding and subsequent exposure of polar side chains at the protein's surface.
- O **B.** protein misfolding and subsequent exposure of non-polar side chains at the protein's surface.
- O **C.** increased phosphorylation of Tau.
- O **D.** decreased phosphorylation of Tau.

Question 10

The DNA-activated sensor surface studies allowed researchers to quantify DNA binding interactions between Tau and DNA. Which of the following components of DNA would be most likely to directly bind Tau?

- O **A.** Nitrogenous base
- O **B.** Nitrogenous base pair
- O **C.** Ribose sugar
- O **D.** Phosphodiester backbone

Question 11

A group of researchers develop a treatment strategy to reduce the frequency of neurodegenerative disease. Which of the following strategies would NOT effectively prevent Tau-associated neurodegeneration in humans?

- O **A.** Inhibition of kinases that are responsible for hyperphosphorylation
- O **B.** Activation of Tau-specific phosphatases
- O **C.** Targeted silencing of mRNA transcripts coding for Tau in neuronal cell
- O **D.** Silencing of mRNA transcription of the gene coding for Tau

Question 12

Tau most likely enters the nucleus from the cytosol by:

- O **A.** translation by ribosomes located within the nucleus.
- O **B.** translation by ribosomes located on the membrane of the nucleus.
- O **C.** transport through nuclear pores.
- O **D.** membrane fusion between the nuclear membrane and transport vesicles containing Tau.

Questions 13 through 16 do not refer to a passage and are independent of each other.

Question 13

A researcher wishes to create a transgenic bacterium that will produce a protein of interest that is extremely difficult to isolate using traditional methods. They decide to alter certain genes in non-functional domains to decrease solubility. Which substitution would require the fewest substitutions to achieve the desired affect?

- O **A.** Asp to Ala
- O **B.** Gln to Gly
- O **C.** Ala to Met
- O **D.** Glu to Phe

Question 14

Protein analysis determines that α-helices in a patient's G protein-coupled receptors lack kinks necessary for proper function. A mutation at which amino acid residue is most likely responsible for this error?

- O **A.** V
- O **B.** C
- O **C.** F
- O **D.** P

Question 15

Many amino acids beyond the 20 commonly observed in the human genetic code exist. Which of the following amino acids is likely to have a pI less than 7?

○ **A.**

H
H3C
N
CO2H
O
NH2

○ **B.**

HOOC
COOH
CO2H
NH2

○ **C.**

CH3
+NH
H2N
N
H
CO2H
NH2

○ **D.**

OH
H2N
CO2H
NH2

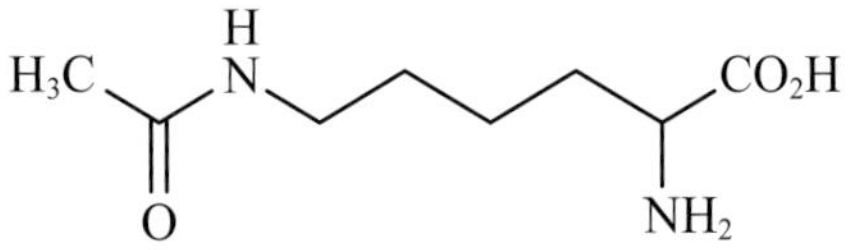

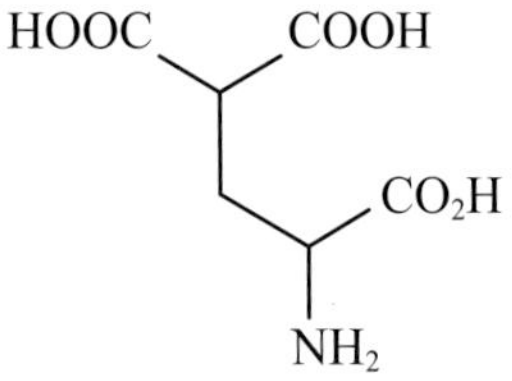

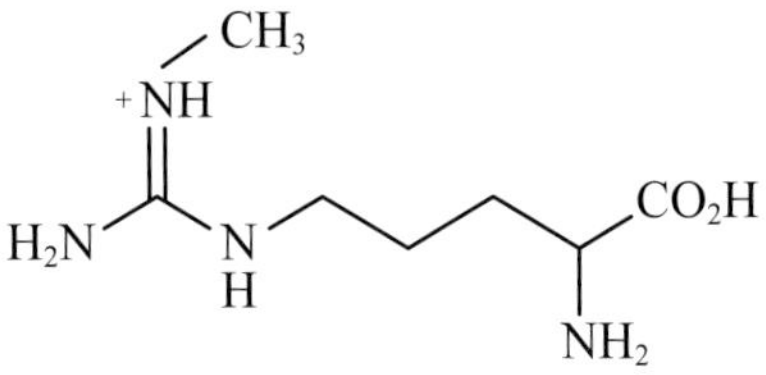

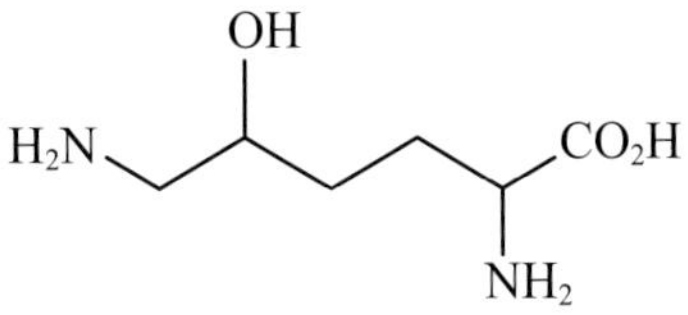

Question 16

A digestive zymogen contains the follow amino acid sequence:

GWRESYNVT

Activation of this zymogen occurs when a peptide bond in this sequence is cleaved at the C-terminus of a basic amino acid residue. Where will this cleavage occur?

○ **A.** Between W and R

○ **B.** Between R and E

○ **C.** Between Y and N

○ **D.** Between N and V

Passage 4 (Questions 17-20)

Excitotoxicity contributes to a wide range of neurological disorders, such as stroke. Pharmacological inhibition of NMDA receptor (NMDAR) ameliorates excitotoxicity-mediated neuronal death and protects the brain after cerebral ischemia. Excitotoxicity takes place primarily as the result of L-glutamate binding to NMDAR. Since glutamate is the major excitatory transmitter in the brain, generalized inhibition of a glutamate receptor subtype like the NMDAR causes side effects that clearly limit the potential for clinical applications.

It is believed that chemical molecules with a relatively fast off rate, and which only transiently block NMDA receptors, promise to be potential drug candidates for excitotoxicity-evoked brain damage. Previous studies showed that 2-(2-benzofuranyl)-2-imidazoline (2-BFI), an imidazoline receptor ligand, dose-dependently protects rodent brains from cerebral ischemia injury (Figure 1). However, the mechanism of action was largely unknown.

In this study, it was found that 2-BFI transiently and reversibly inhibits NMDA in a dose-dependent manner in cultured rat cortical neurons (Figure 2). 2-BFI also transiently and reversibly blocked NMDA receptor-mediated calcium entry to cultured neurons and provided long-term neuroprotection against NMDA toxicity *in vitro*. Collectively, these studies demonstrated a potential mechanism of 2-BFI-mediated neuroprotection and indicated that 2-BFI is an excellent candidate for repositioning as a drug for stroke treatment.

Inhibition fraction
1.0
0.8
0.6
0.4
0.2
0.0
IC50 = 124.33 ± 13.11 μM
k = 1.2 ± 0.1
10
100
1000
[2-BFI] (μM)

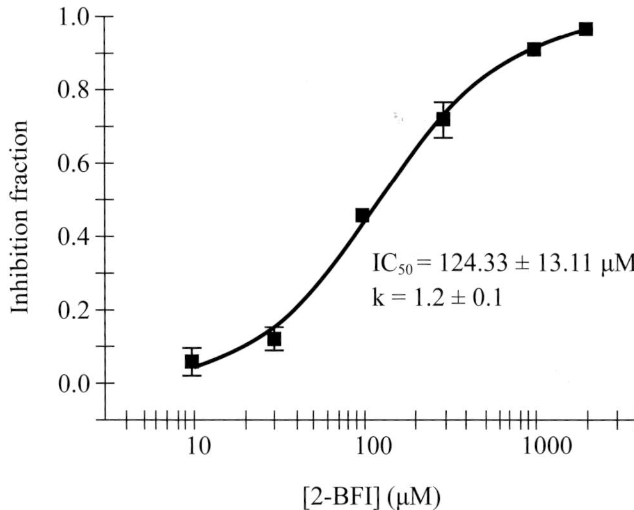

Figure 1 2-BFI concentration-response relationship for inhibition of NMDA currents

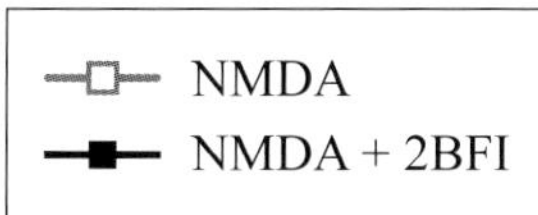

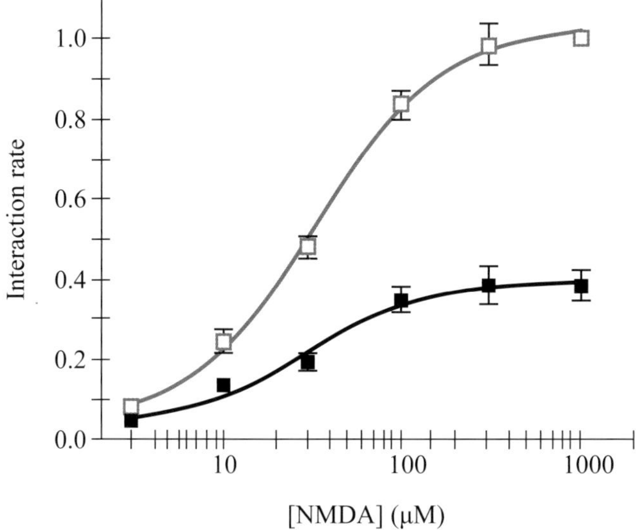

Figure 2 Interaction rate of NMDA receptor opening with and without inhibition by 2-BFI.

Question 17

In a follow-up experiment, investigators attempted to replicate the in vitro experimental conditions to confirm the study results. The findings showed no measurable interaction at the NMDA receptor. Which of the following likely occurred in their experimental set up?

- O **A.** They did not add sufficient concentrations of 2-BFI.
- O **B.** They added too much D-glutamate.
- O **C.** They added less L-glutamate than in the original study.
- O **D.** They added too much L-glutamate.

Question 18

2-BFI is LEAST likely to be:

- O **A.** a mixed inhibitor.
- O **B.** a non-competitive inhibitor.
- O **C.** a covalent modifier.
- O **D.** an uncompetitive inhibitor.

Question 19

Based on data provided in Figure 2, investigators likely concluded that this inhibition could have been all of the following types EXCEPT:

- O **A.** competitive inhibition.
- O **B.** non-competitive inhibition.
- O **C.** uncompetitive inhibition.
- O **D.** mixed inhibition.

Question 20

Nimodipine, a calcium channel blocker, is frequently used to prevent complications of hemorrhagic stroke. This drug binds to the L-type voltage gated calcium channel. Which of the following is likely NOT true about nimodipine?

- O **A.** Nimodipine competitively binds and blocks the calcium binding site.
- O **B.** Nimodipine binds noncompetitively to a structural protein.
- O **C.** Nimodipine blocks net entry of positive charge into the cell where the channel is located.
- O **D.** Nimodipine binds allosterically to a globular protein.

Passage 5 (Questions 21-25)

Thromboembolic (TE) diseases are among the principal causes of mortality in the world and occur when blood clots become lodged in vessels, leading to reductions in blood flow to target tissues. Stroke, heart attacks, and muscle death can all occur as a result of TE disease.

The central role of the serine protease thrombin in thrombosis and hemostasis makes it an attractive target for antithrombotic therapy, which may prevent the formation of the clots that lead to TE. Thrombin catalyzes the conversion of soluble fibrinogen to insoluble fibrin in the clotting cascade (Figure 1).

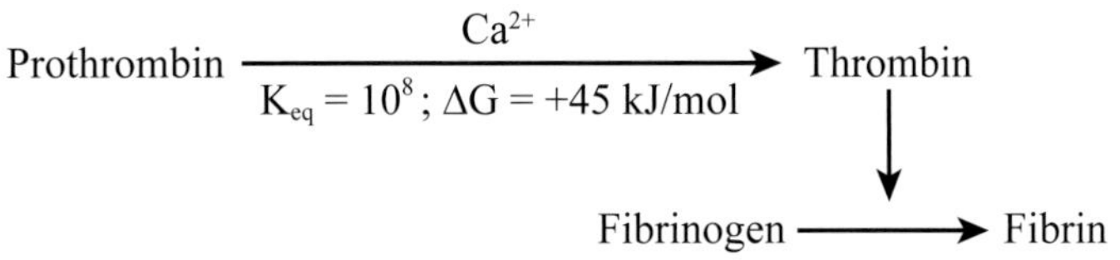

$$\text{Prothrombin} \xrightarrow[K_{eq} = 10^8;\ \Delta G = +45 \text{ kJ/mol}]{Ca^{2+}} \text{Thrombin}$$

$$\text{Fibrinogen} \longrightarrow \text{Fibrin} \quad (\text{Thrombin} \downarrow)$$

Figure 1 The role of thrombin in the conversion of fibrinogen to fibrin

Oral thrombin inhibitors (TI) could provide a new standard of care in anticoagulation therapy. Molecular modeling is a powerful tool to investigate bioactive compounds and their structure-activity relationship (SAR) with the main purpose of identifying the molecular features that contribute to a high bioactivity. Compound 57, a potential TI that bound to the S1, S2, and S3 subsites of the fibrinogen binding site in thrombin, is shown in Figure 2. The $\Delta G°$ of compound 57 binding to thrombin was found to be –5.52 kJ/mol.

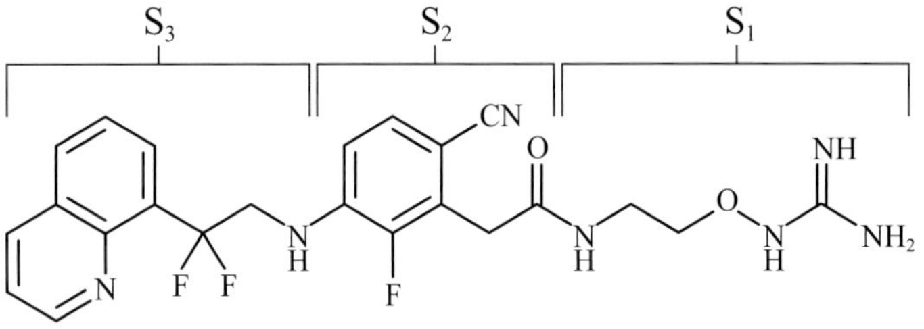

S_3 S_2 S_1

CN O NH NH₂ N H F F F O

Figure 2 Molecular structure of compound 57

Molecular modeling also predicts hydration of TIs in the S1, S2, and S3 sites. Water molecules in S1 often formed hydrogen bonding networks between the ligands and the enzyme. No water molecules were identified in S2, and most water molecules found in S3 had occasional interactions with polar groups forming hydrogen bonds but were relatively free to diffuse out of the enzyme.

This passage was adapted from "Study of the Differential Activity of Thrombin Inhibitors Using Docking, QSAR, Molecular Dynamics, and MM-GBSA." Mena-Ulecia K, Tiznado W, and Caballero J. *PLoS ONE*. 2015. 10(11) doi:10.1371/journal.pone.0142774 for use under the terms of the Creative Commons CC BY 4.0 license (http://creativecommons.org/licenses/by/4.0/legalcode).

Question 21

In addition to its role in blood clotting, thrombin may also have intracellular functions. Considering the molecular structure of compound 57, what is the most likely mechanism for its entry into the cell?

- **A.** Active transport
- **B.** Receptor mediated endocytosis
- **C.** Passive diffusion through the plasma membrane
- **D.** Transport through an ion channel

Question 22

The S1 binding portion of compound 57 closely resembles which amino acid?

- **A.** R
- **B.** K
- **C.** G
- **D.** A

Question 23

Which of the following best describes the role of calcium in the activation of prothrombin to thrombin?

- **A.** Reactant
- **B.** Product
- **C.** Cofactor
- **D.** Prosthetic group

Question 24

In contrast to the reaction catalyzed by thrombin, the K_{eq} of the uncatalyzed reaction converting prothrombin to thrombin is:

- **A.** 10^2.
- **B.** 10^6.
- **C.** 10^8.
- **D.** 10^{12}.

Question 25

The equilibrium constant of the reaction occurring between compound 57 and thrombin at 25°C is approximately:

- **A.** 10.
- **B.** 100.
- **C.** 1,000.
- **D.** 10,000.

Questions 26 through 29 do not refer to a passage and are independent of each other.

Question 26

A peptide sequence is shown below:

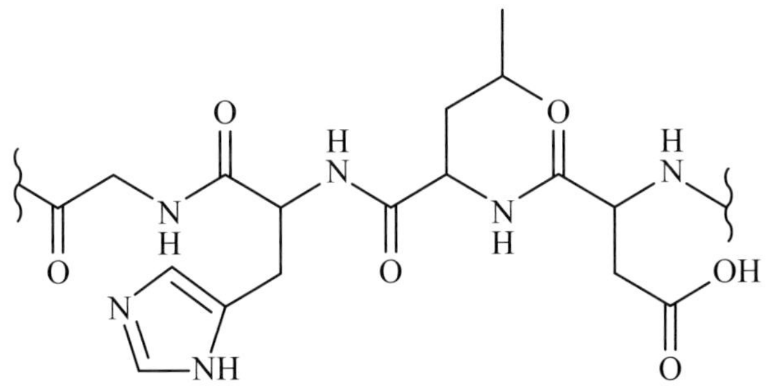

Which of the following correctly codes for this sequence?

- O **A.** DLHG
- O **B.** GHLD
- O **C.** GHIQ
- O **D.** QIHG

Question 27

A chemical equation depicting an esterification is shown below:

$$CH_3COOH + CH_3CH_2OH \xrightarrow{\text{conc } H_2SO_4} CH_3COOH_2CH_3 + H_2O$$

Enzymes are required for esterification reactions to proceed under physiological conditions. Which of the following active sites is LEAST able to catalyze the reaction?

- O **A.** VDSTEC
- O **B.** TYLDID
- O **C.** EVAGLI
- O **D.** LITYGA

Question 28

The amino acid tyrosine can best be described as:

- O **A.** very weakly acidic because it is resonance stabilized at a benzyl position.
- O **B.** neutral because all alcohols have a pK_a approximately equivalent to water.
- O **C.** neutral because the valence shells of each atom of the R-group are filled.
- O **D.** very weakly basic because the aromatic ring can act as an electron donor.

Question 29

The uncommon amino acid shown below, which is not present in the human genetic code, is most likely to have similar chemical properties to which of the following amino acids?

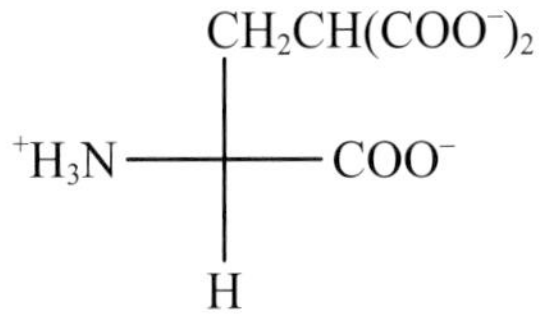

$CH_2CH(COO^-)_2$

^+H_3N—C—COO^-

H

- O **A.** Glu
- O **B.** Gly
- O **C.** Gln
- O **D.** Thr

Passage 6 (Questions 30-33)

The human pathogen *Helicobacter pylori* thrives in the mucous layer covering the gastric epithelium. The pathogen is a common cause of peptic ulcers and gastritis, or inflammation of the stomach lining. Central to the acid adaptation of *H. pylori* is the urease system which is essential for maintaining pH near neutrality when the bacteria are exposed to low pH. The cytoplasmic urease enzyme is a nickel-containing dodecameric heterodimer, which cleaves urea to ammonia and carbon dioxide. Cytoplasmic urease activity is controlled by the inner membrane pH-gated channel UreI, which regulates the access of the substrate to the bacterial cell in response to an acidic pH.

The acidic pH triggers the autophosphorylation of the histidine kinase ArsS and the subsequent phosphorylation of its cognate response regulator ArsR. Phosphorylated ArsR then acts both as an activator and repressor of pH-responsive genes.

Experiment 1

ArsS contains seven histidine residues (H35, H44, H90, H93, H94, H118, H126) in the periplasmic domain. ArsS sensor activity requires the protonation of amino acids to trigger a conformational change of the protein stimulating its histidine kinase activity. The gene hp0119 encodes an *H. pylori*-specific protein of unknown function. Phosphorylated ArsR binds to its promoter region and initiates transcription. This experiment analyzed the transcription of the gene in mutant strains with glutamine substitutions for all seven ArsS histidine residues (H_7Q) or for H94 (H94Q) specifically (Figure 1).

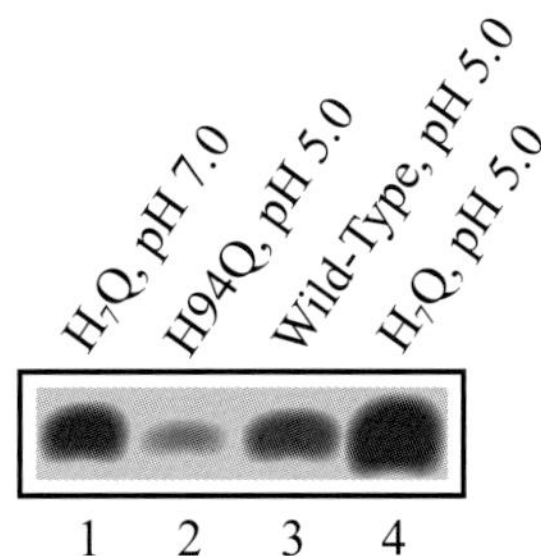

Figure 1 Analysis of transcription of the acid-responsive gene hp0119 in three *H. pylori* strains at various pH values

Experiment 2

Differential expression of the pH-responsive gene hp1432 was observed when *H. pylori* is shifted from neutral pH to pH 5.0 in *H. pylori* strains expressing ArsS proteins with individual histidine to glutamine mutations in the periplasmic domain (Figure 2).

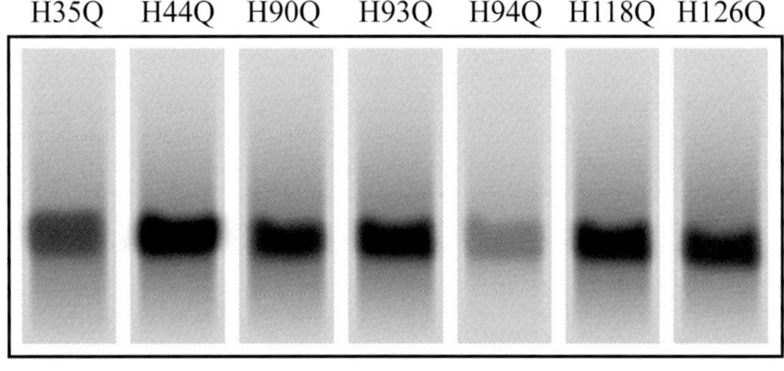

Figure 2 Analysis of transcription of the acid-responsive gene hp1432 in *H. pylori* mutant strains

Experiment 3

This experiment tested for the transcription of hp0119 in the *H. pylori* strains from the previous experiment (Figure 3).

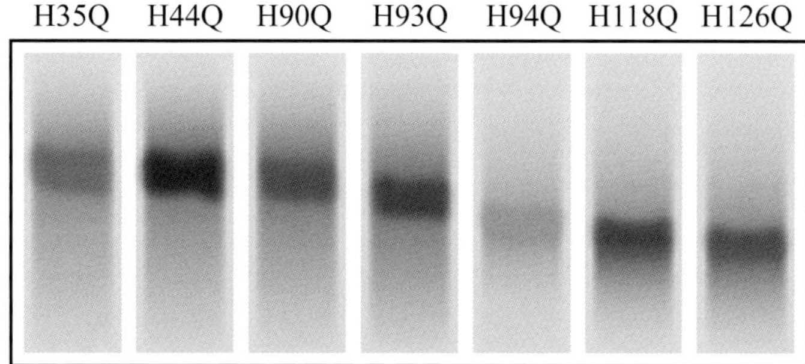

Figure 3 Analysis of transcription of the acid-responsive gene hp0119 in *H. pylori* mutant strains

Question 30

Which of the following reflects the structure of the H94 histidine residue of ArsS at pH 5.0?

- **A.** A nitrogen atom in the heterocyclic ring is bound to a hydrogen atom.
- **B.** Two nitrogen atoms in the heterocyclic ring are bound to hydrogen atoms.
- **C.** An oxygen atom in the heterocyclic ring is bound to a hydrogen atom.
- **D.** The amine group connected to the heterocyclic ring is bound to three hydrogen atoms.

Next ▶

Question 31

Based on the data in the passage, the amino acid residue LEAST likely to bring about the autophosphorylation of ArsS as a result of a change in pH is given by the code:

- O **A.** Lys.
- O **B.** Arg.
- O **C.** Pro.
- O **D.** His.

Question 32

Urea is a product of protein degradation produced by liver hepatocytes. The information in the passage most directly suggests that urea is:

- O **A.** hydrophobic, because it is broken down by urease to carbon dioxide, which is nonpolar.
- O **B.** hydrophobic, because it is found in the cytoplasm only when bound to the protein urease.
- O **C.** hydrophilic, because it contains a carboxylic acid group, which is converted by urease.
- O **D.** hydrophilic, because it is transported by the protein UreI, which is regulated by pH.

Question 33

Based on the data in the passage, which experiment may lend support to the finding that amino acid residues other than histidine contribute to the tertiary structural changes observed at pH 5.0?

- O **A.** Experiment 1
- O **B.** Experiment 2
- O **C.** Experiment 3
- O **D.** None of the experiments indicate this point.

Passage 7 (Questions 34-37)

The human adult hemoglobin (HbA) is a tetrameric protein containing two α- and two β-chains, each associated with a heme molecule. A defect in the production of one of the globin chains in the red blood cell (RBC) precursors results in various degrees of anemia and thalassemia syndromes, such as α-thalassemia in the case of reduced α-globin production. It is now accepted that the α and β subunits do not associate spontaneously to form $\alpha 2\beta 2$ Hb. The scheme of Hb biosynthesis is the following: first, alpha hemoglobin stabilizing protein (AHSP) binds to the α-globin (without the heme molecule) or α-Hb (with heme), maintaining it in a soluble state. Second, AHSP is replaced by β-hemoglobin chains (β-Hb) to form an αβ dimer, and tetramers in a further step. Unlike the free β-Hb, which are soluble and form homologous tetramers, freshly synthesized α-Hb chains are unstable molecules.

In human α-thalassemia, the reduced availability of α-globin chains may be due to several molecular mechanisms. In a study, it has been reported that two elongated α-Hb variants, Hb Constant Spring and Pakse associated with an α-thalassemia phenotype, led to an impaired binding to AHSP. The mutated mRNA α-globin of this variant was present at normal levels in the reticulocytes but no abnormal chains were detected.

AHSP specifically recognizes the G and H helices of α-Hb, a region which also binds to the β-Hb subunit. The region 95–137 of α-Hb, composed by G and H helices, plays a predominant role in the interaction between α-Hb and AHSP. In addition, the region 103–124 allows together the binding to AHSP and to β-Hb. Some amino acids interact with AHSP, others only with β-Hb within an $\alpha 1\beta 1$ dimer and three (103, 117, 119) are involved in both contacts.

Question 34

Researchers hypothesized that a deletion of a leucine in the region 95-137 of α-Hb would inhibit the binding of AHSP. Which finding would best support this hypothesis?

- O **A.** AHSP contains a hydrophilic aspartate in the region that binds α-Hb.
- O **B.** AHSP contains a hydrophobic valine in the region that binds α-Hb.
- O **C.** The deletion of leucine prevents α-Hb from fitting in the allosteric site of AHSP.
- O **D.** The substitution of valine for leucine does not change the K_D.

Question 35

The G and H helices of α-Hb are primarily stabilized by:

- O **A.** cystine bonds.
- O **B.** hydrogen bonding.
- O **C.** hydrophobic interactions.
- O **D.** ion pairs.

TEST 1B

Question 36

Scientists conducted a study to test if AHSP exhibited typical Michaelis-Menten kinetics. Which experimental manipulation would serve as the best indicator of AHSP's activity profile?

- **A.** Increasing the concentration of AHSP and monitoring α-Hb usage.
- **B.** Increasing the concentration of β-Hb and monitoring αβ dimer formation.
- **C.** Increasing the concentration of α-Hb and monitoring αβ dimer formation.
- **D.** Increasing the concentration of AHSP and monitoring β-Hb usage.

Question 37

Which property of α-Hb is a likely reason that it spontaneously denatures when not bound to AHSP?

- **A.** The protein lacks a hydrophobic core.
- **B.** AHSP is required for essential hydrogen bond formation of α1β1.
- **C.** The solvation layer surrounding the protein is small.
- **D.** AHSP is required for essential ion pair formation in the tertiary α2β2.

Passage 8 (Questions 38-42)

In 2012, there were 1.82 million new cases and 1.56 million deaths due to lung cancer. Globally, lung cancer is the leading cancer in terms of incidence and mortality. Lung cancer can be divided into two major histopathological groups: non-small-cell lung cancer (NSCLC) and small-cell lung cancer (SCLC). NSCLC (80% of lung cancers) has a very limited response rate to current chemotherapeutic agents with a 2-year survival rate of between 10% and 16%. The present study examines the use of a customized biological peptide (CB1a) as a prospective therapy for lung cancer.

In nature there are many cationic, lytic peptides. Cecropin is a cationic, lytic peptide found in silkworms. Among the cecropin family, cecropin B (CB) is known to have the highest level of antimicrobial activity and, previous studies have shown that CB can lyse not only bacteria, but also cancer cells. A custom peptide, CB1a, has been derived from CB in an attempt at better selectivity and efficacy. CB1a has three repeats of the terminal ten amino acids found at the N-terminus of CB, which are: Lys-Trp-Lys-Val-Phe-Lys-Lys-Ile-Glu-Lys. The second and third repeats are linked by a hinge bridge motif (Ala-Gly-Pro or AGP).

The IC_{50} is the concentration of CB1a that produces a 50% cell survival rate. The IC_{50} of CB1a for normal lung cells (NLC), SCLC, and NSCLC are recorded in Table 1. CB1a was also compared to docetaxel, a currently approved treatment for lung cancer with a severe side effect profile, including extreme weight loss.

Table 1 IC_{50} of CB1a shown for three different lung cell lines

	NLC			SCL	NSCLC			
Cell line	WI-38	MRC-5	HEL-299	NCI-H146	A549	NCI-H209	NCI-H460	NCI-H520
IC_{50}	> 300	84	158	4	29	5	25	5

This passage was adapted from "Inhibition Effect of a Custom Peptide on Lung Tumors." Huang C-Y, Huang H-Y, Forrest MD, Pan Y-R, Wu W-J, et al. *PLoS ONE*. 2014 9(10): e109174. *doi:10.1371/journal.pone.0109174* for use under the terms of the Creative Commons CC BY 4.0 license (http://creativecommons.org/licenses/by/4.0/legalcode).

Question 38

If arginine were joined to the N-terminal lysine of CB, the reaction would result in the formation of which functional group?

- **A.** Amine
- **B.** Amide
- **C.** Carbonyl
- **D.** Carboxylic acid

Next ▶

Question 39

The hinge bridge amino acids would likely form which secondary structure?

- O **A.** Alpha helix
- O **B.** Beta turn
- O **C.** Beta sheet
- O **D.** Beta conformation

Question 40

CB1a binds to an enzyme that undergoes conformational changes in lung cells. Based on the data in Table 1, which of the following rankings most likely corresponds to the K_m of the enzyme in the respective cell types?

- O **A.** NLC>NSCLC>SCLC
- O **B.** NLC>SCLC>NSCLC
- O **C.** SCLC>NSCLC>NLC
- O **D.** SCLC>NLC>NSCLC

Question 41

Based on the amino acid sequence, which of the following interactions does NOT stabilize the tertiary structure of the N-terminus of CB1a?

- O **A.** Electrostatic interactions
- O **B.** Van der Waals forces
- O **C.** Disulfide bridges
- O **D.** Hydrophobic bonding

Question 42

The data presented below show tumor weight after treatment with saline, CB1a, or Docetaxel. Based on the passage and figure, which of the following is true of CB1a?

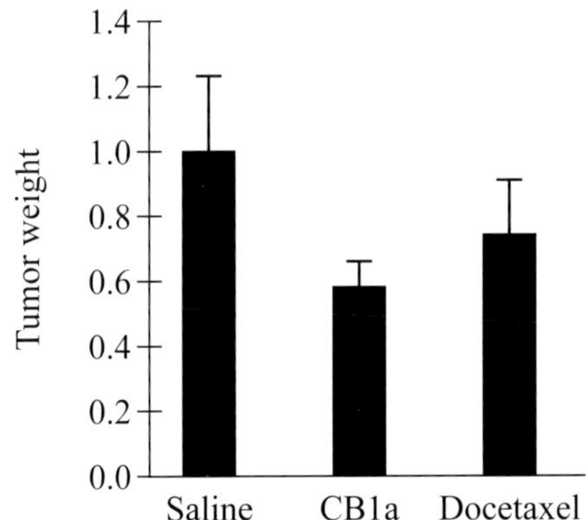

- O **A.** CB1a kills NLC more effectively than docetaxel.
- O **B.** CB1a peptide denatures at temperatures found inside the human body.
- O **C.** CB1a binds more selectively to lung cancer cells than docetaxel.
- O **D.** CB1a binds SCLC more selectively than NSCLC.

Questions 43 through 46 do not refer to a passage and are independent of each other.

Question 43

Individuals with a rare deficiency in small, hydrophobic amino acids are enrolled in a clinical trial to test the effects of amino acid supplementation. People who were administered which of the following likely served as experimental controls?

- O **A.** D-Ala
- O **B.** L-Ala
- O **C.** D-Gly
- O **D.** L-Gly

Question 44

In amyloidosis conditions, protein plaques are formed outside of cells consisting of a dense, degradation resistant, insoluble fibers. Which would you not expect to see?

- O **A.** O-linked glycosylation
- O **B.** Covalent R group modification such as formylation
- O **C.** Blocked amino terminus
- O **D.** Racemization

Question 45

In the classical pathway of the complement cascade, a protein called C1q has globular domains which non-permanently bind to hinge regions of IgM antibodies which are only exposed after these antibodies have multivalently bound to a target. These hinge regions are rich in Cysteine and Proline. What type of chemical interactions would be most likely to dominate these interactions?

I. Hydrogen bonding
II. Ionic interactions
III. Disulfide bonds

- O **A.** I and II
- O **B.** I and III
- O **C.** II and III
- O **D.** III only

Question 46

Kartagener syndrome is a rare genetic disorder that is characterized by recurrent respiratory infections and male infertility. The mechanism of infertility is immobility of sperm. A mutation in which of the following proteins is likely to cause Kartagener syndrome?

- O **A.** Dynein, a component of cilia
- O **B.** Adenosine deaminase, an enzyme of the immune system
- O **C.** SRY protein, a protein encoded on the Y chromosome responsible for determining sex
- O **D.** Lysozyme, an enzyme capable of destroying bacterial cell walls

Passage 9 (Questions 47-51)

Classical homocystinuria is an autosomal recessive disease that is caused by a mutation in the gene that codes for cystathionine beta synthase. Cystathionine beta synthase (CBS) is the rate-limiting enzyme responsible for the de novo synthesis of cysteine. Patients with CBS deficiency have greatly elevated plasma total homocysteine (tHcy), decreased levels of plasma total cysteine (tCys), and often a marfanoid appearance characterized by thinness and low body-mass index (BMI). CBS deficiency is also known to increase the risk of intellectual disabilities and blood clots.

Researchers characterized the growth and body mass characteristics of CBS deficient TgI278T Cbs$^{-/-}$ mice and show that these animals have significantly decreased fat mass and tCys compared to heterozygous sibling mice, as shown in Figure 1. The decrease in fat mass is accompanied by a 34% decrease in liver glutathione (GSH) along with a significant decrease in liver mRNA and protein for the critical enzyme Stearoyl CoA desaturase-1 (Scd-1). Because plasma tCys has been positively associated with fat mass in humans, researchers tested the hypothesis that decreased tCys in TgI278T Cbs$^{-/-}$ mice was the cause of the lean phenotype by placing the animals on water supplemented with N-acetyl cysteine (NAC) from birth to 240 days of age. Although NAC treatment in TgI278T Cbs$^{-/-}$ mice caused significant increase in serum tCys and liver GSH, there was no increase in body fat content or in liver Scd-1 levels.

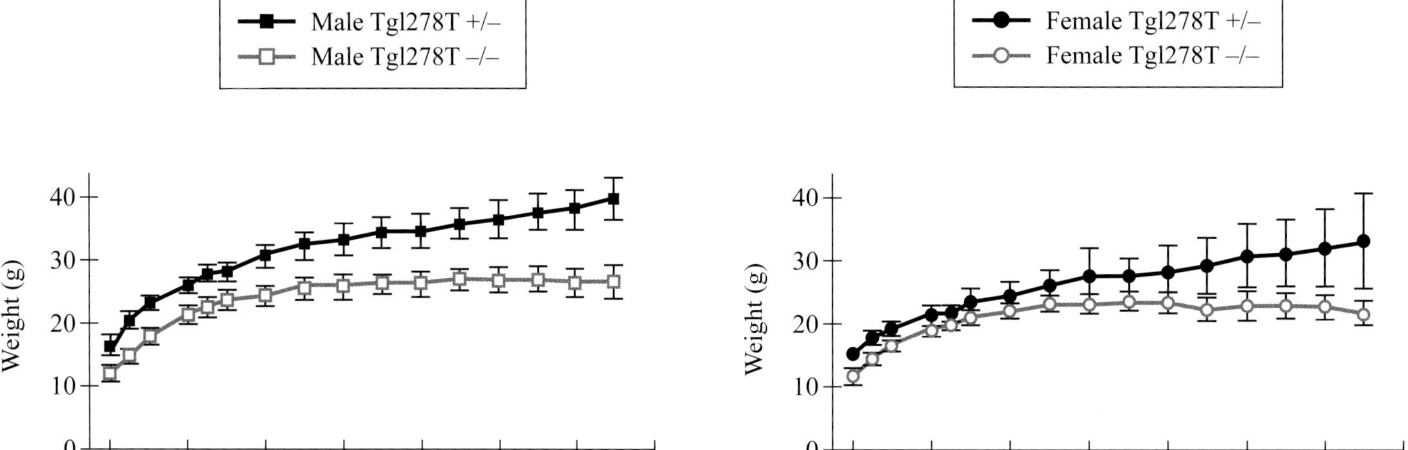

Figure 1 Comparison of the weight of CBS deficient TgI278T Cbs$^{-/-}$ mice with age and gender matched control TgI278T Cbs$^{+/-}$ mice

Question 47

Homocysteine is likely synthesized from which amino acid?

- O **A.** H
- O **B.** I
- O **C.** M
- O **D.** V

Question 48

Based on information in the passage, Stearoyl CoA desaturase is most likely involved in:

H
|
$^{+}H_3N$ — C — COO^-
|
CH_2 — CH_2 — SH

- O **A.** glycogenolysis.
- O **B.** fatty acid metabolism.
- O **C.** peptide synthesis.
- O **D.** transcription.

Question 49

NAC is used to treat a variety of diseases including cystic fibrosis and psychiatric disorders and the biological effects are assumed to be through NAC's antioxidant properties. How can NAC act as an antioxidant?

- **A.** The thiol group can be oxidized, thus preventing oxidative damage to the cell.
- **B.** The disulfide group can be oxidized, thus preventing oxidative damage to the cell.
- **C.** The thiol group can be reduced, thus preventing oxidative damage to the cell.
- **D.** The disulfide group can be reduced, thus preventing oxidative damage to the cell.

Question 50

Which of the following conclusions can be drawn from Figure 1?

- **A.** The effect of genotype on weight is more significant as mice age.
- **B.** TgI278T $Cbs^{+/-}$ mice are at greater risk for heart disease.
- **C.** Genotype has a more significant effect on male mice than female mice.
- **D.** TgI278T $Cbs^{+/-}$ mice are at greater risk for oxidative stress.

Question 51

A diet rich in pyridoxine and folic acid has been an effective treatment for people with homocystinuria. These molecules are important cofactors for metabolic enzymes. Pyridoxine and folic acid are most likely:

- **A.** minerals.
- **B.** fat soluble vitamins.
- **C.** water soluble vitamins.
- **D.** macronutrients.

Passage 10 (Questions 52-56)

Hydroxylation of Phe to Tyr is the committed step in Phe catabolism and therefore requires strict regulation to ensure homeostasis of the essential amino acid Phe. Dysfunction of phenylalanine hydroxylase (PAH) causes phenylketonuria (PKU), a well-examined genetic disease leading to mental retardation upon accumulation of Phe. Recent studies found immune activation and inflammation to be associated with an increase in the ratio of Phe to Tyr in blood of patients suffering from trauma, sepsis, carcinoma, and infection, suggesting an inhibition of PAH. As immune activation of macrophages is paralleled by the release of toxic reactive oxygen species (ROS) and neopterin, oxidative stress is discussed as chemical background for PAH deactivation consistent with studies correlating PKU with oxidative stress.

The catalytic mechanism of PAH involves the reduction from ferric (III) to ferrous (II) form by the cofactor BH_4. Ferrous iron is subsequently oxidized by molecular oxygen to a Fe(IV)O intermediate, which in turn hydroxylates Phe to Tyr. Eukaryotic PAH is found as a homotetramer, where each subunit contains three distinct domains: an N-terminal autoregulatory domain (residues 1–142), the catalytic domain (residues 143–410) and a tetramerization domain stabilizing the quaternary structure (residues 411–452). BH_4 acts as an allosteric regulator of PAH activity by stabilizing an inactive form, whereas the enzyme is activated by phosphorylation of Ser16 as well as binding of Phe. The positive cooperativity of Phe binding allows for fast responses to increased Phe levels in order to avoid damages to the brain.

The exposed surface area and the volume of the active site of PAH has been determined in its native and oxidized state (Table 1).

Table 1 Surface area and volume of active site of PAH_{nat} and PAH_{ox} (note: SD is the standard deviation)

Average (SD)	PAH_{nat}	PAH_{ox}
Area [$Å^2$]	15.74 (1.16)	9.40 (1.97)
Volume [$Å^3$]	155.87 (35.11)	66.58 (22.73)

Question 52

Scientists discovered two reduced cysteine residues located within the native PAH protein. Is cystine bond formation consistent with the hypothesis that ROS formation may lead to PKU?

- **A.** Yes; oxidation of cysteine residues leads to tertiary structure alteration.
- **B.** Yes; oxidation of cysteine residues stabilizes the secondary structure of PAH_{ox}.
- **C.** No; oxidation of cysteine residues results in the breaking of a cystine bond.
- **D.** No; oxidation of cysteine residues results in stabilization of PAH_{nat}.

Question 53

How many unique tertiary structures can be found in PAH?

- A. 1
- B. 2
- C. 3
- D. 4

Question 54

What will happen to the level of Tyr when high concentrations of BH_4 and Phe are both present?

- A. Increased Tyr concentration
- B. Tyr concentration remains the same
- C. Decreased Tyr concentration
- D. Tyr concentration cannot be determined

Question 55

Which finding would most strongly challenge the hypothesis that ROS formation is the primary cause of an increased Phe to Tyr ratio in patients suffering from trauma?

- A. Patients suffering from trauma show high level of macrophage activity.
- B. Patients suffering from trauma show high concentrations of BH_4.
- C. Patients suffering from trauma show abnormal PAH conformations.
- D. Patients suffering from trauma show negative cooperativity in their PAH enzymes.

Question 56

Iron plays an essential role in the conversion of Phe to Tyr. What is the most accurate description of its function?

- A. Substrate
- B. Cofactor
- C. Allosteric regulator
- D. Coenzyme

Questions 57 through 59 do not refer to a passage and are independent of each other.

Question 57

Hexokinase and glucokinase are independently responsible for the phosphorylation of glucose to glucose-6-phosphate. Glucokinase is found only in the liver and pancreas and hexokinase is found in all other tissues. Compared to hexokinase, glucokinase most likely:

- A. has lower K_m and lower V_{max}.
- B. has lower K_m and higher V_{max}.
- C. has higher K_m and higher V_{max}.
- D. has higher K_m and lower V_{max}.

Question 58

Scientists studying a tetrameric enzyme found that under low substrate concentration there was almost no activity. Upon the addition of substrate, the reaction velocity increased exponentially until a maximum rate was achieved. Why did scientists continue to add substrate after they found little activity?

- A. Some enzymes exhibit delayed reactions that take time to manifest.
- B. Certain enzymes require initial substrate binding in order to function effectively.
- C. The enzyme to substrate ratio was too large to allow for enzyme activity.
- D. Additional substrate was added to displace an inhibitor.

Question 59

Tetrahydrobiopterin is a non-vitamin cofactor involved in hydroxylation reactions. Which of the following is true?

- A. Tetrahydrobiopterin is able to lower the activation energy of hydroxylation reactions.
- B. Tetrahydrobiopterin is necessary but not sufficient for hydroxylation reactions.
- C. Tetrahydrobiopterin is a coenzyme meaning it is covalently bound to an enzyme.
- D. Tetrahydrobiopterin can be used to make high energy molecules like ATP.

STOP. If you finish before time is called, check your work. You may go back to any question in this test.

ANSWERS & EXPLANATIONS for Test 1B can be found on p.188.

Biological Molecules and Enzymes

TEST 1C

Time: 50 minutes
Questions 1–31

DIRECTIONS: Most questions in the Biological and Biochemical Foundations of Living Systems test section are grouped with a descriptive passage. Select the best answer to each question using background knowledge and the given passage. A portion of this test section is comprised of discrete questions, which are independent of any passage and one another. Select the best answer for each discrete question. Indicate your selection by blackening the corresponding oval on your answer document. If you are unsure of the answer, rule out incorrect choices and select from the remaining options. You may access a periodic table found on the last page of this book at any point during this test section.

TEST 1C

Passage 1 (Questions 1-5)

Low extracellular pH (pHe), which is characteristic of many tumors, tends to reduce the uptake of weakly basic drugs, such as doxorubicin, thereby conferring a degree of physiological resistance to chemotherapy. It has been assumed that the effect of intracellular pH (pHi) is symmetrically opposite. Doxorubicin, like other anthracyclines, targets DNA and intercalates between adjacent nucleotide base pairs to stall DNA polymerase during S phase replication. Stalling of the replication fork leads to activation of the DNA damage response and cellular apoptosis.

To understand the importance of pH on the chemotherapeutic activity of doxorubicin, doxorubicin uptake into colon HCT116 cells via the doxorubicin carrier CDR5 was measured using the drug's intrinsic fluorescence under conditions that alter pHi and/or pHe. It was important for the scientists to use colon HCT116 cells, as these have relatively low expression levels of the drug resistance-conferring P-glycoprotein and the proposed doxorubicin pump SLC22A16.

Acutely, doxorubicin influx across the cell-membrane (Figure 1) was correlated directly with the mean fluorescence intensity and with the trans-membrane pH-gradient (ΔpH = pHe - pHi). Once inside cells, doxorubicin bound to nuclear proteins that allowed for slow release of the drug into the nuclear space. Additionally, the scientists noted that the ability of doxorubicin to associate with these nuclear proteins decreased with pHi and could not be overcome by the addition of additional doxorubicin. The efficacy of doxorubicin-induced cell killing was quantified in terms of the dose required to reduce cell proliferation by 50% (EC_{50}). The scientists found that the greatest levels of killing occurred upon modulation of both pHi and pHe.

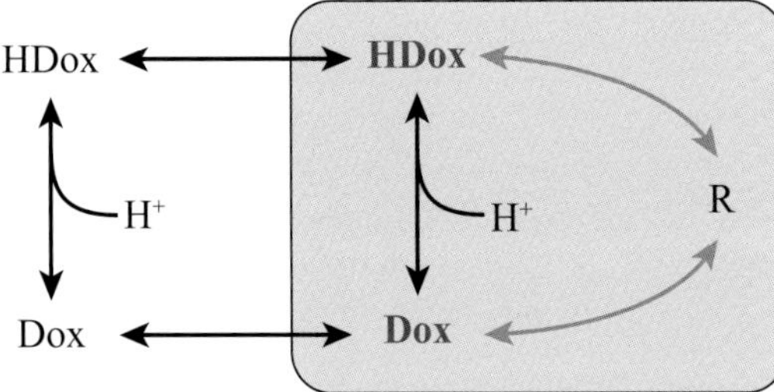

Figure 1 pH-dependent transport of doxorubicin (Dox). R represents the reservoir of doxorubicin stored in sub-nuclear sites

Question 1

According to the experimental data, doxorubicin diffusion across the phospholipid plasma membrane would be maximized under what pH circumstances?

- O **A.** Low extracellular $[H^+]$ and high intracellular $[H^+]$
- O **B.** High extracellular $[H^+]$ and low intracellular $[H^+]$
- O **C.** High extracellular $[H^+]$ and high intracellular $[H^+]$
- O **D.** Low extracellular $[H^+]$ and low intracellular $[H^+]$

Question 2

Carbonic anhydrase inhibitors can markedly alter extracellular pH by inhibiting the conversion of carbon dioxide and water first to carbonic acid and then to hydronium and bicarbonate. What effect would a carbonic anhydrase inhibitor have on doxorubicin uptake into colon cancer HCT116 cells?

- O **A.** The uptake of doxorubicin would decrease.
- O **B.** The uptake of doxorubicin would increase.
- O **C.** The uptake of doxorubicin would remain the same.
- O **D.** The effect on the uptake of doxorubicin cannot be predicted without additional information.

Question 3

The binding of doxorubicin to the nuclear proteins responsible for the slow release of the drug into the nuclear space most likely characterized by what value of K_m?

- O **A.** A high K_m
- O **B.** A low K_m
- O **C.** An intermediate K_m
- O **D.** The K_m value cannot be predicted

Question 4

Based on the passage, at physiological pH doxorubicin is most likely characterized by a:

- O **A.** positive net electric charge.
- O **B.** negative net electric charge.
- O **C.** double negative net electric charge.
- O **D.** neutral net electric charge.

Question 5

Why was it important for the scientists to use HCT116 cells deficient in the proposed doxorubicin pump SLC22A16?

- O **A.** The carrier protein could interact with the nuclear doxorubicin-binding proteins to hamper measurements of the EC_{50}.
- O **B.** SLC22A16 does not requires ATP to move doxorubicin, which would limit the usefulness of the HCT116 cells.
- O **C.** SLC22A16 could also transport hydrogen ions, diminishing the pH gradient.
- O **D.** The intracellular fluorescence of doxorubicin could be directly correlated with its ability to cross the plasma membrane.

Passage 2 (Questions 6-9)

The methionine salvage pathway is responsible for regenerating methionine from its derivative, methylthioadenosine (MTA). This pathway is highly conserved in all domains of life and is essential for maintaining sufficient methionine levels. Methionine deficiency can lead to increased histamine, fluid retention and toxin levels. Despite its importance, the pathway has only been fully described in one eukaryotic organism, yeast. To further understand the pathway, researchers attempted to identify the enzymes of the methionine salvage pathway in another eukaryote, *Tetrahymena thermophila*. In this organism, the pathway has a fused gene, MTNBD. This fusion gene, composed of the complete sequence of two or more other genes, produces an enzyme, mtnBD, which catalyzes two different single steps of the pathway in other organisms. The reaction catalyzed by mtnBD is shown in Figure 1.

S-methyl-5-thio-D-ribulose 1-phosphate (MTRuP)

mtnBD: O_2 → H_3PO_4, HCOOH

4-methylthio-2-oxobutanoate

Figure 1 mtnBD converts S-methyl-5-thio-D-ribulose-1-phosphate to 4-Methylthio-2-oxobutanoate in *Tetrahymena thermophila*

In yeast, mtnB and mtnD catalyze non-consecutive steps in the pathway. Interestingly the gene that codes for the intervening enzyme in the pathway, mtnC, is missing from the genome of Tetrahymena. Sequence similarities to mtnB and mtnD and the lack of an mtnC homolog suggest that the fusion protein, mtnBD, might be able to perform the functions of mtnC in addition to those of mtnB and mtnD in Tetrahymena. To determine if this hypothesis was correct, researchers investigated the *in vivo* function of the *Tetrahymena thermophila* fused gene by doing complementation studies in yeast cells. A synthetic gene that codes for the same amino acid sequence as the mtnBD fusion from Tetrahymena, but with codon usage optimized for expression in yeast cells, was inserted into a pGREG505 plasmid. The plasmid (pGREG505/MTNBD) was transformed into three different yeast strains that had the genes that code for the enzymes mtnB, mtnC and mtnD of the methionine salvage pathway individually deleted. The results are shown in Figure 2.

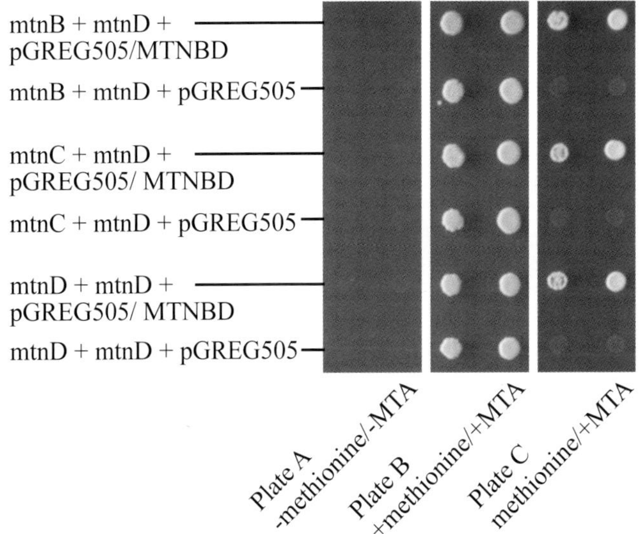

Figure 2 The diagram shows growth of the different yeast cell lines in three different mediums.

Question 6

In Figure 2, Plate A and Plate B are acting as:

- ○ **A.** a positive control plate and a negative control plate, respectively.
- ○ **B.** a control plate and an experimental plate, respectively.
- ○ **C.** a negative control plate and a positive control plate, respectively.
- ○ **D.** an experimental plate and a control plate, respectively.

Question 7

The results of the yeast complementation study suggest which of the following is true about mtnBD?

- ○ **A.** mtnBD is a trifunctional enzyme.
- ○ **B.** mtnBD only catalyzes the reactions that mtnB and mtnD catalyze in yeast.
- ○ **C.** The reaction following the one catalyzed by mtnB is catalyzed by mtnC in yeast cells.
- ○ **D.** mtnBD cannot function without methionine.

Question 8

In yeast, lack of the mtnB enzyme would result in which of the following outcomes?

- ○ **A.** The mtnD enzyme would compensate for mtnB.
- ○ **B.** The activation energy of the reaction catalyzed by mtnB would increase.
- ○ **C.** The reaction catalyzed by mtnB would never occur.
- ○ **D.** The affinity of mtnD for MTRuP would increase.

TEST 1C

Question 9

The researchers hypothesize that the mtnBD enzyme is regulated by noncompetitive inhibition. To test their theory they add the inhibitor to the enzyme and measure the K_m and V_{max}. Which of the following experimental findings would support their theory?

- ○ **A.** K_m increases and V_{max} increases
- ○ **B.** K_m increases and V_{max} decreases
- ○ **C.** K_m does not change and V_{max} decreases
- ○ **D.** K_m decreases and V_{max} does not change

Passage 3 (Questions 10-14)

Retinopathy of prematurity (ROP) is a major cause of vision loss in premature infants. 50% of infants born weighing less than 1700 g develop ROP. Premature infants are often given oxygen to support their underdeveloped lungs. Exposure of immature retinal blood vessels to relative hyperoxia damages the immature retinal capillaries and impairs vascular development. The resulting vascular insufficiency results in a condition of relative hypoxia as development of the retina continues. This up-regulates growth factors, such as vascular endothelial growth factor (VEGF), leading to pathological angiogenesis, or new blood vessel formation.

Disruption of amino acid metabolism may be involved in ROP development. Preterm infants have been shown to be deficient in L-arginine, which is nutritionally essential for neonatal development. L-arginine is the substrate of both nitric oxide synthase (NOS) and arginase. NOS catalyzes L-arginine to produce NO and L-citrulline, whereas arginase uses L-arginine to produce urea and ornithine. Hepatic urea production is crucial for ammonia detoxification. Ornithine is processed to form L-proline and polyamines, important for collagen synthesis and cell growth, respectively.

To determine whether the arginase pathway is involved in hyperoxia-induced retinal vascular injury, researchers conducted experiments that knocked out the pathway using two methods.

Experiment 1

An arginase inhibitor, 2(S)-amino-6-boronohexanoic acid (ABH), was administered in vitro to a group of cells under conditions of normoxia or hyperoxia. The percentage of apoptosis, or cell death, was measured. The results are shown in comparison to a group of cells not given ABH (Figure 1).

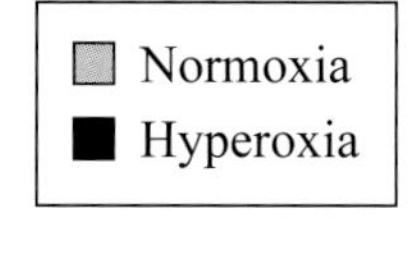

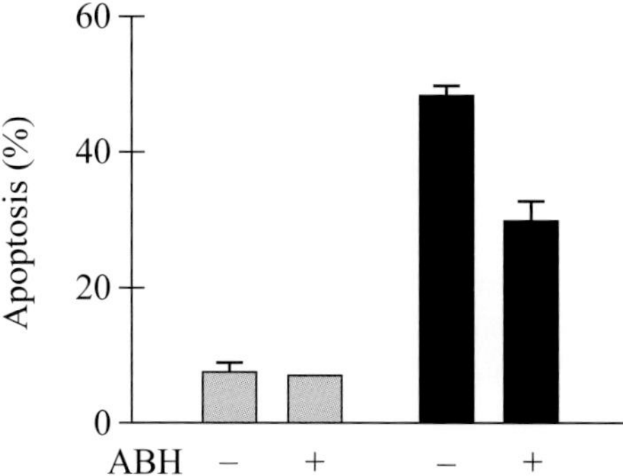

Figure 1 The percentage of apoptosis in cells given ABH or not in hyperoxic or normoxic conditions

Experiment 2

The area of the neovascularization tuft, or collection of new blood vessels, was measured in wild type mice, mice with only one copy of the arginase gene (A+/–) and complete arginase knock out mice (A–/–) under conditions of hyperoxia (Figure 2).

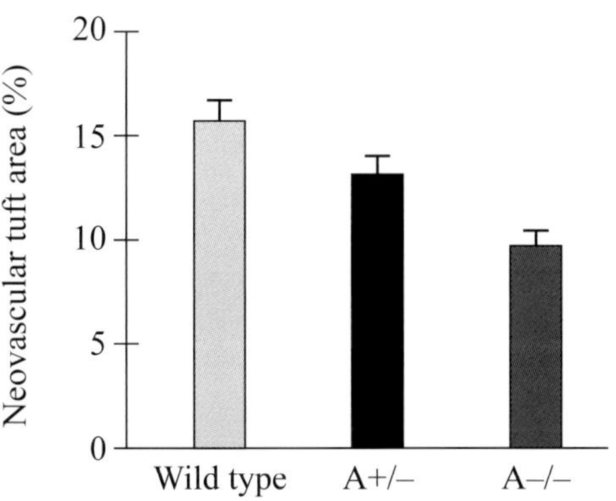

Figure 2 Neovascular tuft area percentage in wild type, A+/– and A–/– mice under conditions of hyperoxia

This passage was adapted from "Arginase 2 Deficiency Prevents Oxidative Stress and Limits Hyperoxia-Induced Retinal Vascular Degeneration." Suwanpradid J, Rojas M, Behzadian MA, Caldwell RW, Caldwell RB. *PLoS ONE*. 2014. 9(11) doi: 10.1371/journal.pone.0110604 for use under the terms of the Creative Commons CC BY 4.0 license (https://creativecommons.org/licenses/by/4.0/legalcode).

Question 10

L-arginine deficiency can lead to all of the following outcomes EXCEPT:

- O **A.** excessive ammonia leading to organ dysfunction.
- O **B.** excessive NO levels leading to hypotension.
- O **C.** impaired cell growth.
- O **D.** impaired collagen synthesis.

Question 11

One of the researchers proposes that ABH must have structure that is very similar to L-arginine. What is the appropriate response to this proposal?

- O **A.** Agree, ABH must have a similar structure to L-arginine to bind to the active site to inhibit it.
- O **B.** Agree, ABH must have a similar structure
- O **C.** Disagree, there are multiple ways to inhibit an enzyme other than competitive inhibition.
- O **D.** Disagree, there are multiple ways to inhibit an enzyme other than noncompetitive inhibition.

Question 12

Babies who are born preterm and have a dysfunctional vitamin C metabolism do not develop ROP. Which of the following provides the best explanation for this finding?

- O **A.** Vitamin C acts as a competitive inhibitor of arginase.
- O **B.** Vitamin C acts as a coenzyme for arginase.
- O **C.** Vitamin C can act as a substitute for L-arginine.
- O **D.** Vitamin C acts as a cofactor for arginase.

Question 13

L-proline likely contributes what property to the structure of collagen?

- O **A.** Polarity
- O **B.** Enzymatic function
- O **C.** Secondary structures like alpha helices
- O **D.** Kinks in the protein structure

Question 14

The crystal structure of L-arginine appears different when it is crystallized independently from when it is crystallized while complexed with arginase. This can be explained by:

- O **A.** enzyme specificity.
- O **B.** the activation energy of arginase.
- O **C.** the lock and key model.
- O **D.** the induced fit model.

TEST 1C

TEST 1C

Questions 15 through 18 do not refer to a passage and are independent of each other.

Question 15

Which of the following is consistent with the lock and key model of enzyme-substrate binding?

- A. This model provides an alternative to the enzyme specificity model.
- B. The model suggests that the active site and substrate change shape upon binding.
- C. It explains the interactions between all substrates and enzymes.
- D. It supports the idea that each enzyme has a small set of compatible substrates.

Question 16

A metabolic pathway is catalyzed by an enzyme found only to be active in the presence of its substrate, a complex aldose sugar. Which of the following is NOT true?

- A. The enzyme could be controlled by noncompetitive inhibition
- B. The enzyme could be controlled by competitive inhibition
- C. If the enzyme and its substrate were placed in a test tube, with sufficient time the concentration of the substrate would be zero
- D. If the enzyme and its substrate were placed in a test tube, with sufficient time the concentration of the substrate would form an equilibrium with the product

Question 17

An enzyme and substrate are added to a test tube, which of the following Lineweaver-Burk plots shows the effect of adding a noncompetitive inhibitor?

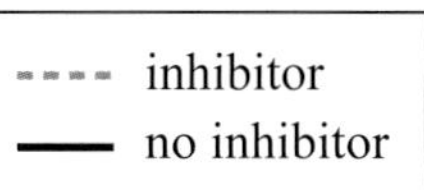

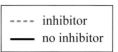

A.

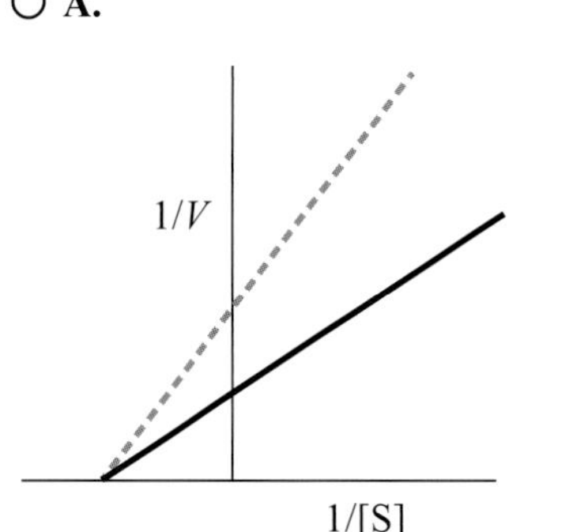

B.

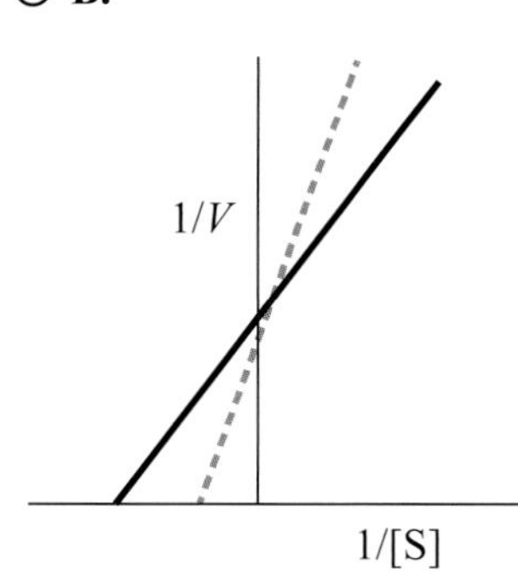

C.

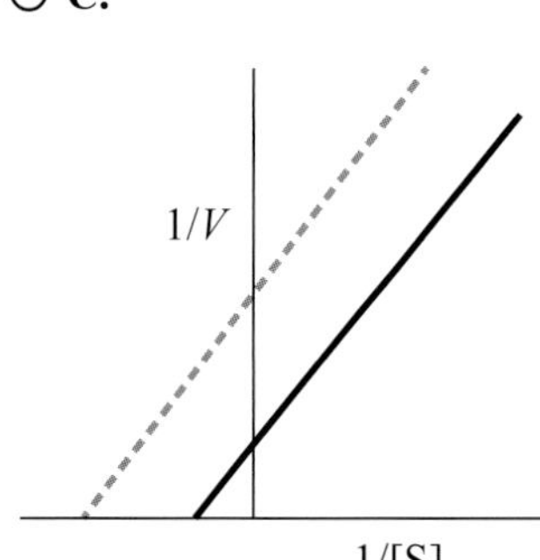

D.

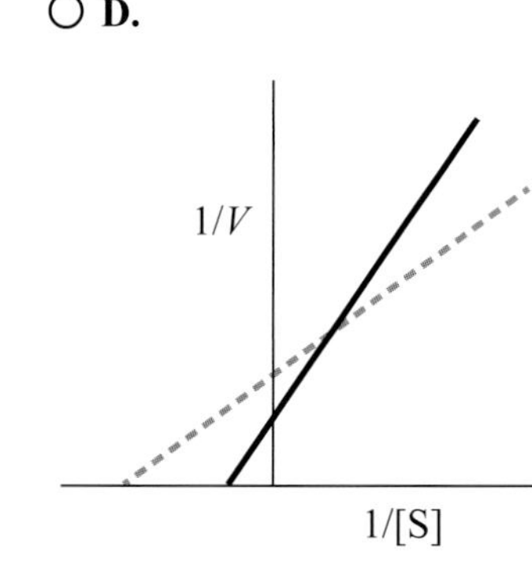

Question 18

Investigators performed an experiment using an unknown inhibitor. They found that this inhibitor caused the K_m and V_{max} to decrease. Which of the following conclusions would be supported by this data?

- A. This inhibitor works by binding the enzyme's active site directly.
- B. The first step in the inhibition is the inhibitor binding the enzyme.
- C. The inhibitor can bind the enzyme or the enzyme-substrate complex.
- D. The equilibrium constant of the inhibitor contains the enzyme-substrate complex concentration.

Next ▶

Passage 4 (Questions 19-23)

The *PTEN* gene located at human chromosome 10q23 encodes the tumor suppressor enzyme PTEN. *PTEN* is thought to be mutated in 50–80% of sporadic human cancers. By catalyzing the dephosphorylation of PIP_3 to PIP_2, PTEN antagonizes the phosphatidylinositol-3- kinase (PI3K) Akt pathway, mediating cell proliferation and apoptosis.

Previously, researchers reported on a form of PTEN called PTEN-L (64.9 kDa), which is translated from a conserved CUG codon. The alternative form has 173 additional N-terminal amino-acid residues, including a secretion signal sequence and an Arg6 motif that enables extracellular protein to enter the cytosol. PTEN-L has enzymatic activity, but its catalysis is even less well characterized than that of wild-type PTEN.

Experiment 1

Using a continuous assay, researchers tested whether salt concentration has a marked influence on catalysis by PTEN. When researchers refrained from adding salt to the assay solution, they discover that PTEN exhibits Michaelis–Menten kinetics (Figure 1).

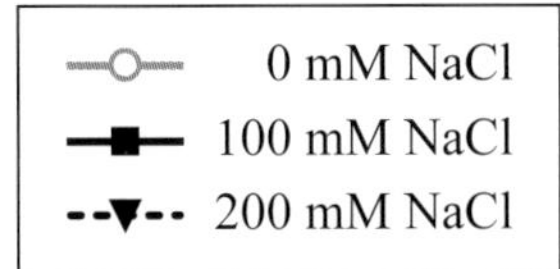

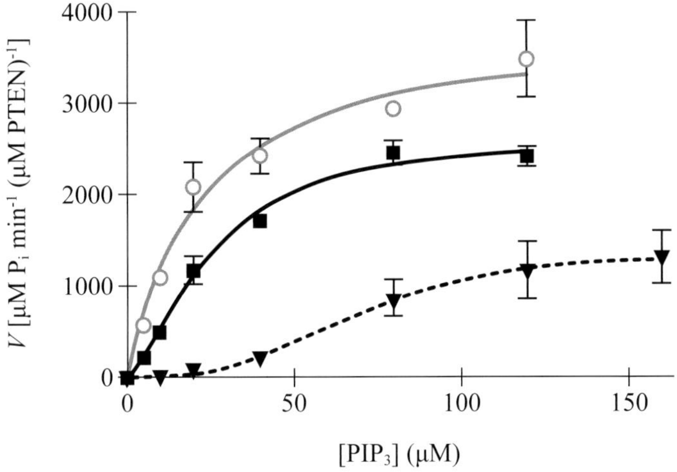

Figure 1 PTEN catalysis at 0 mM, 100 mM, and 200 mM NaCl concentrations

Experiment 2

Scientists hypothesized that N-terminal binding to the PIP_2 product that is generated from the dephosphorylation of PIP_3 enhances the affinity of PTEN for a PIP_3 substrate (Figure 2).

	6	7	8	9	10	11	12	13	14
PTEN	K	E	I	V	S	R	N	K	R
PIP_2-binding motif	K/R	X	X	X	X	K/R	X	K/R	K/R

Figure 2 PIP_2-binding motif

Experiment 3

Due to the location of the additional residues on the N terminus of PTEN-L, scientists tested whether the added domain affects the activating effect of PIP_2. The results are shown in Figure 3.

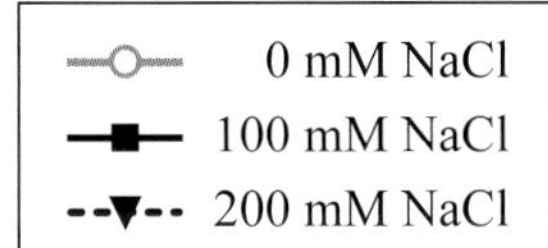

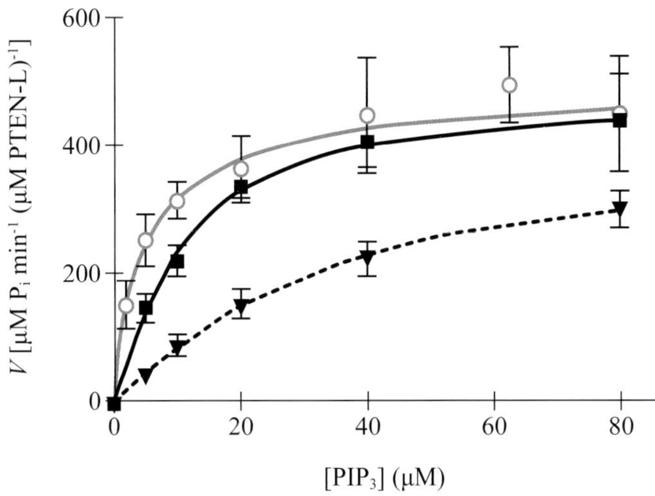

Figure 3 PTEN-L catalysis at 0 mM, 100 mM, and 200 mM NaCl concentrations

Question 19

Does the passage data support the conclusion that allosteric PIP_2 binding causes PTEN to have a greater PIP_3 binding affinity than PTEN-L at 0 mM NaCl?

- **A.** Yes; PTEN has a greater V_{max} than PTEN-L.
- **B.** Yes; the K_m of PTEN is lower than that of PTEN-L.
- **C.** No; PTEN-L has a lower V_{max} than PTEN.
- **D.** No; the K_m of PTEN is greater than that of PTEN-L.

Question 20

The addition of a molecule that reversibly binds to the active site of PTEN will cause the curves in Figure 1 to:

- **A.** decrease in peak height but maintain initial slope.
- **B.** maintain peak height but decrease initial slope.
- **C.** decrease in peak height and initial slope.
- **D.** maintain peak height but increase initial slope.

Question 21

How is PIP_2 likely to bind PTEN in order to best facilitate increased μM/min P_i ?

Molecule of PIP_2

- O **A.** Hydrophobic interactions in active site to stabilize the active PTEN conformation
- O **B.** Ionic interactions with the N terminus allosteric site to alter PTEN conformation
- O **C.** Hydrophobic interactions in N terminus allosteric site to enhance the PTEN active site
- O **D.** Ionic interactions in the PTEN active site to increase PIP_3 binding affinity

Question 22

At 200 mM NaCl there was limited turbidity in the assay solutions. The researchers hypothesized that the K_m of PTEN was increased due to:

- O **A.** the enzyme aggregating or "salting out."
- O **B.** the high affinity of PTEN for PIP_3.
- O **C.** the increased binding of ions to the substrate and active site.
- O **D.** the strict requirement for constant solution pH.

Question 23

After an initial experiment was conducted at 0 mM NaCl, researchers realized that they had accidently doubled the quantity of PTEN. Which of the following results would have been found?

- O **A.** K_m would be higher due to an increased quantity of bound PIP_3.
- O **B.** V_{max} would be higher and K_m would be lower due to increased catalysis.
- O **C.** K_m would be lower due to the increased affinity for PIP_3.
- O **D.** V_{max} would be higher due to increased total capacity.

Passage 5 (Questions 24-27)

The incidence of type 2 diabetes (T2DM) and obesity is associated with the consumption of fructose, typically in the form of sucrose and high fructose sweeteners. Fructose and sweeteners are associated with adverse effects including weight gain, insulin resistance, and cognitive decline.

Fructose and glucose have distinct effects in the central nervous system (CNS). In healthy lean adults, ingestion of fructose leads to a unique pattern of cerebral blood flow to brain regions associated with appetite and reward compared to blood flow patterns following ingestion of glucose.

Glucose can be converted to fructose via the polyol pathway (glucose → sorbitol → fructose), an alternate glucose pathway that bypasses the control points of hexokinase and phosphofructokinase. Glucose is reduced to sorbitol by the action of aldose reductase, and sorbitol is oxidized to fructose through sorbitol dehydrogenase.

Researchers studied women in the late stages of pregnancy and divided them into three groups: lean, overweight/obese, and diabetic women. Because aldose reductase is highly expressed in the placenta, researchers sought to evaluate the effects of maternal glucose levels on fetal exposure to sorbitol and fructose by measuring cord venous blood levels of these metabolites, reflecting blood from placenta to fetus. The presence of polyol pathway activity was evaluated in the CNS through cerebrospinal fluid (Figure 1), and cord blood (Figure 2) during the late stages of pregnancy, a time of increased maternal energy requirements to meet the increased energy demands of the fetus and placenta.

— median ratio
● diabetic individuals
■ lean individuals
▼ overweight/obese individuals

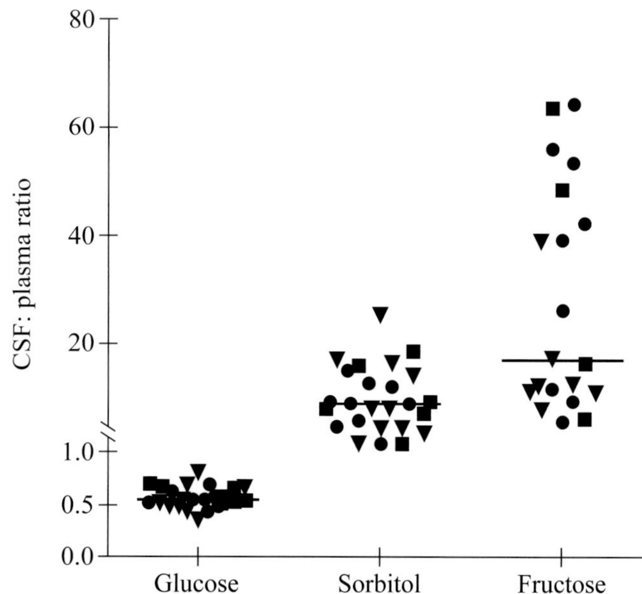

Figure 1 Cerebrospinal fluid to plasma ratios of glucose, sorbitol and fructose

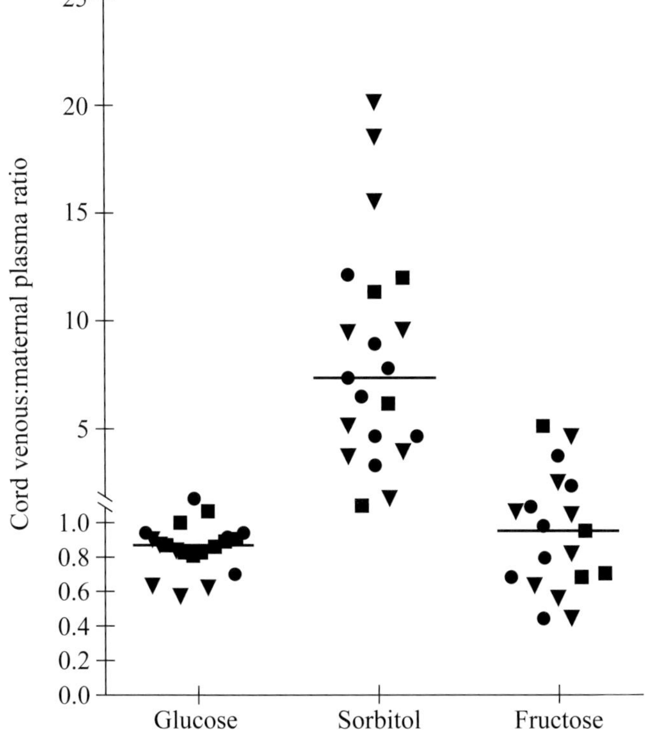

Figure 2 Cord venous blood to maternal plasma ratios of glucose, sorbitol and fructose

Plasma and CSF fructose and sorbitol levels were measured using gas chromatography-liquid mass spectrometry. Fructose levels were below detection limits for 5 maternal plasma (3 obese, 1 lean, 1 DM subject) and 4 cord plasma samples (3 obese, 1 lean subject) and were excluded. Glucose levels were measured enzymatically with glucose oxidase.

Question 24

Based on the passage, the maximum rate of conversion from sorbitol to fructose is most directly limited by:

- O **A.** the concentration of sorbitol dehydrogenase, which is a catalyst.
- O **B.** the concentration of aldose reductase, which is a catalyst.
- O **C.** the concentration of fructose, which is the product of the reaction.
- O **D.** the pH within the cell.

Question 25

Based on the passage, which of the following enzymes is likely regulated allosterically?

- O **A.** Aldose reductase, because its expression can be increased in the placenta
- O **B.** Aldose reductase, because the maximum rate of the reaction is affected by the concentration of substrate
- O **C.** Phosphofructokinase, because its expression can be lowered in the placenta
- O **D.** Phosphofructokinase, because it is at a control point

Question 26

A change from adenine to guanine in the gene encoding hexokinase is expected to be most severe:

- O **A.** when it results in a change from Lys to Arg in the active site.
- O **B.** when it results in a change from Asn to Ser in the active site.
- O **C.** when it results in a change from Asp to Gly in the allosteric site.
- O **D.** when it results in a change from Thr to Ala in the active site.

Question 27

The researchers consider a new experiment testing the effects of an aldose reductase inhibitor. Which of the following would be the most important alteration to the experiment?

- O **A.** Utilize a negative control group that would help to cancel out other variables.
- O **B.** Utilize a rodent model.
- O **C.** Enroll a large number participants to increase the likelihood of significance.
- O **D.** Test the effects of a high fructose diet on fructose levels in fetuses.

Questions 28 through 31 do not refer to a passage and are independent of each other.

Question 28

The K_m of the enzyme represented in the table below is:

Concentration	Rate (in mEqs/s)
0.01 nM	0.27
0.05 nM	0.33
1 nM	0.37
5 nM	0.41
0.01 μM	0.49
0.05 μM	0.53
0.1 μM	0.68
0.5 μM	0.84
1.0 μM	0.88
5.0 μM	0.86

- **A.** 1.0 nM
- **B.** 5.0 nM
- **C.** 0.01 μM
- **D.** 0.5 μM

Question 29

The mechanism of action for the antiepileptic drug Vigabatrin involves the formation of a covalent bond between the drug molecule and GABA transaminase, the enzyme responsible for breakdown of an essential inhibitory neurotransmitter. Vigabatrin is a(n):

- **A.** mixed inhibitor.
- **B.** uncompetitive inhibitor.
- **C.** noncompetitive inhibitor.
- **D.** irreversible inhibitor.

Question 30

Arg 327 most likely stabilizes the inhibitor in the enzyme active site through:

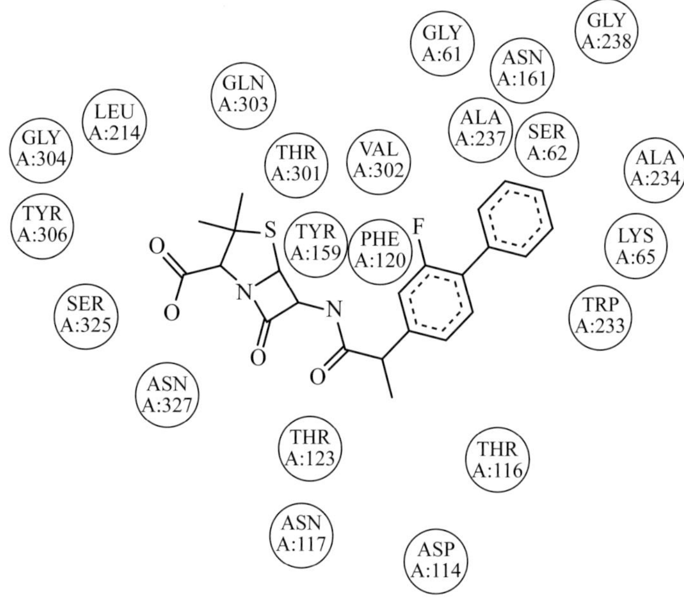

This image was adapted from "Novel Penicillin Analogues as Potential Antimicrobial Agents; Design, Synthesis and Docking Studies." Ashraf Z, Bais A, Manir M, and Naizi U. *PLoS ONE*. 2015. 10(8) doi:10.1371/journal.pone.0135293 for use under the terms of the Creative Commons CC BY 4.0 license (http://creativecommons.org/licenses/by/4.0/legalcode).

- **A.** covalent bonds.
- **B.** electrostatic interactions.
- **C.** van der Waals attractions.
- **D.** a metal cofactor interaction.

Question 31

The reaction between two amino acids in the peptidyltransferase site of the ribosome is best described as a:

- **A.** hydrolysis reaction.
- **B.** condensation reaction.
- **C.** carboxylation reaction.
- **D.** decarboxylation reaction.

STOP. If you finish before time is called, check your work. You may go back to any question in this test.

ANSWERS & EXPLANATIONS for Test 1B can be found on p.188.

Genetics

TEST 2A

Time: 95 minutes
Questions 1–59

DIRECTIONS: Most questions in the Biological and Biochemical Foundations of Living Systems test section are grouped with a descriptive passage. Select the best answer to each question using background knowledge and the given passage. A portion of this test section is comprised of discrete questions, which are independent of any passage and one another. Select the best answer for each discrete question. Indicate your selection by blackening the corresponding oval on your answer document. If you are unsure of the answer, rule out incorrect choices and select from the remaining options. You may access a periodic table found on the last page of this book at any point during this test section.

TEST 2A

Passage 1 (Questions 1-4)

Danshen, an oxygen-containing cyclic aromatic compound of the tanshinone family, has been widely used in traditional Chinese medicine practice for centuries in the treatment of coronary artery disease and cerebrovascular diseases with minimal side effects. Given danshen's effects on modulating cell death in atherosclerotic diseases, scientists also wished to characterize its effects in cancer treatment. Danshen treatment showed dose-dependent effects on the growth inhibition of breast cancer cells by significantly down-regulated cyclin D and cyclin B protein levels and induced breast cancer cell apoptosis by downregulation of Aurora A. The Aurora proteins are responsible for adding phosphates to other proteins, and are involved in the processes of cell division. Aurora A is localized on duplicated centrosomes and spindle poles during mitosis and is required for proper formation of a bipolar mitotic spindle by regulating centrosome maturation, separation, and microtubule nucleation activity.

Epigenetic alterations of the genome such as DNA promoter methylation, acetylation, and chromatin remodeling play an important role in forming tumors. Scientists further investigated possible epigenetic mechanisms that might be responsible for Aurora A overexpression in breast cancer cells and for explaining danshen activity in downregulating Aurora A expression. When breast cancer cells were treated with 5-AZA, a DNA demethylating regent, Aurora A gene expression was not altered. Breast cancer cells treated with sodium butyrate (SB), a histone deacetylase inhibitor, had an increased level of Aurora A gene expression by 4-fold. The presence of SB reduced the growth inhibition activity of danshen by 25%.

Question 1

Decreasing Aurora A levels unpredictably increased the activity of histone methyltransferase, which is responsible for methylating the individual histones of nucleosomes around locus X. Expression of genes in locus X would most likely:

- O **A.** increase.
- O **B.** decrease.
- O **C.** remain the same.
- O **D.** Gene expression is not dependent upon methylation status.

Question 2

In order to better characterize the role of Aurora A in breast cancer cells, the scientists should most likely perform what follow-up experiment?

- O **A.** Use non-coding RNAs to reduce the expression of Aurora A in colon cancer cells.
- O **B.** Fully characterize the acetylation of chromatin in the genome.
- O **C.** Completely knock out the expression of Aurora A in breast cancer cells.
- O **D.** Overexpress Aurora A in breast cancer cells.

Question 3

Additional genome sequencing identified a mutation that completely eliminated the expression of Aurora A in a subset of clinical breast cancers. The mutation identified could have occurred in which region(s) of the Aurora A gene?

I. Promoter
II. Enhancer
III. Repressor
IV. Intron

- O **A.** I and II
- O **B.** I and IV
- O **C.** II and III
- O **D.** II, III, and IV

Question 4

Decreases in Aurora A expression would most likely prevent the cell from entering which phase of mitosis?

- O **A.** Prophase
- O **B.** Metaphase
- O **C.** Anaphase
- O **D.** Telophase

Passage 2 (Questions 5-8)

Chromatin modifications are among the most common epigenetic changes in cancer and allow the transcriptional enhancement or repression of many oncogenes and tumor suppressor genes. Nucleosome remodeling is mediated by the SWI/SNF proteins of chromatin modifying complexes (CMCs), but some members of these families and the role they play in disease are poorly understood.

CMCs are multi-subunit complexes that use the energy of ATP hydrolysis to modify DNA-histone interactions. These multi-protein complexes control access to chromatin DNA by regulating the structure, the type of histone variants and nucleosome positioning. CMCs also impinge on various other chromatin-related modifications, such as acetylation, methylation, phosphorylation and ubiquitination, which are also important for regulation of gene expression. Furthermore, CMCs may be able to mediate the formation of chromatin loops to modulate gene expression. These loops, which join the 5′ and 3′ ends of a single gene, are proposed to allow an efficient recycling of the RNA polymerase II (RNA Pol II) from the termination site back to the promoter.

In order to better understand the role of the SWI/SNF proteins, scientists used the model organism *Arabidopsis* to investigate how chromatin modifications control progression through the cell cycle. They analyzed the molecular function of one accessory subunit, BAF60, which had been shown to prevent the formation of local chromatin loops. In the presence of BAF60, transcription of two cell cycle genes, *IPT3/7* and *KRP7* is inhibited and cell cycle progression can occur. When BAF60 is knocked down with siRNA, transcriptional looping occurs and *IPT3/7* and *KRP7* are transcribed, preventing cell cycle progression (Figure 1).

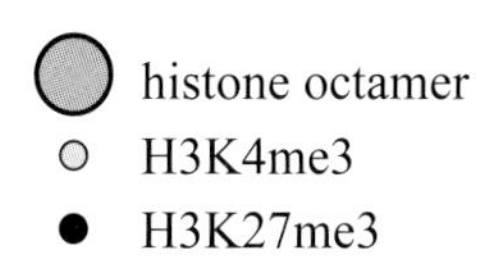

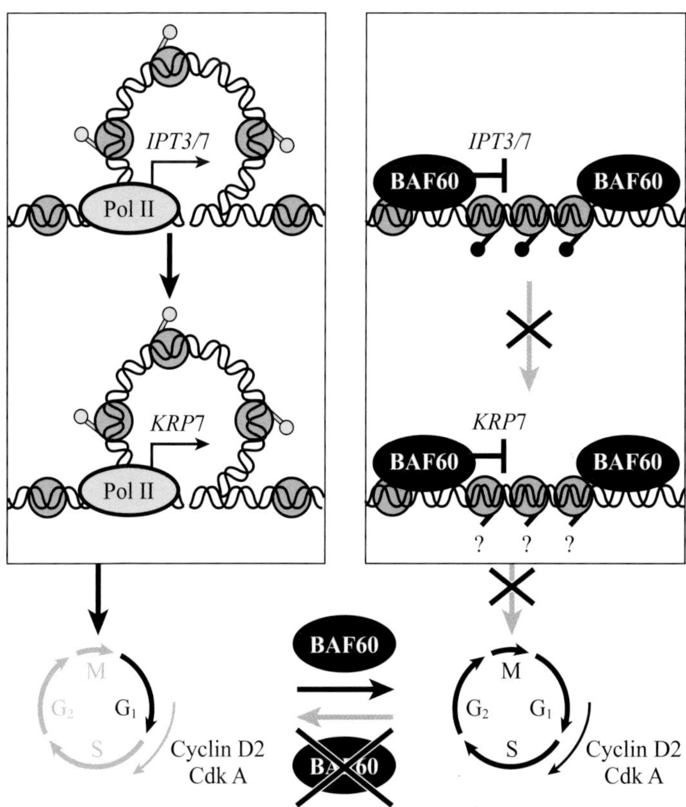

Figure 1 Model for the role of BAF60 in cell cycle progression

Question 5

Which of the following amino acids is LEAST likely to be found in high concentrations in histones?

- **A.** K
- **B.** N
- **C.** E
- **D.** H

Question 6

Which experimental result would support the role of Xist, a long non-coding RNA, in maintaining heterochromatin?

- O **A.** Anti-sense nucleotides complementary to Xist decrease the global protein content of the cell.
- O **B.** Xist is found to associate with one X chromosome in women.
- O **C.** Anti-sense nucleotides complementary to Xist result in increased chromosome condensation.
- O **D.** Glucose-6-phosphatase protein levels increase upon Xist knockdown.

Question 7

The SWI/SNF complex likely serves to:

- O **A.** inhibit the transcription of cyclin D2.
- O **B.** activate the transcription of cyclin-dependent kinase A.
- O **C.** increase the concentration of ATP in the cell.
- O **D.** associate with non-coding RNA to increase the rate of translation.

Question 8

Chromosomal looping serves to increase transcription by:

- O **A.** increasing the A:T content of the promoter.
- O **B.** increasing the frequency of RNA polymerase II association with the transcription start site.
- O **C.** increasing the rate of nucleotide addition by RNA polymerase II.
- O **D.** decreasing the number of repressor elements that prevent transcription.

Passage 3 (Questions 9-12)

Preeclampsia is characterized by uncontrolled maternal high blood pressure that can progress to organ failure, seizures , and maternal death. A precise etiology of preeclampsia is unknown but is linked to impaired vascular development, known as angiogenesis, of the placenta. Angiogenic growth factors such as vascular endothelial growth factor (VEGF) and placental growth factor (PLGF) are required for invasion of the spiral artery and proper placentation.

Genome-wide hypomethylation has been observed in placental tissue from preeclamptic women. As CpG methylation can influence the expression of genes and subsequently proteins, it may be a major contributor to disease. Scientists analyzed relationships between changes in CpG methylation in placental tissue from women with preeclampsia compared to controls, and the associated functional changes in gene expression levels. The methylation status of 390,452 distinct CpG probes corresponding to 20,452 individual genes was analyzed across all placentas. Most (80.7%) of the probes identified hypomethylation in the preeclamptic placenta versus the normotensive placenta, while only 19.3% were hypermethylated. The methylation and expression data for angiotensin receptor associated protein, *AGTRAP,* is shown in Figure 1.

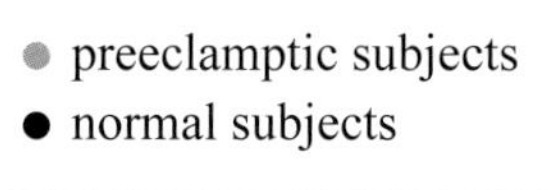

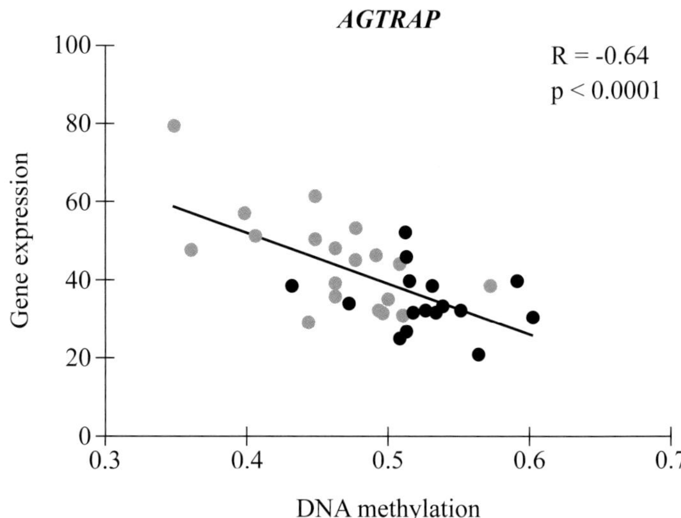

Figure 1 Plots of CpG methylation levels and gene expression levels across all subjects

In addition to *AGTRAP*, scientists identified significant hypomethylation in a second gene, *TGF-β*. *TGF-β* is elevated in the serum of preeclamptic patients and is known to inhibit the angiogenic factor VEGF in many tissues. Enrichment analysis for transcription factors known to associate with TGF-β identified Kidney-enriched Kruppel-like factor 15 (KLF15), Myeloid Zinc Finger Protein 1 (MZF1), and Kruppel-like Zinc Finger protein 219 (ZNF219). All three factors are predicted to contribute to blood vessel development.

Question 9

Methylation of C bases in the genome most likely acts to:

- O **A.** decrease translation of genes by inhibiting the ribosome.
- O **B.** increase the transcription of genes by acting as a transcription factor binding site.
- O **C.** decrease the transcription of genes by increasing DNA association with histones.
- O **D.** increase translation of genes by stimulating an increase in RNA processing.

Question 10

Hypomethylation of the *TGF-β* locus leads to changes in expression of KLF15, which functions by:

- O **A.** binding RNA.
- O **B.** binding DNA.
- O **C.** replicating RNA.
- O **D.** replicating DNA.

Question 11

What additional experimental evidence would support the authors' assertions that epigenetic regulation of angiogenesis-related genes was correlated with preeclampsia?

- O **A.** Women treated with DNA methyltransferase inhibitor 5-AZA had increased incidence of preeclampsia.
- O **B.** Women with preeclampsia often have first degree relatives whom also had preeclampsia.
- O **C.** Increased expression of KLF15 correlated with increased incidence of preeclampsia.
- O **D.** Prior use of anti-VEGF antibodies used to treat cancer in some women led to increased incidence of preeclampsia.

Question 12

In a second methylation experiment, scientists found that 4.4% of the hypomethylated probes, such as the one associated with locus 257358, were associated with gene silencing, as shown below. Which statement best explains these findings?

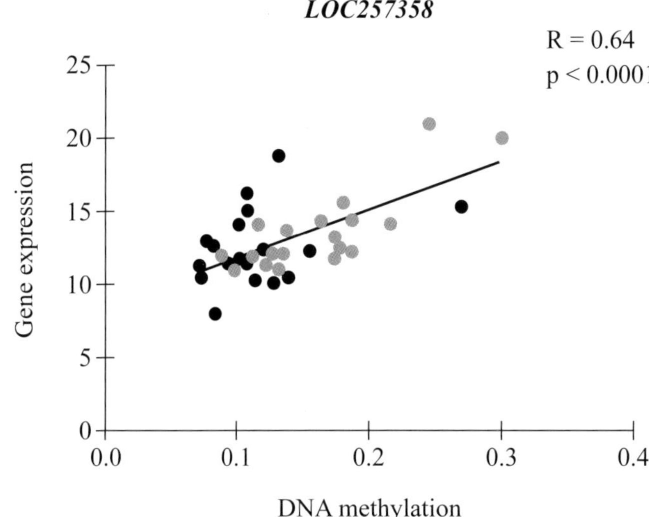

- O **A.** Hypomethylation increased the interaction between histone H4 and DNA.
- O **B.** Hypermethylation decreased the interaction between RNA and the ribosome.
- O **C.** Hypomethylation results in the transcription of small interfering RNAs.
- O **D.** The finding likely represents experimental artifacts inherent to methylation sequencing.

Questions 13 through 16 do not refer to a passage and are independent of each other.

Question 13

Scientists interested in identifying the specific locus of a gene would most likely use:

- O **A.** PCR.
- O **B.** fluorescence *in situ* hybridization (FISH).
- O **C.** DNA isolation and gel electrophoresis.
- O **D.** western blotting.

TEST 2A

Question 14

Which of the following does NOT describe an epigenetic change?

- O **A.** Acetylation of histone H3
- O **B.** Methylation of histone H4
- O **C.** Methylation of A nucleotides
- O **D.** Synonymous mutation of C to T

Question 15

GAPDH is a 335 amino acid protein that is regularly transcribed in living cells. Which of the following mutations will likely have the smallest effect on synthesis of this protein?

- O **A.** Deletion of the 35th nucleotide in the mRNA sequence.
- O **B.** Substitution of adenine for cytosine at the 25th nucleotide by the RNA polymerase
- O **C.** Replacing a guanine with an adenine so the new codon for the 30th amino acid residue is UGA
- O **D.** Substitution of adenine for guanine at the 33rd nucleotide in the mRNA transcript

Question 16

CpG dinucleotides in the genome are often methylated compared to C in another nucleotide context. Methylated CpG sites would be expected around:

I. centromeres.
II. transcriptionally active genes.
III. heterochromatin.

- O **A.** I only
- O **B.** I and II only
- O **C.** I and III only
- O **D.** I, II, and III

Passage 4 (Questions 17-20)

Breast cancer cells penetrate blood and lymph through intravascular system and proliferate in distant tissues whereby new vessels are formed by a process of angiogenesis. The expression of vascular endothelial growth factor (VEGF) by invasive tumors has been shown to correlate with vascularity and cell proliferation.

Small non-coding RNAs known as microRNAs (miRNAs), such as miR-15 and miR-16, bind to 3′ untranslated region (3′ UTR) of the target mRNAs and specifically inhibit translation. Scientists investigated the mechanistic aspects of chemotherapeutics cisplatin, etoposide, and C-10 to understand how they modulate expression of micro-RNAs associated with angiogenesis and regulates cell proliferation.

Cells treated with cisplatin, etoposide, or C-10 were incubated for 24 hours and subjected to endogenous miRNA expression studies visualized by a northern blot (Figure 1).

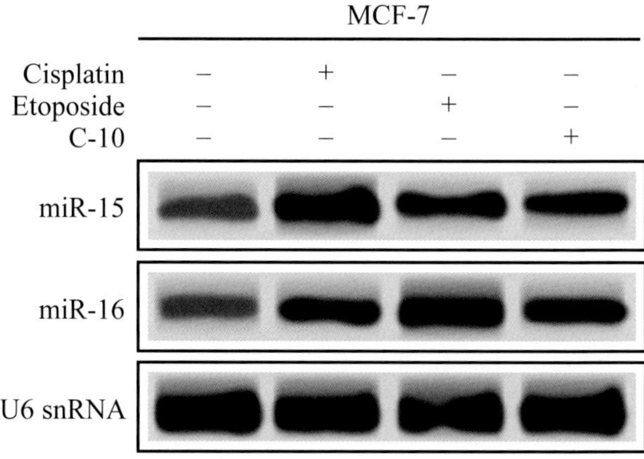

Figure 1 Role of cisplatin, etoposide, and C-10 in modulating miRNA levels in breast cancer

To discover which proteins were regulated by miR-15 and miR-16, a western blot was used to visualize the expression of the nuclear mRNA processing enzyme Drosha and the cytoplasmic endonuclease Ago-1 in MCF- 7 breast cancer cells (Figure 2).

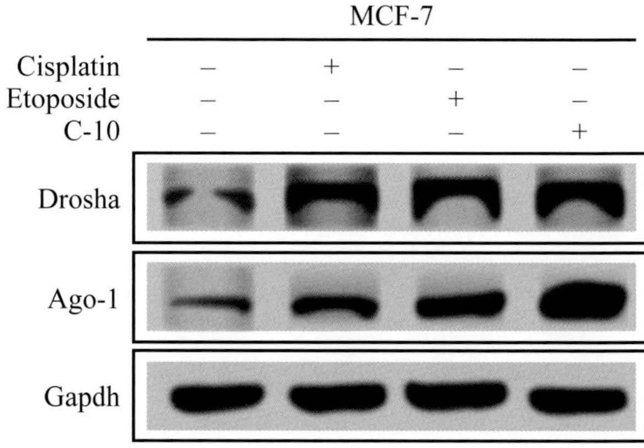

Figure 2 Western blot for the regulation of Drosha and Ago-1 expression by cisplatin, etoposide, and C-10-induced miRNAs

Because chemotherapeutics modified miRNA and protein expression related to regulating the protein levels of VEGF, scientists were interested to study the transcriptional regulation of VEGF promoter. Scientists cloned the VEGF promoter sequences in a vector containing a luciferase reporter gene and exposed MCF-7 cells to etoposide or C-10. An shRNA directed against STAT3, one of the transcription factors known to regulate VEGF expression, was used as a positive control. The results are shown in Figure 3.

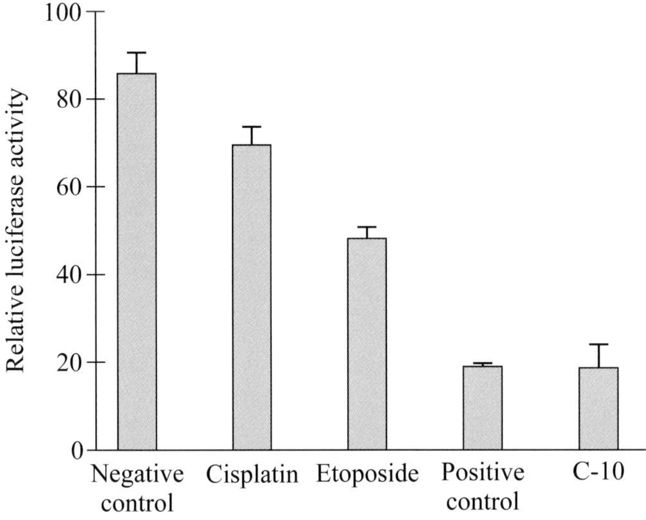

Figure 3 Effect of cisplatin, etoposide, and C-10 on VEGF promoter activity

Scientists conclude that the strong antiangiogenic effect caused by cisplatin, etoposide, and C-10, in combination with miR-15 and 16, demonstrate clear evidence for the therapeutic potential of these compounds for treatment of breast cancer.

Question 17

Which of the following curves best describes how methylation affects miR-15 expression?

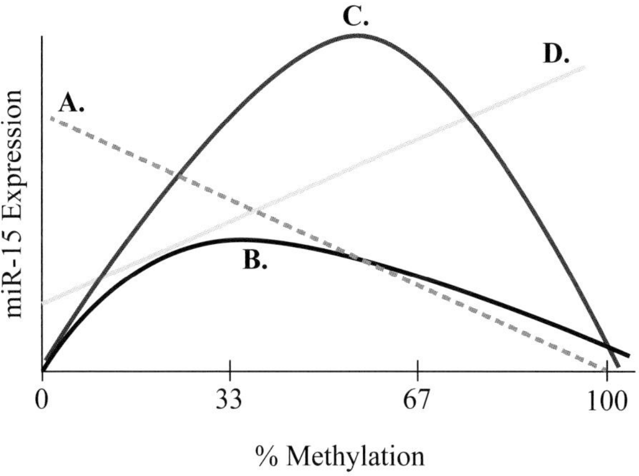

- O **A.** A
- O **B.** B
- O **C.** C
- O **D.** D

Question 18

Which of the following likely predicts the best pairing between the 3′ UTR of the VEGF mRNA and miR-15?

- O **A.** 5′- ^{7}me-G-TGCATGCA-3′ and 5′-TGCATGCA-3′
- O **B.** 5′-UGCAUGCC-3′ and 5′-GGCAUGCA-3′
- O **C.** 5′-TAAATAAA-3′ and 5′-TTTATTTA-3′
- O **D.** 5′- ^{7}me-G-UGGCUCCG-3′ and 5′-CGGAGCCA-3′

Question 19

miR-16 modulation of intracellular VEGF levels suggests that it acts as a(n):

- O **A.** oncogene.
- O **B.** tumor suppressor.
- O **C.** transcription factor.
- O **D.** ribozyme.

Question 20

Which of the following statements is best supported by the authors' experimental findings?

- O **A.** Etoposide but not cisplatin increases miR-15 expression, which increases STAT3 signaling.
- O **B.** Cisplatin but not C-10 increases miR-16 expression, which decreases STAT3 signaling.
- O **C.** Etoposide and cisplatin increase miR-15 expression, which decreases STAT3 signaling.
- O **D.** C-10 but not etoposide decrease miR-16 expression, which increases STAT3 signaling.

Passage 5 (Questions 21-25)

HIV-1 utilizes −1 programmed ribosomal frameshifting to translate structural and enzymatic domains in a defined proportion required for replication. A slippery sequence, U UUU UUA, and a stem-loop are well-defined RNA features modulating −1 frameshifting in HIV-1. The GGG glycine codon immediately following the slippery sequence (the 'intercodon') contributes structurally to the start of the stem-loop in natural isolates of HIV but it is unknown if it contributes to the frameshift mechanism.

As shown in Figure 1, significant slippage occurs when the intercodon is in the ribosomal A site. Normal translation fidelity can be superseded by programmed ribosomal frameshifting (PRF). PRF involves tRNA slippage either 5′ (−1) or 3′ (+1) relative to the mRNA followed by continued translation in the new reading frame. In the HIV-1 mRNA, −1 PRF results in translation of enzymatic domains and determines a specific ratio of enzymes to structural proteins critical for virus infectivity.

Experiment 1

Scientists sought to characterize the effect of the intercodon on frameshifting by making multiple substitutions of the natural glycine codon, as presented in Figure 2. Additionally, over-expression of the eukaryotic release factor, eRF1, decreased frameshift efficiency while cognate suppressor tRNA increased frameshifting in competition with endogenous eRF1. The data suggest that the GGG intercodon of the HIV-1 frameshift element influences frameshifting in at least two ways by promoting the lower stem structure and increasing the chance for −1 PRF to occur.

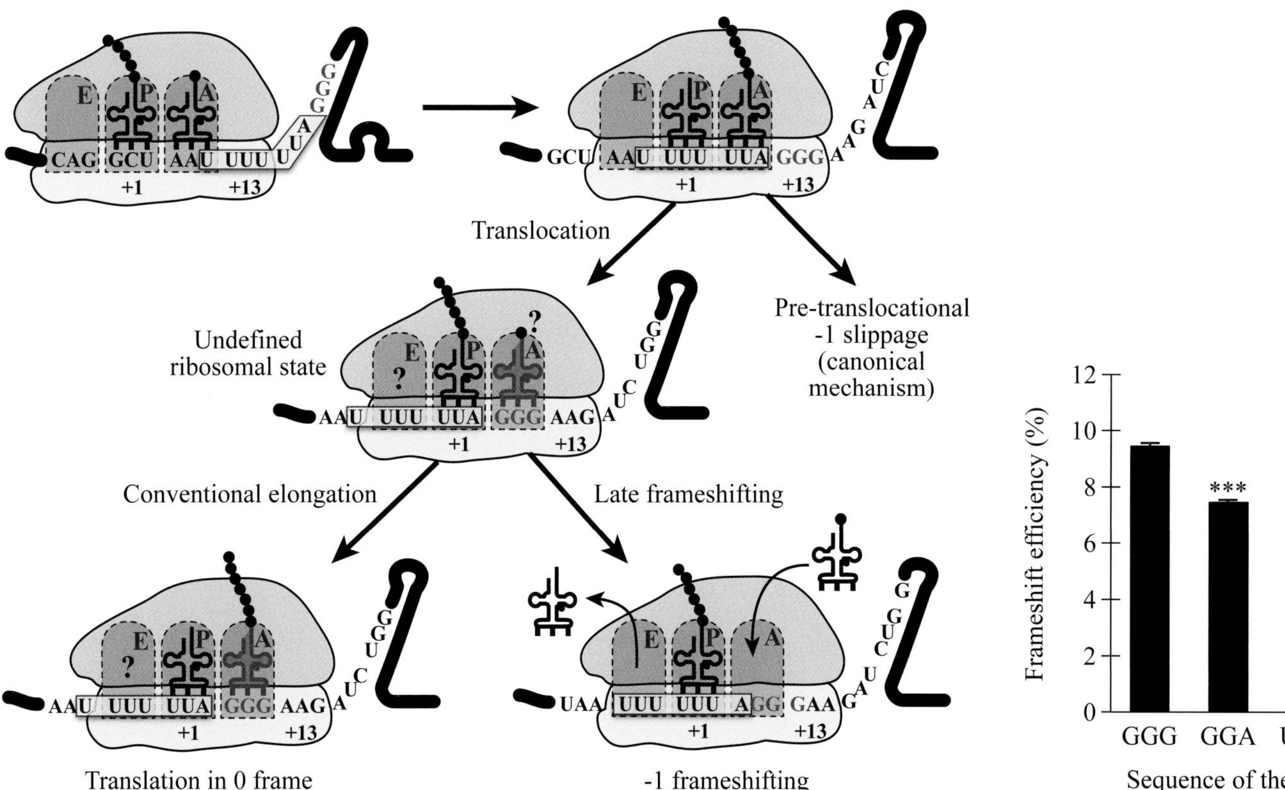

Figure 1 Schematic of ribosomal translation with in-frame elongation and late frameshifting

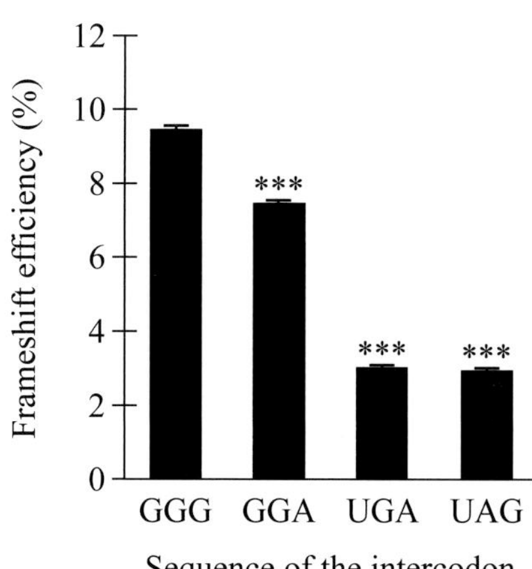

Figure 2 The sequence of the intercodon influences -1 frameshift efficiency. ***$p < 0.001$ compared to the GGG intercodon

This passage was adapted from "The Highly Conserved Codon following the Slippery Sequence Supports -1 Frameshift Efficiency at the HIV-1 Frameshift Site." Mathew SF, Crowe-McAuliffe C, Graves R, Cardno TS, McKinney C, et al. *PLoS ONE*. 2015. 10(3) doi:10.1371/journal.pone.0122176 for use under the terms of the Creative Commons CC BY 4.0 license (http://creativecommons.org/licenses/by/4.0/legalcode).

Question 21

The nucleolus is the site of synthesis for what component of translation?

- O **A.** RNA polymerase
- O **B.** Ribosome
- O **C.** mRNA
- O **D.** tRNA

Question 22

According to the passage, the nucleotide sequences immediately following the HIV slippery sequence are LEAST likely to contain:

- O **A.** tyrosine codons.
- O **B.** methionine codons.
- O **C.** thymine nucleotides.
- O **D.** ribosomal binding sites.

Question 23

Which of the following codons is LEAST likely to be recognized by the host cell eRF1?

- O **A.** UAG
- O **B.** UGA
- O **C.** UAA
- O **D.** UGG

Question 24

The tRNA carrying the tyrosine amino acid crucial to the structure of the CCR5 receptor that HIV uses to infect human T cells most likely binds to what site in the ribosome?

- O **A.** The tRNA binding site
- O **B.** The A site
- O **C.** The P site
- O **D.** The E site

Question 25

Changing the intercodon from a glycine codon to a codon recognized by eRF1 is most likely to:

- O **A.** increase the frameshift efficiency by 70%.
- O **B.** decrease the frameshift efficiency by 70%.
- O **C.** have no effect on the frameshift efficiency.
- O **D.** decrease the frameshift efficiency by 10%.

Questions 26 through 28 do not refer to a passage and are independent of each other.

Question 26

Binding of a four ring compound to a cytoplasmic receptor is likely to:

- O **A.** increase the transcription of glucose 6-phosphatase.
- O **B.** increase the transcription of DHEA.
- O **C.** decrease the transcription of Na^+/H^+ genes.
- O **D.** decrease the transcription succinate dehydrogenase.

Question 27

All of the following are plausible reasons for prokaryotic gene regulation EXCEPT:

- O **A.** generating motor proteins to move away from noxious chemicals.
- O **B.** expressing a pilus when another prokaryote is detected nearby.
- O **C.** transcribing enzymes to breakdown nearby monosaccharides.
- O **D.** maintaining the internal temperature of the cytoplasm.

Question 28

Hydrolysis of the 5’ cap on mRNA is most likely to impair:

I. alternative splicing.
II. poly-A tail addition.
III. nuclear export.

- O **A.** I only
- O **B.** III only
- O **C.** I and III only
- O **D.** II and III only

TEST 2A

Passage 6 (Questions 29-32)

Huntington's disease (HD) is a progressive neurodegenerative disorder resulting from a trinucleotide CAG repeat expansion in the *Huntingtin* gene. Pathologically, HD is characterized by neuronal death in the caudate-putamen regions of the brain and HD patients suffer a triad of movement, cognitive, and behavioral issues which worsen throughout the course of the disease. Currently, there are no effective treatments and the key pathogenic mechanisms responsible for causing progressive neurodegeneration are unknown.

Transcriptional dysregulation is a characteristic of the disease process in humans. Abnormalities in transcription occur prior to the onset of symptoms and are accompanied by changes in histone acetylation, ubiquitylation, and methylation. In particular, acetylation of the N-terminal tail of histone H3 is an activating mark for gene expression, and increases in histone acetylation precede and facilitate increased transcriptional activity. However, in HD, levels of acetylated histone H3 (AcH3) are decreased, resulting in the downregulation of genes. In a transgenic HD mouse model, mRNA abnormalities were reversed by treatment with inhibitors of histone deacetylases (HDAC), the family of enzymes that remove acetyl groups from histone tails, with concomitant increases in global histone H3 acetylation.

HDAC inhibition is currently being investigated as a potential therapeutic intervention for HD. However, the relationship between histone acetylation and gene expression has not been studied in human HD brains. A DNA microarray was used to determine AcH3-binding events at various gene loci in wild type and transgenic mice with HD. The locations and binding percentages of AcH3 probes are shown in Figures 1 and 2.

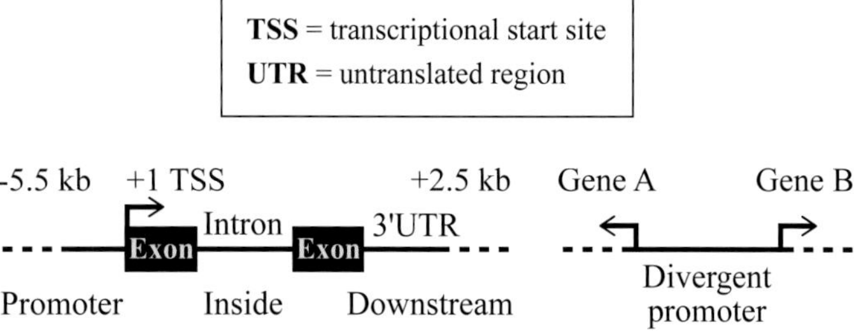

Figure 1 Schematic indicating location of probes

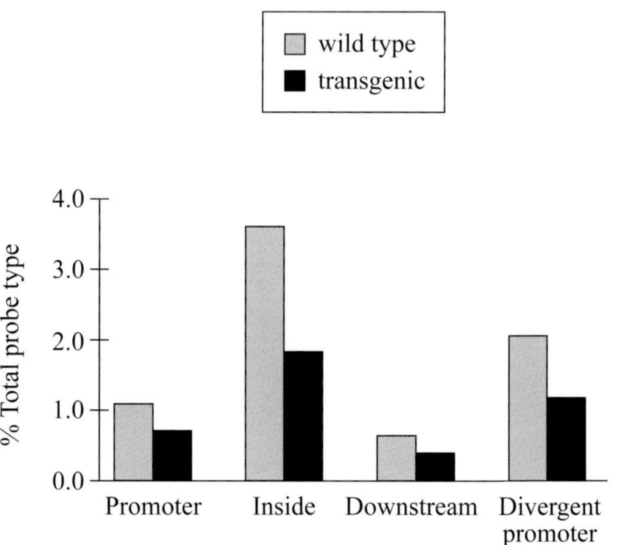

Figure 2 Locations of probes within the gene expressed as percent bound of total probe type within the microarray

This passage was adapted from "Genome-Wide Histone Acetylation Is Altered in a Transgenic Mouse Model of Huntington's Disease." McFarland KN, Das S, Sun TT, Leyfer D, Xia E, et al. *PLoS ONE*. 2012. 7(7) doi:10.1371/journal.pone.0041423 for use under the terms of the Creative Commons CC BY 3.0 license (http://creativecommons.org/licenses/by/3.0/legalcode).

Question 29

Throughout transcription and translation, many genes are modified for regulation purposes. Histone acetylases represent what type of genetic modification?

- **A.** Post-translational
- **B.** Post-transcriptional
- **C.** Epigenetic
- **D.** Pre-translational

Question 30

The microarray results imply that histone acetylases:

- **A.** predominantly associated at coding regions for expressed genes.
- **B.** regulate the majority of transcriptional activity via the promoter.
- **C.** use non-coding DNA to exert considerable influence over transcriptional rates.
- **D.** promote one gene product over another.

Question 31

Several genomic abnormalities can cause reduced gene expression. Which of the following is least likely to result in reduced gene expression in eukaryotes?

- **A.** Mutations in enhancer sequences
- **B.** Elongation of poly-A tail in mRNA transcript
- **C.** Disruption of the transcription bubble
- **D.** Improper attachment of methyl-G cap in mRNA transcript

Next ▶

Question 32

Different clinical trials are exploring treatments for HD. What is the function of histone deacetylase inhibitors as a potential therapy for HD?

- O **A.** To decrease histone acetylation levels, thereby downregulating genes
- O **B.** Decrease histone acetylation levels, thereby upregulating genes
- O **C.** To increase histone acetylation levels, thereby downregulating genes
- O **D.** To increase histone acetylation levels, thereby upregulating genes

Passage 7 (Questions 33-36)

Macrophages destroy bacteria by engulfing them in intracellular compartments, which they then acidify to kill or neutralize the bacteria. However, some pathogenic bacteria, such as *Salmonella enterica*, have evolved to withstand and even grow while within these acidified compartments. Instead of combating the acidification of the Salmonella-containing vacuole (SCV), Salmonella acidifies its own cytoplasm in response to the extracellular low pH. The acidic cytoplasm then acts as a signal to stimulate the secretion of a particular class of Salmonella virulence proteins. These virulence proteins, or effectors, are released into the host cell, where they are able to perturb the immune response. This results in symptoms like nausea, vomiting and diarrhea among others. In the United States, Salmonella is the number one cause of hospitalizations due to foodborne illness.

The acidification of the cytoplasm requires a pair of proteins, EnvZ and OmpR. EnvZ is a sensor kinase that responds to intracellular osmotic stress. When activated, EnvZ phosphorylates OmpR, a DNA-binding protein that regulates the expression of numerous proteins. OmpR regulates the cadC/BA operon, which codes for CadA, CadB and CadC. These three proteins maintain intracellular pH by catalyzing reactions to consume excess protons. The data indicate that OmpR acts as a repressor of this operon; thus, when OmpR is activated in the SCV, it stifles the normal response to low pH stress.

OmpR also regulates Salmonella pathogenicity island 2 (SPI-2), which encodes a nanomachine called the type III secretion system. This nanomachine is composed of a SPI-2 needle complex used to inject bacterial virulence proteins into the host cell. The actions of EnvZ and OmpR in a Salmonella bacteria when it is inside the SCV are shown in Figure 1.

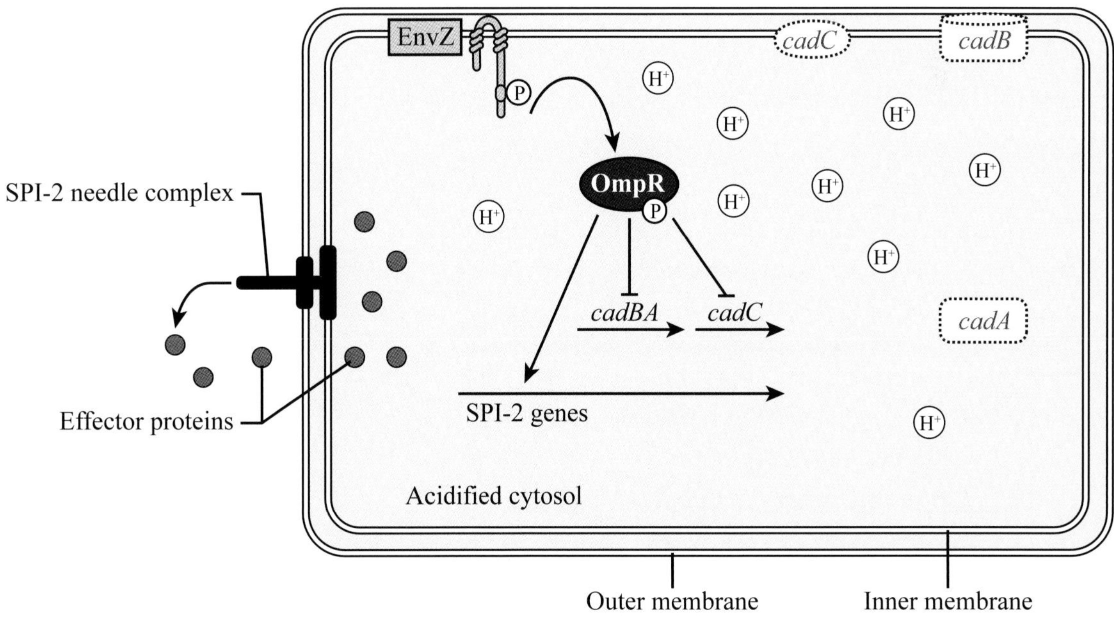

Figure 1 Diagram of EnvZ and OmpR action in Salmonella in SCV

TEST 2A

Question 33

What experimental finding would confirm that the cytoplasmic acidification is a regulated and not passive response?

- **A.** The cytoplasm of Salmonella strains lacking EnvZ or OmpR acidifies in the SCV.
- **B.** The cytoplasm of Salmonella strains with EnvZ and OmpR acidifies in the SCV.
- **C.** The cytoplasm of Salmonella strains lacking EnvZ remains neutral in SCV.
- **D.** The cytoplasm of Salmonella strains lacking OmpR is neutral outside SCV.

Question 34

In a wild type Salmonella existing outside the SCV, the presence of CadC would necessitate the presence of which of the following?

- **A.** CadB, EnvZ, and phosphorylated OmpR
- **B.** CadA, CadB, dephosphorylated OmpR, and SPI-2 gene products
- **C.** CadA and dephosphorylated OmpR
- **D.** CadA, EnvZ, and a low extracellular pH

Question 35

OmpR demonstrates:

I. positive control in prokaryotic gene expression.
II. prokaryotic gene repression.
III. enhancer activity.

- **A.** I only
- **B.** II only
- **C.** I and II only
- **D.** II and III only

Question 36

The researchers observed that a Salmonella did not acidify its cytoplasm while inside the SCV. They collected data on the presence (+) or absence (−) of four bacterial proteins. Based on the data above, which of the following is most likely true?

- **A.** The cadC/BA operon's operator is mutated and dysfunctional.
- **B.** The cadC/BA operon is mutated and dysfunctional.
- **C.** OmpR is mutated and dysfunctional.
- **D.** The cadC/BA operon's promoter is mutated and dysfunctional.

Passage 8 (Questions 37-41)

One process disturbed in cancerous cells is alternative splicing. Alternative splicing consists of joining of certain residual exons of the primary transcript to produce mRNA molecules of different sequences. Alternative splicing is a complicated process, involving a significant number of proteins, including splicing factors called serine-arginine rich proteins (SR proteins). These factors bind to sequences called splicing enhancers, located primarily in exons (exonic splicing enhancers) but also in introns (intronic splicing enhancers).

Binding of SR proteins to splicing enhancers promotes exon inclusion. The splicing reaction is also regulated by a large number of non-SR factors, such as hnRNPs (heterogeneous nuclear ribonucleoproteins) which mainly bind to sequences of splicing silencers and act as splicing repressors. It is known that disturbances in alternative splicing may contribute to carcinogenesis due to production of tumor-suppressive or oncogenic variants of gene transcripts, affecting proliferation, cell motility, and apoptosis susceptibility.

Experiment 1

The expression of two splicing factors belonging to the SR protein family (SF2/ASF and SC35) and one non-SR factor, hnRNP A1 (heterogeneous nuclear ribonucleoprotein A1), was measured in 38 pairs of tumor-control clear cell renal carcinoma (ccRCC) samples by PCR (Figure 1). According to the findings, disturbances in expression of splicing factors occur in at least half (50–60%) of analyzed samples, although the disturbances are diverse and result from both up- and downregulation of splicing factors.

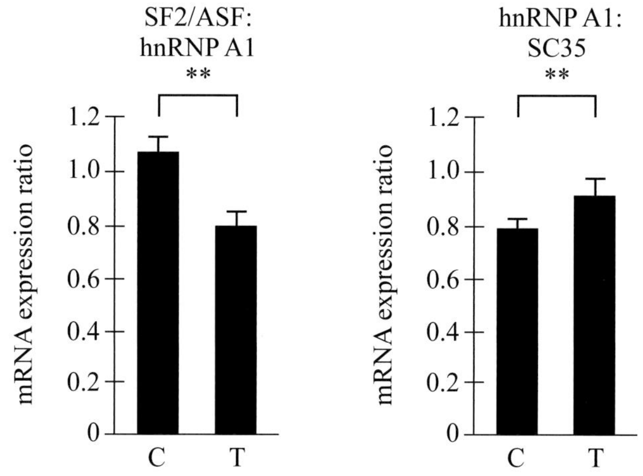

Figure 1 Changes in ratios between splicing factors known to act antagonistically in tissue samples

Next ▶

Question 37

According to the information presented in the passage, binding of SC35 to DNA is most likely to occur:

- **A.** in protein coding regions.
- **B.** in regions that allow for homologous recombination.
- **C.** in the presence of an RNA polymerase.
- **D.** during S phase of the cell cycle.

Question 38

Where is an RNA transcript that is undergoing alternative splicing most likely to be located in cancer cells?

- **A.** Endoplasmic reticulum
- **B.** Golgi body
- **C.** Cytoplasm
- **D.** Nucleus

Question 39

Splicing factors are likely to contain amino acids that have what type of side chain(s)?

- **A.** Basic, negatively charged
- **B.** Acidic, positively charged
- **C.** Polar
- **D.** Aromatic

Question 40

What additional experimental evidence, in combination with the information presented in the passage, would most likely weaken the assertion that hnRNPs repress splicing events?

- **A.** Mutations upstream in genic non-coding sequences increase splicing.
- **B.** Mutation of serine to glutamate in SC35 active site decreases splicing.
- **C.** Mutation of arginine to alanine in the hnRNP active site does not change splicing.
- **D.** hnRNPs are shown to bind to exon regions.

Question 41

In a separate experiment, scientists determined that a separate splicing factor, SP82, was upregulated in a subset of cancers. Which of the following mechanisms is the LEAST likely to account for this finding?

- **A.** Hypermethylation of the SP82 promoter sequence
- **B.** Acetylation of the SP82 enhancer sequence
- **C.** Hypermethylation of the SP82 repressor sequence
- **D.** Hypomethylation of the SP82 enhancer sequence.

Questions 42 through 45 do not refer to a passage and are independent of each other.

Question 42

RNA secondary structure may be caused by repetitive CpG dinucleotides. Repetitive CpG sequences may result in:

- **A.** increased slippage of RNA polymerase on DNA.
- **B.** decreased protein production.
- **C.** increased rates of DNA replication.
- **D.** decreased initiation of translation.

Question 43

An antibody used to isolate the 40S subunit of an actively translating ribosome is likely to pull down:

I. mRNA.
II. tRNA.
III. rRNA.

- **A.** I only
- **B.** II only
- **C.** I and II only
- **D.** I, II, and III

Question 44

The eukaryotic initiation factor eIF2 most likely binds which of the following codons?

- **A.** AUG
- **B.** ATG
- **C.** UAA
- **D.** UGA

Question 45

Scientists notice a single site of partially unwound DNA near the center of a bacterial chromosome. The DNA polymerase is most likely acting at:

- **A.** a promoter.
- **B.** an enhancer.
- **C.** a repressor.
- **D.** an origin of replication.

TEST 2A

TEST 2A

Passage 9 (Questions 46-50)

Multiple sclerosis (MS) is an autoimmune demyelinating dysfunction causing inflammation, oligodendrocyte (OL) cell death and axonal degeneration. Remyelination of axons occurs spontaneously at early stages of MS disease progression, while when disease progresses OLs arrest in a pre-myelination state. The reasons for inadequate CNS remyelination at chronic MS lesions is largely unknown.

To improve the regenerative properties of current MS treatments it is important to clarify how Oligodendrocyte Precursor Cell (OPC) differentiation and maturation occur at demyelinated lesions in the adult brain and to identify novel compounds acting in this process. The Myelin Regulatory Factor (MRF) is a critical transcriptional regulator required for CNS myelination. MRF expression is essential for OL maturation and is required for the expression of the vast majority of the CNS myelin genes.

Global expression profile studies aimed at identifying positive regulators of remyelination show that Retinoic x Receptor gamma (RxRγ) up-regulation is associated with OPC differentiation and remyelination at demyelinated lesions. Members of the glucocorticoid family (FGC), such as halcinonide and clobetasol, are predicted to activate RxRγ by activating Smoothened (Smo). Smo is a member of the seven trans-membrane family of receptors that is activated upon release from Patched (PTCH), a twelve-pass trans-membrane protein that binds to Hedgehog ligands (Figure 1). FGCs may also activate myelin gene expression by binding cytosolic receptors with the help of Heat Shock Proteins (HSP).

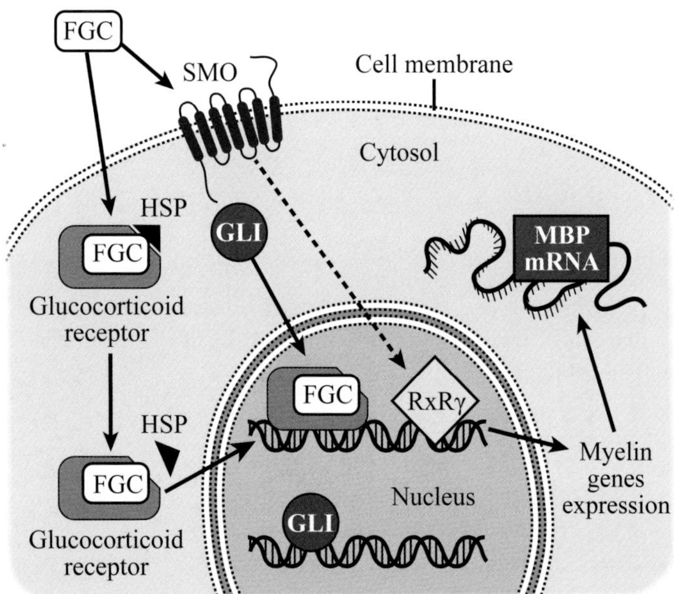

Figure 1 Predicted pathway of glucocorticoid-mediated myelin gene expression

Using Real Time PCR, various glucocorticoids were tested to determine how robustly they activate RxRγ expression by binding Smo. The results are shown in Figure 2.

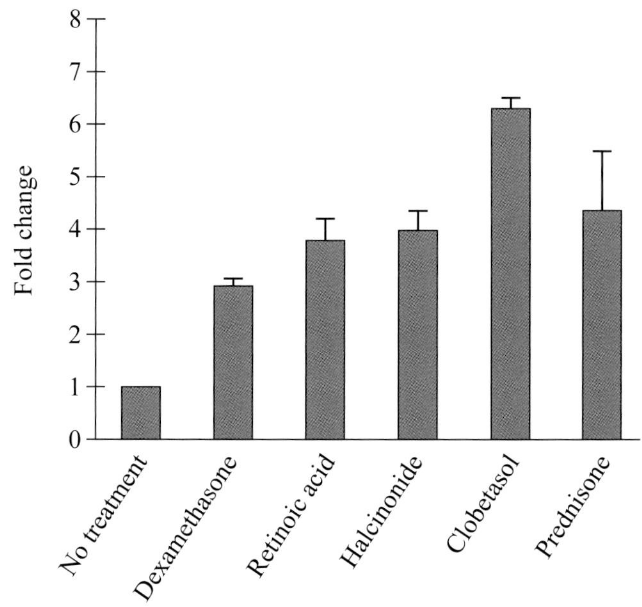

Figure 2 Effect of FGCs on RxRγ expression

Question 46

Upon activation, RXRγ controls myelin gene expression by:

- **A.** binding RNA.
- **B.** binding DNA.
- **C.** replicating RNA.
- **D.** replicating DNA.

Question 47

Glucocorticoids most likely bind which of the following segments of amino acids to activate Smoothened?

- **A.** W-L-P-F
- **B.** R-R-I-L
- **C.** V-D-E-K
- **D.** S-T-F-Y

Question 48

Assuming that no mutations occur to the signaling pathway described by the passage, what event activates RXRγ?

- ○ **A.** Protein cleavage
- ○ **B.** GTP exchange
- ○ **C.** Association with the plasma membrane
- ○ **D.** Phosphorylation

Question 49

According to the passage, what is most likely true about the genes that become expressed upon activation of MRF?

- ○ **A.** They cause disruption of the plasma membrane.
- ○ **B.** They contain a MRF binding site in their TATA box regions.
- ○ **C.** They have gain-of-function mutations that alter their role in myelin formation.
- ○ **D.** They bind to RXRγ in the cytosol.

Question 50

A mutation in the RNA responsible for carrying phenylalanine would result in:

- ○ **A.** decreased transcription of myelin genes.
- ○ **B.** decreased translation of myelin genes.
- ○ **C.** increased transcription of myelin genes.
- ○ **D.** increased translation of myelin genes.

Passage 10 (Questions 51-55)

Nucleic acid secondary structures are widespread genomic regulatory elements capable of modulating gene transcription . Recent studies have shown that transcription of approximately 40% of the human genome is regulated by secondary structures within the 1kb proximal promoter region, including genes involved in Fragile X Syndrome, the most common inherited intellectual disability. Previous work by scientists showed that transcription of tyrosine hydroxylase (Th), the rate-limiting enzyme for catecholamine neurotransmitter biosynthesis, is regulated by secondary structures in its proximal promoter region and that agents to modify nucleic acid secondary structure may serve as treatments for diseases, such as Alzheimer's disease.

One of the most extensively used compounds to manipulate nucleic acid secondary structure stability is TMPyP4, a porphyrin molecule (Figure 1). The molecular mechanism of this inhibition is unknown, but the positively charged nitrogen of the methyl pyridinium group is reminiscent of the charged quaternary amine of acetylcholine.

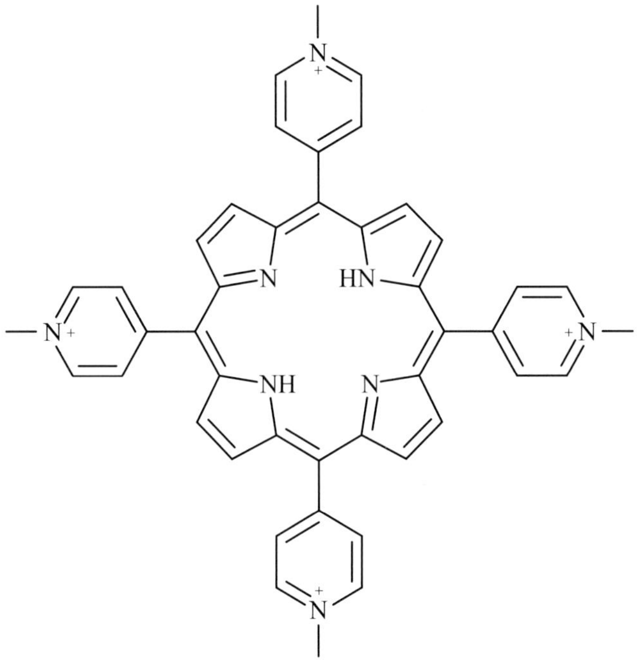

Figure 1 Molecular structures of TMPyP4

TEST 2A

Scientists treated SH-SY5Y neuronal cells with TMPyP4, and TMPyP2, a control compound, While low doses of TMPyP4 reduced Th promoter activity in mouse forebrain slice cultures (Figure 2), administering a high dose resulted in temporary paralysis by inhibiting acetylcholinesterase (AChE), an enzyme that breaks down the neurotransmitter acetylcholine in the synaptic cleft.

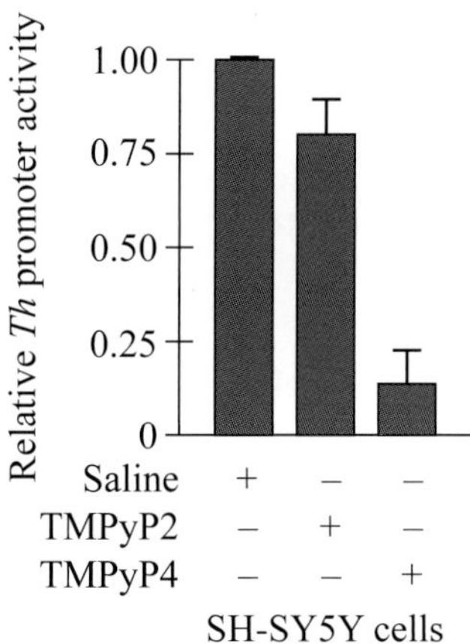

Figure 2 *In vitro* modulation of Th expression by TMPyP4

In an attempt to better understand the mechanism of action of TMPyP4, neurons were pre-treated with hemeoxygenase-2 (HO-2) to determine whether degradation of porphyrin molecules could rescue AChE activity from TMPyP4-mediated inhibition. The results are shown in Figure 3.

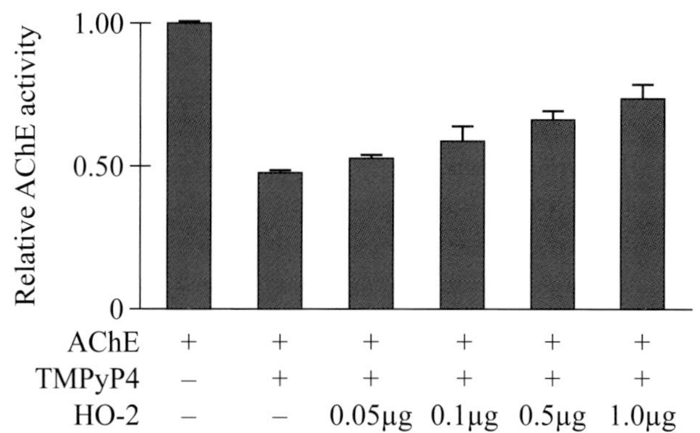

Figure 3 TMPyP4 inhibits AChE activity

Question 51

A previous RNA sequencing experiment utilized AChE mRNA in an attempt to better understand why TMPyP4 inhibited normal levels of AChE protein. What is the most likely reason this failed to yield informative results?

- **A.** AChE mRNA does not include the sequences of the promoter bound by TMPyP4.
- **B.** AChE mRNA did not include a 5′ GMP gap.
- **C.** AChE mRNA did not include a 3′ poly-A tail.
- **D.** AChE mRNA was rapidly degraded by exonucleases after transcription.

Question 52

In a subsequent experiment, *in vitro* incubation of neuronal DNA in a high salt concentration was found to increase the concentration of AChE produced in an *in vitro* transcription and translation assay. These findings likely:

- **A.** refute the authors' conclusion that secondary structure hinders *AChE* transcription.
- **B.** support the authors' conclusions that secondary structure hinders *AChE* transcription.
- **C.** refute the authors' conclusion that secondary structure hinders AChE translation.
- **D.** support the authors' conclusion that secondary structure hinders AChE translation.

Question 53

Control cells that are not treated with TMPyP4 are likely to have:

- **A.** increased concentrations of GTP.
- **B.** decreased concentrations of GTP.
- **C.** increased concentrations of CTP.
- **D.** decreased concentrations of CTP.

Question 54

Pol II activity is most likely:

- **A.** increased in cells treated with TMPyP4.
- **B.** reduced in cells treated with TMPyP4.
- **C.** inactivated in cells with TMPyP4.
- **D.** not affected by TMPyP4.

Question 55

Pre-treatment of neurons with HO-2 would be expected to:

- **A.** decrease the transcription of AChE.
- **B.** increase the transcription of AChE.
- **C.** decrease the transcription and translation of AChE.
- **D.** increase the transcription and translation of AChE.

Questions 56 through 59 do not refer to a passage and are independent of each other.

Question 56

Overexpression of telomerase is most likely to result in:

- O **A.** increased rates of DNA replication.
- O **B.** increased cellular apoptosis.
- O **C.** cellular senescence.
- O **D.** cellular immortality.

Question 57

Nucleoside analogues would be LEAST likely to induce apoptosis in:

I. hematopoietic stem cells.
II. neurons.
III. skeletal muscle.

- O **A.** I only
- O **B.** II only
- O **C.** II and III only
- O **D.** I, II, and III

Question 58

S phase of the cell cycle is LEAST likely to regulate:

- O **A.** the initiation of DNA replication.
- O **B.** duplication of centrioles.
- O **C.** transcription of cyclin proteins that initiate mitosis.
- O **D.** actin polymerization from the centrosome.

Question 59

Which of the following is the most likely reason that cancer cells show overexpression of genes involved in homologous recombination?

- O **A.** Increased rates of double strand breaks necessitate increased homologous recombination during G_1.
- O **B.** Stalling of the replication fork during S phase requires rescue by homologous recombination.
- O **C.** Increased time spent by cancer cells in G_2 requires higher concentrations of proteins involved in homologous recombination.
- O **D.** Increased expression of homologous recombination genes occurs by 2 bp insertions in the first exon of these genes.

STOP. If you finish before time is called, check your work. You may go back to any question in this test.

ANSWERS & EXPLANATIONS for Test 2A can be found on p. 222.

Genetics

TEST 2B

Time: 95 minutes
Questions 1–59

DIRECTIONS: Most questions in the Biological and Biochemical Foundations of Living Systems test section are grouped with a descriptive passage. Select the best answer to each question using background knowledge and the given passage. A portion of this test section is comprised of discrete questions, which are independent of any passage and one another. Select the best answer for each discrete question. Indicate your selection by blackening the corresponding oval on your answer document. If you are unsure of the answer, rule out incorrect choices and select from the remaining options. You may access a periodic table found on the last page of this book at any point during this test section.

Passage 1 (Questions 1-4)

Tight control of gene expression is achieved by numerous transcription factors that result from alternative splicing of a few genes. Alternative splicing allows one isoform of a transcription factor, TFII-I, to activate target gene expression, while other isoforms are involved in transcriptional repression.

In addition to alternative splicing, other proteins may bind TFII-I to change its function. The repressive function of TFII-I is mediated by association with histone deacetylases HDAC1 and HDAC3. Additionally, mouse double minute 2 (Mdm2) is an oncogene in human cancers and negatively regulates p53 levels. p53 halts cell cycle progression upon DNA damage and prevents damaged cells from becoming cancerous. Mdm2 may also interact with TFII-I and have negative effects on TFII-I-dependent transcription in human cells.

Experiment 1

To determine whether expression of TFII-I results in overexpression of Mdm2, scientists co-transfected plasmids containing the TFII-I gene and plasmids containing Mdm2, the deubiquitinating enzyme USP48, and tumor suppressor p14 all under the control of a viral cytomegalovirus (CMV) promoter. Cells were lysed and protein pellets collected for western blot against the co-transfected genes. The results are shown in Figure 1.

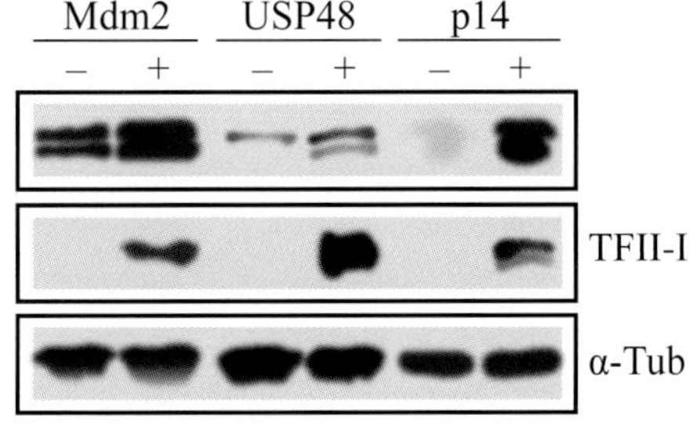

Figure 1 TFII-I affects gene expression from plasmid constructs containing CMV promoter

Experiment 2

DNA vaccines that use a CMV promoter are used to treat cancer and some infectious diseases. Scientists also sought to confirm whether TFII-I bound the CMV promoter of these DNA vaccines. Scientists transfected control plasmids or plasmids containing TFII-I with plasmids containing the full-length CMV promoter or its shorter deletion mutants that controlled the expression of luciferase reporter gene (Figure 2).

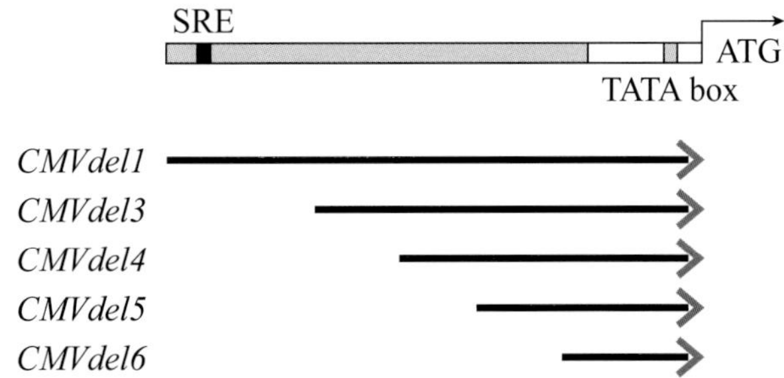

Figure 2 Full length CMV promoter and its shorter deletion mutants

Scientists lysed cells 24 hours after transfection and measured the luciferase protein content by western blot to determine the effects of shortening the CMV enhancer on gene expression. The results are shown in Figure 3.

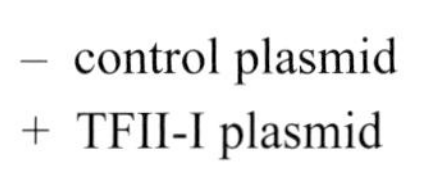

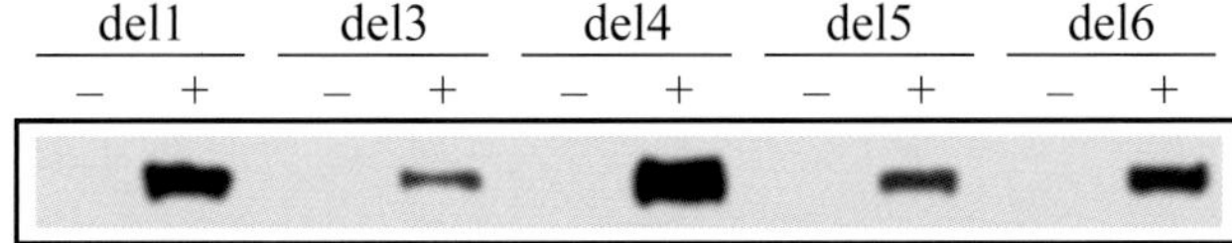

Figure 3 Effect of TFII-I on luciferase expression in full-length CMV promoter and its shorter deletion mutants

Question 1

Non-covalent interaction between TFII-I and HDAC1 most likely:

- O **A.** increases the proportion of euchromatin in the genome.
- O **B.** increases the proportion of heterochromatin in the genome.
- O **C.** increases the expression of genes bound to deacetylated histones.
- O **D.** increases the number of C nucleotides that are methylated.

Question 2

Alternatively spliced TFII-I isoforms are able to mediate opposite effects on gene expression by:

- O **A.** competing for the same DNA consensus binding sequence.
- O **B.** competing for the same RNA consensus binding sequence.
- O **C.** stabilizing or destabilizing aminoacyl-tRNAs.
- O **D.** stabilizing or destabilizing proteins through addition or removal of ubiquitin.

Question 3

What additional experimental evidence would support the role of Mdm2 as an oncogene?

- A. Overexpression of Mdm2 was found to increase the number of cells undergoing apoptosis.
- B. Overexpression of Mdm2 was found to decrease the time required to complete the cell cycle.
- C. A silent mutation in exon 2 of Mdm2 failed to decrease the number of cells in G_0.
- D. A nonsense mutation in exon 1 of Mdm2 decreased Mdm2 protein concentrations in the cytosol.

Question 4

Which of the following sequences is most likely to have been deleted when creating the CMVdel4 mutant?

- A. TFII-I repressor binding site
- B. TFII-I enhancer binding site
- C. TFII-I promoter site
- D. CMV promoter site

Passage 2 (Questions 5-9)

Amyloid plaques are characteristic pathologic features of Alzheimer's disease (AD), a progressive neurodegenerative disorder. Amyloid plaques are formed from the amyloid β peptide (Aβ), which is a proteolytic product of the amyloid precursor protein (APP). Aβ peptides can accumulate and form oligomers that eventually give rise to amyloid plaques.

Early-onset forms of AD arise from mutations leading to elevated Aβ production. This change in Aβ can arise from heightened APP levels due to mutations in APP or from increased APP copy number as observed in Down's syndrome (Trisomy 21). Regulatory sequences within the 3′ UTRs (untranslated regions) of an mRNA can affect its stability, transcription, and translation. Guanine quadruplexes (G-quadruplexes) are RNA secondary structures that contain repeating guanines arranged in a manner that facilitates intra-molecular stacking and may affect transcription and translation. Though bioinformatics analysis, scientists discovered two G-rich regions in the *APP* gene (Figure 1).

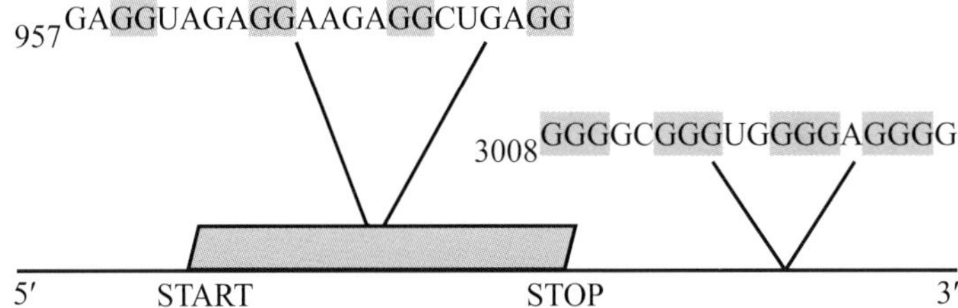

Figure 1 APP contains a putative G-quadruplex in the coding region at position 957 and the G-quadruplex sequence in the 3′UTR at position 3008.

Experiment 1

To investigate the functional significant of the G-quadruplexes, scientists utilized a luciferase reporter construct in which the human APP 3′UTR was inserted after the stop codon of the firefly luciferase gene. They used PCR to measure luciferase mRNA levels in into human embryonic kidney (HEK293) cells transfected with plasmids containing wild type or mutant APP 3′ UTR. The results are shown in Figure 2.

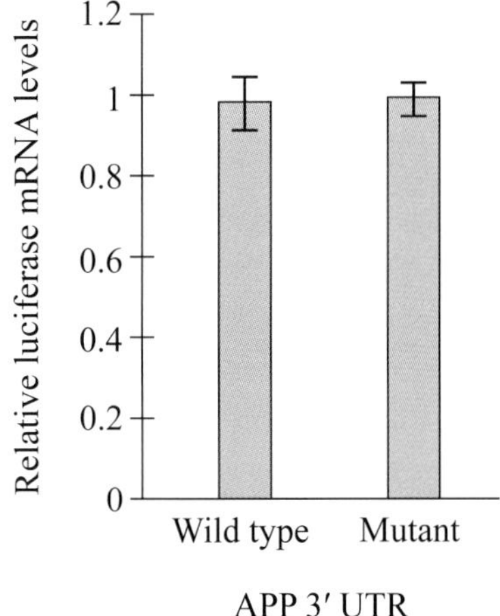

Figure 2 G-quadruplex regulation of Luciferase gene expression

TEST 2B

Experiment 2

To investigate whether the 3′ UTR G-quadruplex impacted translation, the wild type and mutant luciferase reporter constructs were individually transfected into human embryonic kidney (HEK293) cells. 24 hours post-transfection, they measured the luciferase activity as a proxy for luciferase protein expression levels from the two constructs. The results are shown in Figure 3.

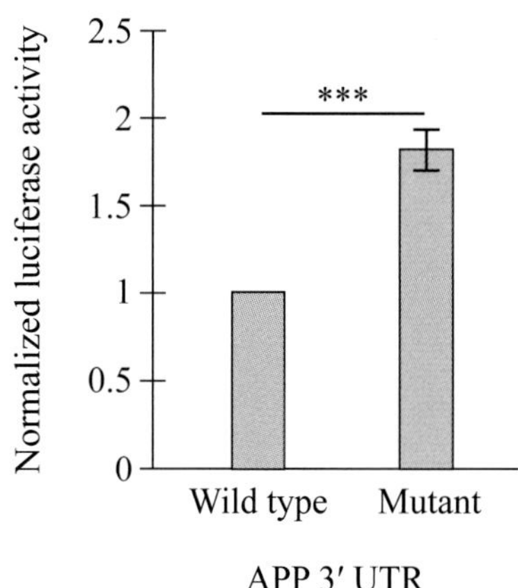

Figure 3 G-quadruplex regulation of Luciferase gene expression

Question 5

G-quadruplexes in the 3′ UTR of *APP* most likely:

- O **A.** decrease the concentration of *APP* in the cytosol.
- O **B.** increase the concentration of *APP* in the cytosol.
- O **C.** decrease the transcription of *APP*.
- O **D.** increase the transcription of *APP*.

Question 6

Misfolded APP proteins can also result from slippage of the ribosome between adjacent codons. Which of the following mRNA molecules represents the DNA sequence that could give rise to misfolded APP in this manner?

- O **A.** 5′- AATTGCTAATTCGTAT – 3′
- O **B.** 3′ – AAUUCCGCGUAGUA – 5′
- O **C.** 5′ – AAUAAUAAUAAUGC – 3′
- O **D.** 5′ – AUCGUGCGAUCGUAA – 3′

Question 7

Upon repeating Experiment 1, scientists failed to detect any luciferase signal resulting from the transcription of the plasmid containing either the wild type or mutant 3′ UTR. Their HEK293 cells most likely contained a nonsense mutation in:

- O **A.** POLδ, a DNA polymerase.
- O **B.** TOP2A, a DNA topoisomerase I.
- O **C.** HIST2H, a histone.
- O **D.** the 50S subunit of the ribosome.

Question 8

The nucleotide sequence of G-quadruplexes is similar to the sequence of:

I. eukaryotic telomeres.
II. prokaryotic operons.
III. eukaryotic DNA replication start sites.

- O **A.** I only
- O **B.** I and II only
- O **C.** I and III only
- O **D.** II and III only

Question 9

Aβ oligomers most likely form between which of the following amino acids?

- O **A.** A
- O **B.** S
- O **C.** Y
- O **D.** E

Passage 3 (Questions 10-13)

The capacity of T cells to recognize all antigens relies on their diverse naïve T cell repertoire. Cells specific for each antigen are rare, but immune responses are efficient because lymphocytes have a remarkable capacity to expand. For example, each individual CD4 T cell may generate up to a 10^{14} progeny. These division properties pose an important paradox. Multiple divisions increase DNA breaks, which must be repaired to allow T cell survival and prevent transformation into blood cancers like leukemia. However, rapid T cell accumulation during immune responses is only possible because T lymphocytes' cycle time is of short duration, reducing the time available for efficient repair.

DNA damage is recognized by histone H2AX. Double strand breaks (DSBs) recruit the MRN complex, which holds the DNA ends together, and recruits ATM. ATM propagates DSB-induced changes in the chromatin structure, phosphorylates H2AX, and recruits the endonuclease ARTEMIS. ATM also activates TP53, which leads to cell cycle arrest. Once the cell cycle is arrested, DNA repair molecules are recruited to the DNA damaged sites.

Previous studies have shown that CD8 accumulation collapses in the absence of CD4 help. By using PCR array-based expression profiling, DNA damage response (DDR) modifications were found to be restricted to the exponential phases of the immune responses. In the presence of CD4 cells, the expression of H2AX was 5-fold increased and the expression of Rad51, which plays a fundamental role in homologous recombination, was 15-fold up-regulated. Without CD4 help, most of the components of MRN complex and ATM were down-regulated. Additionally, TP53 expression was also 3-fold reduced. The prevailing model is that the immune system evolved efficient methods to guarantee timely cell accumulation during immune responses, while preventing T cell transformation in spite of the CD8 extensive division.

Question 10

Phosphorylation of histone H2AX likely results in:

- O **A.** increased association of DNA with the histone complex.
- O **B.** dissociation of DNA from the histone complex.
- O **C.** decreased time for T cell proliferation to occur.
- O **D.** increased translation of the regions surrounding the histone complex.

Question 11

ATM mediates its intracellular signaling by acting as a:

- O **A.** phosphatase.
- O **B.** ligase.
- O **C.** nuclease.
- O **D.** kinase.

Question 12

What additional experimental evidence would support the role of ATM in mediating the DDR?

- O **A.** *ATM*$^{-/-}$ mice show a decreased number of T cells arrested in the G_2 phase upon secondary antigen challenge.
- O **B.** *TP53*$^{-/-}$ mice show an embryonic lethal phenotype.
- O **C.** *ATM*$^{+/+}$ mice show an increased number of T cells arrested in the G_1 phase upon secondary antigen challenge.
- O **D.** *H2AX*$^{-/-}$ mice show an increased incidence of T cell leukemia.

Question 13

In a subsequence experiment, scientists determined that overexpression of *TP53* leads to a dramatic reduction in the proliferation of T cells. *TP53* is likely to act as a(n):

I. transcription factor.
II. tumor suppressor.
III. oncogene.

- O **A.** I only
- O **B.** I and II only
- O **C.** I and III only
- O **D.** II and III only

TEST 2B

Questions 14 through 17 do not refer to a passage and are independent of each other.

Question 14

Activity of which of the following proteins is necessary for progression through prophase?

- O **A.** Laminin-1 kinase
- O **B.** Topoisomerase I
- O **C.** DNA polymerase
- O **D.** Thymidylate synthetase

Question 15

BAF60 allows cell cycle progression beyond G_1. Somatic epithelial cells treated with an inhibitor of BAF60 contain:

- O **A.** 23 chromosomes.
- O **B.** 23 chromatids.
- O **C.** 46 chromosomes.
- O **D.** 92 chromatids.

Question 16

Cri du chat is a genetic disorder characterized by the absence of telomerase reverse transcriptase, a catalytic subunit of the enzyme telomerase. Which of the following is the most likely consequences of this disorder?

- O **A.** An increased rate of cellular aging resulting from a decreased rate of DNA transcription
- O **B.** A decreased rate of fusion between each chromosome and its surrounding chromosomes
- O **C.** A decrease in the number of TTAGGG repeats due to enzyme inactivity
- O **D.** A decrease in the methylation of CpG islands surrounding the kinetochore

Question 17

DNA plasmid vaccines are important tools for experimental gene therapy and replace defective genes in diseases like cystic fibrosis. Replication of the DNA plasmids most likely occurs:

- O **A.** in bacteria by replicating double stranded DNA.
- O **B.** in yeast by replicating double stranded DNA.
- O **C.** in bacteria by replicating single stranded DNA.
- O **D.** in yeast by replicating single stranded DNA.

Passage 4 (Questions 18-21)

A hallmark of solid tumors is hypoxia, which confers resistance to conventional chemotherapy and radiation therapy at oxygen concentrations of 1% or less. As a physiological feature of solid tumors, hypoxia has also shed light on targeting therapy through the development of hypoxia-activated prodrugs (HAPs). HAPs, including the compound Q6, covalently modify DNA in hypoxic cells but are deactivated in normoxic cells (Figure 1).

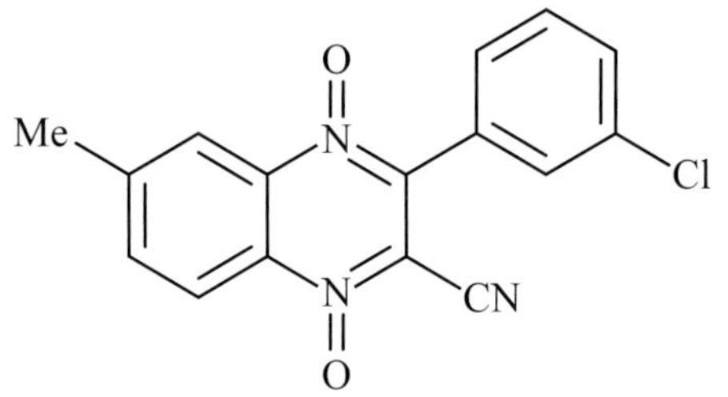

Figure 1 Structure of HAP Q6

Most anticancer drugs can induce DNA damage leading to DNA double-strand break (DSBs) formation. DNA DSBs can also arise from abortive topoisomerase activity. On the basis of selective anti-cancer effects of Q6 in hypoxia, scientists investigated its targeting effects on Topoisomerase II (topo II), and the subsequent effects on the cell cycle. Scientists grew breast cancer cells under normoxic or hypoxic conditions, in the presence and absence of Q6 and stained for cell death. The results are shown in Figure 2.

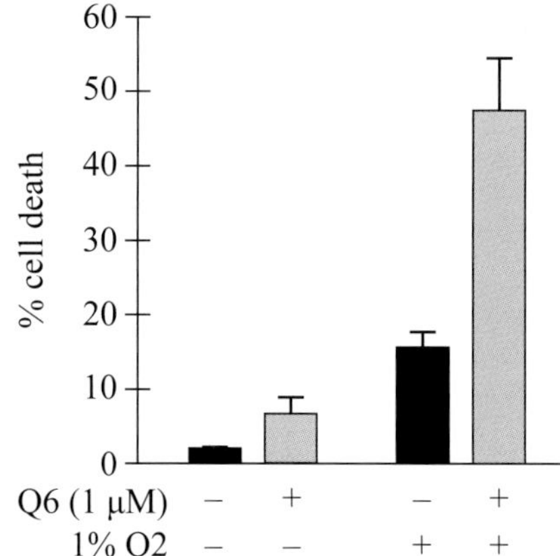

Figure 2 Effect of Q6 and hypoxia on cell death

Structural analysis showed that Q6 could effectively bind to topo II and the DNA binding domain, forming electrostatic interactions with the DNA phosphate groups. Additionally, the aromatic rings of Q6 were found to form hydrophobic interactions with topo II amino acid residues, which further reinforced the interactions between Q6 and topo II DNA complexes.

Question 18

In a follow-up experiment, scientists measured the percentage of cells in each cell cycle phase after treatment with increasing concentrations of Q6. Which of the following statements best describes the results:

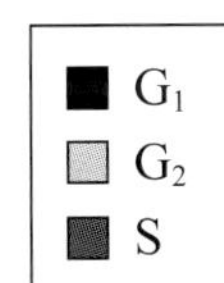

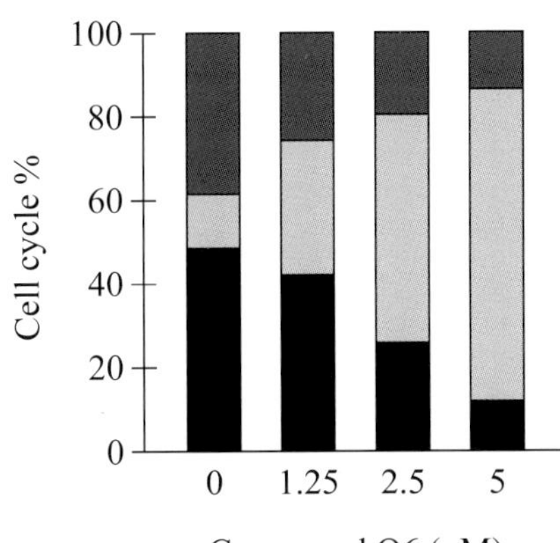

- ○ **A.** 5 μM treatment increases the number of cells with 4 copies of a gene compared to 1.25 μM treatment.
- ○ **B.** 2.5 μM treatment decreases the number of cells undergoing DNA replication compared to 5 μM treatment.
- ○ **C.** 2.5 μM treatment decreases the number of cells in growth phases compared to 1.25 μM treatment.
- ○ **D.** 5 μM treatment decreases the number of cells with duplicated centrioles compared to 1.25 μM treatment.

Question 19

Genome replication is most likely initiated by:

- ○ **A.** binding of RNA polymerase to the TATA box.
- ○ **B.** binding of DNA polymerase to histones.
- ○ **C.** binding of the ribosome to mRNA.
- ○ **D.** binding of telomerase to the ends of DNA.

Question 20

Which of the following enzymes is critical for the final step in repairing DSBs?

- ○ **A.** DNA endonuclease
- ○ **B.** DNA ligase
- ○ **C.** DNA polymerase
- ○ **D.** Nucleoside phosphotransferase

Question 21

The number of apoptotic cells is likely to be greatest in:

- ○ **A.** culture dishes grown in normoxic conditions in the absence of Q6.
- ○ **B.** culture dishes grown in normoxic conditions in the presence of Q6.
- ○ **C.** culture dishes grown in hypoxic conditions in the absence of Q6.
- ○ **D.** culture dishes grown in hypoxic conditions in the presence of Q6.

Passage 5 (Questions 22-26)

Numerous studies have shown that the normal apoptotic process is dysfunctional in colorectal cancer. Dysregulation of apoptosis contributes to the development of resistance to chemotherapy and a poor prognosis. Apoptosis is characterized by a number of morphological changes, including plasma membrane blebbing, chromatin condensation, nuclear fragmentation, formation of apoptotic bodies, and exposure of phosphatidylserine on the outer leaflet of the plasma membrane .

Nucleoside analogues are an important class of chemotherapeutic agents used in the treatment of cancer. Scientists interested in identifying novel nucleoside analogues screened HT-29 colorectal cancer cell lines against a panel of potential compounds. They concluded that three nucleosides had potential anti-tumor activity based on increased apoptosis observed in HT-29 after treatment. A representative nucleoside is shown in Figure 1.

Figure 1 Structure of Nucleoside 1

However, off-target effects of nucleoside analogues are clinically concerning and can include depression of the immune system due to increased leukocyte death. To assess off-target effects, the scientists exposed freshly isolated leukocytes to each of the three nucleoside analogues and to camptothecin, a mammalian topoisomerase I inhibitor and a known inducer of apoptosis. The results are shown in Figure 2.

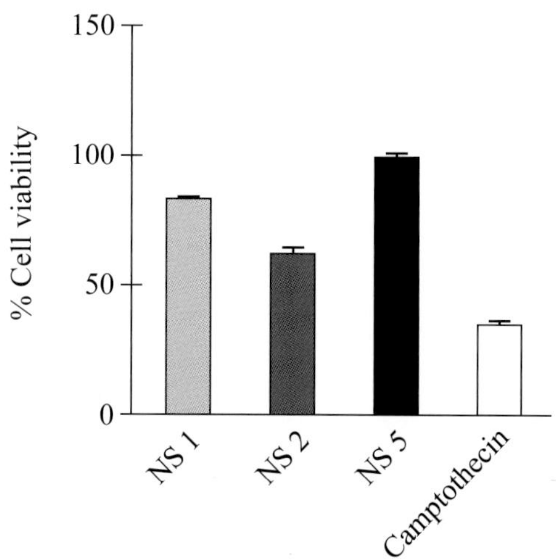

Figure 2 Leukocyte viability 24 hours after treatment with nucleosides (NS) 1, 2, 5, and camptothecin

The scientists concluded that nucleosides 1, 2, and 5 held promise as an anti-tumor drugs due to their ability to cause apoptosis in HT-29 cells while not decreasing immune system functioning. To determine whether cytochrome c, the main intracellular mediator of apoptosis, was released from the mitochondria, scientists measured the mitochondrial membrane voltage ($\Delta\psi$) by flow cytometry with the cationic fluorescent dye JC-1. The results are presented in Table 1.

Table 1 Summary of the mitochondrial membrane potential change induced by the nucleoside analogues and camptothecin in the HT-29 colon cancer cell lines

Cell type	% HT-29 cells with depolarized $\Delta\Psi$m
Untreated cells	10.35
Nucleoside 1	14.39
Nucleoside 2	12.74
Nucleoside 5	12.12
Camptothecin	44.00

Question 22

Which of the following cells is LEAST likely to be affected by nucleoside 1?

- O **A.** Erythrocytes
- O **B.** T cells
- O **C.** B cells
- O **D.** Natural killer cells

Question 23

Chromatin condensation during apoptosis is likely mediated by:

- O **A.** methylation of histone H3.
- O **B.** acetylation of histone H4.
- O **C.** phosphorylation of histone H2A.
- O **D.** ubiquitination of histone H2B.

Question 24

Camptothecin works by preventing:

- **A.** elongation of the DNA replication fork.
- **B.** procession of the ribosome of mRNA.
- **C.** initiation of DNA replication.
- **D.** binding of RNA polymerase to the TATA box.

Question 25

What additional experimental evidence would suggest that nucleoside 2 inhibited colorectal cancer cell growth?

- **A.** Nucleoside 2-treated HT-29 cells showed a 3% increase in $\Delta\psi m$.
- **B.** Cellular consumption of O_2 in nucleoside 2-treated HT-29 cells decreased by 55%.
- **C.** Levels of cyclin D began to rise 10 minutes after treatment of HT-29 cells with nucleoside 2.
- **D.** GLUT2, a glucose transporter, transcription increased in HT-29 cells after treatment with nucleoside 2.

Question 26

Scientists mutated the amino acid responsible for inducing the apoptosis cascade in the cytosol to confirm the role of cytochrome c. Which of the following is the most likely mutation made by the scientists?

- **A.** I to L
- **B.** V to G
- **C.** S to T
- **D.** A to R

Questions 27 through 30 do not refer to a passage and are independent of each other.

Question 27

Telomerase is a ribonucleoprotein complex made of multiple functional subparts that is responsible for lengthening the single-stranded 3′ ends of eukaryotic chromosomes with thousands of TTAGGG repeats. One of the subparts of the telomerase enzyme must function as a(n):

- **A.** helicase.
- **B.** topoisomerase.
- **C.** endonuclease.
- **D.** reverse transcriptase.

Question 28

Nonhomologous end joining (NHEJ) is one mechanism of DNA double strand break repair that operates without a second copy of the genome. The final step in NHEJ is most likely mediated by:

- **A.** DNA ligase.
- **B.** DNA kinase.
- **C.** DNA endonuclease.
- **D.** DNA polymerase.

Question 29

Scientists interested in mutating codon 532 in glucose-6-phosphatase would be most likely to induce:

- **A.** homologous recombination.
- **B.** gene inversion.
- **C.** transposons.
- **D.** gene duplication.

Question 30

The DNA sequence of cellular subclones with a primary tumor most likely contain:

- **A.** no shared mutations between the subclones.
- **B.** a few shared mutations between the subclones but no shared mutations in tumor suppressor genes.
- **C.** a few shared mutations in tumor suppressor and oncogenes between the subclones.
- **D.** completely shared mutations between the subclones.

Passage 6 (Questions 31-34)

Radiotherapy is widely used for the adjuvant treatment of numerous cancers. However, resistance to radiotherapy remains an important concern. Various factors including p53 mutation, overexpression of DNA repair proteins, and tumor microenvironment heterogeneity have been proposed to play roles in radioresistance. p53, a transcription factor that plays a central role in the cellular responses to DNA damage, promotes cell survival via cell-cycle arrest and DNA repair at low levels of DNA damage while it induces cell death at high levels. Mutation of p53 occurs in more than 50% of human cancers, which significantly increases cellular resistance to ionizing radiation.

Experiment 1

Metformin, the mainstay treatment in type II diabetes, has been shown to synergize with ionizing radiation to induce cell death in breast cancer cells by blocking the G_2/M phase and decreasing DNA repair by reducing adenosine triphosphate (ATP) production. To evaluate metformin-p53-dependent cytotoxicity in human colorectal cancer cells, researchers exposed HCT116 $p53^{+/+}$ and $p53^{-/-}$ cells to varying concentrations of metformin for 48 hours and assayed for cell death. The results are shown in Figure 1.

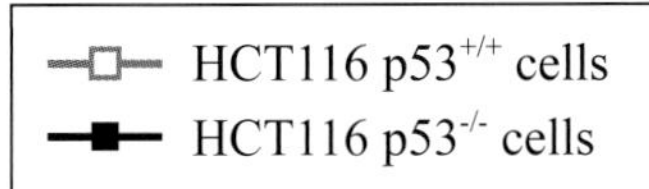

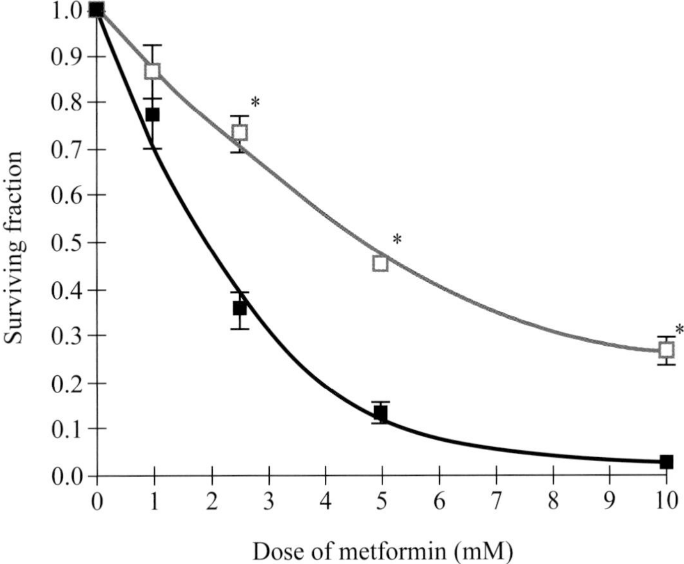

Figure 1 Effect of metformin on p53-deficient compared with p53 wild-type cells

Experiment 2

To determine whether metformin affected IR-induced cell cycle accumulation in the G_2/M phase and the proportion of G_2/M phase cells associated in the presence or absence of p53, scientists analyzed the cell cycle phase distribution of HCT116 $p53^{+/+}$ and $p53^{-/-}$ cells (Figure 2).

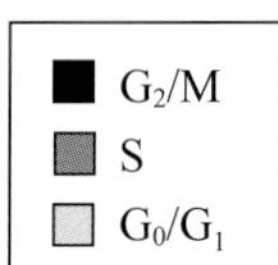

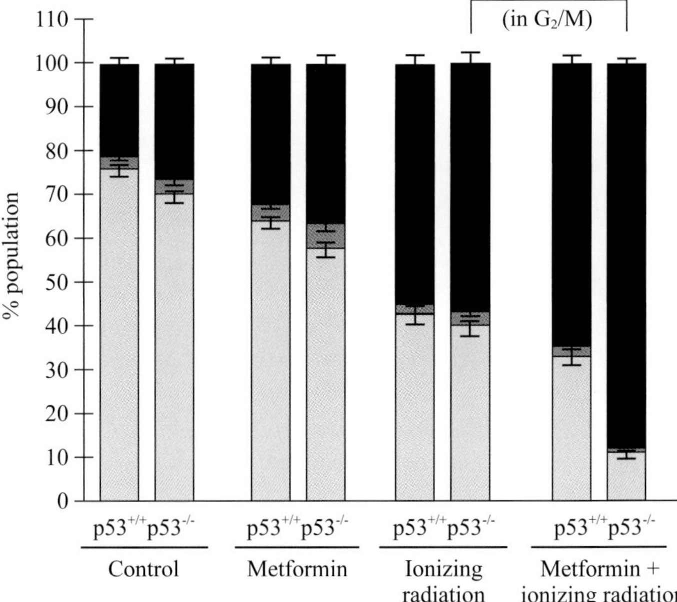

Figure 2 Effect of metformin and ionizing radiation on cell cycle progression in HCT116 $p53^{-/-}$ cells

Question 31

According to information contained in the passage, metformin is also likely to:

I. inhibit the formation of cytoskeletal components.
II. inhibit the oxidation of glucose.
III. inhibit the breakdown of the nuclear membrane.

- **A.** I only
- **B.** II only
- **C.** I and II only
- **D.** II and III only

Question 32

After treating HCT116 cells with ionizing radiation they are LEAST likely:

- **A.** to stain positively for one copy of DNA.
- **B.** be arrested with chromosomes aligned at the metaphase plate.
- **C.** have a partially broken down nuclear membrane.
- **D.** to stain positively for two centrioles.

Next ▶

Question 33

A western blot was used to confirm growth arrest during G_2/M phase. Which protein was most likely assayed?

- O **A.** Cyclin
- O **B.** DNA polymerase
- O **C.** RNA polymerase
- O **D.** Actin

Question 34

Inhibition of which of the following enzymes would be most likely to cause aneuploidy?

- O **A.** GDP kinase, an enzyme required for microtubule polymerization
- O **B.** ADP kinase, an enzyme required for actin polymerization
- O **C.** RNA polymerase, an enzyme required for RNA production
- O **D.** Ribozyme, an enzyme required for protein production

Passage 7 (Questions 35-39)

Genetic analyses of cancer-related genetic instability events have detected regions of the human genome that are hypersusceptible to breakage, which can lead to the deregulation of oncogenes and/or inactivation of tumor suppressors. Interestingly, many such regions contain sequences that can adopt alternative DNA secondary structures, such as cruciform DNA, and several of these modified conformations have been shown to be sources of genetic instability.

Cruciform DNA structures can form at inverted repeat (IR) sequences, where the two symmetric sequences undergo intrastrand base-pairing of at least 5 nucleotides. Long IRs (>500 bp), which are rare in the human genome, have been found at sites of large chromosomal rearrangements and can cause double strand DNA breaks (DSBs) in sperm and egg cells that lead to children born with chromosomal imbalances, such as Trisomy 21 (Down Syndrome). Short IRs (<100 bp) can stimulate DSBs by stalling DNA replication forks, causing DNA deletions. To explore plausible mechanisms of short IR-induced genetic instability, scientists examined the ability of short IRs to impede DNA polymerase in malignant melanoma, an aggressive form of skin cancer that develops from melanocytes in the human epidermis. After DNA replication, two-dimensional (2D) gel electrophoresis was performed to separate DNA replication intermediates to investigate whether short IRs promoted genetic instability in malignant melanoma.

The sequences isolated from gel electrophoresis were then sequenced to quantify the number of short IRs that were necessary to cause cancer by stalling DNA polymerase. The average number of short IRs in the ±100 bp regions surrounding the DNA DSBs was 28.5 ± 4.7 (mean ± SD) in malignant melanoma cells and 21.4 ± 5.0 (mean ± SD) in normal human melanocytes. After extensive research, the scientists concluded that short IRs induce chromosomal translocations in human cancer, likely through the ability to stall replication forks and promoting DNA strand breaks.

Question 35

Were the scientists correct to conclude that short IRs caused chromosomal translocations that lead to the formation of malignant melanoma?

- O **A.** Yes, because the mean number of short IRs in DSB regions was greater in melanoma cells than normal melanocytes.
- O **B.** No, because the mean number of short IRs in DSB regions was greater in the normal melanocytes than in melanoma cells.
- O **C.** Yes, because the confidence interval of the mean number of short IRs in DSB regions was narrower in normal melanocytes cells than melanoma.
- O **D.** No, because the confidence intervals of the mean number of short IRs in DSB regions was overlapping in melanoma cells and normal melanocytes.

TEST 2B

TEST 2B

Question 36

Okazaki fragments contain many short IRs. Which of the following, if true, would best support the claim that short IRs cause cancer by forming cruciform DNA that stalls DNA polymerase?

- O **A.** Melanocytes but not malignant melanoma cells efficiently replicate the leading strand.
- O **B.** Malignant melanoma cells but not melanocytes efficiency replicate the leading strand.
- O **C.** Malignant melanoma cells replicate the lagging strand of DNA with low efficiency.
- O **D.** Melanocytes contain a large genomic fraction of short IRs.

Question 37

How do the DNA polymerases in melanoma recognize the exact location in the genome to begin DNA replication?

- O **A.** DNA polymerases use a DNA primer to recognize the first few nucleotides of a given DNA sequence.
- O **B.** DNA polymerases recognize a consensus $(TATA)_n$ sequence to being replication.
- O **C.** DNA polymerases associate with other transcription factors to begin replication at the correct locus.
- O **D.** DNA polymerases bind other replication factors to begin replication.

Question 38

Which of the following best describes how DNA polymerase reads the parent DNA strand and synthesizes the complementary DNA strand?

- O **A.** Reads $3' \rightarrow 5'$ and synthesizes $5' \rightarrow 3'$
- O **B.** Reads $3' \rightarrow 5'$ and synthesizes $3' \rightarrow 5'$
- O **C.** Reads $5' \rightarrow 3'$ and synthesizes $5' \rightarrow 3'$
- O **D.** Reads $5' \rightarrow 3'$ and synthesizes $3' \rightarrow 5'$

Question 39

Cruciform DNA formation would be most detrimental during what phase of the cell cycle?

- O **A.** M Phase
- O **B.** G_1 Phase
- O **C.** S Phase
- O **D.** G_2 Phase

Passage 8 (Questions 40-43)

Triple negative breast cancer (TNBC) defines a clinical subset of breast cancer negative for estrogen receptors (ER), progesterone receptors (PR), and human epidermal growth factor receptor type 2 (HER2). Triple negative breast cancer is often the most difficult to treat, given the lack of targetable extracellular and intracellular oncogenic proteins. TNBC also has the shortest time to disease recurrence and lowest overall survival. Cancers, including TNBC, often have decreased expression of DNA repair genes, allowing them to escape apoptosis that is driven by interactions of DNA repair genes and mutated DNA. One such DNA repair gene, BRCA1, has a crucial role in the repair of double strand DNA breaks and its mutation leads to cancer predisposition and genomic instability. Characterization of the expression of BRCA1 could have important prognostic and predictive implications, such as the response to the currently used anticancer agents and to novel targeted agents.

Physician-scientists collected tumors that were classified as: luminal A (hormone receptor positive) and triple-negative (ER, PR, and HER2 negative). RNA was isolated and quantified from each of the tumors and was reverse transcribed to cDNA. Gene expression levels of BRCA1 and other DNA repair genes were correlated with recurrence and overall survival and the results are presented in Figures 1 and 2. The levels of expression of p53, a known tumor suppressor, were also characterized in the tumors.

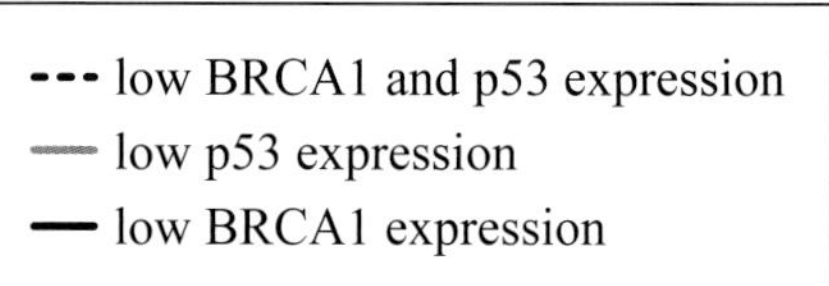

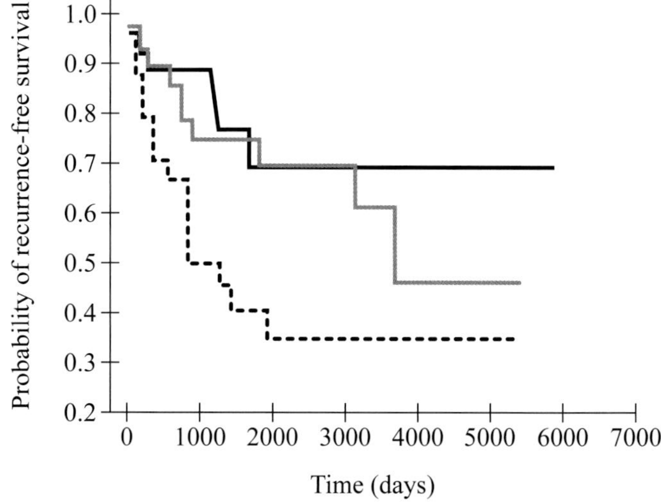

Figure 1 Recurrence-free survival (RFS) relative to mRNA levels of DNA repair genes

Next ▶

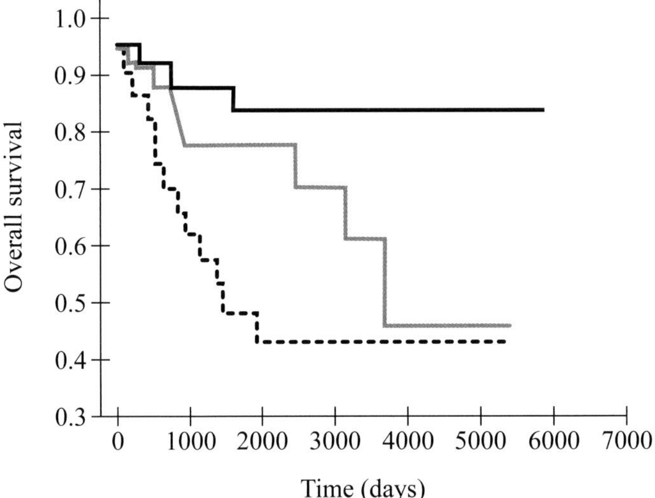

Figure 2 Overall survival (OS) relative to mRNA levels of DNA repair genes

Question 40

BRCA1 can only repair DNA in which a single base pair is mismatched but is surrounded by at least three nucleotides upstream and downstream that are correctly paired. Which of the following DNA sequences is BRCA1 most likely to repair?

- **A.** 5′-TCGATCGATCGA-3′
  3′-TCGATCGATCGA-5′
- **B.** 5′-TCGATCGATCGA-3′
  3′-AGCTACCTAGCT-5′
- **C.** 5′-TCGATCGATCGA-3′
  3′-GTCTAGCTAGCT-5′
- **D.** 5′-TCGATCGATCGA-3′
  3′-AGCTAGCTAGCT-5′

Question 41

Suppose a separate study was conducted that measured RFS and OS of ER+/PR+ breast cancer. How would those survival curves compare to the data derived from TNBC?

- **A.** Both RFS and OS will be similar between ER+/PR+ breast cancer and TNBC.
- **B.** RFS and OS will both be decreased in ER+/PR+ breast cancer compared with TNBC.
- **C.** RFS and OS will both be increased in ER+/PR+ breast cancer compared with TNBC.
- **D.** RFS will decrease and OS will increase in ER+/PR+ breast cancer compared with TNBS.

Question 42

After isolation of cellular mRNA, the RNA isolated from the TNBC cells was reverse transcribed to cDNA. The cDNA is likely to lack which sequences that would be found in genomic DNA?

I. Introns
II. Exons
III. Gene promoters

- **A.** I only
- **B.** II and III only
- **C.** I and III only
- **D.** I, II, and III

Question 43

Based on the disease progression and survival data presented in Figure 1, it can be concluded that:

- **A.** simultaneous mutations in BRCA1 and p53 correlate with the worst overall survival.
- **B.** simultaneous mutations in BRCA1 and p53 correlate with the best overall survival.
- **C.** a BRCA1 mutation but not a p53 mutation correlates with worse overall survival.
- **D.** p53 but not BRCA1 mutations correlates with worse overall survival.

Questions 44 through 47 do not refer to a passage and are independent of each other.

Question 44

Ionizing radiation has been shown to cause an increase in radical oxygen species that can react with the phosphodiester backbone of DNA. Ionizing radiation is most likely to cause which of the following mutations?

- O **A.** Missense mutations
- O **B.** Sense mutations
- O **C.** Deletions
- O **D.** Insertions

Question 45

DNA sequencing of a child's genome reveals that the paternal chromosomes are exactly identical to the grandfather's chromosomes. This is likely due to:

- O **A.** failure of the formation of tetrads.
- O **B.** the father's sperm contributing to the formation of the zygote.
- O **C.** failure of the zygote to divide and grow properly.
- O **D.** chance.

Question 46

An environmental toxin that inhibited formation of the synaptonemal complex would likely have which of the following effects?

- O **A.** Inability to progress through mitosis
- O **B.** Decreased cancer risk for cells in the digestive tract
- O **C.** Unexpectedly high or low coefficient of relatedness between siblings
- O **D.** Cell arrest in prophase II

Question 47

Which of the following examples describes a postzygotic barrier to reproduction?

- O **A.** A mutation that inhibits ATP production by the mitochondria of sperm.
- O **B.** Mating between a father with 23 chromosomes and a mother with 22 chromosomes.
- O **C.** Abnormal acidification of the vagina that degrades the acrosomes of sperm.
- O **D.** An oncogene mutation that gives rise to colon cancer in the fifth decade of life.

Passage 9 (Questions 48-51)

A 28-year-old female notices an abnormality in her breast tissue and reports to her physician for follow-up. She receives a mammogram, a radiologic test that detects increased density in tissues that suggests cancer. Additionally, a genetic test for a susceptibility to cancer helps diagnose her with early breast cancer, which she was predisposed to by a germline heterozygous mutation in *BRCA1*, a gene on chromosome 17.

Mutations can arise from errors during replication, such as the incorporation of a non-complementary nucleotide opposite an intact template nucleotide during DNA synthesis, or from DNA damage caused by exogenous mutagens or endogenous reactions at any time during normal growth of a cell. If uncorrected by the next round of DNA replication, these lesions will lead to arrested replication and cell death (Figure 1).

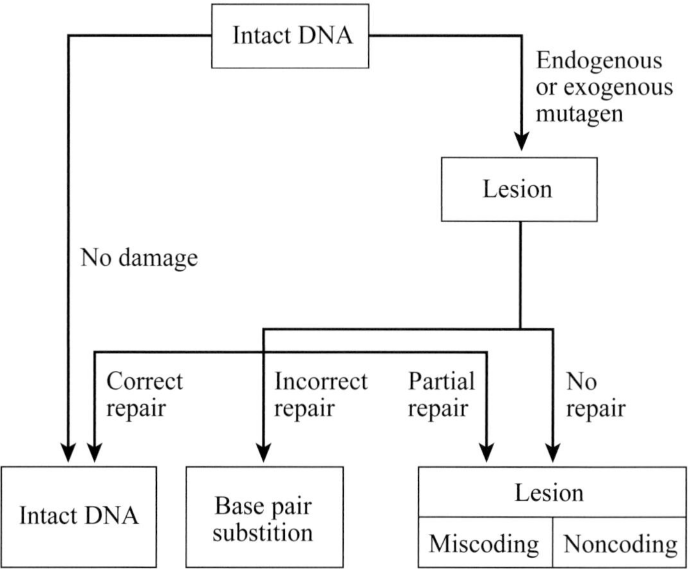

Figure 1 An overview of the mutagenesis process, which involves DNA damage, repair, and replication

DNA regions that contain high CpG content contain a large number of mutations, believed to be due primarily to the spontaneous deamination of C to 5-methylcytosine (5mC). 5mC is later converted to uracil. Deamination at CpG sites make substantial contribution to mutations in almost all cancer types and accumulates at constant yearly rates that appear to be positively correlated with the turnover rates of the corresponding normal tissues.

Question 48

Deamination of C bases is likely to lead to a:

○ **A.**

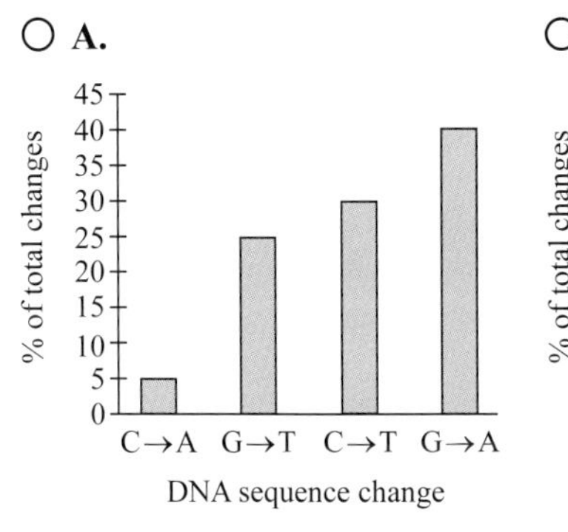

○ **B.**

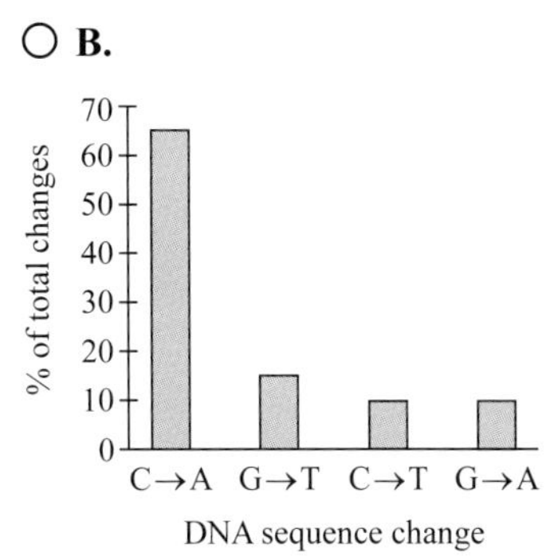

○ **C.**

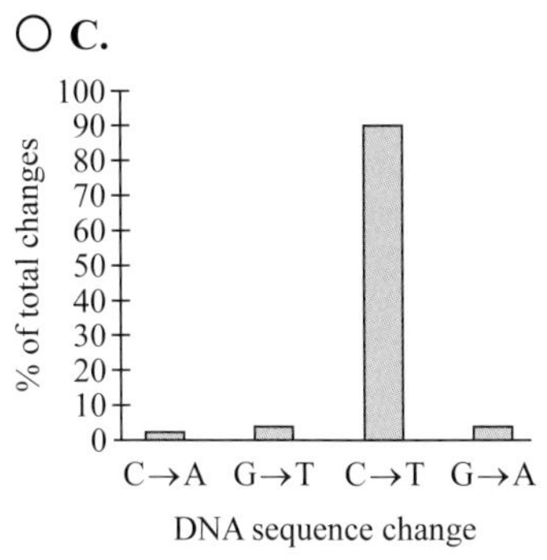

○ **D.**

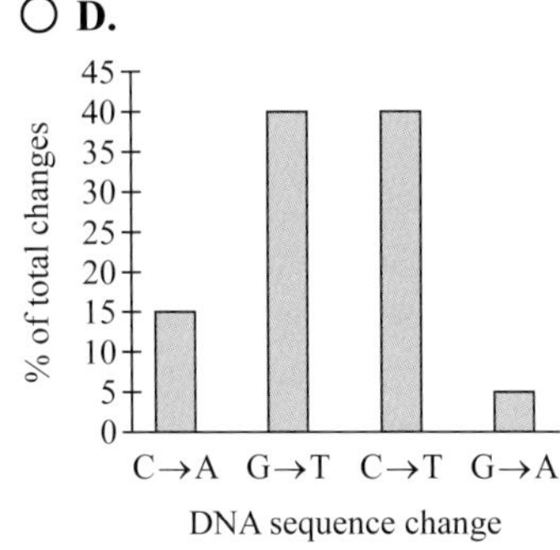

Question 49

BRCA1 most likely acts as a(n):

○ **A.** tumor suppressor gene.
○ **B.** oncogene.
○ **C.** promoter.
○ **D.** ribozyme.

Question 50

Decreases in CpG content surrounding *BRCA1* are LEAST likely to cause:

○ **A.** an increase in BRCA1 protein concentrations.
○ **B.** a decrease in the transcription of the *BRCA1* gene.
○ **C.** a decrease in the association of histone H3 to the *BRCA1* gene.
○ **D.** an increase in the number of nucleosomes containing the *BRCA1* gene.

Question 51

Over the lifetime of an individual, the greatest number of mutations in CpG sites are expected to accumulate in which of the following cells?

○ **A.** Skin epithelial cells
○ **B.** Blood vessel endothelial cells
○ **C.** Hematopoietic stem cells
○ **D.** Gastric mucosal cells

Passage 10 (Questions 52-56)

In mammalian oocytes, synapsis and meiotic recombination occur during fetal development, after which the oocyte enters prophase I arrest. This arrest in oocytes may last for several months or years in the follicular microenvironment depending on the species. In humans, the oocyte completes meiosis I just before ovulation. Meiotic resumption is morphologically characterized by geminal vesicle breakdown (GVBD). After GVBD, chromosomes regulate the assembly of spindle microtubules during prometaphase, and the spindle is then maintained in prometaphase I with chromosomes maintained in the spindle's central region. Subsequently, the chromosomes align at the metaphase plate and anaphase I ensues, followed by extrusion of first polar body. The meiotic cell cycle becomes arrested again at metaphase II until fertilization.

In mitosis, erroneous kinetochore–microtubule attachment, with either both sister kinetochores attached to the same pole (syntelic attachment), or both poles attached to the same kinetochore (merotelic attachment), can result in inaccurate segregation of sister chromatids and subsequent aneuploidy. Extracellular signal-regulated kinase 3 (ERK3) is generally known as an atypical member of the mitogen-activated protein (MAP) kinase family. Despite nearly 50% identical to ERK1/2 in the kinase domain, ERK3 presents striking differences in structure from classical MAPKs.

It is widely known that the MAPK signaling pathway plays a critical role in the regulation of mouse oocyte maturation, while the roles of ERK3 are unclear. To elucidate its role, ERK3-deleted and control oocytes were cultured for 8.5 h, and then transferred to medium which was pre-cooled to 4°C and cultured for 10 minutes. Imaging by fluorescent microscopy revealed that all chromosomes were attached to microtubules in control oocytes; interestingly, chromosomes in ERK3-deleted oocytes were disordered; further magnification showed that some chromosomes were not attached to microtubules (Figure 1).

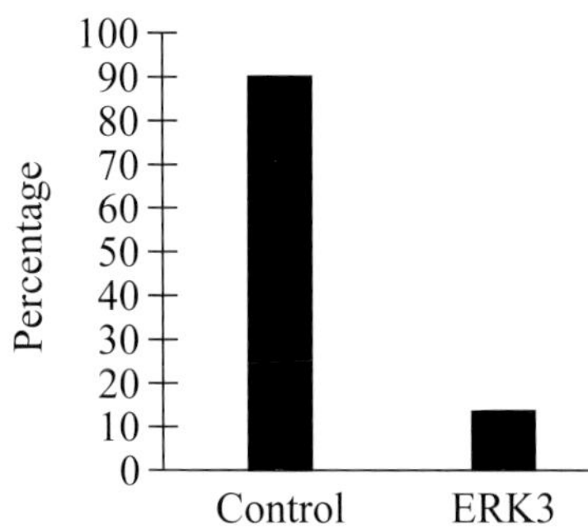

Figure 1 Attachment of microtubule attachment to chromosomes in control and ERK3 knock-out mouse oocytes

TEST 2B

Question 52

Researchers most likely incubated oocytes in pre-cooled culture media for 10 minutes before imaging in order to:

- O **A.** prevent present bacteria from reproducing and contaminating samples.
- O **B.** lower the activation energy necessary meiotic processes.
- O **C.** raise the activation energy necessary for meiotic processes.
- O **D.** to slow cells from undergoing further changes before imaging.

Question 53

ERK3 oocytes would be more likely than wild type oocytes to contain:

I. one extra chromosome.
II. one less chromosome.
III. more than two copies of the same chromosome.

- O **A.** I only
- O **B.** II only
- O **C.** I and II only
- O **D.** I, II, and III

Question 54

Wild-type oocytes that contain chromosomes attached to spindles are least likely to be in:

- O **A.** prophase I.
- O **B.** metaphase I.
- O **C.** metaphase II.
- O **D.** anaphase I.

Question 55

Which of the following enzymes would be required to facilitate genetic recombination?

I. DNA ligase
II. DNA polymerase
III. Endonuclease

- O **A.** I only
- O **B.** I and III only
- O **C.** II and III only
- O **D.** I, II, and III

Question 56

Which of the following events would be more likely to occur in an ERK3 oocyte than a wild type oocyte?

- O **A.** Cell cycle arrest
- O **B.** Genetic recombination
- O **C.** Nondisjunction
- O **D.** Frameshift mutations

Questions 57 through 59 do not refer to a passage and are independent of each other.

Question 57

In contrast to flies, where the sex of the offspring is determined by the ratio between X chromosomes and autosomes, sex in humans is determined by:

- O **A.** the Mullerian inhibiting substance gene on chromosome 19.
- O **B.** the testes determining factor gene on the Y chromosome.
- O **C.** the follicle stimulating hormone gene on chromosome 6.
- O **D.** the luteinizing hormone gene on chromosome 19.

Question 58

Evolutionary analysis has revealed that myelin genes evolved by genetic recombination. What portion of a gene is most likely to mediate evolution by recombination?

- O **A.** Exon
- O **B.** Promoter
- O **C.** Enhancer
- O **D.** Intron

Question 59

Blood-typing is a necessary preparatory step in most surgeries. Which classification best applies to blood-typing?

- O **A.** Complete dominance
- O **B.** Incomplete dominance
- O **C.** Co-dominance
- O **D.** Partial penetrance

STOP. If you finish before time is called, check your work. You may go back to any question in this test.

ANSWERS & EXPLANATIONS for Test 2B can be found on p. 222.

Genetics

TEST 2C

Time: 50 minutes
Questions 1–31

DIRECTIONS: Most questions in the Biological and Biochemical Foundations of Living Systems test section are grouped with a descriptive passage. Select the best answer to each question using background knowledge and the given passage. A portion of this test section is comprised of discrete questions, which are independent of any passage and one another. Select the best answer for each discrete question. Indicate your selection by blackening the corresponding oval on your answer document. If you are unsure of the answer, rule out incorrect choices and select from the remaining options. You may access a periodic table found on the last page of this book at any point during this test section.

Passage 1 (Questions 1-4)

Aneuploidy, the presence of extra or missing chromosomes, is a numerical chromosomal abnormality. It contributes to spontaneous abortions, stillbirths, and aneuploid births with severe congenital defects in humans. Aneuploid zygotes that survive beyond implantation are either sex chromosome aneuploids or one of three types of autosomal trisomies (chromosomes 13, 18, and 21). These aneuploidies arise as *de novo* mutations or structural rearrangements either during the meiosis of oogenesis or spermatogenesis or during mitosis after fertilization. Embryos formed from aneuploid spermatozoa tend to have a demonstrable background level of aneuploidy and chromosome breakage.

Surprisingly, 25% or more of the gametes involved in assisted reproductive technology-derived pregnancies are aneuploid. Most autosomal aneuploidy is maternal in origin. Nevertheless, approximately 80% of aneuploidies associated with sex chromosomes are paternal in origin. Determining whether a relationship exists between sperm viability and nondisjunction requires simultaneous study of both viability and chromosome composition in individual spermatozoa.

Researchers cultured spermatozoa for 3 days, then assessed viability status and chromosomal constitution in each spermatozoon. In order to assess for aneuploidy, fluorescence *in situ* hybridization (FISH) was used. This process uses directly labeled DNA probes specific to sequences on chromosomes 18, X, and Y in order to investigate both the autosomes and the sex chromosomes. The probes carried fluorescent markers in three different colors, one for each of the chromosomes analyzed. The results are presented in Figures 1 and 2.

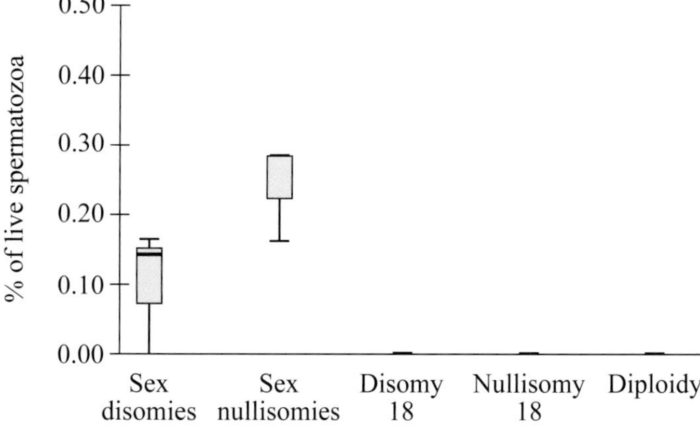

Figure 1 Aneuploidy of live spermatozoa in Day 0 (Note: bolded horizontal bars within the boxes represent the mean.)

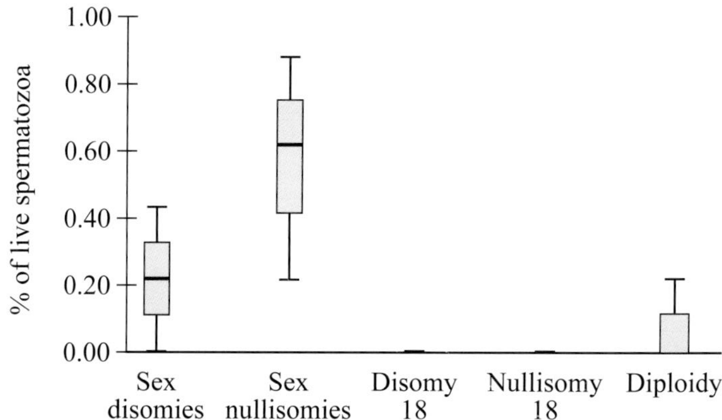

Figure 2 Aneuploidy of live spermatozoa in Day 3 (Note: bolded horizontal bars within the boxes represent the mean.)

Question 1

Which of the following is true of metaphase II in the primary spermatocytes that give rise to the cells analyzed in this experiment?

- **A.** There is a haploid number of chromosomes.
- **B.** Chromosomes line up as homologous pairs.
- **C.** Crossing over occurs along homologous regions of chromosomes.
- **D.** It is not detectable by light microscopy.

Question 2

Which of the following accurately describes the pattern of division in oogenesis as it differs from spermatogenesis?

- **A.** There is an equal division of cytoplasm to accommodate more viable eggs that can form future zygotes.
- **B.** There is an unequal division of chromosomes to accommodate one egg that will form the future zygote.
- **C.** There is an unequal division of cytoplasm to accommodate one egg that will form the future zygote.
- **D.** There is an unequal division of mitochondria only to accommodate one egg that will form the future zygote.

Question 3

Would the information in the passage support the use of spermatozoa with sex disomies to fertilize eggs missing an X or Y chromosome as a means of producing a healthy baby?

- **A.** Yes, because the embryos could be screened for other aneuploidy before implantation.
- **B.** Yes, because the embryos would have the same number of chromosomes as normal embryos.
- **C.** No, because the embryos would have sex chromosomes derived from one parent.
- **D.** No, because the embryos would be at additional risk of carrying mutations.

Question 4

Why would the researchers forgo testing for specific aneuploidy in chromosome 1?

- **A.** This is an uncommon abnormality.
- **B.** Only small chromosomes experience aneuploidy.
- **C.** There is no reason not to test for such an abnormality.
- **D.** This abnormality is incompatible with life.

Passage 2 (Questions 6-9)

Choroid plexus carcinomas (CPC) are tumors that originate from the epithelium lining the brain ventricles and are typically found in children. CPC are very aggressive tumors with an unfavorable prognosis and typically appear in the first decade of life. Considering the high mortality rate for CPC, it is important to identify biologic markers that may be relevant to understanding risk stratification, tumor formation mechanism, and prognosis.

The most common mechanism involved in CPC formation is related to dysfunction in the tumor suppressor gene p53, found on chromosome 17, with up to 50% of the patients being positive for a germline TP53 mutation. Scientists were interested in understanding the genetics and identity of the TP53 mutation in CPC and investigated 29 patients diagnosed with CPC. Patient genomic DNA was isolated from two 2 mm punch biopsies of the skin. A 447 base pair (bp) PCR product corresponding to a fragment of TP53 exon 10 was generated using the forward primer, 5′-CTG AGG CAC AAG AAT CAC-3′, and the reverse primer 5′-TCC TAT GGC TTT CCA ACC-3′. The amplified product was digested with the restriction enzyme Hha1, yielding 293 bp and 154 bp fragments in an agarose gel if the R337H point mutation was not present. Figure 1 shows a representative pedigree depicting affected and unaffected family members, as well as the RFLP analysis of the patient after digestion of the PCR product with Hha1.

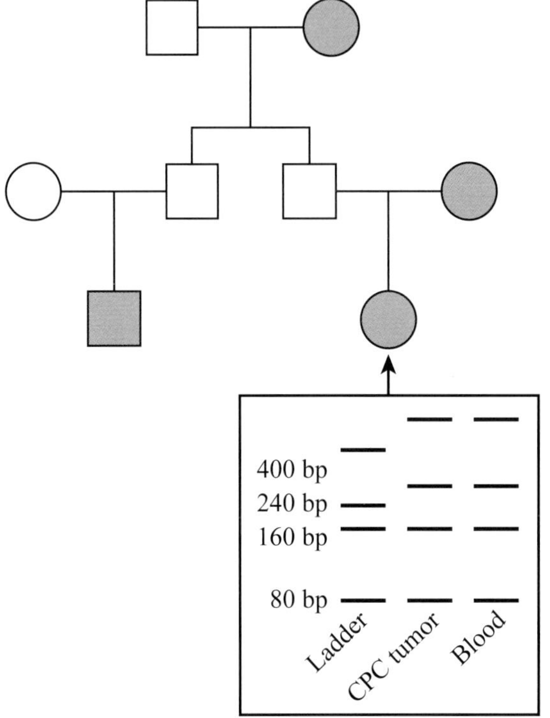

Figure 1 Pedigree and *TP53* RFLP assay of a patient with a germline *TP53* R337H mutation

TEST 2C

Question 5

Scientists are able to separate DNA of various sizes because:

- O **A.** DNA is uniformly negatively charged.
- O **B.** DNA does not contain uracil bases.
- O **C.** DNA is first treated with SDS, a compound that denatures cysteine bonds.
- O **D.** a magnetic field is applied to the agarose gel.

Question 6

The frequency of the R337H allele is 10% in the general population. What percentage of the population are carriers for the allele causing CPC?

- O **A.** 10%
- O **B.** 18%
- O **C.** 28%
- O **D.** 90%

Question 7

According to information contained in the passage, what is the most likely mode of inheritance of CPC?

- O **A.** Autosomal dominant
- O **B.** Autosomal recessive
- O **C.** Sex-linked dominant
- O **D.** Sex-linked recessive

Question 8

Suppose the following inheritance pattern was found. The F1 male is not a carrier.

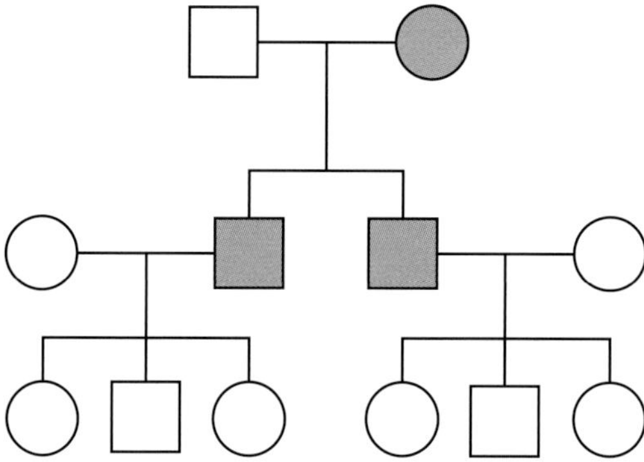

How would this impact the assertion by the authors that the R337H mutation in *TP53* was responsible for CPC?

- O **A.** It would undermine the authors' findings because the mutation would not be found on chromosome 17.
- O **B.** It would undermine the authors' findings because not enough affected individuals were present to draw conclusions.
- O **C.** It would support the authors' findings that the disease was autosomal recessive.
- O **D.** It would support the authors' findings that the disease was sex-linked dominant.

Question 9

The R337H *TP53* mutation associated with CPC is most likely a(n):

- O **A.** sense mutation.
- O **B.** inversion.
- O **C.** conservative missense mutation.
- O **D.** duplication.

Passage 3 (Questions 10-14)

Aurora kinases play a crucial role in cellular division by controlling chromatid segregation. Deregulation of Aurora kinase activity can result in mitotic abnormality and genetic instability, leading to defects in centrosome function, spindle assembly, chromosome alignment, and cytokinesis, ultimately resulting in cancer. Despite similarities in sequences and structures, Aurora kinases vary in their subcellular distribution. Aurora A localizes around the centrioles from the end of S phase to the beginning of the next G_1 and spreads along spindle microtubules during mitosis. In contrast, Aurora B remains in the nucleus and moves to centromeres from prometaphase to metaphase.

Because Aurora A and Aurora B have partially overlapping functions, understanding of the evolution of the kinases may help predict future changes that could be countered with drugs to improve cancer therapy. Evolution can affect the phenotype either by modifying the sequences of proteins or by changing their pattern of expression. Selection can modulate gene sequence evolution by constraining potential changes of amino acid sequences or by favoring new and adaptive genetic variants.

At any given moment of time, positive selection, which favors uncommon alleles, affected only a small fraction of sites in the Aurora A and B genes. In the process of evolution, a previously non-existent allele arose by mutation and became fixed in the population. The Aurora A I57V mutation arose roughly 1 million years ago and has become highly penetrant, prevailing in 84.4% of human populations. This suggests that the Aurora A I57V mutation is likely to induce significant gain in the functional activity of protein. Chemotherapies designed specifically against Aurora A kinases with the I57V mutation could lead to better outcomes for patients with cancer.

Question 10

By using PCR to selectively amplify only the Aurora A and Aurora B genes for DNA sequencing, scientists are LEAST likely to observe:

- ○ **A.** evolutionary changes in the promoter of Aurora A.
- ○ **B.** evolutionary changes in the *cis*-enhancer sequences of Aurora B.
- ○ **C.** evolutionary changes in the *trans*-genes regulating Aurora A.
- ○ **D.** evolutionary changes in the introns of Aurora B.

Question 11

In a follow-up experiment, scientists determined that the Aurora A I57V mutation is found at a prevalence of up to 90% in certain cancer types. This mutation most likely:

- ○ **A.** results in increased rates of cell proliferation.
- ○ **B.** results in decreased rates of cell survival.
- ○ **C.** results in an increased number of cells in G_2.
- ○ **D.** results in an increased number of cells in G_1.

Question 12

Nitrosamines, DNA alkylating compounds that are found in cigarette smoke, most commonly result in what type of mutation in DNA?

- ○ **A.** Missense mutation
- ○ **B.** Nonsense mutation
- ○ **C.** Insertion
- ○ **D.** Deletion

Question 13

Early in tumorigenesis a mutation in Aurora B created a novel allele that was found in 10% of tumor cells. After the tumor had grown larger, the allele was found at a frequency of 6%. This finding is an example of:

- ○ **A.** positive selection.
- ○ **B.** genetic drift.
- ○ **C.** heterozygous advantage.
- ○ **D.** incomplete dominance.

Question 14

The Aurora A I57V mutation lengthens the time a cell spends in mitosis because it prevents proper separation of chromosomes. The diversity of mutations in a cancer cell population:

- ○ **A.** decreases over time due to increased cell death.
- ○ **B.** decreases over time due to increased DNA replication.
- ○ **C.** increases over time due to frequent synapsis.
- ○ **D.** increases over time due to activation of DNA damage repair pathways.

TEST 2C

Questions 15 through 18 do not refer to a passage and are independent of each other.

Question 15

A biologist interested in determining the genotype of an organism showing a dominant phenotype would design an experiment using which of the following analytical methods?

- O **A.** Chi-square test
- O **B.** Test cross
- O **C.** Crossover frequency analysis
- O **D.** Hardy Weinberg analysis

Question 16

A female with a widow's peak, freckles, and curly hair has children with a male with a straight hairline, no freckles, and straight hair. If one of their children has wavy hair, a straight hairline, and no freckles, which of the following is most likely true about the inheritance pattern of each of these traits?

I. Hairline displays incomplete dominance.
II. The allele for freckles is co-dominant.
III. Hair texture displays incomplete dominance.

- O **A.** I only
- O **B.** II only
- O **C.** III only
- O **D.** I and III only

Question 17

DNA sequencing of the *TP53* gene revealed that 7 of 10 patients with a germline C to G mutation in codon 562 developed stage IV brain cancer during their fifth decade of life. This mutation is best characterized as:

- O **A.** partially penetrant.
- O **B.** completely dominant.
- O **C.** partially expressive.
- O **D.** heterozygous.

Question 18

A three-year-old male child presents with coarse facial features, stiffness, and developmental delay. Both parents and the child's two sisters are unaffected. The mother states that her brother and her sister's son experienced similar conditions. The mother is currently pregnant. What are the chances that her newborn will be affected?

- O **A.** 0%
- O **B.** 25%
- O **C.** 50%
- O **D.** 75%

Passage 4 (Questions 19-22)

In both cardiovascular disease (CVD) and stroke, atherosclerosis is the underlying pathology. Genetic factors explain a proportion of the observed inter-individual variability in atherosclerosis progression, which is exemplified by the observed 30–60% heritability in twin studies.

Both common and rare genetic variants contribute to the heritability. A recent meta-analysis of Genome Wide Association Studies (GWAS) of nearly 64,000 cases with CVD has identified 46 common single nucleotide polymorphisms (SNPs) of small effect size, which account for about 10.6% of the estimated heritability. Some SNPs have also been identified in several pedigrees with Mendelian forms of atherosclerosis. A well-known example of such a monogenic dominant disorder, that underlies atherosclerosis, is Familial Hypercholesterolemia (FH), caused by loss of function (LOF) causing mutations in the genes encoding for the low-density lipoprotein receptor (LDLR) or Apolipoprotein B (APOB), or gain of function (GOF) mutations in Pro-protein Convertase Subtilisin/Kexin Type 9 (PCSK9). Carriers of mutations in these genes are characterized by high plasma levels of LDL-cholesterol (LDL-c) and early onset atherosclerosis. A pedigree of a family with premature atherosclerosis is shown in Figure 1. PCR and DNA sequencing identified a previously unknown non-synonymous mutation in the Keratocan (KERA) gene, which encodes the extracellular proteoglycan KERA.

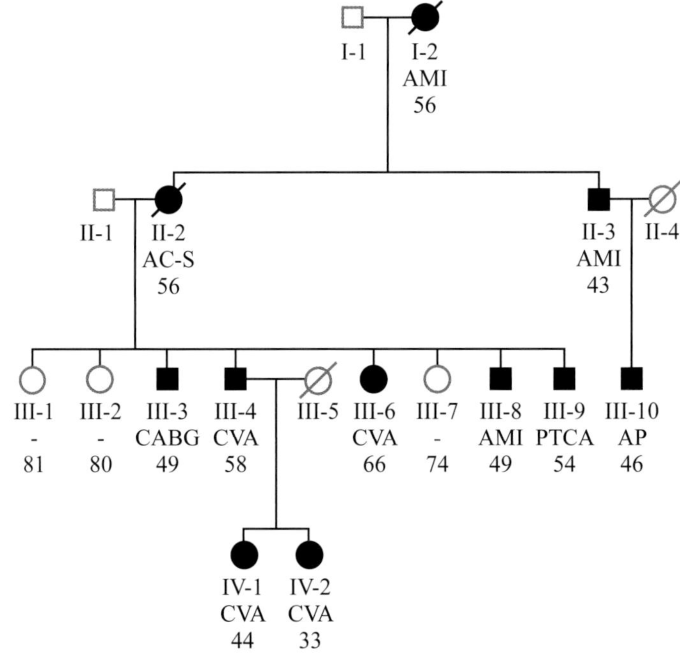

Figure 1 Pedigree corresponding to a family with premature atherosclerosis

The Ser307Cys mutation is localized in the C-terminal part of KERA and is flanked by cysteine residues at positions 303 and 343. The mutation at residue 307 may form a preferred bond with Cys303, resulting in Cys343 being unpaired and becoming more exposed to the solvent than in the wild-type KERA protein, enabling novel protein-protein interactions.

Next ▶

This passage is adapted from "Mutation in KERA identified by linkage analysis and targeted resequencing in a pedigree with premature atherosclerosis." Maiwald S, Sivapalaratnam S, Motazacker MM, van Capelleveen JC, Bot I, et al. *PLoS ONE*. 2014. 9(5) doi:10.1371/journal.pone.0098289 for use under the terms of the Creative Commons CC BY 4.0 license (http://creativecommons.org/licenses/by/4.0/legalcode).

Question 19

The mutation in *KERA* predisposing the family of the pedigree in Figure 1 most likely segregates in a(n):

- **A.** autosomal recessive manner.
- **B.** autosomal dominant manner.
- **C.** X-linked recessive manner.
- **D.** Y-linked manner.

Question 20

Confirmatory DNA sequencing of the *KERA* gene revealed that 6 of 12 patients with a germline A to T mutation developed hyperlipidemia during their life. This mutation is best characterized as:

- **A.** partially penetrant.
- **B.** completely dominant.
- **C.** partially expressive.
- **D.** heterozygous.

Question 21

The UCA codon is responsible for coding for serine, while the UGU codon produces cysteine. The UCA codon is best described as:

- **A.** the wild type allele and the UGU codon as the mutant allele.
- **B.** the mutant allele and the UGU codon as the wild type allele.
- **C.** the wild type allele, along with UGU.
- **D.** the mutant allele, along with UGU.

Question 22

A male with the *KERA* Ser307Cys mutation and an APOB V2R mutation mates with a *KERA* and *APOB* wild type female. One of their six grandchildren has a *KERA* Ser307Cys mutation and wild type *APOB*. During gametogenesis, chromosome 16 likely underwent:

- **A.** no recombination between the *KERA* and *APOB* genes.
- **B.** a single crossover between *KERA* and *APOB* genes.
- **C.** a double crossover between *KERA* and *APOB* genes.
- **D.** a quadruple crossover between *KERA* and *APOB* genes.

Passage 5 (Questions 23-27)

Type 1 von Willebrand disease (VWD) is a common highly heterogeneous bleeding disorder that is characterized by a partial quantitative deficiency of functionally normal von Willebrand factor (VWF) that initiates platelet clotting. The ability to diagnose it is complicated by incomplete penetrance of the disease and the wide variability in plasma VWF levels which are influenced by environmental and genetic factors, such as age and ABO blood group, respectively. The majority of VWF sequence variations predict missense substitutions in VWF and the likelihood of identifying a variation is greater in those patients having more severe deficiency of the protein.

However, some type 1 von Willebrand disease patients have no identifiable mutations in the VWF protein. The search for genetic factors that may explain the bleeding tendency in these 35% of patients has focused mainly on the identification of modifier genes that have a role in influencing plasma VWF levels. Several G-protein coupled receptors (GPCRs) expressed on the cell surface of platelets modulate platelet recruitment and aggregation at sites of vessel injury. The *F2R* and *F2RL3* genes encodes two GPCRs PAR1 and PAR2, respectively, that are coupled to GS proteins to stimulate adenylyl cyclase, raising cAMP levels and leading to activation of protein kinase A (PKA). PKA is able to induce pathways involved in clotting and alter the transcription of key clotting factor genes.

In order to determine whether variation in *F2R* or *F2RL3* affected PAR1 and PAR4 functioning, the DNA of patients with type 1 von Willebrand disease was sequenced to determine single nucleotide variations (SNVs) that might affect GPCR structure and function. Five candidate SNVs are shown in Table 1.

Table 1 GPCR gene variations identified in type 1 VWD patients and their predicted effects

Gene	Protein	SNV	Effect on protein
F2R	PAR1	c.-67 G>C	N/A
F2R	PAR1	c.1063 C>T	p.L355F
F2RL3	PAR4	c.65 C>A*	p.T22N
F2RL3	PAR4	c.402 C>G	p.A134
F2RL3	PAR4	c.1029 G>C	p.V343

SNV = single nucleotide variation
MAF = minor allele frequency
* co-inherited SNVs identified in Index case P3

This passage is adapted from "Identification and characterization of novel variations in platelet G-protein coupled receptor *(GPCR)* genes in patients historically diagnosed with Type 1 von Willebrand disease." Stockley J, Nisar SP, Leo VC, Sabi E, Cunningham M, et al. *PLoS ONE*. 2015. 10(12) doi:10.1371/journal.pone.0143913 for use under the terms of the Creative Commons CC BY 4.0 license (http://creativecommons.org/licenses/by/4.0/legalcode).

TEST 2C

Question 23

Phylogenetic analysis among families with type 1 von Willebrand disease that do not have mutations in VWF often shows a penetrance of nearly 100%. This most likely supports the role of:

- O **A.** a particular nucleotide sequence in mediating risk of VWD.
- O **B.** an environmental toxin in mediating risk of VWD.
- O **C.** four to five nucleotide sequences in mediating risk of VWD.
- O **D.** an environmental exposure that changes a nucleotide sequence in mediating risk of VWD.

Question 24

The C to G SNV in *F2RL3* is a synonymous change in the DNA sequence. This SNV most likely:

- O **A.** creates a new allele of the *F2RL3* gene.
- O **B.** creates a truncated protein product of the *F2RL3* gene.
- O **C.** creates a single amino acid change in the protein product of the *F2RL3* gene.
- O **D.** creates multiple amino acid changes in the protein product of the *F2RL3* gene.

Question 25

One man carrying a G at position 67 in *F2R* and a C at position 65 in *F2RL3* has children with a woman with a C at position 67 in *F2R* and an A at position 65 in *F2RL3*. After gametogenesis in the children, assuming no mitotic recombination, what is the probability a germ cell will have a G at position 67 in *F2R* and an A at position 65 in *F2RL3*, if the recombination frequency is 25 cM between *F2R* and *F2RL3*?

- O **A.** 1/8
- O **B.** 1/4
- O **C.** 1/2
- O **D.** 1

Question 26

F2RL3 is LEAST likely to be found on:

- O **A.** the Y chromosome.
- O **B.** the X chromosome.
- O **C.** chromosome 21.
- O **D.** chromosome 19.

Question 27

TBXA2R and *PTGIR*, on chromosomes 5 and 10, respectively, were also found to be associated with a decreased risk of developing type 1 VWD. The father inherited an A at position 54 in *TBXA2R* from his father and a C at position 54 in *PRGIR* from his mother. After meiosis, these alleles were found to have a 50% chance of being in the same sperm. This probability results from:

- O **A.** chromosomal nondisjunction.
- O **B.** incomplete dominance.
- O **C.** independent assortment.
- O **D.** linkage disequilibrium.

Questions 28 through 31 do not refer to a passage and are independent of each other.

Question 28

Marcus' brother has Zellweger's syndrome, an autosomal recessive disease with incidence approximately 1/8100 across all ethnic groups which inhibits the formation of properly functioning peroxisomes. He shows no signs of the disease, and his wife has an affected sibling. The chances that Marcus is a carrier is closest to:

- O **A.** 1/3.
- O **B.** 1/4.
- O **C.** 2/3.
- O **D.** 1/16.

Question 29

An experimental biologist designing a dihybrid cross believes that two independently assorting genes of interest exhibit dominant epistasis, where the dominant allele at one location masks the expression at a second locus. Which of the following ratios of F2 genotypes would be expected?

- O **A.** 9:3:3:1
- O **B.** 12:3:1
- O **C.** 9:3:4
- O **D.** 1:2:1

Question 30

A father with a heterozygous mutation in *PARKIN*, a gene that predisposes people to early onset Alzheimer's disease when inherited in an autosomal recessive manner, mates with a female with wild type *PARKIN*. What is the probably that their child will have early onset Alzheimer's disease?

- O **A.** 0%
- O **B.** 25%
- O **C.** 50%
- O **D.** 75%

Question 31

The *BRCA1* gene helps monitor DNA for damage and initiates DNA damage repair to prevent cancer. Patients with a germline mutation in *BRCA1* are predisposed to developing breast cancer because:

- O **A.** the patients already have the mutation in a recessive state.
- O **B.** the patients already have the mutation in a dominant state.
- O **C.** the patients already have a homozygous recessive mutation.
- O **D.** the patients already have a homozygous dominant mutation.

STOP. If you finish before time is called, check your work. You may go back to any question in this test.

ANSWERS & EXPLANATIONS for Test 2C can be found on p. 222.

Metabolism

TEST 3A

Time: 90 minutes
Questions 1–59

DIRECTIONS: Most questions in the Biological and Biochemical Foundations of Living Systems test section are grouped with a descriptive passage. Select the best answer to each question using background knowledge and the given passage. A portion of this test section is comprised of discrete questions, which are independent of any passage and one another. Select the best answer for each discrete question. Indicate your selection by blackening the corresponding oval on your answer document. If you are unsure of the answer, rule out incorrect choices and select from the remaining options. You may access a periodic table found on the last page of this book at any point during this test section.

Passage 1 (Questions 1-5)

Pancreatic cancer is one of the most deadly solid malignancies in the United States and generally responds poorly to conventional treatment modalities such as chemotherapy and radiation therapy. However, recent epidemiological studies support the premise that diets rich in some spices may be protective against various human malignancies. Capsaicin, a homovanillic acid derivative (N-vanillyl-8-methylnonenamide) is an active and spicy component of hot chili peppers and has been used as a food additive, particularly in South Asian and Latin-American countries.

Mitochondria are major physiological sources of radical oxygen species (ROS), which are generated due to incomplete reduction of oxygen during normal mitochondrial respiration. Most cancer cells have higher levels of ROS that help in proliferation and cell growth. However, due to elevated ROS levels, cancer cells are highly dependent on their antioxidant system to maintain redox balance and hence are more susceptible to further oxidative stress. Capsaicin has been shown to suppress the growth of cancer cells by increasing the number of ROS generated, ultimately causing cell-cycle arrest. Scientists devised the following experiment to further understand how capsaicin affected pancreatic epithelial cancer cell viability.

Two cell lines, a control cell line and BxPC-3, a pancreatic cancer cell line, were plated at 37°C and 5% CO_2 for 24 hours. The cells in both flasks were harvested and resuspended in growth medium that contained a combination of 150 μM capsaicin, catalase, an enzyme responsible for eliminating free radicals, and/or EUK, a manganese compound that neutralizes radical oxygen species. Scientists then measured complex-V (ATP synthase) activity as an indirect measure of cancer cell viability. The results are shown in Figure 1.

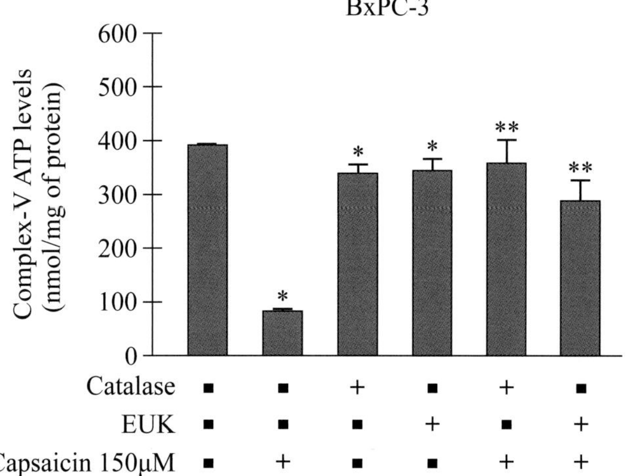

Figure 1 Effect of capsaicin on mitochondrial ATP-synthase (complex V) activity

Question 1

Cancer cells are more likely than normal cells to have a mutation in which of the following complexes of the electron transport chain?

- O **A.** Complex I
- O **B.** Complex II
- O **C.** Complex III
- O **D.** Complex IV

Question 2

Cyanide is a potent inhibitor of complex IV of the electron transport chain. Early research into the use of cyanide as a chemotherapeutic agent was likely discarded because:

- O **A.** cyanide increases the proton electrochemical gradient, injuring mitochondria.
- O **B.** cyanide collapses the proton electrochemical gradient, preventing ATP synthesis.
- O **C.** cyanide releases cytochrome c into the cytoplasm, inducing apoptosis.
- O **D.** cyanide directly inhibits ATP synthase.

Question 3

Which of the following cell lines was most likely chosen as the control cell line in this experiment?

- O **A.** PBC, a pancreatic beta-cell line
- O **B.** PEC, a pancreatic epithelial cell line
- O **C.** HEK, a skin epithelial cell line
- O **D.** SR, a striated muscle cell line

Question 4

According to information in the passage, which of the following is the most likely reason the scientists chose to add EUK to the growth medium of normal and pancreatic cancer cells?

- O **A.** To confirm that ATP levels restored by catalase were due to elimination of ROS.
- O **B.** To test whether an enzyme could be used as a potential cancer treatment.
- O **C.** To identify whether addition of metals to cancer cells increased ATP production.
- O **D.** To determine whether or not capsaicin directly interacted with either molecule.

Question 5

Reduction in the availability of which of the following molecules would have the greatest effect on cancer cell viability?

- O **A.** NADH
- O **B.** $FADH_2$
- O **C.** AMP
- O **D.** Pyruvate

Passage 2 (Questions 6-10)

Two members of the lipase family, lipoprotein lipase (LPL) and hepatic lipase (HL) are known to influence plasma lipoprotein metabolism and risk of atherosclerosis in humans. Atherosclerosis is the narrowing of blood vessels due to the accumulation of lipid droplets in the arterial walls. Endothelial lipase (EL) is a more recently discovered member of this family of lipases. Similar to HL and LPL, it is secreted and binds to the endothelial surface. In vitro, EL effectively hydrolyzes high-density lipoprotein (HDL) phospholipids. In mice, EL has a major influence on HDL metabolism. HDL is commonly referred to as "good cholesterol."

Several genetic association studies have suggested that rare variants and common polymorphisms in the human EL gene might be associated with variation in HDL concentrations. However, these studies have not been conclusive and were not accompanied by direct measurement of EL concentrations . The goal of the current study is to elucidate the association between EL mass and HDL concentration.

Previous studies indicated that EL, like HL and LPL, is an avid heparin-binding protein, and it was suspected that it would be released by injection of heparin in humans. A preliminary study in 60 individuals with normal lipid profiles indicated an approximately 3- to 4-fold increase in EL mass concentrations from pre-heparin to post-heparin plasma. The association of EL mass with various cardiovascular risk factors is given below for samples before and after treatment with heparin (Table 1). The R value is a measure of correlation, and a high positive value (0.28) indicates a strong association between the two factors.

Table 1 Association of EL Mass with Cardiovascular Risk Factor

Variable	Total R pre-heparin	Total R post-heparin
Age	0.14	0.048
BMI	0.28	0.22
Waist circumference	0.28	0.26
Blood pressure	0.18	0.24
Fasting glucose	0.11	0.16
HOMA-IR	0.27	0.24
Triglycerides	0.22	0.133
Total cholesterol	0.14	0.11
LDL-C	0.12	0.07
ApoB	0.22	0.21
HDL-C	– 0.11	– 0.18
ApoA-I	– 0.042	– 0.05

TEST 3A

This passage was adapted from "Endothelial Lipase Concentrations Are Increased in Metabolic Syndrome and Associated with Coronary Atherosclerosis." Badellino KO , Wolfe ML, Reilly MP, and Rader DJ. *PLoS Medicine.* 2006. 3(2) doi: 10.1371/journal.pmed.0030022 for use under the terms of the Creative Commons CC BY 2.0 license (http://creativecommons.org/licenses/by/2.0/legalcode).

Question 6

When someone consumes a large meal with a high fat content, which of the following correctly describes how dietary lipids are processed by the gut?

- O **A.** Lipids are taken up by intestinal epithelial cells where they are broken down and free fatty acids are released into the blood.
- O **B.** Intestinal epithelial cells package lipids in HDL particles to send to the liver and then to other tissues.
- O **C.** Lipids are packaged in chylomicrons by intestinal epithelial cells from which the particles are sent to the lymphatics.
- O **D.** Dietary lipids are broken down and are predominantly used as fuel by intestinal epithelial cells.

TEST 3A

Question 7

Based on the graph below, which of the following is likely true of patients with the greatest degree of artery calcification?

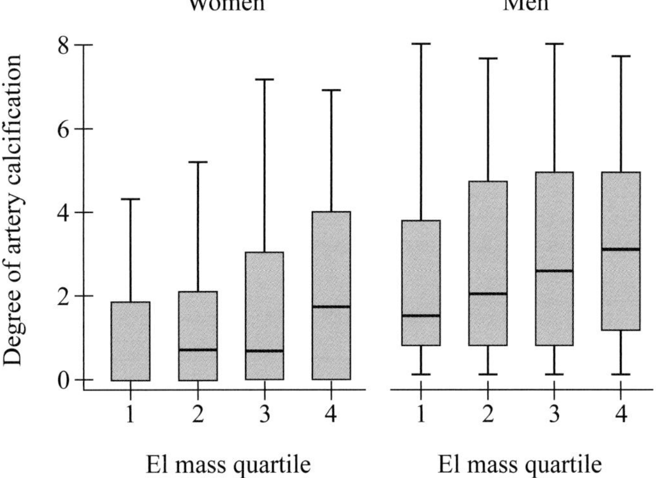

- O **A.** They have a high level of endothelial lipase and a high level of HDL in the blood.
- O **B.** They have a low level of endothelial lipase and a low level of HDL in the blood.
- O **C.** They have a low level of endothelial lipase and high level of HDL in the blood.
- O **D.** They have a high level of endothelial lipase and a low level of HDL in the blood.

Question 8

During a prolonged fast, which of the following continues to use glucose in addition to ketone bodies for energy?

- O **A.** The brain
- O **B.** Red blood cells
- O **C.** The liver
- O **D.** Skeletal muscle

Question 9

After reviewing the data from the initial experiment, the researchers chose to save time testing blood samples and abridged their experiment. Which of the following involves a plausible scenario and explanation for this choice?

- O **A.** They tested only pre-heparin samples because they saw that the post-heparin results were less conclusive.
- O **B.** They tested only pre-heparin samples because heparin binds endothelial lipase and increases the level of endothelial lipase.
- O **C.** They tested only post-heparin levels because heparin binds endothelial lipase and would be a more sensitive measure of endothelial lipase.
- O **D.** They tested only post-heparin levels because the endothelial lipase levels in this case are closer to those seen in circulation.

Question 10

PCSK9 is a protein that binds to the LDL receptor and pulls it from the membrane to be degraded in lysosomes. People with mutations in PCSK9 that renders it ineffective would be expected to have:

I. low serum LDL.
II. high serum HDL.
III. low serum endothelium lipase.
IV. increased risk of atherosclerosis.

- O **A.** I only
- O **B.** II only
- O **C.** II and IV only
- O **D.** I and IV only

Passage 3 (Questions 11-14)

Parkinson disease (PD) is one of the most common neurodegenerative disorders, affecting about 1% of people over 50 years old. It is caused by the progressive loss of dopaminergic (DA) neurons. Chemicals that inhibit the mitochondrial electron transport complex I or that elicit production of reactive oxygen species (ROS) can induce PD in humans. This suggests that mitochondria, which not only produce cellular energy but also control cell death, play a major role in human PD. Inhibition of complex I results in enhanced production of ROS, and increased ROS levels may in turn inhibit complex I, resulting in a vicious cycle of oxidative stress and impaired mitochondrial respiration.

For both neurons and non-neuronal cells, mitochondrial membranes are the battleground on which opposing signals combat to seal the cell's fate by mitochondrial membrane permeabilization (MMP). Once MMP occurs, hydrolases and activators of caspases are released. The destructive action of these enzymes, as well as the cessation of the vital bioenergetic and redox functions of mitochondria, cause cell death . Excessive cell death leads to tissue dysfunction and ultimately organ failure.

Mutations in PTEN-induced putative kinase 1 (PINK1), a mitochondrial enzyme, are the second-most common cause of autosomal recessive PD. The failure of PINK1 to phosphorylate one particular substrate, TRAP1, during oxidative stress can sensitize cells to the lethal effects of ROS. This process is shown in Figure 1.

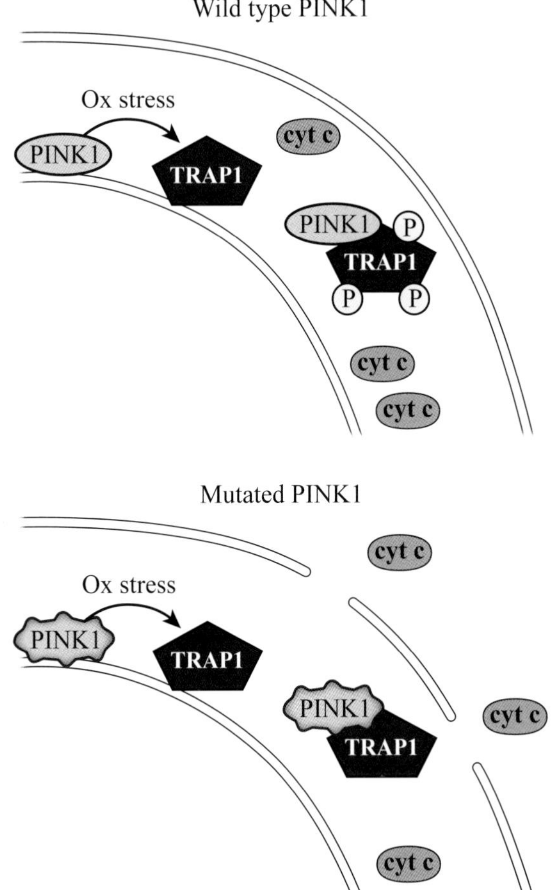

Figure 1 Mechanism of PD pathogenesis caused by mutated PINK1

Oxidation and degradation of the neurotransmitter dopamine may induce oxidative stress, and this may be the underlying reason for the selective vulnerability of DA neurons.

Question 11

Based on the information in the passage, which of the following could be administered as a therapeutic agent for patients suffering from PD caused by mutations in PINK1?

- O **A.** Inhibitors of the phosphatase that dephosphorylates TRAP1
- O **B.** PINK1 inhibitors
- O **C.** Complex I inhibitors
- O **D.** Molecules that enhance the release of cyt c

Question 12

A flavoprotein that functions to reduce oxidative stress is identified in the inner mitochondrial membrane. In order to control the activity of this enzyme, the researcher could manipulate which of the following experimental parameters?

- O **A.** The concentration of free radicals
- O **B.** The concentration of flavin
- O **C.** The pH of the environment
- O **D.** The temperature of the environment

Question 13

Which of the following is the most likely mechanism of cell death initiated by inhibition of complex I?

- O **A.** Cyt c release
- O **B.** Caspase activator release
- O **C.** Decreased ROS species leading to further complex I inhibition
- O **D.** ATP depletion

Question 14

A group of researchers discover that people with a partially functional PINK1 enzyme have a significantly reduced risk of Parkinson disease if they consume a diet high in antioxidants, which oppose spikes in oxidative stress. The most likely explanation for this finding is that:

- O **A.** the antioxidants can also phosphorylate TRAP1.
- O **B.** the antioxidants inhibit caspase activators.
- O **C.** the partially functioning PINK1 can maintain a sufficient concentration of phosphorylated TRAP1 to oppose MMP.
- O **D.** the partially functioning PINK1 can function at full capacity in the presence of antioxidants.

Questions 15 through 18 do not refer to a passage and are independent of each other.

Question 15

A doctor notices that a patient's blood test comes back indicating a high level of acetone. What can she conclude about the patient's metabolic status?

- A. The patient is producing a surplus of acetyl CoA from B-oxidation.
- B. There is a buildup of glucose-6-phosphate from glycogen breakdown.
- C. Uric acid is building up in the blood from DNA metabolism.
- D. Serum levels of beta-hydroxybutyrate may be elevated because of ongoing ketogenesis.

Question 16

An increase in the concentration of ATP observed during glycolysis most likely occurs by what mechanism?

- A. Transfer of electrons between sequentially arranged redox centers.
- B. Transfer of phosphates residing on cellular proteins to ADP.
- C. Substrate-level phosphorylation from organic phosphate and ADP.
- D. Transport of extracellular ATP into the cytosol by ATP symporters.

Question 17

Consider an experiment in which scientists were interested in understanding the role of electron carriers in inducing apoptosis in normal and cancerous cells. Which of the following molecules would be chosen by researchers to explore first?

- A. ATP synthase (complex V)
- B. Ubiquinone
- C. Cytochrome c
- D. Succinate dehydrogenase (complex II)

Question 18

Which of the following lipids when metabolized can produce a substrate for effective gluconeogenesis?

- A. Stearic acid (18 carbons)
- B. Palmitic acid (16 carbons)
- C. Pentadecanoic acid (15 carbons)
- D. While glucose can be converted to fatty acids, the opposite is not possible in humans.

Passage 4 (Questions 19-22)

Multiple myeloma is a hematological malignancy characterized by the clonal proliferation of plasma cells that exhibit an elevated rate of lipogenesis. Increased lipogenesis is mainly supported by de novo fatty acid synthesis (FAS) rather than by dietary fatty acids and primarily occurs through an elevated activity of fatty acid synthase (FASN), a multi-enzyme that catalyzes the conversion of malonyl-CoA into fatty acids through the de novo fatty acid synthesis pathway. The newly synthesized free fatty acids can be esterified and stored into neutral lipids (such as triacylglycerol), transformed into membrane lipids (such as cholesterol or phospholipids), or converted into signaling lipids (such as prostaglandin E2). In addition, endogenous fatty acid catabolism through increased beta-oxidation also seen in cancer can provide an alternative pathway to support cancer cell growth and survival. The following two experiments were designed to characterize fatty acid metabolism and the impact of its pharmacological inhibition in myeloma cells.

Four cell lines, including a control and three multiple myeloma cell lines, were treated with orlistat, a Food and Drug Administration-approved anti-obesity drug that specifically inhibits FASN activity. 5×10^8 cells per group were plated and supplied with growth medium spiked with radioactive ^{14}C. Following a 24-hour growth period, cells were treated with either 20 μM orlistat or 0-20 μM orlistat for 10 days.

After a 24-hour post-treatment recovery period, a scintillator was used to measure the levels of ^{14}C incorporated into newly synthesized lipids. Additionally, information on the effect of orlistat treatment on cell viability was measured by a trypan blue stain. Averaged results of three or more independent experiments describing lipogenesis and cell viability are shown in Figures 1 and 2, respectively.

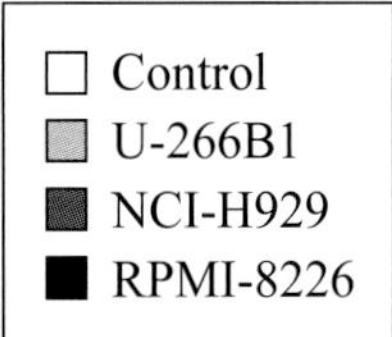

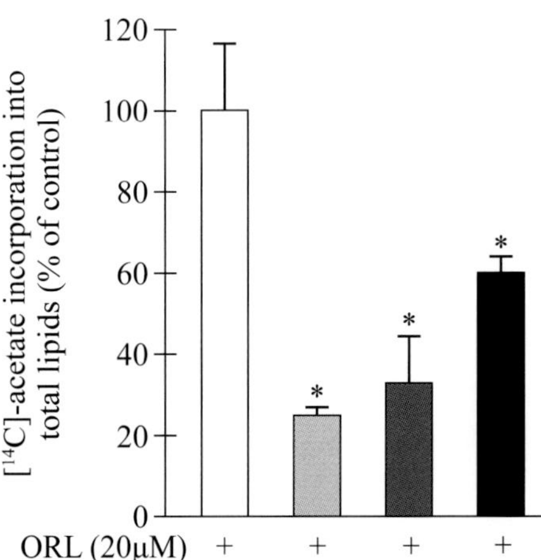

Figure 1 Effects of orlistat on fatty acid metabolism in myeloma cell lines

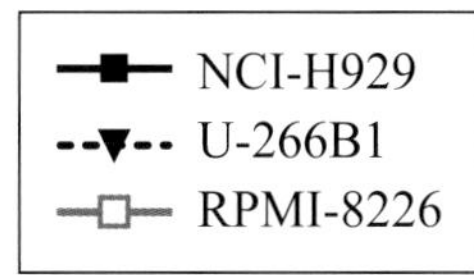

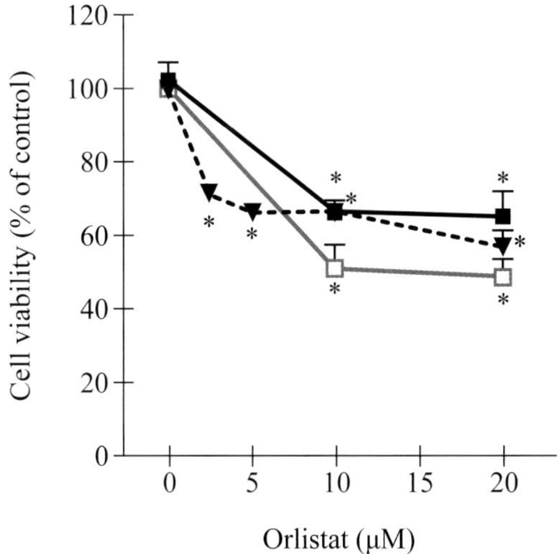

Figure 2 Effect of orlistat on cell viability in myeloma cell lines

Question 19

According to information in the passage, which of the following organelles would be found in higher abundance in cancer cells than in normal cells?

I. Nucleolus
II. Mitochondria
III. Lysosomes
IV. Rough Endoplasmic Reticulum

O **A.** II only

O **B.** I and II

O **C.** III and IV

O **D.** I, II, and III

Question 20

Information in the passage implies that:

O **A.** cancer cells have a more rigid plasma membrane than normal cells.

O **B.** cancer cells have a more fluid plasma membrane than normal cells.

O **C.** cancer cells have reduced stores of triglycerides compared to normal cells.

O **D.** cancer cells cause less inflammation than normal cells.

Question 21

Which of the following cell lines would have the lowest amount of ^{14}C in its plasma membranes when treated with 20 μM orlistat?

O **A.** Control

O **B.** U-266B1

O **C.** NCI-H929

O **D.** RPMI-8226

Question 22

According to the passage, which of the following cell lines is most dependent upon lipogenesis for survival?

O **A.** U-266B1

O **B.** NCI-H929

O **C.** RPMI-8266

O **D.** None of the cell lines are dependent upon lipogenesis.

TEST 3A

Passage 5 (Questions 23-26)

Researchers isolated samples of adipocytes, or fat cells, from a human body and studied the samples with regard to their structure and unique properties. The samples were designated as Samples A, B, and C. While two of the samples (Sample A and Sample B) were easily identified by their known properties, researchers were able to classify the final sample (Sample C) by process of elimination.

The specimen from Sample A, when visualized under the microscope, had large cells with a hollowed out appearance. Small nuclei were seen along the cell border edges. When running a protein expression assay on the cells, researchers noticed that the cells produced a significant number of insulin receptors as well as leptin, which is a hormone that signals satiety.

The cells of Sample B, by contrast, had a darker appearance with what appeared to be multiple lipid droplets within each cell. Under high-powered electron microscopy, they could make out numerous mitochondria. In a protein expression assay, they noticed the cells produced high levels of uncoupling protein 1 (UCP1), which is crucial to non-shivering thermogenesis and the ability to use excess energy in the body. Non-shivering thermogenesis is accomplished by uncoupling the proton gradient of oxidative phosphorylation from ATP synthesis to release energy instead as heat. In developmental studies, they noticed that these cells would arise from unique precursor cells as compared to those in Sample A.

They noticed that both Sample A cells and Sample B cells produced high levels of the protein adiponectin, which is made by all adipocytes and is important in regulating glucose levels in the body. The protein *HOXC9* is uniquely expressed beige adipocytes.

The researchers used the observations above along with the information in Table 1 to classify the cells from each of the samples.

Table 1 Biochemical and physiologic differences in adipose subtypes

Property	Adipose subtype		
	White	Beige	Brown
Appearance under microscope	Cell with a washed-out center	Cell with multiple circular droplets	Cell with multiple circular droplets
Presence in the body	Predominant type under skin	Colonies within white adipocyte populations	In the neck and along the spine
Age distribution	More abundant in adults	Present in non-obese children	Predominantly in newborns and infants
Metabolic activity	Storage and release of lipids and free fatty acids	Fuel metabolism for heat production	Fuel metabolism for heat production
Developmental origin	*Myf5*- cells	*Myf5*- cells	*Myf5*+ cells

This passage was adapted from "Direct Evidence of Brown Adipocytes in Different Fat Depots in Children." Rockstroh D, Landgraf K, Wagner IV, Gesing J, Tauscher R, et al. *PLoS Medicine.* 2015. 10(2) doi: 10.1371/journal.pone.0117841 for use under the terms of the Creative Commons CC BY 4.0 license (http://creativecommons.org/licenses/by/4.0/legalcode).

Question 23

Which of the following steps of glucose metabolism generate ATP through substrate-level phosphorylation?

I. The production of glucose-6-phosphate from glucose
II. The movement of protons through ATP synthase
III. The conversion of acetyl-CoA to carbon dioxide
IV. The metabolism of glucose-6-phosphate to pyruvate
V. The conversion of NADH to NAD+ by electron donation
VI. The conversion of citrate to oxaloacetate

- **A.** I, II, and III only
- **B.** II, V, and VI only
- **C.** II, IV, and V only
- **D.** III, IV and VI only

Question 24

Adding insulin to the cells in culture would have which of the following effects?

- **A.** Release of free fatty acids following lipolysis in brown adipocytes
- **B.** Increased storage of ketone bodies in brown adipocytes
- **C.** Increased storage of triglycerides in white adipocytes
- **D.** Release of free fatty acids through the action of hormone sensitive lipase in white adipocytes

Question 25

Which of the following may account for obesity in individuals with large deposits of white adipose tissue under the skin?

- **A.** There is an overproduction of leptin causing an increased appetite and overeating.
- **B.** There is an underproduction of leptin causing less satiety after meals and overeating.
- **C.** There is an underproduction of leptin as new white adipocytes put pressure on existing adipocytes due to limited space.
- **D.** There is an overproduction of leptin leading to leptin resistance.

Question 26

Which of the following is a logical experimental setup to classify an unknown sample after first visualizing it under a light microscope?

- **A.** It should be tested for expression of *HOXC9.*
- **B.** It should be tested for expression of adiponectin and then for *HOXC9.*
- **C.** It should be first tested for expression of insulin receptor and then for *HOXC9.*
- **D.** It should be visualized by electron microscopy for the presence of mitochondria.

Questions 27 through 30 do not refer to a passage and are independent of each other.

Question 27

Beta -oxidation of which of the following fatty acids would yield the most ATP?

- O **A.** Palmitic acid, a 16-carbon saturated fatty acid
- O **B.** Palmitoleic acid, a 16-carbon cis-monounsaturated fatty acid
- O **C.** Crotonic acid, a 4-carbon trans-monounsaturated fatty acid
- O **D.** Myristoleic acid, a 14-carbon cis-monounsaturated fatty acid

Question 28

A patient presents to the ER with hypoglycemia as well as an enlarged liver. Which metabolic pathway is most likely defective?

- O **A.** Beta-oxidation
- O **B.** Gluconeogenesis
- O **C.** Glycolysis
- O **D.** Glycogenolysis

Question 29

Humans can synthesize 5 amino acids at all times, and only an additional 6 based on environmental conditions. This makes the other 9 that are used 'essential' amino acids. Which of the following describe a process by which the essential amino acid lysine could be obtained?

- O **A.** UV light dependent peptide synthesis
- O **B.** By breaking the disulfide bonds of a lysine rich protein
- O **C.** By breaking the peptide bonds of a lysine rich protein
- O **D.** The Stretcher amino acid synthesis

Question 30

Exercise and diet are known to affect the rate of oxidative phosphorylation in the cell. Compared to an individual at rest, the rate of oxidative phosphorylation would be:

- O **A.** higher in a muscle cell in the leg of a runner that becomes depleted of oxygen during a one-mile race.
- O **B.** lower when the relative amount of ADP in a hepatocyte is high.
- O **C.** the same as that in a fasting individual following consumption of a large meal full of carbohydrates.
- O **D.** lower as the ratio of NADH to its oxidized form in a cardiac cell decreases.

Passage 6 (Questions 31-34)

Salmonella is one of the most common food-borne bacterial pathogens and the disease outcomes range from a self-limited gastroenteritis to typhoid fever in humans. *S. typhimurium* causes an estimated 20 million cases of typhoid and 200,000 human deaths worldwide per annum. Typhoid infection involves transmission of *Salmonella* via the ingestion of contaminated food and water followed by bacterial penetration of the small intestinal barrier by invading gut epithelial cells, causing bloody diarrhea. Subsequently, Salmonella can enter the mesenteric lymph nodes and invade phagocytic cells such as macrophages.

Recent research has been directed towards establishing the role of central metabolic pathways in the virulence of pathogenic bacteria. Scientists were interested in investigating the effect of disrupting the TCA cycle on the ability of *S. typhimurium* to replicate within murine 4/74 macrophages by deleting genes encoding TCA cycle enzymes. Specifically, the researchers deleted the *sucAB, sucCD,* and *sdhCDAB* genes that encode 2-ketoglutarate dehydrogenase, succinyl-CoA synthetase, and succinate dehydrogenase, respectively (Figure 1). The number of intracellular bacteria in HeLa cells was quantified and the results are presented in Figure 2.

Bacteria that harbor an incomplete TCA cycle retain the ability to generate 2-ketoglutarate, oxaloacetate, and succinyl-CoA from pyruvate via the glyoxylate shunt. The glyoxylate shunt bypasses reactions of the TCA cycle in which CO_2 is released and conserves 4 carbon compounds, including glycolytic intermediates, for biosynthesis (Figure 1). The pathway is active during growth on 2-carbon compounds when glucose is unavailable and 4-carbon TCA cycle intermediates need to be conserved.

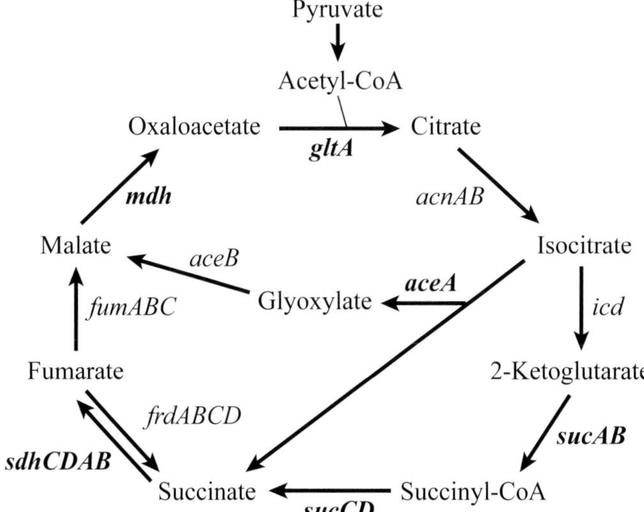

Figure 1 TCA cycle and glyoxylate shunt showing intermediate products and genes encoding enzymes within the pathway. Genes deleted by the scientists are shown in bold.

TEST 3A

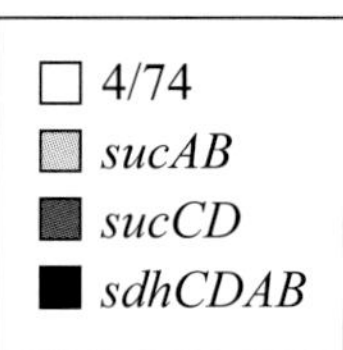

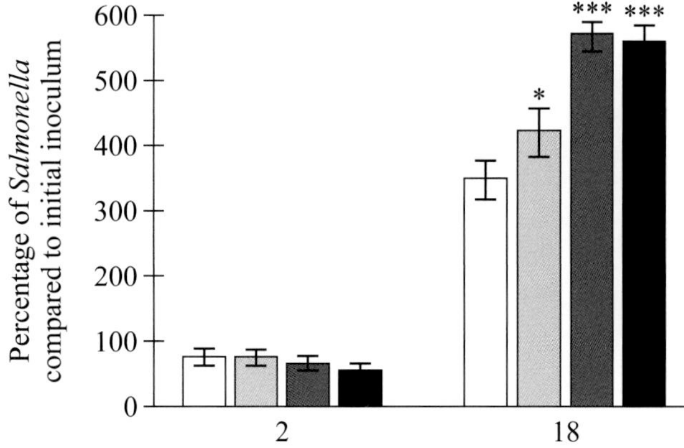

Figure 2 Number of intracellular *S. typhimurium* in macrophages. The various bars represent specific gene deletions in *S. typhirmurium.* The significant differences between the control and experimental strains are shown by asterisks: $p < 0.05$, * $p < 0.05$, ** $p < 0.01$, and *** $p < 0.001$.

This passage was adapted from "An incomplete TCA cycle increases survival of *Salmonella* typhimurium during infection of resting and activated murine macrophages." Bowden S, Ramachandran V, Knudsen G, Hinton J, Thompson A. *PLoS ONE.* 2010. 5(11) doi:10.1371/journal.pone.0013871 for use under the terms of the Creative Commons CC BY 3.0 license (http://creativecommons.org/licenses/by/3.0/legalcode).

Question 31

Based on the passage, using the glyoxylate shunt to bypass intermediates of the TCA cycle most likely benefits *Salmonella* by:

- O **A.** increasing its ability to be phagocytized by macrophages.
- O **B.** providing additional metabolic reactants for biosynthetic pathways.
- O **C.** decreasing the amount of glucose required to maintain cellular replication.
- O **D.** increasing invasion into the mesenteric lymph system.

Question 32

Bacteria that harbor an incomplete TCA cycle could most likely produce what number of ATP per glucose molecule oxidized?

- O **A.** 2
- O **B.** 12
- O **C.** 30
- O **D.** 36

Question 33

According to information in the passage, which of the following statements describes the primary role of the TCA cycle in *Salmonella*?

- O **A.** The TCA cycle primarily provides metabolic intermediates for synthesis of amino acids.
- O **B.** The TCA cycle primarily provides metabolic intermediates for synthesis of heme.
- O **C.** The TCA cycle primarily provides NADH for ATP production.
- O **D.** The TCA cycle primarily provides $FADH_2$ for ATP production.

Question 34

The glyoxylate pathway is most likely to be active when which of the following molecules is the primary source of cellular ATP?

- O **A.** Fatty Acids
- O **B.** Amino Acids
- O **C.** Glucose
- O **D.** Lactate

Passage 7 (Questions 35-39)

The worldwide increase in obesity and diabetes mellitus type 2 has brought new interest to the mechanisms by which dietary monosaccharides are absorbed in the intestine and to what extent these systems undergo diet-dependent regulation. Glucose derived either from hydrolysis of starch or from sucrose is taken up into the epithelial cell predominantly by the sodium-dependent glucose co-transporter (SGLT1). Its pivotal role in glucose absorption is demonstrated by the inability of animals lacking SGLT1 to survive on glucose-containing diets. However, *Sglt1* knockout mice maintained on a glucose-free/galactose-free diet are viable, healthy, and fertile although they exhibit impaired intestinal glucose absorption. Efflux of glucose from enterocytes into blood is thought to be mediated by GLUT2 as a facilitative transporter with a low affinity but high transport capacity.

With the availability of mice lacking SGLT1, the contribution of the transporter to intestinal glucose transport as well as its role in incretin hormone secretion can be assessed under experimental conditions. Intragastric administration of D-glucose including radiolabeled glucose was used, and tracer contents in intestinal tissues along the entire small intestine (Figure 1) were determined.

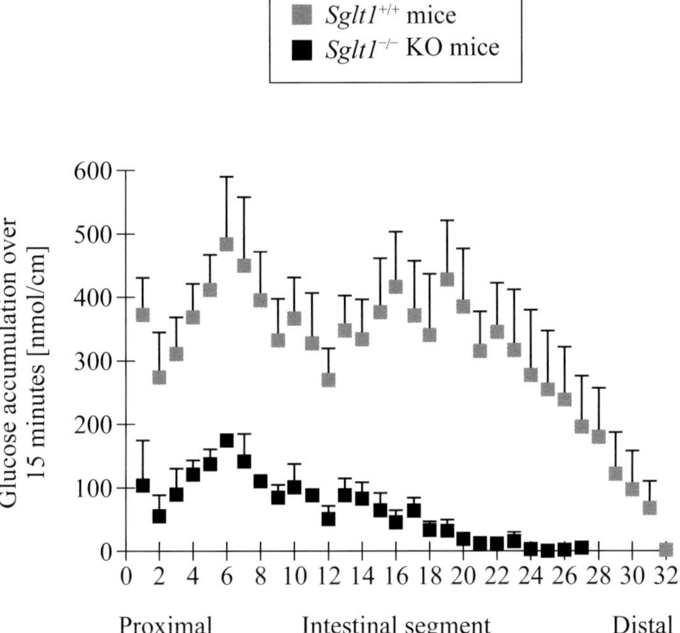

Figure 1 Glucose accumulation in the intestine following intragastric glucose administration.

Besides their role in glucose transport, both SGLT1 and GLUT2 are proposed to function as glucose sensors in enteroendocrine cells leading or contributing to glucose-induced secretion of the incretins glucose-dependent insulinotropic peptide (GIP) and glucagon-like-peptide 1 (GLP-1). GLP-1 stimulates insulin release while also inhibiting glucagon release. The relationship between SGLT1 and incretin concentration is shown in Figures 2 and 3.

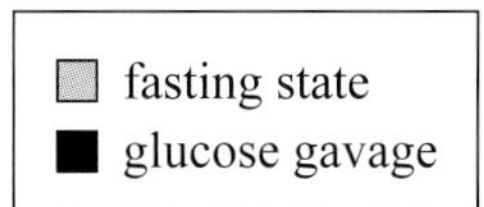

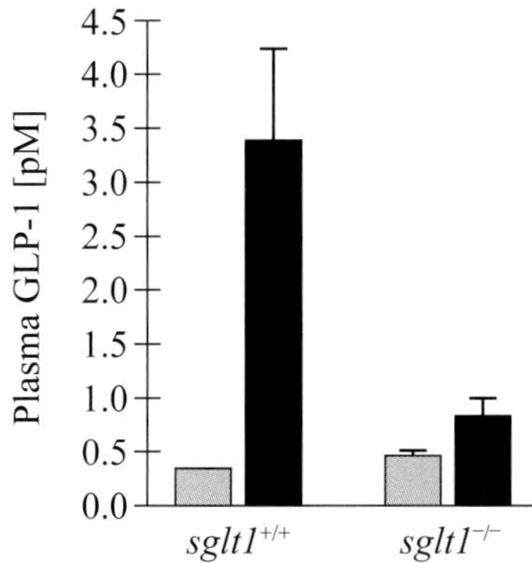

Figure 2 Change in plasma GLP-1 levels after intragastric glucose administration.

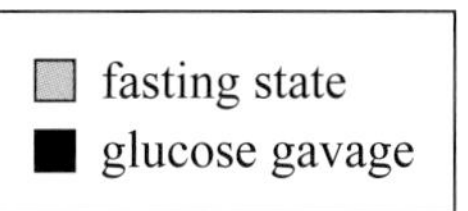

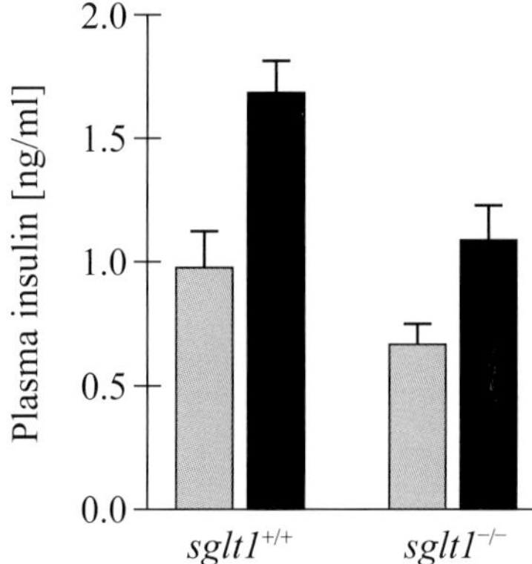

Figure 3 Change in plasma insulin levels after intragastric glucose administration.

Question 35

In Figure 1, which combination of intestinal segment and genetic background (wild-type or *Sglt1* knock-out) would lead to the least insulin release following the intragastric glucose administration?

- O **A.** Intestinal segment 6 in the wild-type background
- O **B.** Intestinal segment 6 in the *Sglt1* knock-out background
- O **C.** Intestinal segment 10 in the wild-type background
- O **D.** Intestinal segment 30 in the wild-type background

TEST 3A

Question 36

GLUT2 deficiency is likely to result in which of the following outcomes?

- O **A.** A higher glucose concentration in blood
- O **B.** A higher glucose concentration in intestinal cells
- O **C.** A higher glucose concentration in the stool
- O **D.** An increase in glycogen synthesis in the liver

Question 37

Based on the passage, which of the following is expected to be lower in nonfasting wild-type mice than in nonfasting SGLT1 deficient mice?

- O **A.** Glucose uptake in skeletal muscle
- O **B.** Blood glucose levels
- O **C.** Glucose uptake in red blood cells
- O **D.** Insulin release from the pancreas

Question 38

Which of the following would explain the use of *Sglt1* knock-out mice to test the effects of the transporter on insulin release instead of a potent sodium-dependent glucose co-transporter (SGLT) inhibitor for their research?

- O **A.** The inhibitor while potent may still not fully block the transporter.
- O **B.** The inhibitor compound may have undesired consequences in the mice.
- O **C.** The inhibitor may block similar transporters such as SGLT2 in the kidney.
- O **D.** There is better control over the variables of the experiment using the genetically modified mice.

Question 39

Research suggests that the current obesity epidemic and rise in insulin secretion disorders are the result of increased fructose consumption. Which of the following supports this hypothesis?

- O **A.** Fructose is transported into intestinal cells through the action of GLUT5 not SGLT1.
- O **B.** GLP-1 levels are higher following intragastric fructose administration compared to glucose administration.
- O **C.** Fructose entry to the glycolysis pathway is less tightly regulated than is glucose entry leading to more fat synthesis.
- O **D.** Fructose has been shown to be a risk for non-alcoholic fatty liver disease that causes insulin resistance through impaired cell signaling.

Passage 8 (Questions 40-43)

Epidemiological studies have provided evidence for a role of chronic hepatitis B virus (HBV) infection in the development of hepatocellular carcinoma (HCC). Reports have also established that cancer cells frequently display high rates of anaerobic glycolysis, despite normal oxygen levels in comparison to their non-transformed counterparts. Previous studies based on HBV-infected mice have also revealed a metabolic alteration of hepatocytes from the glycogen-storage state toward a glycogen-depleted state characterized by an increase of glycolysis, with HBV protein pre-S2 possibly mediating the switch.

The mammalian target of rapamycin (mTOR) is a highly conserved serine/threonine kinase that controls cell growth and proliferation. In addition to its better-known functions in promoting protein synthesis, mTOR is now emerging as a key regulator of cellular metabolism and cancer. Activated mTOR can upregulate Yin Yang 1 (YY1), a transcription factor involved in cell proliferation and regulation of oncogenes.

Given the overlap between HBV pre-S2 and activated mTOR phenotypes, scientists sought to investigate whether pre-S2 mutant-induced mTOR activation may regulate aerobic glycolysis and glycogen storage through YY1 in HBV-related tumorigenesis. Cell staining for glycogen in 1-, 3-, 6-, and 12-month-old control mice and transgenic mice with pre-S2 deleted is shown in Figure 1.

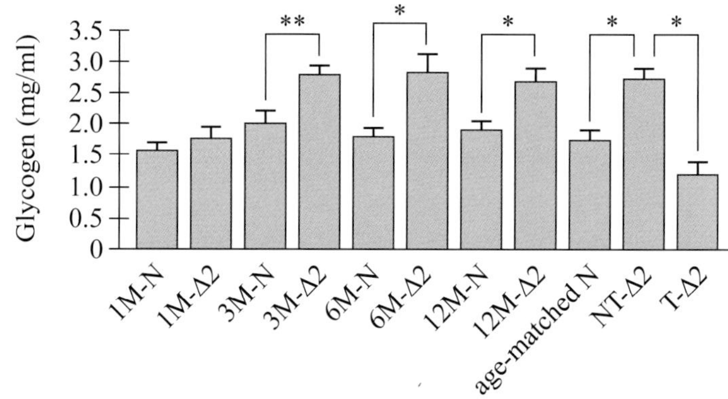

Figure 1 Glycogen levels in mice livers. Shown are representative results from different months (M) of pre-S2 mutant (Δ2) and non-transgenic (N) livers, non-tumorous livers (NT), and tumors (T). * denotes $p < 0.05$. ** denotes $p < 0.01$.

Question 40

Based on the passage, switching from oxidative phosphorylation to anaerobic respiration most likely benefits cancer cell growth by:

- O **A.** providing an increased supply of macromolecules.
- O **B.** increasing the number of free radicals produced in the electron transport chain.
- O **C.** reducing the amount of glucose used for ATP production.
- O **D.** providing a supply of NADH for anabolic processes.

Question 41

The information in the passage supports the hypothesis that overexpression of which of the following genes is most likely to contribute to metabolic alteration in HBV-infected mice?

- O **A.** *GYS1*, the glycogen synthase gene
- O **B.** *PYG*, the glycogen phosphorylase gene
- O **C.** *PDH*, the pyruvate dehydrogenase gene
- O **D.** *G6P*, the glucose-6 phosphatase gene

Question 42

According to information in the passage, which of the following is LEAST likely to describe the metabolic state of hepatocellular carcinoma (HCC)?

- O **A.** Increased activity of glycogen synthase
- O **B.** Increased activity of glucokinase
- O **C.** Increased activity of glycogen phosphorylase
- O **D.** Decreased activity of succinate dehydrogenase

Question 43

According to the passage, glucose is most likely to be stored in the livers of:

- O **A.** mice with a non-synonymous mutation in YY1.
- O **B.** mice with overactivation of mTOR.
- O **C.** mice with mutated pre-S2.
- O **D.** wild-type mice.

Questions 44 through 47 do not refer to a passage and are independent of each other.

Question 44

Reduced glucose absorption in skeletal muscle, heart, and adipose tissue leads to which immediate compensatory response in patients with Type 2 diabetes?

- O **A.** Increased production of acetyl-CoA through beta oxidation
- O **B.** Internalization of insulin receptors due to sensitization
- O **C.** Cell apoptosis in response to insufficient energy precursors
- O **D.** Shuttling of additional insulin receptors to the cell surface

Question 45

Tyrosine is least likely to contribute to:

- O **A.** neurotransmitters that elicit action potentials in neighboring neurons.
- O **B.** hormones that regulate metabolism.
- O **C.** the fluidity of the plasma membrane.
- O **D.** the ability of the body to deliver oxygen to tissues.

Question 46

Researchers are examining a molecule that could potentially act as a substitute for ATP based on its energy profile. Which of the following experimental findings would best support their hypothesis?

- O **A.** The molecule has a phosphate group.
- O **B.** The molecule has a hydrolysis $\Delta G < 0$.
- O **C.** The molecule has adenosine.
- O **D.** The molecule had a hydrolysis $\Delta G > 0$.

Question 47

Which of the following statements best describes the molecular output of the citric acid cycle and electron transport chain?

- O **A.** The number of ATP produced from NADH is greater than the number produced from $FADH_2$.
- O **B.** The number of GTP produced is equal to the number of ATP produced.
- O **C.** The number of GTP produced is greater than the number of ATP produced.
- O **D.** The number of ATP produced from NADH is less than the number produced from $FADH_2$.

Passage 9 (Questions 48-52)

Alzheimer's disease (AD) is the most common form of dementia. It is estimated that AD affects more than 35 million patients worldwide and its incidence is expected to increase with the aging of the population. Although extensive investigations of AD have taken place over the past few decades, its pathogenesis has yet to be elucidated. Currently no treatment is available to prevent or halt the progression of AD and the clinical diagnosis of AD is not possible until a patient reaches the dementia phase of the disease. The dementia phase is characterized by a decline in mental ability that significantly affects the patient's quality of life. A more accurate and earlier diagnosis of AD could enable the use of potential disease-modifying drugs, which emphasizes a need for biological markers for the early stages of AD.

Metabolic alterations have been proposed to be involved in AD from the early stages of the disease. Perturbations in mitochondrial function have long been observed in AD patients, including decreased activity of key mitochondrial enzymes and a reduction in the intracellular concentration of oxygen. Impaired glucose transport has also been reported in AD brains.

The pathway predicted to decrease most significantly in AD is the carnitine shuttle. The carnitine shuttle is a carnitine-dependent transport of fatty acids into the mitochondria for the production of energy via β-oxidation (Figure 1). Brain acyl-carnitines can function in synthesizing lipids, altering and stabilizing membrane composition, and enhancing cholinergic neurotransmission. Decreased activity of carnitine acyl-transferase (CAT) has been measured in the temporal cortex of AD patients and it has been demonstrated that acetyl-carnitine administration can improve the cognitive performance in patients with mild AD.

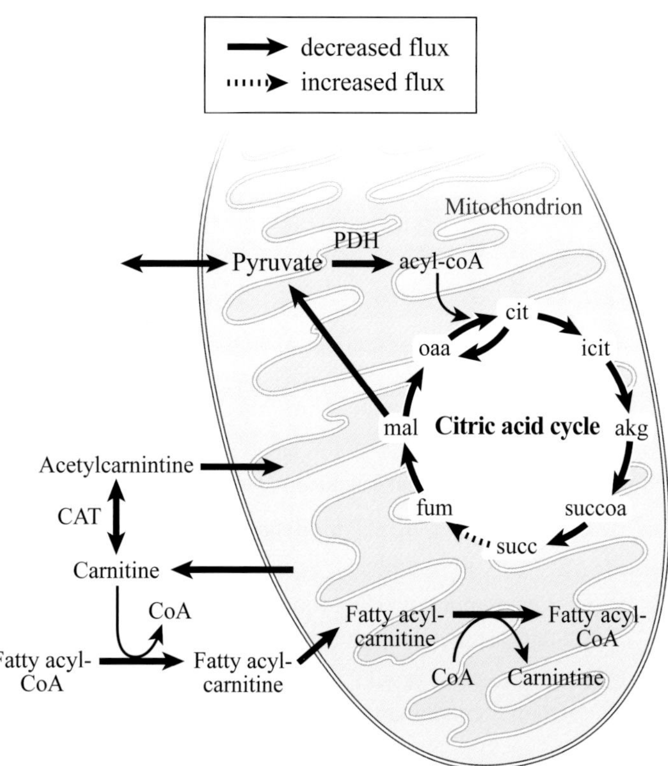

Figure 1 Key metabolic flux alterations in AD versus normal

Question 48

Compared to normal individuals, patients with Alzheimer's disease are likely to have:

- O **A.** decreased glycogen stores in temporal lobe neurons.
- O **B.** increased flux through the pentose phosphate pathway in temporal lobe neurons.
- O **C.** increased β-oxidation of long-chain fatty acids in temporal lobe neurons.
- O **D.** decreased conversion of succinate to fumarate in temporal lobe neuron mitochondria.

Question 49

AD patients may also be at an increased risk for a stroke which is caused by blood vessel occlusion that occurs in the brain. Which of the following statements best describes the flux of α-ketoglutarate in neurons near the region of a stroke compared to normal neurons?

- O **A.** The flux of α-ketoglutarate is lower in normal neurons than stroke-associated neurons
- O **B.** The flux of α-ketoglutarate is higher in normal neurons than stroke-associated neurons
- O **C.** The flux of α-ketoglutarate is the same in normal and stroke-associated neurons
- O **D.** The flux of isocitrate is lower in normal neurons than stroke-associated neurons.

Question 50

Compared to normal individuals, patients with AD are likely to show decreased oxidation of fatty acids in:

I. the mitochondria.
II. the peroxisome.
III. the smooth endoplasmic reticulum.

- O **A.** I only
- O **B.** I and II
- O **C.** II and III
- O **D.** I, II, and III

Question 51

Which of the following intermediates of the citric acid cycle can be used for glucose synthesis?

- O **A.** Isocitrate
- O **B.** Succinyl-CoA
- O **C.** Fumarate
- O **D.** Oxaloacetate

Question 52

Which of the following figures best describes the change in free energy occurring between intermediates of the citric acid cycle in AD and normal patient neurons?

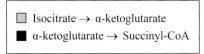

Isocitrate → α-ketoglutarate
α-ketoglutarate → Succinyl-CoA

A.

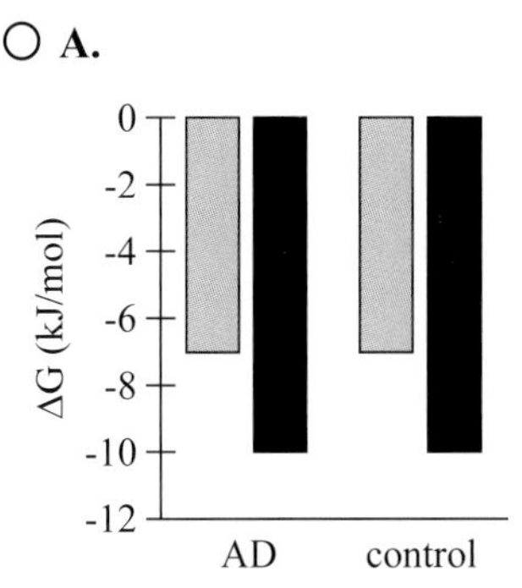

B.

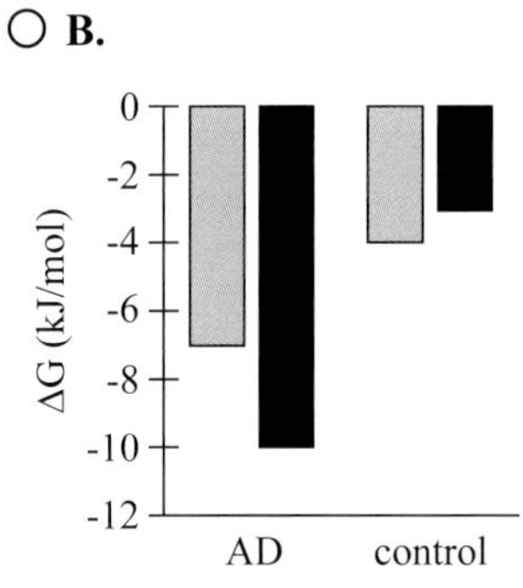

C.

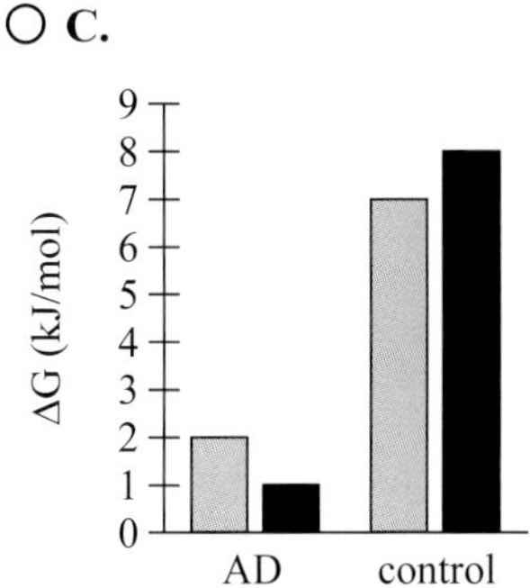

D.

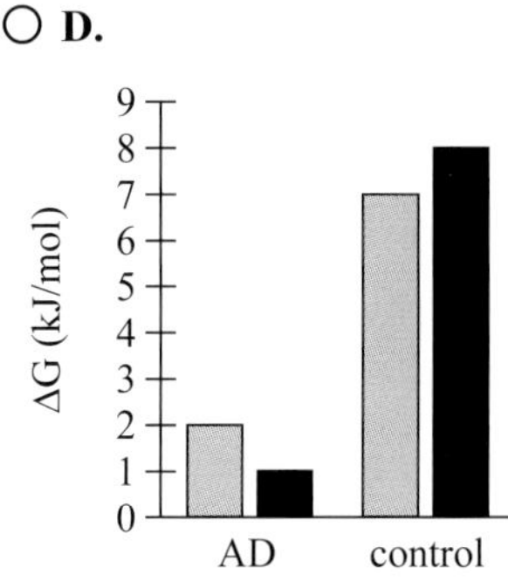

Passage 10 (Questions 53-56)

Every enzyme in human metabolism has the potential to be improperly assembled secondary to changes in the sequence of DNA. These mutant enzymes may be incapable of performing their usual task, resulting in the buildup of metabolic intermediates. If there is a major mutation in one of the enzymes of glycolysis, the results are fatal *in utero*. If the mutation occurs in a less essential metabolic pathway, specific disease patterns will result. One famous example is alkaptonuria (AKU), also known as black urine disease.

Alkaptonuria is often diagnosed clinically with episodes of dark urine, biochemically by the accumulation of peripheral homogentisic acid (Figure 1), and molecularly by the presence of mutations in the homogentisate 1,2-dioxygenase gene (HGD).

Alkaptonuria is invariably associated with HGD mutations, which consist of single nucleotide variants and small insertions/deletions. The presence of deletions beyond a few nucleotides among over 150 reported deleterious mutations has not been described, raising the suspicion that this gene might be protected against the detrimental mechanisms of gene rearrangements.

The quest for an HGD mutation in a patient with AKU revealed with a single nucleotide polymorphism (SNP) array two large regions of homozygosity (5–16 Mb), the smaller of which includes the HGD gene (Figure 2). A homozygous deletion of 649 bp deletion that encompasses the 72 nucleotides of exon 2 and surrounding DNA sequences in flanking introns of the HGD gene was unveiled in a patient with AKU. The nature of this deletion suggests that this in-frame deletion could generate a protein without exon 2.

Researchers modeled the tertiary structure of the mutant protein structure to determine the effect of exon 2 deletion. While the two β-pleated sheets encoded by exon 2 were missing in the mutant structure, other β-pleated sheets are largely unaffected by the deletion. However, nine novel α-helical coils substituted the eight coils present in the native HGD crystal structure (Table 1). Thus, this deletion results in a deleterious enzyme, which is consistent with the known phenotype. Screening for mutations in the HGD gene, particularly in the Middle East, ought to include this exon 2 deletion in order to determine its frequency and uncover its origin.

TEST 3A

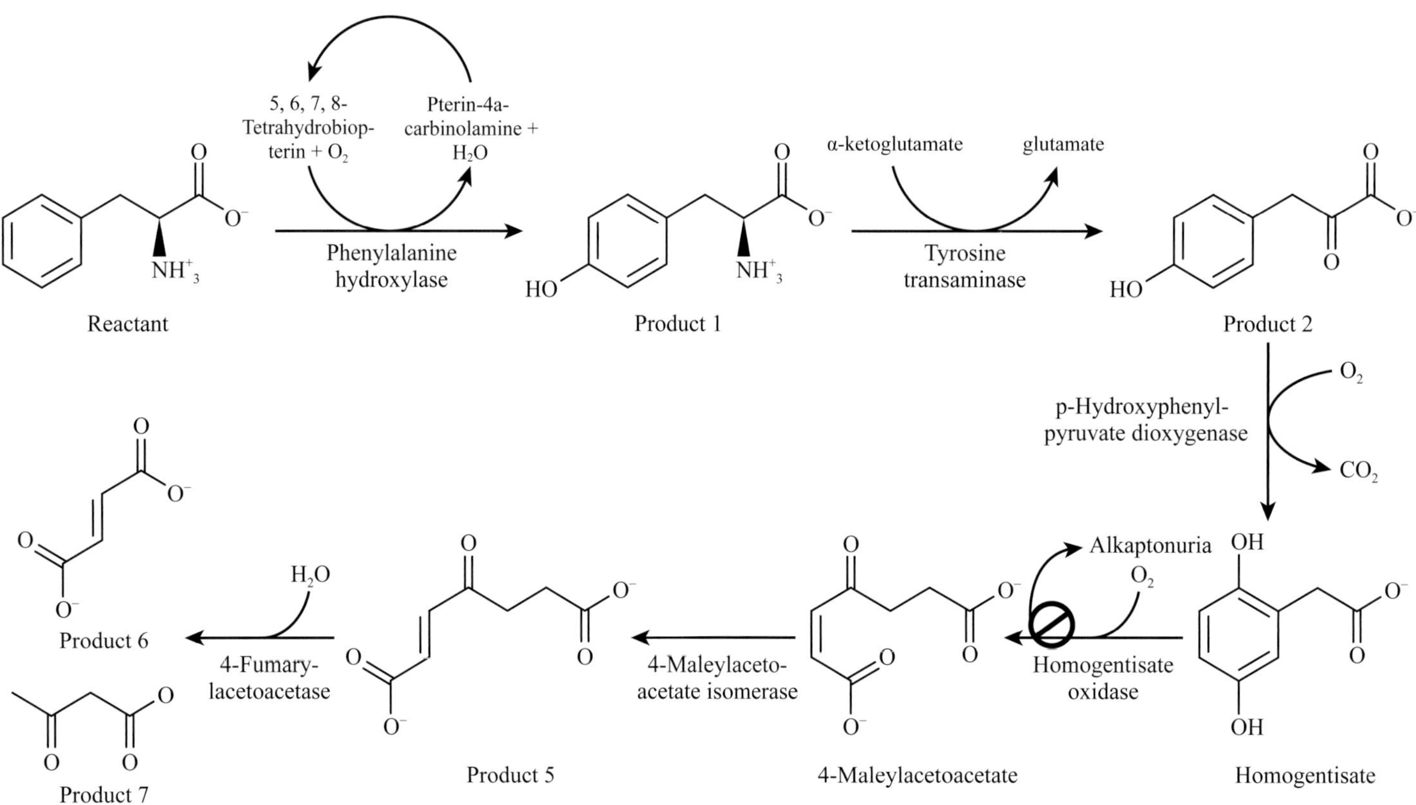

Figure 1 Alkaptonuria metabolic defect

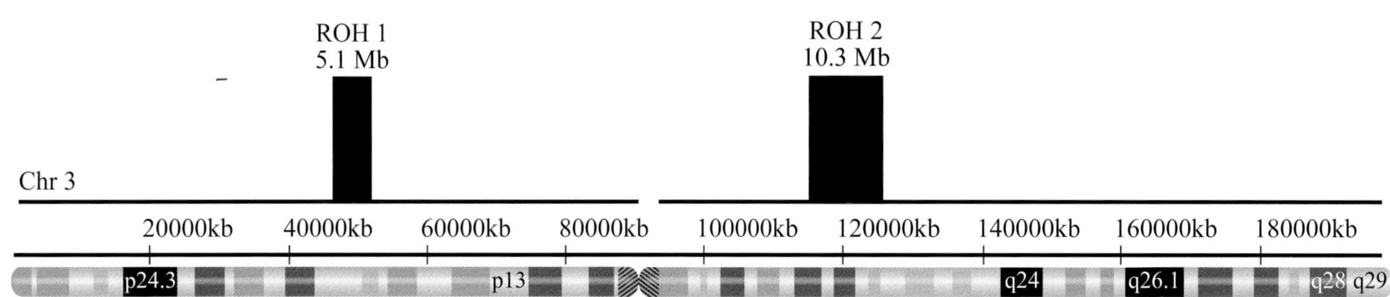

Figure 2 Regions of Homozygosity (ROH) derived from the patient in the SNP array

	Normal	Mutant
α-helical coils	CPYNL	WDE
	PRSTNK	ASQ
	NPR	IKS
	Absent	YHKC
β-pleated sheets	YIS	Deleted
	FLIP	Absent
	GGGSLH	GGGSLH

Table 1 Selection of amino acid sequences of α-helical coils and β-pleated sheets in the normal and mutated HGD proteins

Question 53

A patient with alkaptonuria would be expected to have which of the following results if intermediates of the pathway were measured?

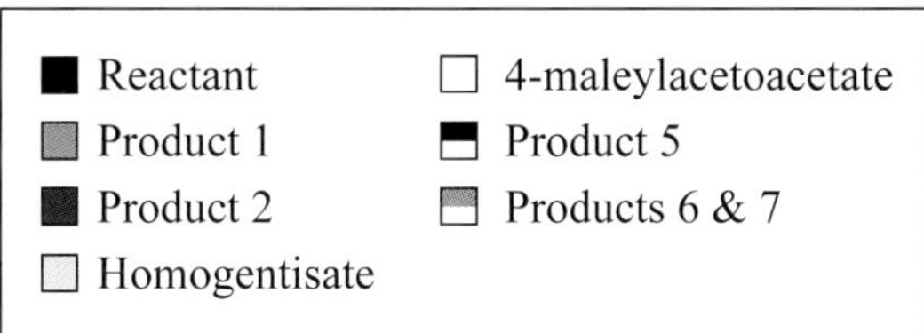

○ **A.**

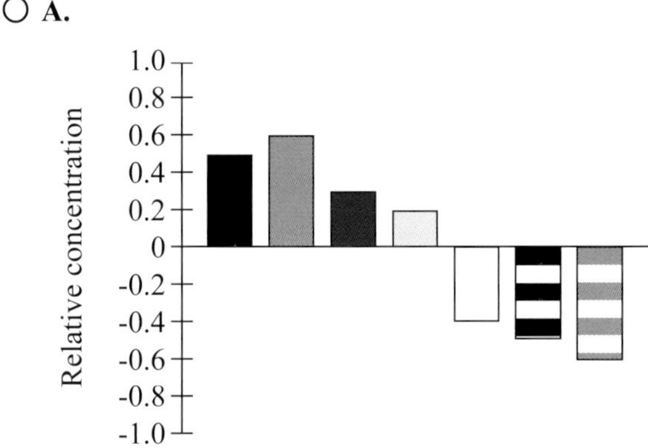

○ **B.**

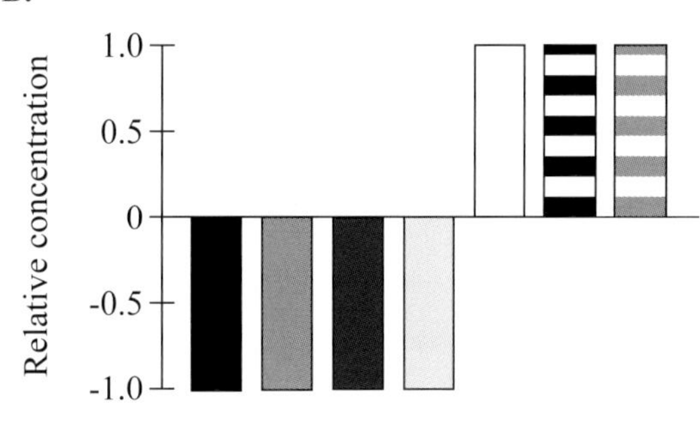

○ **C.**

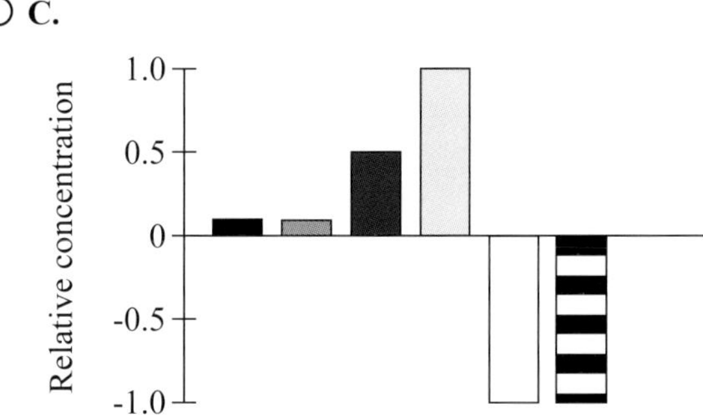

○ **D.**

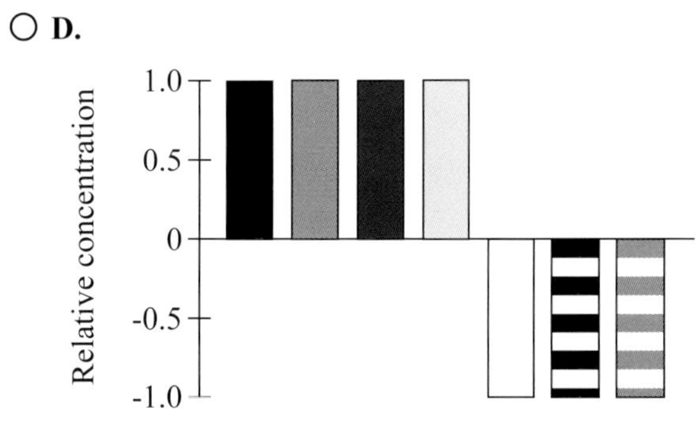

Question 54

The reactant in the metabolic pathway affected by alkaptonuria would most likely be found:

○ **A.** in the interior of the enzymes used for glycolysis.

○ **B.** in the interior of the enzymes used for protein synthesis.

○ **C.** on the exterior of the enzymes used for glycolysis.

○ **D.** on the exterior of the enzymes used for protein synthesis.

Question 55

One of the final products of phenylalanine metabolism:

○ **A.** is an intermediate of glycolysis.

○ **B.** will have difficulty entering a mitochondrion.

○ **C.** can be used to generate reducing agents in the tricarboxylic acid pathway.

○ **D.** cannot be used for gluconeogenesis.

Question 56

The production of Product 2 is coupled with:

○ **A.** formation of a Krebs cycle intermediate.

○ **B.** destruction of a Krebs cycle intermediate.

○ **C.** formation of a protein.

○ **D.** destruction of a protein.

Questions 57 through 59 do not refer to a passage and are independent of each other.

Question 57

Lipids can serve as a source of cellular energy alongside glucose, undergoing beta oxidation into Acetyl-CoA. Which statement correctly describes the relationship between molecular conformation and energy content?

- O **A.** Saturated lipids generate more net gain of ATP due to their greater reducing potential
- O **B.** Unsaturated lipids generate more net gain of ATP due to their increased number of double bonds
- O **C.** Saturated lipids generate more net gain of ATP due to their greater molecular weight
- O **D.** Unsatruated lipids generate less net gain of ATP due to their tendency to disrupt cohesion between phospholipids in plasma membranes.

Question 58

Suppose scientists synthesize a compound that renders cancer cells unable to produce enough cholesterol to maintain fluidity in their plasma membranes. Which of the pathways occurring in the cytosol is most likely inhibited?

- O **A.** Glycogenolysis
- O **B.** Pentose Phosphate Pathway
- O **C.** Glycolysis
- O **D.** The Citric Acid Cycle

Question 59

Diet supplementation with which of the following cofactors is most likely to increase the flux of electrons through the electron transport chain complexes?

- O **A.** Riboflavin
- O **B.** Iron
- O **C.** Zinc
- O **D.** Vitamin C

STOP. If you finish before time is called, check your work. You may go back to any question in this test.

ANSWERS & EXPLANATIONS for Test 3A can be found on p. 256.

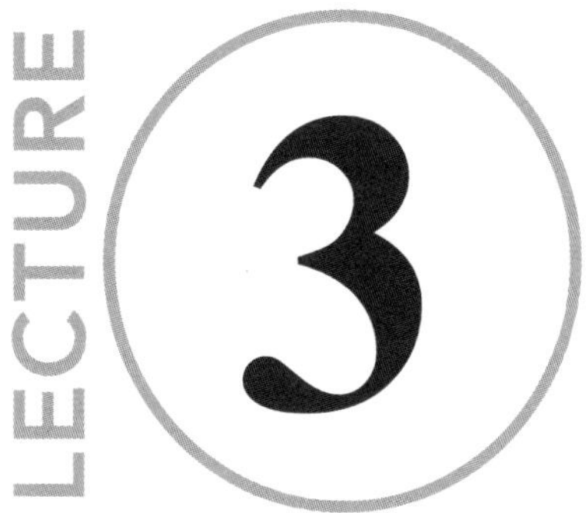

Metabolism

TEST 3B

Time: 90 minutes
Questions 1–59

DIRECTIONS: Most questions in the Biological and Biochemical Foundations of Living Systems test section are grouped with a descriptive passage. Select the best answer to each question using background knowledge and the given passage. A portion of this test section is comprised of discrete questions, which are independent of any passage and one another. Select the best answer for each discrete question. Indicate your selection by blackening the corresponding oval on your answer document. If you are unsure of the answer, rule out incorrect choices and select from the remaining options. You may access a periodic table found on the last page of this book at any point during this test section.

Passage 1 (Questions 1-5)

Second-hand tobacco smoke (SHS) is a cardiovascular disease (CVD) risk factor that significantly increases individual risk of developing a heart attack or stroke. While CVD is often thought of as an adult disease, studies clearly show that atherogenesis, or the buildup of lipid plaques in the arteries, can begin early in life. Cigarette smoke exposure is associated with increased lesion formation in these individuals. Cotinine is a metabolite of nicotine, and the serum level can be used to measure cigarette smoke exposure. It is estimated that 59% of children between the ages of 3 and 11 years of age have been exposed to SHS based upon serum cotinine levels. Additionally, 13.2% of women continue to smoke during pregnancy.

In order to determine the effects of prenatal and neonatal SHS exposure on adult CVD development, hypercholesterolemic apolipoprotein E null mice were exposed to SHS *in utero* or neonatally (birth to 3 weeks of age). Apolipoprotein E is a major protein constituent of chylomicrons, and mice lacking the apoE gene are at high risk for atherosclerosis when fed a high-fat diet. The mice were assessed as adults at 12–14 weeks of age for atherosclerotic lesion development, oxidative stress, mitochondrial DNA copy number, and mitochondrial DNA deletions. It was found that both *in utero* and neonatal SHS exposure resulted in significantly increased adult atherosclerotic lesion development.

Because oxidative stress is known to play an important role in atherosclerosis initiation and progression, oxidant load assessment was performed by quantifying aconitase activity in aortic homogenates. Aconitase is a redox sensitive, citric acid cycle enzyme that is specifically inactivated by superoxide (O_2^-) and peroxynitrite ($ONOO^-$). The results of this experiment are shown below in Figure 1.

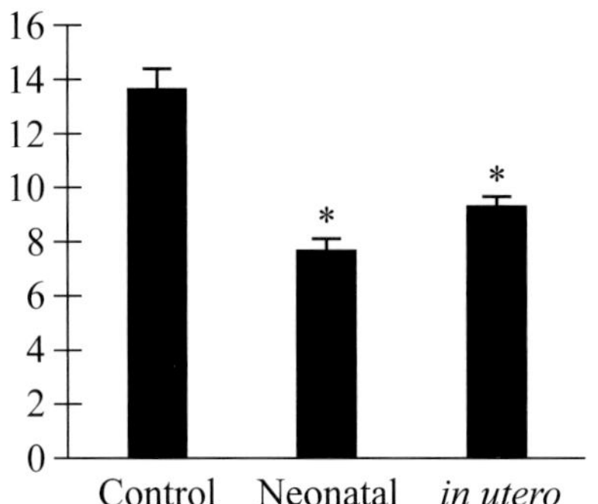

Figure 1 Aconitase activity measured after extraction from aorta homogenates from mice exposed to filtered air, neonatal SHS, or *in utero* SHS. (Note: an asterisk indicates a significant difference from the control).

Question 1

Based on the passage, what may account for the relative obesity of the mice used in the experimental setup?

- O **A.** The loss of ApoE results in an inability to metabolize triglycerides in peripheral tissues.
- O **B.** The loss of ApoE results in an inability to absorb fatty acids by the intestinal cells.
- O **C.** The loss of ApoE results in an inability to transfer lipid particles to the liver.
- O **D.** The loss of ApoE results in an inability to convert lipids to glucose for use by the brain.

Question 2

Which of the following measurements would account for the values of enzyme activity collected in the experiment in Figure 1?

- O **A.** The production of carbon dioxide, which is generated from the decarboxylation of isocitrate
- O **B.** The loss of citrate, which is converted to isocitrate during the citric acid cycle
- O **C.** The production of ATP, which comes as a result of the oxidation of isocitrate
- O **D.** The generation of isocitrate, which is a structural isomer of citrate

Question 3

In another experiment, mice are exposed to second-hand smoke and are examined at multiple intervals. Which group of mice is LEAST likely to show results similar to the first experiment?

- O **A.** Mice with impaired LDL receptor function
- O **B.** Mice given an intestinal lipase inhibitor
- O **C.** Mice with decreased HDL particle formation
- O **D.** Wild-type mice

Question 4

What short-term effect would be seen when the mice previously exposed to filtered air are subjected to high amounts of cigarette smoke?

- A. They will show atherosclerosis in some arteries.
- B. There will be an increase in ketone body formation during starvation.
- C. They will have high serum triglyceride levels.
- D. They will develop lung cancer as a result of oxidative stress in lung cells.

Question 5

A defect in each of the following proteins would be expected to impair the transition from pyruvate to the tricarboxylic acid cycle with the EXCEPTION of:

- A. the outer mitochondrial membrane pyruvate transporter.
- B. the inner mitochondrial membrane pyruvate transporter.
- C. the inner mitochondrial membrane NADH transporter.
- D. pyruvate carboxylase.

Passage 2 (Questions 6-9)

Altered energy metabolism has been proven to be widespread in cancer. Cancer cells have elevated rates of glucose consumption and high lactate production in the presence of oxygen, known as the Warburg Effect. Despite its wide clinical applications, the mechanisms underlying the Warburg effect remain largely elusive.

Mutations of key components of metabolic enzymes may play significant roles in cancer metabolic reprogramming. Pyruvate kinase (PK) is a key rate-limiting enzyme which catalyzes the final step of glycolysis. During tumorigenesis, tissue-specific isoform PKM1 expression gradually diminishes and is replaced by PKM2 expression. PKM2 is considered a key regulator of the Warburg effect but can also function as a transcriptional co-activator to regulate tumorigenesis. A schematic of the role of PKM2 in metabolism and tumorigenesis is presented in Figure 1.

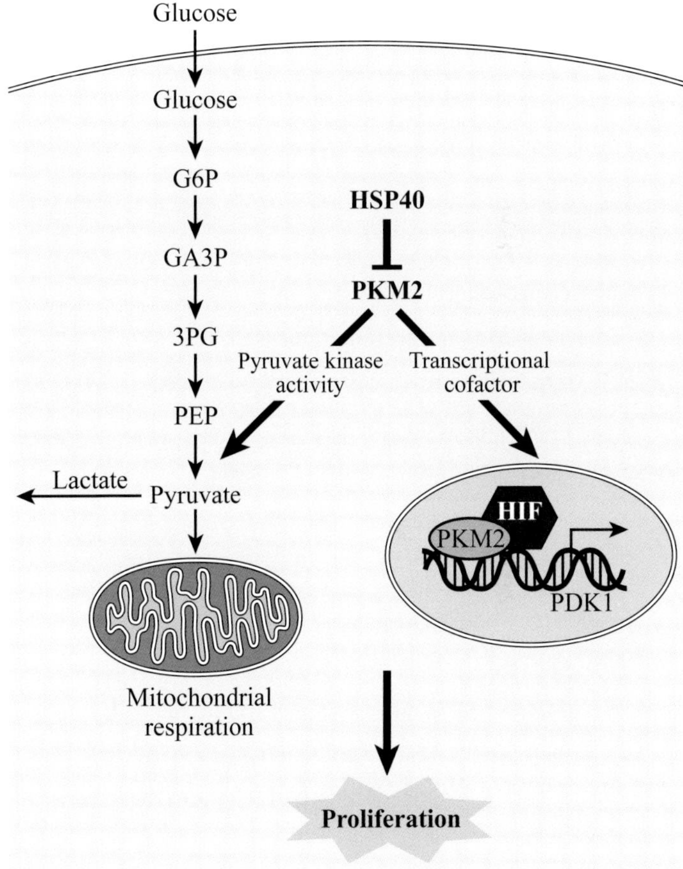

Figure 1 The role of HSP40 and PKM2 in cellular metabolism and tumorigenesis.

Scientists set out to further clarify the molecular mechanisms underlying the regulation of PKM2 by characterizing its interaction with heat shock proteins (HSPs). HSPs are a class of proteins expressed during oxygen deprivation that are indispensable for protein translation, folding, unfolding, translocation, and degradation. Their results showed that HSP40 knockdown enhanced glucose consumption and lactate production and promoted oxidative phosphorylation. Thus, the scientists hypothesized that HSP40 and PKM2 may interact.

TEST 3B

In a subsequent experiment, a plasmid encoding HSP40 was transfected into HeLa cells, a cervical cancer cell line. Ten days after transfection, the scientists determined relative levels of mRNA of PDK1. The results are shown in Figure 2.

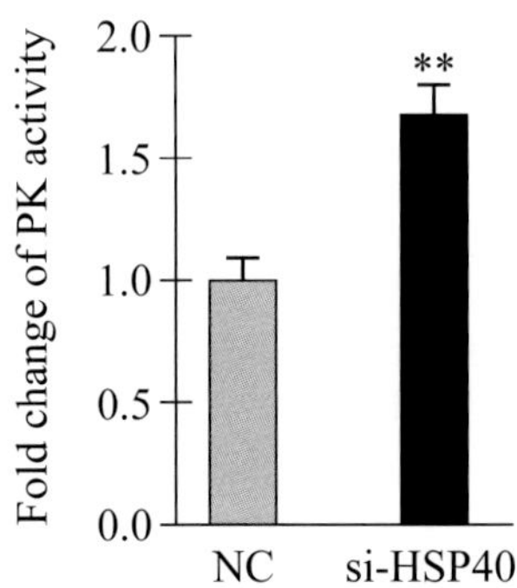

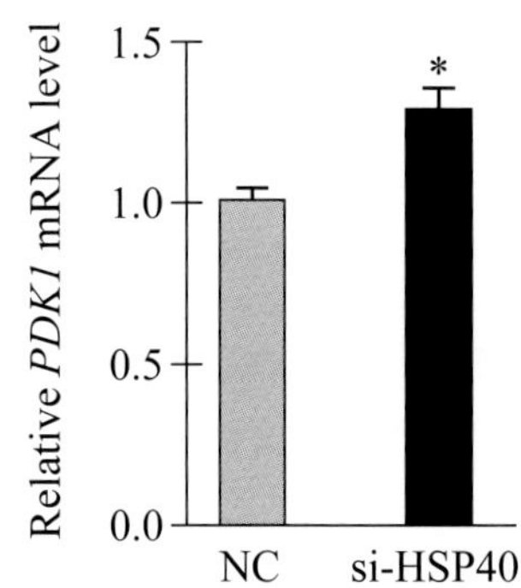

Figure 2 HSP40 impairs PKM2 functions in HeLa cells. * denotes $p < 0.05$, while *** denotes $p < 0.01$.

Question 6

Scientists determined the effect of HSP40 knockdown on oxidative phosphorylation by:

- O **A.** measuring intracellular glucose levels.
- O **B.** measuring intracellular glycogen levels.
- O **C.** measuring intracellular oxygen levels.
- O **D.** measuring intracellular ATP levels.

Question 7

Knockdown of HSP40 in HeLa cells undergoing aerobic metabolism would most likely:

- O **A.** increase the concentration of PEP in the cell.
- O **B.** decrease the concentration of PEP in the cell.
- O **C.** increase the concentration of lactate in the cell.
- O **D.** decrease the concentration of lactate in the cell.

Question 8

What additional experiment would most likely help confirm the role of HSP40 in regulating the transcription in cells demonstrating the Warburg Effect?

- O **A.** Overexpression of HSP40 in HeLa cells.
- O **B.** Knockdown of HSP40 in HeLa cells.
- O **C.** Overexpression of PKM2 in HeLa cells.
- O **D.** Knockdown of PKM2 in HeLa cells.

Question 9

In cancer cells that are under the Warburg Effect, levels of lactic acid in the cell are likely to:

- O **A.** decrease.
- O **B.** increase.
- O **C.** remain constant.
- O **D.** first increase then decrease.

Passage 3 (Questions 10-13)

Niemann-Pick Type C (NPC) disease is an autosomal recessive neurodegenerative disorder caused in most cases by mutations in the *NPC1* gene. The function of the *NPC1* gene product is shown in Figure 1.

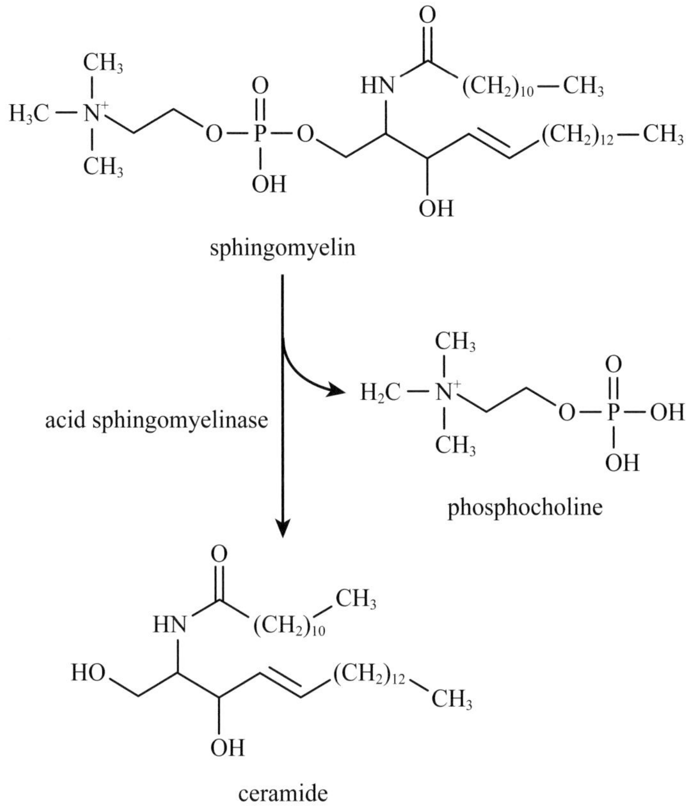

sphingomyelin

acid sphingomyelinase

phosphocholine

ceramide

Figure 1 Metabolism of sphingomyelin

NPC1-deficiency is characterized by late endosomal accumulation of cholesterol, impaired cholesterol homeostasis, and a broad range of other cellular abnormalities. The most severe consequence of *NPC1*-deficiency is a near complete loss of Purkinje neurons in the cerebellum. Increased oxidative stress in symptomatic NPC disease, increases in mitochondrial cholesterol, and alterations in autophagy/mitophagy suggest that mitochondria play a role in NPC disease pathology.

To investigate early metabolic alterations that could affect NPC disease progression, researchers performed metabolomics analyses of different brain regions from age-matched wildtype and $Npc1^{-/-}$ mice. The results are shown in Figure 2.

TEST 3B

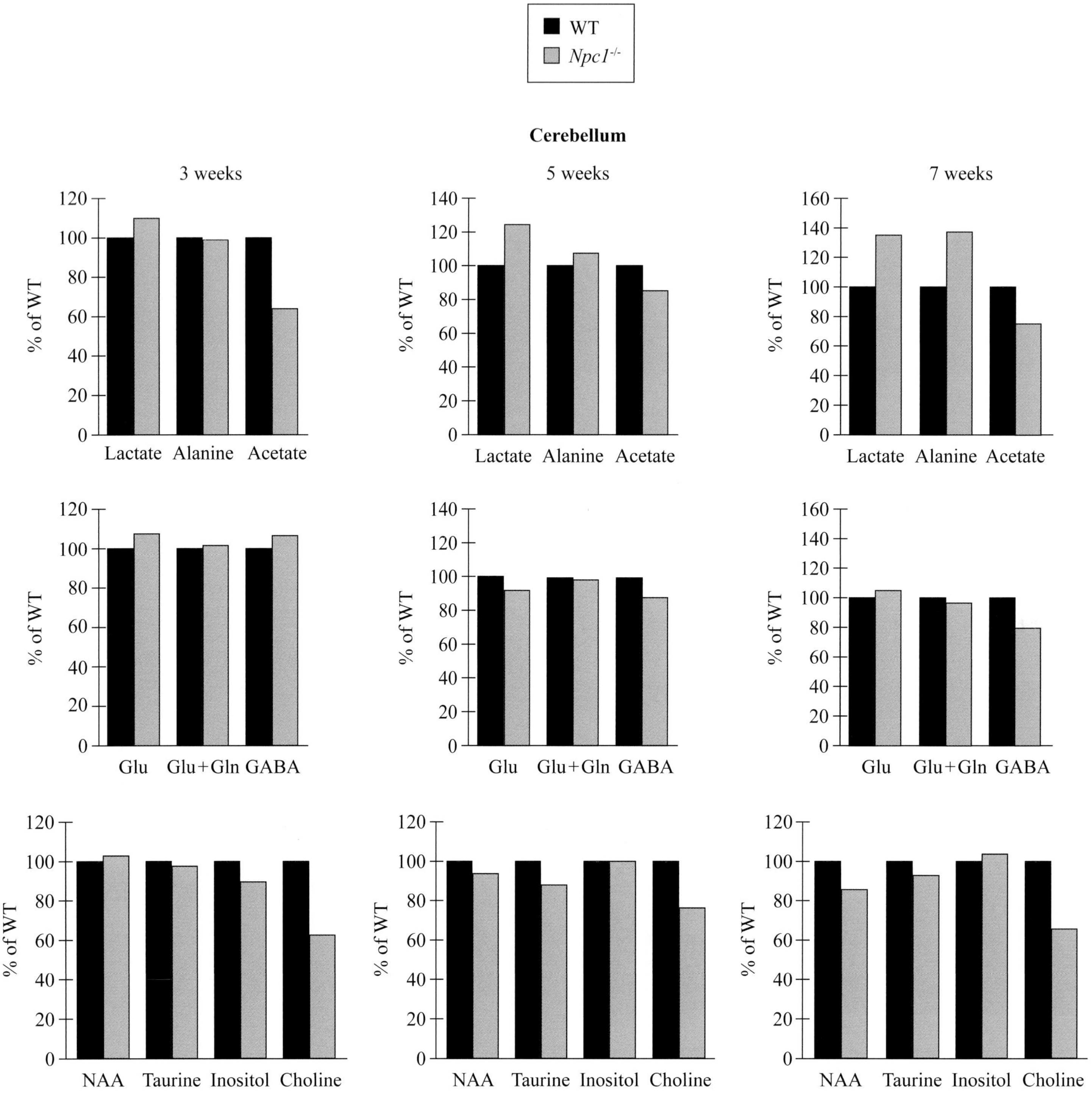

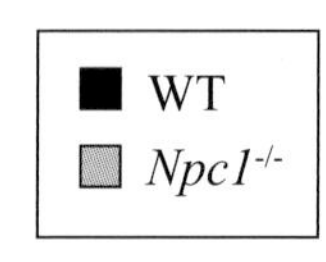

Figure 2 Altered Energy Metabolism in the cerebellum of *NPC1*$^{-/-}$ mice

This passage was adapted from "Pre-Symptomatic Activation of Antioxidant Responses and Alterations in Glucose and Pyruvate Metabolism in Niemann-Pick Type C1-Deficient Murine Brain." Kennedy BE, LeBlanc VG, Mailman TM, Fice D, Burton I, et al. *PLoS ONE.* 2013. 8(12) doi:10.1371/journal.pone.0082685 for use under the terms of the Creative Commons CC BY 4.0 license (https://creativecommons.org/licenses/by/4.0/legalcode).

Question 10

Sphingomyelin can be described as:

- A. a zwitterion.
- B. amphipathiC.
- C. a phosphoglyceride.
- D. a wax.

Question 11

How could the body obtain energy from catabolism of ceramide?

- A. Substrate level phosphorylation will yield large amounts of ATP.
- B. Ceramide can be modified for use in the proteins used for glycolysis.
- C. Ceramide is too large to be metabolized by human enzymes but may be a fuel source for symbiotic bacteria.
- D. The alkyl chains can be used to make acetyl CoA which can provide reducing agents for oxidative phosphorylation.

Question 12

According to Figure 2, *Npc1*$^{-/-}$ mice may exhibit:

- A. difficulty walking due to overuse of aerobic respiration.
- B. difficulty walking due to overuse of anaerobic respiration.
- C. difficulty breathing due to overuse of aerobic respiration.
- D. difficulty breathing due to overuse of anaerobic respiration.

Question 13

Which of the following may explain the initial elevation in glutamate levels in *Npc1*$^{-/-}$ mice?

- A. Damage to inhibitory neurons
- B. Synthesis of proteins
- C. The citric acid cycle is slowed
- D. There is no elevation in glutamate

Questions 14 through 16 do not refer to a passage and are independent of each other.

Question 14

Mitophagy is the selective destruction of damaged mitochondria. Which of the following may trigger mitophagy?

I. Loss of the proton gradient in the intermembrane space
II. Buildup of NAD^+ and FAD
III. Excess of cAMP

- A. II only.
- B. I and III only.
- C. II and III only.
- D. I, II and III.

Question 15

Which of the following explains why unsaturated fats are considered to be more healthy than saturated fats?

- A. Unsaturated fats store more calories per unit as compared to saturated fat.
- B. Unsaturated fats are broken down in the body and do not build up in fat stores.
- C. Unsaturated fats store fewer calories per unit as compared to saturated fat.
- D. Unsaturated fats can be converted to glucose to be easily used by muscle.

Question 16

α-glucosidase inhibitors are used as treatments for diabetes because they lower blood sugar levels. What hormone does this activity most closely mimic?

- A. Calcitonin
- B. PTH
- C. Glucagon
- D. Insulin

Passage 4 (Questions 17-20)

A 32-year-old patient presents to the Emergency Department with symptoms of memory loss and increased aggression that has developed over three to four weeks since an operation to remove gallstones. The physician learns that the hospital recently had three other similar cases and suspects that a prion disease is to blame, possibly being transmitted by contaminated operating room instruments.

Several diseases are caused by mutations that generate aberrant proteins with adverse cytotoxic consequences. Most disease-causing mutations that result in misfolded proteins are eliminated by cellular quality control (QC) pathways. In other instances, mutants fail to be efficiently recognized by QC and consequently accumulate excessively. Prion diseases, such as Creutzfeldt-Jakob disease (CJD), are one example of disorders in which the generation of aberrant misfolded proteins has dire consequences for the cell. These neurodegenerative diseases can be acquired by a transmissible route, sporadically, or through an inherited mutation. In each case, the central event involves aberrant metabolism of the cell surface prion protein (PrP).

In transmissible prion diseases, a misfolded conformer of PrP (termed PrP^{Sc}) directs the templated conversion of normal cellular PrP into additional PrP^{Sc}. How or why PrP^{Sc} accumulation leads to neurodegeneration remains largely unknown. Disease-causing PrP^{Sc} mutations use a QC pathway that culminates in lysosomal degradation, which has several potential implications for inherited prion disease pathogenesis. The most important implication is that reduced lysosomal function leads to accumulation of misfolded PrP^{Sc} species. This could represent a mechanism of neuronal cytotoxicity in prion disease, causing the confusion, memory loss, and mood changes seen early on in the disease progression.

Question 17

Increased breakdown of normal cellular PrP is LEAST likely to co-occur with:

- O **A.** oxidation of glucose to pyruvate.
- O **B.** synthesis of glucose from oxaloacetate.
- O **C.** oxidation of fatty acids to acetyl-CoA.
- O **D.** synthesis of ketones from acetyl-CoA.

Question 18

Which of the following reactions is most likely inhibited in CJD patients?

- O **A.** $\text{Peptide}_n + H_2O \xrightarrow{H+} \text{Peptide}_{n-1} + \text{Amino Acid}$
- O **B.** $\text{Peptide}_n + H_2O \xrightarrow{OH-} \text{Peptide}_{n-1} + \text{Amino Acid}$
- O **C.** $\text{Peptide}_n + H_2O \xrightarrow{\text{Carboxypepidase}} \text{Peptide}_{n-1} + \text{Amino Acid}$
- O **D.** $\text{Peptide}_n + H_2O \xrightarrow{H2O} \text{Peptide}_{n-1} + 3\ \text{Amino Acid}$

Question 19

Failure to cleave which of the following amino acid sequences likely leads to aggregation of PrP^{Sc}?

- O **A.** AAVVAVLIPM
- O **B.** RAKVADLIPE
- O **C.** TAYYAVFISM
- O **D.** CAVCASLIHM

Question 20

Which of the following figures best presents the cytosolic and lysosomal pH of normal versus Creutzfeldt-Jakob disease (CJD) patients?

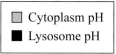

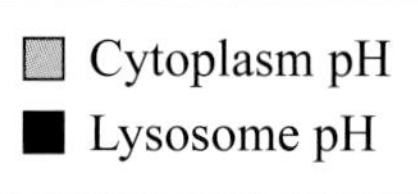

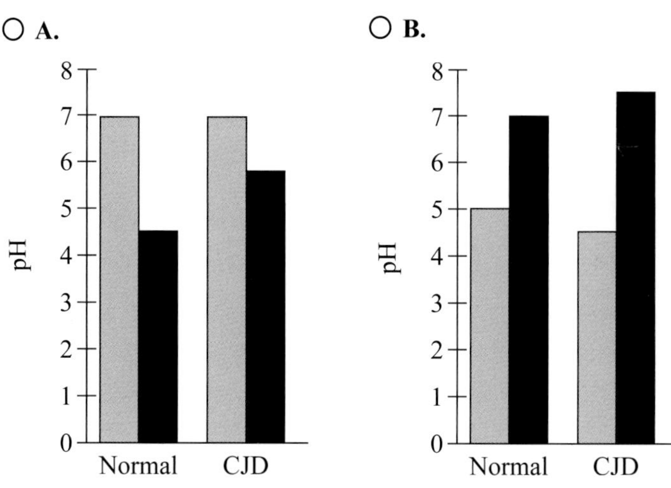

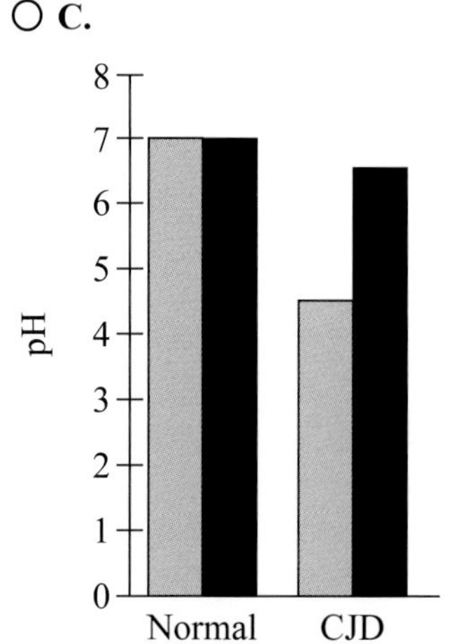

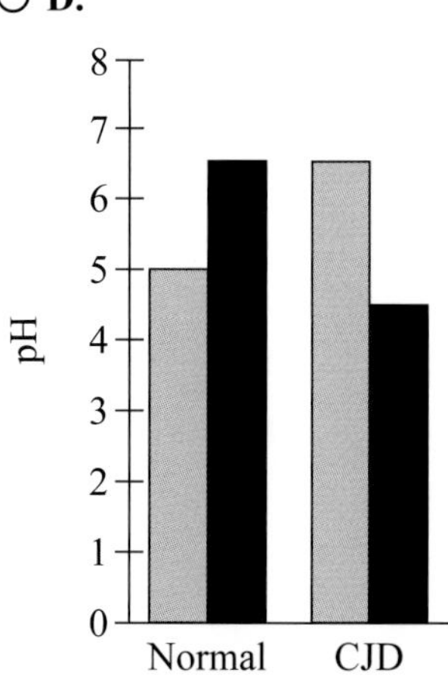

Passage 5 (Questions 21-25)

Hyperglycemia in type 2 diabetes is characterized by enhanced glucose production. In the presence of insulin resistance, enhanced glucose output by the liver contributes to hyperglycemia together with reduced glucose deposition in skeletal muscle, heart, and adipose tissue. Inhibition of hepatic glucose production contributes to glycemic control in the diabetic patients through traditional insulin sensitizers. Berberine (BBR, $C_{20}H_{18}NO_4$) is an isoquinoline alkaloid originally isolated from the Chinese herb Coptis chinensis. BBR is widely used to reduce blood glucose in type 2 diabetes in China but its mechanism of action is insulin-independent. In cultured hepatocytes, BBR inhibits oxygen consumption and reduces intracellular adenosine triphosphate (ATP) levels.

Insulin inhibits expression of phosphoenolpyruvate carboxykinase (PEPCK) and glucose-6-phosphatase (G6Pase), two rate-limiting genes in gluconeogenesis. PEPCK converts oxaloacetate to phosphoenol pyruvate and G6Pase converts glucose-6-phosphate to glucose to be released into the blood. These genes are induced by glucagon and reduced by insulin. Activation and inhibition of transcription factors including forkhead transcription factor O1 (FoxO1), hepatic nuclear factor 4 (HNF4), and peroxisome proliferator-activated receptor-c coactivator-1a (PGC-1a) are the underlying mechanism of the hormone actions. Figure 1 shows the effects of BBR.

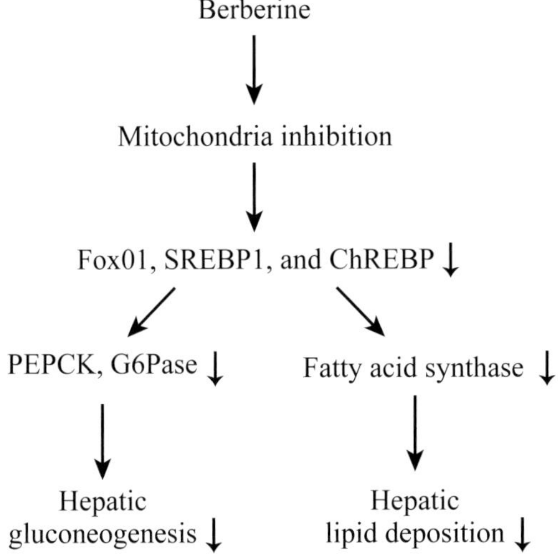

Figure 1 Diagram of Berberine action in a hepatic cells

Question 21

Using the information in the graph below, which physiological state best describes the rate of hepatic gluconeogenesis and the concentration of blood glucose after the administration of Berberine?

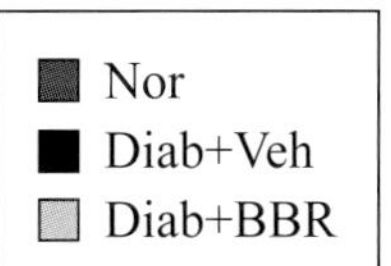

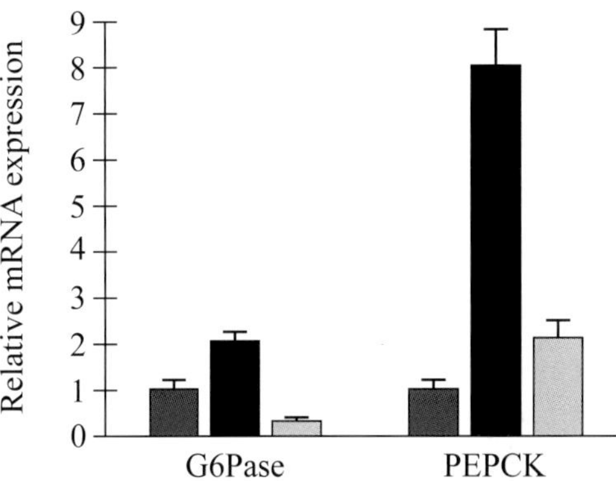

- ○ **A.** Gluconeogenesis decreases and blood glucose concentration increase
- ○ **B.** Gluconeogenesis increases and blood glucose concentration decreases
- ○ **C.** Gluconeogenesis and blood glucose concentration decrease
- ○ **D.** Gluconeogenesis and blood glucose concentration remain unchanged

Question 22

FoxO1, HNF4, and PGC-1a are modulated by intracellular ATP levels in the liver. Which condition will lead to the greatest activity of these transcription factors?

- ○ **A.** Fed state and high ATP
- ○ **B.** Fasting state and high ATP
- ○ **C.** Fed state and low ATP
- ○ **D.** Fasting state and low ATP

TEST 3B

Question 23

Where will glucose-6-phosphatase will act on its substrate in person with diabetes?

- O **A.** Inner mitochondrial matrix of a hepatic cell
- O **B.** Cytosol of a kidney cell
- O **C.** Cytosol of a muscle fiber
- O **D.** Inner mitochondrial matrix of a kidney cell

Question 24

The scientists chose to examine mRNA levels of PEPCK and G6Pase rather than the enzyme activity that is responsible for the reactions of gluconeogenesis. Why was enzyme activity not studied?

- O **A.** These gluconeogenic enzymes are primarily controlled by allosteric regulators.
- O **B.** Hormones always regulate enzymes through transcriptional control.
- O **C.** Enzyme activity cannot directly be measured.
- O **D.** Hormonal activation of transcription factors does not affect enzyme activity.

Question 25

Under which physiological condition would administration of Berberine and inhibition of FoxO1 be particularly harmful?

- O **A.** During periods of high blood glucose concentration
- O **B.** During periods of fatty acid metabolism
- O **C.** During periods of low brain glucose concentration
- O **D.** During periods of low muscle glucose concentration

Questions 26 through 29 do not refer to a passage and are independent of each other.

Question 26

Nitrogen elimination from the breakdown of glucokinase into its constituents:

- O **A.** occurs in the mitochondria and cytosol and is eliminated in the bile.
- O **B.** occurs in the nucleus and peroxisome and is eliminated in the bile.
- O **C.** occurs in the nucleus and peroxisome and is eliminated in the kidney.
- O **D.** occurs in the mitochondria and cytosol and is eliminated in the kidney.

Question 27

Researchers notice that a flavoprotein deficiency is the cause of an increased production of lactate in a cell culture plate. Which of the following experimental designs would effectively mimic the underlying issue?

- O **A.** Supplement the cells with FAD and then use a pyruvate dehydrogenase inhibitor.
- O **B.** Supplement the cells with FAD and then use a pyruvate carboxylase inhibitor.
- O **C.** Supplement the cells with riboflavin and then use a phosphofructokinase inhibitor.
- O **D.** Supplement the cells with riboflavin and then use a glucose-1-phosphate uridyltransferase inhibitor.

Question 28

Researchers analyzing the role of insulin on the conversion of glucose-1-phosphate to glycogen should carry out all of the following procedures except:

- O **A.** measuring the concentration of glycogen synthase in cells before and after insulin exposure.
- O **B.** measuring the ratio of glycogen synthase bound to insulin to free glycogen synthase in cells before and after insulin exposure.
- O **C.** measuring the concentration of glucose-6-phosphate in cells before and after insulin exposure.
- O **D.** measuring the ratio of phosphorylated to dephosphorylated glycogen synthase in cells before and after insulin exposure.

Question 29

The following graph describes the relative levels of:

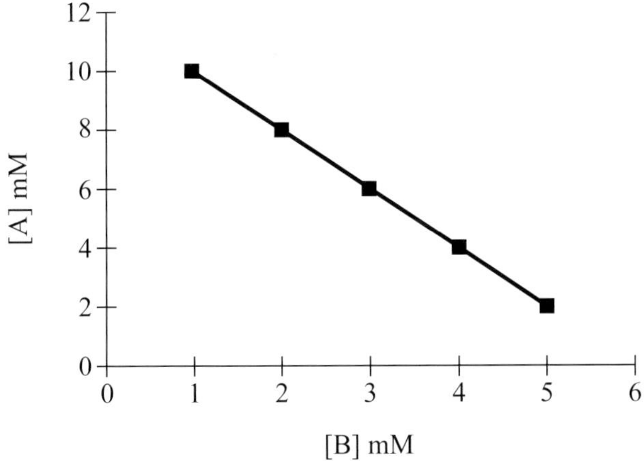

- O **A.** NADPH and NADH.
- O **B.** $FADH_2$ and GTP.
- O **C.** pyruvate and glucose.
- O **D.** 5-ribulose and NADPH.

Passage 6 (Questions 30-33)

Celiac disease (CD) is an inflammatory bowel disease of the small intestine that develops upon exposure to the polypeptide gluten in genetically susceptible individuals (HLA-DQ2 or -DQ8 carriers). Isotretinoin (also known as 13-*cis*-retinoic acid) is a synthetic form of vitamin A, which is primarily used to treat severe acne that fails to respond to other treatments such as oral antibiotics. Isotretinoin regulates cell proliferation and differentiation by activating nuclear retinoic acid receptors.

There is controversy in the literature as to whether isotretinoin exposure could be linked to inflammatory intestinal diseases. While one case-control study has found an association between isotretinoin exposure and development of inflammatory bowel disease, the majority of reports fail to demonstrate a link between the two.

Isotretinoin exposure was compared across overt CD patients and their age- and gender-matched control from the same pool. To evaluate the risk of latent CD with isotretinoin exposure, patients were overlapped with a community-based list of patients with serum samples that were tested for CD through blood-work serology, excluding those with overt CD (2006–2011). Isotretinoin exposure was defined as the use of isotretinoin prior to CD diagnosis or serology. The results are shown in Table 1.

Table 1 Effect of isotretinoin exposure on celiac disease

Variable		Exposed	Unexposed	p-value
Age		31.0±8.7	29.0±8.9	<0.001
Female		60.9%	70.8%	<0.001
Race:	Non-white	6.3%	8.4%	0.311
	White	89.3%	88.3%	
	Unknown	4.3%	3.3%	
Indication:				<0.001
	Non-acne	3.4%	8.2%	
	Acne	96.6%	91.8%	
Positive CD serology		1.8%	1.4%	0.474

Question 30

Which of the following is a therapeutic option for a person with celiac disease?

- O **A.** Avoidance of all glucose-containing foods
- O **B.** Destruction of white blood cells
- O **C.** Administration of a protease with any gluten containing meal
- O **D.** Supplementation with vitamins and minerals.

Question 31

Where is isotretinoin likely catabolized?

- A. In the cytosol
- B. In the mitochondria
- C. In the smooth ER
- D. Outside the cell

Question 32

Which of the following conclusions can be drawn from the research presented in the passage?

- A. The authors controlled for temporality and there was no relationship between isotretinoin and celiac disease.
- B. The authors controlled for temporality and there was a relationship between isotretinoin and celiac disease.
- C. The authors did not control for temporality and there was no relationship between isotretinoin and celiac disease.
- D. The authors did not control for temporality and there was a relationship between isotretinoin and celiac disease.

Question 33

Which of the following is NOT true of isotretinoin?

- A. It behaves like a steroid hormone.
- B. It is absorbed in the GI tract and transported in a lipoprotein.
- C. Its metabolism may lead to production of ketone bodies
- D. It must first be metabolized by lipase.

TEST 3B

Passage 7 (Questions 34-38)

Oxidative stress and mitochondrial function are key elements of many pathological conditions including high fat diet induced insulin resistance, neurodegenerative disease, disuse atrophy, and sarcopenia. The role of reactive oxygen species (ROS) in cellular function is most commonly associated with damage to DNA, proteins, and lipids. ROS are also involved in the regulation of several cellular processes including mitochondrial biogenesis. Interaction between mitochondrial function and oxidative stress appears to play an important role in controlling cell health and disease. The control of *in vivo* mitochondrial function and cell energetics by oxidative stress remains unclear.

Researchers treated wild type mice for 2 weeks with paraquat (PQ) to test the effect of oxidative stress on *in vivo* mitochondrial function in skeletal muscle. Mice were injected either once (PQ1) or twice (PQ2) a week for two weeks with 10 mg PQ/kg body weight, while controls (C) received volume-matched doses of saline. The results are shown in Figure 1.

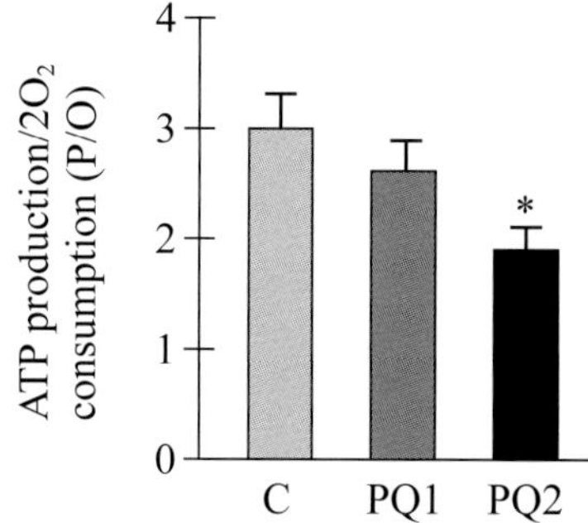

Figure 1 P/O following treatment. Note: * indicates significance.

Resting *in vivo* mitochondrial oxygen consumption in the hindlimb skeletal muscle increased significantly with PQ treatment and the resting rate of mitochondrial ATP production was unchanged. In addition, resting *in vivo* myoglobin saturation was negatively correlated with oxygen consumption due to the increased oxygen demand of the muscle.

Researchers determined *in vivo* ATP_{max} by measuring the rate of recovery of phosphocreatine (PCr) from ischemia, deprivation of oxygen to the tissue, in the mouse hindlimb (Figure 2).

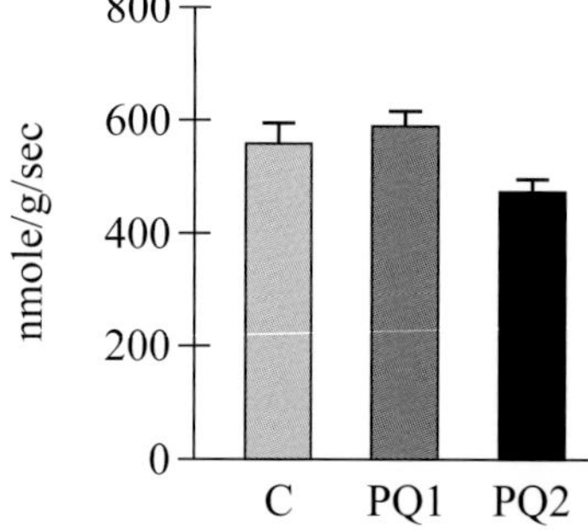

Figure 2 Maximum ATP production following treatment.

This passage was adapted from "Reduced Coupling of Oxidative Phosphorylation *In Vivo* Precedes Electron Transport Chain Defects Due to Mild Oxidative Stress in Mice." Siegel M, Kruse S, Knowels A, Salmon A, Beyer R, et al. *PLoS ONE.* 2011. 6(11) doi: 10.1371/journal.pone.0026963 for use under the terms of the Creative Commons CC BY 3.0 license (http://creativecommons.org/licenses/by/3.0/legalcode).

Question 34

The hydrolysis of the phosphoester bond in PCr has a significantly negative ΔG and can couple to the production of other high energy molecules. Why is the recovery rate of PCr used as an indicator of ATP_{max} in the experiment?

- O **A.** During ischemia, PCr donates P_i for the ATP synthase to use as a substrate.
- O **B.** After ischemia, oxidative phosphorylation produces ATP and PCr recovers.
- O **C.** All substrate-level phosphorylation uses PCr due to its significantly negative ΔG.
- O **D.** PCr serves as a cellular marker for a properly functioning electron transport chain.

Question 35

Protons will be pumped into which region of the cell prior to passing through the ATP synthase after recovery of PCr concentration?

- O **A.** Mitochondrial matrix
- O **B.** Cytosol
- O **C.** Mitochondrial intermembrane space
- O **D.** Extracellular space

Question 36

Which finding would provide further evidence that oxidative stress causes a reduction in P/O while maintaining ATP_{max}?

- O **A.** Cells treated with PQ show an abnormally high turnover rate of NADH to NAD^+.
- O **B.** Oxidative stress results in an increase in the transcription of ATP synthase mRNA.
- O **C.** Cells treated with PQ show a conversion of pyruvate to lactic acid.
- O **D.** Oxidative stress results in an increased expression of glucose transporters.

Question 37

Scientists hypothesized that oxidative stress causes some protons to become uncoupled from the electron transport chain. Does the evidence in the passage support this conclusion?

- O **A.** Yes, maintained ATP_{max} with increased oxygen consumption is evidence.
- O **B.** Yes, the decline in $^{P}/_{O}$ is characteristic of dissipation of the proton gradient.
- O **C.** No, maintained ATP_{max} cannot be achieved with a disrupted proton gradient.
- O **D.** No, the decline in $^{P}/_{O}$ suggests that oxidative stress damages the electron transport chain.

Question 38

If twice the amount of soluble electron carriers are present but ATP production remains the same, how does the P/O ratio change?

- O **A.** $(2)^{P}/_{O}$
- O **B.** $^{P}/_{O}$
- O **C.** $(\frac{1}{2})^{P}/_{O}$
- O **D.** $(\frac{1}{4})^{P}/_{O}$

TEST 3B

Passage 8 (Questions 39-42)

Mutations in the KRAS oncogene are known to modulate a number of major metabolic pathways, including glycolysis, tricarboxylic acid (TCA) cycle, pentose phosphate pathway (PPP), and glucose transport, as shown in Figure 1. The ubiquitin proteasome system processes the majority of cellular proteins, including proteins involved in growth, cell cycle regulation and apoptosis, and integrates with other major metabolic pathways to provide substrates for anabolism. Cancer cells have an elevated need for protein quality control and may have a greater reliance on proteasome function for survival compared to other cell types.

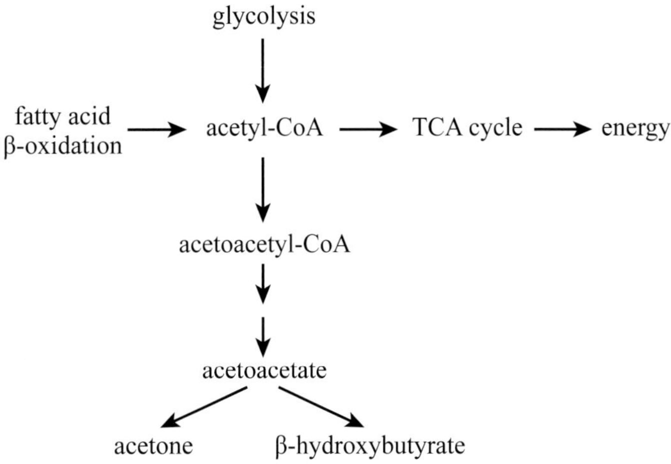

Figure 1 Common pathways altered in KRAS G12D mutant tumors

Previous research has shown that KRAS G13D mutant tumors are more reliant on proper proteasome functioning than KRAS wild type (WT) tumors. To further understand the differences between KRAS WT and KRAS mutant tumors and their response to ixazomib, a proteasome inhibitor, scientists injected 1×10^6 cancer cells into mice and treated the mice with a control compound or ixazomib. They measured the volume of the tumor over 20 days. The results are shown in Figure 2.

In a second experiment, mass spectrometry was used to analyze the metabolic effects of ixazomib on KRAS WT and mutant tumors. Compared to KRAS WT tumors, KRAS G13D mutant tumors showed decreased levels of glycogen intermediates, such as maltose and glucose, higher levels of free fatty acids, and an acute drop in levels of many individual amino acids following ixazomib treatment.

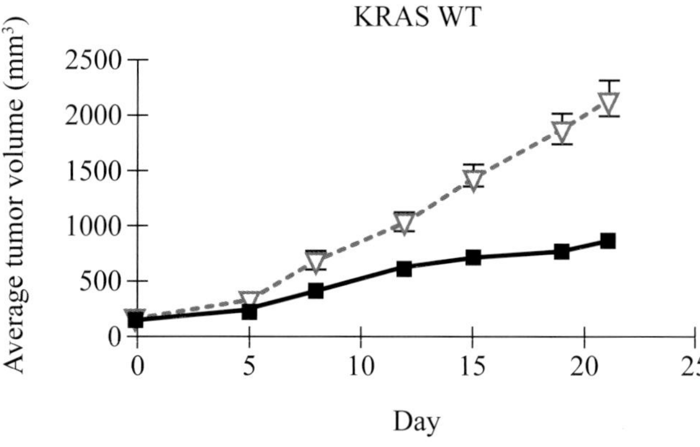

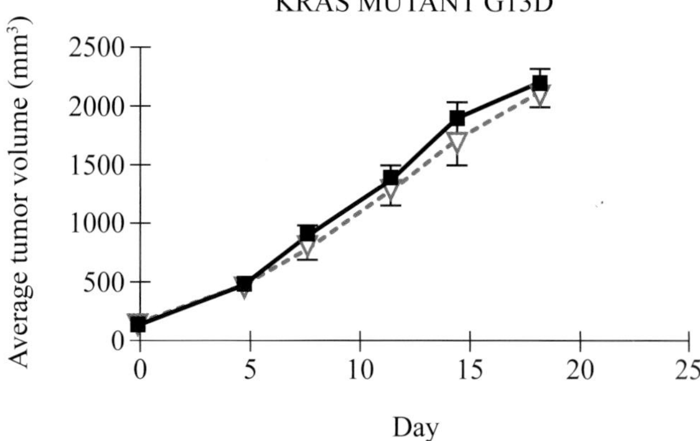

Figure 2 Effect of ixazomib on tumor volume in KRAS WT and G13D mutant tumors

Question 39

KRAS G13D mutant tumors display increased activity of the pentose phosphate pathway. What reasoning best explains this finding?

- O **A.** Increased NADH formation fuels oxidative phosphorylation to generate ATP
- O **B.** Increased NAD^+ formation allows glycolysis to continue in the cytosol
- O **C.** Increased NADPH formation provided reducing equivalents to anabolic reactions
- O **D.** Increased $NADP^+$ formation aids in β-oxidation

TEST 3B

Next ▶

Question 40

Which of the following findings would best support the data in Figure 2?

I. Compared to KRAS wild type cancer cells treated with ixazomib, KRAS G13D mutant cancers treated with ixazomib show increased uptake of radiolabeled CTP

II. Compared to KRAS wild type cancer cells treated with ixazomib, KRAS G13D mutant cancers treated with ixazomib show increased uptake of ^{13}C-labeled cholesterol

III. Compared to untreated KRAS wild type cancer cells, untreated KRAS G13D show decreased concentrations of NADPH

- **A.** I only
- **B.** I and II
- **C.** II and III
- **D.** I, II, and III

Question 41

The metabolic effects of ixazomib treatment most closely resemble the physiologic effects of which of the following hormones?

- **A.** Glucagon
- **B.** Insulin
- **C.** PTH
- **D.** LH

Question 42

The G13D mutation in KRAS makes the enzyme constitutively active, regardless of its phosphorylation status. This finding suggests that KRAS acts as a(n):

- **A.** oncogene.
- **B.** tumor suppressor.
- **C.** phosphatase.
- **D.** transcription factor.

Questions 43 through 46 do not refer to a passage and are independent of each other.

Question 43

Which of the following is NOT a function of riboflavin (vitamin B2)?

- **A.** As a flavoprotein in the electron transport chain.
- **B.** As a metalloprotein in the electron transport chain.
- **C.** As a reducing agent.
- **D.** As an oxidizing agent.

Question 44

Each successive electron receptor in the electron transport chain of the mitochondria has a greater:

- **A.** oxidative potential.
- **B.** Gibbs free energy.
- **C.** reduction potential.
- **D.** electronegativity.

Question 45

Excess acetyl-CoA is LEAST likely to:

- **A.** provide a reserve fuel source for erythrocytes.
- **B.** stimulate the activity of fatty acid synthase.
- **C.** increase the uptake of low density lipoprotein (LDL) particles.
- **D.** increase the intracellular ATP:ADP ratio.

Question 46

Which of the following is a potential use for an amino acid?

I. Gluconeogenesis

II. Ketogenesis

III. Hormone

- **A.** I only
- **B.** III only
- **C.** II and III
- **D.** I, II, and III

Passage 9 (Questions 47-50)

Gastric cancer is one of the most common malignancies in the world. In the economically developing countries, gastric cancer is the second cause of cancer-related death. In spite of the improvement in surgical and multimodal therapy, the overall 5-year survival rate is still low (15% to 35%) because of the high recurrence rates, invasion, and metastases.

L-Carnosine is a naturally occurring dipeptide that is synthesized by endogenous carnosine synthetase. It is widely distributed in mammalian brain, skeletal muscle, stomach, kidneys, heart, and skin. Carnosine may also have an anti-tumorigenic effects. For example, carnosine has been reported to possess the ability to inhibit malignant gliomas growth, and this effect may be mediated by an influence on glycolytic energy metabolism. Tumor cells exhibit the Warburg effect, where they undergo massive amount of glycolysis without the same levels of aerobic respiration.

In the case of human gastric cancer cells, little information is available to what extent glycolysis and mitochondrial oxidative phosphorylation contribute to the cellular energy production and rapid proliferation. Whether carnosine can inhibit the growth of human gastric cancer cells remains unknown. Researchers explored the effects of carnosine on the metabolism and growth of human gastric cancer cells and to further characterize the bioenergetic profile of cultured human gastric cancer cells and the roles of carnosine energy metabolism. To do this, they measured the extracellular acidification rate (ECAR) in gastric cancer cells following exposure to carnosine. The results are shown in Figures 1 and 2.

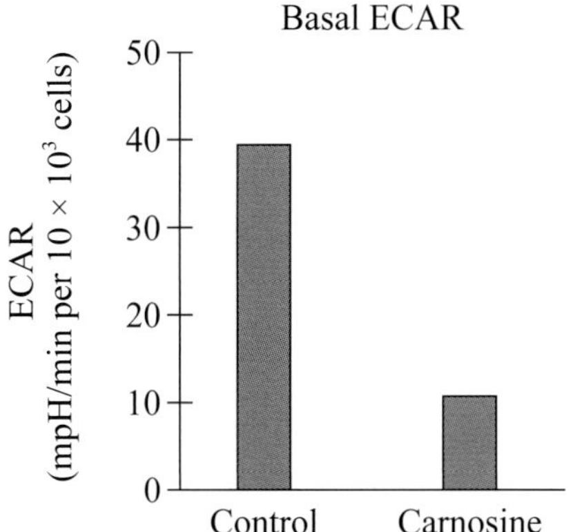

Figure 1 ECAR following carnosine treatment

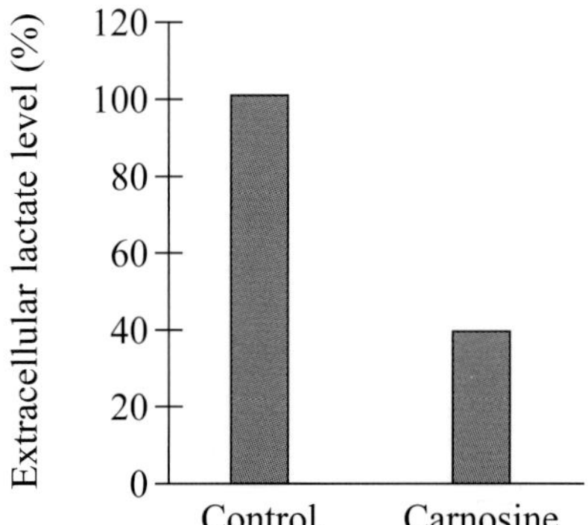

Figure 2 Extracellular lactate levels following carnosine exposure.

Question 47

Based on the results of Figures 1 and 2, which of the following is true?

- O **A.** The results support each other because lactic acid dissociates, resulting in lactate and a proton.
- O **B.** The results support each other because lactate acid dissociates, resulting in lactic acid and a proton.
- O **C.** The results contradict each other because lactic acid dissociates, resulting in lactate and a proton.
- O **D.** The results contradict each other because lactate dissociates, resulting in lactic acid and a proton.

Question 48

Which of the following would be most effective in causing increased aerobic respiration in gastric cancer cells?

- O **A.** Administration of reduced electron carriers to the cytoplasm
- O **B.** Administration of pyruvate to the cytoplasm
- O **C.** Administration of glucose to the cytoplasm
- O **D.** Administration of protons to the cytoplasm

Question 49

Where does the majority of ATP production occur in cells that match the definition of the Warburg effect?

- O **A.** Nucleus
- O **B.** Cytoplasm
- O **C.** Mitochondria
- O **D.** Vacuole

Question 50

Which of the following is most likely the effect of carnosine on gastric cancer cell proliferation?

- O **A.** Increased growth due to increased ability to undergo glycolysis.
- O **B.** Increased growth due to reduced ability to undergo glycolysis.
- O **C.** Reduced growth due to increased ability to undergo glycolysis.
- O **D.** Reduced growth due to reduced ability to undergo glycolysis.

Passage 10 (Questions 51-55)

Dengue virus is endemic in peninsular Malaysia. The clinical manifestations vary depending on the incubation period of the virus as well as the immunity of the patients. Glucose-6-phosphate dehydrogenase (G6PD) deficiency is also prevalent in Malaysia where the incidence is 3.2%. G6PD deficiency is associated with an inability to regenerate the antioxidant GSH. It has been noted that some G6PD-deficient individuals suffer from a more severe clinical presentation of dengue infection.

Researchers investigated the oxidative responses of DENV2-infected monocytes from G6PD-deficient individuals.

First they identified participants with true G6PD deficiency. The results are shown in Figure 1.

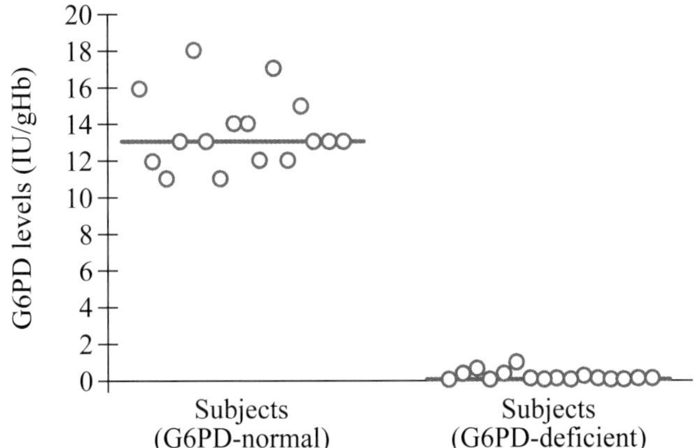

Figure 1 G6PD levels

Then, monocytes from G6PD-deficient individuals were infected with DENV2 and infection rate, levels of oxidative species, nitric oxide (NO), superoxide anions (O_2^{2-}), and oxidative stress were determined and compared with normal controls. The results are shown in Figures 2 and 3. An altered redox state of DENV-infected monocytes from G6PD-deficient individuals appears to augment viral replication in these cells. DENV-infected G6PD-deficient individuals may contain higher viral titers, which may be significant in enhanced virus transmission. Furthermore, granulocyte dysfunction and higher viral loads in G6PD-deificient individuals may result in a severe form of dengue infection.

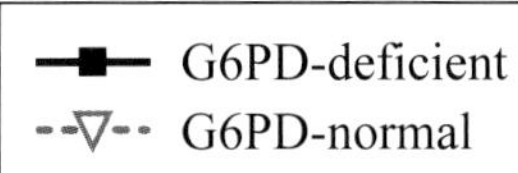

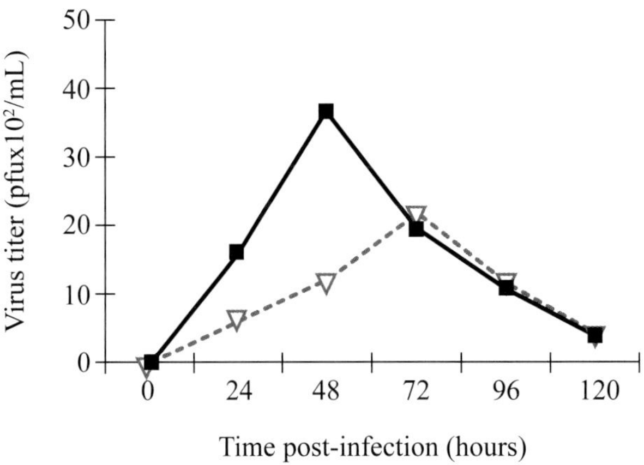

Figure 2 Dengue virus titer in G6PD deficient and control participants

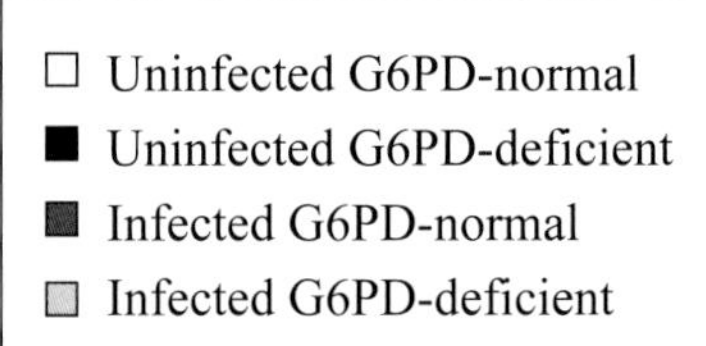

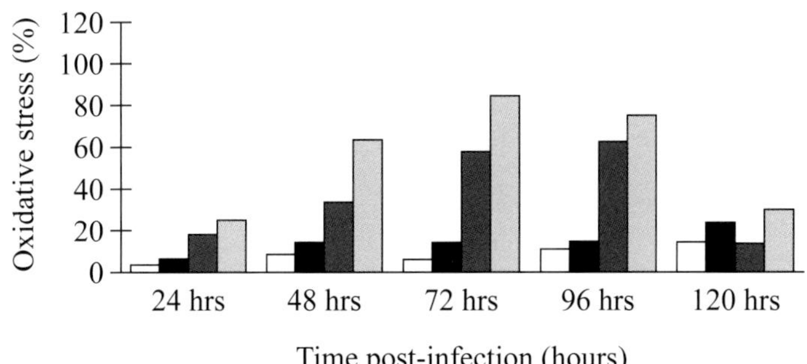

Figure 3 Oxidative stress in cells

TEST 3B

Question 51

What would be the expected enzymatic product from G6PD?

O **A.** O **B.**

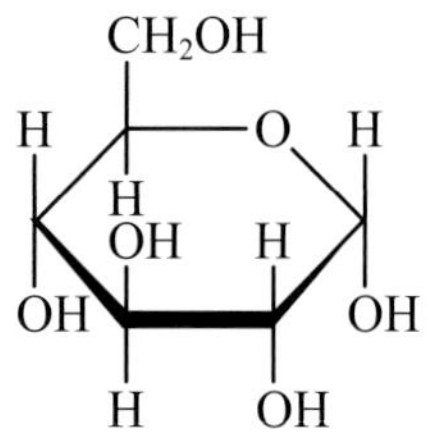

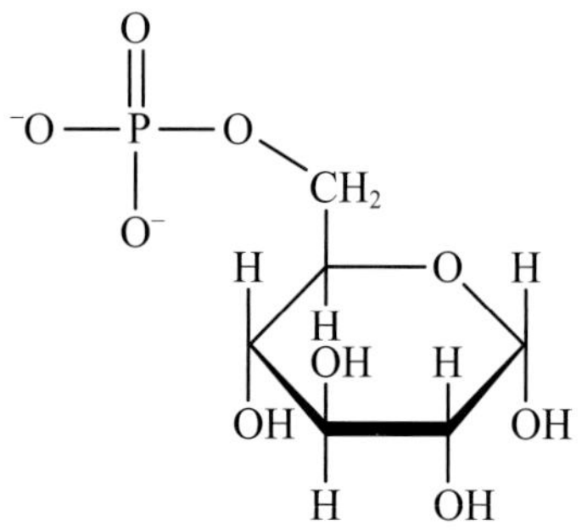

O **C.** 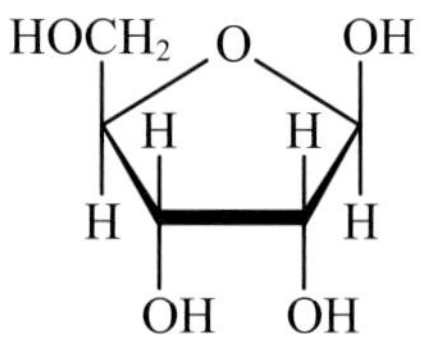 O **D.**

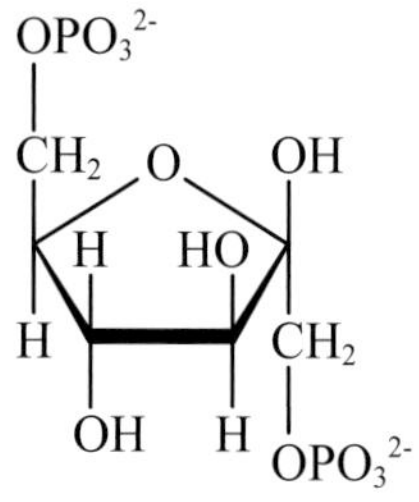

Question 52

What ethical considerations were important in this experimental design?

O **A.** Researchers used phagocytes because it would be unethical to infect patients with dengue virus.

O **B.** Researchers used granulocytes because it would be unethical to infect patients with dengue virus.

O **C.** Researchers used phagocytes because dengue virus is specific for those cells.

O **D.** Researchers used granulocytes because dengue virus is specific for those cells.

Question 53

Which of the following serves as an explanation for the findings in Figure 3?

O **A.** Patients with dengue virus are at risk for destruction of red blood cells and white blood cells.

O **B.** G6PD deficiency may serve as a protective mutation against dengue virus susceptibility.

O **C.** G6PD deficiency patients are unable to respond appropriately to oxidative stress due to lack of antioxidant GSH.

O **D.** G6PD deficiency and dengue virus both cause oxidative stress.

Question 54

Which of the following statements best explains why G6PD is not fatal?

O **A.** The pentose phosphate pathway is not essential to life.

O **B.** The enzyme is still partially functional.

O **C.** Some cells possess normal enzyme.

O **D.** The mutation is autosomal dominant.

Question 55

Which enzyme from glycolysis is most similar in mechanism to G6PD?

O **A.** Hexokinase

O **B.** Phosphoglucoisomerase

O **C.** Pyruvate dehydrogenase

O **D.** Glyceraldehyde-3-phosphate dehydrogenase

Next ▶

TEST 3B

Questions 56 through 59 do not refer to a passage and are independent of each other.

Question 56

What are the roles of the oxidative and non-oxidative phases of the pentose phosphate pathway?

- O **A.** Generation of reducing equivalents and production of 5-carbon sugars, respectively.
- O **B.** Generation of NAD^+ and energy production, respectively.
- O **C.** Antioxidant production and generation of NADPH, respectively.
- O **D.** Generation of nucleotides and glucose production, respectively.

Question 57

The conversion of one molecule of ATP to cAMP by adenylate cyclase requires cleavage of a phosphate group at the:

- O **A.** α-position
- O **B.** β-position
- O **C.** γ-position
- O **D.** δ-position

Question 58

The compound carboxin blocks the action of Complex II, also known as succinate dehydrogenase, in the electron transport chain. Somatic cells treated with carboxin will most immediately:

- O **A.** halt the citric acid cycle because of the inability to reduce the intermediate product succinate.
- O **B.** reverse the citric acid cycle with loss of function of its major regulatory enzyme.
- O **C.** shut down chemiosmotic coupling given its inability to reduce oxygen.
- O **D.** experience a reduction in the proton gradient formed in the mitochondrial intermembrane space.

Question 59

Which of the following pathways is associated with a positive ΔG value?

- O **A.** Gluconeogenesis in the absence of ATP
- O **B.** Beta-oxidation in the absence of cellular glucose and ATP
- O **C.** Oxidation of pyruvate in the absence of acetyl CoA
- O **D.** The pentose phosphate pathway in the absence of cellular ribose

---

STOP. If you finish before time is called, check your work. You may go back to any question in this test.

ANSWERS & EXPLANATIONS for Test 3B can be found on p. 256.

TEST 3B

Metabolisn

TEST 3C

Time: 50 minutes
Questions 1–31

DIRECTIONS: Most questions in the Biological and Biochemical Foundations of Living Systems test section are grouped with a descriptive passage. Select the best answer to each question using background knowledge and the given passage. A portion of this test section is comprised of discrete questions, which are independent of any passage and one another. Select the best answer for each discrete question. Indicate your selection by blackening the corresponding oval on your answer document. If you are unsure of the answer, rule out incorrect choices and select from the remaining options. You may access a periodic table found on the last page of this book at any point during this test section.

Passage 1 (Questions 1-5)

Patients with metabolic syndrome, symptoms of which include abdominal obesity and dyslipidemia, have a five-fold increased risk of developing type 2 diabetes mellitus and show a decreased capacity for exercise. Atherosclerotic plaques formed by foam cell macrophages occlude blood vessels and are often the cause of exercise intolerance.

During foam cell formation, macrophages take up considerable amounts of lipids. Transcription factors of the peroxisome proliferator-activated receptor (PPAR) family are critical for adaptation to lipid overload by increasing mitochondrial and peroxisomal fatty acid oxidation (FAO). Additionally, AMP-activated protein kinase (AMPK) senses metabolic stresses via its activation by increased AMP/ATP and ADP/ATP ratios. Activated AMPK shuts off energy-consuming processes, while inducing protein, carbohydrate, and fat catabolism.

Scientists explored the transcriptome of human macrophages under conditions of single and combined activation of AMPK and PPARδ. They found enhanced activation of FAO-associated genes, including pyruvate dehydrogenase kinase 4 (PDK4), by combined AMPK/PPARδ agonism. The mRNA and protein expression levels of PDK4 under various combinations of AMPK and PPARδ agonism are shown in Figures 1 and 2, respectively. The scientists concluded that a combination of PDK4 and AMPK agonism may help reduce cardiovascular disease in patients with metabolic syndrome.

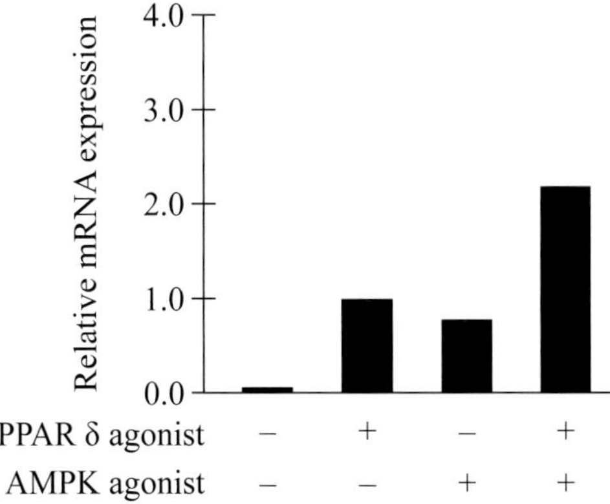

Figure 1 Pharmacological AMPK and PPARδ activation affects mRNA expression of PDK4

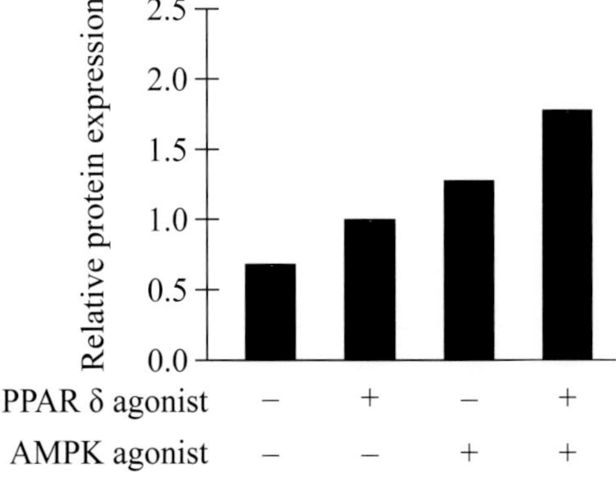

Figure 2 Pharmacological AMPK and PPARδ activation affects protein expression of PDK4

Question 1

In a separate experiment, scientists measured oxygen consumption in the presence of PDK4 and AMPK agonism. CO_2 production is the greatest in which of the following conditions?

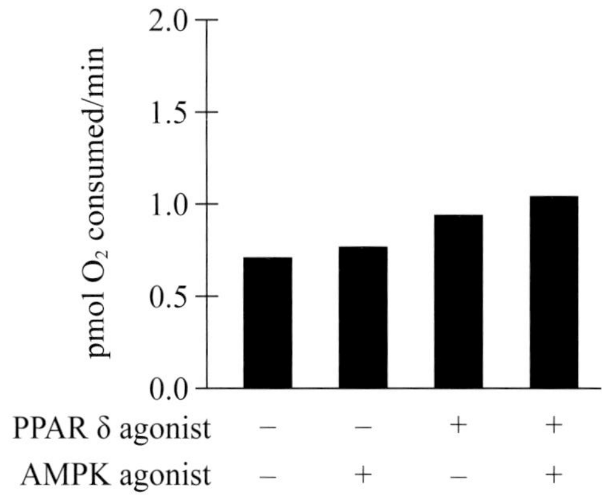

- A. PPARδ Agonism
- B. AMPK Agonism
- C. PPARδ Agonism and AMPK Agonism
- D. Cannot be determined

Question 2

Why might FAO not increase robustly even though dual PPARδ and AMPK agonism increased the protein concentration of corresponding enzymes involved in Fatty Acid Oxidation reactions?

- A. FAO is determined to a major extent by the ATP demand.
- B. The mRNA coding for PDK4 was degraded immediately after transcription.
- C. The AMPK agonist served as an antagonist of PDK4.
- D. FAO levels are independent of the concentrations of enzymes involved in FAO reactions.

Question 3

PDK4 is a mitochondrial kinase that phosphorylates and inactivates pyruvate dehydrogenase. What effect would PDK4 overexpression most likely have on the four-carbon reactant for gluconeogenesis?

- **A.** PDK4 overexpression would increase the concentration of the reactant for gluconeogenesis.
- **B.** PDK4 overexpression would decrease the concentration of the reactant for gluconeogenesis.
- **C.** PDK4 overexpression would have no effect on the concentration of the reactant for gluconeogenesis.
- **D.** The effect of PDK4 overexpression cannot be determined.

Question 4

Which of the following statements could explain the disparity between PPARδ and AMPK agonism in influencing PDK4 mRNA and protein levels?

- **A.** PPARδ agonism causes an increase in ribosome synthesis.
- **B.** AMPK agonism destabilizes RNA transcripts in the nucleus
- **C.** AMPK agonism causes rapid degradation of mRNA transcripts after translation.
- **D.** PPARδ and AMPK agonism causes proteolysis of ribosomes.

Question 5

mRNA levels in Figure 1 could have been normalized to which of the following gene transcripts?

I. GAPDH, an enzyme that catalyzes a reaction in glycolysis
II. 8S rRNA, a key RNA in the 30S ribosome
III. Actin, a structural protein in eukaryotic cells

- **A.** I only
- **B.** I and II
- **C.** I and III
- **D.** I, II, and III

Passage 2 (Questions 6-10)

Prior to activation, T lymphocytes (T cells) are quiescent and use only low rates of metabolism to fuel migration and homeostatic proliferation. Once activated, CD4 and CD8 T cells proliferate rapidly and undergo differentiation into diverse effector cell populations. These effector cells optimize the immune response for specific pathogenic challenges. Activated CD4 T cells can differentiate into T helper (T_h) subpopulations, while activated CD8 T cells can differentiate into cytotoxic T cells (T_c).

Activation and the transition from immature to effector lymphocyte greatly alters cellular metabolic demands, as cells require both ATP and biosynthetic components to fuel various processes. *In vitro* generated T_h CD4 T cells are highly glycolytic, performing high rates of glycolysis and minimal fatty acid oxidation. In contrast, inducible CD4 regulatory T cells exhibit low rates of glucose uptake, with high rates of fatty acid oxidation. Similarly, CD8 cytotoxic T cells have been shown to adopt a highly glycolytic metabolism, but transition to fatty acid oxidation as memory cells.

The net result of early lymphocyte metabolic reprogramming is a switch towards a highly glycolytic metabolism, wherein cells undertake high rates of glycolysis but perform comparatively low rates of oxidative phosphorylation (OXPHOS), and preferentially secreting glucose-liberated carbon as lactate. Recently, it was shown that in mice with a T cell specific deletion of the glucose transporter Glut1, CD4 T_h cells were significantly affected by the deletion, while CD8 cytotoxic T cells were not. Along this line, researchers compared the metabolic profiles of CD4 and CD8 lymphocytes following activation. The results are shown in Figures 1, 2, and 3 below.

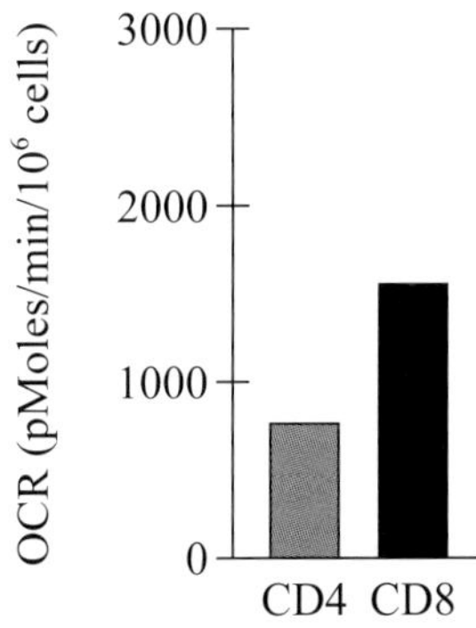

Figure 1 Oxygen consumption rate (OCR) of CD4 and CD8 cells

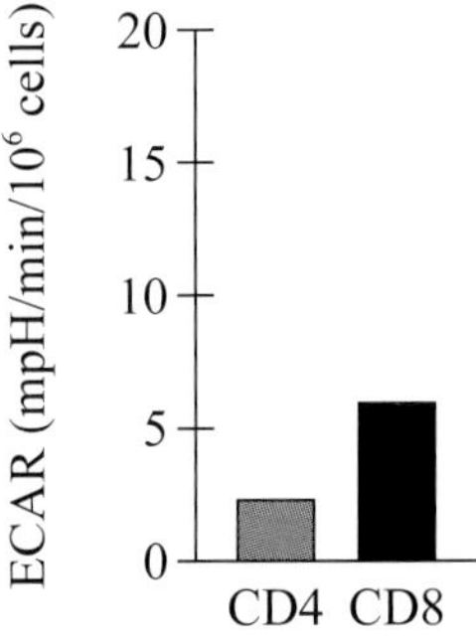

Figure 2 Extracellular acidification rate (ECAR) of CD4 and CD8 cells

TEST 3C

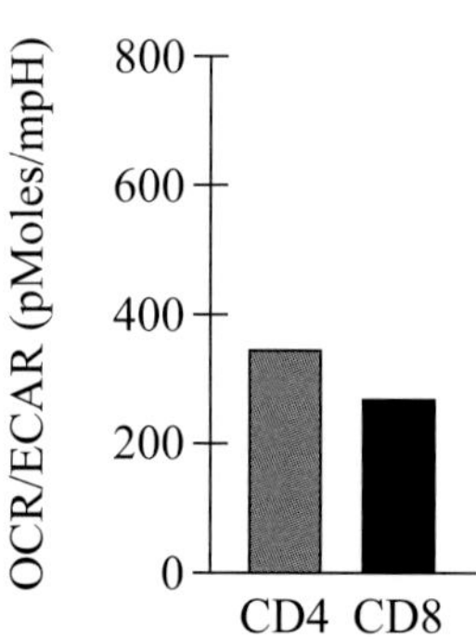

Figure 3 OCR/ECAR of CD4 and CD8 cells

Question 6

What does the difference in Glut1 deletion between CD4 T_h and CD8 cells indicate?

- O **A.** Different dependence on glycolysis, with CD4 T_h being more dependent
- O **B.** Different dependence on glycolysis, with CD8 T_c being more dependent
- O **C.** Higher overall glycolysis in CD4 T_h
- O **D.** Same dependence on glycolysis in both types of cells

Question 7

Which of the following is closest to what OCR/ECAR measures?

- O **A.** Ratio of gluconeogenesis to glycolysis
- O **B.** Ratio of glycogenesis to glycogenolysis
- O **C.** Ratio of aerobic to anaerobic metabolic processes
- O **D.** Ratio of anaerobic to aerobic metabolic processes

Question 8

Based on the passage OCR and ECAR results, which of the following is most likely true?

- O **A.** CD8 cells experience faster growth compared to CD4 cells following activation as indicated by increased OCR and ECAR.
- O **B.** CD8 cells experience faster growth compared to CD4 cells following activation as indicated by decreased OCR and ECAR.
- O **C.** CD8 cells experience slower growth compared to CD4 cells following activation as indicated by increased OCR and ECAR.
- O **D.** CD8 cells experience slower growth compared to CD4 cells following activation as indicated by decreased OCR and ECAR.

Question 9

Which of the following best summarizes the results of Figures 1 and 2?

- O **A.** CD8 cells have decreased overall metabolic rate and growth, and CD4 cells depend more on aerobic respiration relative to glycolysis.
- O **B.** CD8 cells have decreased overall metabolic rate and growth, and CD4 cells depend less on aerobic respiration relative to glycolysis.
- O **C.** CD8 cells have increased overall metabolic rate and growth, and CD4 cells depend more on aerobic respiration relative to glycolysis.
- O **D.** CD8 cells have increased overall metabolic rate and growth, and CD4 cells depend less on aerobic respiration relative to glycolysis.

Question 10

Which of the following compounds would most strongly facilitate the expansion of CD8 cells following activation?

- O **A.** Lipase
- O **B.** Trypsin
- O **C.** Glucagon
- O **D.** Cortisol

Passage 3 (Questions 11-14)

Breast cancer susceptibility gene 1 (BRCA1) is a major breast cancer suppressor gene and the most frequently mutated gene in hereditary breast cancer. The BRCA1 protein plays a critical role in the cellular response to stress and functions as a sensor of DNA damage. BRCA1 is implicated in DNA double-strand break repair, cell cycle control, and resistance to anticancer agents. The impact of BRCA1 on tumor cell metabolism, however, remains unclear.

BRCA1 has been shown to regulate *de novo* fatty acid synthesis, β-oxidation, and protect tumor cells against oxidative stress. Previous studies have also found that wild-type BRCA1 transfection in mutant cells induces numerous modifications of glucose metabolism, involving glycolysis, the TCA cycle, and oxidative phosphorylation.

Experiment 1

Scientists used control breast cancer cells (SUM1315) and genetically modified breast cancer cells that contained a homozygous deletion of the *BRCA1* locus (SUM1315ΔBRCA1) to determine the relative production and consumption of lactate and glucose, respectively, over 24 hours. The results are shown in Figure 1.

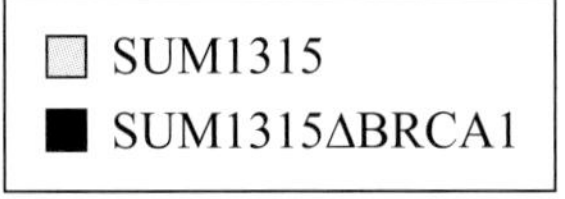

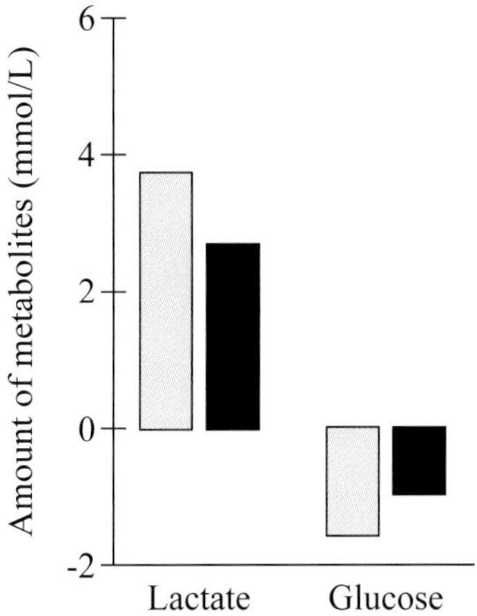

Figure 1 Role of BRCA1 in energetic metabolism

Experiment 2

Scientists also measured the proportion of saturated, monounsaturated, and polyunsaturated fatty acids in SUM1315 and SUM1315ΔBRCA1 cells using a fluorescent dye that associates with the carboxyl end of the various fatty acids. The results are presented in Figure 2.

BRCA1 deletion also induced a global increase in cellular ATP levels compared to control breast cancer cells. The scientists used PCR to measure the relative levels of mRNA transcripts of genes involved in the citric acid cycle and determined that succinate dehydrogenase was upregulated in SUM1315ΔBRCA1. They reasoned that a specific inhibitor of succinate dehydrogenase could hinder growth and proliferation of SUM1315ΔBRCA1 cells compared to BRCA1 wild type cancer cells.

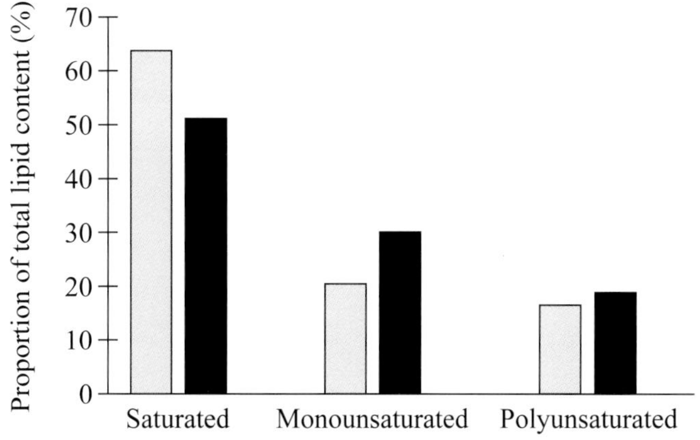

Figure 2 Relative proportion of saturated, monounsaturated, and polyunsaturated fatty acids in SUM1315 and SUM1315ΔBRCA1

Question 11

Based on the data presented in Figure 1, which of the following ratios best estimates the cytosolic NADH in SUM1315 versus SUM1315ΔBRCA1 cells?

- O **A.** 1:1
- O **B.** 2:5
- O **C.** 4:3
- O **D.** 10:1

Question 12

Based on data contained in the passage, which of the following statements best describes the relative pH of cells with an inactivating mutation of *BRCA1?*

- O **A.** The pH of breast cancer cells with a frameshift mutation in *BRCA1* is 3 units higher than in wild type cells.
- O **B.** The pH of breast cancer cells with a frameshift mutation in *BRCA1* is less than 1 unit higher than in wild type cells.
- O **C.** The pH of breast cancer cells with a nonsense mutation in *BRCA1* is 2 units lower than in wild type cells.
- O **D.** The pH of breast cancer cells with a synonymous mutation in *BRCA1* is 1 unit lower than in wild type cells.

Question 13

Scientists observed that *BRCA1* deletion induced a global increase in cellular ATP levels. Which of the following statements best explains this finding?

- O **A.** Increased glycogenolysis increased ATP production through glycolysis
- O **B.** Increased gluconeogenesis increased ATP production through breakdown of glucose
- O **C.** Increased β-oxidation increased ATP production through the TCA cycle
- O **D.** Increased fatty acid synthesis increased ATP production through oxidative phosphorylation

Question 14

An increase in glycolysis is most likely to be under the allosteric control of:

- O **A.** ADP.
- O **B.** acetyl-CoA.
- O **C.** malate.
- O **D.** NADH.

TEST 3C

Questions 15 through 18 do not refer to a passage and are independent of each other.

Question 15

The dissolution of the phosphoanhydride bond in the hydrolysis of ATP to ADP is expected to be:

- O **A.** coupled to an exergonic process for a combined process with a negative change in Gibbs free energy.
- O **B.** coupled to an endergonic process for a combined process with a negative change in Gibbs free energy.
- O **C.** coupled to an exergonic process for a combined process with a positive change in Gibbs free energy.
- O **D.** coupled to an endergonic process for a combined process with a positive change in Gibbs free energy.

Question 16

In some pre-cancerous cells, the presence of reactive oxygen species carrying unstable electron groups are expected to impair normal cell processes such as:

- O **A.** the conversion of dihydroxyacetone phosphate to glyceraldehyde-3-phosphate by triose phosphate isomerase.
- O **B.** the conversion of glucose-6-phosphate to fructose-6-phosphate by phosphoglucose isomerase.
- O **C.** the conversion of adenosine diphosphate to adenosine triphosphate by ATP synthase.
- O **D.** the conversion of oxaloacetate and acetyl CoA to citrate by citrate synthase.

Question 17

Which of the following statements is NOT true of the electron transport chain?

- O **A.** The proton gradient in the intermembrane space can meet energetic needs of the body besides ATP production.
- O **B.** ATP is generated through oxidative phosphorylation.
- O **C.** Cytochrome C gets oxidized in a final step of the process.
- O **D.** Electrons are distributed to complexes with increasingly higher oxidation potentials.

Question 18

Which of the following is a lipid-soluble electron carrier?

I. Cytochrome C
II. Ubiquinone
III. NADH

- O **A.** I only
- O **B.** II only
- O **C.** II and III only
- O **D.** I and II only

Passage 4 (Questions 19-22)

In adipocytes and hepatocytes, lipid droplets (LD) are structures specialized for lipid storage in support of energy production. Related structures called lipid bodies (LB) are found in leukocytes and are additionally specialized as reservoirs of bioactive lipid precursors. LB numbers are regulated in macrophages and other granulocytes in response to bacterial and parasitic infections. Recently, scientists have found a link between lipid bodies and susceptibility to life-threatening systemic bacterial infection.

Diabetic patients appear disproportionally susceptible to sepsis, a systemic manifestation of severe bacterial infection. Prior to cellular insulin resistance that occurs late in the disease course of type II diabetes, insulin elevation may cause LB expansion in leukocytes, leading to dysregulation of the immune response to infection. The only hormone previously shown to regulate LB numbers in an immune system cell is leptin. However, it is unknown whether LB structures are primarily reservoirs of absorbed dietary lipid or of de novo synthesized lipids induced by leptin, insulin, or other innate stimuli in granulocytes. Scientists were interested in characterizing LBs to determine whether inhibitors of fatty acid synthesis or fatty acid absorption could reduce susceptibility to sepsis in diabetic patients.

Scientists cultured mast cells under absent, medium, and high levels of insulin and observed enrichment of LBs, ER lipid accumulation, and ER stress in mast cells. After isolating the LBs by ultra-centrifugation, they used HPLC-mass spectrometry to characterize how the populations of lipids changed from low insulin to high insulin environments (Figure 1). Additionally, they found that high levels of LBs correlated with increased apoptosis of innate immune system cells.

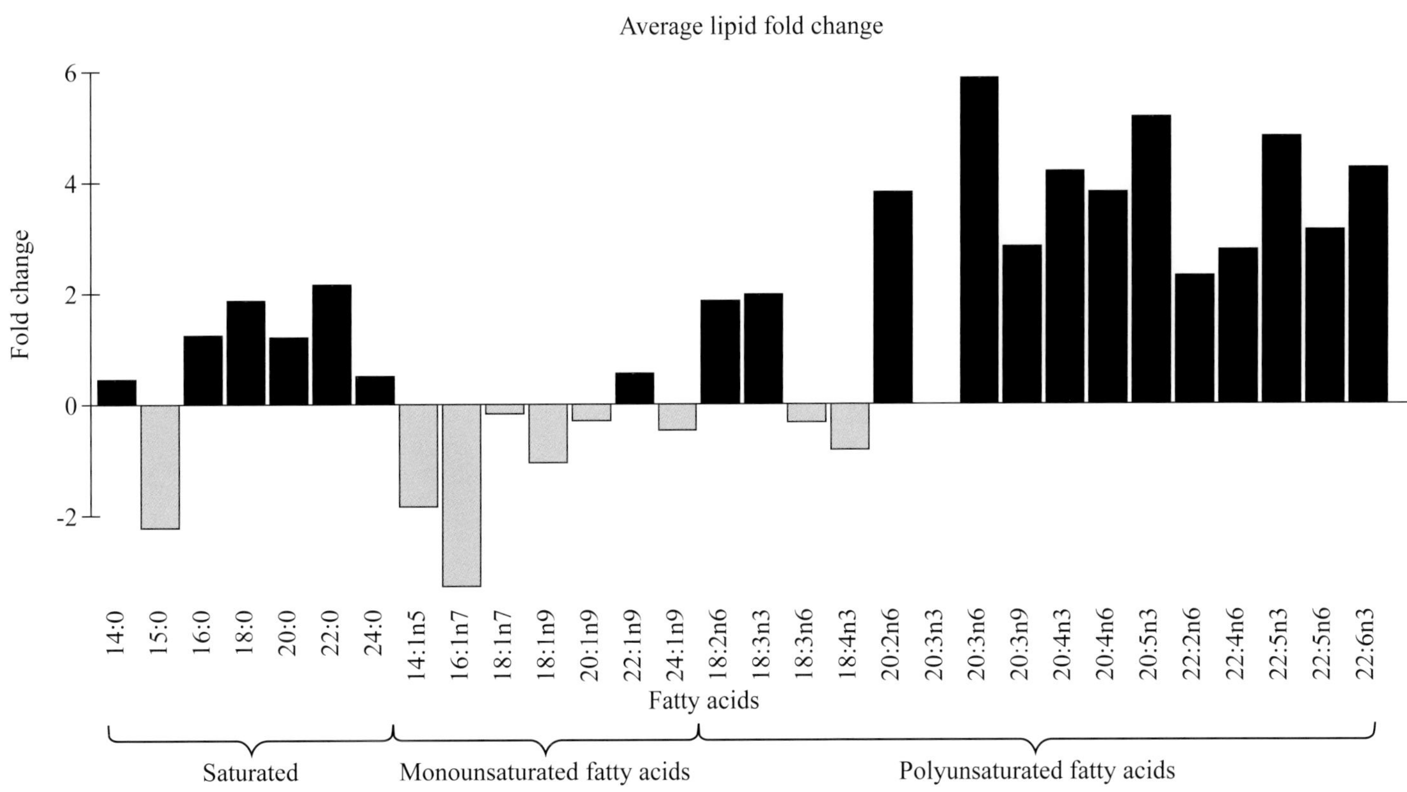

Figure 1 Changes in the whole cell lipidome of mast cells cultured under high insulin conditions relative to control.

Question 19

High circulating insulin levels in patients without Type II diabetes are likely to result in:

- O **A.** skeletal muscle cells that have reached their saturation point for glycogen.
- O **B.** increased secretion of glucagon from pancreatic alpha cells.
- O **C.** reduced bone mineralization.
- O **D.** an decreased concentration of *cis*-unsaturated fatty acids.

Question 20

Which assertion would best support a medical recommendation that encourages reducing the content of palmitate, a 16-carbon saturated fatty acid, in the diet?

- O **A.** Palmitate produces more energy than palmitoleic acid.
- O **B.** Palmitate contains a carbonyl functional group, whereas palmitoleic acid does not.
- O **C.** The increased number of carbons in palmitate over palmitoleic acid requires additional amylases to break down.
- O **D.** Palmitate is often stored in α-1,4 linkages in the cell as an energy reserve.

Question 21

According to information contained in the passage, an increased number of which of the following molecules would lead to the greatest increase in mast cell membrane fluidity?

- O **A.** HDL
- O **B.** IDL
- O **C.** LDL
- O **D.** VLDL

Question 22

Which of the following explanations best explains why scientists saw drastic changes in PUFA levels but only marginal changes in triacylglycerol levels?

- O **A.** Triacylglycerols are restricted to one polyunsaturated fat per molecule.
- O **B.** The identity of a triacylglycerol is determined by the molecule that links ester groups.
- O **C.** Dehydrogenase activity does not require presence of free fatty acids.
- O **D.** Increased chylomicron concentrations have been noted in the blood of type II diabetic patients.

Passage 5 (Questions 23-27)

Glycogen is an essential source of energy when fasting. Numerous enzymes are involved in glycogen anabolism and catabolism and mutations in each enzyme are known to cause disease. Glycogen catabolism is initiated by hormone binding to a membrane bound GPCR that utilizes adenylate cyclase and protein kinase A to effectively reverse the directionality of glycogen metabolism enzymes.

Pompe disease, also known as glycogen storage disease (GSD) type II, is caused by deficiency of lysosomal acid α-glucosidase (GAA). The resulting glycogen accumulation causes a spectrum of disease severity ranging from a rapidly progressive course that is typically fatal by 1 to 2 years of age to a slower progressive course that causes significant morbidity and early mortality in children and adults.

Knockout mice for S6K1 (S6K1$^{-/-}$) and S6K2 (S6K2$^{-/-}$) were crossed to Pompe mice to give the double knockouts (GAA$^{-/-}$ × S6K1$^{-/-}$) and (GAA$^{-/-}$ × S6K2$^{-/-}$). Researchers evaluated glycogen metabolism in heart, triceps, quadriceps, and liver from wild type and knockout mice strains. The results are shown in Figure 1. Next, the GAA$^{-/-}$ mice were treated with recombinant human GAA (rhGAA) which led to a dramatic reduction in the levels of glycogen, glycogen synthase, glycogenin, and glucose-6-phostphate. Analysis of phosphorylase activity confirmed a previous report that, although phosphorylase protein levels are identical in muscle lysates from wild type and GAA$^{-/-}$ mice, phosphorylase activity is suppressed in the GAA$^{-/-}$ mice in the absence of AMP. This reduction in phosphorylase activity likely exacerbates lysosomal glycogen accumulation and disease symptoms. If the dysregulation in glycogen metabolism observed in the mouse model of Pompe disease also occurs in Pompe patients, it may contribute to the observed broad spectrum of disease severity.

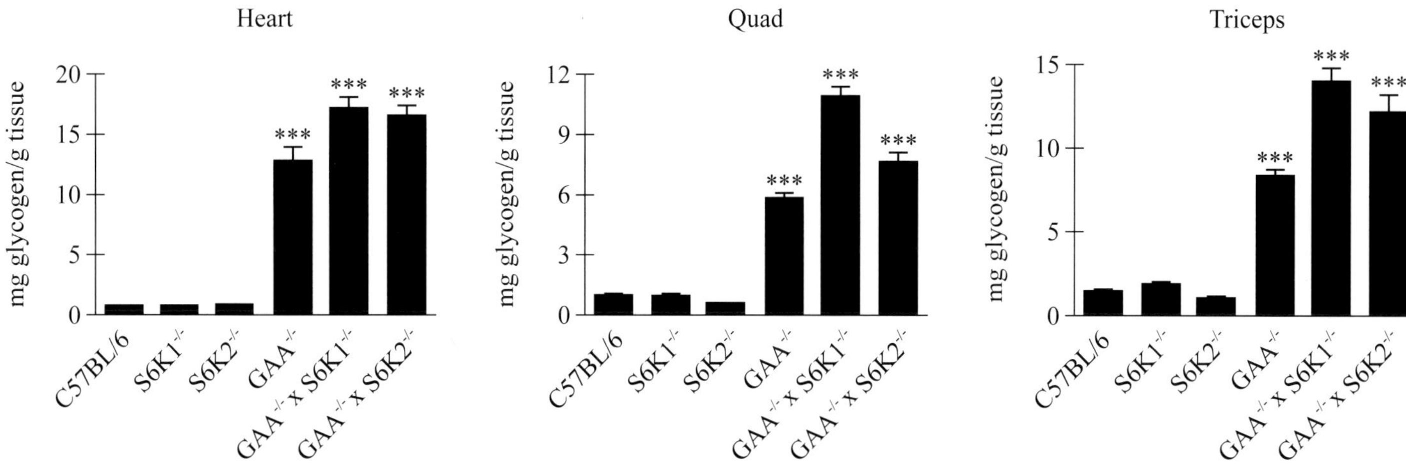

Figure 1 Glycogen levels in mice of different genotypes. ***P,0.001.

This passage was adapted from "Dysregulation of Multiple Facets of Glycogen Metabolism in a Murine Model of Pompe Disease" Taylor KM, Meyers E, Phipps M, Kishnani PS, Cheng SH, et al. *PLoS ONE.* 2013. 8(2) doi:10.1371/journal.pone.0056181

Question 23

Lysosomal acid α glucosidase is also known as:

- **A.** α-1,4-glucosidase.
- **B.** α-1,5-glucosidase.
- **C.** α-1,6-glucosidase.
- **D.** β-1,4-glucosidase.

Question 24

According to Figure 1, which genotype is the most likely to experience the greatest elevation in glucagon while fasting?

- **A.** C57BL/6
- **B.** $S6K2^{-/-}$
- **C.** $GAA^{-/-}$
- **D.** $GAA^{-/-} \times S6K1^{-/-}$

Question 25

In terms of biomolecular cause, which of the following diseases is most similar to Pompe disease?

- **A.** Sickle cell anemia, in which a mutation changes the structure of hemoglobin
- **B.** Cystic fibrosis, in which a mutation prevents proper trafficking of a membrane-bound ion-transport protein
- **C.** Phenylketonuria, in which a mutation prevents proper metabolism of phenylalanine
- **D.** Diabetes Mellitus, in which insensitivity to insulin results in elevated blood glucose

Question 26

Base of the findings in Figure 1, which of the following is likely to occur?

- **A.** $GAA^{-/-}$ mice may experience spontaneous hydrolysis of glycogen.
- **B.** $S6K2^{-/-}$ mice may experience spontaneous hydrolysis of glycogen.
- **C.** $GAA^{-/-}$ mice have a lesser activation energy for glycogen hydrolysis than $S6K2^{-/-}$ mice.
- **D.** $S6K2^{-/-}$ mice have a more negative δG for glycogen hydrolysis than $GAA^{-/-}$ mice.

Question 27

People with Pompe disease are reliant on which of the following processes for energy?

- **A.** Gluconeogenesis and glycogenolysis
- **B.** Gluconeogensis and ketogenesis
- **C.** Ketogenesis and the pentose phosphate pathway
- **D.** Glycogenoslysis and the pentose phosphate pathway.

Questions 28 through 31 do not refer to a passage and are independent of each other.

Question 28

Which of the following steps in glycogen catabolism is the most spontaneous?

- **A.** Glycogen → glucose
- **B.** Glucose → glucose-6-phostphate
- **C.** Dihydroxyacetone phosphate → glyceraldehyde-3-phosphate
- **D.** 3-phosphoglycerate → 2-phosphoglycerate

Question 29

Which of the following best describes the mechanism of action of compound A in cells?

[Compound A]	Transmembrane potential (ΔΨ)	[ATP]
0 nM	-40 mV	79 mM
10 nM	0 mM	14 mM

- **A.** Compound A creates an ion pore through the inner mitochondrial membrane.
- **B.** Compound A hydrolyzes ADP to AMP.
- **C.** Compound A inhibits the Na^+/K^+ pump on the plasma membrane.
- **D.** Compound A inhibits ATP synthase.

Question 30

Cyanide blocks cytochrome c oxidase, one of the final electron carriers in the electron transport chain. What is the likely result of cyanide poisoning in the cell?

- **A.** Pyruvate will build up in the cytosol due to an inability to carry out the remainder of glucose metabolism.
- **B.** There will be a lack of ADP as a result of poor recycling of ATP.
- **C.** Cells will produce an organic acid to recycle a key coenzyme.
- **D.** The increase in substrates for oxidative phosphorylation will compete for binding to the cytochrome.

Question 31

Which of the following is most likely during the time closely following a meal?

- **A.** Fatty acids are converted into triglycerides, and glucose is converted to glycogen.
- **B.** Triglycerides are converted into fatty acids, and glucose is converted to glycogen.
- **C.** Fatty acids are converted into triglycerides, and glycogen is converted into glucose.
- **D.** Triglycerides are converted into fatty acids, and glycogen is converted to glucose.

STOP. If you finish before time is called, check your work. You may go back to any question in this test.

ANSWERS & EXPLANATIONS for Test 3C can be found on p. 256.

Laboratory Techniques

TEST 4A

Time: 90 minutes
Questions 1–59

DIRECTIONS: Most questions in the Biological and Biochemical Foundations of Living Systems test section are grouped with a descriptive passage. Select the best answer to each question using background knowledge and the given passage. A portion of this test section is comprised of discrete questions, which are independent of any passage and one another. Select the best answer for each discrete question. Indicate your selection by blackening the corresponding oval on your answer document. If you are unsure of the answer, rule out incorrect choices and select from the remaining options. You may access a periodic table found on the last page of this book at any point during this test section.

Passage 1 (Questions 1-5)

Diabetes is one of the most important health issues facing the world in the twenty-first century. Alpha-glucosidase inhibitors have been used for about 20 years to lower blood glucose. These compounds show reasonably good efficacy comparable with other oral blood glucose-lowering drugs and, in some parts of the world, are the most commonly prescribed oral diabetes medication, especially in Asian countries. In recent years, investigations of herbal medicines have become increasingly important in the search for new, effective, and safe α-glucosidase inhibitors for diabetes treatment.

Phlomis tuberosa L. is an Asian folk medicine used as a general medicine for intoxication, tuberculosis, pulmonary diseases, cardiovascular diseases, and rheumatoid arthritis. The ethyl acetate fraction of *P. tuberosa* extracts shows significant inhibitory activity against α-glucosidase (IC50 = 100 μg/mL). Repeated column chromatography over silica gel is frequently used for purification of bioactive compounds from medicinal herbs. However, this separation method can be a tedious process requiring long time frames and large volumes of organic solvents. Irreversible adsorption of samples onto the solid phase, which sometimes results in reductions or disappearance of active compounds, may also occur. Better purification strategies to assure the efficacy and reliability of α-glucosidase inhibitor identification from *P. tuberosa* are necessary.

High pressure liquid chromatography (HPLC) and TLC have led to the isolation of many new compounds, including two new diterpenoids (compounds 1 and 2 of Figure 1) from *P. tuberosa*. The α-glucosidase inhibitory activities of the isolated compounds were subsequently determined (Table 1).

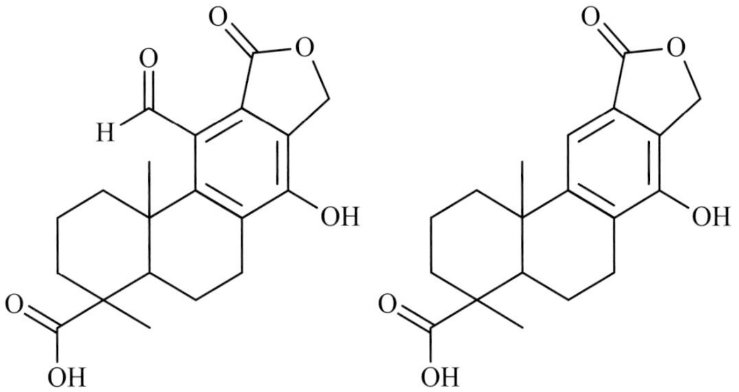

Figure 1 Compounds 1 and 2 isolated from *P. tuberosa*

Table 1 IC_{50} (concentration to inhibit 50% of α-glucosidase activity) of various compounds isolated from *P. tuberosa*

Compound	IC_{50} (mM)
1	0.379 ± 0.016
2	0.624 ± 0.026
3	0.721 ± 0.037
4	0.067 ± 0.003
5	0.482 ± 0.019

Question 1

Which of the following statements is true regarding compounds 1 and 2 in HPLC?

- O **A.** Compound 1 is more polar, so it will elute faster during HPLC.
- O **B.** Compound 1 is more polar, so it will elute slower during HPLC.
- O **C.** Compound 2 is more polar, so it will elute faster during HPLC.
- O **D.** Compound 2 is more polar, so it will elute slower during HPLC.

Question 2

Which of the following would be observed in an IR spectroscopy of Compound 1?

I. 1700 band
II. 2500-3500 stretch
III. 3300 band

- O **A.** I only
- O **B.** II only
- O **C.** I and II
- O **D.** II and III

Question 3

Which of the following is true regarding UV spectroscopy for the compounds isolated from *P. tuberosa*?

- O **A.** Neither compound 1 nor 2 will show absorbance.
- O **B.** Compound 1, but not compound 2, will show absorbance.
- O **C.** Compound 2, but not compound 1, will show absorbance.
- O **D.** Both compounds 1 and 2 will show absorbance.

Question 4

Why is ethyl acetate effective at separating compounds 1 and 2 from other compounds?

- O **A.** Compounds 1 and 2 are both polar and will be soluble in ethyl acetate.
- O **B.** Compounds 1 and 2 are both polar and will be insoluble in ethyl acetate.
- O **C.** Compounds 1 and 2 are both nonpolar and will be soluble in ethyl acetate.
- O **D.** Compounds 1 and 2 are both nonpolar and will be insoluble in ethyl acetate.

Question 5

Which of the following separation techniques would most effectively distinguish between compounds 1, 2, and other aromatic compounds?

- O **A.** Western blot
- O **B.** Southern blot
- O **C.** Northern blot
- O **D.** None of the above

Passage 2 (Questions 6-9)

Tuberculosis (TB) is a sub-acute or chronic infectious disease caused by *Mycobacterium tuberculosis* (Mtb), a bacillus that infects approximately one-third of the world's population. Traditional diagnostic approaches require the patient to make repeated trips to the clinic, which often is cost-prohibitive for the patient, resulting in the failed opportunity for early diagnosis and treatment. Among the bacterial products, lipoarabinomannan (LAM) has received intense attention in developing non-sputum based diagnostic platforms. LAM is one of the three major groups of interrelated lipoglycans within the mycobacterial cell wall which are non-covalently linked to the plasma membrane and/or outer membrane via a phosphatidylinositol anchor and extend to the surface.

LAM with terminal mannose caps on the D-arabinan end (ManLAM) is characteristic of pathogenic, slow-growing mycobacterial species such as *M. tuberculosis, M. leprae*, and *M.bovis*. The average molecular weight of LAM has been found to be approximately 17.3 kDa, with a broad distribution on either side that reflects considerable molecular heterogeneity with regard to size, pattern of branching of the arabinan side-chains, capping, acylation, and branching of the mannan backbone.

In order to determine whether LAM could be used as a diagnostic marker for TB in human clinical samples, gas chromatography/mass spectrometry (GC/MS) analyses were conducted using urine of TB-infected individuals and controls. The scientists assumed that D-arabinose is only present in the mycobacteria and is absent among eukaryotes. Using a hydrophobic interaction column, arabinose was isolated from patients' urine and subjected to mass spectrometry to detect D-arabinose. The results are shown in Figure 1.

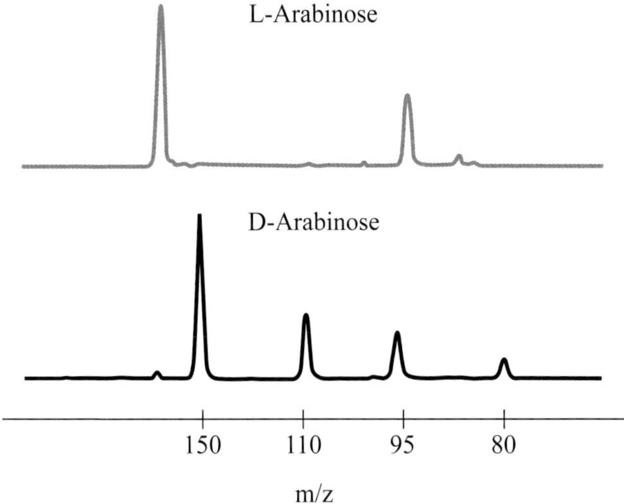

Figure 1 Differences in peak patterns and retention times in GC/MS chromatogram for D- and L-arabinose

This passage was adapted from "Estimation of D-Arabinose by Gas Chromatography/Mass Spectrometry as Surrogate for Mycobacterial Lipoarabinomannan in Human Urine." De P, Amin A, Valli E, Perkins M, McNeil M, et al. *PLoS ONE*. 2015. 10(12) doi:10.1371/journal.pone.0144088 for use under the terms of the Creative Commons CC BY 4.0 license (http://creativecommons.org/licenses/by/4.0/legalcode).

TEST 4A

Question 6

The ^{13}C NMR for D-arabinose is shown below. How many chemically distinct carbons are likely to be found in L-arabinose?

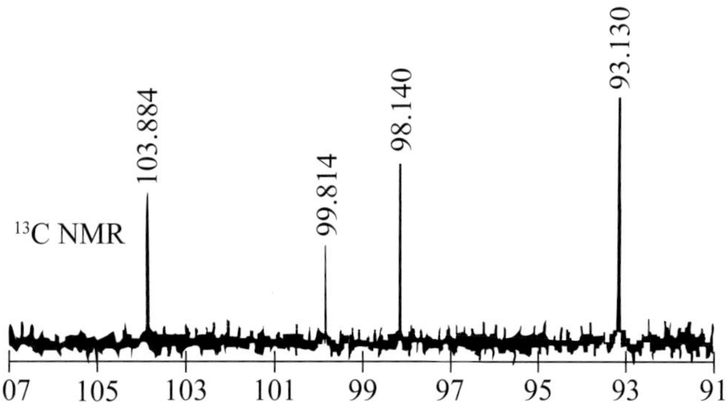

- O **A.** 2
- O **B.** 4
- O **C.** 8
- O **D.** 16

Question 7

Which of the following peaks in Figure 1 most likely corresponds to D-arabinose$^+$?

- O **A.** m/z of 150
- O **B.** m/z of 110
- O **C.** m/z of 95
- O **D.** m/z of 80

Question 8

Which of the following forces most likely mediates separation of L-arabinose and D-arabinose in gas chromatography as described in the passage?

- O **A.** Covalent bonding
- O **B.** Electrostatic forces
- O **C.** Van der Waals interactions
- O **D.** Hydrogen bonding

Question 9

LAM modified with only 2 mannose residues was shown in a subsequent experiment to be the most specific predictor of TB infection. Purification of (Mannose)$_2$-LAM would be best accomplished by:

- O **A.** size exclusion chromatography.
- O **B.** mass spectrometry.
- O **C.** ^{1}H NMR.
- O **D.** gel electrophoresis.

TEST 4A

Passage 3 (Questions 10-13)

Chronic alcohol consumption results in approximately 12,000 deaths per year attributed to alcoholic liver disease. β-oxidation and lipid biosynthesis are directly regulated by cell autonomous circadian clocks, and recent studies suggest that disruption of daily rhythms in metabolism facilitates the development of alcoholic fatty liver. However, it is not known whether ethanol disrupts the core molecular clock in the liver, nor whether this, in turn, alters rhythms in lipid metabolism. To understand the effect of alcohol consumption on liver cell autonomous circadian clocks, researchers aimed to monitor the activity of Nocturnin, a circadian deadenylase.

Deadenylases specifically catalyze the removal of the poly(A) tail at the 3′-end of eukaryotic mRNAs and release AMP as the product. There are currently two methods to run a deadenylase assay. One is based on radioactive isotopic labeled RNA substrates. This method has high sensitivity but is radioactive and time-consuming. The other method utilizes commercially available poly(A) as the substrate and is based on methylene blue colorimetry. The methylene blue molecules can insert into the polynucleotide chain, which shifts the absorbance maximum in the UV spectrum. However, this method is not accurate when short oligoadenylic acid (oligoA) acts as the substrate since oligoA has a relatively low methylene blue binding affinity.

Size-exclusion chromatography (SEC) is one of the most widely used methods to separate or identify molecules with different molecular sizes or shapes. Researchers decided to explore the possibility of using SEC as a deadenylase assay method. They used 2-mer oligoA (A2), 6-mer oligoA (A6), and 20-mer olgioA (A20) as substrates. The 5′ phosphate was removed from each of these substrates. Deadenylase was mixed with each substrate and SEC was performed. The elution volume of each substrate during SEC is shown in Figure 1.

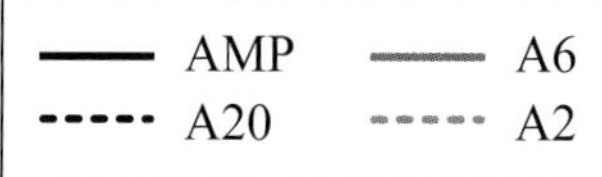

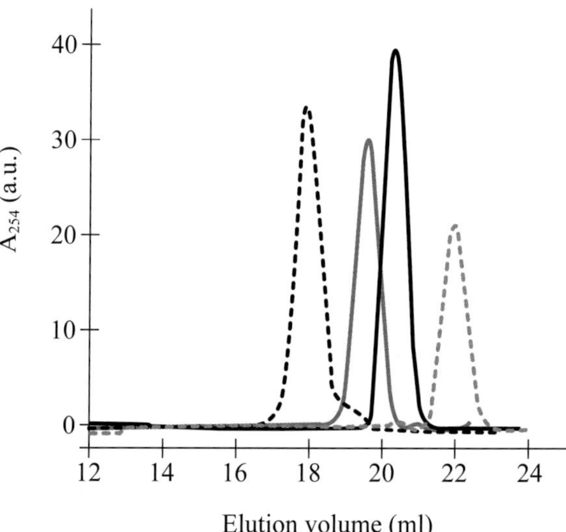

Figure 1 Elution volumes of A2, A6, A20 and AMP after SEC

Next ▶

This passage was adapted from "A Deadenylase Assay by Size-Exclusion Chromatography." He G-j and Yan Y-B. *PLoS ONE*. 2012. 7(3) doi: 10.137/journal.pone.0033700 and from "Chronic Ethanol Consumption Disrupts the Core Molecular Clock and Diurnal Rhythms of Metabolic Genes in the Liver without Affecting the Suprachiasmatic Nucleus." Filiano AN, Millender-Swain T, Johnson R Jr, Young ME, Gamble KL, et al. *PLoS ONE*. 2013. 8(8) doi: 10.1371/journal.pone.0071684 for use under the terms of the Creative Commons CC BY 3.0 license (http://creativecommons.org/licenses/by/3.0/legalcode).

Question 10

Of the three substrates used, which substrate would be least suitable for a deadenylase assay?

- O **A.** A2
- O **B.** A20
- O **C.** A6
- O **D.** AMP

Question 11

AMP levels in Figure 1 represent which of the following parameters?

- O **A.** The enzymatic activity of deadenylase
- O **B.** The speed of the enzymatic reaction
- O **C.** The specificity of the enzymatic activity
- O **D.** The control variable

Question 12

Based on Figure 1, which of the following best describes the relationship between elution volume and the elution time of the mRNAs measured?

- O **A.** Elution volume is inversely related to elution time.
- O **B.** Elution volume is directly related to elution time.
- O **C.** Elution volume is unrelated to elution time.
- O **D.** Elution volume is double the elution time.

Question 13

The product(s) of a deadenylase reaction when A2 is the substrate is(are):

- O **A.** AMP.
- O **B.** AMP and adenosine.
- O **C.** adenosine.
- O **D.** AMP, adenosine, and deadenylase.

Questions 14 through 17 do not refer to a passage and are independent of each other.

Question 14

Which of the following accurately describes the difference between a western blot and a DNA microarray?

- O **A.** A western blot more directly measures protein levels, while a DNA microarray measures gene expression on a larger scale.
- O **B.** A DNA microarray more directly measures protein levels, while a western blot measures expression on a larger scale.
- O **C.** A western blot more directly measures RNA levels, while a DNA microarray measures expression on a larger scale.
- O **D.** A DNA microarray more directly measures RNA levels, while a western blot measures expression on a larger scale.

Question 15

The conjugation of double bonds in lycopene, a molecule predicted to support cardiac health, allows it to absorb blue-green light. What color will lycopene appear to be?

- O **A.** Blue-green
- O **B.** Yellow-orange
- O **C.** Red-orange
- O **D.** Blue-violet

Question 16

Which technique would most efficiently identify a molecule as containing a carbonyl?

- O **A.** ^{1}H NMR spectroscopy
- O **B.** IR spectroscopy
- O **C.** Ultraviolet spectroscopy
- O **D.** Mass spectrometry

Question 17

Which of the following statements best describes the effect of temperature on the efficiency of crystallization?

- O **A.** High temperatures are most effective at promoting crystal formation.
- O **B.** Low temperatures are most effective at promoting crystal formation.
- O **C.** High and low temperatures are equally effective at promoting crystal formation.
- O **D.** Temperature does not affect the efficacy of crystal formation.

Passage 4 (Questions 18-21)

Despite significant improvements in the diagnosis and treatment of breast cancer, tumor dormancy followed by distant recurrences accounts for 90% of all cancer deaths. Stat3 is a transcription factor which is known for its role as an integrator of cytokine and growth factor signaling. Activated Stat3 translocates to the nucleus where it binds to consensus promoter sequences of target genes and regulates their transcription. Inhibition of Stat3 activation in breast cancer cells inhibits growth and neoangiogenesis, and potentiates a response to the chemotherapeutic agent doxorubicin.

Autotaxin (ATX), a secreted glycoprotein with lysophospholipase D activity, promotes cell migration, metastasis, and angiogenesis through the generation of lysophosphatidic acid (LPA), a lipid mitogen and motility factor that acts on several G protein-coupled receptors. Significantly, enforced expression of ATX in metastatic models of breast cancer enhances osteolytic bone metastases while reduced expression of ATX inhibits bone metastases through regulation of osteoclasts. Furthermore, it has recently been shown that over-expression of either ATX or LPA to the mammary gland mediates *de novo* tumorigenesis, suggesting the oncogenic nature of this pathway. In order to investigate the regulation of ATX, scientists examined primary breast cancer samples with matched axillary lymph nodes. The protein levels of phosphorylated Stat3 (pStat3), Stat3, ATX, and Tubulin were measured by western Blot for six highly malignant breast cancer cell lines. The transcript levels of ATX and actin were examined by using radioactive oligonucleotide probes complementary to a gene-specific nucleotide sequence. The results are presented in Figure 1.

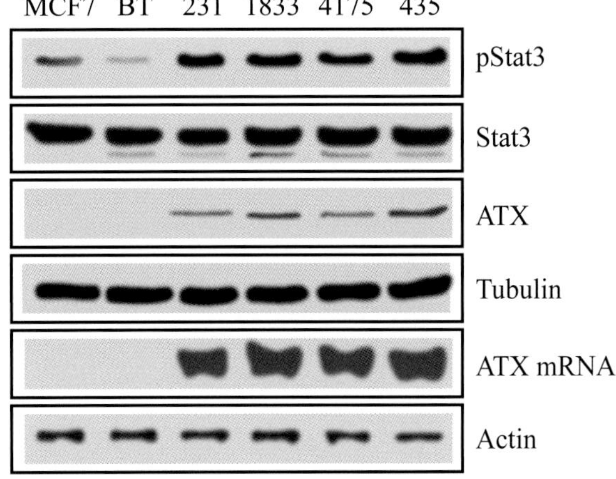

Figure 1 Stat3 regulates ATX expression in breast cancer cells

After measuring transcription and translation of the assayed genes, the scientists observed the effect of pStat3 overexpression on cell migration patterns by overexpressing Stat3 in normal breast epithelial cells and measuring the distance the cells travel through an agarose medium. pStat3 levels were found to correlate with increased cellular migration.

This passage was adapted from "Stat3 mediates expression of autotaxin in breast cancer." Azare J, Doane A, Leslie K, Chang Q, Berishaj M, et al. *PLoS ONE.* 2011. 6(2) doi:10.1371/journal.pone.0027851 for use under the terms of the Creative Commons CC BY 3.0 license (http://creativecommons.org/licenses/by/3.0/legalcode).

Question 18

Binding of an anti-Stat3 antibody to its target protein most likely utilizes which of the following interactions?

I. Hydrogen bonds
II. Disulfide bonds
III. Van der Waals interactions

- **A.** I
- **B.** I and III
- **C.** II and III
- **D.** I, II, and III

Question 19

Tissue staining with specific antibodies, known as immunohistochemical analysis, did NOT show levels of pStat3 consistent with Figure 1. What explanation is LEAST likely to account for this finding?

- **A.** pStat3 is denatured during the tissue preparation process.
- **B.** Low grade primary tumors were stained instead of malignant tumors.
- **C.** Anti-pStat3 antibody also recognizes pStat5.
- **D.** A secondary antibody-enzyme conjugate was not used in the experiment.

Question 20

Scientists interested in further characterizing the epitope recognized by the anti-pStat3 antibody noted that the three amino acid epitope had an overall isoelectric point of 10.25. Which of the following epitopes is most likely recognized by anti-pStat3?

- **A.** RRK
- **B.** VIL
- **C.** DDD
- **D.** EED

Question 21

According to the passage, which statement most accurately describes the relationship between pStat3 and breast cancer cell migration?

- **A.** pStat3 mediates ATX up-regulation and enhanced migration of breast cancer cell lines.
- **B.** Stat3 activates ATX, enhancing migration of breast cancer cells.
- **C.** Tubulin activates Stat3, leading to decreased migration of breast cancer cells.
- **D.** ATX activates Stat3, leading to increased migration of breast cancer cells.

TEST 4A

Next ▶

Passage 5 (Questions 22-25)

Japanese cedar (Cj) pollinosis is a serious type I allergic disease in Japan. More than 25% of Japanese citizens suffer from Cj pollinosis and the number of patients has constantly increased over the years. Type I allergic diseases are characterized by the elevation of immunoglobulin E (IgE) levels and mast cell degranulation, followed by the release of histamine and other chemical mediators of allergy. Immunotherapy using allergen-specific T-cell epitopes is thought to be a safe and effective treatment for the control of IgE-mediated allergic diseases.

Two cedar pollen proteins, Cry j 1 (45 kDa) and Cry j 2 (32 kDa), were identified as major pollen allergens. After the complementary DNA (cDNA) clones encoding Cry j 1 and Cry j 2 were isolated and sequenced, the dominant human T-cell epitopes were identified. Among them, seven major human T-cell epitopes derived from Cry j 1 and Cry j 2 were selected to construct an artificial protein (7crp) used for vaccination as shown in Figure 1. Genetically manipulated (GM) chickens producing 7crp fused with chicken egg white lysozyme (cLys-7crp) were generated using a retroviral vector. The cLys-7crp-containing egg white was orally administered to Cj pollinosis model mice to investigate its therapeutic effects.

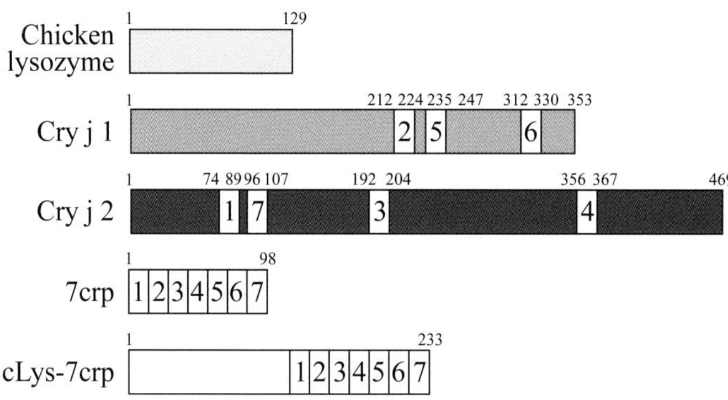

Figure 1 Generation of cLys-7crp from chicken lysozyme and Cry j 1 and 2

Retroviral sequences were detected by PCR using genomic DNA extracted from the chicken blood cells as a template and specific primers for the retroviral packaging signal region. cLys-7crp and Enhanced Green Fluorescent Protein (EGFP) genes were co-expressed bicistronically mediated by IRES under the control of the ubiquitous chicken β-actin promoter. Transgene expression was visually detectable by the EGFP expression in the blood cells of GM chickens.

The oral administration of cLys-7crp-containing egg white exhibited a therapeutic effect in Cj pollinosis mice. As a follow up study, researchers measured the total IgE content in the serum of each mouse before and after the repeated administration of cLys-7crp-containing or normal egg white (Figure 2).

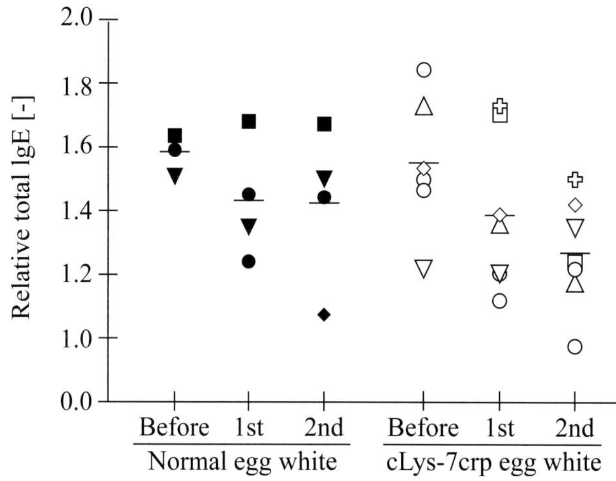

Figure 2 Relative total IgE of individual mice

Question 22

In order for the GM chickens to produce cLys-7crp, specific allergens needed to be isolated. The scientists most likely used which technique to separate the allergens?

- **A.** Size-exclusion chromatography
- **B.** DNA sequencing
- **C.** NMR structural analysis
- **D.** Western blot

Question 23

In a further study, why would researchers incorporate a poly-histidine tag on the cLys-7crp protein?

- **A.** Egg white has a pH of 9 so cLys-7crp could be isolated using a negatively charged ion-exchanger.
- **B.** The poly-histidine tag enlarges the protein and allows it to be isolated using gel-electrophoresis.
- **C.** Egg white has a pH of 9 so cLys-7crp could be isolated using a positively charged ion-exchanger.
- **D.** The poly-histidine tag enlarges the protein and allows it to be isolated using size-exclusion chromatography.

TEST 4A

Question 24

A 5′-CGGGCTGCAGGAATTCG-3′ primer corresponding to the retroviral vector sequence was added into the PCR setup immediately following:

- O **A.** the denaturing of the recombinant DNA.
- O **B.** hybridization of the DNA strands.
- O **C.** the addition of complementary cLys primers.
- O **D.** the reannealing of complementary strands.

Question 25

Which feature of EGFP makes it a suitable indicator of cLys-7crp expression in the blood of GM chickens?

- O **A.** The EGFP fluoresces under the acidic conditions of the red blood cells.
- O **B.** The small conjugated chromophore contained within the barrel structure fluoresces under infrared light.
- O **C.** The small conjugated chromophore contained within the barrel structure fluoresces under ultraviolet light.
- O **D.** The barrel structure of EGFP allows it to absorb red light and fluoresce green light.

Questions 26 through 29 do not refer to a passage and are independent of each other.

Question 26

The relative number of acidic and basic amino acids in a protein can most reasonably be assessed by determining which of the following characteristics of a protein?

- O **A.** pI
- O **B.** pH
- O **C.** Number of α-helices
- O **D.** Number of β-pleated sheets

Question 27

Column chromatography with a palmitate stationary phase and an acetonitrile/water mobile phase is LEAST likely to separate:

- O **A.** D-arabinose and L-arabinose.
- O **B.** D-glucose and L-mannose.
- O **C.** D-fructose and D-glucose.
- O **D.** D-lactose and D-arabinose.

Question 28

Co-expression of reverse transcriptase in a eukaryotic cell transfected with the RNA of an anti-viral gene would result in:

- O **A.** increased translation of the transfected RNA by allosteric activation of the ribosome.
- O **B.** increased replication of the RNA transcript in the cytosol of the eukaryotic cell.
- O **C.** integration of the RNA transcript into the eukaryotic cell genome.
- O **D.** decreased survival of the resulting cell line to challenge with a virus.

Question 29

Gel electrophoresis that occurs prior to a Southern blot separates:

- O **A.** DNA fragments by charge.
- O **B.** DNA fragments by size.
- O **C.** RNA fragments by charge.
- O **D.** RNA fragments by size.

Passage 6 (Questions 30-33)

Amyotrophic lateral sclerosis (ALS), the most common adult onset motor neuron disease, is characterized by degeneration of both lower and upper motor neurons, leading to death within 2–5 years of onset. The lack of biological tools to diagnose ALS together with the non-specificity and heterogeneity of clinical symptoms lead to difficulty in making the diagnosis in early stages. Metabolomic studies are a powerful approach to ascertaining metabolic signatures from a combination of small molecules in biological fluid and could lead to the identification of diagnostic or prognostic biomarkers for ALS.

Because NMR spectroscopy appears to be cost-effective and is useful in routine care and screening, researchers searched for a metabolic signature of ALS in the cerebral spinal fluid (CSF) using high resolution NMR spectroscopy. After the ^{1}H NMR spectra of CSF samples was collected from ALS patients and from patients without a neurodegenerative disease, the researchers analyzed 17 CSF metabolites in ALS and non ALS patients (Figure 1). Some of the metabolites included: amino-acids (alanine, glutamine, tyrosine), organic acids (citrate and acetate), ketone bodies (acetone and acetoacetate), glucose, fructose, metabolites involved in glucose metabolism (pyruvate and lactate), and the anti-oxidant molecule ascorbate.

Three metabolites were identified with mean CSF concentrations that were characteristic of each molecule. There were higher concentrations of ascorbate and pyruvate in ALS patients compared to non-ALS patients. The lactate/pyruvate ratio was also lower in ALS patients than in controls ($p = 0.0029$). Acetone concentrations trended to be higher in patients with ALS.

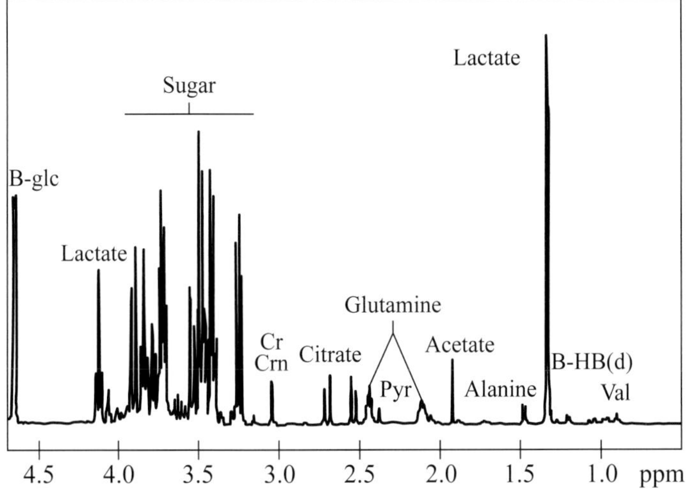

Figure 1 CSF spectrum by ^{1}H NMR from an ALS patient

This passage was adapted from "^{1}H-NMR-Based metabolomics profiling of CSF in early amyotrophic lateral sclerosis." Blasco H, Corcia P, Moreau C, Veau S, Fournier C, et al. *PLoS ONE.* 2010. 9(5) doi:10.1371/journal.pone.0013223 for use under the terms of the Creative Commons CC BY 3.0 license (http://creativecommons.org/licenses/by/3.0/legalcode).

Question 30

Ascorbate is produced as an indirect byproduct of mitochondrial electron transfer and has been shown to scavenge hydrogen peroxide and superoxide free radicals in the neurons of patients with ALS. Which of the following describes the levels of oxidative stress in ALS versus non-ALS patients?

- **A.** The level of oxidative stress is lower in ALS patients than in non-ALS patients.
- **B.** The level of oxidative stress is higher in ALS patients than in non-ALS patients.
- **C.** The level of oxidative stress in ALS and non-ALS patients is similar.
- **D.** The level of oxidative stress cannot be determined without additional information.

Question 31

Based on the information in the chart below, which of the following statements best describes the metabolite levels measured by NMR in ALS versus non-ALS patients?

Metabolites (μmol/L)	ALS	Non ALS	p
Alanine	56	61	0.74
Acetate	53	104	0.0002
Lactate	2076	2020	0.81
Glutamine	716	785	0.24
Pyruvate	68	17	0.002
Citrate	283	285	0.51
Glucose	3240	3174	0.98
Fructose	428	419	0.82
Ascorbate	25	0	0.003
Tyrosine	12	8	0.35
Formate	28	30	0.35

- **A.** Amino acid levels are higher in non-ALS patients as compared to ALS patients.
- **B.** Pyruvate levels are lower in non-ALS patients as compared to ALS patients.
- **C.** Carbohydrate levels are lower in non-ALS patients as compared to ALS patients.
- **D.** Citric acid cycle intermediates are higher in non-ALS patients as compared to ALS patients.

TEST 4A

Question 32

^{1}H-NMR peaks representing glucose that are shifted downfield are most likely neighbored by which of the following functional groups?

- A. $-CO_2H$
- B. $-CH_3$
- C. $-CH_2-$
- D. $-O(CH_3)_3$

Question 33

Which statement would most likely weaken the finding that ALS patients had higher levels of ascorbate than non-ALS patients?

- A. The lactate peak at 1.3 ppm is found in the NMR spectrum of an isolated neuron.
- B. The creatinine peak at 3.05 ppm is identical to the creatinine peak in astrocytes.
- C. The pyruvate peak at 2.4 ppm is not found in the NMR spectrum of an isolated neuron.
- D. The glutamine peaks at 2.1 and 2.4 ppm are also found in oligodendrocytes.

TEST 4A

Passage 7 (Questions 34-39)

Ribosomes are central to cellular function in bacteria as evidenced by the number of effective antibiotics which target their function. The complexity of their composition, structure and function requires the implementation of a range of analytical techniques and most rely on the isolation of ribosomes using density gradient centrifugation. Chromatography has been used in the past in an attempt to accelerate and simplify the isolation process. High backpressures caused by the size of ribosomes severely limit the maximum flow rate that can be attained, thus greatly increasing the overall time taken to obtain ribosomal fractions.

Monolith columns are a new class of chromatographic stationary phase, based on a highly cross-linked porous monolithic polymer. Unlike conventional chromatography columns packed with porous particles, the monolithic column is a single piece of porous structure of uninterrupted and interconnected channels. The absence of matrix packing leads to low backpressures allowing high flow rates to be achieved. Strong anion exchange chemistry is used, as there are significant areas of exposed negatively charged rRNA on the surface of the ribosome. Initial attempts, using a linear NaCl gradient to elute the bound material, revealed that bacterial cell lysates could be fractioned into two main components on quaternary amine (QA) monolithic columns (termed fractions QA1-2. Proteins extracted in the two elutions were run through a polyacrylamide-SDS gel and were stained with Imperial Blue (Figure 1).

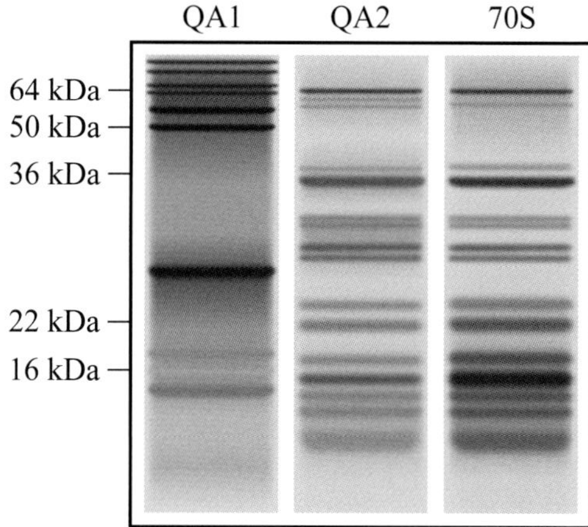

Figure 1 Precipitated proteins from QA1 and QA2 compared to sucrose-purified ribosomes (70S) by SDS-PAGE

Mass spectrometry was used for analysis of fractions QA1 and QA2. QA1 was found to contain a number of cytosolic proteins, as well as membrane and cell wall associated proteins when spectra were compared to the ProteinPilot database. Fraction QA2, on the other hand, contained a large number of different ribosomal proteins as well as a few ribosome-associated proteins and some cytosolic proteins.

Question 34

Which of the following techniques serves as the most conclusive proof based on external means that the second elution fraction contains ribosomal proteins?

- O **A.** The use of the SDS-PAGE gel for 70S ribosomes
- O **B.** The use of mass spectrometry on the fractions
- O **C.** There was no conclusive test to show this result.
- O **D.** The use of density gradient centrifugation

Question 35

Which type of solution could have been used instead to elute the ribosomes from the column in a similar way?

- O **A.** A polar solution
- O **B.** A nonpolar solution
- O **C.** A salt solution
- O **D.** A nonpolar solution using high pressure

Question 36

Using knowledge of gel electrophoresis, what effect would an increased voltage have on the separation of proteins in the SDS-PAGE gel?

- O **A.** The compounds of the control ladder would be expected to move faster than those in the sample mixture.
- O **B.** The compounds of the control ladder would be expected to move slower than those in the sample mixture.
- O **C.** The compounds of the control ladder would be expected to move faster and in proportion to those in the sample mixture.
- O **D.** The compounds of the control ladder would be expected to move slower and in proportion to those in the sample mixture.

Question 37

The retention time of a compound undergoing high pressure liquid chromatography (HPLC) is known to be influenced by a number of factors. Which of the following would NOT affect the retention time?

- O **A.** The pressure applied to the column
- O **B.** The temperature of the column
- O **C.** The particle size for the stationary phase
- O **D.** The amount of sample mixture

Question 38

When performing the separation for the first time, researchers found that the ribosomal proteins were eluted in the first fraction (QA1). This result is likely to be associated with which of the following findings?

- O **A.** A high concentration of NaCl in the mobile phase used at the start of the elution
- O **B.** A low concentration of NaCl in the mobile phase used at the start of the elution
- O **C.** A high pressure used on the column at the start of the elution
- O **D.** A faulty monolith column with beads instead of the solid matrix

Question 39

After using the monolith column to isolate ribosomal proteins, the researchers carried out experiments testing which antibiotics could effectively bind to the proteins. Which of the following may be a fault with this approach?

- O **A.** The proteins may be denatured in the process of isolating them.
- O **B.** The NaCl buffer may be an unnatural contaminant.
- O **C.** Other separation techniques may be needed prior to these experiments.
- O **D.** The antibiotics may be able to bind other cellular proteins.

Passage 8 (Questions 40-43)

Wilson's disease (WD) is an autosomal recessive illness characterized by excessive accumulation of copper in the liver, brain, and other tissues. WD is attributed to a defect in the ATP7B gene (on chromosome 13), which encodes the ATP-dependent copper transporting transmembrane protein mainly expressed in the liver. A defect in the ATP7B function leads to the accumulation of copper, primarily in the liver and subsequently in the brain, eye and other organs.

Presently, penicillamine (PA), a copper-binding agent, is a common choice of treatment due to the preferred excretion effect of copper through the urine, although it is known to lead to numerous side effects. Comprehensive examinations of metabolic patterns of biological samples from WD patients with or without drug treatment are crucial for explaining the metabolic response to copper toxicity, which can be done through a metabolomics analysis. NMR-based metabolomics combine NMR spectroscopy with pattern recognition techniques and quantitatively measure the multiparametric metabolic response to the changes in both endogenous and exogenous factors of integrated living systems.

In one study, rats were fed a copper-laden diet to model the behavior of copper deposits in their organs. Using high resolution ^{1}H NMR spectroscopy, the biochemical variations of serum from these experimental copper-laden rats were investigated (Figure 1).

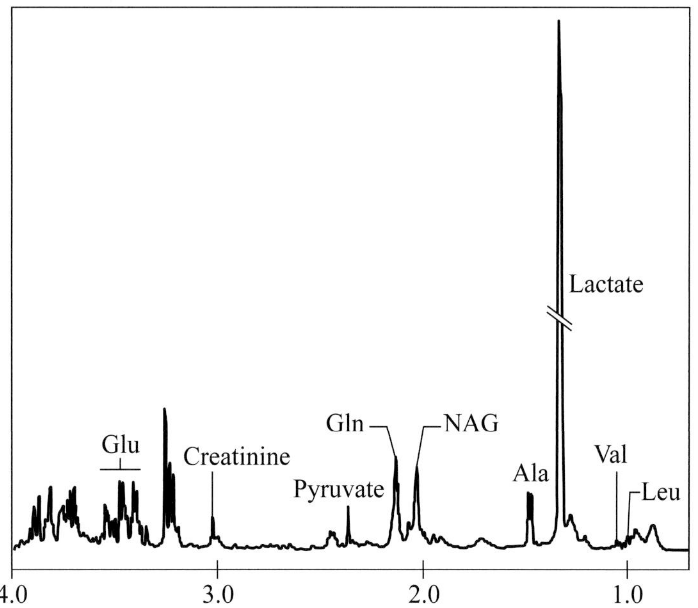

Figure 1 ^{1}H NMR spectrum of serum obtained from the copper-laden rats

Penicillamine was selected to treat the copper-laden rats based on preferred copper clearance and drug-induced variations in their biological metabotypes. The copper concentration in the urine and liver was separately examined by atomic absorption spectrophotometry for the three study populations indicated below (Table 1).

Table 1 Copper contents of control group, copper-laden model group, and model+PA group

Copper content	Control	Copper-laden model	Model + PA
Urinary copper (μg/24hr)	36.98 ± 6.72	156.83 ± 34.03*	380.31 ± 46.08*
Hepatic copper (μg/g)	5.54 ± 0.74	108.15 ± 12.60*	43.84 ± 19.41*

Question 40

Which feature of lactate would lend evidence to the conclusion that lactate is significantly elevated in rats fed with a high copper diet?

- O **A.** The rightward chemical shift for the lactate peak in the ^{1}H NMR spectrum
- O **B.** The height of the lactate peak in the ^{1}H NMR spectrum
- O **C.** The area under the curve for the lactate peak in the ^{1}H NMR spectrum
- O **D.** The ^{1}H NMR spectrum would not indicate this conclusion.

Question 41

If the methyl group of pyruvate is replaced with an aldehyde group, the chemical shift of the peak for the aldehyde hydrogen will:

- O **A.** be downfield relative to the present pyruvate peak.
- O **B.** be upfield relative to the present pyruvate peak.
- O **C.** not change relative to the present pyruvate peak.
- O **D.** be lowered relative to the present pyruvate peak.

TEST 4A

Question 42

The peak labeled as alanine in Figure 1 is composed of two peaks side by side. What can be concluded about the formation of this peak?

- O **A.** It is formed by a splitting pattern resulting from one hydrogen on an adjacent carbon.
- O **B.** It is formed by a splitting pattern resulting from two hydrogens on an adjacent carbon.
- O **C.** It is formed by a splitting pattern resulting from two identical hydrogens on the same carbon.
- O **D.** It is formed by a splitting pattern resulting from two different hydrogens, each on a carbon adjacent to the other.

Question 43

When combined with the information in Figure 2, which information regarding the treatment of Wilson's Disease can be used to devise other possible treatments?

- O **A.** The solubility of the penicillamine-copper complex in oil
- O **B.** The solubility of the penicillamine-copper complex in water
- O **C.** The binding affinity of penicillamine for copper
- O **D.** The solubility of copper in water

Questions 44 through 47 do not refer to a passage and are independent of each other.

Question 44

Amino acids used in *in vitro* translation experiments must be synthesized *de novo* and added to the reaction mix to allow the ribosome to create polypeptides. Synthesis of these α-amino acids most likely occurs by:

- O **A.** an aldehyde carrying the sidechain reacting with an electrophilic cyanide molecule.
- O **B.** an aldehyde carrying the sidechain reacting with a nucleophilic cyanide molecule.
- O **C.** a ketone carrying the sidechain reacting with an electrophilic alcohol.
- O **D.** a ketone carrying the sidechain reacting with a nucleophilic alcohol.

Question 45

Which of the following best describes how a fluorescent probe in real-time PCR binds its target sequence?

- O **A.** Binding between a probe and its target is mediated by three hydrogen bonds between A and T and two hydrogen bonds between G and C.
- O **B.** RNA polymerase carries the probe and polymerizes its incorporation into the growing DNA strand.
- O **C.** Formation of intermolecular bonds between the probe and its target allow for specific binding.
- O **D.** The fluorescent molecule directly intercalates between adjacent nucleotides of its target sequence.

Question 46

After denaturing a double stranded piece of DNA, which of the following manipulations is needed for reannealing to occur?

- O **A.** Raise the temperature.
- O **B.** Lower the temperature.
- O **C.** Add DNA ligase.
- O **D.** Add DNA primers

Question 47

The stationary phase of a gas chromatography column is comprised primarily of dodecane. Which of the following would be the best mobile phase to separate various halogen modifications of phospholipids?

- O **A.** $CH_3–(CH_2)_2–CH_3$
- O **B.** $NH_3–(CH_2)_7–CH_3$
- O **C.** $OH–(CH_2)_2–CH_3$
- O **D.** CCl_4

Passage 9 (Questions 48-51)

p53 is one of the most well studied tumor suppressor proteins and is regarded as the guardian of the genome. The p53 gene has been found to be mutated in most human cancers. This protein mediates cell-cycle arrest, apoptosis in response to myriads of cellular stresses including DNA damage via its transcriptional, as well as non-transcriptional roles. p53 suppresses tumorigenesis by preventing propagation and transmission of damaged DNA with potentially harmful mutations.

p53 is known to bind to a specific sequence, the p53 response element (p53RE), present in the promoter regions of p53 target genes. Previous studies implicated ATP binding to the C terminus of p53 in modulating the release of p53 from the p53-DNA complex. This study investigated the ATPase activity associated with purified p53 protein.

Experiment 1

Using a real time assay, ATPase activity of GST tagged recombinant human p53 was studied. Figure 1 shows decline in absorbance at 340 nm as a function of time. The absorbance decline accounts for NADH decomposition, which is a measurable read-out for the ATPase reaction.

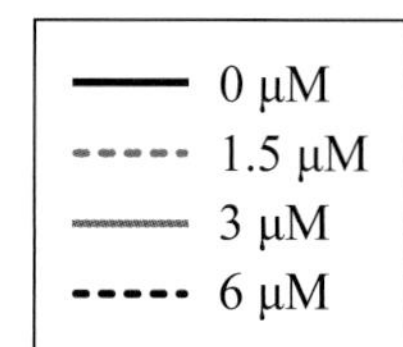

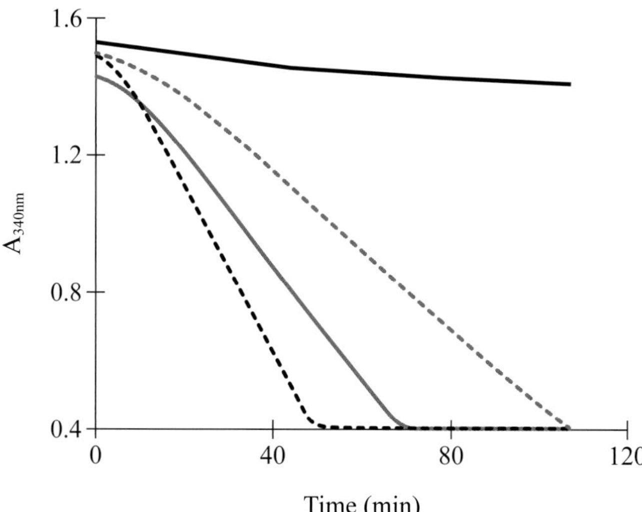

Figure 1 Absorbance at 340nm as a function of time

Experiment 2

In order to further validate the ATPase activity of p53, researchers analyzed the ATPase rates of various p53 deletion mutants (Figure 2).

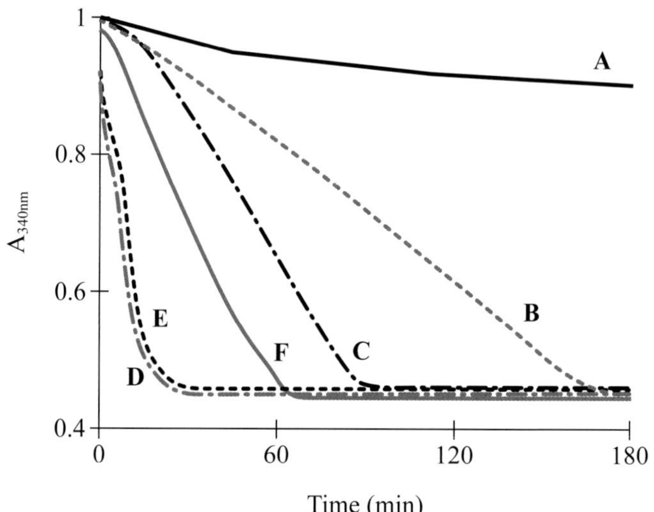

Figure 2 Absorbance at 340nm as a function of time for mutant p53 proteins

Experiment 3

Purified N-terminal GST tagged human p53 protein was electrophoresed on SDS-PAGE (12%) gel (Figure 3). After electrophoresis, the gel was stained and analyzed for ATPase activity. The protein was allowed to recover its conformation and was then incubated at 30°C for 24 hrs in Buffer A, which contains 20% methanol and 0.075% lead nitrate, until the white ATPase activity band appeared as a result of lead phosphate precipitate formation within the gel.

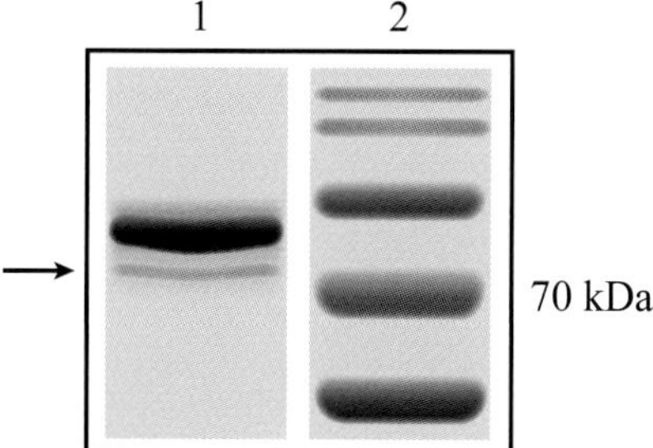

Figure 3 SDS-Page of active p53 protein (arrow indicates unexpected band)

Question 48

In Experiment 2, which absorbance spectrum is indicative of the non-mutated p53 protein and saline solution, respectively?

- A. E and A
- B. F and A
- C. A and E
- D. C and E

Question 49

Which additional piece of evidence would help researchers confirm that the human p53 protein hydrolyzes a phosphoanhydride bond in order to stabilize its binding to p53RE?

- O **A.** DNA sequencing of p53 is consistent with other proteins containing ATPase activity.
- O **B.** NMR structural analysis shows an ATP binding domain on the C-terminus of p53.
- O **C.** NADH concentration becomes exceedingly low in cells with active p53.
- O **D.** Defective p53 and high levels of ATP are found in cancer cells.

Question 50

The absorbance data from the oxidation of NADH to NAD^+ can be found if which of the following variables are known?

I. Concentration of NADH
II. Length of light path
III. Frequency of light
IV. Molar absorptivity

- O **A.** I and II
- O **B.** I, II, and IV
- O **C.** I, III, and IV
- O **D.** I, II, III, and IV

Question 51

In Experiment 3, purified p53 protein was isolated using electrophoresis. Which aspect of the p53 protein allows it to migrate on the gel independently of contaminants?

- O **A.** Primary structure
- O **B.** Secondary structure
- O **C.** Tertiary structure
- O **D.** Quaternary structure

Passage 10 (Questions 52-56)

Lung cancer is the leading cause of cancer-related mortality and the most frequently diagnosed cancer worldwide. Surgery is often the key treatment for tumor masses, but the difficulty of determining an exact etiologic diagnosis prior to the surgery leads to resection of more surrounding tissue than necessary. Real-time confirmation methods are therefore required to guide the surgeon in tissue resection and to optimize treatment.

Proteomics are used to study the large spectrum of genome encoded proteins present at a given time. Hypothesizing that rapid mass spectrometry (MS) analysis of a crude crushed tissue sample could be informative, scientists evaluated the reliability of MS to rapidly classify a crude lung tissue sample of unknown origin as cancerous or non-cancerous. A protocol with a minimal sample volume and a simple preparation method was used in order to test the feasibility of performing the test in the operating room.

For the classification of cancer and non-tumor entities, 290 samples were analyzed corresponding to 138 patients. Representative MS spectra from a primary tumor, a metastatic tumor, and a non-tumor tissue are shown in Figure 1. A total of 40 m/z peaks generated from the samples were considered significantly different between tumor samples ($p<0.001$). Further analysis of blinded samples (40 primary tumors and 8 metastatic tumors) accurately detected 68.7% and 66.7% of primary and metastatic tumors, respectively. Among the potential peaks of the spectra, numerous proteins related to cell cycle progression, DNA damage response, and cellular migration were detected at peaks 4963.85, 8563.21, and 9952.85, corresponding to Cyclin D, p53, and actin. Infrared (IR) absorption and ultraviolet (UV) spectroscopy were also performed on the crude samples to confirm the functional groups on the peaks identified in MS. The IR spectrogram showed a sharp dip at 1659 cm^{-1} and broad dip from 3156 – 3567 cm^{-1}.

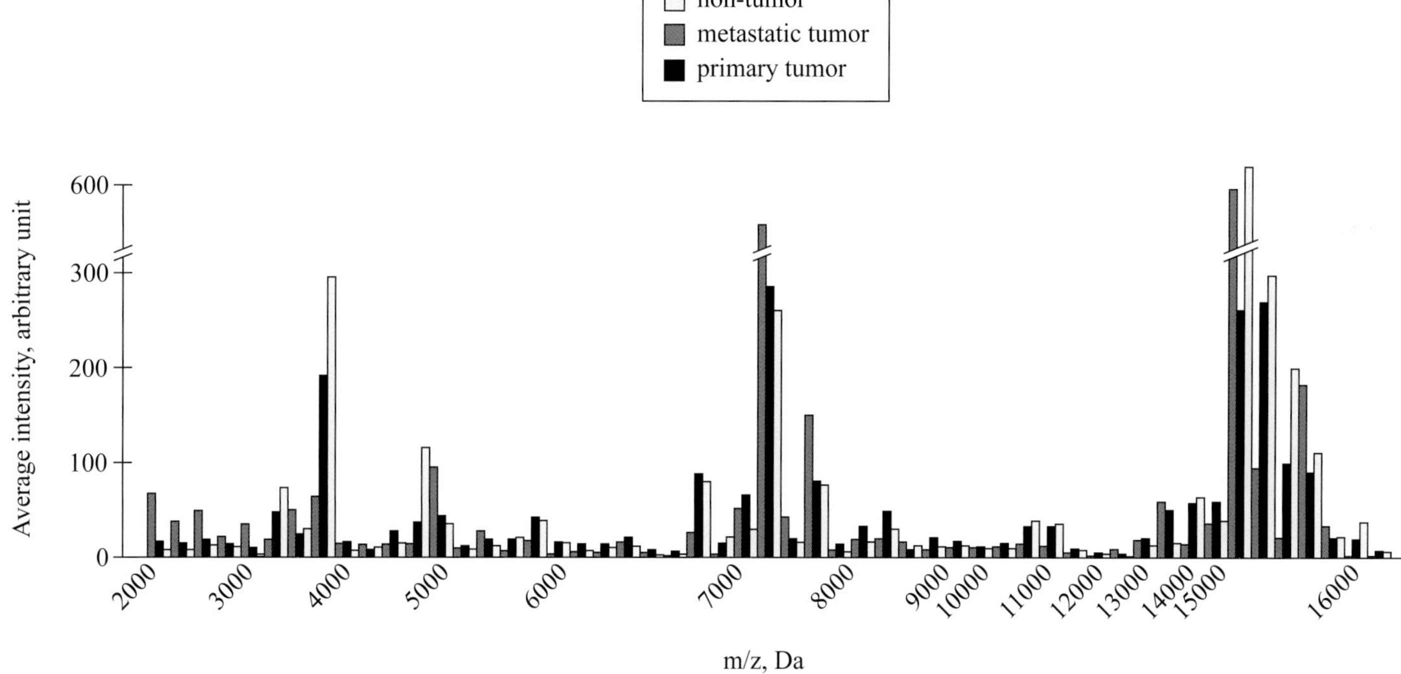

Figure 1 Average intensity versus mass-to-charge ratio of 49 peaks significantly different between Non-Tumor, Primary Tumor, and Metastatic Tumor samples

Question 52

Scientists were unable to identify a known functional group containing conjugated double bonds at the 5000 peak with UV spectroscopy. Which experiment are the scientists most likely to perform next to identify the functional group?

- **A.** Perform visible light spectroscopy.
- **B.** Perform ^{1}H-NMR.
- **C.** Use a second sample from the 4963.85 peak for UV spectroscopy.
- **D.** Perform IR spectroscopy.

Question 53

According to information in the passage, which of the following is most likely the identity of the functional group characterized by IR spectroscopy?

- **A.** Aldehyde
- **B.** Carboxylic acid
- **C.** Ketone
- **D.** Alcohol

Question 54

In a subsequent experiment, researchers performing IR absorption spectroscopy noticed a predominance of sharp dips between 200 and 1000 cm^{-1}. The scientists are most likely observing which components of a molecule?

- O **A.** Complex carbon-carbon bond vibrations
- O **B.** An alcohol functional group
- O **C.** Contamination by Br_2 contained in the mass spectrometry preparation medium
- O **D.** An amine functional group

Question 55

Which of the following samples served as controls in this experiment?

I. Purified actin protein
II. Non-tumor tissue
III. Purified cyclin A

- O **A.** I only
- O **B.** I and II
- O **C.** II and III
- O **D.** I, I, and III

Question 56

Detection of a carboxylic acid functional group, $-CO_2H$, by MS is required to identify whether actin is present or absent in a given tissue sample. Which of the following peaks could correspond to actin, assuming it is the most abundant protein in a metastatic cell?

- O **A.** 15000
- O **B.** 7000
- O **C.** 4250
- O **D.** 2000

Questions 57 through 59 do not refer to a passage and are independent of each other.

Question 57

Using a microarray, scientists are able to detect significantly lower RNA levels of *Rb* in breast ductal cancer tissue versus breast epithelium tissue. Which additional finding would support this data?

- O **A.** Breast ductal cancer contains frequent nonsynonymous mutations in RNA polymerase.
- O **B.** *Rb* is hypomethylated in breast ductal cancer.
- O **C.** Breast ductal cancer contains histones with higher levels of glutamate than histones in breast epithelium.
- O **D.** The *Rb* sequence contains a synonymous mutation in a glutamine codon in exon two.

Question 58

Which technique would provide a quick and accurate distinction between a vial of hydrocarbon and a vial of phenol?

- O **A.** Using thin-layer chromatography, match the high R_f value to the hydrocarbon and the low R_f to the phenol.
- O **B.** Using thin-layer chromatography, match the larger distance traveled to the phenol and the smaller distance traveled to the hydrocarbon.
- O **C.** Using thin-layer chromatography, match the high R_f value to the phenol and the low R_f to the hydrocarbon.
- O **D.** Smell each vial because phenol has a very characteristic, sweet scent which would differentiate these two compounds.

Question 59

Which of the following is true of the R_f factor in paper chromatography?

- O **A.** It can be used to identify an unknown compound.
- O **B.** It is normally greater than 1.
- O **C.** It is an absolute measure of polarity.
- O **D.** The denominator for the ratio is the distance to the solvent line.

STOP. If you finish before time is called, check your work. You may go back to any question in this test.

ANSWERS & EXPLANATIONS for Test 4A can be found on p. 290.

Laboratory Techniques

TEST 4B

Time: 95 minutes
Questions 1–59

DIRECTIONS: Most questions in the Biological and Biochemical Foundations of Living Systems test section are grouped with a descriptive passage. Select the best answer to each question using background knowledge and the given passage. A portion of this test section is comprised of discrete questions, which are independent of any passage and one another. Select the best answer for each discrete question. Indicate your selection by blackening the corresponding oval on your answer document. If you are unsure of the answer, rule out incorrect choices and select from the remaining options. You may access a periodic table found on the last page of this book at any point during this test section.

Passage 1 (Questions 1-5)

A chromosomal abnormality is detected in 1 of 140 births and the most common aneuploidy is trisomy 21 (Down syndrome). There are a variety of prenatal tests that can indicate increased risk for fetal aneuploidy. Although invasive diagnostic tests such as amniocentesis are the current gold standard, they are associated with a non-negligible risk of fetal loss.

A common method of determining the aneuploidy is by Digital Karyotyping, where gene-specific fluorescent oligonucleotides are hybridized to patient DNA. However, scientists cannot survey the whole genome due to limitations on the number of fluorescent probes that can be used in a single karyotype. In contrast, whole genome sequencing has the unbiased ability to detect aneuploid status. In order to decrease the time and cost of using whole genome sequencing for aneuploidy testing, scientists developed a new method, named Fast Aneuploidy Screening Test-Sequencing System (FAST-SeqS).

FAST-SeqS uses primers that anneal to a subset of retroviral-derived repeated regions dispersed throughout the genome. To investigate whether FAST-SeqS could distinguish patient samples, scientists performed experiments using DNA from patients with trisomy 21 and normal individuals. In a first experiment, researchers mixed 5%, 10%, and 25% trisomy 21 DNA into normal white blood cell DNA and found a correlation between the expected and observed fractions of extra chromosome 21 ($r = 0.997$). In a second experiment, researchers evaluated mixtures that contained 4% or 8% trisomy 21 DNA. There was a clear distinction between the samples containing 4% trisomy 21 DNA vs. those from normal individuals. The samples containing 8% trisomy 21 DNA were even more easily distinguishable when compared to the euploid group ($p = 4 \times 10^{-6}$).

Question 1

DNA sequencing machines make an error in correctly identifying the base at a genomic location once in every 1000 bases. Which of the following tests would most likely account for the DNA sequencing error in Experiment 2?

- **A.** One-tailed t-test
- **B.** Two-tailed t-test
- **C.** Linear regression
- **D.** ANOVA

Question 2

Nucleic acid sequencing allows scientists to determine the order of nucleotides in a given sample down to the base-pair level. In which of the following scenarios is DNA sequencing LEAST likely to be used?

- **A.** Detection of missense mutations in the *SMAD4* gene in patients with Alzheimer's disease
- **B.** Quantification of protein levels of *TP53*, a tumor suppressor gene in breast cancer
- **C.** Identification of alternative splicing variants of *XBP1*, a DNA repair gene
- **D.** Detection of silent mutations in DNA polymerase

Question 3

Scientists claimed that FAST-SeqS could be used to identify copy number changes, in addition to chromosomal abnormalities. The evidence in the passage that best supports this statement is that:

- **A.** FAST-SeqS had a tight correlation between expected and observed fractions of trisomy 21 DNA.
- **B.** FAST-SeqS provides a less expensive alternative to Digital Karyotyping.
- **C.** Digital Karyotyping is unable to identify all genes due to the limitation on the number of fluorescent probes.
- **D.** FAST-SeqS can amplify repeated regions in the human genome.

Question 4

Which of the following describes an ethical consideration of FAST-SeqS?

- **A.** FAST-SeqS is not 100% accurate at detecting chromosomal alternations.
- **B.** FAST-SeqS is able to detect changes in gene copy number.
- **C.** FAST-SeqS can be applied to both autosomes and sex chromosomes.
- **D.** FAST-SeqS has been shown to have a false positive rate of 5%.

Question 5

In a separate experiment, scientists were interested in measuring the levels of gene expression for 50 genes in patients with trisomy 21. Which of the following techniques would the scientists be most likely to utilize?

- **A.** Southern blot
- **B.** Western blot
- **C.** DNA microarray
- **D.** Northern blot

TEST 4B

Passage 2 (Questions 6-10)

Accumulative evidence supports the hypothesis that a small number of undifferentiated stem or stem-like cells, called cancer stem cells (CSC), are responsible for tumor initiation and therapeutic resistance. Among the colorectal CSC markers, lgr5 is a G-protein coupled receptor (GPCR) that has been reported to promote cancer cell proliferation, migration, and tumorigenicity. Lgr5 deficiency also induced premature differentiation of Paneth cells, which are at the bottom of intestinal crypts.

DNA methylation has been demonstrated as an important epigenetic mechanism for inactivating genes during tumorigenesis. Scientists interested in the epigenetic control of cancer stem cells examined the methylation status of CpG islands within the immediate promoter region of lgr5 gene in colorectal cancer cell lines. After isolating DNA from seven colon cancer cell lines, they conducted PCR that was designed to specifically amplify methylated DNA. They ran the PCR products on a gel and the results are shown in Figure 1.

M = methylated
U = unmethylated

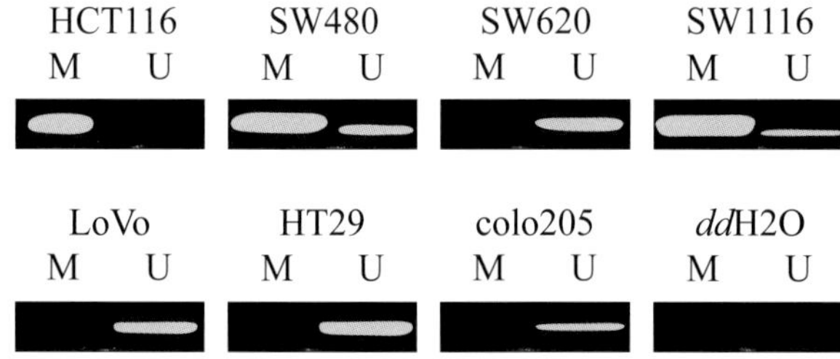

Figure 1 Methylation of Lgr5 in seven colon cancer cell lines

In a follow-up experiment, scientists transfected small interfering RNA (siRNA) against lgr5 into HCT116 colon cancer stem cells and measured the mRNA levels and protein levels of lgr5 24 hours after transfection. The results are shown in Figure 2.

A.

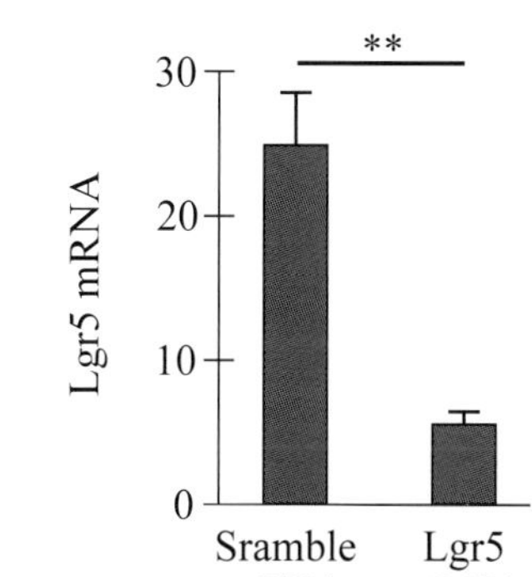

B.

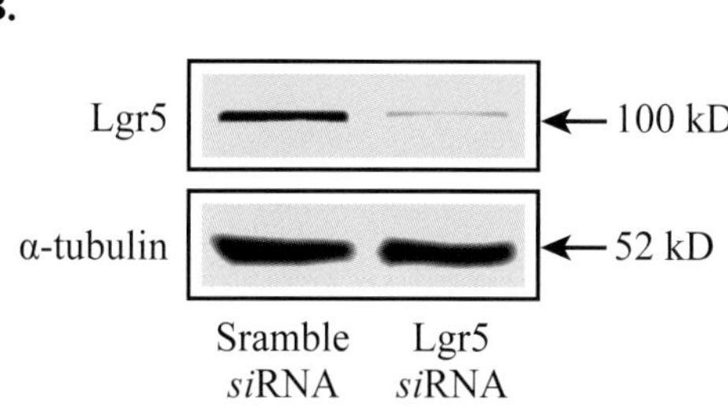

Figure 2 Lgr5 mRNA and protein levels 24 hours after transfection with lgr5-specific siRNA

To evaluate the clinical significance of lgr5 methylation, scientists also analyzed the association between lgr5 promoter methylation status and severity of disease in patients. They identified a significant reverse correlation between lgr5 methylation and higher tumor size, indicating that lgr5 methylation was an independent predictive biomarker for good prognosis of colorectal cancer.

Question 6

Decreased Paneth proliferation results in loss of colorectal microvilli, which is LEAST likely to impair absorption of:

I. glucose.
II. amino acids.
III. H_2O.

- **A.** I only
- **B.** III only
- **C.** I and II only
- **D.** II and III only

Question 7

In order to determine methylation status in the seven colorectal cancer cell lines, scientists use a technique called bisulfite conversion to change all unmethylated C to U prior to PCR. What effect is this likely to have on the PCR protocol?

- O **A.** A higher DNA denaturation temperature will be required.
- O **B.** A lower annealing temperature will be required.
- O **C.** A higher extension temperature will be required.
- O **D.** A lower number of PCR cycles will be required.

Question 8

Lgr5 siRNA most likely decreases expression of the lgr5 protein by:

- O **A.** preventing the peptidyltransferase reaction in the ribosome.
- O **B.** inhibiting the procession of the DNA polymerase.
- O **C.** binding mRNA and increasing its degradation.
- O **D.** catalyzing the addition of ubiquitin to lgr5.

Question 9

Which experiment would the scientists be most likely to perform next?

- O **A.** Inject a plasmid containing lgr5 siRNA into mice with colorectal cancer and measure tumor growth.
- O **B.** Create an agonist antibody against lgr5 and measure Paneth cell proliferation.
- O **C.** Design an siRNA against α-tubulin and measure Paneth cell migration.
- O **D.** Sequence DNA of differentiated Paneth cells to discover other target GPCRs.

Question 10

Transfection of a plasmid containing the lgr5 gene under a constitutively active promoter would be most likely to:

- O **A.** decrease the transformation of normal Paneth cells into cancer cells.
- O **B.** decrease the proliferation of colon epithelial cells.
- O **C.** increase the differentiation of CSCs.
- O **D.** increase the migration of undifferentiated Paneth cells.

Passage 3 (Questions 11-14)

Tuberculosis (TB) caused by drug-resistant strains of *Mycobacterium tuberculosis* is considered one of the most critical public health issues. The early diagnosis of drug-resistant tuberculosis via a rapid and reliable method can facilitate the administration of effective anti-tuberculosis drugs and prevent the further spread of drug-resistant strains. Nucleic acid amplification technique (NAAT) is currently the most rapid and sensitive molecular diagnostic tool to detect drug-resistant tuberculosis. 95% of rifampin (RFP)-resistant strains contain mutations localized in the *rpoB* gene that encodes the β-subunit of the bacterial RNA polymerase.

Scientists interested in developing a robust and reliable probe-based real-time PCR assay generated six fluorescent probes (LNA1 – LNA6) that can discriminate one-base mutations. The 6 probes, which each contained a different fluorophore, were designed to identify a total of 23 common *rpoB* mutations associated with RFP-resistant *M. tuberculosis*, including high frequency mutations at codons 516, 526, and 531.

Plasmid DNA templates, including the wild-type template and the corresponding mutant templates, were used to determine the specificity of each LNA probe. The reaction was run under the following conditions: 95°C for 5 min, followed by 45 cycles at 95°C for 15 s then 65°C for 30 s. Fluorescence intensity measurements were made at 65°C during each of the 45 cycles. An internal amplification control (IAC) based on *B. globigii* was used to monitor PCR inhibitors in each tube. The IAC system consists of specific primers and a probe labeled with a different fluorophore, which was targeted at a conserved segment in a different gene, *BgSP*. The experimental set-up is shown in Figure 1.

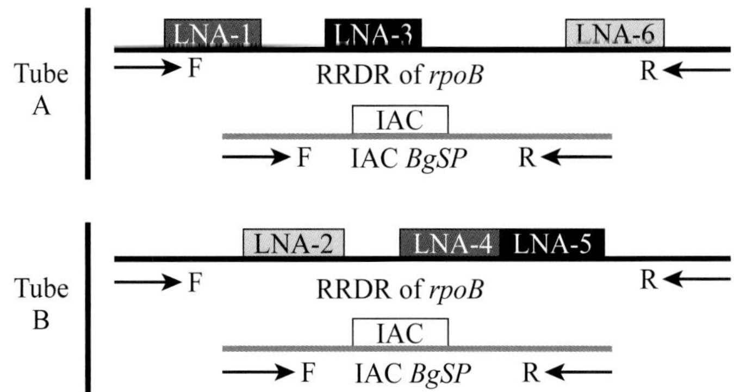

Figure 1 Schematic description of the assay and mutation discrimination capability of the six LNA probes

Scientists confirmed their LNA panel in a set of 154 clinical isolates with well-defined information on drug susceptibility and known *rpoB* gene sequence. Their results are shown in Table 1.

TEST 4B

Next ▶

Table 1 Assay performance with 154 clinical isolates

Sample types	Amount of samples	Amount of samples detected
not *M. tuberculosis*	12	12 (100%)
RFP-susceptible *M. tuberculosis*	88	88 (100%)
RFP-resistant *M. tuberculosis*	54	52 (96.3%)
Total	154	152 (98.7%)

Question 11

Each LNA probe was designed to assay for multiple missense mutations within its binding region. Which of the following best describes the probe design?

- **A.** LNA-2 contains a degenerate base that is able to bind either a purine or a pyrimidine.
- **B.** LNA-6 is designed to be complementary to the wild type sequence.
- **C.** Multiple distinct LNA-1 probes are required to detect each missense mutation.
- **D.** LNA-5 requires binding of nearby LNA-4 to detect missense mutations.

Question 12

Based on the passage, rifampin most likely targets:

- **A.** the phosphodiester transferase reaction occurring between two nucleic acids.
- **B.** the aminotransferase reaction occurring between two amino acids.
- **C.** unwinding of DNA at a gene promoter.
- **D.** procession of the ribosome between the A and P sites.

Question 13

Considering the structure of rifampin, what is the most likely assay used to detect its concentration *in vitro*?

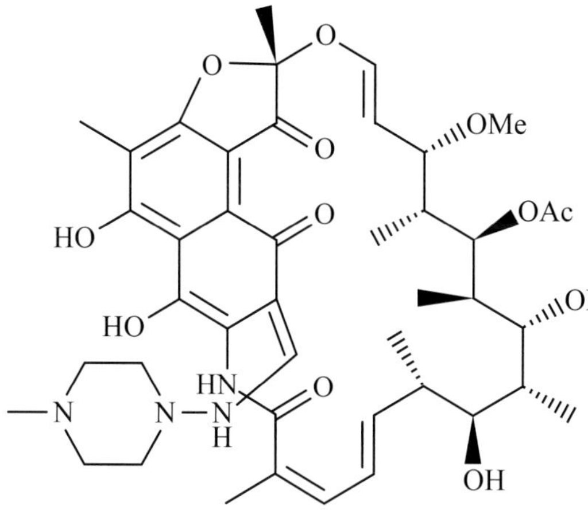

O O O O HO HO OMe OAc OH OH HN N N N H O

- **A.** Column chromatography
- **B.** NMR
- **C.** UV spectroscopy
- **D.** Mass spectrometry

Question 14

In a follow-up genetic experiment, scientists discover mutations in *sst1* and *lpr1* that mediate resistance to the innate immune system. How does this new information impact the authors' conclusions?

- **A.** It strengthens the authors' conclusion because missense mutations in *sst1* can be detected by LNA1-6.
- **B.** It strengthens the authors' conclusion because nonsense but not missense rifampin-resistant mutations may be found in *lpr1.*
- **C.** It weakens the authors' conclusion because missense rifampin-resistant mutations may be found in *sst1.*
- **D.** It weakens the authors' conclusion because LNA1-6 cannot detect mutations in *sst1.*

TEST 4B

Questions 15 through 18 do not refer to a passage and are independent of each other.

Question 15

A 20-cycle PCR amplification of a 67 bp region of the *APP* gene, a gene implicated in Alzheimer's progression, would produce how many amplified regions of interest?

- O **A.** 20
- O **B.** 40
- O **C.** 400
- O **D.** 1 million

Question 16

Generation of a nucleotide sequencing library to measure the levels of gene expression involves:

- O **A.** reverse transcription from single stranded RNA to double stranded DNA.
- O **B.** reverse transcription from double stranded RNA to double stranded DNA.
- O **C.** replication of single stranded RNA to double stranded RNA.
- O **D.** replication of single stranded DNA to double stranded DNA.

Question 17

Low concentrations of which molecule are LEAST likely to be detected by IR spectroscopy?

- O **A.** Br_2
- O **B.** HCl
- O **C.** H_2O
- O **D.** H_3PO_4

Question 18

UV spectroscopy is most likely to detect which of the following amino acids?

- O **A.** Leucine
- O **B.** Alanine
- O **C.** Aspartic acid
- O **D.** Tyrosine

Passage 4 (Questions 19-22)

Human trefoil factor 3 (hTFF3) is a small-molecule peptide with potential medicinal value. Its main pharmacological function is to alleviate gastrointestinal mucosal injuries and promote the repair of damaged mucosa. hTFF3 is a small polypeptide specifically secreted by the intestinal goblet cells. There is a special core structural domain within the 59-amino acid sequence, in which six cysteines are connected to each other by disulfides bridges in a specific order, forming a three-cyclic structure, whereby the whole peptide chain is bent and folded and shaped like a "clover." hTFF3 occupies an important niche in the self-protection and repair mechanisms of the intestinal mucosa. Regulation of hTFF3 is complex and precise, and, although a variety of substances are known to be involved in the regulation of hTFF3 expression, the basal regulation of hTFF3 transcription is still unclear.

An approximately 1,826-bp fragment upstream of hTFF3 was successfully amplified using genomic DNA extracted from whole blood, and its core promoter region was determined to be located from 2300 bp to 2280 bp through truncation analysis. Mutational analysis confirmed that the minimum sequence required for maintaining basic transcriptional activity was accurately positioned from 2300 bp to 2296 bp. Bioinformatic analysis confirmed that this area contained an Spl binding site. Researchers used Spl over-expression by DNA incorporation and siRNA knockdown of Spl, or targeted destruction mRNA using the complementarity of nucleic acids, to investigate the impact of Spl on the hTFF3 promoter and hTFF3 expression. The results are shown in Figures 1 and 2.

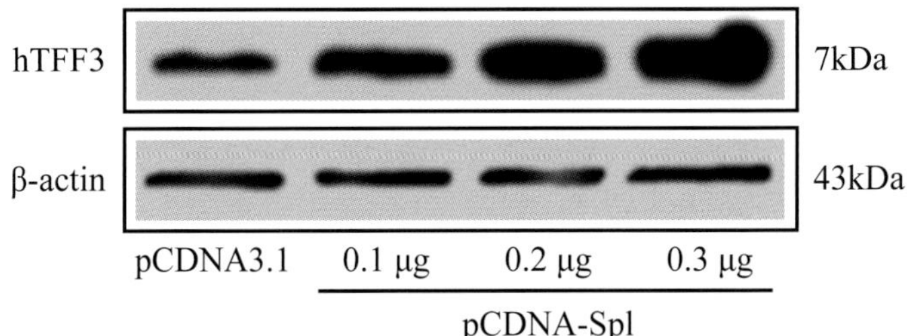

Figure 1 hTFF3 protein levels following transformation with Spl DNA

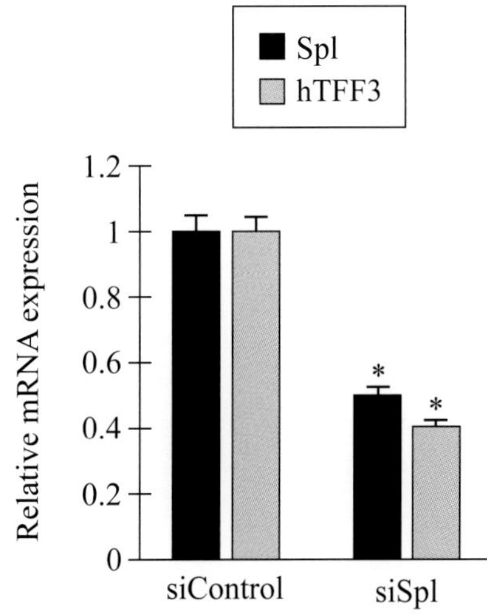

Figure 2 Expression of Spl and hTFF3 following siSpl knockdown

This passage was adapted from "Cloning and Characterization of the Human Trefoil Factor 3 Gene Promoter." Sun Y, Wang L, Zhou Y, Mao X, and Deng X. *PLoS ONE*. 2014. 9(4) doi:10.1371/journal.pone.0095562 for use under the terms of the Creative Commons CC BY 4.0 license (http://creativecommons.org/licenses/by/4.0/legalcode).

Question 19

What does Figure 1 show about relationship between Sp1 and hTFF3?

- **A.** Sp1 expression is inversely correlated with hTFF3 expression.
- **B.** Sp1 expression is directly correlated with hTFF3 expression.
- **C.** Sp1 changes hTFF3 expression in an unknown way.
- **D.** Sp1 expression is not related to hTFF3 expression.

Question 20

Results of Figure 2 are most likely obtained by which of the following techniques?

- **A.** Southern blot
- **B.** Northern blot
- **C.** Western blot
- **D.** Microarray

Question 21

Which of the following would show the direct relationship between Sp1 and hTFF3 expression?

- **A.** Sp1 increases expression of a protein known to induce hTFF3 expression.
- **B.** Sp1 increases expression of a protein known to inhibit hTFF3 expression.
- **C.** Sp1 is visualized binding to a protein that inhibits hTFF3 expression.
- **D.** Sp1 is visualized binding at the promoter of hTFF3.

Question 22

Which of the following is true of actin and hTFF3?

- **A.** Actin travels faster through a gel during gel electrophoresis due to its larger molecular weight.
- **B.** Actin travels faster through a gel during gel electrophoresis due to its smaller molecular weight.
- **C.** hTFF3 travels faster through a gel during gel electrophoresis due to its larger molecular weight.
- **D.** hTFF3 travels faster through a gel during gel electrophoresis due to its smaller molecular weight.

Passage 5 (Questions 23-27)

Gastric cancer is a common tumor of the digestive system with a mortality rate that ranks third in the world. Chemotherapy is one of major treatments for gastric cancer patients, but more than 50% of patients will progress to chemotherapy resistance. A recent study found that microRNAs (miRNAs) play an important role in gastric cancer chemotherapy drug resistance.

Lin28 is an RNA-binding protein that participates in maintaining stem cell-like cells in cancer. Lin28 promotes tumorigenesis by repressing tumor suppressor miRNAs, which are associated with drug resistance. MiR-107 regulates downstream genes that are involved in proliferation and the formation of blood vessels and is predicted to play a role in gastric cancer progression.

Experiment 1

In order to determine the expression of Lin28 and topoisomerase II (TOPOII), a target gene of MiR-107, a 20 μL reaction mixture containing 2 μL of cDNA template and 1 μL each of sense and anti-sense primers (Table 1) designed to amplify the full length gene was amplified as follows: 95°C for 10 min and 40 cycles of 95°C for 30 s, 60°C for 30 s, and 72°C for 40 s. After gel electrophoresis and blotting, results showed that Lin28 was overexpressed in gastric cancer cells, while topoisomerase II was underexpressed.

Table 1 Forward and reverse primer sequences used to amplify Lin28 and TOPOII

Lin28	Forward	5′-AGCGCAGATCAAAAGGAGACA-3′
	Reverse	5′-CCTCTCGAAAGTAGGTTGGCT-3′
TOPOII	Forward	5′-GCTGTGGATGACAACCTCCT-3′
	Reverse	5′-GCTGTGGATGACAACCTCCT-3′

Experiment 2

MKN45 gastric cancer cells were transfected with either an empty plasmid vector or a vector containing Lin28. Of the transfected cells, half of the cells were lysed after 24 hours, which is before the doubling time for MKN45 cells. Cell lysates were separated by electrophoresis and transferred to a nitrocellulose membrane. Western blots were probed with antibodies against Lin28 and GAPDH (Figure 1).

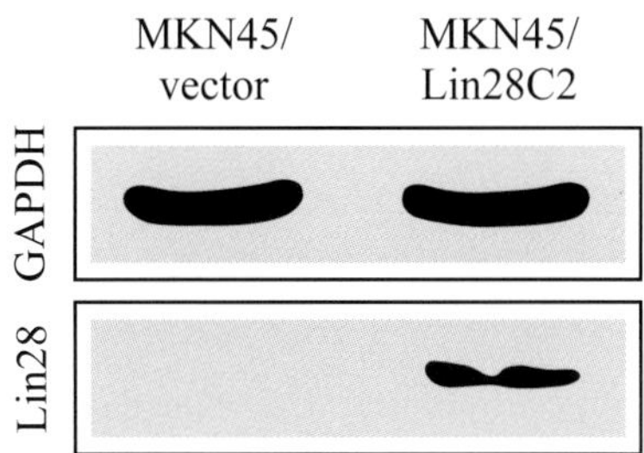

Figure 1 Western blot of GAPDH and Lin28 levels in transfected MKN45 cells

TEST 4B

The survival of the other half of the transfected cells was determined 24 hours after transfection with increasing doses of paclitaxel, a chemotherapeutic that interferes with the breakdown of microtubules during cell division. The results are shown in Figure 2.

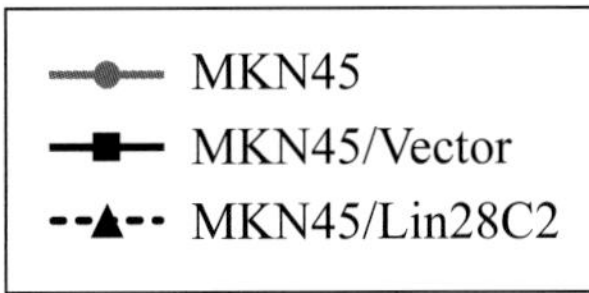

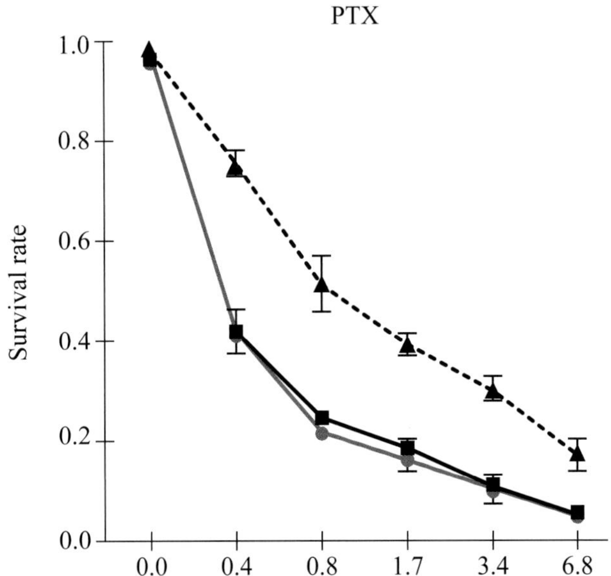

Figure 2 Effect of Lin28 on chemotherapeutic drug resistance in gastric cancer

This passage was adapted from "Overexpression of Lin28 Decreases the Chemosensitivity of Gastric Cancer Cells to Oxaliplatin, Paclitaxel, Doxorubicin, and Fluorouracil in Part via microRNA-107." Teng R, Hu Y, Zhou J, Seifer B, Chen Y, et al. *PLoS ONE.* 2015. 10(12) doi:10.1371/journal.pone.0143716 for use under the terms of the Creative Commons CC BY 4.0 license (http://creativecommons.org/licenses/by/4.0/legalcode).

Question 23

Based on the data presented in the passage, which statement best describes Lin28?

- **A.** Cancer-promoting and regulates GAPDH
- **B.** Cancer-promoting and does not regulate GAPDH
- **C.** Cancer-suppressing and regulates GAPDH
- **D.** Cancer-suppressing and does not regulate GAPDH

Question 24

Which technique would best determine the levels of MiR-107 in MKN45 cells?

- **A.** Northern blot
- **B.** Southern blot
- **C.** Western blot
- **D.** DNA microarray

Question 25

Based on the passage, the level of apoptosis in MKN45 gastric cancer cells is inversely correlated with:

- **A.** the integration of the transfected DNA plasmid into the genomic DNA of MKN45 cells.
- **B.** the integration of the transfected RNA plasmid into the genomic DNA of MKN45 cells.
- **C.** the expression of the transfected DNA plasmid in MKN45 cells.
- **D.** the expression of the transfected RNA plasmid in MKN45 cells.

Question 26

DNA sequencing of the PCR products from Experiment 1 is LEAST likely to reveal:

- **A.** synonymous mutations in exon one of Lin28.
- **B.** a nonsynonymous mutation in intron five of TOPOII.
- **C.** a frameshift mutation in the poly-A tail of Lin28.
- **D.** an insertion or deletion in the promoter of TOPOII.

Question 27

The initial 95°C step in the PCR protocol serves to:

- **A.** denature the two DNA strands.
- **B.** denature the PCR primers from their complementary sequence on the genomic DNA.
- **C.** allow the PCR primers to bind their complementary sequence on the genomic DNA.
- **D.** allow DNA polymerase to extend and replicate the DNA region of interest.

Questions 28 through 31 do not refer to a passage and are independent of each other.

Question 28

Which of the following would make distillation more effective?

I. Distilling two compounds with a larger difference in boiling point

II. Distilling two compounds with a smaller difference in boiling point

III. Using a liquid and a solid

- O **A.** I only
- O **B.** II only
- O **C.** II and III
- O **D.** I and III

Question 29

Crystallization is a commonly used separation technique. Which of the following is true about crystallization?

- O **A.** It is based on pure substances crystallizing more efficiently, and is exothermic for most salts.
- O **B.** It is based on pure substances crystallizing more efficiently, and is endothermic for most salts.
- O **C.** It is based on impure substances crystallizing more efficiently, and is exothermic for most salts.
- O **D.** It is based on impure substances crystallizing more efficiently, and is endothermic for most salts.

Question 30

A cooling step follows the denaturation of DNA during PCR. Which step directly follows the cooling step?

- O **A.** Primer hybridization
- O **B.** Primer detaching
- O **C.** Polymerase activation
- O **D.** Polymerase deactivation

Question 31

During cationic exchange chromatography, a negatively charged solute in a solution would:

- O **A.** be fully retained by the stationary phase.
- O **B.** flow through the column.
- O **C.** be partially retained by the stationary phase.
- O **D.** move towards the top of the column.

Passage 6 (Questions 32-35)

Resveratrol consists of two phenolic rings linked by a double bond and occurs naturally in grape skins, peanuts, and some berries. Resveratrol appears to have promising biological effects in glioblastoma, the most common and deadly adult brain cancer. Resveratrol may act as an anti-inflammatory and/or antioxidant agent through activation of Sirt1, the NAD^+-dependent protein deacetylase, which regulates a wide variety of signaling pathways.

In humans, orally ingested resveratrol is absorbed by diffusion and rapidly eliminated due to its low solubility in blood. Several approaches have been adopted to increase the maximal plasma resveratrol concentration, though no viable current strategy exists.

Scientists hypothesized that high-density lipoproteins (HDL) containing apolipoprotein E3 (apoE3) and phospholipids would solubilize resveratrol, while still allowing it to be delivered to target cells. The lipid bilayer shields hydrophobic compounds, while apoE3 acts as a ligand to bind cell surface localized LDL receptors (LDLr) in glioblastoma cells. In experiment 1, HDL and HDL with resveratrol were exposed to UV-visible spectroscopy in order to determine how efficiently resveratrol integrated into HDL molecules (Figure 1). A greater absorbance indicates greater resveratrol incorporation into HDL.

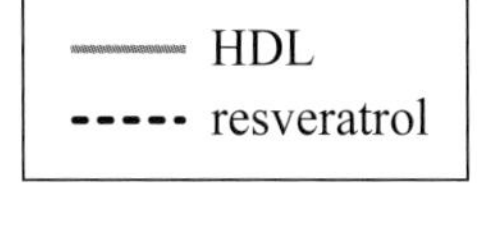

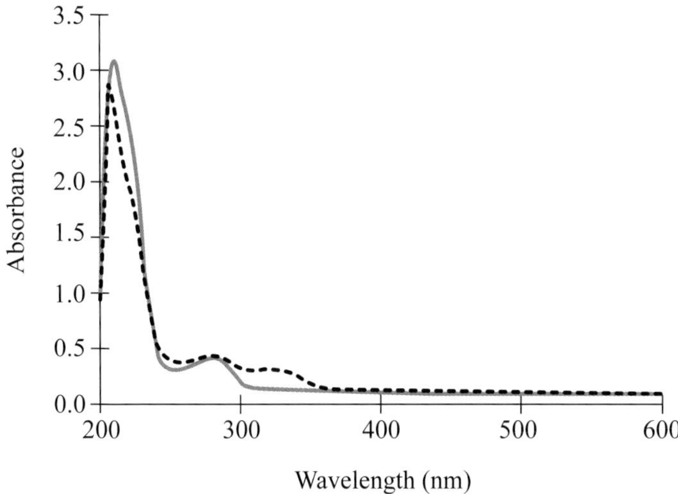

Figure 1 Absorbance spectra of HDL and HDL with resveratrol

To determine if the presence of resveratrol in HDL (HDL/res) hinders the LDLr binding ability of apoE3, a western blot was performed. An antibody against apoE3 was blotted against apoE3 alone (Lane 1), HDL alone (Lane 2), or HDL/res with LDLr (Lane 3). The results are shown in Figure 2.

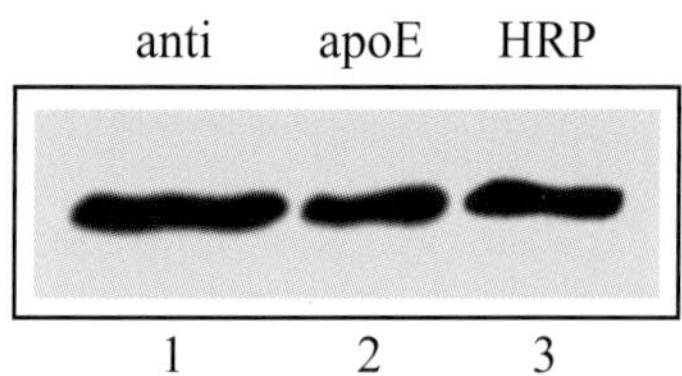

Figure 2 Effect of resveratrol on LDLr binding activity of apoE3

The scientists concluded that HDL serves as an effective vehicle to transport resveratrol across the cellular membrane to endocytic sites via an LDLr mediated endocytosis pathway.

Question 32

In vitro reduction in Sirt1 activity is best induced by:

- **A.** supplementing cell media with malonyl-CoA, the starting molecule for fatty acid synthesis.
- **B.** moving cells to a low oxygen incubator.
- **C.** removing glucose from the cell media.
- **D.** supplementing cell media with lactate.

Question 33

What is the best interpretation of the western blot show in Figure 2?

- **A.** ApoE3 levels are highest in HDL alone.
- **B.** ApoE3 levels are highest in HDL/res bound to LDLr.
- **C.** ApoE3 levels are comparable between HDL alone and HDL/res bound to LDLr.
- **D.** No interpretation of apoE3 levels can be made.

Question 34

HPLC column chromatography was used to separate HDL and HDL/res after attempted incorporation of resveratrol into HDL. Based on the figure below, what was the most likely combination of mobile and stationary phases?

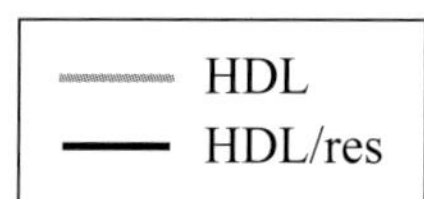

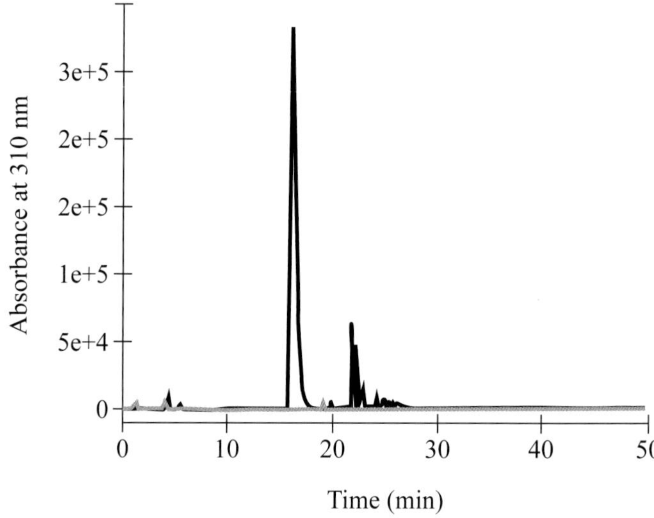

- **A.** Decane as the stationary phase and acetonitrile as the mobile phase
- **B.** Nonane as the stationary phase and CCl_4 as the mobile phase
- **C.** Butane as the stationary phase and nonane as the mobile phase
- **D.** Heptanol as the stationary phase and CCl_4 as the mobile phase

Question 35

The experimental protocol used in Figure 2 relies on the production of protein products from which cell type?

- **A.** $CD4^+$ T cells
- **B.** $CD8^+$ T cells
- **C.** Plasma cells
- **D.** Natural killer cells

Next ▶

Passage 7 (Questions 36-39)

Prostate cancer is the most prevalent cancer in the male population of Western countries. Prostate cancer is highly heterogeneous with variable clinical outcomes: indolent disease tends not to progress even over many years while aggressive disease often progresses quickly to produce metastases which inevitably result in premature death. Hence, there is an urgent need for better diagnostic and prognostic tests for prostate cancer.

Evolving evidence points to the input of highly versatile metabolic pathways in fueling carcinogenesis. Detailed analysis of the tumor-associated metabolome may reveal novel biomarkers. There is an urgent need for better diagnostic and prognostic tests for prostate cancer. Urine has some advantages for metabolomics studies since it has a high abundance of metabolites, low content of protein, is collected non-invasively, and requires minimal sample preparation prior to analysis. The introduction of Hydrophilic Interaction Liquid Chromatography (HILIC), in which the retention mechanism utilizes highly nonpolar carbon chains, offers a suitable separation platform for the many metabolites in urine. In addition, HILIC provides a distinct advantage over traditional gas chromatography.

An HILIC column with a mobile phase at a pH of 9.2 has previously been shown to clearly separate the isomers of sarcosine, a compound suggested to serve as a marker of prostate cancer. The creatinine retention time was used as a normalization method by scaling the peak area of each elutant to that of the creatinine concentration of each sample. Results are shown in Table 1.

Table 1 Potential urine biomarkers of prostate cancer as analyzed by HILIC

Retention time (s)	Name	Formula	P-value
8.24	N-hydroxy-2-acetamido-fluorene	$C_{15}H_{13}NO_2$	0.0003
6.74	indolylacryloylglycine	$C_{13}H_{12}N_2O_3$	0.0007
11.66	Ureidoisobutyric acid	$C_5H_{10}N_2O_3$	0.0014
5.01	acetylvanilalinine	$C_{12}H_{15}NO_5$	0.0022
16.48	Caffeic acid sulfate	$C_9H_8O_7S$	0.0026
11.66	Ureidoisobutyric acid	$C_5H_{10}N_2O_3$	0.0030
6.40	Thr-Trp-Pro	$C_{20}H_{26}N_4O_5$	0.0041
15.52	2-oxoglutarate	$C_5H_6O_5$	0.0067
13.21	Dihydro ferulic acid sulphate	$C_{10}H_{12}SO_7$	0.0332
7.77	2,3-diaminosalicylic acid	$C_7H_8N_2O_3$	0.0462

Question 36

Which compound would most likely be found in high abundance as the stationary phase of an HILIC column?

- O **A.** $CH_3(CH_2)_{19}CO_2H$
- O **B.** $CH_3(CH_2)_{19}CH_3$
- O **C.** $CH_3(CH_2)_{14}F$
- O **D.** $CH_3(CH_2)_9CH_3$

Question 37

Scientists further collected 50 urine specimens, 30 from prostate cancer patients and 20 from control patients. Using gas chromatography with a heated argon gas carrier, they were unable to reproduce the data presented in Table 1. Which of the following statements best explains this discrepancy?

- O **A.** Heated krypton gas should have been used instead of heated argon gas.
- O **B.** The scientists did not collect a sufficient number of samples to draw significant conclusions.
- O **C.** Gas chromatography is necessarily limited to volatile compounds.
- O **D.** Gas chromatography is unable to separate polar compounds.

Question 38

Before loading the patient samples into the HILIC column, scientists first eliminated urea, which can confound column retention times. Which of the following molecules was used to extract urea?

- O **A.** $C_6H_8O_7$
- O **B.** HCl
- O **C.** $NaHCO_3$
- O **D.** NaOH

Question 39

According to the passage, how would the following compounds rank in order of polarity, from the most nonpolar to most polar?

I. Acetylvanilalinine
II. Indolylacryloglycine
III. 2-oxoglutarate

- O **A.** I < II < III
- O **B.** II < I < III
- O **C.** III < II < I
- O **D.** III < I < II

TEST 4B

Passage 8 (Questions 40-43)

Paleomicrobiology permits the identification of causative agents of past infectious diseases and the temporal and geographical distribution of infected groups. This discipline also traces the genetic evolution of microorganisms. In 1998 *Yersinia pestis* DNA was first identified in the dental pulp from teeth extracted from victims of the plague. The first confirmation of *Y. pestis* as the agent responsible for the plague during the early medieval pandemic used a technique called suicide PCR, detecting *Y. pestis* DNA in dental pulp of the teeth of children and two adults from the 14th century Black Death pandemic.

Molecular biology techniques are commonly used to detect microorganismal DNA, but the risk of contamination, chemical modification and fragmentation of DNA and the presence of PCR inhibitors in ancient samples have led researchers to explore alternative methods based on antigenic protein detection, including ELISA, a protein detection method. However, ELISA is unsuitable for ancient samples due to a lack of sensitivity and the availability of only small quantities of samples.

To increase the sensitivity of protein detection, researchers used immuno-PCR (iPCR) to detect *Y. pestis* proteins. Technically, the antigens are recognized by a detection antibody that is conjugated to a linker molecule that attaches the antibody-antigen complex to a DNA tag. This DNA tag is subsequently amplified by PCR. Results comparing the sensitivity of PCR, ELISA, and iPCR in detecting *Y. pestis* are shown below (Figure 1).

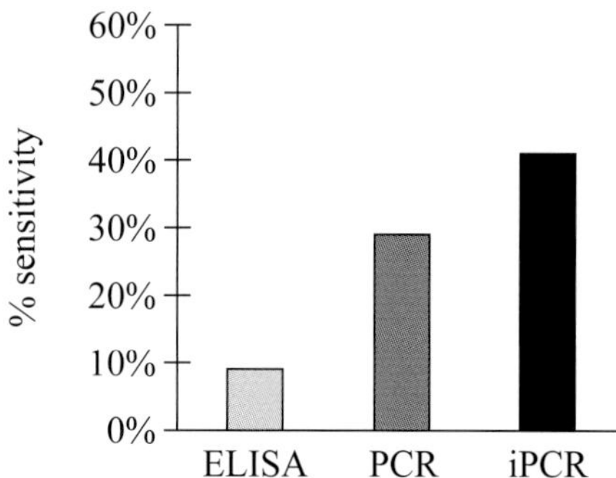

Figure 1 Sensitivity of each method of *Y. pestis* identification

Question 40

If a researcher isolates 10 μg of DNA from a dental pulp sample, and 1,280 μg are required for a particular test, how many PCR cycles must be run?

- **A.** 4
- **B.** 5
- **C.** 6
- **D.** 7

Question 41

Which stage of iPCR most likely causes the reduced need for a large quantity of intact sample relative to other tests?

- **A.** Antibody-antigen interaction
- **B.** Isolation of dental pulp
- **C.** PCR amplification
- **D.** ELISA

Question 42

When analyzing ancient samples, false positives are a significant concern. Which of the following would be most helpful in determining the reliability of a test in terms of its ability to parse out false positives?

- **A.** Using modern *Y. pestis*-free dental pulp samples as positive controls
- **B.** Using modern *Y. pestis* -free dental pulp samples as negative controls
- **C.** Using ancient *Y. pestis* -free dental pulp samples as positive controls
- **D.** Using ancient *Y. pestis* -free dental pulp samples as negative controls

Question 43

Which of the following statements is true regarding the use of DNA and RNA in analyzing ancient samples?

- **A.** DNA is more effective because primers bind more effectively to it.
- **B.** RNA is more effective because primers bind more effectively to it.
- **C.** DNA is more effective because it is more resilient.
- **D.** RNA is more effective because it is more resilient.

Questions 44 through 47 do not refer to a passage and are independent of each other.

Question 44

What is the role of rinsing proteins in a detergent before running them through a gel in electrophoresis?

I. To make the shape of the proteins consistent

II. To make the charge of the protein proportional to length

III. To reduce all proteins to 100 amino acids

O **A.** I only

O **B.** II only

O **C.** I and II

O **D.** II and III

Question 45

All of the following methods can be used to separate enantiomers from a racemic mixture EXCEPT:

O **A.** crystallization.

O **B.** stereospecific enzymes.

O **C.** conversion into diastereomers.

O **D.** size exclusion chromatography.

Question 46

Radioactive tyrosine has been proposed as a way to treat cancer cells that have increased uptake of amino acids to support growth. Synthesis of radioactive iodine-labeled tyrosine could occur by:

O **A.** a carbanion attack on a one carbon methylhalide.

O **B.** a carbocation attack on a one carbon methylhalide.

O **C.** a carbanion attack on a two carbon benzylhydroxyhalide.

O **D.** a carbocation attack on a two carbon benzylhydroxyhalide.

Question 47

Which technique would most specifically allow a researcher to control gene expression in an organism?

O **A.** Total knockout

O **B.** Conditional knockout

O **C.** Treatment with a DNA polymerase inhibitor

O **D.** RNA interference (RNAi)

Passage 9 (Questions 48-52)

Diabetes Mellitus (DM) is a complex metabolic disorder characterized by persistent hyperglycemia, which may cause acute or chronic complications, including blindness, heart disease, and stroke. Type 2 diabetes (T2D) results from the body's ineffective use of insulin and can be treated by some medications.

Ursolic acid (UA) is ubiquitous in traditional medicinal herbs. UA and its analogues exhibit a wide range of biological activities, including anti-diabetic activity. Scientists sought to better understand how derivatives of UA could serve as medications for diabetes. A series of new hydrolyzation analogues were synthesized and their bioactivities against α-glucosidase were evaluated *in vitro*. In a follow-up experiment, computer modeling called Molecular Docking was used to predict the binding of UA analogues in the active site of α-glucosidase to demonstrate that the hydrophilic moieties can interact with the hydrophobic group of the catalytic pocket, as well as form hydrogen bonds with catalytic amino acids.

All the target analogues, including compound 11 (Figure 1), were purified by column chromatography with petroleum ether/ethyl acetate and/or chloroform/methanol as the eluent. Their structures were confirmed by ^{1}H NMR, ^{13}C NMR, and electrospray ionization mass spectrometry (ESI-MS). The results indicated that compound 11 formed hydrogen bonds with the residues of SER222, GLU415, ASP329, and ARG415 of the protein. The researchers predicted that these intermolecular interactions between compound 11 and α-glucosidase might play an important role in enhancing its inhibitory activity by improving binding affinity.

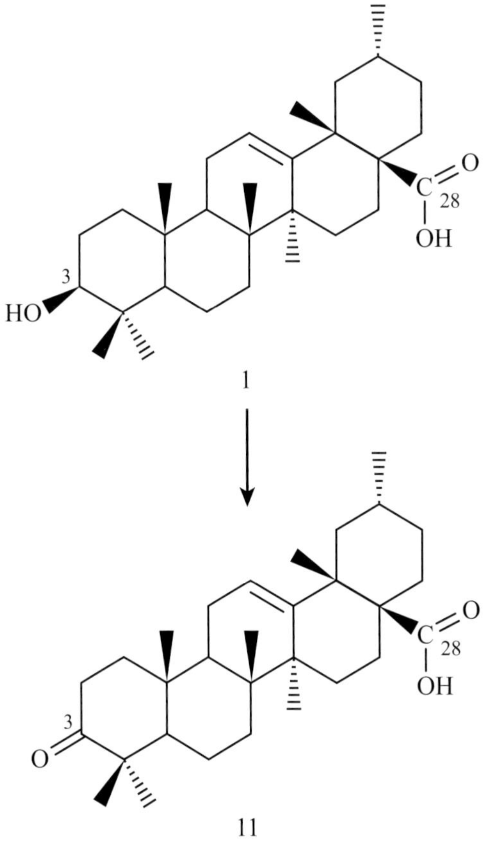

3
HO
C
O
28
OH
1

3
O
C
O
28
OH
11

Figure 1 Synthesis of compound 11 from ursolic acid

Question 48

Structures resembling compound 11 are LEAST likely to contribute to:

- **A.** regulating transcription of rRNA genes.
- **B.** decreasing the concentration of cytosolic receptors.
- **C.** translocation of cytosolic proteins to the nucleus.
- **D.** binding of cell surface receptors.

Question 49

Binding of acarbose to α-glucosidase causes a tryptophan ring to flip from the hydrophobic interior of the protein to the exterior. Binding of acarbose would best be monitored by:

- **A.** UV spectroscopy.
- **B.** mass spectrometry.
- **C.** Bradford assay.
- **D.** molecular docking.

Question 50

Column chromatography using *n*-decane was used to purify the synthesized compounds. Which mobile phase would best allow for separation of the compounds, each of which contains a unique substitution at carbon 3 on compound 1?

- **A.** Methanol
- **B.** Cyclohexane
- **C.** *N*-Nonane
- **D.** CCl_4

Question 51

The peak at 78 ppm in the ^{13}C NMR below represents which carbon in compound 11?

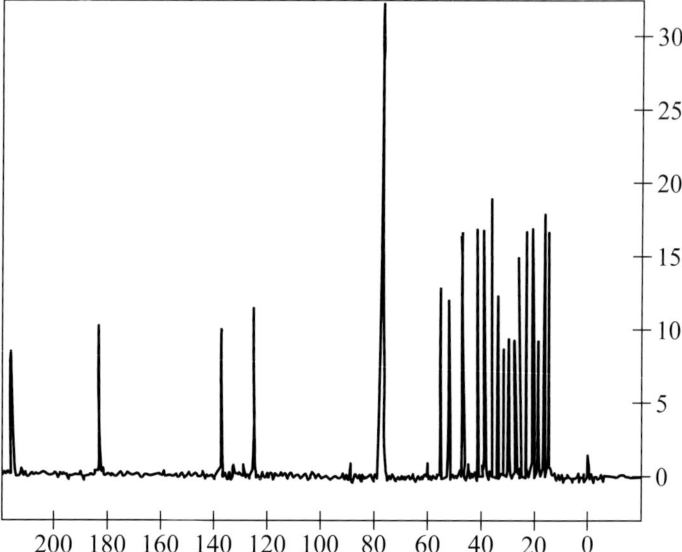

- **A.** $-CH_2-$
- **B.** $-CH_3$
- **C.** $-CH(R)-$
- **D.** $-CH_3(R)$

Question 52

The peaks on the mass spectrogram shown below represent the organic fragments of compound 11 separated by:

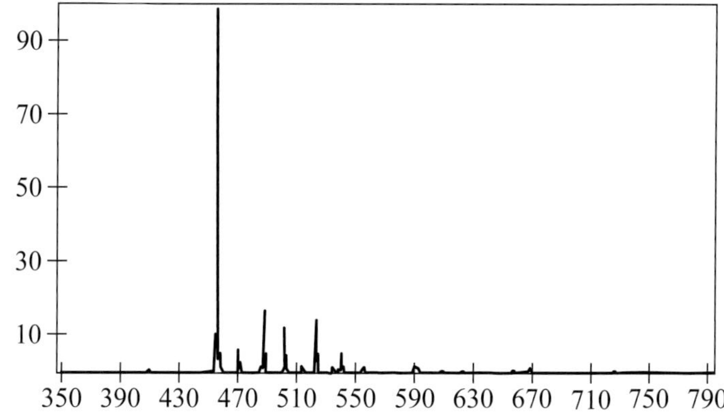

- **A.** size.
- **B.** mass and charge.
- **C.** polarity.
- **D.** boiling point.

TEST 4B

Passage 10 (Questions 53-56)

Infections due to antibiotic-resistant (AbR) enterobacteria are a worldwide cause of morbidity and mortality. As AbR genes disseminate mostly by conjugation, new strategies to control AbR dissemination before infection by targeting AbR plasmid conjugation are being developed. Previously, only unsaturated fatty acids (uFAs) were considered effective compounds to inhibit plasmid conjugation in enterobacteria. Among previously discovered conjugation inhibitors (COINs), uFAs, such as oleic and linoleic acids, have double bonds susceptible to oxidation. Although the triple-bonded fatty acids 2-hexadecynoic acid (2-HDA) and 2-octadecynoic acid (2-ODA) are promising COINs, they have toxicity issues that must be overcome.

COIN application in clinical settings demands non-toxic, chemically and biologically stable molecules. In order to screen for novel COINs, scientists used a collection of clinically representative conjugative plasmids found in *Enterobacteriaceae*, treated the bacteria with various compounds, and measured the conjugation frequency (CF). The results are shown in Figure 1. Three tanzawaic acids (TZAs), TZA-A, TZA-B, and TZA-E, were discovered as natural COINs with reduced toxicity compared to synthetic ones. TZAs are carboxylic acids containing two aromatic rings at the end of an unsaturated aliphatic chain (Figure 2). The scientists concluded that additional modifications of TZA-B may further uncover drugs to prevent the spread of antibiotic resistance.

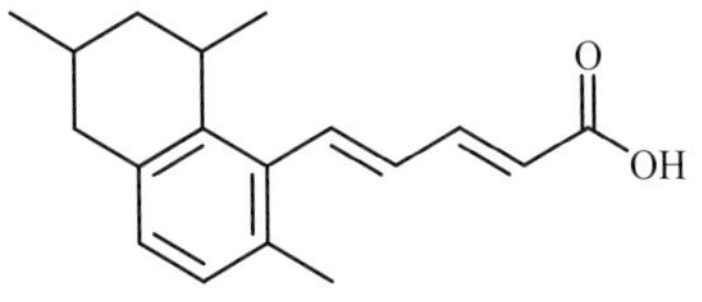

TZA-A

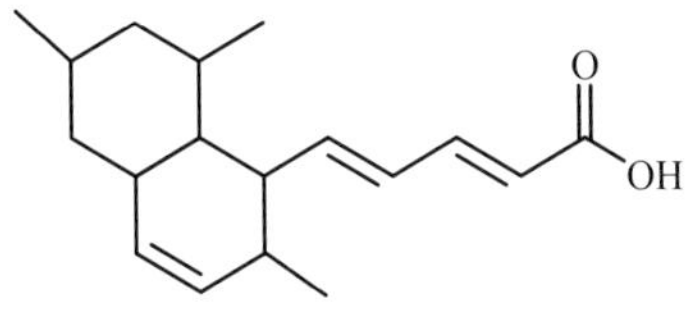

TZA-B

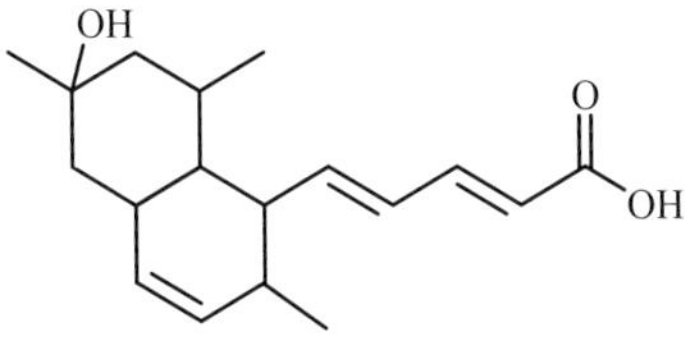

TZA-E

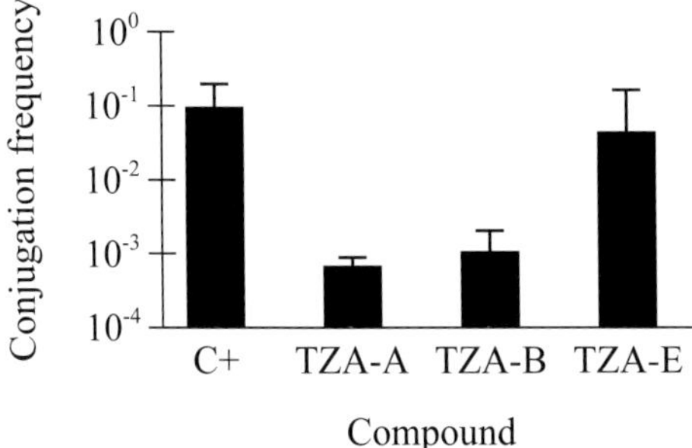

Figure 1 Structure and activity of TZAs A, B, and E

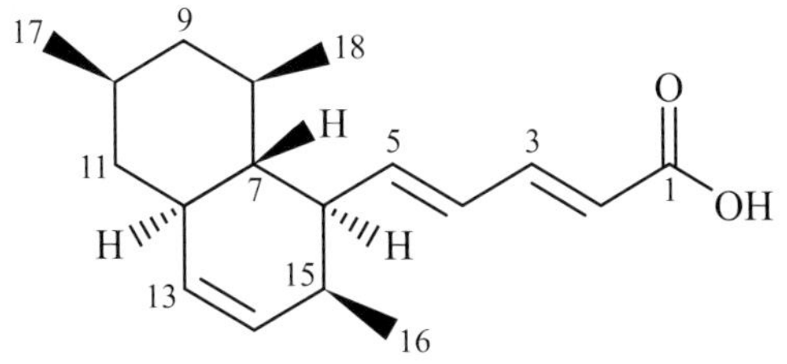

Figure 2 Structural elucidation of TZA-B

This passage was adapted from "Tanzawaic Acids, a Chemically Novel Set of Bacterial Conjugation Inhibitors." Getino M, Fernandez-Lopez R, Palencia-Gandara C, Campos-Gomez J, Sanchez-Lopez J, et al. *PLoS ONE.* 2016. 11(1) doi:10.1371/journal.pone.0148098 for use under the terms of the Creative Commons CC BY 4.0 license (http://creativecommons.org/licenses/by/4.0/legalcode).

Question 53

^{1}H-NMR would most likely illustrate that the hydrogen on carbon 12 in TZA-B is:

- **A.** split into two peaks of equal heights.
- **B.** split into five peaks of symmetric heights.
- **C.** split into six peaks of symmetric heights.
- **D.** not split into multiple peaks.

Question 54

TZA-A may inhibit assembly of membrane phospholipids in bacteria. This process can be modeled in micelles. Which technique would best determine the most effective TZA-A concentration for preventing micelle formation?

- **A.** UV spectroscopy
- **B.** IR spectroscopy
- **C.** ^{13}C NMR
- **D.** Mass spectrometry

Question 55

Which of the following interactions is most crucial for TZA-B efficacy?

- **A.** Van der Waals
- **B.** Electrostatic
- **C.** Dipole-dipole
- **D.** Covalent

TEST 4B

Question 56

The following measurements are made by IR spectroscopy for compound TZA-B.

Bond	Wavenumber (cm^{-1})
C7 to C12	1258
C8 to C9	1200

Which of the following measurements best corresponds to compound TZA-A?

○ **A.**

Bond	Wavenumber (cm^{-1})
C7 to C12	1675
C8 to C9	1900

○ **B.**

Bond	Wavenumber (cm^{-1})
C7 to C12	1681
C8 to C9	1210

○ **C.**

Bond	Wavenumber (cm^{-1})
C7 to C12	620
C8 to C9	1208

○ **D.**

Bond	Wavenumber (cm^{-1})
C7 to C12	1109
C8 to C9	2106

Questions 57 through 59 do not refer to a passage and are independent of each other.

Question 57

A strand of DNA has 5 restriction sites for a particular restriction enzyme. How many fragments are formed when it is exposed to the restriction enzyme?

○ **A.** 5 strands

○ **B.** 6 strands

○ **C.** 10 strands

○ **D.** 4 strands

Question 58

Mass spectrometry is a technique used to characterize molecules from various samples. Which of the following is true of mass spectrometry?

I. It measures the mass to charge ratio of pieces of the parent molecule.

II. The sample is bombarded by neutrons.

III. It can be used to determine molecular mass.

○ **A.** I only

○ **B.** III only

○ **C.** I and III

○ **D.** I, II, and III

Question 59

Which of the following occurs at the highest temperature in atmospheric pressure conditions?

○ **A.** Boiling of water

○ **B.** Denaturing of DNA

○ **C.** Primer annealing

○ **D.** Activation of DNA polymerase

STOP. If you finish before time is called, check your work. You may go back to any question in this test.

ANSWERS & EXPLANATIONS for Test 4B can be found on p. 290.

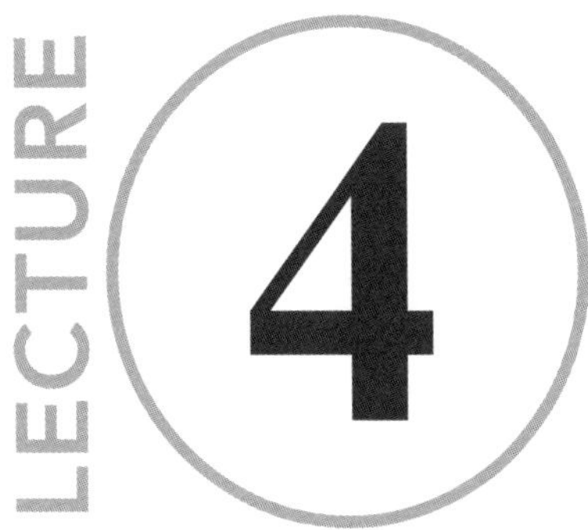

Laboratory Techniques

TEST 4C

Time: 50 minutes
Questions 1–31

DIRECTIONS: Most questions in the Biological and Biochemical Foundations of Living Systems test section are grouped with a descriptive passage. Select the best answer to each question using background knowledge and the given passage. A portion of this test section is comprised of discrete questions, which are independent of any passage and one another. Select the best answer for each discrete question. Indicate your selection by blackening the corresponding oval on your answer document. If you are unsure of the answer, rule out incorrect choices and select from the remaining options. You may access a periodic table found on the last page of this book at any point during this test section.

Passage 1 (Questions 1-5)

Generation of DNA sequencing libraries by ligation of patient DNA into plasmids is used to test for mutations in genes that give rise to a number of diseases, including neurodegenerative diseases. By flanking a PCR (polymerase chain reaction) primer with the recognition sites of the appropriate restriction Type IIP endonucleases (ENase), a DNA fragment taken from a patient can be cloned to virtually any cloning site that is used to linearize the acceptor sequencing vector. The only frequently occurring obstacle arises when the patient DNA fragment to be cloned contains the recognition site(s) of the Type IIP enzyme(s) to be used for cloning.

Physician-scientists interested in bypassing this problem sought to use a Body Double (BD) for the particular enzyme: a Type IIS ENase. Type IIP enzymes generate identical, palindrome overhangs. In contrast, Type IIS enzymes are less frequently employed because they generate overhangs with arbitrary sequences that are not complementary, and, thus, are not suitable for joining.

To explore whether Type IIS ENases could replace Type IIP restriction enzymes, scientists performed cloning reactions involving NcoI that recognizes a CCATGG motif. The cloning site of the pTXB3 acceptor sequencing vector contains an NcoI site that allows seamless incorporation of a patient's DNA fragment immediately following the first ATG triplet. Unfortunately, many of the DNA fragments scientists planned to clone to this vector contain NcoI sites, including the cDNA of *APP*, a protein implicated in the pathogenesis of Alzheimer's disease, and its mutant variants. Thus, they used BsmBI as a Body Double of NcoI to digest the PCR fragments and create a DNA sequencing library (Figure 1).

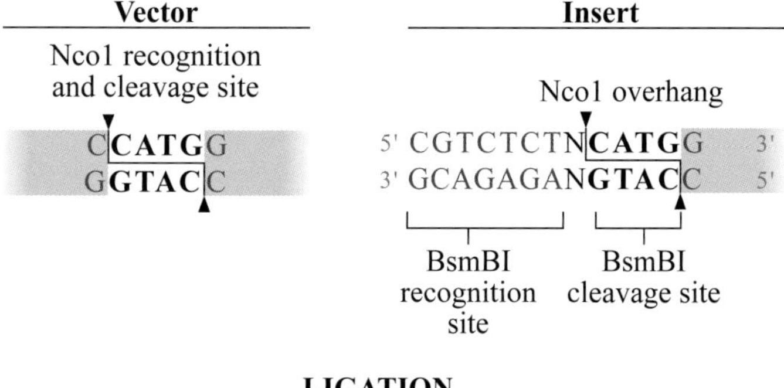

LIGATION

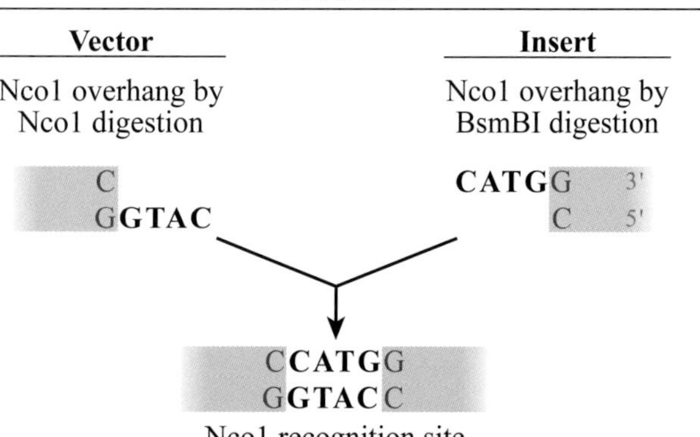

Figure 1 Ligation of NcoI overhangs generated by NcoI and its Body Double BsmBI allows for the formation of a DNA sequencing library

Question 1

Administration of 5-AZA, a DNA demethylating agent, to bacteria during the cloning process with endogenous restriction enzymes would most likely result in:

- **A.** fragmentation of bacterial genomic DNA.
- **B.** inhibition of the endogenous restriction enzymes.
- **C.** prevention of cleavage of the exogenous DNA strand to be ligated into the acceptor vector.
- **D.** inhibition of bacteria DNA polymerase.

Question 2

Which of the following could be an additional use of Body Doubles in the cloning process?

- **A.** Removal of an unwanted cleavage site in the product vector after ligation
- **B.** Creation of additional palindromic ends
- **C.** Repairing the phosphodiester backbone of cleaved DNA
- **D.** Digestion of bacterial genomic DNA

Question 3

Body Doubles useful in preparing DNA sequencing libraries readily accommodate a 18 bp PCR primer. Successful amplification of target sequences therefore occurs when the distance between the recognition and cutting sites of an endonuclease is:

- **A.** 9 bp.
- **B.** 19 bp.
- **C.** 36 bp.
- **D.** 50 bp.

Question 4

According to information contained in the passage, which of the following statements best describes why Type IIP enzymes could not be used to generate a DNA sequencing library?

- O **A.** The enzyme would cleave bacterial genomic DNA.
- O **B.** The enzyme would create non-palindromic sticky ends.
- O **C.** The enzyme would not cleave the acceptor sequencing vector.
- O **D.** The enzyme would cleave the sequence the scientists were interested in ligating into the plasmid.

Question 5

Which of the following criteria must be fulfilled for a Type IIS enzyme to qualify as a Body Double?

I. The Type IIS ENase needs to cut in a predictable manner.

II. Cutting needs to always occur precisely at a given distance from the recognition site.

III. The Type IIS ENase needs to generate protruding ends that can be efficiently religated.

IV. The protruding ends need to be the same length as those of a Type IIP ENase.

- O **A.** I
- O **B.** I and II
- O **C.** II and IV
- O **D.** I, II, III, and IV

Passage 2 (Questions 6-9)

Irinotecan (CPT-11), as shown in Figure 1, is a semisynthetic analogue of the natural alkaloid camptothecin (CPT). It is a pro-drug topoisomerase I inhibitor and it is activated by the enzyme carboxylesterase to 7-ethyl-10-hydroxycamptothecin (SN-38), as shown in Figure 2.

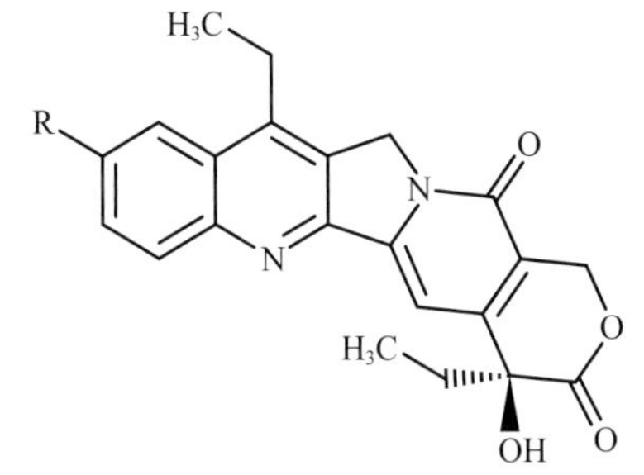

Compound	R
CPT-11	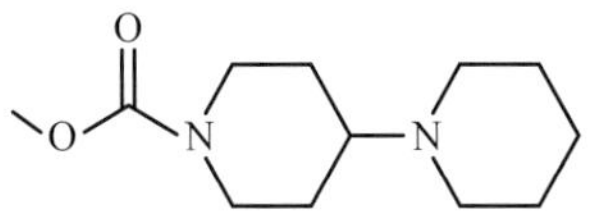
SN-38	–OH
SN-38G	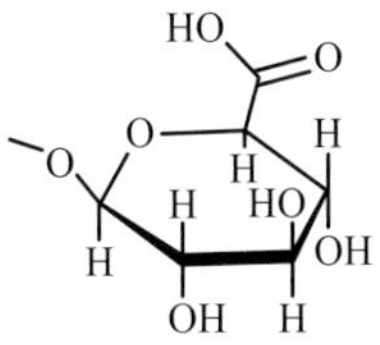
APC	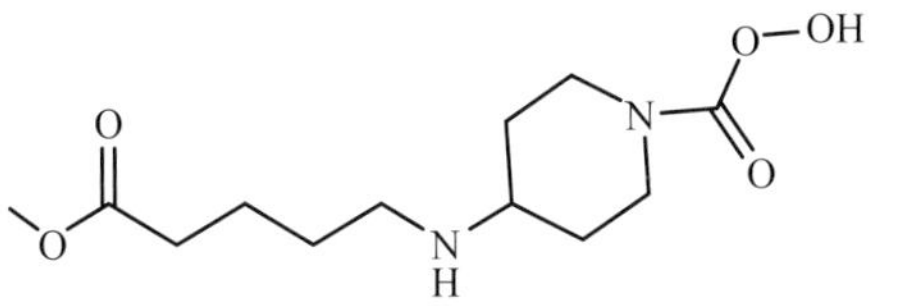
NPC	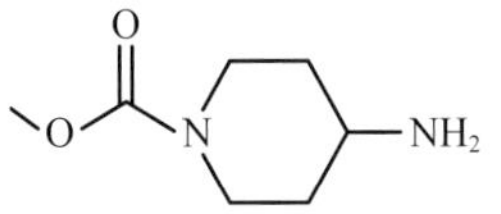

Figure 1 Structure of CPT-11 and its metabolites

TEST 4C

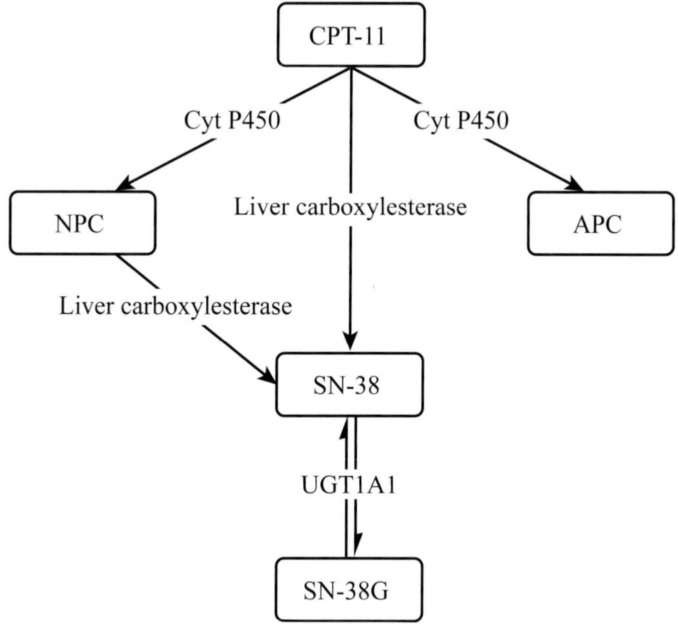

Figure 2 Metabolism of CTP-11 to its metabolites by the liver cytochrome P450 and carboxylesterase enzymes

Compared with the parent drug, SN-38 is 100 to 1000-times more cytotoxic. Recent important advances in the field of pharmacogenetics deserve the inclusion of patient genetic profiling in clinical drug development and in the optimization of antineoplastic chemotherapy. The genetic polymorphisms involved in CPT-11 pharmacokinetics (PK) are considered to be reliable predictors of clinical outcome, both for toxicity and efficacy. In particular, uridine diphosphate glucuronosyltransferase (UGT1A1) is involved in the detoxification process of SN-38 by the formation of SN-38 glucuronide (SN-38G). A polymorphism in the UGT1A1 gene (UGT1A1028/028) has been associated with reduced formation of SN-38G compared with wild-type UGT1A101, leading to variability in PK of SN-38, and in the toxicity profile of irinotecan. To solve the inter-individual variability in PK of irinotecan, Therapeutic Drug Monitoring (TDM) of the parental drug and its metabolites is required.

Scientists developed a combined column chromatography/mass spectrometry method to quantify the levels of each metabolite in blood plasma. After removing HCO_3^- from the blood plasma by separation and extraction, scientists ran the extracted layer on a hydrophobic chromatography column with a 0.1% CH_3COOH acetonitrile/water mobile phase. Each eluted peak was then accelerated in a uniform electric field and the resulting fragments analyzed and quantitated against a known standard.

This passage is adapted from "Development and Validation of a High-Performance Liquid Chromatography-Tandem Mass Spectrometry Method for the Simultaneous Determination of Irinotecan and Its Main Metabolites in Human Plasma and Its Application in a Clinical Pharmacokinetic Study." Marangon E, Posocco B, Mazzega E, and Toffoli G. *PLoS ONE*. 2015. 10(2) doi:10.1371/journal.pone.0118194 for use under the terms of the Creative Commons CC BY 4.0 license (http://creativecommons.org/licenses/by/4.0/legalcode).

Question 6

Electrospray Ionization (ESI) mass spectrometry donates a proton to a metabolite during ionization and can be used to detect the concentration of drugs like SN-38G. Which of the following statements best describes the data presented in the mass spectrogram of SN-38G below?

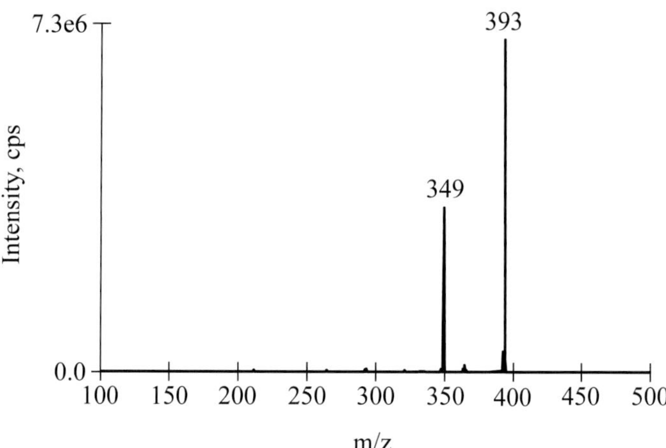

- A. The peak at 393 m/z represents the monoprotonated parent molecule.
- B. The peak at 349 m/z represents the monoprotonated parent molecule.
- C. The peak at 393 m/z represents the diprotonated parent molecule.
- D. The peak at 349 m/z represents the diprotonated parent molecule.

Question 7

Based on the following chromatogram of irinotecan and its metabolites, which of the following compounds is the least polar?

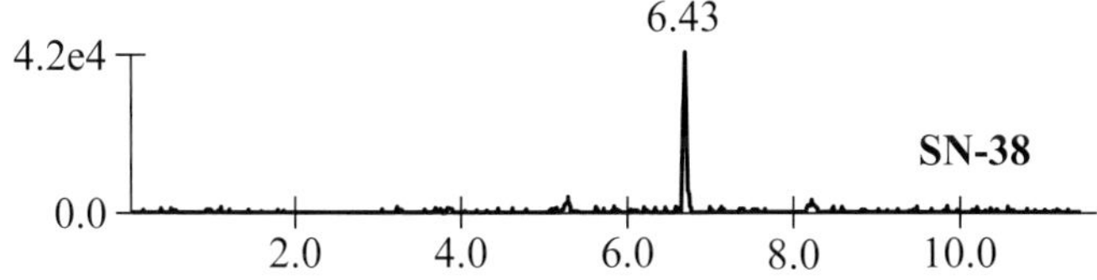

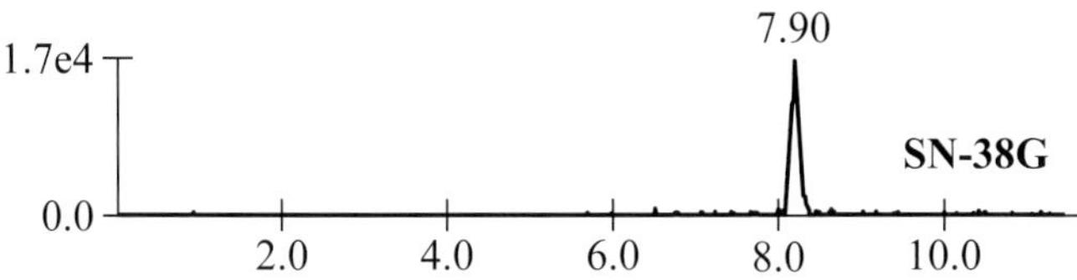

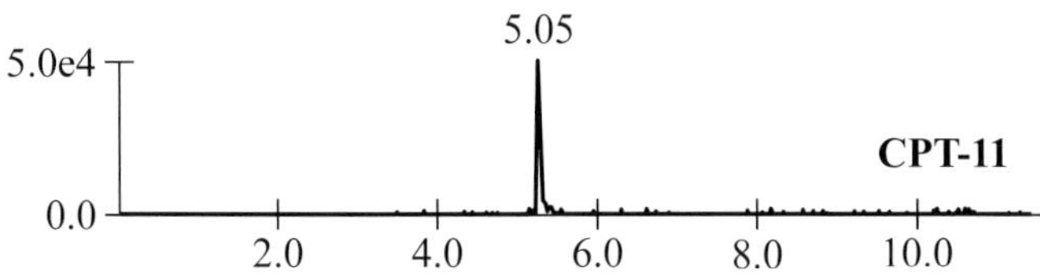

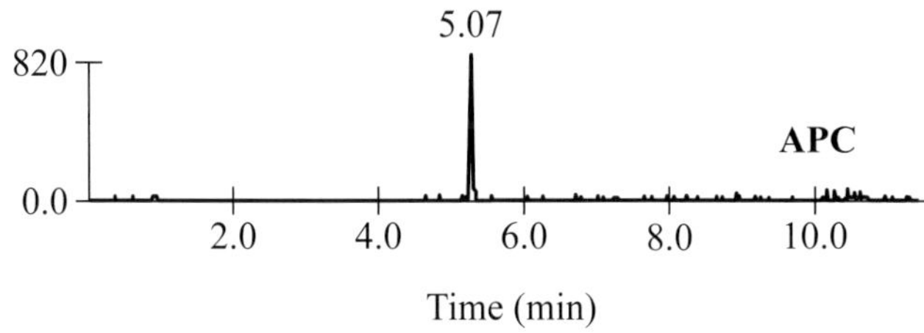

- O **A.** APC
- O **B.** CPT-11
- O **C.** SN-38G
- O **D.** SN-38

Question 8

CPT-11 would be most likely to impair:

- O **A.** DNA replication.
- O **B.** DNA translation.
- O **C.** mRNA translation.
- O **D.** mRNA alternative splicing.

Question 9

The substituent group that characterizes SN-38G most resembles:

- O **A.** cyclic AMP.
- O **B.** glucose.
- O **C.** fructose.
- O **D.** cholesterol.

Passage 3 (Questions 10-14)

Rasburicase, the recombinant form of urate oxidase from *Aspergillus flavus*, is a therapeutic enzyme used to decrease the high levels of uric acid in blood that can occur as a result of chemotherapy. However, impurities introduced during the preparation of the enzyme can lead to immunogenicity and hypersensitivity that cause significant and sometimes fatal adverse reactions to treatment. Therapeutic enzymes like rasburicase are costly and time-consuming to purify by chromatography. In order to establish a new method to purify rasburicase, scientists investigated the possibility of using crystallization as a purification step.

It has been shown with proteins that crystallization can occur from impure solutions, which suggests that crystallization may be an efficient, fast, and cost-effective way to purify and concentrate a protein. Urate oxidase is a 135 kDa tetramer with identical subunits having a molecular mass of about 34 kDa. Selecting the most appropriate crystallization methods for protein purification is vital. A protein can be considered to be a polyelectrolyte, meaning that a decrease in solubility via a pH shift triggers crystallization and makes purification possible. Adding salt can also be an effective way to purify a protein by crystallization via the salting-out effect.

Experiment 1

In order to determine the optimal crystallization conditions, urate oxidase (UOx) was dissolved in a neutral buffer and the solution was subjected to changes in pH and temperature. The concentration of UOx in solution was measured and the results are presented in Figure 1.

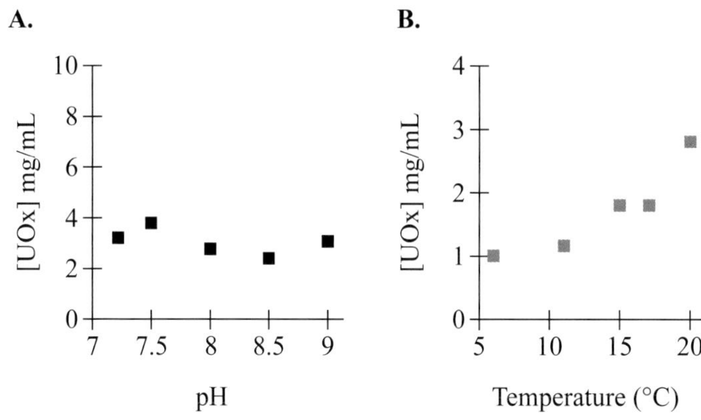

Figure 1 Solubility variations of the recombinant urate oxidase

Experiment 2

The precipitated crystals were re-dissolved in buffer and subjected to size exclusion chromatography to measure the relative purity of the precipitated crystal formation. Each elution pool was subjected to UV spectroscopy. The relative absorbance is plotted in Figure 2.

TEST 4C

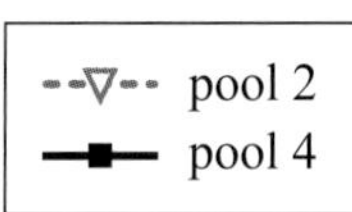

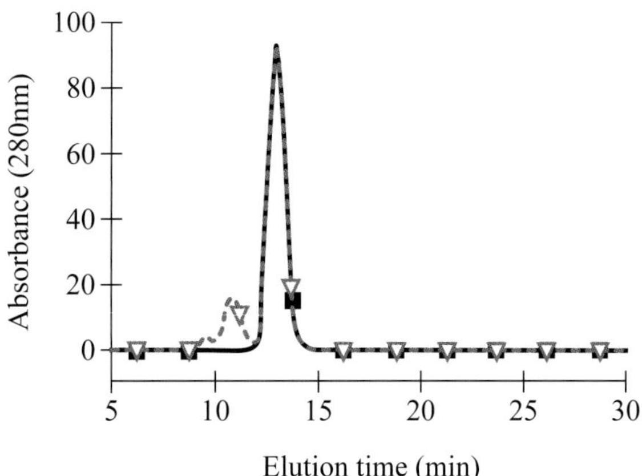

Figure 2 UV spectroscopy of eluted peaks after size exclusion chromatography analysis of urate oxidase crystal content

This passage is adapted from "Urate Oxidase Purification by Salting-in Crystallization: Towards an Alternative to Chromatrography." Giffard M, Ferte N, Ragot F, Hajji M, Castro B, et al. *PLoS ONE.* 2011. 6(5) doi:10.1371/journal.pone.0019013 for use under the terms of the Creative Commons CC BY 3.0 license (http://creativecommons.org/licenses/by/3.0/legalcode).

TEST 4C

Question 10

Crystallization of rasburicase is most effective at:

- O **A.** a slightly basic pH and low temperature.
- O **B.** a slightly acidic pH and high temperature.
- O **C.** a strongly basic pH and high temperature.
- O **D.** a strongly acidic pH and low temperature.

Question 11

Because urate oxidase contains more E and D residues than R and K residues, which pH value should be avoided during crystallization in order to obtain a non-denatured protein?

- O **A.** 4.5
- O **B.** 5.7
- O **C.** 6.8
- O **D.** 7.9

Question 12

Which of the following amino acids is LEAST likely to have contributed to the absorbance readings of the eluted fractions in Figure 2?

- O **A.** Trp
- O **B.** Val
- O **C.** Phe
- O **D.** Tyr

Question 13

Which of the following statements best describes the results of Figure 2?

- O **A.** The purity of pool 2 is 85% and the purity of pool 4 is 99%.
- O **B.** The purity of pool 2 is 99% and the purity of pool 4 is 99%.
- O **C.** The purity of pool 2 is 60% and the purity of pool 4 is 60%.
- O **D.** The purity of pool 2 is 99% and the purity of pool 4 is 50%.

Question 14

In order to differentiate whether the tetramer or monomers formed the precipitated crystals, the scientists would most likely use:

- O **A.** an antibody directed against the UOx protein.
- O **B.** an antibody directed against the UOx gene.
- O **C.** a fluorescent oligonucleotide probe directed against the UOx protein.
- O **D.** a fluorescent oligonucleotide probe directed against the UOx gene.

Next ▶

Questions 15 through 18 do not refer to a passage and are independent of each other.

Question 15

A scientist transfers 0.5 mL of a protein sample to a cuvette for an UV spectrogram reading, and observes that the intensity of the radiation is decreased after passing through the sample. Which of the following statements best explains this observation?

- O **A.** UV photons displaced electrons in a C-C single bond to the highest occupied molecular orbital.
- O **B.** UV photons displaced electrons in a C=C double bond to the highest occupied molecular orbital.
- O **C.** UV photons displaced electrons in a C-C single bond to the lowest unoccupied molecular orbital.
- O **D.** UV photons displaced electrons in a C=C double bond to the lowest unoccupied molecular orbital.

Question 16

A whole genome nucleotide sequencing library prepared using bacterial transformation is most likely to contain:

- O **A.** DNA fragments of repetitive sizes and sequences.
- O **B.** DNA fragments of a specific sequence amplified by PCR.
- O **C.** DNA fragments of non-repetitive sequences and varying sizes.
- O **D.** RNA fragments of non-repetitive sequences and varying sizes.

Question 17

Which of the following most accurately depicts a separation using affinity chromatography?

- O **A.** Attaching antigens to an antibody assay plate
- O **B.** Separating plasma proteins based on affinity to a nonpolar mobile phase
- O **C.** Isolating insulin using a column lined with the alpha binding regions of the insulin receptor
- O **D.** Using electrostatic forces to temporarily attach compounds to the stationary phase

Question 18

Two proteins of identical length are passed through a size-exclusion chromatography column, but they elute at distinct speeds. Which of the following explains this observation?

- O **A.** The proteins are oppositely charged and interact differently with the solvent.
- O **B.** The proteins have distinct tertiary structures and interact differently with the column matrix.
- O **C.** The proteins have different hydrophobicities and interact differently with the column matrix.
- O **D.** The size-exclusion chromatography column is defective and this difference should not have occurred.

Passage 4 (Questions 19-22)

Head and neck cancer is a frequent cause of speech and swallowing impairment and may metastasize, leading to significant morbidity and mortality. Mitochondrial dysfunction has long been linked to cancer and a number of mechanisms have been reported to be involved in this process. Among these mechanisms, dysregulation of different mitochondrial tumor suppressor (TS) genes have been suggested. Mitochondrial tumor suppressor 1 (MTUS1) is an important TS gene and is localized at 8p22, a chromosomal region frequently deleted in tumors. Alternative splicing of exon 2, exons 2 and 5, and exons 2, 5, and 7 of this gene leads to 3 known transcript variants: ATIP1, ATIP2, and ATIP3.

A study was designed to characterize the expression pattern of selected mitochondrial tumor suppressor genes in head and neck cancer and to investigate the association of *MTUS1* expression with the clinical characteristics and prognosis of head and neck cancer patients. Using quantitative PCR, scientists measured the relative expression of *MTUS1* in controls and patients with head and neck cancer. The electrophoresis gel and quantitative PCR (qPCR) results are presented in Figure 1.

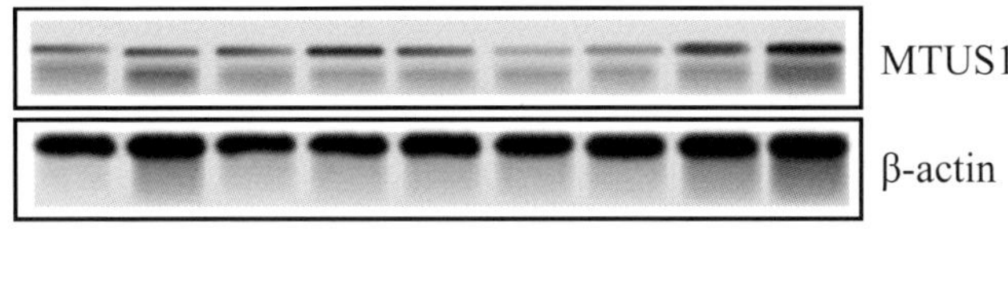

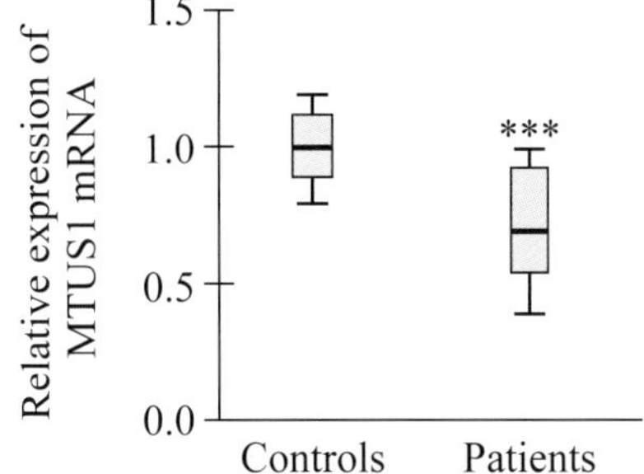

Figure 1 Relative expression of *MTUS1* mRNA in controls and head and neck cancer patients

Scientists also analyzed the expression level of mitochondrial DNA repair gene *OGG1-2a* in head and neck cancer patients and respective controls using qPCR (Figure 2). Accumulating evidence indicates that low hOGG1 expression is associated with increased oxidation of G to 8-oxoG in genomic DNA, which may give rise to a mutator phenotype.

TEST 4C

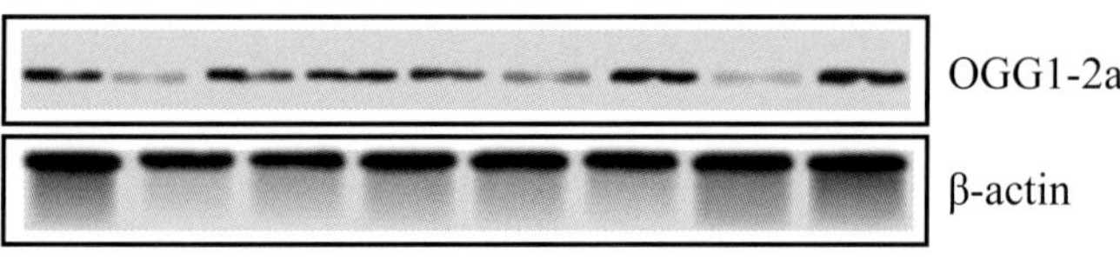

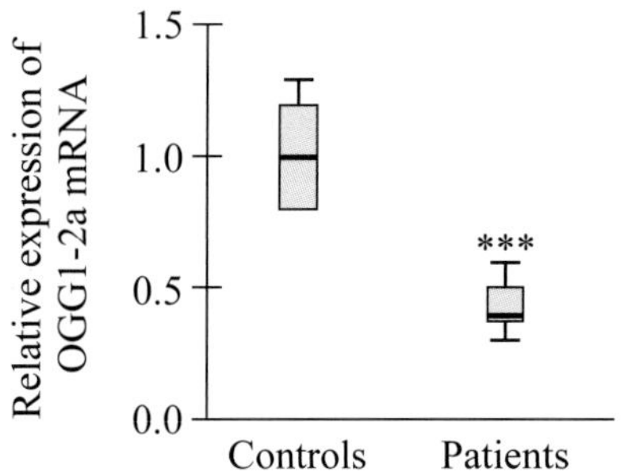

Figure 2 Expression of *OGG1-2a* in head and neck cancer patients and controls

Question 19

Which technique was likely used to determine the presence of *MTUS1* mRNA before qPCR?

- O **A.** Southern blot
- O **B.** Protein microarray
- O **C.** Northern blot
- O **D.** UV spectroscopy

Question 20

Which gel would result from reverse transcription of ATIP1, ATIP2, and ATIP3 mRNA?

O **A.** O **B.**

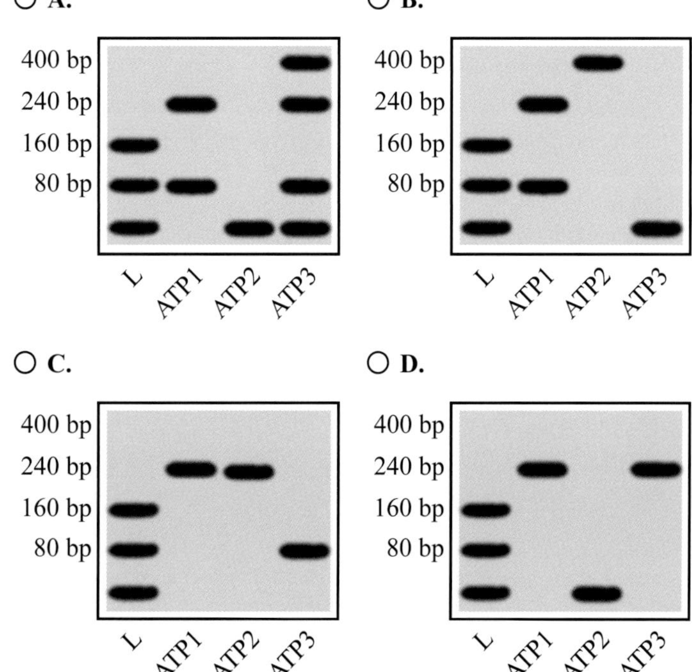

Question 21

Patient 3 of the head and neck cancer cohort did not show loss of 8p22 but had the lowest expression of *MTUS1.* Which of the following statements best explains this finding?

- O **A.** Patient 3 likely had a heterozygous deletion of *POLD1*, which encodes the catalytic unit of DNA polymerase δ.
- O **B.** Patient 3 had a frameshift deletion in a repressor region regulating *MTUS1.*
- O **C.** Patient 3 had increased methylation of the *MTUS1* promoter.
- O **D.** Patient 3 had increased expression of E3-ubiquitin ligase.

Question 22

Loss of the larger q arm of chromosome 17 deletes *TP53*, a gene that controls the cellular response to DNA damage. Chromosomal loss would best be detected by:

- O **A.** fluorescence *in situ* hybridization of unfragmented DNA isolated from cancer cells.
- O **B.** qPCR on fragmented DNA isolated from cancer cells.
- O **C.** DNA sequencing of DNA isolated from normal cells.
- O **D.** RNA sequencing of RNA isolated from cancer cells.

Next ▶

Passage 5 (Questions 23-27)

Tuberculosis (TB) is a global health problem. The World Health Organization estimated 9.4 million incident cases during 2009 and 1.7 million deaths. The challenge in reducing the global burden of tuberculosis is rapid diagnosis followed by appropriate treatment. Current methods of diagnosing TB are inadequate. The most widely used test, microscopic examination of sputum, lacks sensitivity and global cases detection rates remain low. It is estimated that only 63% of incident cases are detected each year. Definitive diagnosis requires isolation and culture of the bacilli which may take weeks and requires considerable laboratory infrastructure to protect against infection.

Detection of lipid moieties, which are essential components of the cell envelope of *Mycobacterium tuberculosis*, offers an alternative approach for diagnosis. Chemical analysis has an advantage over culture methods in that it can be rapid and does not require live organisms. The mycocerosic acid components of the phthiocerol dimycocerosate (PDIM) family of complex lipids are established diagnostic markers for tuberculosis. Fatty acids of this type are found in *M. tuberculosis*, *Mycobacterium bovis*, *Mycobacterium kansasii*, *Mycobacterium leprae*, *Mycobacterium marinum*, *Mycobacterium gastri*, *Mycobacterium haemophilum* and *Mycobacterium ulcerans*. Members of the *M. tuberculosis* complex have a characteristic profile composed of trimethyl C29, tetramethyl C30, and C32 mycocerosates (Figure 1). Analysis of mycocerosates has been performed using gas chromatography (GC) followed by electron capture detection or negative ion chemical ionization MS, including detection in sputum.

C29

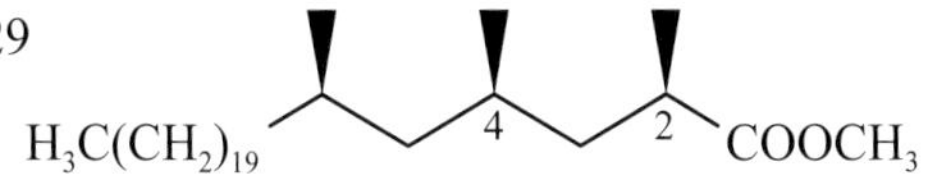

$H_3C(CH_2)_{19}$ — 4 — 2 — $COOCH_3$

C30

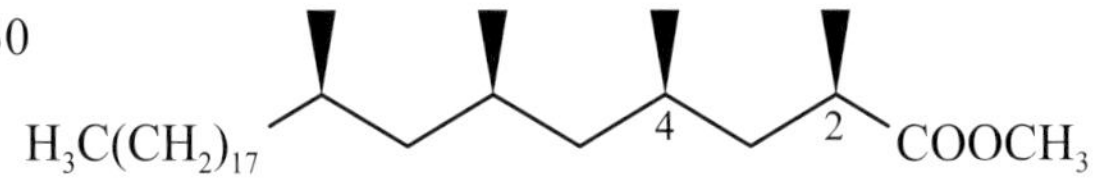

$H_3C(CH_2)_{17}$ — 4 — 2 — $COOCH_3$

C32

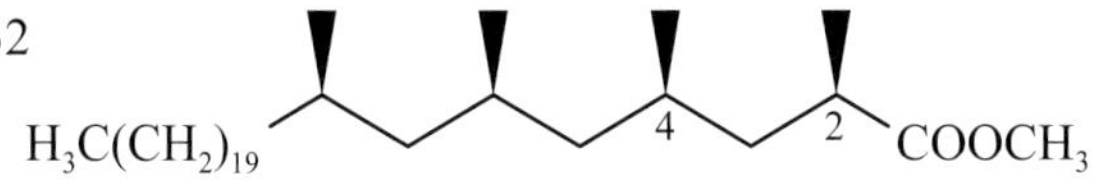

$H_3C(CH_2)_{19}$ — 4 — 2 — $COOCH_3$

Figure 1 Tuberculosis lipids

This passage was adapted from "Detection of Mycobacterium tuberculosis in Sputum by Gas Chromatography-Mass Spectrometry of Methyl Mycocerosates Released by Thermochemolysis." O'Sullivan DM, Nicoara SC, Mutetwa R, Mungofa S, Lee OYC, et al. *PLoS ONE*. 2012. 7(3) doi:10.1371/journal.pone.0032836 for use under the terms of the Creative Commons CC BY 3.0 license (http://creativecommons.org/licenses/by/3.0/legalcode).

Question 23

Which of the three compounds elutes fastest during thin layer chromatography (TLC)?

- O **A.** C29
- O **B.** C30
- O **C.** C32
- O **D.** Cannot be determined

Question 24

Which tuberculosis lipid would have the greatest number of unique hydrogens in a hydrogen NMR?

- O **A.** C29
- O **B.** C30
- O **C.** C32
- O **D.** Equal number of unique hydrogens for all three

Question 25

Which enzyme would most affect the compounds being investigated if contamination occurred?

- O **A.** Pepsin
- O **B.** Lipase
- O **C.** Salivary amylase
- O **D.** Pancreatic amylase

Question 26

Which of the following is true regarding affinity chromatography with isolation of individual tuberculosis lipids?

I. Separation cannot be achieved by a molecule that binds to esters.

II. Separation cannot be achieved by a molecule that binds to carboxylic acids.

III. Separation can be achieved by a molecule that binds to all hydroxyl groups.

- O **A.** I only
- O **B.** I and II
- O **C.** II and III
- O **D.** I, II, and III

Question 27

During liquid-gas chromatography, a sample is dissolved in gas and then cooled. Each component reaches equilibrium with the liquid phase at a distinct points. How would C32 behave in a liquid-gas chromatography experiment in comparison to C30 and C29?

- O **A.** C32 would reach equilibrium first due to its stronger intermolecular forces.
- O **B.** C32 would reach equilibrium first due to its weak intermolecular forces.
- O **C.** C32 would reach equilibrium last due to its stronger intermolecular forces.
- O **D.** C32 would reach equilibrium last due to its weaker intermolecular forces.

TEST 4C

Questions 28 through 31 do not refer to a passage and are independent of each other.

Question 28

Which of the following would NOT explain why a western blot failed to visualize a protein?

- O **A.** There were over 20 types of proteins in the sample.
- O **B.** The investigator did not add sufficient secondary antibodies.
- O **C.** The primary antibody was contaminated, which prevented the necessary fluorescence.
- O **D.** Transfer of the protein of interest from the electrophoresis gel was unsuccessful.

Question 29

The DNA in the Southern blot depicted was hybridized to a probe specific for *APP,* a protein implicated in Alzheimer's progress. Which of the following is NOT a reasonable interpretation of the blot?

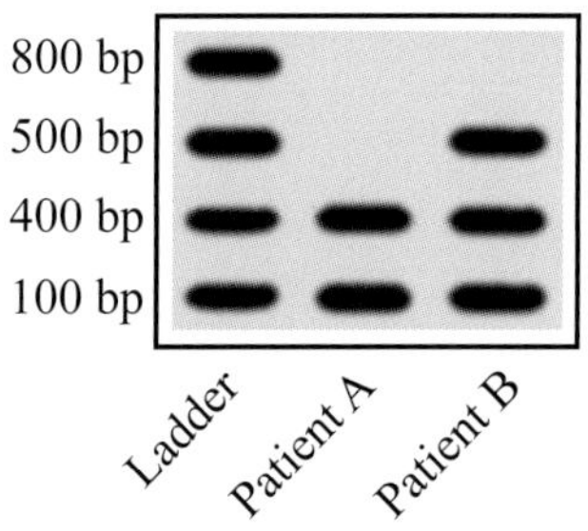

- O **A.** Patient A is homozygous at the *APP* locus.
- O **B.** Patient B is heterozygous at the *APP* locus.
- O **C.** A 500 bp fragment undergoes alternative splicing.
- O **D.** An 800 bp fragment is degraded into smaller fragments.

Question 30

A restriction fragment length polymorphism (RFLP) assay uses which of the following methods to detect a G to C transversion in a 150 bp PCR product of the *SMAD4* gene?

- O **A.** Southern blot
- O **B.** Northern blot
- O **C.** Agarose gel electrophoresis
- O **D.** Western blot

Question 31

Which of the following statements best describes the ethical concerns of DNA sequencing?

I. DNA sequencing may uncover diseases that segregate in families.

II. DNA sequencing may uncover diseases that have no known treatments.

III. DNA sequencing may have deleterious effects on the ability to obtain health insurance.

- O **A.** I only
- O **B.** II only
- O **C.** II and III only
- O **D.** I, II, and III

STOP. If you finish before time is called, check your work. You may go back to any question in this test.

ANSWERS & EXPLANATIONS for Test 4C can be found on p. 290.

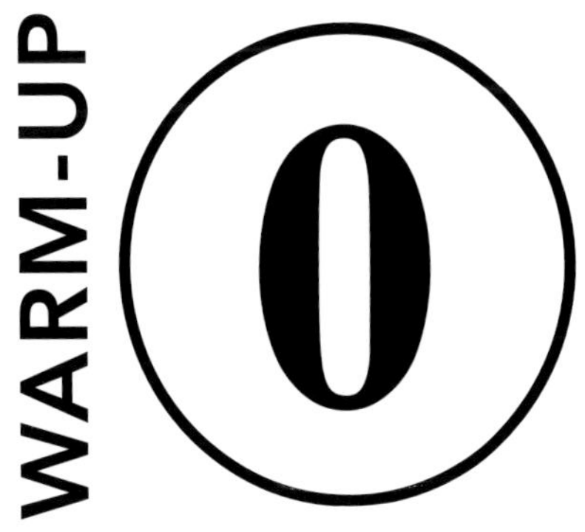

ANSWERS & EXPLANATIONS

Questions 1–5

ANSWER KEY
1. D
2. A
3. B
4. C
5. C

EXPLANATIONS FOR WARM-UP

Passage 1 (Questions 1-5)

1. **D is the best answer.** The question is asking for the process that does not play a role in the development of the disease. The first paragraph mentions that the protein requires activation by a cAMP-dependent kinase, which means that synapsin needs to be phosphorylated to be fully active. Choice B can be eliminated. According to Figure 1, in the disease there is increased expression of PDE, which degrades cAMP and lowers the levels of synapsin. Choice C can be eliminated. In addition, CREB levels are decreased in the disease, resulting in decreased gene expression of Syn. Choice A can be eliminated. Choice D would likely decrease the activity of synapsin, but the passage provides evidence for a reduction in CREB protein levels, rather than inhibition of the protein. Choice D is the best answer.

2. **A is the best answer.** The question asks for the type of inhibition involved between papaverine and PDE, as well as the corresponding LB plot. According to the Figure 2, the structure of papaverine is similar to that of cAMP. Papaverine most likely binds at the active site of the enzyme where cAMP usually binds. This is competitive inhibition. A competitive inhibitor does not affect V_{max}, but it does increase the concentration at which half the maximal rate is achieved (K_m). The LB plot that corresponds to that must have the same y-intercept, but the x-intercept must be closer to the origin. This corresponds to choice A.

   Choice D corresponds to the plot of a noncompetitive inhibitor, where V_{max} is decreased without affecting K_m. Choices B and C are not plots corresponding to inhibition.

3. **B is the best answer.** The question is asking about the drug(s) that will make a person that is HPRT− to produce Synapsin amounts similar to individuals that are HPRT+ and not taking any drugs. In Figure 3, the level produced by an individual that is HPRT+, not taking any drugs is 0.15 (first column). The only other column that shows similar levels is the 7th column, which corresponds to HPRT− treated with Papaverine alone. Choice B is the best answer.

4. **C is the best answer.** The question stem describes cAMP as an activator of PKA. Activating is a type of allosteric interaction. The second part of the question stem describes how binding one activator facilitates the attachment of other activators. This is positive cooperativity. Options I and II are correct. The only choices that includes these two options are choices C and D.

   Option III is positive feedback, where the product of the enzyme can affect the activity of the enzyme. cAMP is not a product of PKA. Option III will not be included in the best answer and choice B can be eliminated.

5. **C is the best answer.** This question is asking about the distinction between nucleotides with purine or pyrimidine rings. The answer must include A and G, but not C or T. Nucleotides that have 2 hydrogen bonds are A and T. Choice A can be eliminated. The nucleotides that have 3 hydrogen bonds are C and G. Choice B can be eliminated. Nucleotides that have a pyrimidine ring are C and T. Choice D can be eliminated. The nucleotides that have a purine ring are A and G. Choice C is the best answer.

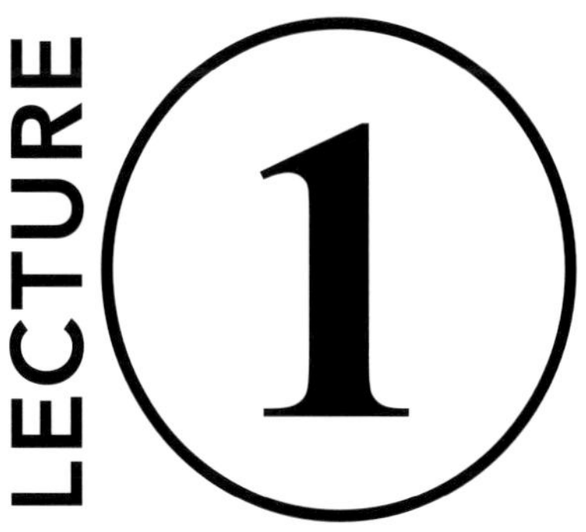

Biological Molecules and Enzymes

TEST 1A

ANSWERS & EXPLANATIONS

Questions 1–59

TEST 1A A&E

LECTURE 1 ANSWER KEY

TEST 1A		TEST 1B		TEST 1C	
1. A	31. B	1. B	31. C	1. A	17. A
2. C	32. B	2. B	32. D	2. B	18. D
3. A	33. D	3. A	33. A	3. B	19. D
4. D	34. B	4. B	34. B	4. A	20. B
5. C	35. C	5. C	35. B	5. D	21. B
6. D	36. A	6. C	36. C	6. C	22. C
7. D	37. B	7. B	37. A	7. A	23. D
8. A	38. A	8. D	38. B	8. B	24. A
9. A	39. A	9. B	39. B	9. C	25. D
10. D	40. A	10. D	40. A	10. B	26. D
11. A	41. D	11. D	41. C	11. C	27. B
12. D	42. D	12. C	42. D	12. B	28. B
13. C	43. D	13. D	43. A	13. D	29. D
14. B	44. C	14. D	44. C	14. D	30. B
15. C	45. D	15. B	45. B	15. D	31. B
16. C	46. A	16. B	46. A	16. C	
17. A	47. A	17. B	47. C		
18. D	48. A	18. C	48. B		
19. C	49. B	19. A	49. A		
20. A	50. A	20. B	50. C		
21. B	51. B	21. A	51. C		
22. D	52. B	22. A	52. A		
23. B	53. C	23. C	53. A		
24. B	54. C	24. C	54. D		
25. B	55. D	25. A	55. B		
26. C	56. C	26. A	56. B		
27. B	57. B	27. D	57. C		
28. C	58. C	28. A	58. B		
29. D	59. C	29. A	59. B		
30. D		30. B			

EXPLANATIONS FOR LECTURE 1

Passage 1 (Questions 1-4)

1. **A is the best answer.** According to the passage, HP-β-CyD is responsible for mediating increased cholesterol efflux from the cells it interacts with. If a patient is given an infusion of HP-β-CyD to treat AML, HP-β-CyD will also interact with other cells of the body. Cholesterol is one key component of lipid rafts, which are plasma membrane components that hold proteins and other cell surface proteoglycans and glycoproteins. Upon activation of an MHC molecule and a T cell or B cell receptor, lipid rafts merge together to bring all the proteins necessary for immune system signaling into the same place. This is one example of how lipid rafts are able to increase the local concentration of proteins, eliminating choice B. Bile salts are made in part from cholesterol. Decreased cholesterol in hepatocytes of the liver would impair the synthesis of bile salts, eliminating choice C. Vitamin D is also made from cholesterol and serves to increase the reabsorption of calcium in the kidneys and intestines. Impaired vitamin D synthesis due to decreased cholesterol would impair calcium homeostasis, eliminating choice D. Thyroid hormone is made from tyrosine, not cholesterol. It is one of the only steroid hormones that is not derived from cholesterol. Decreases in cholesterol are least likely to impact thyroid hormone synthesis, making choice A the best answer choice.

2. **C is the best answer.** Figure 2 provides the first half of the information needed to answer this question. According to Figure 2, increasing the concentration of HP-β-CyD leads to a decrease in the cell number, meaning that more cell death occurred in the groups of cells that were treated at the highest concentrations. Because an increase in cell death, not a decrease, is seen with increasing HP-β-CyD concentrations, choices A and B can be eliminated. Additionally, decreasing the concentration of cholesterol would decrease membrane fluidity, further helping to eliminate choice A. As the concentration of HP-β-CyD increases, the concentration of cholesterol would be expected to decrease. Cholesterol serves two main roles in the plasma membrane by helping modulate the fluidity of the membrane and associating with the hydrophobic tails of the lipids in the membrane to help prevent the diffusion of small molecules across the membrane. Decreased plasma membrane fluidity would likely be seen with decreased cholesterol concentrations, eliminating choice D. As the concentration of cholesterol decreased, increased permeability of the membrane to small molecules would occur, possibly helping to increase the rates of cell death, making choice C the best answer choice.

3. **A is the best answer.** Cholesterol serves a key role in modulating the fluidity of membranes in the cell, including the plasma membrane, mitochondrial membrane, and membranes of the Golgi and endoplasmic reticulum. According to the passage and Figure 3, HP-β-CyD leads to increased cholesterol efflux from the cell, which would decrease the ability of the membrane to respond to changes in temperature, leading to decreased membrane fluidity. Continued efflux of cholesterol should eventually render the cell unable to respond to changes in temperature that could occur with increased exercise or exposure to hot or cold environments. Choice B shows an initial increase in membrane fluidity that is unlikely to occur with decreased cholesterol concentrations, eliminating it as a best answer choice. Similarly, choice C shows an initial increase, also eliminating it as the best answer choice. While the membrane fluidity is low with increasing concentrations of HP-β-CyD, at high concentrations choice D shows high fluidity, which would be unlikely to occur with low cholesterol levels, eliminating choice D as the best answer choice. Choice A shows a proportional decrease in membrane fluidity with increasing HP-β-CyD concentrations, making it the best answer choice.

4. **D is the best answer.** According to the new information provided by mouse models, HP-β-CyD failed to decrease the tumor burden in mice over the course of treatment. This is in contrast to the information presented in the passage, where increasing concentrations of HP-β-CyD decrease the cell number of AML cancer cells. The new finding would not support the authors' conclusions, as HP-β-CyD would be expected to show decreases in tumor burden if it worked the same way in solid tumors versus blood tumors. Choice A can be eliminated. Choice B is a tempting answer choice because the failure to show a decrease in tumor mass appears to weaken the hypothesis of the scientists. However, no information is provided in the in vivo experiment about cholesterol and cholesterol efflux. It is not clear whether or not cholesterol efflux was increased in colorectal cancer cells but this effect did not induce the same level of cell killing as seen in AML. Choice B is less likely to be the best answer. The passage does not go into detail about the use of HP-β-CyD to deliver chemotherapeutic drugs, eliminating choice C as the best answer. The solid tumor model of colorectal cancer is significantly different from the blood cancer model of AML and the in vivo experiment does not provide a reason as to why the treatment of mice with HP-β-CyD failed to show therapeutic effect. Without additional information, the findings of the additional experiment do not strengthen or weaken the authors' conclusions, making choice D the best answer choice.

Passage 2 (Questions 5-9)

5. **C is the best answer.** An enzyme is responsible for catalyzing the reaction between two or more reactants to create products. Overall, an enzyme lowers the activation energy required to facilitate a reaction though a few mechanisms. Activation energy is comprised of three parts – the kinetic energy required to overcome repulsive forces, the orientation of the two or more reactants, and the fact that the enzyme increases the local "concentration" of reactants to make it more likely that they will react. One of the mechanisms is to hold the reactants in an active site, increasing the local concentrations of the reactants and making it increasingly likely that the two will be in close enough proximity to react. Option I is a component of the best answer. Because catalysis decrease the overall activation energy, they decrease the kinetic energy that would be required to facilitate a reaction. Option II is the opposite of what enzymes would do, meaning that it is not a component of the best answer choice. Molecules are only able to react in certain orientations that facilitate the transfer of chemical groups. Enzymes use amino acids in their active sites to position molecules in a specific fashion, meaning that option III is a component of the best answer. Choice A can be eliminated because it does not contain option III. Choice B can be eliminated because it contains option II. Choice D can be eliminated because it contains option II. Choice C is the best answer choice, as it contains options I and III that are characteristics of the mechanisms of enzyme catalysis.

6. **D is the best answer.** Amino acids are able to facilitate reactions between both hydrophobic and hydrophilic compounds. In general, reactions that are between two hydrophobic compounds will involve amino acids that are nonpolar, while reactions that are between two hydrophilic compounds will involve amino acids that are polar or charged. ATP contains a net negative charge and is a highly polar molecule. In order for sphingosine to receive a phosphate to become sphingosine-1-phosphate, sphingosine must have a nucleophilic group, such as a hydroxyl group, to attack the phosphate of ATP. Sphingosine is also polar. Both ATP and sphingosine are hydrophilic on the regions of the molecules that react together. Serine, S, contains a hydroxyl group that could help stabilize hydrophilic molecules, eliminating choice A. Histidine, H, is also polar and contains a nitrogen that could help in the transfer of the phosphate, eliminating choice B. Tyrosine, Y, like serine, also contains a hydroxyl group that could stabilize the hydrophilic ends of the molecules during the reaction. Isoleucine, I, is a nonpolar amino acid that would likely be unable to help transfer the phosphate, as it contains no polarity on its side chain and does not have a nucleophile that could help catalyze the transfer. Isoleucine would be the least likely, making choice D the best answer choice.

7. **D is the best answer.** Amino acids exist as dipolar ions, with the amino group characterized by a positive charge and the carboxylic acid functional group characterized by a negative charge. The peptide bond that forms between amino acids is a reaction between the carboxylic acid and the amino group that is partially facilitated by the attraction between the positive and negative charged. The question is asking about the role of this positive and negative charge in mediating amino acid condensation, the reaction that occurs to join two amino acids. The best answer will be the one that does not impact the charge of the amino or carboxy termini of an amino acid. Phosphoric acid would be able to donate a hydrogen to the carboxy terminus of amino acids, neutralizing the negative charge. This would hinder the electrostatic attraction between amino acids, decreasing peptide formation. Choice A can be eliminated. Bicarbonate could react to remove the hydrogen from the amino terminus, neutralizing the positive charge on the nitrogen. Choice B can be eliminated. Magnesium exists as a positively charged ion in the cell. It can form electrostatic interactions with negative charges, helping to functionally neutralize the negative charge of the carboxy terminus. Decreasing the concentration of positively charged species would allow more negative charge on the carboxy terminus, helping to support peptide production, eliminating choice C. By contrast, increasing levels of positively charged species, such as zinc, would likely neutralize some negative charge on the dipolar amino acid, which would hinder peptide production. Choice D is the best answer choice.

8. **A is the best answer.** According to the last paragraph, ceramide is transported to the Golgi from the ER, allowing it to get metabolized into sphingomyelin and other sphingolipid compounds. These sphingolipids are important in the formation of lipid rafts in the plasma membrane and in the formation of S1P, which is a survival factor according to the passage. According to Figure 1, treatment of CRCs with luteolin increases the concentration of ceramide, which, according to Figure 2, reduces cell viability. Decreased cell viability would imply increased apoptosis, or programmed cell death. Using Figure 3, increased ceramide decreases sphingomyelin, which is formed in the Golgi from the precursor ceramide. Upon treatment with luteolin, ceramide increases but sphingomyelin decreases. The last paragraph notes that ceramide must be transported to the Golgi in order to be processed into sphingomyelin. This does not occur in the smooth endoplasmic reticulum, eliminating choice B. Sphingomyelin does incorporate into membranes but is a key component of the plasma membrane. Additionally, the passage does not provide information about mitochondria, making choice C less likely to be the best answer. Cholesterol allows the plasma membrane to remain fluid at temperature extremes. However, no information is provided about cholesterol and sphingolipids are not synthesized from cholesterol, eliminating choice D. The best answer is the one that can explain how increased levels of ceramide fail to increase levels of sphingomyelin. This would occur if the drug inhibited transport of the precursor ceramide to the Golgi, making choice A the best answer.

9. **A is the best answer.** Lipids, similar to proteins, can act in a paracrine or endocrine manner by acting locally or traveling in the blood, respectively, to affect other cells. Because S1P contains a phosphate, it is a polar molecule that is likely unable to cross membranes by diffusion, requiring it to be exocytosed. Once S1P is exocytosed it can travel to neighboring cells to impact their growth and proliferation by binding receptors on either the plasma membrane or in the cytoplasm. Nonpolar molecules can cross through plasma membranes, which are composed of nonpolar lipids, to bind cytoplasmic receptors. However, S1P is polar, meaning that it would be unlikely to cross the hydrophobic plasma membrane. Because it cannot cross the plasma membrane, S1P cannot bind cytoplasmic receptors, eliminating choice B. A nuclear receptor would require that the polar lipid crossed two membranes, eliminating choice C. Binding of an ER membrane receptor would require that the polar lipid crossed the plasma membrane before binding the ER receptor, eliminating choice D. Polar molecules bind extracellular cell surface receptors to affect intracellular signaling, which could lead to a pro-survival phenotype, making choice A the best answer choice.

Passage 3 (Questions 10-13)

10. **D is the best answer.** The question is asking to explain good and bad cholesterol in terms of flow of cholesterol. In the arteries, cholesterol would help in the formation of atheromas, which are risk factors to CVD. In the liver, cholesterol is metabolized and used up as energy. In the adipocytes, cholesterol would be stored for energy. Removal of cholesterol from both arteries and adipocytes is favorable for decreasing the risk of CVD. "Good" cholesterol will be directed towards the liver away from adipocytes and arteries. HDL will carry cholesterol towards the liver. Choices A, B and C can be eliminated.

11. **A is the best answer.** The question is asking for the relationship between sialidase activity and atherogenesis. Since sialidase is not an enzyme that is taught, its function can be deduced from its name. The suffix "-ase" refers to an enzyme. "Siali" refers to sialic acid. The function of the enzyme must be to remove a sialic acid residue. Increased activity must result in decreased glycosylation. Choices C and D can be eliminated. According to the passage, decreased sialic acid residues were associated with MetSyn, and most likely increase the risk of atherogenesis. Choice B can be eliminated, leaving choice A as the best answer.

12. **D is the best answer.** The question is asking which experiment would inhibit the first step in atherogenesis. The passage describes post-translational modifications as a means to adding carbohydrates to the protein. Inhibiting this step would result in a protein lacking the carbohydrate chain, and cannot interact with the endothelium, effectively disrupting the first step of atherogenesis. Option I is correct, so choice C can be eliminated. The use of antibodies targeting the glycoprotein of lipoproteins or endothelium would also result in interruption of the interaction. Options II and III are also correct. Choices A and B do not include option III as a correct response, and can be eliminated.

13. **C is the best answer.** The question is asking which disaccharides contains only six-membered rings (pyranoses). Of note, the common 6 membered-ring sugars are glucose and galactose. Fructose has a 5-membered ring (furanose). Maltose is composed of two glucose molecules. Lactose is composed of a glucose and a galactose molecule. Sucrose is composed of a glucose and a fructose molecule. Choices A and B can be eliminated since they are partly composed of a furanose. Both maltose and lactose are composed of pyranoses. Choice D can be eliminated since amylose and amylopectin are the components of starch, which are long polymers of glucose rather than disaccharides.

Stand-alones (14-17)

14. **B is the best answer.** The question stem states that Susan is on a low fat diet. There are two types of vitamins, water soluble and fat soluble. The fat soluble vitamins are transported in the body along with fats obtained from the diet. If she has been restricting fats for months, she could very well have a deficiency in her fat soluble vitamins. The fat soluble vitamins are A, D, E, and K. This eliminates choices A, C, and D. Vitamin B is a water soluble vitamin, and restricting fats should have little bearing on this vitamin's status. Choice B is the best answer.

15. **C is the best answer.** While this question appears to require in-depth knowledge of the types of lipids present in the plasma membrane, the biggest clue comes from the specification of the organism's environment. The question stem specifically notes that the mammal lives in a cold environment. Phosphatidylcholine, sphingomyelin, and phosphatidylinositol are key components of the normal plasma membrane and serve to help maintain polarity of the inner and outer leaflet, as well as maintain the diffusion barrier to large, polar molecules. It is less likely that temperature would heavily change their concentrations in the membrane compared to another molecule, cholesterol, making choice A, B, and D less likely to be the best answer. Cholesterol, however, is the most important molecule to modulating membrane fluidity in cold and warm temperatures. In cold temperatures, cholesterol helps maintain membrane flexibility, while in warm temperatures, cholesterol prevents the membrane from dissociating. Cholesterol is the best answer choice, making choice C the best choice.

16. **C is the best answer.** A hexose is a six-carbon sugar. Choice A or L-glucose is a stereoisomer of D-glucose, which is commonly found in living organisms. Stereoisomers differ only in terms of the orientation of the atoms in space, but there are the same number of carbon atoms, or six for glucose. Galactose from choice B has six carbons. It differs from glucose in terms of the bonds formed but not in terms of the overall molecular formula $C_6H_{12}O_6$. Choice C or ribose is the best answer as ribose has only five sugars. It is an example of a pentose and is a derivative of the pentose phosphate pathway. Choice D or fructose has six carbons and is similar to glucose and galactose.

17. **A is the best answer.** Glycoproteins are most commonly found on the plasma membrane and function in extracellular matrix adhesion and interaction with cell surface molecules on other cells, making choice A the best answer. Glycoproteins are proteins that have sugars attached to the underlying protein structure, meaning they are polar and are typically found facing hydrophilic environments like the extracellular matrix. In order to interact with other cells, the proteins would be on the plasma membrane, not in the cytosol, eliminating choice B. In addition, because the nucleus and mitochondria are both intracellular organelles, they do not outwardly face other cells, preventing them from serving as adherence factors. This eliminates choices C and D.

Passage 4 (Questions 18-22)

18. **D is the best answer.** Carbohydrates contain a high concentration of C-H bonds, which allows them to store significant amounts of energy that can be oxidized to produce ATP to power cellular functions. In contrast to carbohydrates, lipids provide the greatest amount of energy per mole due to their increased number of C-H bonds. Option I does not describe the role of carbohydrates. Glycogen is a branched polymer of glucose in the cell that allows for efficient storage of glucose for later oxidation. Option II is a component of the best answer. Carbohydrates can also be added to proteins in the ER and Golgi in order to affect intracellular trafficking of proteins or allow for cell-cell adhesions to occur on the cell surface. Option III is a component of the best answer. Choice A can be eliminated because it contains option I only. Similarly, while option II is correct, the inclusion of option I makes choice B unlikely to be the best answer. As with choice C, option III is correct but the inclusion of option I makes choice C unlikely to be the best answer. Choice D describes two roles of carbohydrates, making it the best answer choice.

19. **C is the best answer.** Polysaccharides are carbohydrate compounds that contain monomers linked together to form longer chains. Polysaccharides are typically broken down by enzymes in the gut prior to absorption by enterocytes. Maltose is a polysaccharide composed of two glucose molecules. The two maltose disaccharides contain four glucose molecules. Because the question stem suggests that fructose is the main carbohydrate used in sperm, choice A can be eliminated. Lactose is a polysaccharide of galactose and glucose. The two lactose molecules contain two galactose and two glucose monosaccharides. It also does not contain fructose, allowing choice B to be eliminated. Galactose is a monosaccharide, not a polysaccharide. Its bonding to lactose means that the polymer in choice D contains two galactose molecules and one glucose molecule. Choice D can be eliminated. Sucrose is a polysaccharide of fructose and glucose. In the sucrose polymer, there are two fructose molecules and two glucose molecules. Because sucrose could supplement fructose in the diet, choice C is the best answer.

20. **A is the best answer.** Figure 2 provides the best information to help answer this question. Upon administration of 10 mM 2-Deoxy-D-Glucose, the intracellular concentration of ATP decreases at a relatively uniform rate over time. This is evidenced by the roughly straight line that decreases over time. 1st order kinetics follows a parabolic decrease and would not show up as a straight line on a graph plotting the concentration of a molecule over time. Choice B can be eliminated. 2nd order and 3rd order kinetics also follow parabolic decreases, though the rate of reduction in ATP concentration decreases with increasing order. Choices C and D can be eliminated. 0th order kinetics is a fixed rate of decrease in the concentration of a reactant over time. The slope of the line is linear and closely resembles the curve for the 10 mM line in Figure 2. Choice A is the best answer.

21. **B is the best answer.** Hexokinase is an enzyme that facilitates the transfer of one phosphate from ATP to glucose to produce glucose-6-phosphate. An enzyme is responsible for lowering the activation energy of a reaction to make it more likely that a reaction will occur. Choice A shows an increase in activation energy, which is the opposite of the effect of an enzyme. The activation energy is the ΔG from the reactants to the top of the curve. Choice A can be eliminated. Choices C and D show curves that do not have a positive activation energy. The role of an enzyme is to lower a high energy of activation to one that can be overcome by correctly orienting reactants and increasing the probability that they will react by concentrating them in the enzyme active site. One feature of biological reactions that are mediated by an enzyme is that they have a positive activation energy. This positive activation energy helps to control which reactions take place and allows a change in enzyme concentration to help dictate the production of products. This helps to eliminate choices C and D. Choice B is the best answer choice because it shows a decrease in the activation energy due to the action of hexokinase.

22. **D is the best answer.** According to the last paragraph, 2-Deoxy-D-Glucose inhibits hexokinase from catalyzing the transfer of a phosphate from ATP to glucose. 2-Deoxy-D-Glucose is most likely a structural analogue of glucose that does not contain an –OH at the 2′ position, meaning that it cannot receive the phosphate. Competitive inhibition occurs when a molecule can bind in the active site to prevent enzymatic action. Competitive inhibitors resemble the structures of the raw substrate, eliminating choice A. Competitive inhibition can be overcome by adding in excess substrate, which in this example, would be glucose. Choice B can be eliminated. Inhibition can also be overcome by increasing the concentration of the enzyme. One way to do this would be to increase the rate of transcription of hexokinase, eliminating choice C. Allosteric inhibitors bind at sites outside of the active site and often do not structurally resemble to normal substrate. Because 2-Deoxy-D-Glucose likely binds in the active site, choice D is the best answer choice.

Passage 5 (Questions 23-27)

23. **B is the best answer.** The breakdown products of lactose are glucose and galactose, and they are shown in Figure 1. It can be noted that the only difference between these two molecules is the position of the hydroxyl group at the C4 carbon. Anomers are two cyclic saccharides that differ in their configuration at the hemiacetal carbon, also known as the anomeric carbon (C1). The anomeric carbon is the carbon that contains the carbonyl group when the sugar is in the straight chain form. Because the differences between glucose and galactose do not occur at the anomeric carbon, choice A can be eliminated. Epimers are two molecules that differ in their configuration at a single stereocenter. The term epimers would correctly describe the relationship between glucose and galactose as they differ in configuration only at the C4 carbon. Stereoisomers are compounds that possess the same molecular formula and arrangement of bonds, but differ in their conformations in space. While glucose and galactose are stereoisomers, epimers is a more specific term that accurately describes these molecules, so choice C is not the best answer. Diastereomers are a type of stereoisomer in which the configuration at one or more, but not all, stereocenters is different. In the same way that glucose and galactose are stereoisomers, they could also be considered diastereomers, but because epimers provides a more specific description of their differences, choice D can be eliminated, and choice B remains as the best answer.

24. **B is the best answer.** The question is testing the function of the enzyme lactase. It is shown in Figure 1 that lactase cleaves lactose to yield glucose and galactose. Carbon rings are numbered based on the open conformation where C1 is the carbon on the end closest to a carbonyl bond. When in the ring form, the above numbering system will be consistent, but the carbonyl carbon has become the anomeric carbon. Using this numbering system, it can be seen that galactose and glucose that make lactose are linked at C1 and C4, respectively. Choices C and D can be eliminated because they improperly identify the carbons involved the linkage. The linkage can either be an alpha or beta linkage. This type of linkage is identified by the position of the hydroxyl group on the anomeric carbon (C1) involved in the bond. In lactose, the anomeric carbon of galactose is in the beta position because the hydroxyl is on the same side of the ring as the CH_2OH group. Since the linkage pictured in Figure 1 is a beta(1,4) linkage between the two monosaccharides, choice A should be eliminated, and choice B should be selected as the best answer.

25. **B is the best answer.** The glycosidic linkage describes the covalent bond that binds a carbohydrate to another molecule. That other molecule could be a carbohydrate or other type of compound. In this case, it is a carbohydrate as the glycosidic linkage is used to form a disaccharide. Individuals with high levels of lactose in their system should have a higher level of glycosidic linkages than those with a low level of lactose, assuming all else is equal. Group 1 is the normal weight, lactose intolerant group. This choice can be eliminated, because they would not be expected to have exceedingly high level of glycosidic linkage in their body following milk deprivation, due to a lack of lactose intake. Group 2 is the overweight, lactose intolerant group. One might expect that following the consumption of milk, the lactose intolerant groups would have a higher level of glycosidic linkage due to their inability to break down lactose, making choice B a strong answer. Group 3 is the overweight, control group. After milk deprivation they would not be expected to have elevated glycosidic linkages within their body due to a lack of lactose intake, eliminating choice C. Group 4 is the normal weight control group, and they would not be expected to have the highest signal of glycosidic linkage following lactose consumption due to their ability to break down these bonds using the enzyme lactase. This eliminates choice D, and leaves choice B as the best answer.

26. **C is the best answer.** The main topic this question aims to test is the common names of disaccharides. The enzyme lactase is named after the common name of the disaccharide it breaks down, lactose. This question requires knowledge of the common name of the disaccharide comprised of two glucose molecules. Sucrose, the molecule that would be broken down by sucrase, is comprised of a glucose and a fructose molecule, so choice A can be eliminated. Fructose is actually a monosaccharide comprised of only itself. Fructase, so named as the enzyme that may break down fructose, would not be responsible for breaking down two glucose molecules, eliminating choice B. Maltase would be the enzyme that breaks down maltose. Maltose is formed from two glucose molecules, making choice C the best answer. It should also be noted that fructase also is not a real enzyme, but fructose is broken down by enzymes known as aldolases. For example, an aldolase is the enzyme responsible for breaking down fructose into glyceraldehyde-3-phosphate and dihydroxyacetone phosphate in glycolysis. Although aldolase is a real enzyme, it does not break down the disaccharide formed by two glucose molecules, so choice D should also be eliminated.

27. **B is the best answer.** This question aims to test the configuration of carbohydrates in nature. Humans are able to digest many naturally occurring carbohydrates. Almost all carbohydrates in nature are found in the D-configuration. This is the opposite configuration as amino acids, which are found in the L-configuration. However it is important to note that D and L are not always the same as R and S. In the case of carbohydrates, D corresponds with R. In the case of amino acids, most of the 20 L amino acids are S, except for cysteine. Choice A can be eliminated because human digestion tolerates the L-form of amino acids and D-form of carbohydrates. Choice B is a strong answer because it is known that carbohydrates have the opposite isomeric configuration from amino acids. Choice C can be eliminated because carbohydrate digestion is a complex process that requires energy and enzymes in order to occur. Choice D can be eliminated because as discussed above, the amino acids that humans digest are in the L-configuration while the carbohydrates are in the D-configuration. This leaves choice B as the best answer.

Stand-alones (28-31)

28. **C is the best answer.** Glycogen is a polysaccharide composed of alpha linkages of only glucose, so choice A can be eliminated. Glycogen is found in many cells, though it is primarily stored in the liver and in muscle where it can be broken down easily to glucose for energy, so choice B can be eliminated. Glycogen is a storage molecule and it is formed when there is abundant glucose in contrast to the fasting state when the glycogen must be broken down to provide glucose, so choice D can be eliminated. Choice C accurately depicts the location where glycogen is formed. It may be easier to remember this fact when considering that muscle is in need of abundant glucose to be readily available during exercise. The liver controls metabolic needs and stores glycogen to provide energy to the body when blood glucose is low.

29. **D is the best answer.** This question is asking about the structure of nucleotides and nucleic acids. First, consider the difference between DNA and RNA. The second carbon of the sugar is deoxygenated, so 2′ must be included in one of the answers. Choice B can be eliminated. Next, consider the structure of the DNA backbone. The hydroxyl group of the third carbon is covalently bound to a phosphate that is connected to the fifth carbon of the next nucleotide. In order to interrupt this bonding, either the 3′ or the 5′ carbon must be missing from a ddNTP. Choice C does not contain either of these, and can be eliminated. If 5′ was missing its hydroxyl group, then there would not be a phosphate attached to the sugar, and the compound would be called a nucleoside rather than a nucleotide. Since ddNTPs are nucleotides, this is not the case, and choice A can be eliminated. This leaves choice D as the best answer.

30. **D is the best answer.** The question refers to the structure of the different DNA nucleotides, but one does not need to memorize the structures to answer this question correctly. The clue in the stem is that there is only one nitrogen-containing ring and a sugar. This fits with the fact that pyrimidines are smaller and have only one such ring in contrast to the purines that have double rings. Since thymine and cytosine are both pyrimidines, and only thymine is given as an answer choice, choice D is the best answer. Pyridoxine in choice A is another name for vitamin B6, which is composed of a heterocyclic ring but no sugar group. Knowledge of this structure is beyond the scope of the MCAT®, but it could be misread as "pyrimidine" which could be selected unintentionally. Adenine and guanine both have larger double rings.

31. **B is the best answer.** Nucleotides are composed of a nitrogenous bases, pentose sugar, and phosphate group. In DNA, the bases come together in the interior of the double stranded helix and the sugar-phosphate backbone remain on the outside of the molecule. The nuclear envelope serves to limit what can and cannot enter the nucleus. The cytosol freely flows through the nuclear envelope and is in direct contact with the DNA. Choice A can be eliminated because the nucleus is an aqueous environment. The sugar-phosphate backbone lines the outside of the DNA molecule. The polar nature of the backbone interacts favorably with the hydrophilic environment of the cell. This interaction helps to shield the hydrophobic bases from the cytosol and provides stability to the DNA. Choice B is a strong answer. Base-pairing between nitrogenous bases helps to stabilize the core of the DNA molecule. However, the hydrophobic nature of the nitrogenous bases remains and they still need to be protected from the cytosol. Choice C can be eliminated because it does not explain how DNA can be stable in a hydrophilic environment. Destabilization of DNA results in death of the cell. DNA is required for the cell to produce proteins so its destabilization would severely impair cellular function. Choice D can be eliminated because DNA is stable within cells and does not require constant regeneration. Choice B is the best answer because it explains how DNA can remain stable in a polar environment.

Passage 6 (Questions 32-35)

32. **B is the best answer.** The data presented in Figure 1 is most directly related to this question. Figure 1 presents the results of a Western Blot, an analytical technique that is used for quantifying protein concentrations. Notice that two different fractions are measured – a lipid raft fraction and a non-lipid raft fraction. In the non-raft fraction, upon stimulation of the cells by EDLF, the intensity of the band for Fas/CD95 decreases, indicating that the level of protein decreased. Choice B is the best answer. Choice A can be eliminated because the EDLF-stimulated band would be darker and thicker than the control if the protein level increased. Choice C can be eliminated because the bands would have the same intensity if the protein levels remained the same. Figure 1 quantifies protein concentrations, eliminating choice D.

33. **D is the best answer.** The question asks for the type of interaction that forms secondary structures in proteins, such as alpha helices and beta-pleated sheets. Hydrogen bonds are primarily responsible for maintaining these protein shapes. Choices A and B can be eliminated because covalent and ionic bonding occur between directly adjacent atoms within a molecule, not between different domains of a protein. The exception to this are disulfide bonds, but disulfide bonds are not critical in maintaining the shape of alpha helices. Electrostatic interactions primarily play a role in tertiary and quaternary structure, eliminating choice C.

34. **B is the best answer.** This question asks for the RNA sequence complementary to 5′-UGCAUGCA-3′. RNA uses uracil (U) bases in place of thymine (T) bases, so choices A and D can be eliminated. Choice B is the best answer because it contains U instead of T and each base from 5′ to 3′ pairs correctly with the bases in the mRNA, read 3′ to 5′. Choice C can be eliminated because the base pairing does not match. A always pairs with U and C always pairs with G between RNA strands. Choice C mistakenly pairs each nucleotide with its same nucleotide on the opposite strand (A with A, C with C, G with G, and U with U).

35. **C is the best answer.** This question hints at the stability of a DNA double helix. Remember that A pairs with T via two hydrogen bonds, while G pairs with C via three hydrogen bonds. Breaking three hydrogen bonds would require more heat than breaking two hydrogen bonds; the best answer would contain the greatest number of C and/or G nucleotides. Choice A contains 2 C/G nucleotides, choice B contains 4 C/G nucleotides, choice C contains 6 C/G nucleotides, and choice D contains no C/G nucleotides. Choice C contains the most C/G nucleotides, giving it the largest number of hydrogen bonds to break, and would require the highest denaturation temperature.

Passage 7 (Questions 36-39)

36. **A is the best answer.** The nucleoside analog in the figure has two fused rings. This is characteristic of purines. Pyrimidines have one ring. Uracil, cytosine and thymine are all pyrimidines. One way to remember this is: "pyrimidine" contains a "y," and so do "cytosine" and "thymine." Uracil replaces the thymine in RNA, so it must also be a pyrimidine. Adenine is a purine. The best answer is choice A.

37. **B is the best answer.** As stated in the passage, long term exposure to NRTIs leads to the inhibition of DNA polymerase γ, which synthesizes mitochondrial DNA. This eventually leads to oxidative stress and mitochondrial dysfunction. Because HAD is a form of HAND, one would expect a decrease in HAD to decrease the incidence of HAND, not increase it. This eliminates choice A. If neurons displayed a higher sensitivity to mitochondrial dysfunction than other types of cells, this may account for the increasing incidence of HIV associated neurocognitive disorders with increasing exposure to NRTIs. For this reason choice B is a strong answer choice. The purpose of NRTIs is to inhibit reverse transcriptase, an enzyme only present in infected human cells. It is the cross reactivity of NRTIs with other enzymes that use nucleosides or nucleotides as substrates which leads to unwanted side effects like HAND. Because choice C describes the intended effect of NRTIs, it does not explain the rise in HAND and is not the best answer. NRTIs can only form 3′ phosphodiester bonds when they have been converted to active triphosphates. In their inactive form, they can neither inhibit reverse transcriptase nor interfere with DNA polymerase γ. Choice D does not answer the question because it cannot explain the rise in HAND. Since both choice C and choice D could not explain the rise in HAND, choice B is the best answer choice.

38. **A is the best answer.** Based on the information in the passage, NRTIs are nucleoside analogs, which require activation by cellular enzymes to their active forms. A nucleoside is a nitrogenous base fused to a pentose sugar. Nucleotides are nucleoside plus a phosphate group. When DNA polymerases and reverse transcriptases are building DNA strands, they form a bond between the hydroxyl of the 3' sugar on the existing strand and the 5′ phosphate on the incoming nucleotide. In order for a nucleoside to be an active drug it must be converted into a nucleotide. As described in the passage, the host cell enzymes take care of this through phosphorylation. What the question is really asking is why the NRTI is inactive. Choice A, the absence of a phosphate group, describes what distinguishes the NRTI from its nucleotide, or active, form. This makes choice A the best answer. Choice B and C can be eliminated because a nucleoside consists of these two components. Choice D can be eliminated because it describes the purpose of the prodrug once it is activated.

39. **A is the best answer.** Mitochondria are responsible for ATP generation. RNA polymerase is responsible for the transcription of cellular proteins. DNA polymerase III is responsible for DNA replication during cell division. Data that would support heightened sensitivity of DNA polymerase γ over DNA polymerase III would show signs of distress due to mitochondrial processes before processes related to DNA replication and cell division. ATP depletion is a sign of mitochondrial failure. Cell death in an otherwise healthy cell would indicate that the NRTI affected the DNA polymerase γ. Option I should be include in the best answer, eliminating choices C and D. The absence of cytoplasmic kinase mRNAs would indicate a problem with transcription, the regulation of gene expression or post transcriptional destruction of mRNA, but nothing to do with DNA polymerase III. Option II will not be included in the best answer, eliminating choice B. Recall that during the life cycle of a cell, cellular growth will occur in preparation for cellular division. This stage is called G_1 and proceeds the S phase where DNA is replicated. If there was a problem with the DNA polymerase III, the cells would grow in G_1 but fail to complete S phase and divide. Abnormally large cells likely indicate NRTI inhibition of DNA polymerase III rather than DNA polymerase γ. Option III should not be included in the best answer. Choice A is the best answer.

Passage 8 (Questions 40-44)

40. **A is the best answer.** The DNA molecule is a double-helix, meaning that two helices curve around each other. This question is asking about how the DNA maintains its secondary structure by binding itself, not how GAPDH binds the DNA itself. Each half of the double helix is one strand of single strand DNA joined together by the phosphodiester backbone. Upon correct base pairing between A and T and G and C, the two strands join to form a double helix with a major and a minor groove that allow for binding of proteins to DNA. DNA bases are polar due to the presence of nitrogen atoms and carbonyl bonds. Van der Waals attractions form between nonpolar molecules, eliminating choice B. Disulfide bonds form between cysteine amino acids. Amino acids are components of proteins, not nucleic acids, eliminating choice C. Electrostatic attractions form between opposite charges. The DNA bases themselves are not charged, though the backbone is negatively charged. Choice D can be eliminated. Hydrogen bonds form between A and T and G and C. These hydrogen bonds allow the two strands to join to form the double helix. Choice A is the best answer choice.

41. **D is the best answer.** The chemistry of nucleic acid polymerization that is catalyzed by DNA polymerase or RNA polymerase allows the 3′ hydroxyl of the deoxyribose to serve as a nucleophile to attack the first phosphate of an incoming nucleotide, which contains the triphosphate moiety. The 5′ end of the deoxyribose is not responsible for the nucleophilic attack. Additionally, nucleosides are the base plus the sugar and do not contain phosphate molecules. Choice A can be eliminated. The 3′ hydroxyl serves to link the growing nucleic acid chain together, freeing the β and γ phosphates to help drive the reaction. If the γ phosphate were attacked, two phosphate molecules would be found between bases, which is not the case, eliminating choice B. The base does not serve as a nucleophile and the nucleoside contains no phosphate molecules, eliminating choice C. Choice D is the best answer because attack of the alpha phosphate allows for one phosphate molecule to separate the nucleosides in a DNA molecule.

42. **D is the best answer.** The alpha carbon of an amino acid is bound to hydrogen, the carboxylic acid, the amino group, and the side chain that gives the amino acid its biological properties. Because it is bound for four chemically distinct groups, it is optically active and can rotate plane polarized light. Another way of saying this is that the alpha carbon is chiral. Alanine is a nonpolar amino acid that could help stabilize the aromatic ring of SA. However, eukaryotic amino acids are L configurations at the alpha carbon, not D configurations, which would be the opposite chirality. Option I would be unlikely to stabilize SA in human GAPDH because human GAPDH would not contain D-Alanine. Threonine is a polar amino acid that contains a hydroxyl group that could hydrogen bond with the hydroxyl and carboxylic acid groups. In addition, option II is an L amino acid. Because L-Threonine is both an L amino acid and could hydrogen bond, option II would stabilize SA, eliminating it as the best answer choice. Serine is a polar amino acid that could hydrogen bond with the hydroxyl and carboxylic acid of SA. Option III is a D amino acid, however, not an L amino acid, meaning that human GAPDH would not contain D-Serine. Option III would be part of the best answer. Choice A can be eliminated because D-Serine would also not be found in eukaryotic GAPDH and could not stabilize HA. Choice B can be eliminated because L-threonine could stabilize SA. Choice C can be eliminated for the same reason. Choice D is the best answer because eukaryotic GAPDH would not contain D amino acids and could not stabilize SA.

43. **D is the best answer.** Amino acids are the building blocks of proteins. Proteins contain many of the 20 common amino acids all linked together via dehydration reactions into polypeptides. Each amino acid has a unique functional group, called its side chain or R group. These groups determine how the protein interacts with substrates, like SA. The various structures of the R groups also allow them to stabilize other parts of the protein or link multiple polypeptides into larger protein structures. Nucleic acids are the building blocks of DNA and RNA. Because GAPDH is a protein, choice A can be eliminated. Carbohydrates are broken down to supply the cell with energy and can also be attached to various proteins to form glycoproteins that are often found on the extracellular parts of the plasma membrane. GAPDH is not composed primarily of carbohydrates, eliminating choice B. Fatty acids store energy within cells and also can be broken down to provide a supply of ATP. They do not make up proteins, eliminating choice C. Because amino acids are the building blocks of proteins, they are most likely to compose GAPDH, making choice D the best answer choice.

44. **C is the best answer.** Figure 3 and a knowledge of how antibodies function in western blot experiments is needed to begin answering this question. Antibodies are polypeptides that recognize specific sequences of amino acids called an epitope. While antibodies do not catalyze enzymatic reactions, they do allow immune system cells like macrophages and dendritic cells to phagocytize pathogens like bacteria and viruses. MNNG serves to drive GAPDH to translocate to the nucleus. As the concentration of glycyrrhizin increases, the bands of the western blot become less dense, meaning that a lower amount of GAPDH protein is found in the nucleus, eliminating choice A. If a lower amount of GAPDH is found in the nucleus, there would be a decrease, not increase, in binding of GAPDH to DNA, eliminating choice B. The information contained in the passage does not suggest that GAPDH binds RNA directly. It most likely acts to help initiate transcription in the nucleus, according to paragraph two. Figure 3 shows that less antibody against GAPDH is binding the nuclear fraction with increasing concentrations of glycyrrhizin, making choice C the best answer choice.

Stand-alones (45-48)

45. **D is the best answer.** Since only chiral molecules rotate plane polarized light, this question can be rewritten to say "Which amino acid is not chiral?" Since all amino acids have an acid group, an amine group and a hydrogen, the R group will determine chirality. Chiral molecules must have all unique substituents originating from an atom, so if the R group matches the acid, amine, or hydrogen, then it is not chiral. Isoleucine, valine and proline all have four different substituents and are chiral. Glycine has a hydrogen as the fourth substituent. Since there are two hydrogens on the α carbon, glycine is achiral and does not rotate plane polarized light, so choice D is the best answer.

46. **A is the best answer.** Under physiologic pH, amino acids exit as zwitterions. A polypeptide will have a C-terminus that is negatively charged and an N-terminus that is positively charged. Each acidic amino acid with a pKa below approximately 7 will be negatively charged because the acid will donate its proton to the solution. Basic amino acids will be positively charged because they will gain a proton from the solution. All other amino acids are neutral. Overall, chain A will have a net charge of 2-, and chain B will have a net charge of 3+. Since the chains are connected by disulfide bonds, they are covalently bound and will not dissociate during migration. Choice D can be eliminated. Overall the molecule is positively charged (+3 and -2 will give +1). It will migrate towards the negative pole, so choice A is the best answer.

If the molecule had been negatively charged it would travel to the positive pole. Choice B can be eliminated. If the molecule were neutral, it would not travel to either pole. Choice C can be eliminated.

47. **A is the best answer.** Cooperativity occurs when the binding of a substrate at one active site increases the affinity for the substrate at another active site. The saturation curve begins with a low slope to reflect the affinity of the enzyme for the initial substrate. Once the first active site is bound, the slope of the curve dramatically increases to reflect the higher affinity of the substrate for the subsequent active sites. In other words, the steeper slope shows that the second, third and fourth oxygen molecules bind to hemoglobin at faster rates than the preceding oxygen molecule. An allosteric inhibitor would alter the conformation of a protein and prevent it from binding any substrate. Choice B is not the best answer because the pH of blood causes shifts in the curve left or right, but does not cause the sigmoidal shape. Choice C is necessary for cooperativity to occur, but multiple binding spots alone does not mean that cooperativity occurs. For example, an enzyme may be able to bind two substrates, but the affinity for the substrate would not change. An isoform refers to two or more proteins that are functionally, but not structurally identical. Choice D is not the best answer because the saturation curves of each of the isoforms would be considered separately if they had differing mechanisms of saturation.

48. **A is the best answer.** Choice A is the condensed molecular formula for mercaptoethanol, which disrupts disulfide bonds by reduction. Even without identifying the reagent, it is still possible to deduce the best answer. The most notable bonding activity of cystine is a covalent disulfide bond. This occurs between two sulfur atoms of the thiol groups that form its side chain. Recognizing that the reagent in choice A contains sulfur suggests that it would be most likely to interfere with this activity. Choice B is the formula for dichloromethane, an organic solvent that might disrupt hydrophobic interactions, but would have no effect on a covalent bond. Choice C is the molecular formula for urea, which disrupts hydrogen bonds, but it is unlikely to break a covalent bond. Choice D is acetic acid, and could play a role in disrupting various electrostatic bonds by protonating the negatively charged member, but would not break covalent bonds.

Passage 9 (Questions 49-52)

49. **B is the best answer.** The structures of compounds A-D contain many conjugated benzene rings and its derivatives. The amino acids that contain cyclic portions on their side chains or contain highly conjugated systems would likely structurally resemble compounds A-D. Tyrosine, Y, contains a hydroxyl-substituted benzene ring, eliminating choice A as the best answer choice. Phenylalanine, F, contains a benzene ring on its side chain, eliminating choice C as the best answer choice. Tryptophan contains two rings, one that is a benzene and one that is a pyrrole, eliminating choice D. Cysteine, C, contains an –SH on its side chain and no conjugation or cyclic structures, making it the least likely to resemble compounds A-D. Choice B is the best answer choice.

50. **A is the best answer.** The third paragraph describes how compound C binds only to the active site of AChE. Competitive inhibitors compete with the true substrate for the enzyme active site, resulting in an increase in K_m with no corresponding change in Vmax. Option I characterizes compound C. Noncompetitive inhibitors bind to sites other than the active site of the enzyme, leading to a decrease in V_{max} with no change in K_m. Because compound C binds in the active site, option II can be eliminated. Uncompetitive inhibitors bind to the enzyme-substrate complex but not to the active site of the enzyme. They can change both the K_m and the V_{max}. Because compound C does bind the active site, it is not an uncompetitive inhibitor, eliminating option III. The best answer choice will contain only option I, making choice A the best answer.

51. **B is the best answer.** Paragraph three describes how compound E functions by binding in the active site of AChE, which makes it a competitive inhibitor. In the Lineweaver-Burk plot presented above, a competitive inhibitor would raise K_m and maintain V_{max}. The x-intercept represents $1/K_m$, so the best answer will show an intercept with a value closer to zero, or the origin on the graph provided. With a competitive inhibitor, the K_m would increase, meaning that the value of $1/K_m$ would decrease and become closer to zero. The y-intercept represents $1/V_{max}$, so it should not change. Choice A represents a non-competitive inhibitor that decreases V_{max} and keeps K_m constant. Choice A can be eliminated because the y-intercept is higher in A versus the no competition, meaning that the value of $1/V_{max}$ is larger, making V_{max} smaller. Choice A can be eliminated. Choices C and D represent allosteric activators of the protein, as V_{max} is increased and K_m is maintained. V_{max} is increased in both of these choices because the value of the y-intercept, $1/V_{max}$, is reduced, meaning that V_{max} is higher. Choices C and D can be eliminated. Additionally, there is no way to distinguish between choices C and D from the information provided in the passage, so the answer choices may also be eliminated this way. Choice B is the best answer because it shows the same y-intercept, maintaining V_{max}, while showing an increased K_m.

52. **B is the best answer.** Endocytosis involves invagination of the plasma membrane and transport of membrane bound receptors or endocytosed particles to the endosome and then the lysosome as the endosome acidifies. ACh receptors would be found on the cell surface of the neuron synapse to allow for ACh binding to trigger an action potential in the receiving dendrite. It is reasonable that ACh receptors may be endocytosed upon binding ACh, eliminating choice A. Phosphatidylcholine and sphingomyelin are both components of the plasma membrane and are lipids that help maintain membrane fluidity and a barrier to diffusion of large, polar molecules. Because the plasma membrane is pinched off and used to transport molecules, it is reasonable to assume that some membrane lipids would be in the lysosome membrane, eliminating choices C and D. Heavily glycosylated molecules are surrounded by a large hydration shell that helps protect them from the acidic lumen of the lysosome. Specific knowledge of the neuron and the lysosome are not required to choose the best answer choice for this question. It is important to know that adding sugars to molecules allows water to associate and protect them from hydrolysis, making choice B the best answer.

Passage 10 (Questions 53-56)

53. **C is the best answer.** Table 2 shows the kinetics for the mutant and wild type G6PD enzymes. For the MCAT® it is important to know the effect each type of inhibitor has on the V_{max} and K_m. Competitive inhibitors increase the K_m without changing the V_{max}. This is not what is shown in Table 2 so choice A can be eliminated. Uncompetitive inhibitors decrease both the K_m and the V_{max}. This is also not shown in Table 2 so choice B can be eliminated. Mixed inhibitors decrease the V_{max} and can either increase or decrease the K_m. Table 2 shows a large decrease in V_{max} and an increase in K_m which matches the effects of mixed inhibitors. So, choice C is the best answer. Noncompetitive inhibitors decrease the V_{max} without changing K_m so choice D can be eliminated. Table 2 contains more information than is needed to answer the question. It may be tempting to try to use the K_i's listed in the table. The K_i is the inhibitor constant and is an indicator of how potent the inhibitor is. Table 2 shows how potency of inhibitors is changed in the G6PD mutation. However, K_i data cannot be used to determine the type of inhibition occurring so this data is not helpful in answering this question.

54. **C is the best answer.** Table 1 shows the second most common mutation is the Chinese-4 mutation, cause by Gly131Val. According to the table description, mutations are written as the original amino acid, followed by the position, followed by the new amino acid. Glycine is the smallest amino acid because it lacks a side chain. It is considered nonpolar because the side chain lacks any polar groups. Valine is a larger, branched amino acid with an isopropyl side chain. Valine is also nonpolar. Choices A and B can be eliminated because both Gly and Val are nonpolar. Choice C is a strong answer because it correctly defines the characteristics of glycine and valine. Choice D can be eliminated because glycine is not aromatic. The aromatic amino acids are tyrosine and phenylalanine.

55. **D is the best answer.** Enzymes are usually named for their reactant. So, glucose 6 phosphate dehydrogenase has glucose-6-phosphate as a substrate. Glucose and phosphate are both polar groups so the active site should have polar amino acid residues. The polar amino acids are serine (S), threonine (T), cysteine (C), asparagine (N), tyrosine (Y) and glutamine (Q). The only answer choice with only polar amino acids listed is choice D, so this is the best answer. To remember the one letter codes of amino acids, it is helpful to realize how they were assigned. The smallest (based on molecular weight) amino acids took priority for the codes. So, glycine is G (as opposed to glutamine or glutamate), alanine is A (as opposed to asparagine, aspartate, or arginine), leucine is L (as opposed to lysine), proline is P (as opposed to phenylalanine) and threonine is T (as opposed to tyrosine or tryptophan). Then, the following mnemonics can be helpful: Qlutamine, glutamEEc acid (E), asparDic acid (D), aRginine (R), Fenylalanine (F), tYrosine (Y), and tWyptophan (W). For lysine, K is alphabetically after L so lysine's letter is K. For asparagine, it is the smallest amino acid with an amino side chain so its letter is N.

56. **C is the best answer.** Hydrolases are enzymes that use water to break a bond, that is they catalyze hydrolysis reactions. There is no information in the passage to suggest this occurs, so choice A is not a strong answer. Lyases are enzymes that cleave bonds without water. This means that lyases are used to catalyze reactions in which functional groups are added to double bond. In terms from organic chemistry, hydrolases do substitution reactions with water as the nucleophile. Alternatively, lyases do elimination reactions. Like choice A, there is no information to support choice B so it is not a strong answer. G6PD stands for glucose 6 phosphate dehydrogenase and involves NADPH. NADPH is oxidized to $NADP^+$ through electron transfer which is characteristic of oxidoreductase type enzymes. Dehydrogenase enzymes are always oxidoreductases. So, choice C is the best answer. Transferases transfer functional groups from one molecule to another. There is no information in the passage to suggest this occurs so choice D is not the best answer.

Stand-alones (57-59)

57. **B is the best answer.** Based on the information provided in the question stem, peptides are mounted based on their association with these residues. Choice A is a possible answer because it has two similar substitutions, however one comes in the last position, which would mean that the end of the peptide is not secured in the groove. Choice B has only one similar difference, which means closer approximation of function, and that position is in the middle of the sequence. This allows for greater security than if the first or last position were compromised. Choices C and D both have two substitutions, making them weaker answer choices. In choice C this is the middle two residues, and in choice D the first and last residues. Since choice B has only one substitution, and it is more likely to be able to compensate for the error, it is the best answer.

58. **C is the best answer.** This question does not require any knowledge of the structure of immunoglobulins. The goal of the experiment is to isolate the chains from one another to analyze them. The isolation process should be as direct and careful as possible to maintain as much of the protein structure as possible. Choice A is problematic because heat has the effect of breaking all types of bonds and is not at all specific. It can dramatically alter the proteins in the process. Choice B is also a bit extreme as urea would destroy the hydrogen bonds that are the foundation of a protein's secondary structure with regards to α-helices and β-sheets. Choice C is the best answer, since it represents a direct approach to dissolve the disulfide bonds that are fundamental to the attachment of large chains to one another. The benefit of this approach is that there would be no effect on secondary structure or other aspects of the tertiary structure. Organic solvents would disturb the hydrophobic interactions without disrupting the covalent disulfide bonds, eliminating choice D.

59. **C is the best answer.** The solubility of proteins is dependent on the distribution of their hydrophilic and hydrophobic groups. All of the answers exchange an amino acid with a more hydrophilic alternative. The actual change in solubility must be balanced with the change in conformation based on the size of the R group. Choice A substitutes the amide group of glutamine for the guanidium group of arginine. This is significantly longer and is charged, making it an unlikely candidate despite both possessing nitrogenous groups. Choice B substitutes a nonpolar isoleucine for glutamate. While this will increase the solubility, this change will likely significantly change the conformation of the protein, so choice B can be eliminated. Choice C and D are similar in that they change a soluble hydroxyl group to an amide group, which is more soluble. Both choices also change a smaller amino acid for a larger one. Choice C, threonine to asparagine, has a smaller increase in size and is less likely to significantly change the conformation of the protein than choice D, serine to glutamine. Choice C is the best answer.

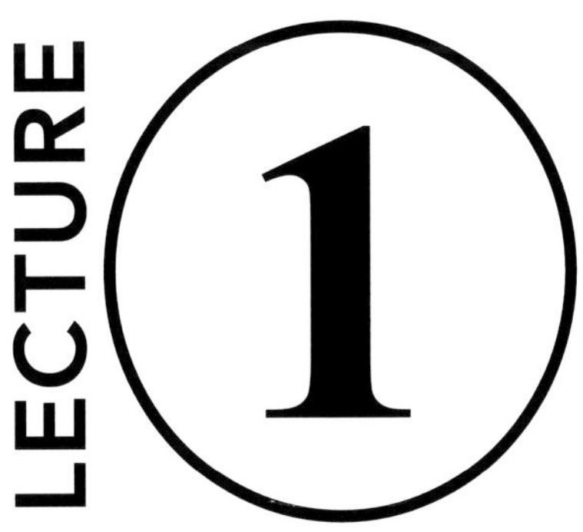

Biological Molecules and Enzymes

TEST 1B

ANSWERS & EXPLANATIONS

Questions 1–59

Passage 1 (Questions 1-4)

1. **B is the best answer.** The first paragraph notes that cancer immunotherapy relies on the expression of neo-antigen only on cancer cells, not normal cells. It can be assumed that the utility of immunotherapy to specifically target cancer cells would be reduced if the neo-antigen were expressed on normal cells, eliminating choices C and D. The question stem reveals that SSX2, the antigen being targeted, is only expressed on normal cells when local inflammation is occurring. Without nearby inflammation, SSX2 would not appear on the surfaces of normal cells. Only in the instances of inflammation does the utility of targeting SSX2 for immunotherapy decrease.

2. **B is the best answer.** Arginine is a basic amino acid that is positively charged at physiologic pH, while threonine is a polar amino acid that has no net charge at physiologic pH. A codon that substitutes arginine for threonine would be a non-conservative amino acid substitution and likely change the conformation of the TCR to prevent the neo-antigen from binding the TCR. The second paragraph says that a TCR must recognize a neo-antigen to kill mutated cells. If the TCR could not recognize the antigen, the T cell would not be activated, and the ability of the T cells to lyse cancer cells would decrease. Choice A states the opposite and can be eliminated. An amino acid substitution would affect the ability of the T cell to lyse breast cancer cells, eliminating choice C. Choice D is also unlikely because enough information is provided in the second paragraph and the question stem to predict the outcome of a non-conservative amino acid substitution.

3. **A is the best answer.** cDNA is the reverse transcript product of mRNA. The mRNA that is reverse transcribed has already undergone splicing to eliminate introns, making choice A the best answer choice. The mRNA was alternatively spliced to eliminate unnecessary exons that could have been used to code for other proteins, eliminating choice D. Alternative splicing is the process that occurs on the primary RNA transcript that joins adjacent or non-adjacent exons together. Exons that do not code for a protein necessary in a specific cell type, for example, will be spliced out. Additionally, eukaryotic mRNA does not code for multiple proteins on the same mRNA transcript in the same way prokaryotes can when an operon is transcribed. Choice B is unlikely because enhancer elements are not transcribed into mRNA, while choice C is also less likely because all DNA is double stranded.

4. **B is the best answer.** The lower intracellular pH level indicates that excess hydrogens are available to protonate negatively charged amino acids like glutamate and aspartate. Protonation of these amino acids neutralizes their charges and causes proteins to denature, decreasing their activity. Denaturation of lysozyme and granzyme would decrease the killing of breast cancer cells. The question stem notes that the low pH is caused by increased glycolysis, which is ultimately derived from the energy stored in carbohydrates, making choice B the best answer. Amino acids, fatty acids, and nucleic acids do not provide substrates to glycolysis, making choices A, C, and D can be eliminated.

Passage 2 (Questions 5-8)

5. **C is the best answer.** Paragraph two notes that the base of the V3 loop is maintained by a bond between two cysteine residues. A disulfide bond forms between the two sulfur atoms in cysteine and is characteristically a covalent bond. The best answer choice will be the compound that can disrupt covalent bonding. Mercaptoethanol is the only solvent listed that has the ability to disrupt covalent bonds in proteins, making choice C the most likely answer. Urea, changing pH, and organic solvents can all disrupt secondary structure of proteins maintained by hydrogen bonds, electrostatic bonds, and hydrophobic interactions, respectively. However, none of these agents can disrupt covalently linked atoms, making choices A, B, and D unlikely to be the best answer choice.

6. **C is the best answer.** Paragraph two of the passage notes that the anti-parallel sheet and the alpha helix are linked via a kinked linker. The only amino acid that cannot hydrogen bond is proline, making it the ideal amino acid to cause kinks in linker chains. The five-membered ring structure of proline also distorts the helix, preventing efficient hydrogen bonding. Choice C is the best answer choice. Hydrogen bonds form between the hydrogen of one amino acid and the nitrogen or oxygen of another amino acid. Aspartic acid, glutamic acid, and lysine all have the ability to hydrogen bond and are unlikely to cause kinks in protein chains and more likely to contribute to secondary structures like alpha helices and anti-parallel sheets. Choices A, B, and D are unlikely to be the best answer choice. Another strategy to answering this question would be to choose the unique answer if three of them are similar. Lysine, Aspartic Acid, and Glutamic Acid can all commonly hydrogen bond. Even if a student was not aware that proline was specifically prohibited from hydrogen bonding, it could be eliminated because it was dissimilar to choices A, B, and D.

7. **B is the best answer.** Cofactors are additional atoms or molecules that are required for enzymes to function or proteins to maintain tertiary or quaternary structure. The most common metal cofactors in the human body are iron, copper, manganese, zinc, magnesium, and calcium. As choices A, C, and D could likely be contained in the enzyme required for CCR5 folding, they are unlikely to be the best answer. Tin is not regularly used as a cofactor and is the best answer choice.

8. **D is the best answer.** A synonymous mutation is one that does not change the identity of an amino acid, even though the nucleotide sequence giving rise to the codon encoding the amino acid does change. According to Figure 1, a mutation from R to K will decrease infectivity. However, because the question stem indicates a synonymous mutation, the arginine will remain and not mutate to a lysine, making a synonymous mutation of any of the three V3 loop residues equivalent by having no effect on infectivity. Choice D is the best answer choice. If a non-synonymous mutation from R to K occurred, then choices A, B, and C would be considered. Looking at Figure 1, mutations in the first amino acid (the one near the N terminus) have more of an effect than either the middle or C-terminus residues. However, because the mutation was synonymous, choices A, B, and C can be eliminated.

Passage 3 (Questions 9-12)

9. **B is the best answer.** To aggregate means "to cluster together", the best answer choice will probably explain a potential reason why individual Tau proteins would stick to one another. Phosphorylation and dephosphorylation reactions often alter activity of proteins, but because the passage does not present any information in regard to how these reactions affect Tau, both choices C and D can be eliminated. Proteins within a cell are dissolved in the aqueous cytosol, and consequently the amino acids exposed at the surface of the protein are hydrophilic, or polar. Protein misfolding can expose hydrophobic, or nonpolar, amino acid residues at the protein's surface and would likely induce hydrophobic interactions with other exposed nonpolar residues, eliminating choice A and making choice B the best answer.

10. **D is the best answer.** The passage does not reveal specific information about the location of Tau binding to DNA, but MCAT® background knowledge is sufficient to answer this question. Double-stranded DNA is composed of two complementary strands that bind together and curl into a double helix. The hydrogen bonding that occurs between complementary bases (A and T; C and G) is responsible for holding the DNA strands together, preventing the nitrogenous bases from being exposed to the outside of the DNA strand and making nitrogenous bases and base pairs unlikely targets for direct protein binding. Choices A and B can be eliminated. The sugar-phosphate backbone is exposed to the outside of the DNA and would be a more likely target for protein binding, making choice D the best answer. Choice C can be eliminated because DNA contains deoxyribose sugars, not ribose sugars.

11. **D is the best answer.** The passage states that hyperphosphorylation of Tau leads to increased neuronal degeneration. Decreasing the rate of Tau phosphorylation would reduce hyperphosphorylation, eliminating choice A. Similarly, increasing the rate of dephosphorylation of Tau would also reduce hyperphosphorylation, eliminating choice B. Although Tau is responsible for increased neuron degradation, the passage states that Tau also plays roles in microtubule stabilization and organization system. These processes are necessary in a healthy eukaryote, and inhibiting Tau completely would halt normal cell processes and harm the organism, making choice D an inviable treatment option in humans and the best answer. Choice C also inhibits Tau function, but by targeting only neuronal cells, it has less of a negative impact on the organism overall, so choice D is a better answer than choice C.

12. **C is the best answer.** Proteins that bind to DNA, including Tau, must enter the nucleus through nuclear pores, making choice C the best answer. Ribosomes are manufactured in the nucleolus but never translate mRNA into protein within the nucleus, eliminating choice A. Similarly, ribosomes do not bind to the nuclear membrane during translation, eliminating choice B. Although transport vesicles budding from the Golgi complex can fuse with various membranes in the cell, including the plasma membrane, lysosomes, and endosomes, these vesicles do not fuse with the nuclear membrane, eliminating choice D.

Stand-alones (13-16)

13. **D is the best answer.** The solubility of proteins is dependent on the distribution of their hydrophilic and hydrophobic groups. The process of separating proteins by altering their solvation potential is a common one, however it is usually accomplished with reagents or immunoprecipitation rather than genetic engineering. The key to this question is comparing the R groups of the various residues. The pair that has the largest decrease in solubility will be the best answer. Choice A substitutes aspartate for alanine. This is a strong possible answer as this replaces a carboxyl group with a methyl group which is nonpolar. Choice B replaces glutamine, which is polar with an amide group, with glycine which is somewhat nonpolar. So far choice A is stronger than choice B since alanine is more nonpolar than glycine. Choice C replaces alanine's methyl group with methionine, which is nearly identical in polarity. Choice C can be eliminated. Choice D replaces the carboxyl group of glutamate with the large, steric, benzene ring on phenylalanine. This substitutes a strongly hydrophilic hydrogen bond donor and acceptor with a large steric nonpolar group. This would be the largest change in solubility, and is the best answer.

14. **D is the best answer.** It can be intimidating to see the one-letter amino acid codes on Test Day, so consider writing out the names of each on the scratch paper. The choices, in order, refer to valine, cysteine, phenylalanine, and proline. Now consider how each contributes to the secondary structure of proteins, which includes α-helices. Valine does not have any particular contribution to secondary structure, so choice A can be eliminated. Cysteine is responsible for disulfide bonds in proteins, but these do not result in kinks in α-helices. Choice B is a weak choice. Phenylalanine does not contribute to secondary structure in any systematic way, so choice C can be eliminated. Proline stands out among amino acids because its R-group is bound to its N-terminus. This configuration results in kinks in the protein structure. Choice D is the best answer.

15. **B is the best answer.** The pI is the isoelectric point, the pH at which no net charge exists on a molecule. Acidic amino acids carry negative charges because they tend to donate protons. Basic amino acids carry positive charges because they accept protons. The isoelectric point of an acidic amino acid is less than 7 because, in acidic conditions, protons will be in excess. In that environment, the acidic side chain will not donate protons as readily to the surroundings and no charge will develop. Without the charge on the side chain, the amino acid will be a zwitterion. In other words, the pI describes the pH at which an amino acid exists as a zwitterion (zero net charge). The amino acid needed to answer the question will have a negative charge. Choice A is neutral. There is no acidic hydrogen present in the R-group, so choice A can be eliminated. The amino acid in choice B has two negatively charged carboxylic acid residues, so this is an acidic molecule. Choice B is a strong choice. Choice C is basic because it has developed a positive charge. That choice can be eliminated. Choice D is also basic because of the positive charge on the molecule. The alcohol group in this molecule is only very weakly acidic because loss of its hydrogen would result in a very strong base. Choice D can be eliminated. Notice that an excess of protons would not eliminate the positive charges in choices C and D. A high pH environment would be required to remove these charges. Choice B is the best answer.

16. **B is the best answer.** Remember that protein structure is written from the N-terminus to the C-terminus. Choices A and B both have R (arginine) and choices C and D both have N (asparagine). Asparagine contains nitrogen, but it is not basic. Choices C and D can be eliminated for that reason. To decide between choices A and B, consider the termini. The C-terminus of arginine will occur to the right of it as written in the sequence. That means that the zymogen will be activated when the peptide bond between R and E is cleaved. Choice A would result in a cleavage at the N-terminus, so it can be eliminated. Choice B is the best answer.

Passage 4 (Questions 17-20)

17. **B is the best answer.** This question is testing knowledge of binding affinities. If this study group found that there was no interaction occurring at the NMDA receptors, this could mean one of two things. The first is that the substrate, glutamate, did not bind at sufficient amounts to cause an interaction at the NMDA receptor. Alternatively, it could mean that so much inhibitor was bound to the NMDA receptor that no interaction was able to take place. Choice A is not the best answer because adding too little inhibitor, 2-BFI, would have the opposite effect in comparison to the *in vitro* experiment. If too little inhibitor was added, not all of the NMDA receptors would have an inhibitor bound to them, allowing them to continue to interact with the substrate molecules and an interaction to be observed. Choice B might be a tempting answer to eliminate because it states that adding too much substrate would yield zero interaction, which is inconsistent with the analysis provided above. However, remember that the amino acid substrates that are compatible with human consumption and use are in the L-form. The D-glutamate should theoretically not interact at the NMDA receptor even at the highest quantities. Choice C states that adding less substrate than in the original *in vitro* interaction could yield an immeasurable reaction at NMDA. While this might be true for some substrate levels, the answer choice does not give information to decide how much less, so choice B is a better answer. Choice D can be eliminated because adding too much of the proper substrate, L-glutamate, in the absence of any inhibitor should not manifest in zero interaction occurring at NMDA receptors. This eliminates choice D, and choice B is left as the best answer. An important takeaway from this question is that the concept being tested is which configuration of amino acid is used by the body, but the question stem makes this less clear by asking about inhibition and experimental set ups. Keep in mind that MCAT® questions are often designed to test concepts that differ from what the question appears to ask.

18. **C is the best answer.** The principles of inhibition for the MCAT® are taught with regard to enzyme structure and function. However, there are many biological molecules that can be subject to inhibition. The NMDA receptor provides a good example of this. When this receptor is activated, an ionic current is transmitted through the open channel, and the addition of an inhibitory molecule can alter the amount of current that is able to pass through. Concepts related to types of inhibition will still apply to these non-enzymatic molecules. Paragraph 3 states that 2-BFI is a reversible inhibitor that transiently binds the NMDA receptor. Choice A can be eliminated because typically mixed inhibition is reversible. Mixed inhibitors bind either the enzyme or the enzyme-substrate complex. Choice B is not the best answer because, although it is less clear mechanistically, these inhibitors also bind non-covalently to a site on the enzyme other than the active site. Since non-covalent binding is more typical of reversible inhibition, choice B is not the best answer. Choice C, a covalent modifier, is a strong answer because in most scenarios, covalent modification is associated with irreversible and toxic effects. Choice D can be eliminated because uncompetitive inhibitors bind reversibly to the enzyme-substrate complex and an allosteric site. Choice C is the best answer.

19. **A is the best answer.** The principles of inhibition for the MCAT® are taught with regard to enzyme structure and function. However, there are many biological molecules that can be subject to inhibition. Ionotropic receptors provide a strong example of this principle because when activated, an ionic current is transmitted through the open channel, and the addition of an inhibitory molecule can alter the amount of current that is able to pass through. Concepts related to types of inhibition will still apply to these non-enzymatic molecules. Figure 2 displays what looks very much like a reaction rate curve for NMDA-glutamate binding with and without inhibitor 2-BFI. Rather than measuring a reaction rate, what is being measured is the amount of current passing through the NMDA receptor for a given amount of substrate and inhibitor. This is depicted by plotting "Interaction Rate" on the y-axis. The inhibitor curve shows a markedly diminished interaction rate. It is known that this type of inhibition lowers the V_{max}. Looking to the answer choices, the best answer for this question will be a type of inhibition that does not yield a diminished V_{max}. Choice A, competitive inhibition, is a strong answer because it is known that this type of inhibition can be overcome by additional substrate addition. This means that at a high enough concentration of glutamate, NMDA should be able to achieve the same current as without 2-BFI. Because this was not observed, choice A is inconsistent with the data shown in Figure 2. The remaining choices are not the best answers for this question because inhibition that cannot be overcome by additional substrate will always have a diminished V_{max}. Choices B, C, and D, can be eliminated, leaving choice A as the best answer.

20. **B is the best answer.** The question stem indicates that nimodipine is a calcium channel blocker that binds to the L-type voltage gated calcium channel. Although this question is not describing an enzymatic reaction, remember that the principles of enzyme inhibition apply to other biological molecules, including receptors and channels. Because the principles of enzyme inhibition apply, nimodipine could bind competitively and block the calcium binding site of this channel, eliminating choice A. While nimodipine could bind in a noncompetitive fashion to a site on the channel that is not the calcium binding site, nimodipine would not be binding to a structural protein. Structural proteins are usually long fibrous proteins that provide strength to the cell and matrix. Structural proteins do not typically function as receptors or channels, making choice B a strong answer. Nimodipine blocks the entry of calcium through the L-type calcium channel, which would diminish the positive charge allowed to enter the cell, eliminating choice C. Nimodipine could work through an allosteric mechanism, and it would most likely bind to a globular protein given that it is known to bind to a calcium channel, and ion channels are most commonly comprised of globular proteins. This eliminates choice D, leaving choice B as the best answer.

Passage 5 (Questions 21-25)

21. **A is the best answer.** Figure 2 shows the structure of compound 57. Compound 57 contains many polar and electronegative groups, such as F and CN, and is likely positively charged a physiologic pH at the end of the molecule containing the terminal amine. As the compound is synthetic and does not mimic the structure of the fibrinogen protein, it is unlikely to have a cognate receptor in the body, preventing receptor mediated endocytosis. Choice B can be eliminated. Because it is highly polar and positively charged, it would associate with water, meaning that it is hydrophilic, not hydrophobic. Hydrophilic molecules do not diffuse through the plasma membrane, eliminating choice C. Ions channels allow small atoms like calcium, potassium, and sodium to travel across the plasma membrane. Compound 57 is much larger than these ions, preventing it from entering those channels, eliminating choice D. Active transport, using the energy of ATP or the diffusion gradient of another molecule, would allow compound 57 to move into the cell, making choice A the best answer choice.

22. **A is the best answer.** Figure 2 shows the portions of compound 57 that bind in different portions of the thrombin molecule. The end of the molecule that binds in the S1 site contains three nitrogen atoms in various bonding configurations in what is called a guanidinium group. Lysine, K, contains an amine at the end of its side chain that is positively charged, making it a basic amino acid. However, it does not contain the other two nitrogen moieties, eliminating choice B. Glycine, G, is a nonpolar amino acid with a hydrogen as its side chain. As it does not have a nitrogen on its side chain, choice C can be eliminated. Alanine, A, contains a methyl group as its side chain. Because it also does not have a nitrogen, choice D can be eliminated. Arginine contains a side chain that also has a guanidinium group at its end, making it most closely resemble the S1 binding portion of compound 57. Choice A is the best answer.

23. **C is the best answer.** According to Figure 1, calcium is required for the activation of prothrombin to thrombin. Prothrombin is what is known as a zymogen, or an inactive version of an enzyme. A zymogen must typically be cleaved into a smaller protein in order to become active. Calcium does not appear on the left of the reaction arrow and the passage does not indicate that prothrombin needs to react with calcium directly to generate a produce, eliminating choice A. Calcium does not appear on the right of the reaction arrow, meaning it is unlikely to be a product, eliminating choice B. A prosthetic group remains covalently bound to an enzyme throughout a reaction and, like the enzyme, emerges from the reaction unchanged. Prosthetic groups are larger molecules that can undergo covalent bonding with the enzyme. Calcium is a metal, meaning that is can bond ionically or associate with negatively charged amino acids like glutamate but it cannot undergo covalent bonding, as it is not a nonmetal. Choice D can be eliminated for this reason. A cofactor is a small molecule, typically an ion, which functions to assist the enzyme in coordinating the chemistry of a reaction. Typically, metals hold parts of the enzyme together or help draw in water to do hydrolysis reactions. Choice C is the best answer choice.

24. **C is the best answer.** An enzyme is important for facilitating a reaction between two or more reactants that has a non-spontaneous, or positive, ΔG. Enzymes lower the activation energy, making it significantly more likely that a reaction will occur. An enzyme cannot change the equilibrium constant, K_{eq}, of a reaction because the equilibrium is determined by thermodynamics, not kinetics. Choice A represents a decreased equilibrium constant and can be eliminated because it is not equal to the 10^8 shown in Figure 1. Choice B can be eliminated for the same reason. Choice D shows an equilibrium constant that is higher than that shown in Figure 1, eliminating it as a possible answer choice. Because the enzyme cannot change the equilibrium constant, it should remain the same in either the presence or absence of an enzyme, making choice C the best answer.

25. **A is the best answer.** The relationship between the equilibrium constant and the free energy, $\Delta G°$ is the main concept of this question. Mathematically, $\Delta G° = -2.3 \cdot R \cdot T \cdot \log(K_{eq})$ where R is the universal gas constant with a value of 8.314 J/mol·K and T is the temperature in Kelvin. 25°C is 293K. The $\Delta G° = -5.52$ kJ/mol for the reaction between compound 57 and thrombin is also needed to solve this question. Rounding the gas constant to 8 J/mol · K and the temperature to 300 K greatly simplifies the math and is a useful skill on test day.

$$- 5.52 \text{ kJ/mol} = -2.3 \cdot (8 \text{ J/mol} \cdot \text{K}) \cdot (300 \text{ K}) \cdot \log(K_{eq})$$

$$-5.52 \text{ kJ/mol} = -5520 \text{ J/mol} \cdot \log(K_{eq})$$

$$-5520 \text{ J/mol} = -5520 \text{ J/mol} \cdot \log(K_{eq})$$

$$1 = \log(K_{eq})$$

$$10^1 = 10^{\log(Keq)}$$

$$10 = K_{eq}$$

Choice B can be eliminated because it is 10 times higher than the calculated equilibrium constant. Similarly, choice C is 100 times higher and choice D 1,000 times higher than the calculated equilibrium constant, eliminating choices C and D as possible answer choices. Because the equilibrium constant is closest to 10, choice A is the best answer.

Stand-alones (26-29)

26. **A is the best answer.** This question shows a sequence of four amino acids. It would help to identify each one by the R-groups and then associate the one-letter abbreviation with each. The order from left to right is: glycine (G), histidine (H), leucine (L), aspartic acid (D). Choices C and D contain two amino acids not present in the figure: isoleucine (I) and glutamine (Q). Those choices can be eliminated. Choices A and B contain the same amino acids but are written in inverse directions. Remember that amino acids need to be written from the N-terminus to the C-terminus. The figure shows the sequence from the C-terminus to the N-terminus, so the best answer will be the inverse of the figure as drawn. Choice B is in the same order as the figure, so it can be eliminated. Choice A is the best answer because it identifies the amino acids in the correct N-terminus to C-terminus order.

27. **D is the best answer.** Many reactions are unfavorable under physiological conditions. The purpose of enzymes is to create conditions that allow these reactions to proceed *in vivo*. This occurs through holding reagents in proximity with the appropriate orientation and/or the creation of acidic or basic microenvironments. This question gives no information about structural configuration, but the esterification equation does show that acidic conditions catalyze the reaction. Start the problem by looking at the answer choices and identifying which have acidic R-groups. The best answer will be unlikely to provide acidic conditions. The only two acidic amino acids are aspartic acid (D) and glutamic acid (E). Choice A contains two acidic groups, so it may be able to catalyze the reaction. Choice B may also catalyze the reaction with the presence of two acidic groups. Choice C contains only one acidic group, so choices A and B can be eliminated since they are more acidic. Choice D, however, contains no acidic groups, so it is least likely to provide the acidic conditions required for esterification. Choice C can be eliminated since choice D is even less acidic. Choice D is the strongest answer.

28. **A is the best answer.** In most tables of amino acids, tyrosine is listed as neutral. Look at the structure to consider the answer choices. Choice A appears to conflict with these tables because tyrosine is not usually described as an acidic amino acid, but if the alcohol group lost its hydrogen, the resulting negative charge would be stabilized by three additional resonance structures thanks the aromatic ring. Choice A seems possible. Choice B's justification that alcohols have a similar pK_a to water is usually sound, but tyrosine's R group is not a typical alcohol since it is at a benzyl position – that is, adjacent to an aromatic ring – which increases its acidity. While it is true that tyrosine's atoms have filled valence shells, resonance destabilization is the driver of its acid-base properties, so choice C can be eliminated. Choice D mischaracterizes tyrosine as a basic molecule. The justification is also weak: an aromatic compound will be resistant to any change that disrupts its aromaticity such as electron donation. Choice D can be eliminated. Now use organic chemistry knowledge to decide between choices A and B. Most alcohols have the same acidity as water. Putting the alcohol group adjacent to an aromatic ring will enhance the acidity of the molecule somewhat, so calling this compound "very weakly acidic" is appropriate. Choice B's justification falls short of this reasoning because not all alcohols, as seen in tyrosine, have a pK_a that is equivalent to water. Choice A is a stronger choice than choice B.

29. **A is the best answer.** The chemical properties of amino acids differ with respect to their R-groups. It may help to write out the full names of each of the answer choices along with sketches of their R-groups. Notice that the question stem gives the structure of an L-amino acid in a Fischer projection. The R-group is at the top point of this projection, and it may help to sketch out its R-group in bond-line structure, too. Notice that the R-group consists of four carbons, the last two of which are carboxylate anions bound to the γ-carbon. Choice A, glutamate, also has a carboxylate anion bound to a γ-carbon, so that is a strong choice. Glycine does not have any carbons in its R-group, so choice B is not a strong answer. Glutamine is similar in that a carbonyl is bound to the γ-carbon, but glutamine contains an amide rather than a carboxylate group. Choice A is stronger than choice C because glutamine has acidic properties, which is closer to the chemical properties of the molecule shown in the question stem. Choice C can be eliminated because glutamine is neutral. Choice D, threonine contains an alcohol group bound to the β-carbon. This alcohol group is not charged at physiological pH, so it is unlikely to have similar chemical properties to the amino acid shown in the question stem. Choice D is a weak answer. Choice A is most similar to the amino acid in the question and is the best answer.

Passage 6 (Questions 30-33)

30. **B is the best answer.** Histidine is a basic amino acid with a heterocyclic five-membered ring with two nitrogen atoms. One of the nitrogen atoms is regularly bound to a hydrogen atom, whereas the other is bound only to carbon atoms on either side. In acidic conditions, as the question indicates, the second nitrogen atom is protonated. Choice A is true but is not the best answer because it leaves out any mention of the second nitrogen. Choice B is a better answer, since at pH 5.0, both nitrogen atoms are attached to hydrogen atoms. Choice C is inaccurate, since there is no oxygen in the ring. Monosaccharides commonly have an oxygen within their rings. Choice D is inaccurate, since there is no amine group connected to the heterocyclic ring. The other basic amino acids, arginine and lysine, by contrast, have additional amine groups in their side chains.

31. **C is the best answer.** The passage indicates that at pH 5.0, there is an autophosphorylation of ArsS that is triggered by the acidic pH. The second and third figures point to the concept that histidine is likely responsible for this effect, since where histidine in position 94 is substituted, there is a loss of the acid response. The effect of histidine is likely due to its ability to bind protons as a basic amino acid, thereby bringing about a conformational change. Choice A, or lysine, is an example of another basic amino acid, and it could be expected to respond to the acidic environment by taking up a proton. Choice B, or arginine, is also a basic amino acid, and it could be expected to function in a similar capacity. Choice C, or proline, is the best answer because as the only nonpolar amino acid in a list of bases, it would not be expected to alter the protein conformation through a change in pH. Choice D, or histidine, is the primary example in this passage of an amino acid that contributes to the autophosphorylation, and so this choice can be eliminated.

32. **D is the best answer.** The answers come in two parts and require one to classify urea by its polarity and to explain how one would know this based on information in the passage. The passage indicates that urea is broken down by urease to carbon dioxide and ammonia. This information on its own is not necessarily a determinant of the polarity of urea. Choice A is misleading, because while it is true that carbon dioxide is nonpolar, the carbon dioxide is derived from a polar carbonyl group in this case. Choice B is inaccurate, since while this is true for some hydrophobic molecules, there is nothing in the passage to support this assumption. Choice C is misleading because it lacks a foundation from the passage. Also, urea is used to dispose of nitrogen through amino groups and would not be expected to contain a carboxylic acid group. Choice D is a better answer, since the passage indicates that urea is transported to the cytoplasm by UreI, which indicates that it cannot freely cross the hydrophobic plasma membrane. This provides support from the passage that urea is hydrophilic.

33. **A is the best answer.** For this question, it is best to carefully analyze the figures. Figure 1 shows an experiment where all seven histidine residues are substituted, and yet, one can see that transcription of the acid-responsive gene is increased from pH 7.0 to pH 5.0 for the H_7Q sample. It is possible that other basic amino acids such as lysine or arginine in the active site may also become protonated and change the tertiary structure of the protein as a result of new electrostatic interactions or hydrogen bonds. The tertiary structure refers to the three dimensional shape of the peptide chain that is formed by the folding of the chain through various intermolecular bonds between side chain groups. A protonated group may form new electrostatic bonds to a side chain with a carboxyl group. This type of bond allows for a folding pattern based on the new bond that is created by this protonation. Because the acid response persists without histidine, it is likely that it may also be mediated by these or other amino acids that are affected by the change in pH. Choice A is the best answer, since Experiment 1 indicates that amino acids other than histidine play a role in the acid-response, since where all histidine residues are substituted, there is nevertheless a response. Choice B or Experiment 2 only provides data on individual histidine residues, but it cannot be extrapolated to provide information for other amino acids. Choice C or Experiment 3 also has the same limitation. Choice D is misleading, since one may assume that this is true given that all the experiments deal with histidine exclusively. Still, the point of the first experiment is to show that histidine alone cannot account for the whole effect.

Passage 7 (Questions 34-37)

34. **B is the best answer.** It is stated in the passage that the region 95-137 of α-Hb is important for the binding of AHSP. In proteins, hydrophobic residues generally do not exist on the exterior surface due to the polar environment of the cell. In order to overcome the unfavorable interactions, hydrophobic residues associate with each other so that water can be excluded. Choice A can be eliminated because a hydrophilic residue will not interact with the hydrophobic leucine due to unfavorable interactions. If there was a hydrophobic valine on AHSP, it is likely that there are favorable hydrophobic interactions that are taking place between it and the leucine on α-Hb so choice B is the best answer. Choice C introduces new information regarding the allosteric site of AHSP. The passage provides no guidance whether α-Hb interacts with AHSP allosterically. Also, allosteric interactions can potentially increase OR decrease binding affinity, so without more information this choice cannot be the best answer. Valine and leucine are very similar amino acids, differing by only a CH_2. They would be expected to behave in a very similar manner, so no change in the K_D (dissociation constant) would be expected if the residues were exchanged. In other words, the affinity of AHSP would not be expected to change with the substitution of valine for leucine, so choice D does not add new information, and can be eliminated.

35. **B is the best answer.** A cystine bond is a covalent linkage between the sulfur atoms of two cysteine residues. These bonds do not stabilize α-helices, so choice A can be eliminated. In a protein α-helix, hydrogen bonding between the carbonyl of one amino acid and the amine group of another provide the most stability to the structure so choice B is the best answer. Choice C can be eliminated because while hydrophobic interactions of residues 3-4 away from each other contribute to stability, hydrogen bonding is more important. This also applies to ion pairs, so choice D can be eliminated.

36. **C is the best answer.** In order to follow Michaelis-Menten kinetics, substrate concentration needs to be proportional to reaction rate until the maximum is reached. AHSP can be thought of in terms of Michaelis-Menten kinetics because it has a binding affinity for α-Hb and leads to αβ-Hb formation. Choice A can be eliminated because increasing the concentration of AHSP would give less information than increasing the concentration of α-Hb. By increasing the concentration of AHSP, the maximum velocity cannot be determined because AHSP never becomes saturated with α-Hb subunits. Choice B can be eliminated because AHSP interacts with α-Hb and not β-Hb. Increasing the concentration of β-Hb would not help scientists determine how AHSP interacts with α-Hb. Choice C is the best answer because by increasing α-Hb and monitoring αβ-Hb dimer formation, the rate of product formation as a function of reactant concentration as well as the maximum velocity can be determined. Choice D can be eliminated because by increasing the AHSP concentration, information about the maximum velocity is lost.

37. **A is the best answer.** When proteins are in solution, a solvation layer forms which normally forces hydrophobic residues into the interior of the protein, creating a hydrophobic core. In the case of α-Hb, the hydrophobic residues are stabilized by AHSP which allows them to remain on the surface. Without AHSP, the protein is not stable. Choice A, αHb lacks a hydrophobic core, is a reasonable answer. Choice B can be eliminated because this refers to the formation of dimers, rather than the spontaneous denaturing of α-Hb. Choice C can be eliminated because it mistakenly applies the principle of a solvation layer. Small solvation layers are favorable because it means that the hydrophobic residues are buried in the protein and protected from the polar environment of the cell. Choice D can be eliminated for the same reason as choice B, leaving choice A is the best answer.

Passage 8 (Questions 38-42)

38. **B is the best answer.** Chains of amino acids are linked together to form polypeptides via peptide linkages. The type of reaction required to form a peptide is a dehydration reaction in which water is eliminated and the amine of an amino acid is joined to the carboxylic acid group of another amino acid. The functional group that results from this reaction would have to contain a nitrogen bound to carbonyl carbon. The amine functional group is a derivative of ammonia, where one or more of the 3 hydrogens bound to the nitrogen can be replaced by alkyl groups. While this answer might be tempting because the reaction leads to a nitrogen forming a bond with a carbon, it does not best describe a linkage of a nitrogen to a carbonyl carbon specifically, so choice A can be eliminated. An amide linkage describes a linkage of a nitrogen atom to a carbonyl carbon, so choice B is consistent with the reaction described in the question stem. A carbonyl was present before and after the reaction, eliminating choice C. While the hydrolysis of a peptide does result in a newly formed carboxylic acid, the opposite reaction is being described here, and choice D can be eliminated, leaving choice B as the best answer.

39. **B is the best answer.** The hinge bridge amino acids are alanine, glycine, and proline. To answer this question, first consider the properties of these individual amino acids. Alanine is unremarkable, and in general does not provide unique information for answering amino acid questions. Glycine is the smallest amino acid, and has the most rotational flexibility. This allows glycine to participate in turns, and it also is not found in abundance in alpha helices due to adding too much rotational instability. Proline is often found in kinks due to its cyclic structure, and is rarely found in alpha helices. Choice A can be eliminated. Beta sheets are group of beta conformations together, so choices C and D can be eliminated. It is also a good general principal that proline residues participate in turns, making choice B the best answer.

40. **A is the best answer.** The K_m, or Michaelis constant, is a measure of how much substrate is required in order to reach ½ V_{max}. If a higher concentration of substrate is needed, the enzyme must have lower affinity for the substrate. The lower the K_m, the higher the affinity of the enzyme for the substrate. Table 1 lists the IC_{50} for CB1a associated with three different types of lung cells. In the passage it states that the IC_{50} measures concentration of CB1a, which in this case is the substrate, required for a 50% cell survival rate. To answer this question, it must be assumed that this is analogous to K_m. Based on the results, the NLC requires the highest concentration of CB1a to cause cell death, followed by NSCLC, and finally SCLC requires the smallest concentration of CB1a to cause cell death. Only choices A and B list NLC as having the highest K_m, so both choices C and D can be eliminated. Choice A lists SCLC as having the lowest K_m, which corresponds with Table 1, so choice B can be eliminated and choice A should be selected as the best answer.

TEST 1B A&E

41. **C is the best answer.** This question requires knowledge of the different types of amino acids as well as the various factors that contribute to tertiary structure. The sequence of the N-terminus is: Lys-Trp-Lys-Val-Phe-Lys-Lys-Ile-Glu-Lys. Within this sequence there are both acidic (Glu) and basic (Lys) amino acids and hydrophobic amino acids (Trp, Val, Phe, Ile). Using this information, it is possible to determine which interactions could be contributing to the tertiary structure. Electrostatic interactions occur between side chains of charged amino acids. Acidic amino acids possess a terminal carboxylic acid in their R group and basic amino acids have R groups with terminal amines. Depending on the pH, these groups can protonate and deprotonate, resulting in a net charge on the amino acid. This charge on one amino acid can interact with the opposite charge on another amino acid, forming what is known as an electrostatic interaction. Since there are two charged amino acids in the sequence, choice A can be eliminated because it is possible that electrostatic interactions are occurring between the glutamate and/or lysine. Van der Waals forces are attractive and repulsive forces that occur between molecules and within molecules. Because they are occurring virtually everywhere, presumably they are occurring in this molecule too, so choice B is not the best answer and can be eliminated. Disulfide bridges occur between two cysteines within the same molecule. The terminal thiols bind together to form and S-S bond. There are no cysteines in the N-terminal sequence, so it would not be possible for the N-terminus to be supported by disulfide bridges. Hydrophobic bonding occurs when hydrophobic side chains are pushed toward the interior of the protein so as to not come into contact with water. There are hydrophobic amino acids in the N-terminus, so choice D can be eliminated, leaving choice C as the best answer.

42. **D is the best answer.** This question tests understanding of the passage and figure shown to determine what is true about the peptide CB1a. The data provided in the figure demonstrate the efficacy of CB1a in reducing tumor volume. The Y-axis plots tumor weight after treatment with one of the regimens on the x-axis: CB1a, docetaxel, or saline (control). The figure suggests that after treatment with CB1a, tumor volume is reduced to levels below those observed with saline treatment and docetaxel treatment. This demonstrates that CB1a is having the desired effect on tumor size. NLC cells, as defined by the passage, are normal lung cells. The passage offers no comparison between CB1a and docetaxel for NLC, so choice A can be eliminated. Choice B can be eliminated based on the information in the passage and figure, since there is no information to suggest that the peptide is denatured within the human body. Table 1 shows that CB1a binds selectively to lung cancer cells over normal lung cells, but it does not discuss CB1a binding compared to docetaxel, so choice C is not the best answer. Table 1 also shows that a lower concentration of CB1a is needed to produce a 50% cell survival rate in SCLC compared to NSCLC, meaning that it is more selective for SCLC. Choice D is the best answer.

Stand-alones (43-46)

43. **A is the best answer.** This question tests amino acids and their absolute configuration. Absolute configuration is assigned to chiral centers based on the molecule glyceraldehyde. For the MCAT®, it will be important to know that for activity in the human body, amino acids with chiral centers (all but glycine) have the L configuration while carbohydrates with chiral centers take the D configuration. The question stem asks which of the amino acids in the answer choices served as the control. In order for the amino acid to potentially serve as a control, it would have to be in a form that is inactive in the human body. Choice A, D-Ala, is a chiral amino acid in the D-configuration and, since it is not active in the human body it could serve as a control. L-Ala is a chiral amino acid in the proper configuration for the human body, so administration of this molecule would not be suitable as an experimental control, and choice B can be eliminated. Glycine is the only amino acid that does not have a chiral center so classifying it as D or L is not appropriate. However, because glycine is achiral this means that any form of glycine administered would be biologically active, so choices C and D can be eliminated, leaving choice A as the best answer.

44. **C is the best answer.** Knowledge of the specific condition is not required to answer this question. Many different features of a protein affect its ability to be enzymatically degraded. Choice A, glycosylation, is a tactic demonstrated by a wide range of proteins that operate in environments within the body that feature high rates of enzymatic degradation. Lysosomes particularly, are lined by proteins and lipids that are extensively glycosylated. Choice B also changes the R groups and three dimensional conformations, which is a common tactic to evade enzyme recognition. Peptides can be cleaved anywhere along their length, so a blocked amino terminus will not necessarily add degradation resistance. Choice D racemization is probably the most effective tactic. Since only L amino acids are used in proteins, barring a few exceptional bacteria, enzymes are specific to them. This makes choice C the best answer as it is not a common tactic to avoid degradation.

TEST 1B A&E

45. **B is the best answer.** This question is easier than it appears on first reading, and knowledge the specific system of molecules is not required to find the best answer. The best strategy to approach this question is to think about the structure of proline and cysteine and review the type of bonds they are capable of forming. Option I, hydrogen bonding, is a strong possibility. Proline can accept H-bonds, and cysteine can donate them. Option II, ionic interactions, can be eliminated as neither amino acid is charged under biological conditions. Salt bridges are formed usually only between acidic and basic amino acids. Option III is another good possibility, as the disulfide bond is the characteristic feature of cysteine. Since both are possible, and there is no way to distinguish one of these from the other based on the information provided, and both are possible, so choice B is the best answer.

46. **A is the best answer.** The MCAT® does not specifically test the proteins listed in the answer choices but is it important to be able to reason to the best answer. The question stem states that Kartagener syndrome is associated with sperm immobility. Sperm are propelled by the flagellar proteins dynein which are also present in the cilia of the respiratory tract. Choice A is a good answer. Adenosine deaminase is an enzyme involved in the immune system. A mutation in this enzyme may result in recurrent infections including those of the respiratory tree but it could not account for the sperm immobility so choice B is not the best answer. SRY protein is involved in display of the male phenotype. A mutation in SRY may cause infertility but not necessarily due to immobile sperm so choice C is not the best answer. Lysozyme digests bacterial cell walls. A mutation in lysozyme may cause infection but would not clearly be related to infertility so choice D is not the best answer.

Passage 9 (Questions 47-51)

47. **C is the best answer.** Homocysteine is synthesized from methionine before conversion to cysteine. The image of homocysteine shows that the structure is very similar to methionine (M) but the final methyl is missing in homocysteine. H, or histidine, has an imidazole ring that is not present in homocysteine so choice A is not the best answer. I, or isoleucine, has a branched aliphatic structure. Choice B is a possible answer but unlikely because homocysteine has two less carbons than isoleucine. M, or methionine, is a good answer because if the final $-CH_3$ is removed from methionine, the structure is identical to homocysteine so choice C is a good answer. V, or valine, is similar to isoleucine in that it is a branched aliphatic amino acid. As with choice B, choice D is not the best answer because homocysteine does not have a branch point.

48. **B is the best answer.** Fatty acids are long hydrophobic chains with carboxylic acid heads that are used for energy in the cell. It is important to know the names of some common fatty acids there is no reason to believe stearoyl CoA is relevant to transcription, so choice D is not a good answer. In reality, stearoyl CoA desaturase is used in fatty acid biosynthesis, particularly in the synthesis of fatty acids stored in triglycerides. Decreased levels of this enzyme may explain why patients with homocystinuria are thin. This level of detail is not required by the MCAT® but the reasoning used to get to the best answer is important.

49. **A is the best answer.** To answer this question, first rule out the answers that are chemically impossible. Thiol groups (−SH) can be oxidized to disulfide (−S−S−) groups and disulfide groups can be reduced to thiol groups. So, choices B and C are impossible and can be eliminated. Between choices A and D, it is necessary to determine is NAC has a thiol group or a disulfide group. NAC stands for N-acetyl cysteine. This means NAC is a cysteine with a secondary amine that is substituted with an acetyl group. Like cysteine, NAC has a thiol group so choice A is the best answer.

50. **C is the best answer.** Figure 1 shows the effect of the TGL278T Cbs genotype on mice. The TgI278T $Cbs^{+/-}$ mice are heavier than the TgI278T $Cbs^{-/-}$ mice. The caption indicates that bars marked with increasing numbers of "*" indicate more statistically significant results where "*" is $p<0.05$; "**" is $p<0.01$; and "***" is $p<0.001$. As the female mice age, there are less "*" so choice A is inaccurate. Choice B may be a true statement. The TgI278T $Cbs^{+/-}$ mice are heavier than the TgI278T $Cbs^{-/-}$ mice so they may be at greater risk for heart disease. However, these conclusions cannot necessarily be drawn from the graph so there is likely a better answer. When looking at the graph for male mice, there are consistently "***" meaning the results are highly statistically significant. This means the data suggests the TgI278T Cbs genotype has a more significant effect on male mice than female mice so choice C is an accurate conclusion from Figure 1. Choice D is a distractor that requires extensive reasoning to rule out. The TgI278T $Cbs^{-/-}$ mice lack the ability to make cystathionine beta synthase which is used to synthesize cysteine. Cysteine has a free thiol group which can be oxidized meaning cysteine can act as an antioxidant. Since choice D mistakenly pairs oxidative stress with TgI278T $Cbs^{+/-}$ mice, it is not a good answer. This leaves choice C as the best answer.

51. **C is the best answer.** Minerals are inorganic ions that may act as cofactors for enzymes. Examples include iron, copper, and zinc. They are all found on the periodic table. Pyridoxine and folic acid are organic molecules, not ions so choice A is not a good answer. The fat soluble vitamins are A, D, E and K. They are each important but are not used significantly as cofactors for metabolism so choice B is not a good answer. The water soluble vitamins include the B vitamins and vitamin C. In fact, pyridoxine is vitamin B6 and folic acid is vitamin B9. They act as cofactors for metabolic enzymes and are important in promoting metabolism. So, choice C is a strong answer. Macronutrients are molecules that are ingested for energy whereas micronutrients are vitamins and minerals. So, choice D is not the best answer.

Passage 10 (Questions 52-56)

52. **A is the best answer.** In the passage, ROS formation is described as one type of oxidative stress. When cysteine residues are oxidized and in close proximity, they are able to form a cystine bond. A cystine bond is a covalent linage between two oxidized cysteine residues. In PAH, the formation of this bond will disrupt the native conformation and lead to dysfunction of the enzyme so choice A is the best answer. Choice B can be eliminated because cystine bonds do not stabilize secondary structures, such as alpha helices and beta pleated sheets. The oxidation of the cysteine residues result in a cystine bond which stabilizes the tertiary structure of the inactive PAH_{ox}. Choice C can be eliminated because oxidation of cysteine residues results in the formation of a cystine bond, not the breaking of one. Choice D can be eliminated because if oxidation of cysteine residues stabilized PAH_{nat}, it would result in enhanced activity rather than an inhibition of the enzyme. Choice A is better than choice D because the question stem states that the cysteine residues are reduced in the native PAH protein. It can be assumed that by oxidizing these residues and forming a cystine bond, the shape of the protein will be altered and affect its function.

53. **A is the best answer.** In the passage it states that PAH is a homotetramer. This means that each of its four subunits are identical so choice A is the best answer. Choice B, C, and D can be eliminated because they mistakenly identify how many unique subunits are contained in the enzyme. Choice C is a trap answer because in the passage it states that each subunit contains three domains. For this question, it is important to understand that a domain is a part of a tertiary structure whereas a subunit is the entire tertiary structure.

54. **D is the best answer.** In the passage it states that BH_4 stabilizes an inactive form of PAH. This means that BH_4 is an inhibitor and will cause PAH to stop converting Phe to Tyr. The passage also states that PAH is activated by binding to Phe. This will cause PAH to increase the conversion of Phe to Tyr. By having high concentrations of both an enzyme activator and inhibitor, the overall enzyme kinetics cannot be determined and the level of Tyr cannot be assessed. Choice A can be eliminated because it cannot be determined whether the inhibitor or the activator will have a greater effect on PAH. Choice B can be eliminated because the concentration of Tyr cannot be determined. The addition of an inhibitor and an activator may cancel each other out if they are added in the correct proportions; however, the information presented in the question stem does not indicate that this is the case. Choice C can be eliminated because the question stem does not indicate that there is more inhibitor than activator. There is not enough information to determine how the concentration of Tyr will be effected. Choice D is the best answer because it takes into account that both inhibitor and activator were present. No information about the concentration of Tyr can be gained because the exact concentrations of inhibitor and activator are unknown.

55. **B is the best answer.** PAH is responsible for the conversion of Phe to Tyr. An increased ratio of Phe to Tyr indicates that PAH is not working properly. Choice A can be eliminated because it states in the passage that macrophage activity is paralleled with ROS formation. High levels of macrophage activity are expected to cause a lot of ROS formation which will negatively impact PAH. In the passage it states that BH_4 is an allosteric inhibitor of PAH. If patients suffering from trauma show an increased concentration of this inhibitor, then it challenges the hypothesis that PAH is being damaged by ROS formation. It is more likely that PAH activity is being effected by the presence of an inhibitor so choice B is the best answer. Choice C can be eliminated because it is likely that reactive oxygen species will damage PAH and cause a conformation change that can affect its kinetics. Choice D can be eliminated for the same reason. Reactive oxygen species will damage the conformation of PAH and may result in negative cooperativity of the enzyme. Choice B is better than the other answer choices because it provides an accurate alternative explanation that does not involve actual damage to the enzyme or oxidative stress.

56. **B is the best answer.** Choice A can be eliminated because substrate is always transformed during a reaction. It is the reactant in the reaction catalyzed by the enzyme. Iron does not undergo a net change during the reaction and cannot be considered substrate. A cofactor is a non-protein part of an enzyme. Iron is described as first being reduced and then being oxidized during the conversion of Phe to Tyr. It is an essential part of the reaction, but it is not part of PAH. Choice B is the best answer because it accurately describes the role that iron plays in the reaction. Choice C can be eliminated because an allosteric regulator effects the rate of the reaction but does not take part during it. Iron is clearly described as being important for the movement of electrons. Choice D can be eliminated because a coenzyme is defined as an organic cofactor. Choice B is better than choice D because iron is an inorganic ion so it cannot be classified as a coenzyme.

Stand-alones (57-59)

57. **C is the best answer.** Both enzymes have the same function (catalyzing the phosphorylation of glucose) but the key difference is the concentration of the substrate (glucose), in their respective physiological locations. Glucose is relatively abundant in the liver and pancreas as compared to other tissues (e.g. skeletal muscle). Accordingly, glucokinase functions in an environment of high glucose concentration, whereas hexokinase functions in an environment of low glucose concentration. In order to handle the greater substrate load, glucokinase will have a higher capacity (i.e. higher V_{max}) but a lower affinity for glucose (i.e. higher K_m). In contrast, for maximum enzymatic efficiency in low substrate conditions, hexokinase will have a higher affinity for glucose (lower K_m) but not a higher capacity (lower V_{max}). This makes choice C the best answer and eliminates choices A, B and D.

58. **B is the best answer.** Enzymes increase the rates of reactions by many thousands of times. It is highly unlikely that there would be a delay of such length that the scientists would have time to add more substrate into the solution. Choice A can be eliminated because it is not the best answer. Choice B is the best answer because it is describing positive cooperativity. Certain enzymes function best after they have bound to a substrate. This initial substrate binding changes the enzyme's conformation in such a way that it increases the binding affinity for additional substrate. Choice C can be eliminated because a high enzyme to substrate ratio would result in a very fast reaction rate. The substrate would bind to an enzyme rapidly and be converted into product very quickly. Choice D can be eliminated because adding more substrate to displace an inhibitor is helpful in determining the type of inhibition, but the aim of the experiment was to characterize the cooperativity given by the sigmoidal shape of the curve.

59. **B is the best answer.** A cofactor is an atom or molecule that assists an enzyme. The enzyme lowers the activation energy and since the cofactor assists then enzyme it may be thought of as lowering the activation energy. So, choice A is possible but not completely accurate. A cofactor is necessary for the enzyme to function meaning the enzyme will not work without it. Additionally, the cofactor alone cannot perform the reaction so the cofactor is not sufficient. Choice B is an accurate statement. A coenzyme is an organic or metalorganic molecule, but coenzymes do not have to be covalently bound. A cofactor that is covalently bound is called a prosthetic group. So choice C is not a strong answer. Coenzymes are used in some pathways to make high energy molecules like ATP but there is no reason to believe tetrahydrobiopterin functions this way from the information given, so choice D is not a strong answer.

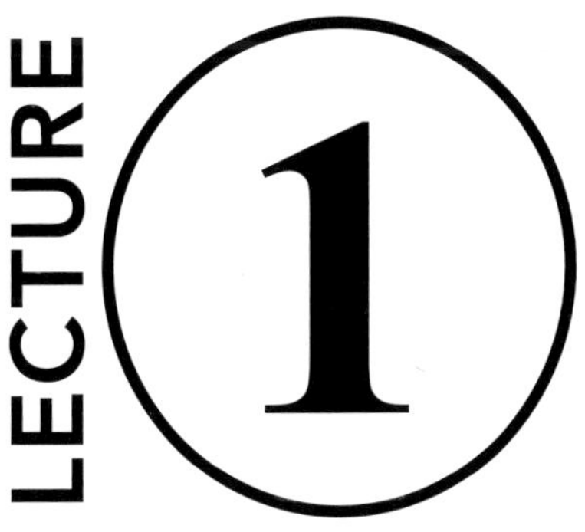

Biological Molecules and Enzymes

TEST 1C

ANSWERS & EXPLANATIONS

Questions 1–31

Passage 1 (Questions 1-5)

1. **A is the best answer.** According to paragraph three, the flux of doxorubicin across the membrane through the carrier CDR5 into the cell is directly proportional to the trans-membrane pH gradient, defined by the equation as $\Delta pH = pHe - pHi$. A high pHe and a low pHi would maximize the transmembrane pH gradient and the doxorubicin uptake into the cell. Since a high pH corresponds to low $[H^+]$ and a low pH corresponds to high $[H^+]$, choice A is the best answer. Choices C and D are less likely because this would minimize the pH gradient. Choice B would generate a gradient, but the gradient established would be in the opposite direction.

2. **B is the best answer.** The third paragraph informs us that doxorubicin uptake is proportional to the trans-membrane pH gradient, defined by $\Delta pH = pHe - pHi$. According to the question stem, a carbonic anhydrase inhibitor prevents the formation of the hydronium ion, which is a free proton in an aqueous solution. With a carbonic anhydrase inhibitor, the pH will be higher due to fewer free protons. This would increase the pHe, leading to an increased pH gradient and increase the uptake of doxorubicin. The extracellular pH rises with a carbonic anhydrase inhibitor instead of falls, eliminating choice A. Because the pHe will change, changing the gradient and the uptake of the drug, choice C is also unlikely. Only the pH gradient needs to be known to predict the change in doxorubicin uptake, making choice D a less attractive answer than choice B.

3. **B is the best answer.** The passage notes that doxorubicin immediately associates with the nuclear proteins and is released slowly over time throughout the nucleus. K_m, or the Michaelis-Menten Constant, is the substrate concentration at which the reaction rate is equal to ½ V_{max}. A low K_m indicates low dissociation of the drug from the protein, meaning it would be released slowly into the nucleus. Choice A is unlikely because a high K_m would indicate high dissociation of the drug and rapid diffusion into the nucleus, while an intermediate K_m would also not show slow release, making choice C also unlikely. Choice D is not an attractive answer because the K_m value can be predicted by knowing that the drug is released slowly into the nucleus.

4. **A is the best answer.** In the first paragraph, the passage states that doxorubicin associates with DNA, which has an overall negative charge. In order to associate with DNA, doxorubicin is most likely positively charged. The first paragraph also describes doxorubicin as weakly basic. Weak bases tend to be neutral molecules that acquire a positive charge when protonated. Choices B, C, and D are unlikely to be the answer because a negatively or neutrally charged drug would most likely not associate with negatively charged DNA. Electrostatic interactions are driven by associations between positively charged ions and negatively charged ions. In this instance, the drug would be positively charged and the DNA negatively charged.

5. **D is the best answer.** In order to correlate movement of doxorubicin across the membrane only dependent on pH, doxorubicin must not be transported by additional mechanisms other than a carrier. A carrier allows molecules to move down their concentration gradients and would allow doxorubicin to move into the cell depending on the pH gradient. Choice A is unlikely to be the answer because a plasma membrane carrier protein would most likely not interact with a nuclear protein. Choice B is also less likely because, while the pump would prevent a correlation between pH and ability to cross the membrane, a pump does require the use of ATP to move a substrate. Choice C is not an attractive choice because all enzymes are highly specific to a substrate and would likely not be able to transport both a large drug like doxorubicin and small ions like hydrogen.

Passage 2 (Questions 6-9)

6. **C is the best answer.** To answer this question, it is helpful to consider the way the experiment is designed. The goal of the experiment is to see if the presence of the mtnBD protein allows MTA to be converted to methionine in yeast cells that have lost mtnB, mtnC, or mtnD. To control for confounding variables, the researchers create two controls: one to show that none of the yeast cells will grow in the absence of MTA and methionine and another to show that all of the yeast cells will grow if they are provided MTA and methionine. The experimental plate removes the methionine to determine if the methionine can be synthesized from the MTA via the salvage pathway. Choice B and D can be eliminated because neither Plate A nor Plate B are the experimental plate. Because Plate A does not have methionine or MTA, the yeast cells do not have a chance to survive regardless of the cell line mutation present and can be considered the negative control. Because Plate B has both methionine and MTA, all the yeast cells survive regardless of the cell line mutation present and can be considered the positive control. This makes choice C the best answer.

7. **A is the best answer.** To answer this question, Figure 2 must be examined. In Plate C, the experimental plate, only the cell lines with pGREG505/MTNBD survive, while those with the pGREG505 plasmid alone do not survive. This means that the yeast cells are able to survive in the presence of the mtnBD protein even if mtnB, mtnC or mtnD are absent. From this information, it is possible to conclude that mtnBD can perform the function of all three enzymes. This makes choice A the best choice. Choice B is not the best answer because as shown in column 1, methionine is still produced in the mtnC knock out. Choice C is true, but it does not answer the question because it does not describe something about mtnBD. Choice D can be eliminated because mtnBD is part of a pathway to generate methionine from MTA. mtnBD is functional in Plate C, which does not have methionine.

8. **B is the best answer.** One of the main purposes of enzymes is to decrease the activation energy of a reaction. Choice A is not the best choice because enzymes normally have a very high specificity for their substrates, and it is unlikely that mtnD could work on mtnB's substrate. If this was true, the yeast cell line in column 4 of Figure 2 would grow since mtnD and mtnC are present. Choice C is not the best answer because it is still possible for the reaction to occur uncatalyzed, but it would take a significantly longer amount of time. Choice D can be eliminated because MTRup, shown in Figure 1, is a substrate for mtnBD not mtnD. This makes choice B the best answer.

9. **C is the best answer.** V_{max} is the maximum rate of reaction of the enzyme. K_m is the concentration of substrate needed to reach half of the V_{max} and is inversely proportional to substrate-enzyme affinity. If an enzyme has a high affinity for its substrate, a low amount of substrate is needed to reach half of the V_{max} and K_m will be a small number. If an enzyme has a low affinity for its substrate, a high amount of substrate is needed to reach half of the V_{max} and K_m will be a large number. Noncompetitive inhibitors bind to enzymes at a location other than the active site and bind to enzymes regardless of the presence of the substrate. In other words, the affinity of the substrate to the enzyme is not affected. K_m is not changed. This would rule out all choices except choice C. In addition, V_{max} will decrease because the inhibitor cannot be displaced by a high saturation of substrate. The more enzymes are inhibited the more the V_{max} will decrease. This rules out choice A and D and makes choice C the best answer.

Passage 3 (Questions 10-14)

10. **B is the best answer.** L-arginine acts as a substrate for both NOS and arginase. NOS catalyzes the formation of NO and L-citrulline, while arginase catalyzes the formation of urea and ornithine. As stated, urea is necessary for ammonia detoxification. Choice A, excessive ammonia leading to organ dysfunction, would occur due to L-arginine deficiency. L-arginine deficiency would decrease the levels of NO and L-citrulline. Choice B, excessive levels of NO leading to hypotension, is the opposite of what one might expect from decreased availability of L-arginine as an NOS substrate. For this reason choice B is the best answer. Ornithine is ultimately used to form L-proline, which is important for collagen synthesis, and polyamines, which is important for cell growth. Without L-arginine, there would not be ornithine and subsequently, L-proline and polyamines would be decreased. This would result in choice C, impaired cell growth, and choice D, impaired collagen synthesis. Both choice C and choice D would be expected outcomes of an L-arginine deficiency.

11. **C is the best answer.** Competitive inhibition occurs when another molecule takes the place of the substrate. This is achieved by using a molecule that has enough similarities with the substrate to fit into the active site. In the question stem, the researcher implies that ABH is a competitive inhibitor. While this is a plausible mechanism of inhibition for ABH, its status as an inhibitor does not necessarily mean it uses competitive inhibition. Enzyme inhibition can be competitive, noncompetitive, mixed and uncompetitive among others. This allows for elimination of choices A and B. Noncompetitive inhibition occurs when an inhibitor binds to an enzyme at a location other than the active site. Its structure does not need to resemble the substrate. Since the researcher implies competitive inhibition, choice C is a better answer than choice D.

12. **B is the best answer.** Based on the data from Figure 1 and Figure 2, arginase is involved in the development of ROP. Its absence does reduce apoptosis and decrease neovascularization. The question is asking the student to determine a role for vitamin C that makes it essential for arginase to function. In other words, because vitamin C is not available in these babies, the arginase cannot promote the development of ROP. Choice A, a competitive inhibitor, would prevent arginase from working. A deficiency in vitamin C would only increase the likelihood that these babies would develop ROP. Choice A can be eliminated. A cofactor is a metal ion that some enzymes need to reach optimal capacity. A coenzyme is an organic molecule that is required for catalysis. Vitamin C is an organic molecule and in this scenario could be acting as a coenzyme. This allows for elimination of choice D and makes choice B the best answer. Enzymes typically have high specificity for their substrates. It is unlikely that arginase could bind to both vitamin C and L-arginine, especially since their structures are nothing alike. Choice C can be eliminated.

13. **D is the best answer.** L-proline is a nonpolar amino acid with an R group that binds to the amine group, causing it to be more rigid than a typical amino acid. Because of its structure, it can create a kink in the structure of a protein. This makes choice D the best answer. Because L-proline is nonpolar, choice A can be eliminated. Collagen is a structural protein, not an enzyme. This eliminates choice B. The kinks that are formed by proline disrupt both beta conformations and alpha helices. This eliminates choice C.

14. **D is the best answer.** Enzyme specificity, choice A, refers to the idea that enzymes act on their substrates in an almost exclusive manner. This concept alone does not explain why L-arginine might appear differently when complexed with arginase. Choice B, the activation energy of arginase, would not have an impact on the structure of the L-arginine. The concept of enzyme specificity can be explained by choice C, the lock and key model, which describes the active site as having a specific shape in which only a substrate of a matching shape can fit. The induced fit model, choice D, is another model to explain enzyme specificity and states that both the enzyme and substrate change shape when the two bind. This model could be an explanation for why L-arginine is crystallized as two apparently different structures. This makes choice D the best answer.

TEST 1C A&E

Stand-alones (15-18)

15. **D is the best answer.** This question tests concepts related to models of enzyme-substrate binding. The lock and key model suggests that each enzyme has a specific substrate or set of substrates with which is binds, the enzyme serving as the lock and the substrate as the key. This model is proposed under the umbrella of enzyme-substrate specificity. Choice A can be eliminated because this model does not provide an alternative to enzyme specificity, but is a possible explanation of how enzyme specificity occurs. Choice B is consistent with the induced fit model of enzyme specificity, not the lock and key model. The lock and key model of enzyme-substrate specificity provides an explanation for specificity that applies to many, but not all enzyme-substrate interactions. It is important to be wary of MCAT® answers that involve extremes like "all" or "none". Choice C can be eliminated. Choice D is consistent with the lock and key model and is the best answer.

16. **C is the best answer.** An enzyme catalyzes both the forward and reverse reaction of a given pathway. In biological systems this is frequently complemented by additional pathways that continuously clear the product, keeping the reaction running forward. With only the substrate and the product being produced from it in the test tube, eventually a dynamic equilibrium will be formed. This makes choice C untrue and consequently the best answer. Choices A and B are both related to the control of the enzyme's activity. The question does not reference inhibition, or provide a mechanism for it, so these are not the best answers. Remember, the best answers on the MCAT® must answer the question, be objectively true, and match the question/passage if associated with one. Choice D accurately represents the formation of a dynamic equilibrium, which makes it accurate, and can be eliminated.

17. **A is the best answer.** This question is testing the ability of the test taker to read Lineweaver-Burk plots. The two features that can help delineate types of inhibition are K_m and V_{max}. On these plots, the X-intercept is equal to $-1/K_m$ and the Y-intercept is equal to $1/V_{max}$. A helpful next step is to think of what is known to be true about each type of inhibition. In noncompetitive inhibition, the K_m does not change while the V_{max} decreases. Choice A shows that with the inhibitor the Km remains the same because the x-intercept does not change. It also shows that the V_{max} is decreased because 1/V is larger. Both of these features are consistent with noncompetitive inhibition. In competitive inhibition, the K_m increases while the V_{max} remains the same. Choice B shows that with inhibitor the K_m increased (this is what happens when X-intercept gets smaller) while the V_{max} is slightly decreased. These features are consistent with competitive inhibition, and choice B can be eliminated. In uncompetitive inhibition, both the K_m and the V_{max} decrease. Choice C shows a decreased K_m and V_{max} by an equal amount, which is typical of uncompetitive inhibition, eliminating choice C. In mixed inhibition, V_{max} will be decreased to some extent while the effect on K_m is variable depending on the type of mixed inhibitor. Choice D shows that with the inhibitor there is a decreased K_m and a decreased V_{max} by an unequal amount, which can be best explained by a mixed inhibition mechanism. Choice D can be ruled out, leaving choice A as the best answer.

18. **D is the best answer.** Both the K_m and V_{max} can be helpful in identifying types of inhibitors, and the question stem states that both of these values are decreased when the unknown inhibitor is added to solution. This is characteristic of uncompetitive inhibition. Choice A is characteristic of competitive inhibition. However, in competitive inhibition, the inhibitor binding to the active site causes a decrease in affinity of the enzyme for the substrate, thereby increasing the K_m. Because this does not match the information provided in the question stem, choice A can be eliminated. Choice B states that the first step in the cascade is the inhibitor binding the enzyme. This can occur in mixed and noncompetitive inhibition, but not uncompetitive inhibition. In uncompetitive inhibition, the inhibitor binds the enzyme-substrate complex, which can only occur after the enzyme binds the substrate. Choice B can be eliminated. Choice C also describes mixed or noncompetitive inhibition and can be eliminated. Choice D is left as the best answer. Note that choice D contains material that is unlikely to be expected knowledge, but with a solid understanding of the characteristics of inhibition, the other three answer choices can be eliminated. To conceptualize choice D, the inhibitor equilibrium constant will be an equilibrium constant just like any other: $\left[\frac{\text{products}}{\text{reactants}}\right]$. Since the inhibitor binds the enzyme substrate complex only, [ES] must be contained in the equilibrium constant. Choice D is the best answer.

Passage 4 (Questions 19-23)

19. D is the best answer. Figures 1 and 3 are both needed in order to answer this question. The binding affinity of an enzyme can be measured by the K_m value. The K_m can be found by finding the substrate concentration associated with half of the V_{max}. Low K_m values mean that only a small concentration of substrate is needed in order for the enzyme to function at half its maximum rate. This means that the enzyme has a high affinity for the substrate. High K_m values indicate that a large concentration of substrate is needed for the enzyme to function at half its maximum rate. This means that the enzyme has a low affinity for the substrate. Choice A can be eliminated because the maximum rate of an enzyme is not a direct measure of the binding affinity of an enzyme to a substrate. Choice B can be eliminated because the K_m of PTEN is higher than the K_m of PTEN-L. The maximum velocity of PTEN can be found on Figure 1 and is about 3500 μM P_i min^{-1}. Half of this rate is 1750 μM P_i min^{-1} which corresponds to a substrate concentration of about 20 μM of PIP_3. The maximum velocity of PTEN-L can be found on Figure 3 and is about 425 μM P_i min^{-1}. Half of this rate is 212.5 μM P_i min^{-1} which corresponds to a substrate concentration of about 5 μM of PIP_3. Choice C can be eliminated because the maximum reaction velocity is not a direct indicator of substrate affinity. While PTEN-L does have a lower V_{max}, this is not the best answer. Choice D is the best answer because the higher K_m of PTEN indicates that it has a lower substrate binding affinity than PTEN-L.

20. B is the best answer. A molecule that reversibly binds in the active site is called a competitive inhibitor. It will compete with PIP_3 for the active site of PTEN. Competitive inhibitors do not change the maximum reaction velocity because they can be outcompeted by increasing the substrate concentration. However, at low substrate concentration they cause the reaction to proceed slowly because the enzyme spends a greater amount of time bound to the inhibitor than the substrate. Choice A can be eliminated because competitive inhibitors do not change the maximum reaction velocity. Additionally, competitive inhibitors do change the enzyme affinity so the slope would change. Choice B is the best answer because it correctly identifies both the height and the slope of a reaction in the presence of a competitive inhibitor. The height is maintained because the maximum velocity stays the same. The initial slope is decreased because at lower concentrations of PIP_3 the rate of reaction will be lower than without the competitive inhibitor. Choice C can be eliminated because the maximum reaction velocity will not decrease in the presence of a competitive inhibitor. Choice D can be eliminated because it states that the maximum reaction velocity will increase in addition to an increased affinity in the presence of an inhibitor. This does not agree with competitive inhibition and can be eliminated.

21. B is the best answer. The question is asking how a molecule of PIP_2 binds to the PTEN enzyme. The passage indicates that the binding of PIP_2 may enhance the affinity of PTEN for PIP_3. Figure 2 contains the amino acid sequence needed for PIP_2 to effectively bind. The molecule of PIP_2 shown in the question stem reveals that it contains both a hydrophilic sugar as well as a hydrophobic fatty acid. Choice A can be eliminated because if PIP_2 was able to bind to the active site, it would most likely act as an inhibitor. Any molecule other than substrate that binds in the active site will reduce the rate of catalysis because it prevents the substrate from binding. Choice B states that ionic interactions at the allosteric site are responsible for the enhanced reaction rate. Figure 2 reveals that lysine (K) and arginine (R) are both present in the N-terminus allosteric site. Both of these residues are basic and possess a positive charge that will form ionic bonds with the negative charges of PIP_2. Choice B is the best answer because it explains the correct type of bond formation as well as the proper location of the bond. Choice C can be eliminated because the positively charged N terminus allosteric site will not be able to form hydrophobic interactions with PIP_2. Choice D can be eliminated because PIP_2 binding in the active site would inhibit the binding of PIP_3. This would result in a decrease in the rate of catalysis of PTEN.

22. C is the best answer. Figure 1 shows that PTEN at 200 mM NaCl behaves differently than PTEN at 100 mM and 0 mM NaCl. PTEN at 200 mM NaCl requires a large quantity of PIP_3 to increase the rate of catalysis whereas PTEN at other NaCl concentrations increases its rate of catalysis immediately. Choice A can be eliminated because the researchers noted limited turbidity, or cloudiness, which would be seen if the enzyme precipitated out of solution. Choice B can be eliminated because a high affinity for PIP_3 would be expected to show a decrease in K_m rather than an increase. Choice D can be eliminated because the pH of the solution does not change at various PIP_3 or NaCl concentrations. Since the pH is constant, it cannot be the reason that the efficiency of PTEN is changing. Choice C is the best answer because additional binding of ions beyond what is optimal for the substrate and active site could reduce the affinity of the enzyme for its substrate. Enzymes have their own optimal ion concentration necessary for catalysis, and too high or too low concentrations can inhibit the binding of enzyme and substrate.

23. D is the best answer. For a molecule that follows Michaelis-Menten kinetics, the K_m value remains constant for all enzyme concentrations. K_m is a property of an enzyme that measures its affinity for its substrate. Changing the quantity of the enzyme will not alter its binding affinity. Alternatively, increasing the amount of enzyme will increase the maximum reaction rate. If more enzyme is present, it can bind to more substrate before it becomes saturated. This allows it to increase the maximum velocity. Choice A can be eliminated because the K_m of any enzyme cannot be changed by altering its concentration. The only way to change K_m is by changing the environment that the enzyme is in. Choice B can be eliminated because K_m would not change. The V_{max} would increase but this has no effect on K_m. Choice C can be eliminated because it does not accurately describe what happens when you increase enzyme concentration. An increased binding affinity does decrease K_m, but increasing the enzyme concentration would not cause binding affinity to change. Choice D is the best answer because increasing the enzyme concentration would only increase the maximum rate of the reaction.

Passage 5 (Questions 24-27)

24. **A is the best answer.** The passage indicates that sorbitol dehydrogenase is an enzyme that oxidizes sorbitol to fructose. Because it is an enzyme, it should follow basic enzyme kinetics, and there is no evidence in the passage that this enzyme is an exception. The maximum rate of the reaction is proportional to the concentration of the enzyme because without the tool to carry out the conversion, the amount of substrate is irrelevant. If there is too little enzyme, then even if there is a lot of substrate such as sorbitol in this case, the available enzymes will be quickly saturated and the reaction will be stalled. Choice A is the best answer because it identifies this relationship. Choice B identifies an enzyme earlier in the pathway which may affect the concentration of the reactant, but choice A more likely since it is the enzyme catalyzing the reaction in question. Choice C can be eliminated because the concentration of the product is not the primary influence on the maximum rate of the reaction.. Choice D is misleading, because while it is true that the enzyme carries out a redox reaction, there is no basis for such an assumption from the passage. While the environment of the cell may have an effect on the ability of the enzyme to function, it would not have an ability to influence the degree to which it functions. The question is asking for what makes the reaction go the fastest it can go and not what allows the reaction to happen in the first place.

25. **D is the best answer.** The passage makes a passing reference to hexokinase and phosphofructokinase in the third paragraph, describing them as "control points." Some enzymes can be constantly active whereas other enzymes are only active where necessary. Key enzymes such as hexokinase and phosphofructokinase can be activated or deactivated by multiple allosteric regulators because these enzymes control whether or not glucose is broken down by glycolysis. Choice D is the best answer. Choice A can be eliminated since control over expression does not indicate whether allosteric regulation also occurs. Choice B can be eliminated because the concentration of substrate can limit the maximum rate when the enzyme is fully saturated. This does not give any indication that allosteric regulation occurs. Choice C is unsupported by the passage, and can be eliminated for the same reason as choice A.

26. **D is the best answer.** This question is asking what small change to an enzyme would be expected to have the greatest impact on its ability to function. The active site is the primary region of enzyme activity. A significant substitution can affect the ability to bind the substrate such as glucose in this case. The amino acid change that is most significant would be expected to have the greatest impact on function. Lysine and Arginine in choice A are both positively charged amino acids, so the change is not likely to be significant, and this choice can be eliminated. Asparagine and serine are both polar amino acids with uncharged side groups, so choice B can be eliminated. Aspartate to Glycine in choice C is a significant change from a negatively charged amino acid to an uncharged one, but the change is in the allosteric site, which while significant, is not as significant as the active site. Choice D is a better answer because a change to the active site will render an enzyme useless if it cannot bind substrate. The change of threonine to alanine is a change from a polar side group to one that is hydrophobic.

27. **B is the best answer.** This is a research question and involves some thought. The passage indicates in the third paragraph that aldose reductase is highly expressed in the placenta and goes on to comment that this is at a time where energy requirements are high for the fetus. This indicates that high fructose in the fetuses is not abnormal but is in fact important for growth as fructose provides abundant energy for the fetuses. Blocking the enzyme that allows for the conversion of glucose to fructose can be negatively impactful for the fetus, and such an experiment would have serious ethical concerns. Choice A is true for all experiments, but it is not the best answer in this case. Choice B is the best answer because it acknowledges that the current study population is not compatible with such an experiment, since fructose may be vital to the life of the fetus. The experiment would first need to be tested in a rodent model, to avoid the possibility of damaging fetuses in a human population. Choice C is also a valid suggestion but is not the best answer given the issue of the study population. Choice D is a distractor as it provides a new direction for the experiment, though it doesn't answer the question regarding a suggestion for an aldose reductase inhibitor experiment.

Stand-alones (28-31)

28. **B is the best answer.** In Michaelis-Menten enzyme kinetics, the K_m is defined as the substrate concentration at one half V_{max}, and while it has a wide range of different applications to inhibition and substrate saturation, the basic definition is all that is needed to solve this problem. This data is frequently encountered as a plot, and it may be beneficial to draw one out on scratch paper. V_{max}, the saturation kinetic state is reached at or around 0.5 μM, as the rates stabilize around 0.85. This would correspond to a plateau on a graph. From there, identify the rate closest to half this value, and look for the answer choice that most closely matches that concentration. Choice A is far below the half value point. Choice B has a rate of 0.41 which is very close to ½ 0.85, making it a strong choice. Choice C is also close, but 0.53 is further from 0.425 than 0.41, so it is not as strong an answer. Choice D is at the V_{max} plateau, and may be chosen if the definitions are confused. Choice B is the closest to ½ V_{max}, making it closest to the expected value of K_m and the best answer.

29. **D is the best answer.** Inhibitors that form covalent bonds with substrates are irreversible inhibitors, making choice D the best answer. A covalent bond is a strong bond that preventing it from carrying out its function permanently. A reversible inhibitor does not bind to the enzyme covalently but interacts through weaker bonds that do not permanently alter its function. Choices A, B, and C are all types of inhibitors that are reversible. Vigabatrin is a suicide inhibitor which begins down the catalytic pathway of an enzyme but cannot proceed all the way through, ultimately staying covalently bound and rendering the enzyme ineffective. The question stem does not provide enough information to determine the type of inhibition other than that it is irreversible, which leaves choice D as the best answer.

30. **B is the best answer.** The image shows various amino acids arranged in the active site around a molecule in the active site of the enzyme. The fact that the molecule is an inhibitor does not contribute to the answer. Arg is a basic amino acid that is positively charged at physiological pH. Finding Arg on the bottom left corner of the figure shows that it is interacting with a carboxylic acid functional group that is negatively charged. Covalent bonds are within a molecule. Because the amino acid and the inhibitor are not chemically linked by sharing electrons, as in a covalent bond, choice A can be eliminated. Van der Waals attractions occur between hydrophobic amino acids. Because Arg is a basic, charged amino acid, not a hydrophobic amino acid, choice C can be eliminated. While a metal cofactor could help stabilize the molecule-amino acid interaction, no molecule is present in the figure. Additionally, metal cofactors tend to be positively charged and would likely repel away from the positive charge of Arg, eliminating choice D. Electrostatic interactions occur between amino acids and other molecules that have opposite charges. The positive charge on the Arg and the negative charge of the carboxylic acid would have an electrostatic attraction, making choice B the best answer choice.

31. **B is the best answer.** The ribosome catalyzes the addition of one amino acid to the growing chain of a polypeptide. The lone pair on the nitrogen attacks the electropositive carbonyl carbon of the receiving amino acid, releasing water in the process. A hydrolysis reaction instead uses water to break apart one molecule into two. Choice A can be eliminated. A carboxylation reaction involves adding a carbon dioxide group to a molecule. The reaction occurring in the ribosome is making a peptide bond, not adding CO_2, eliminating choice C. Decarboxylation reactions occur when carbon dioxide gas is released. Because the question stem does not provide any indication that carbon dioxide is released, choice D is unlikely to be the best answer choice. Condensation would be the joining of two molecules with the specific release of water as a product. Choice B is the best answer choice.

Genetics

TEST 2A

ANSWERS & EXPLANATIONS

Questions 1–59

LECTURE 2 ANSWER KEY

TEST 2A		TEST 2B		TEST 2C	
1. B	31. B	1. B	31. C	1. A	17. A
2. D	32. D	2. A	32. A	2. C	18. B
3. A	33. C	3. B	33. A	3. D	19. B
4. C	34. C	4. A	34. A	4. D	20. A
5. C	35. C	5. A	35. D	5. A	21. A
6. D	36. A	6. C	36. C	6. B	22. B
7. B	37. A	7. B	37. D	7. B	23. A
8. B	38. D	8. A	38. A	8. A	24. A
9. C	39. C	9. A	39. C	9. C	25. A
10. B	40. C	10. B	40. B	10. C	26. A
11. A	41. A	11. D	41. C	11. A	27. C
12. C	42. B	12. A	42. C	12. A	28. C
13. B	43. D	13. B	43. A	13. B	29. A
14. D	44. A	14. A	44. C	14. C	30. A
15. D	45. D	15. C	45. A	15. B	31. A
16. C	46. B	16. C	46. C	16. C	
17. A	47. A	17. A	47. B		
18. B	48. B	18. A	48. C		
19. B	49. B	19. B	49. A		
20. C	50. B	20. B	50. B		
21. B	51. A	21. D	51. C		
22. C	52. B	22. A	52. D		
23. D	53. B	23. A	53. C		
24. B	54. B	24. A	54. A		
25. B	55. D	25. B	55. B		
26. A	56. D	26. D	56. C		
27. D	57. C	27. D	57. B		
28. B	58. D	28. A	58. D		
29. C	59. B	29. A	59. C		
30. C		30. C			

EXPLANATIONS FOR LECTURE 2

Passage 1 (Questions 1-4)

1. **B is the best answer.** Increasing the activity of histone methyltransferase would increase the proportion of histones that were methylated. Methylation is a form of epigenetic regulation, meaning that gene expression is controlled by means other than elements of the primary DNA sequence. Promoters, enhancers, and repressors are part of the primary DNA sequence and would not be considered epigenetic regulation. Methylation forms heterochromatin, causing the DNA to become more tightly wound and limiting gene expression. The expression of genes in the methylated region would decrease, making choice B the best answer. Choice A is less likely to be correct because the expression should decrease, not increase. Choice C is also unlikely to be the answer because the expression decreases instead of remaining the same. Choice D can be eliminated because gene expression does depend on methylation status.

2. **D is the best answer.** Paragraph one describes that the scientists reduced the expression of Aurora A in breast cancer cells and noted that this corresponded to an increase in apoptosis. The follow-up experiment should be to overexpress the Aurora A protein and observe whether or not apoptosis decreased, making choice D the best answer. Choice A can be eliminated because the scientists are concerned with breast cancer cells, not colon cancer cells. Oftentimes, differences in cell types can correspond to different protein functions that cannot be compared. Choice B is less likely to be correct because, as an epigenetic modification, acetylation increases transcription of genes but would not help the scientists understand what gene increased to cause an increase/decrease in apoptosis. Choice C can also be eliminated because knocking out Aurora A expression entirely would be similar to the experiments the scientists already performed, adding less new information.

3. **A is the best answer.** A mutation that eliminates the expression of Aurora A would prevent an mRNA transcript from being synthesized. The best answer will contain the regions that, when rendered non-functional by a mutation, prevent transcription from beginning. The promoter is required for transcriptional initiation and an enhancer increases the likelihood of transcription occurring by helping the DNA-dependent RNA polymerase find the promoter. Options I and II are possible, making choice A the best answer. Mutations rendering a repressor non-functional should increase the rate of Aurora A expression, making option III a less likely answer. Mutations in introns do not affect transcription or translation, as they would be spliced out during the splicing process. Option IV is less likely. Choice A is the only answer that contains the combination of options I and II that are most likely to affect expression, making it the best answer choice.

4. **C is the best answer.** According to paragraph one, Aurora A expression is required for proper formation of a bipolar mitotic spindle. The mitotic spindle forms and assembles with the centrally aligned chromatids during metaphase. The cell could enter into metaphase but not complete it, making choice B less likely. If the mitotic spindle could not form, the cell would not progress to anaphase, when chromosomes are separated, making choice C the best. Prophase is when chromatin condenses into chromosomes, making choice A less likely. Choice D is also not likely because telophase is when the nuclear envelope reforms.

Passage 2 (Questions 5-8)

5. **C is the best answer.** Histones are globular proteins that are wrapped by DNA to compact the DNA in the nucleus. As DNA is negatively charged due to the phosphodiester backbone, histones contain positively charged amino acids in high proportion in order to allow association of the DNA with the protein. Lysine, K, is positively charged at physiologic pH and would be able to tightly associate with DNA, eliminating choice A. Asparagine, N, is polar and uncharged. While it will not repel DNA, due to its neutral change, it may be able to have transient polarization that allows it to associate with the negatively charged backbone of DNA, eliminating choice B. As with lysine, histidine, H, is usually positively charged and could associate with the negatively charged backbone of DNA. Histidine is one of the main amino acids involved in acid/base catalysis due to its pK_a being close to the physiologic pH of the cell. Choice D can be eliminated. Glutamate, E, is negatively charged and the least likely to be contained in high proportions in the histone because the negative charge of glutamate would repel the negative charge of DNA, preventing association. Choice C is the best answer choice.

TEST 2A A&E

6. **D is the best answer.** According to the question stem, Xist may play a role in maintaining heterochromatin, the portion of chromatin that is found in a tightly wound state that represses transcription of genes. Anti-sense oligonucleotides that are complementary to Xist would serve to decrease Xist levels in the cell. If Xist levels were decreased, less heterochromatin would form on the X chromosome, resulting in higher euchromatin percentages. Euchromatin is the portion of DNA that is not tightly bound to histones and is open for transcription. Higher euchromatin would result in increased protein content due to increased RNA transcribed from the X chromosome, eliminating choice A. Xist does associate with one X chromosome in women but this finding does not provide additional evidence that Xist serves to increase heterochromatin, making choice B less likely to be the best answer. Increased chromosome condensation would correlate with heterochromatin. If Xist levels were decreased by anti-sense oligonucleotides, an increase in euchromatin would be expected, not an increase in heterochromatin. Choice C can be eliminated. Glucose-6-phosphatase is a gene located on the X chromosome. If Xist levels were decreased, more of the X chromosome would likely be open for transcription, resulting in higher RNA and protein content of the genes on the X chromosome, including glucose-6-phosphatase. Choice D is the best answer choice.

7. **B is the best answer.** Figure 1 provides the best information to help answer the question. According to paragraph three and Figure 1, knockdown of BAF60, a member of the SWI/SNF chromatin remodeling complex, prevents progression through the cell cycle. In order to proceed through the cell cycle, high levels of cyclin-cyclin-dependent kinase complexes are needed. On the right-hand side of Figure 1, cyclin D2 and cdk A allow for progression from G_1 into S phase for DNA and centromere replication. Cyclin D2 and cdk A levels must be high. If transcription of cyclin D2 were inhibited, the protein levels would be low and no cell cycle progression would occur, eliminating choice A. Paragraph two helps provide information about choice C. SWI/SNF complexes use ATP, hydrolyzing it to ADP to drive rearrangements of chromatin. SWI/SNF action should decrease ATP concentrations in the cell over time, not increase them. Choice C and be eliminated. The passage does not provide any information that suggests that the SWI/SNF complex associates with non-coding RNA, making choice D less likely to be the best answer. Because BAF60 activity allows for cell cycle progression, transcription of cdk A would be activated, making choice B the best answer choice.

8. **B is the best answer.** According to paragraph two, the looping of the chromosome occurs between the 5′ and 3′ ends of genes and allows for the efficient recycling of RNA polymerase II from the end of the gene to the promoter. While the promoter is rich in A and T nucleotides, the passage does not provide any evidence that the actual sequence of the DNA is changed, eliminating choice A. The rate of nucleotide addition is a function of the chemistry mediated by RNA polymerase II. The looping of chromatin does not structurally alter the RNA polymerase, meaning that the chemistry is likely unchanged. Choice C is less likely to be the best answer choice. The passage does not discuss the identity of DNA elements included in the chromosome loops. While it is possible that fewer repressor elements are included, the passage does not provide any information that would support this idea, making choice D less likely to be the best answer. Paragraph two notes that the RNA polymerase II is allowed to move from the 3′ end of the gene back to the promoter with increased efficiency. This would allow for increased transcription, as the RNA polymerase would begin transcribing the gene faster, making choice B the best answer choice.

Passage 3 (Questions 9-12)

9. **C is the best answer.** Methylation is an epigenetic change on cytosine bases in DNA and acts to create a tighter association between DNA and histones, the proteins that condense DNA in the nucleus. Because methylation acts on C bases of DNA, it should not affect the translation of a gene but the transcription. The passage does not provide evidence that it inhibits ribosomes, eliminating choice A. According to Figure 1, an increase in methylation corresponds to a decrease in gene expression, meaning that transcription decreased. Choice B can be eliminated. As with choice A, translation is not affected by methylation on DNA, as translation acts on RNA, eliminating choice D. Methylation increases the association of DNA with histones, creating a tightly wound coil of DNA on the histone proteins. The tighter winding prevents transcription factors and RNA polymerase from accessing promoter sites, leading to decreases in transcription. Choice C is the best answer.

10. **B is the best answer.** According to paragraph three, TGF-β is able to increase the transcription of other transcription factors like KLF15, which may play a role in the errors in angiogenesis in preeclampsia. Transcription factors are primarily responsible for binding sites on DNA, increasing the transcription of particular genes, leading to higher levels of the target protein. Transcription factors are unlikely to bind single stranded RNA over double stranded DNA, eliminating choice A. Replication of RNA occurs by an RNA-dependent RNA polymerase, which some viruses contain. Eukaryotic cells do not undergo RNA replication directly, eliminating choice C. DNA polymerases, not transcription factors, are responsible for replicating DNA, eliminating choice D. Transcription factors bind specific sequences of DNA, helping to recruit the machinery responsible for DNA transcription. Increased transcription leads to increases in the concentration of the protein levels, making choice B the best answer choice.

11. **A is the best answer.** According to information contained in the passage, the epigenetic regulation that defines the role of angiogenesis-related genes is methylation. Their main assertion is that hypomethylation of certain angiogenesis-related genes leads to an increased risk of preeclampsia. If women with preeclampsia also had first degree relatives whom had preeclampsia, this would not lend experimental evidence either for or against the authors' assertions. Preeclampsia is relatively common at ~ 8%, so a woman could have a relative with preeclampsia by chance. Additionally, a relative with a disease indicates a genetic component but not specifically an epigenetic component, making choice B less likely to be the best answer. Changes in the promoter sequence, addition of enhancer sequences, or removal of repressor sequences could all increase the expression of KLF15. Increased KLF15 expression does not necessarily correspond to epigenetic changes, making choice C less likely to be the best answer. Prior use of an anti-angiogenesis antibody would support the angiogenesis-related theory of preeclampsia but not lend specific evidence to the role of epigenetics in the disease. Choice D can be eliminated. If women were treated with a DNA methyltransferase inhibitor, DNA would be hypomethylated, leading to a similar scenario as seen in the passage. If this were correlated with increased incidence of preeclampsia, choice A would be the best answer to support the authors' assertions.

12. **C is the best answer.** In general, methylation of a sequence results in the decrease in transcription of a target locus. Hypomethylation or decreased methylation would decrease, not increase, the interaction between histones and DNA, eliminating choice A. Methylation occurs on DNA, not RNA, as described by the passage. Hypermethylation of RNA is not relevant to answering the experimental questions of the passage, eliminating choice B. The passage provides no information that calls into doubt the findings of the researchers. Additionally, the p value shown in the figure is significant, as it is below 0.05. It is unlikely this finding represents an experimental artifact, making choice D less likely to be the best answer. If hypomethylation resulted in the expression of small interfering RNAs (siRNAs) that degraded mRNA of their target genes, then lower levels of methylation of these negative regulators of gene expression would lead to lower gene expression. As seen in the figure, if DNA methylation were increased at these negative regulation loci, then the siRNAs would not be expressed, leading to increases in gene expression. Choice C is the best answer choice.

Stand-alones (Questions 13-16)

13. **B is the best answer.** The locus of a gene is its specific location on the DNA chromosome, down to the base pair range that it occupies on the whole of the chromosome. In order to find the specific locus of a gene, scientists would be interested in designing oligonucleotide sequences that bind to a specific region of the gene and detect these regions in the cell. PCR allows for the amplification of a sequence of DNA but is unable to physically show its locus, eliminating choice A. DNA isolation and gel electrophoresis may show the size of the gene but would be unable to predict its location in the genome, eliminating choice C. A western blot is used to detect specific proteins, not specific nucleic acid sequences, eliminating choice D. FISH uses fluorescently tagged nucleotides that are complementary to a specific sequence of DNA. The hybridization of the tagged nucleotide would be the best way to identify the specific locus. Choice B is the best answer.

14. **D is the best answer.** Epigenetic changes are those changes on the DNA that do not involve the DNA sequence itself but can modify the histones, the proteins around which DNA associates, and the DNA base itself. Histone acetylation creates permissively active chromatin to increase transcription but does not change the DNA sequence itself, eliminating choice A. Methylation causes DNA to bind tighter to the histone, decreasing transcription, eliminating choice B. Addition of a methyl group to A nucleotides may increase transcription, as this may act as the reciprocal change to methylation of C residues. However, this would not change the actual sequence of DNA, eliminating choice C. If a mutation occurred that changed a C to a T, this would change the DNA sequence, making choice D not an epigenetic change and the best answer.

15. **D is the best answer.** A single deletion of a nucleotide, especially early in the mRNA sequence, is likely to have a major effect on the final protein synthesized. A single deletion causes a frameshift mutation, or a shift in the reading frame that a ribosome uses during translation, and rarely will result in a normally functioning protein, so choice A is a weaker answer. Choices B and D describe a similar mutation since the RNA polymerase is responsible for creating the mRNA transcript. The important difference between the two answers is the position at which the mutation occurs. The 25th nucleotide represents the first nucleotide of a codon while the 33rd nucleotide corresponds to the last nucleotide of a codon. This is important because alterations in the first nucleotide of a codon are much more likely to cause a change in the amino acid used in translation for that codon. For this reason, choice B is more likely to cause an effect than choice D, so choice B can be eliminated. By changing the original codon from UGG to UGA, a stop codon is created early in the transcript. This will end translation prematurely and the protein synthesized will be shorter than the normal protein, so choice C can be eliminated. The wobble effect describes the phenomenon observed when a substitution of the third nucleotide of a codon does not change the amino acid for which it codes. Since the substitution is occurring at the third nucleotide of a codon, choice D is the best answer.

16. **C is the best answer.** CpG dinucleotides are often methylated in the human genome, which is a type of epigenetic change that helps "mute" transcription of genes nearby. Additionally, methylation tends to allow the DNA to associate more tightly with histones, which prevents active transcription. Centromeres are locations on the chromosome that help attach to microtubules during cell division. Centromeres are one location that is heavily composed of tightly bound DNA to histones, making option I true. Methylation creates regions of the DNA that are not transcriptionally active, which is the opposite of option II. Heterochromatin is composed of DNA that is more tightly wound around histones compared to euchromatin, which is considered transcriptionally active chromatin. Option III is part of the best answer. Choice A can be eliminated because heterochromatin is methylated to prevent gene transcription in this region. Choice B can be eliminated because transcriptionally active regions contain low levels of methylation, not high levels. Choice D can be eliminated for the same reason. Choice C is the best answer because high CpG content implies higher levels of DNA methylation, which would be found around centromeres and in regions that have repressed gene transcription, called heterochromatin.

Passage 4 (Questions 17-20)

17. **A is the best answer.** Methylation of cytosine bases tends to make DNA transcriptionally inactive, which can be remembered by methylation "mutes" transcription. Methylation does this by allowing DNA to associate more tightly with its associated histones. Choice B can be eliminated because between 0 and 33% methylation, the expression should fall, not rise. Choice C can similarly be eliminated because as methylation increases from 0 to 67%, expression should fall. Choice D predicts a linear relationship between expression and methylation. However, this is the opposite of what would be expected. As methylation increases, expression should decrease, eliminating choice D as the best answer choice. Choice A predicts falling expression as the levels of methylation increase. Choice A is the best answer choice.

18. **B is the best answer.** Small non-coding regulatory RNAs, such as small interfering RNAs (siRNAs) and miRNAs, bind to their complementary sequences on other mRNA molecules to target them for degradation. The best pairing will be at the 3′ end of the VEGF mRNA, as this is where the passage notes that miRNAs bind, and will be the correct pairing between AU and GC. RNA does not contain T but instead contains U. Choice A can be eliminated because the VEGF sequence presented is at the 5′ end of the molecule, not the 3′ end, as indicated by the presence of the 5′ methyl-guanine cap. Additionally, choice A contains T, which is not found in RNA. Choice C can also be eliminated because it contains T instead of U. Choice D can be eliminated because the VEGF mRNA presented is at the 5′ end of the molecule, as indicated by the 5′ cap. Choice B is the best answer because the RNA contains U, instead of T, and the VEGF mRNA and miR-15 sequences are complementary when matched.

19. **B is the best answer.** According to information contained in the passage, VEGF expression leads to angiogenesis, a necessary component of cancer progression. Decreased VEGF expression, as mediated by miR-16, would lead to decreased blood formation and impairment of metastasis. An oncogene is responsible for driving cancer progression. miR-16 would be considered an oncogene if its overexpression increased angiogenesis and metastasis. Because the opposite effect is expected, choice A can be eliminated. Transcription factors are proteins that bind DNA to increase the rates of transcription of target genes. As miR-16 is an RNA molecule, not a protein, choice C can be eliminated. Ribozymes are nucleic acids that catalyze reactions themselves. While the miRNA is necessary to direct targeting of the Ago-1 endonuclease to a particular mRNA, it does not mediate the nuclease reaction itself. Choice D can be eliminated. Overexpression of miR-16 leads to the decrease in VEGF expression due to decreased VEGF mRNA levels. miR-16 acts to impair cancer progression by limiting angiogenesis, making it a tumor suppressor. Choice B is the best answer choice.

20. **C is the best answer.** Both Figures 1 and 3 are necessary to answer this question. Figure 1 presents a northern blot, which is used to detect the presence and relative abundance of RNA sequences. In this instance, the northern blot is used to detect miRNA expression. Upon treatment with etoposide, cisplatin, and C-10, the bands for miR-15 and miR-16 increase in brightness, indicating that the relative concentration of these increased due to treatment. Figure 3 shows the activity of STAT3 in inducing VEGF signaling on the reporter gene system. Treatment with all three chemotherapeutics decreased STAT3 signaling, as the relative expression read out was lower than the control for all drugs. Choice A can be eliminated because cisplatin increased miR-15 expression and resulted in decreased STAT3 signaling. Choice B can be eliminated because C-10 increased miR-16 expression. Choice D can be eliminated because C-10 increased, not decreased miR-16 expression and resulted in decreased STAT3 signaling. Choice C is the best answer because etoposide and cisplatin both increased miR-15 expression, as seen by the brighter bands on the northern blot, and decreased STAT3 signaling, as seen by the reduced luciferase values in Figure 3.

Passage 5 (Questions 21-25)

21. **B is the best answer.** The nucleolus is the sub-nuclear compartment where ribosome synthesis and assembly takes place, making choice B the best answer. Here, ribosomal RNA (rRNA) and ribosomal proteins are assembled into the large and small subunit that will go on to provide the machinery for translation. RNA polymerase is involved in transcription, not translation, making choice A an unlikely answer. While both mRNA and tRNA are involved in translation, they are cytosolic and assemble with the formed ribosome to synthesize proteins. Because mRNA and tRNA are not synthesized in the nucleolus, choices C and D, respectively, can be eliminated.

22. **C is the best answer.** According to paragraph one, a glycine codon immediately follows the 7 nucleotide HIV slippery sequence on the RNA molecule. The most likely answer to the presented question will be a factor that would not be contained in an RNA sequence. As thymine (T) nucleotides are a component of DNA, not RNA, they would be not be found in RNA, making choice C the best answer. Codons representing tyrosine, a polar amino acid, could be a component of the HIV mRNA sequence, making choice A unlikely. It is not unreasonable that a tyrosine amino acid could be coded for in HIV RNA. Methionine is always the first amino acid coded for in RNA transcripts. A methionine codon would be contained at the beginning of the mRNA sequence, making choice B an unlikely answer. Given that the RNA would be used to code for HIV proteins, it must contain ribosomal binding sites, making choice D also less likely to be the correct answer.

23. **D is the best answer.** According to paragraph three, eRF1 is a eukaryotic release factor, meaning the protein is responsible for releasing the ribosome from the mRNA transcript after translation has been completed. The signal for the end of translation is a stop codon contained on the mRNA transcript. The most likely answer choice will be a codon that does not encode a stop codon. In eukaryotic cells, UGA, UAA, and UAG are the three stop codons and would be most likely to be recognized by the eukaryotic eRF1 protein, eliminating choices A, B, and C. UGG is not a stop codon and would be unlikely to be recognized by eRF1, making choice D the best answer.

24. **B is the best answer.** While this question stem provides some extraneous information, the best answer choice will be the location that a non-initiator (non-methionine) tRNA binds its anti-codon to the codon of the mRNA. tRNAs carrying amino acids can bind either the A site (aminoacyl-tRNA site) or the P site (peptidyl-tRNA). The P site only binds new aminoacyl-tRNAs when the tRNA is carrying the initial methionine amino acid that begins eukaryotic proteins. Given that the tRNA in the question stem is tyrosine, it is unlikely to bind in the P site, eliminating choice C. The A site binds all other incoming aminoacyl-tRNAs as the peptide is growing, making choice B the best answer. The E site is where the tRNA, now with its amino acid removed, exits the ribosome, making choice D an unlikely answer. The ribosome does not contain an explicit tRNA binding site, making choice A less likely than choice B.

25. **B is the best answer.** Figure 2 provides the best direct means of answering this question. According to paragraph one, the glycine codon is GGG. Paragraph three details how the eukaryotic release factor eRF1 recognizes the stop codons, which are UGA, UAA, and UAG. The question is asking about a change in the codon from GGG to any of the stop codons. According to Figure 2, changing the codon from glycine to a stop codon decreases the frameshift efficiency, making answer choices that indicate an increase in efficiency or no change in efficiency less plausible. Choices A and C can be eliminated. The GGG codon appears to have around a 10% frameshift efficiency, while the stop codons have around a 3% frameshift efficiency. The reduction from 10% to 3% is a 70% decrease, making choice B the best answer choice. Given that the frameshift efficiency decreases by more than 10%, choice D can be eliminated in favor of choice B.

Stand-alones (Questions 26-28)

26. **A is the best answer.** A steroid is a molecule with four fused rings that can easily cross the plasma membrane by diffusion, binding a cytoplasmic receptor and translocate to the nucleus. Once in the nucleus, the steroid hormone receptor can bind DNA, increasing the transcription of target genes. DHEA is an androgen like testosterone, which are both steroids. Since steroids are not transcribed, choice B can be eliminated. Steroids tend to increase, not decrease gene transcription, eliminating choices C and D. One steroid hormone is cortisol that is produced in the adrenal glands. Cortisol is known to increase blood glucose levels, in part by stimulating gluconeogenesis. The last step in gluconeogenesis is removal of the phosphate on glucose, allowing glucose to be transported out of the cell. Choice A is the best answer.

27. **D is the best answer.** The main purpose of gene regulation in prokaryotes is for the organism to be able to react and adjust to its environment. This is in contrast to gene regulation in multicellular eukaryotes which is meant to maintain homeostasis. Choices A, B and C describe scenarios in which the Salmonella would be reacting to something in its immediate environment. Choice D describes a scenario in which gene regulation would be used to keep a parameter at a constant state. This is less characteristic of gene regulation in prokaryotes and is the best answer.

28. **B is the best answer.** The 5′ cap and the poly-A tail are added onto an RNA transcript and are necessary for export from the nucleus to the cytosol and initiation of translation. Hydrolysis would remove the 5′ cap after it was added. Alternative splicing to link exons could still occur, eliminating option I. The poly-A tail is added at the end of transcription and could still be polymerized, eliminating option II. Nuclear export requires both the 5′ cap and poly-A tail. Without the 5′ cap, the mRNA could not be exported, making option III a component of the best answer. Choice A can be eliminated because alternative splicing could still occur. Choice C can be eliminated for the same reason. Nuclear export would be impaired but poly-A tail addition would not, eliminating choice D and making choice B the best answer.

Passage 6 (Questions 29-32)

29. **C is the best answer.** The passage states that histone acetylases are involved in facilitating increased transcriptional activity. Their job is to influence the rate of transcription but as the passage states, they do not take any direct role in modulating the actual genetic transcript that is processed in transcription and translation. They are not post-transcriptional or post-translational modifiers, so choice A and B are unlikely to be correct. Their influence on the rate of transcription is best described as epigenetic modification (think "above genome"), making choice C the best answer. Choice D is a trap answer; pre-translational modification is not a real term, though it may sound legitimate. In fact, pre-translational is synonymous with post-transcriptional, and the only post-transcriptional modifications are mRNA splicing (removal of introns), adding of 5′-methylguanine cap, and adding a 3′ poly-A tail. Choices B and D mean the same thing and can both be eliminated.

30. **C is the best answer.** Figure 2 contains the results of the microarray while Figure 1 explains the spatial relationship between the various locations. In summary, Figure 2 shows where the AcH3 probes bind, indicating histone acetylases increase transcriptional activity in places with better binding. Choice A is not the best all the locations where the AcH3 probes bind are non-coding, and no probes actually bind at the exon. Choice B is an unlikely conclusion because according to Figure 2, more probes bind at "Inside" rather than the "Promoter," suggesting that histone acetylases regulate transcriptional activity more at introns. Choice C is the best answer because it identifies the non-coding regions as being instrumental in determining transcription rates. Choice D is too vague to be the best answer. While there is AcH3 binding at the divergent promoter, there is not enough information to suggest that histone acetylases cause one gene product to be produced over another.

31. **B is the best answer.** This question is asking what does not cause reduced gene expression. The answer choices mix up aspects of both transcription and translation, so it is important to keep them straight when approaching this question. Since there is very little passage information on this, process of elimination is the best approach. Choice A identifies an aspect of transcription; enhancer sequences are DNA sites where activator proteins bind, increasing transcription. If there is a mutation in the enhancer sequence, there will be less gene transcription. Choice A can be eliminated for this reason. Choice C identifies another component of transcription. The transcription bubble is the format in which RNA polymerase unzips the DNA double helix. If RNA polymerase fails to unzip due to a disruption of this bubble, it will also lead to reduced gene expression. Choice C can be eliminated. Choice D involves a post-transcriptional modification that influences translation. The 5' cap plays an important role in guiding the mRNA transcript to the ribosome. If it were not attached, it would lead to decreased gene expression. Only choice B would not lead to reduced gene expression. An elongated poly-A tail is abnormal but the purpose of the poly-A tail is to prevent degradation of the mRNA transcript in the cytoplasm by enzymes. The longer the tail, less likely the chance of DNA degradation. This makes choice B least likely to result in reduced gene expression.

32. **D is the best answer.** Histone deacetylase inhibitors inhibit the action of histone deacetylases. This means they work to promote histone acetylation. This rules out choices A and B, as they do not decrease histone acetylation levels. According to the passage, histone acetylation is necessary for gene expression, and in patients with HD, there is not enough histone acetylation. There is a positive relationship between histone acetylation levels and expression of genes, which rules out choice C which shows a negative relationship. Choice D is the best answer that captures both parts of the relationship.

Passage 7 (Questions 33-36)

33. **C is the best answer.** To prove that cytoplasmic acidification is a regulated process, the absence of the regulators should eliminate the acidification response when the Salmonella is in a low pH environment. Choice A, acidification in the SCV without the regulator proteins, indicates that the process is passive rather than regulated. Choice A is the opposite of what the best answer choice should be. Choice B, acidification in the SCV with the regulator proteins, gives no new information as this is what is originally described in the passage and what normally happens. Choice C and choice D both describe a scenario in which one of the regulators is absent from the Salmonella and there is a subsequent lack of acidification. However, choice D describes the state of the Salmonella outside the SCV. It is not clear then if the cytoplasmic neutrality would still occur due to the absence of OmpR if the Salmonella's environment became acidic. Choice C shows that the absence of the regulator when the Salmonella is in the SCV results in a failure of the Salmonella to acidify its cytoplasm. This makes choice C the best answer.

34. **C is the best answer.** An operon consists of an operator, promotor and the genes that translate into a single mRNA. Unlike eukaryotes, prokaryotes have polycistronic mRNA, which can code for more than one protein in a single mRNA strand. In the case of the cadC/BA operon, the mRNA strand codes for CadA, CadB and CadC. If the mRNA is translated all three proteins will be present. Although EnvZ, an environmental sensor, is most probably a constitutive protein in the Salmonella, the presence of CadC cannot be used as a marker for the presence of EnvZ. Phosphorylated OmpR suppresses the cadC/BA operon, and its presence would prevent the transcription of the operon's mRNA. For these reasons choice A can be eliminated. Based on the passage, SPI-2 gene products would most likely be present when the Salmonella is inside the SCV, OmpR is phosphorylated and the cadC/BA operon is suppressed. Since the protein that suppresses the transcription of the CadC gene is the same protein that promotes the transcription of SPI-2 genes, namely OmpR, the presence of CadC would most likely necessitate that SPI-2 gene products are not present. This eliminates choice B. Choice C is the best choice because the proteins translated are consistent with the operon model and the operon is not being suppressed. A low extracellular pH would cause EnvZ to phosphorylate OmpR, which would subsequently suppress the cadC/BA operon and not permit the presence of CadC. Choice D can be eliminated.

35. **C is the best answer.** Positive control refers to when a gene expression regulator binds to the DNA and causes the gene to be translated. Gene repression occurs when the regulator binds to the DNA and prevents the expression of the gene. An enhancer is a piece of DNA that promotes the transcription of a gene that is not necessarily adjacent to it. Enhancers are only present in eukaryotes. OmpR is an interesting gene expression regulator because it has both positive control and gene repression qualities. It promotes the expression of SPI-2 genes and prevents the expression of the cadC/BA operon. Option I and option II will be in the best answer, and option III will not. Choice C is the best answer.

36. **A is the best answer.** An operon consists of a promotor, an operator, and the genes that contribute to a single strand of mRNA. The operator is the part of the operon that serves as the binding location for regulator proteins. For example, OmpR would bind to the operator of the cadC/BA operon to control the operon. If the operator were removed, there would be no way for OmpR to bind to the cadC/BA operon and exert control over it. Without its repressive effect, the operon could be transcribed freely. That would cause CadA, CadB and CadC, the protein products of the cadC/BA operon, to always be present. According to the passage, SPI-2 genes are activated by OmpR as a positive controller. OmpR is phosphorylated and activated when the pH of the external environment is sensed by EnvZ to be low. The absence of an operator for the cadC/BA operon would not affect this process. Taken together, the data supports choice A. Choice B is supported by the data because CadA, CadB and CadC are present inside the SCV when they shouldn't be. When compared to choice A though, choice B is not as strong an answer choice because it is less specific. Because OmpR also regulates SPI-2, the presence of the SPI-2 needle complex at the appropriate times indicates that OmpR is still functional as a positive controller. Choice C is a weaker answer choice than choice A because there is not a good reason to assume OmpR is still functional for SPI-2 but not the cadC/BA operon. The promotor acts as a place for RNA polymerase to bind to the operon and initiate transcription. It is not likely that CadA, CadB and CadC would be present constitutively if the promoter was mutated and unable to bind RNA polymerase. This eliminates choice D.

Passage 8 (Questions 37-41)

37. **A is the best answer.** According to the end of paragraph one, SR proteins are factors that primarily bind to splicing enhancer regions that are located in exons. Exons are protein coding regions that are maintained after splicing in the mature mRNA and are decoded in the ribosome to generate an amino acid strand, making choice A the best answer. Introns, regions of DNA located between exons that are spliced out, allow for homologous recombination during DNA replication and during mitosis. Homologous recombination is the process in which complementary DNA on homologous chromosomes crosses over and becomes integrated into the corresponding chromatid. Homologous recombination is a mechanism to generate diversity in genes. As SC35 binds to exons more than introns, choice B not as strong as choice A. While SC35 may be more likely to bind to DNA in the presence of the RNA polymerase, the passage does not provide any information in either an affirmative or negative direction, making choice C also unlikely. Synthesis (S) phase is the portion of the cell cycle when DNA replication is occurring. Transcription primarily occurs in the growth phases of the cell cycle, G_0 and G_1, not in the DNA synthesis phase, making choice D less likely.

38. **D is the best answer.** An RNA transcript that is actively undergoing alternative splicing is still a primary RNA transcript. Splicing to remove introns and alternative splicing to remove selected exons are two modifications to a primary RNA transcript before it becomes mature mRNA. Only mRNA that has been spliced and given a 5′ cap and poly-A tail is exported from the nucleus. As the splicing is still occurring, the transcript will still be in the nucleus, making choice D the best answer. The endoplasmic reticulum, Golgi body, and cytoplasm are all located outside of the nucleus, making them unlikely locations to contain a primary transcript that is undergoing splicing.

39. **C is the best answer.** According to paragraph one, the splicing factors are serine-arginine rich proteins. The side chains of amino acids can be grouped into one of four categories: basic, acidic, polar, and non-polar. Amino acids containing a conjugated ring are additionally considered aromatic. Serine contains an alcohol functional group at the end of its side chain that makes it polar. The most likely answer choice is a polar side chain, making choice C the best answer. Arginine is a basic amino acid but would be positively charged at cellular pH, eliminating choice A. Neither serine nor arginine is an acidic amino acid like glutamate or aspartate, making choice B unlikely to be the best answer. Additionally, arginine and serine do not contain ring structures, eliminating choice D.

40. **C is the best answer.** According to paragraph two of the passage, hnRNPs bind to splicing silencers to repress splicing events. In order to determine the scenario that would weaken the assertion by the authors that hnRNPs suppress splicing, the best answer would include a change to a protein that would not affect the level of splicing that occurs. A non-conservative mutation from arginine to alanine in the hnRNP active site would theoretically prevent splicing from occurring. However, if no change in splicing level were noted, this would support an idea that hnRNPs do not affect splicing level, making choice C the best answer choice. Non-coding sequences in genic regions are called introns. Mutations in introns that would prevent hnRNPs from binding would increase splicing events, making choice A unlikely because this outcome would strengthen the idea that hnRNPs repress splicing. SC35 is not an hnRNP protein and does not affect splicing repression, making choice B less likely. Even if hnRNPs are found to bind to exons, this does not help answer the question about repression of splicing, eliminating choice D.

41. **A is the best answer.** Upregulation of the SP82 splicing factor implies that transcription of the SP82 gene is increased in the subset of cancers. The best answer choice will be the one that decreases transcription, as the question asks for the least likely mechanism of upregulation. The answer choices provided reference the epigenetic state of a cell's DNA. Epigenetic regulation is any regulation of transcription that is not dependent upon the DNA sequence itself. Methylation tends to reduce transcription, while acetylation increases transcription. Promoter and enhancer sequences increase transcription, while repressor sequences decrease transcription. Hypermethylation of a promoter sequence would decrease transcription, making choice A the best answer choice, as this would not lead to upregulation of SP82. Acetylation of an enhancer would increase transcription, making choice B less likely than choice A to be the correct answer. Hypermethylation of a repressor sequence would mute the repressor, increasing transcription. Choice C can be eliminated. A reduction in methylation, also known as hypomethylation, of an enhancer sequence would also increase transcription, eliminating choice D.

Stand-alones (Questions 42-45)

42. **B is the best answer.** Repetitive CpG nucleotides may fold back on themselves to form RNA secondary structure, as suggested by the question stem. RNA polymerase can slip on repetitive sequences that are AT rich, due to the decreased number of hydrogen bonds between A and T compared to C and G. The three hydrogen bonds between C and G form strong associations and would be less likely to slip, eliminating choice A. CpG repeats tend to slow down DNA replication, as they can form DNA secondary structure, eliminating choice C. The secondary structure likely prevents transcriptional elongation, rather than initiation, when the secondary structure forms, eliminating choice D. Formation of secondary structure that would prevent translation elongation would decrease protein production, making choice B the best answer choice.

43. **D is the best answer.** The eukaryotic ribosome has two components, a large subunit of 60S and a small subunit of 40S. The small subunit contains the mRNA to which the tRNA is bound through codon:anticodon interactions. The large subunit contains rRNA that catalyzes the peptidyltransferase reaction to add the amino acid from the tRNA to the growing peptide chain. mRNA would be pulled out with the small subunit, making option I a component of the best answer. tRNA would be bound to the mRNA attached in the small subunit, making option II a component of the best answer. rRNA, in addition to helping catalyze the reaction in the large subunit, helps to hold the protein components of the ribosome together like glue. The small subunit also has rRNA, making option III a component of the best answer. Choice A can be eliminated because tRNA and rRNA are also found in the small subunit. Choice B can be eliminated because mRNA and rRNA are found in the small subunit. Choice C can be eliminated because rRNA holds the protein components of the small subunit together. Choice D is the best answer because all three RNA components are necessary for the function of the small subunit.

44. **A is the best answer.** Initiation factors, including eIF2, are responsible for bringing the first aminoacyl-tRNA holding methionine to the mRNA to begin translation. These are distinct from transcription factors. mRNA does not contain T bases, eliminating choice B. UAA is a stop codon, not an initiation codon, eliminating choice C. UGA is also a stop codon, eliminating choice D. AUG is the initiation codon that codes for methionine, making choice A the best answer.

45. **D is the best answer.** Origins of replication are the sites where DNA replication begins and are primarily found at the center of a bacterial chromosome to allow bidirectional replication in the most efficient manner, making choice D the best answer choice. If the scientists were instead observing the process of transcription occurring at a promoter, they would most likely observe many genes being transcribed simultaneously. They would see many unwound regions instead of only one instance of partially unwound DNA, making choice A less likely. A DNA polymerase also does not specifically act at enhancer or repressor regions, though these regions do affect the rate and probability of transcription. Choices B and C can be eliminated.

Passage 9 (Questions 46-50)

46. **B is the best answer.** According to the passage, glucocorticoids can function by binding the Smoothened receptor on the plasma membrane, leading to the activation of RXRγ. Using the pathway shown in Figure 1 as a guide, RXRγ translocates to the nucleus upon activation and serves as a transcription factor to increase the expression of myelin genes. Transcription factors bind DNA in the nucleus, leading to increased transcription, eliminating choice A. Replication of RNA is not used to increase gene expression in eukaryotes, eliminating choice C. DNA replication occurs during S phase and is used when cells are progressing through the cell cycle to produce daughter cells via mitosis. This does not increase myelin gene expression, eliminating choice D. Binding of DNA and recruitment of other transcription machinery is the main role of transcription factors like RXRγ, making choice B the best answer.

47. **A is the best answer.** Figure 1 helps to answer what amino acid epitope glucocorticoids would bind. According to the figure, glucocorticoids can cross the plasma membrane and associate with a heat shock protein and glucocorticoid receptor in the cytosol. They can also bind Smo on the plasma membrane. If the glucocorticoids can cross the plasma membrane by diffusion, they must be hydrophobic, also known as nonpolar. They would likely bind nonpolar amino acid residues in Smo as well. Arginine, R, is a polar amino acid that is positively charged. It would be hydrophilic and unlikely to associate with hydrophobic molecules, eliminating choice B. Aspartate, D, and glutamate, E, are negatively charged and hydrophilic while lysine, K, is positively charged and hydrophilic. These hydrophilic amino acids would not associate with hydrophobic compounds like glucocorticoids, eliminating choice C. Serine, S, Threonine, T, and Tyrosine, Y, are polar amino acids that are hydrophilic. They are also unlikely to associate with hydrophobic compounds, eliminating choice D. Tryptophan, W, leucine, L, proline, P, and phenylalanine, F, are all hydrophobic amino acids that would be able to associate with hydrophobic compounds, making choice A the best answer choice.

48. **B is the best answer.** According to paragraph three, Smo is a 7 helix trans-membrane protein that associates with other proteins inside the cell. Binding of glucocorticoids on the extracellular surface allows for the activation of RXRγ. Seven helix trans-membrane proteins are known as G-protein coupled receptors (GPCRs) and help exchange GDP for GTP in the proteins associated on the cytosolic face. Protein cleavage would occur by the proteasome on proteins that are ubiquitin tagged. The passage does not suggest that RXRγ needs to be cleaved like a zymogen in order to be activated, eliminating choice A. RXRγ translocates to the nucleus and does not become associated with the plasma membrane, eliminating choice C. Because Smo is a GPCR, not a kinase, it is unlikely to phosphorylate target proteins to activate them, eliminating choice D. GPCRs help catalyze the exchange of GDP for GTP, which activates proteins intracellularly, making choice B the best answer.

49. **B is the best answer.** MRF is described as a transcription factor, which means that it binds to certain regions of DNA that contain consensus sequences called binding sites. These binding sites are within promoter regions, which also include the TATA box, a stretch of nucleotides rich in T and A bases that are easier to unwind. Myelin helps insulate neurons and should help stabilize the plasma membrane, eliminating choice A. The passage does not imply that mutations occur in the myelin genes in order to allow them to function, eliminating choice C. Transcription factors bind their consensus sequences in the nucleus, not the cytosol, eliminating choice D. A conserved binding site would be found for MRF for all the genes controlled for by the transcription factor. This binding would recruit the transcription machinery like helicases and RNA polymerase, making choice B the best answer choice.

50. **B is the best answer.** In addition to mRNA, two other types of RNA are transfer RNA (tRNA) and ribosomal RNA (rRNA). tRNA is responsible for bringing the appropriate amino acid to the ribosome, pairing with the mRNA at the correct codon:anticodon match, and donating the amino acid to the growing peptide. A mutation that prevented an amino acid like phenylalanine from reaching the ribosome would likely prevent the protein product from being synthesized. Because translation involves tRNAs and amino acids, choices A and C, which relate to transcription of DNA to RNA, can be eliminated. The lack of phenylalanine being delivered to the ribosome would decrease, not increase, translation, making choice B the best answer choice and eliminating choice D.

Passage 10 (Questions 51-55)

51. **A is the best answer.** According to information contained in the passage, TMPyP4 stabilizes secondary structure up to 1000 bp prior to the transcription start site in the promoter. A mature mRNA contains a 5′ GMP cap and 3′ poly-A tail, which are both necessary to ensure proper initiation of translation, and only contains exons of the AChE enzyme. All introns and some exons that were alternatively spliced would have been removed from the RNA as it was maturing. The passage does not provide any information that would suggest that there was a failure of the 5′ cap or the 3′ poly-A tail, making choices B and C, respectively, less likely to be the best answers. Additionally, while an exonuclease would break down AChE mRNA over time, the passage does not provide any evidence to show that AChE mRNA is unstable, eliminating choice D. Paragraph one notes that TMPyP4 works to stabilize secondary structure upstream of the transcription start site. As mRNA does not include non-coding sequences, analyzing mRNA in previous experiments would fail to uncover how TMPyP4 exerts its mechanism of action. Choice A is the best answer choice.

TEST 2A A&E

52. **B is the best answer.** Secondary structure refers to higher order DNA structure, such as alpha helices and beta-pleated sheets. According to paragraph one, secondary structure is common throughout the genome and can impact transcription, the process of creating RNA from DNA. Secondary structures are maintained by hydrogen bonds between amino acids that contain O and N elements. High salt conditions are able to disrupt these bonds, preventing the formation of secondary structure in nucleic acids. The best way to answer this question is to first determine whether the additional evidence supports or refutes the authors' claims. High salt prevents secondary structure formation, which the authors' in the first paragraph suggest prevents transcription of *AChE*. The new finding supports the authors' claim, eliminating choices A and C. The passage also directly states that transcription is inhibited, not translation, eliminating choice D and making choice B the best answer choice.

53. **B is the best answer.** While this question appears to require in-depth knowledge of the energy currency of the cell, this question is actually asking about how mRNA is processed. mRNA contains a 5′ GMP cap and a 3′ poly-A tail that is added before the mRNA is allowed to exit the nucleus. GMP is added to the mRNA in a reaction that utilizes GTP, using the pyrophosphate produced to drive the reaction. If GTP were used for this reaction, the concentration of GTP in the cell would decrease in control cells since they have higher levels of expression of Th than those treated with TMPyP4, eliminating choice A. mRNA processing does not use CTP, but instead uses GTP. Choices C and D can be eliminated. GTP would be used to add GMP to the 5′ end of maturing RNA, decreasing its concentration and making choice B the best answer choice.

54. **B is the best answer.** According to information contained in the passage, the secondary structure induced by TMPyP4 prevents normal transcription of proteins. RNA polymerase II is responsible for transcribing DNA to RNA, which then can be translated into proteins. Increased secondary structure mediated by TMPyP4 would hamper transcription, lowering Pol II activity, eliminating choice A. As implied by the passage, not all gene transcription is affected by secondary structure. Some genes are expected to be transcribed, even in the presence of TMPyP4, eliminating choice C. As an aside, be careful on the MCAT® about choice that seem extreme. Those choices that imply a "none-or-all" criterion should be given extra attention, as biology is almost never "all-or-none." The secondary structure would prevent proper activity of Pol II, lowering the amount of transcription. This effect can be seen in Figure 2, where addition of TMPyP4 shows lower transcript levels than the no treatment or the control TMPyP2, eliminating choice D. Secondary structure acts like a roadblock to RNA polymerase II that is moving along DNA to transcribe a gene into mRNA. Preventing the procession of RNA polymerase II by adding structural roadblocks would lower its activity, making choice B the best answer choice.

55. **D is the best answer.** According to Figure 3, pre-treatment of neurons with HO-2 in increasing concentrations results in increased AChE activity, meaning that the concentration of ACh in the synaptic or neuromuscular cleft decreases faster than under conditions of AChE inhibition. The protein content of an enzyme is a function of both its transcription and its translation. Increases in AChE content would likely require increases in both the processing of DNA to RNA and the processing of RNA to protein. Decreases in the transcription of AChE would lower the amount of protein activity, as fewer enzymes would be present to mediate catalysis. As Figure 3 shows that activity increases, not decreases, choice A can be eliminated. Increases in transcription could help explain some of the increase in activity. However, if translational activity were not also increased, no increase in protein content would be seen. Choice B contains half of the explanation but is not the best explanation. Decreases in both transcription and translation would drastically lower the available protein content, resulting in a decrease in overall activity. As Figure 3 shows an increase, not a decrease, in activity with HO-2, choice C can be eliminated. As described above, an increase in the overall activity of a protein population depends in part on its concentration. Concentration is affected by both transcriptional and translational rate, making choice D the best answer choice.

Stand-alones (Questions 56-59)

56. **D is the best answer.** Telomerase is an enzyme that adds six nucleotide units at the ends of chromosomes to protect the chromosomes from being shortened during DNA replication. Remember that the lagging strand of DNA requires an RNA primer that could not be removed and DNA synthesized if additional DNA sequences did not follow the RNA primer. The rate of DNA replication is based on the catalysis of nucleotide addition by DNA polymerase and is a function of the polymerase itself, not of the presence or absence of telomerase, eliminating choice A. Decreases in telomerase, giving shorter telomeres, triggers apoptosis due to the DNA damage response. Overexpression of telomerase would decrease cellular apoptosis, eliminating choice B. Cellular senescence, or cellular aging, occurs during periods of low nutrients or in the setting of DNA damage. As telomerase helps prevent the DNA damage response triggered by chromosomes that have short telomeres, it is unlikely that cells with telomerase overexpression would become quiescent, eliminating choice C. Cells undergo apoptosis once they have undergone mitosis too many times. Although telomerase helps add telomeres to the ends of chromosomes, the chromosomes get progressively shorter during the lifetime of a cell. Increasing the length of telomeres would help prevent this, making the cell immortal. Telomerase overexpression is one way that cancer cells become immortal.

57. **C is the best answer.** Apoptosis is the process of cell death that occurs when the cell becomes too stressed to survive or proliferate. Nucleoside analogues would likely be the most important during DNA replication that occurs during mitosis, as new nucleosides would be incorporated into newly synthesized DNA during S phase of the cell cycle. Hematopoietic stem cells constantly undergo mitosis to generate new white and red blood cells. If DNA replication were inhibited in this population, apoptosis would occur due to failure to progress through the cell cycle. Option I can be eliminated. Neurons and skeletal muscle do not undergo mitosis at an appreciable rate. They are found in the G_0 phase of the cell cycle and would not undergo DNA replication, as they do not divide. Inhibitors of DNA replication would have little effect on these cells, making the cell types of options II and III least likely to undergo apoptosis. Choice A can be eliminated because the hematopoietic stem cells of option I would be likely to undergo apoptosis. Choice B can be eliminated because skeletal muscle, like neurons, also undergoes limited proliferation, meaning that it would likely be unaffected by nucleoside analogues. Choice D can be eliminated because it contains option I. Choice C is the best answer choice because neurons and skeletal muscle are primarily in the G_0 state and do not undergo proliferation.

58. **D is the best answer.** S phase of the cell cycle is when DNA is replicated, eliminating choice A. Centrioles are the protein components of centrosomes which are responsible for helping separate the sister chromatids during mitosis. Centrioles also replicate with DNA during S phase, eliminating choice B. In order to prevent premature entry into mitosis, the levels of cyclin proteins that initiate M phase are likely to be repressed during S phase. Choice C can be eliminated. Microtubule polymerization, not actin, occurs during metaphase of mitosis to help align the chromosomes along the metaphase plate. This occurs during mitosis, not during S phase, making choice D the best answer choice.

59. **B is the best answer.** Homologous recombination is one mechanism of DNA damage repair, where the sister chromatid is used as a source of the missing DNA that has been lost in a double strand break. Homologous recombination can only occur after DNA replication. Cells have not replicated their DNA in G_1, meaning that homologous recombination does not occur then, eliminating choice A. Cancer cells would likely spend less time on genome maintenance in G_2, opting to continue proceeding through the cell cycle to increase proliferation. Choice C is less likely to be the best answer. A 2 bp insertion would shift the reading frame of the protein, making an insertion mutation. Shifting the reading frame is likely to render the protein product nonfunctional. Overall expression would be lower, not higher, eliminating choice D. During DNA replication, a second copy of a gene may be available and be able to serve as a template for lost DNA by homologous recombination. In order to avoid apoptosis, cancer cells likely need to repair their DNA, which would increase the need for proteins involved in homologous recombination. Choice B is the best answer.

Genetics

TEST 2B

ANSWERS & EXPLANATIONS

Questions 1–59

Passage 1 (Questions 1-4)

1. **B is the best answer.** According to paragraph two, TFII-I is able to bind other proteins, in addition to serving as a transcription factor in the nucleus. Paragraph two states that TFII-I is able to mediate repression of genes by interacting with HDAC1, a histone deacetylase. Epigenetic changes are changes that affect gene expression and function but do not involve the DNA sequence itself. Acetylation helps to neutralize the positive change on histones, allowing the negatively charged DNA to become less associated with the histone proteins and more available for transcription. Acetylation increases transcription. Euchromatin contains DNA that is open for transcription, meaning the genes in euchromatic DNA have higher transcription rates. This is the opposite of what is mediated by HDAC1, eliminating choice A. Because acetylation increases transcription, deacetylation would decrease transcription, which is the opposite of the effect stated in choice C. Choice C can be eliminated. HDAC1 mediates acetylation and deacetylation of histones, not methylation of DNA bases like C, eliminating choice D. Heterochromatin is DNA that is transcriptionally repressed either through methylation of C nucleotides or deacetylation of histones, making choice B the best answer choice.

2. **A is the best answer.** According to the passage, TFII-I is an example of a transcription factor that has many isoforms that can each exert a unique effect on gene transcription. Some isoforms of TFII-I increase the expression of genes, while other isoforms inhibit the expression of genes. Transcription factors are responsible for binding DNA, not RNA, to either increase or decrease transcription, eliminating choice B. Because transcription factors function in the nucleus they are unlikely to interact with aminoacyl-tRNAs that are carrying amino acids to the ribosome, which is in the cytosol. Choice C can be eliminated. Ubiquitin-tagged proteins are targeted for degradation in the proteasome. While this one mechanism of affecting gene transcription, transcription factors act in the nucleus, not the cytosol, eliminating choice D. A DNA consensus sequence is the stretch of nucleotides that a transcription factor binds in order to increase or decrease transcription of a specific gene, making choice A the best answer choice.

3. **B is the best answer.** Mdm2 is described as an oncogene in paragraph two, meaning that it helps normal cells transform into cancer cells. Typically, oncogenes are overexpressed in cancer and increase the rates of cell growth, survival, or proliferation. If overexpression of Mdm2 correlated with an increased number of cells undergoing programmed cell death, or apoptosis, this would suggest that Mdm2 is acting as a tumor suppressor, rather than an oncogene, eliminating choice A as the best answer. A silent, also known as synonymous, mutation changes the nucleotide sequence but does not change the resulting amino acid sequence. A decrease in the number of cells in the non-proliferating and non-dividing phase of the cell cycle called G_0 would imply that the cells were proliferating. Choice C states that a mutation failed to decrease the number of cells in G_0. A synonymous mutation, however, is not predicted to have a drastic effect on protein function, as the amino acid sequence does not change. Choice C can be eliminated because it does not provide evidence either for or against Mdm2 functioning as an oncogene. A nonsense mutation creates a stop codon that is expected to render a protein nonfunctional, resulting in its degradation by the proteasome. A nonsense mutation would decrease protein concentrations of Mdm2, but this fact does not provide any additional evidence that Mdm2 serves as an oncogene, eliminating choice D. The proliferation rate can be considered as the time to complete one round of the cell cycle. If Mdm2 overexpression decreased this time, it would increase proliferation, providing additional evidence that Mdm2 acted as an oncogene and making choice B the best answer choice.

4. **A is the best answer.** Information from both figures two and three is needed to answer this question. Figure 2 shows the deletion mutants have a shorter nucleotide sequence upstream of the CMV promoter, indicated by the TATA box. The ATG is the transcription start site and comes downstream of the CMV promoter. TFII-I is a transcription factor that is co-transfected, meaning that it is the protein that binds the CMV promoter. The TFII-I promoter is not shown in Figure 2, eliminating choice C as the best answer. In all the deletion mutants, the nucleotides upstream of the TATA box are deleted but the TATA box, which is found in the promoter, remains intact, eliminating choice D. Figure 3 shows a western blot of the amount of luciferase in the lysed cells. Notice that the CMVdel4 mutant has the most intense band, meaning that it has the most luciferase. An enhancer is a sequence that increases the transcription of a gene, which would result in lower luciferase expression when deleted. Because the CMVdel4 mutant is the most intense, it is unlikely that an enhancer was deleted, eliminating choice B. A repressor is a sequence that decreases the transcription of a gene, which would result in higher luciferase expression than the other deletion mutants when deleted. Because CMVdel4 shows the greatest expression, it is most likely that a repressor sequence was deleted, making choice A the best answer choice.

Passage 2 (Questions 5-9)

5. **A is the best answer.** mRNA results from the transcription of a gene into an RNA transcript that then undergoes splicing to remove introns, gains a 5′ cap, and has a poly-A tail polymerized onto its RNA sequence. mRNA codes for the protein product of a gene. According to the passage, G-quadruplexes can affect both transcription and translation. Figure 2 shows that when the 3′ UTR is mutated to remove the G-quadruplex structure, there is no apparent difference in mRNA transcript levels, eliminating choices C and D. The best answer will be one that pertains to translation. According to Figure 3, mutating the G-quadruplex structure results in higher luciferase activity, which is a proxy for the protein content according to the last paragraph of the passage. The Wild Type bar is lower than the mutant bar, meaning that translation is impaired with the normal G-quadruplex structure, resulting in a decrease in protein concentration. Choice B can be eliminated and choice A is the best answer.

6. **C is the best answer.** According to the question stem, a misfolded protein can also result from the slippage of the ribosome between adjacent codons. Repetitive sequences in DNA that are transcribed into RNA result in repetitive sequences in RNA. When the ribosome encounters repetitive sequences that are particularly AU rich, it has the potential to slip between codons due to a decreased number of hydrogen bonds that form between A and U compared to G and C. Remember that A and U form two hydrogen bonds, while G and C form three. The best answer will be the mRNA molecule that contains repetitive copies of a DNA sequence that form a codon. Choice A can be eliminated because it contains T instead of U. Remember that uracil is the nucleic acid that substitutes for T in mRNA. By convention, nucleic acid sequences are always written 5′ to 3′, helping to eliminate choice B. Additionally, choice B does not contain repetitive codons. Choice D is written in the correct orientation and contains U instead of T. However, it does not contain repetitive codons that are AU rich, making it less likely to result in ribosome slippage. Choice D can be eliminated. Choice C is written in the correct orientation and contains U instead of T. Additionally, it contains a repetitive codon AAU four times. Upon encountering the sequence, the polymerase may slip between adjacent nucleotides, especially with two A bases in a row. Choice C is the best answer.

7. **B is the best answer.** During both DNA replication and transcription, a polymerase moves along a DNA strand in order to synthesize a copy of DNA during DNA replication or an mRNA transcript during transcription. As the polymerase moves along the DNA it creates positive supercoils in front of the polymerase and negative supercoils behind the polymerase. Unless these supercoils are relieved, the polymerase cannot generate enough force to continue replication or transcription. A nonsense mutation is one that creates a stop codon, which would result in a truncated and nonfunctional protein. A mutation in DNA polymerase would affect DNA replication but not necessarily transcription. Because mRNA transcripts were not seen, choice A can be eliminated. A nonfunctional histone gene would prevent DNA from winding around a protein component, leaving it open for binding by transcription factors and RNA polymerase. Most likely, increased mRNA levels, not decreased mRNA levels, would be seen, eliminating choice C. A mutation in a ribosome would hinder translation, but the question stem refers to experiment 1 where transcription is measured. Also, the 50S subunit is seen in prokaryotes rather than eukaryotes. Choice D can be eliminated. The topoisomerase protein cuts the DNA backbone to allow the supercoils to unwind. If a topoisomerase gene were rendered nonfunctional, eventually too many supercoils would build up in front of and behind a processing RNA polymerase. This would prevent the formation of mRNA transcripts, regardless of whether the transcript contained a wild type or mutant 3′ UTR. Choice B is the best answer choice.

8. **A is the best answer.** Using Figure 1 and the information contained in the passage, G-quadruplexes consist of repetitive DNA sequences that result in the formation of secondary structure. The key to answering this question is noticing that the DNA sequences are highly repetitive. Telomeres form the ends of DNA and contain hundreds to thousands of copies of a specific six nucleotide repeat. Telomeres contain repeating DNA sequences, making option I a component of the best answer. Operons are sequences of multiple genes that are clustered together under the control of a single promoter. An operon is too complex to be considered a repeating nucleotide sequence, so option II will not be included in the best answer. DNA replication in eukaryotes is not dependent upon a specific DNA sequence like it is in prokaryotes but is instead directed by histones, the proteins that DNA wraps around. No specific DNA sequence is known to be the site of DNA replication. Option III is not a component of the best answer. Choice B can be eliminated because it contains option II. Choices C and D can be eliminated because they contain option III. Choice A is the best answer choice because it contains option I only.

9. **A is the best answer.** According to paragraph one, APP Aβ plaques form due to oligomerization. The most likely cause of oligomerization in the cytosol or extracellular environment would be association of hydrophobic amino acids that do not like to associate with water. Strings of hydrophobic amino acids would be the most likely to cause the oligomers. Serine, S, contains a hydroxyl group and is a polar amino acid. It is hydrophilic and would not participate in hydrophobic interactions. Choice B can be eliminated. Tyrosine, Y, also contains a hydroxyl group and is polar, eliminating choice C. Glutamate, E, is a polar, acidic amino acid that contains a carboxylic acid functional group, meaning that it is hydrophilic. Choice D can be eliminated because it is unlikely to participate in hydrophobic interactions. Alanine, A, is a hydrophobic amino acid that would participate in hydrophobic interactions with other alanine residues in the cytosol. Choice A is the best answer choice.

Passage 3 (Questions 10-13)

10. **B is the best answer.** Phosphorylation adds a negative charge to the histone H2AX protein, which would likely result in increased repulsion by the negatively charged phosphodiester backbone of DNA. This negative-negative repulsion would lead to increased dissociation, not association, of DNA with the histone, eliminating choice A. Phosphorylation of H2AX, according to paragraph two, is activated by ATM which also activates TP53 and arrests the cell cycle. This would most likely increase the time for cell proliferation to occur, eliminating choice C. Translation occurs in the cytosol, not the nucleus, and involves RNA to protein. Choice D can be eliminated because the process involved is DNA replication. The negative-negative repulsion between the negatively charged histone and the negatively charged phosphodiester backbone would lead to increased dissociation of DNA, making choice B the best answer choice.

TEST 2B A&E

11. **D is the best answer.** Paragraph two provides the best information to help answer this question. One of the responsibilities of ATM is to phosphorylate H2AX to allow for the recruitment of the DDR proteins to the site of the break. Phosphorylation occurs when a phosphate is transferred from ATP to a receptor protein and is mediated by enzymes called kinases. A phosphatase mediates the opposite reaction that removes a phosphate by hydrolysis. Choice A can be eliminated. A ligase seals the phosphodiester backbone of DNA but does not transfer phosphate molecules to receptor molecules, eliminating choice B. A nuclease is responsible for removing individual nucleotides from a longer chain. Because ATM phosphorylates target proteins and does not break down nucleic acid chains, choice C can be eliminated. Choice D is the best answer.

12. **A is the best answer.** According to paragraph two, ATM is responsible for helping transduce the DSB signal generated by H2AX localization to regions of DNA damage. In animal models, remember that the genotype of the gene is symbolized by +, which represents wild type, and – which represents a null allele, also known as a nonfunctional gene. The mouse in choice B has a homozygous deficiency of TP53, which would prevent it from responding appropriately to DSB. However, this information does not suggest the role of ATM, which is acting upstream of TP53, eliminating choice B. The mouse in choice C is wild type for ATM. According to the passage, ATM acts during DNA replication to allow time to fix double strand breaks when they occur. Because the genome has not been replicated in G_1 it is less likely that wild type mice should show an increase in the number of cells stuck in the G_1 phase of the cell cycle, eliminating choice C. As with choice B, information about H2AX, which acts upstream of ATM, does not directly provide information about the role of ATM in the DSB repair pathway, eliminating choice D. The mice in choice A have a homozygous loss of ATM. This would decrease the ability of the cell to recognize and respond to DSB if they occur. Fewer cells would be stuck in G_2 than expected, making choice A the best answer choice.

13. **B is the best answer.** According to paragraphs two and three, TP53 is activated during DNA damage and helps stop cell cycle progression. It is reasonable to conclude that inhibition of cell cycle progression and initiation of DSB repair requires the transcription and translation of many proteins. If TP53 acted as a transcription factor, it would be able to bind a set sequence of DNA and increase the transcription of target genes necessary to prevent cancerous transformation, making option I a component of the best answer. Genes that prevent cancer from forming are called tumor suppressor genes. TP53 inhibits cell cycle progression in order to prevent cell proliferation, making it a tumor suppressor. Option II is a component of the best answer. An oncogene drives cancer by allowing the cell to have growth, survival, and proliferation advantages. TP53 has the opposite effect and it is unlikely that it acts as a tumor suppressor, eliminating option III from the best answer. Choice A can be eliminated because P53 is also a tumor suppressor, while choice C can be eliminated because TP53 is not an oncogene. Similarly, while P53 is a tumor suppressor, it is not an oncogene, eliminating choice D. Choice B is the best answer because it describes P53 as both a transcription factor and a tumor suppressor.

Stand-alones (Questions 14-17)

14. **A is the best answer.** Topoisomerase I allows for supercoils in DNA to be released in order to complete DNA replication. DNA replication occurs during S phase, not prophase of mitosis, eliminating choice B. DNA polymerase expression is important during S phase when DNA is being duplicated, eliminating choice C. Thymidylate synthetase is the enzyme necessary to synthesize T from U. This is necessary for DNA synthesis, which is more important during S phase, eliminating choice D. Laminin is a component of the nuclear membrane. Phosphorylation of laminin breaks down the nuclear membrane during prophase of mitosis, making choice A the best answer choice.

15. **C is the best answer.** In humans, before DNA replication, cells contain 23 pairs of chromosomes, one from each parent. Because G_1 arrested cells contain 23 pairs of chromosomes, they have 46 total chromosomes, not 23, eliminating choice A. Cells in G_1 have not been replicated, so sister chromatids have not been synthesized, eliminating choice B. A somatic cell has 92 chromatids after DNA replication in S phase and in G_2. Because cells treated with BAF60 inhibitors arrest in G_1 and do not proceed to replicate DNA, they will not contain 92 chromatids, eliminating choice D. Somatic cells contain 23 pairs of chromosomes, or 46 chromosomes overall. Choice C is the best answer choice.

16. **C is the best answer.** The question is asking for the function of the enzyme telomerase. Choice A is partially correct, as lack of telomerase would increase the rate of cellular aging. The reason for increased aging is not a direct result of a decrease in DNA transcription, eliminating choice A. Choice B can be eliminated since a lack of telomerase would increase the rate of fusion between chromosomes. Choice D can be eliminated, since methylation is not a function of telomerase. Choice C is the best answer since it represents a consequence of an absence of telomerase activity.

17. **A is the best answer.** Plasmids are double stranded circular DNA molecules that often contain genes that scientists are interested in replicating. Plasmids are double stranded, not single stranded, eliminating choices C and D. Bacteria are the main organisms used to replicate plasmids because they have fast proliferation. Because bacteria also have no nucleus, it is easier to replicate the plasmid because replication can occur in the cytosol instead of the nucleus, making choice A better than choice B.

Passage 4 (Questions 18-21)

18. **A is the best answer.** The figure provided in the question shows the relative percentages of cells in the various phases of the cell cycle. As the concentration of Q6 increases, more cells remain in G_2, at the expense of S phase and G_1. DNA replication occurs during the S phase of the cell cycle. The 2.5 μM treatment has a greater percentage of cells in S phase compared to the 5 μM treatment, eliminating choice B. G_2 is increased in the 2.5 μM treatment compared to the 1.25 μM treatment, meaning more cells are in the growth phase, eliminating choice C. In addition to DNA duplication, centrioles duplicate in S phase. The 5 μM treatment has more cells in G_2, which is after S phase, meaning that all cells in G_2 would have duplicated centrioles, eliminating choice D. During S phase, the chromosomes of the DNA duplicate. Each chromosome contains two copies of a gene, meaning that when the chromosome replicates, it now has 4 copies of a gene. Because the 5 μM treatment has a greater number of cells in G_2, more cells have genes with four copies. Choice A is the best answer.

19. **B is the best answer.** DNA replication is the process that allows the DNA genome to be replicated during S phase to allow two daughter cells to each contain one copy of the genome. RNA binding to a TATA box initiates transcription, which is the process by which DNA becomes RNA, eliminating choice A. Binding of ribosomes to mRNA initiates translation, which is where mRNA becomes a protein that gives a phenotype, eliminating choice C. Telomeres are important structures that protect the ends of DNA from degradation that occurs at the ends of chromosomes each time DNA replicates. They are also added during S phase but are not the initiating events, eliminating choice D. In contrast to bacteria and other prokaryotes where DNA polymerase binds specific nucleotide sequences called origins of replication, DNA polymerase recognizes certain histone structures in eukaryotes, making choice B the best answer.

20. **B is the best answer.** Repair of mutations, including double strand breaks that split apart DNA, require many proteins that can correct the damage. When a double strand break occurs, it is usually not a clean break and some single stranded DNA hangs over the 5′ or 3′ end of the double stranded DNA. In order to trim this single stranded DNA back to two double stranded ends, DNA endonuclease is one of the first enzymes to arrive and serves to trim nucleotides of DNA that do not match the complementary strand, eliminating choice A. DNA polymerase is the next enzyme that arrives and helps synthesize the bases that are missing in the complementary strand of DNA. Nucleoside phosphotransferase helps transfer phosphate molecules to nucleosides to create nucleotides, which can be used by DNA polymerase to synthesize complementary DNA strands, eliminating choice D. After all of the DNA ends are trimmed and the necessary bases are added to the complementary strand, the phosphodiester backbone must be sealed in order to create a continuous DNA strand. DNA ligase serves this purpose, making choice B the best answer.

21. **D is the best answer.** Figure 2 provides the best information to answer this question. Apoptosis is programmed cell death that occurs when cells experience significant stress. Apoptosis can be the result of failed DNA replication, an increase in stalled transcription on a genome-wide level, or other insults to DNA like radiation damage. Both hypoxia, defined in paragraph one as cells grown in less than 1% oxygen, and the presence of Q6 increase cell death. Cells grown with normal oxygen and in the absence of Q6 likely have the lowest levels of apoptosis. This condition would be the control condition and is marked – for Q6 and – for 1% O_2 in Figure 2, eliminating choice A. Another way of stating – 1% O_2 would be atmospheric O_2 levels. While treatment with Q6 increases the number of cells undergoing cell death, growth in normal oxygen levels is unlikely to have greatest effect, eliminating choice B. While hypoxia increases the number of cells undergoing apoptosis, the absence of Q6 prevents the maximum cell death from occurring, eliminating choice C. The combination of hypoxia and treatment with Q6 causes the greatest percentage of cell death, meaning the greatest numbers of cells are undergoing apoptosis and making choice D the best answer choice.

Passage 5 (Questions 22-26)

22. **A is the best answer.** According to paragraph three, the three nucleosides can be clinically concerning, as they can induce death in leukocytes that constitute the innate and adaptive immune systems. T cells assist in the direct killing of infected or abnormal cells, such as cancer cells. They are a component of the adaptive immune system and undergo rapid proliferation upon stimulation with their cognate antigen. Nucleoside analogues would prevent the DNA replication needed to rapidly proliferate, eliminating choice B. B cells help secrete antibodies against particular antigens and are from the adaptive immune system. Similar to T cells, B cells undergo rapid proliferation when stimulated by their cognate antigen. Nucleoside analogues would likely hinder the rapid proliferation of B cells, eliminating choice C. Natural killer cells are cells of the innate immune system and do not recognize particular antigens but instead kill virally infected cells and cancer cells due to altered expression of MHC Class I. They are a component of the immune system, making choice D less likely to be the best answer. Erythrocytes have lost both their mitochondria and nucleus during their maturation process in the bone marrow. They do not undergo mitosis but instead serve to transport oxygen and carbon dioxide in the blood. As they do not proliferate, they are unlikely to be affected by nucleoside analogues, making choice A the best answer choice.

23. **A is the best answer.** Chromatin condensation occurs when DNA winds tighter around its associated histones and the adjacent histones clump together for form DNA condensation visible by microscopy. All of the changes listed are epigenetic changes, meaning that the architecture of the DNA-histone complex is altered but the actual DNA sequence itself is not. Acetylation tends to "activate" transcription by lessening the attraction between DNA and its histone. This affect would lead to less association, which is the opposite of what is seen during apoptosis. Choice B can be eliminated. Phosphorylation is a negative charge and would repel the negative charge of DNA. This would weaken the association between DNA and its histone, which is the opposite of that seen in apoptosis. Choice C can be eliminated. Ubiquitination is a protein that helps target other proteins for degradation by the proteasome. Ubiquitination of histones should lead to increased degradation of histone proteins, depleting the pool of available protein that can bind DNA. This would be the opposite of the increased clumping of DNA and protein in apoptosis, eliminating choice D. Methylation tends to "mute" transcription by making the DNA more tightly associated with histones. It is reasonable to assume that methylation would assist in clumping DNA together on its histones during apoptosis as well, making choice A the best answer choice.

24. **A is the best answer.** According to paragraph three, camptothecin is a topoisomerase I inhibitor. During DNA replication, as the DNA polymerase moves along the DNA strand, positive supercoils are created in front of the polymerase and negative supercoils are created behind the DNA polymerase. Once enough resistance builds up, the DNA polymerase is unable to proceed in replicating DNA. Topoisomerases relieve supercoils by cutting one or both strands of DNA and allowing the supercoils to unwind. Translation is the process of the ribosome moving along mRNA. Because the mRNA is single stranded and not fixed at either end, supercoils do not form, eliminating choice B. DNA replication initiation does require unwinding of the two strands of DNA. However, this is mediated by a helicase, not a topoisomerase, eliminating choice C. Similarly, RNA polymerase requires unwinding of the two DNA strands to initiate transcription. This is also mediated by a helicase instead of a topoisomerase, eliminating choice D. Once enough resistance in the form of positive supercoils builds up in front of the proceeding replication fork, DNA replication will stall, making choice A the best answer choice.

25. **B is the best answer.** According to Table 1 and the information contained in the passage, treatment of HT-29 cells with the various nucleoside analogues did not drastically alter the mitochondrial membrane potential. The membrane potential would change if protons created by the electron transport chain were able to exit the mitochondria into the cytosol. A small increase could occur due to changes in cellular energy levels and may suggest increased growth, as more ATP would be needed to support this growth, causing cellular metabolism to increase. Choice A can be eliminated. Cyclin D is one of the factors that allows progression through the cell cycle. Increases in cyclin D would suggest proliferation, not inhibition, eliminating choice C. GLUT2 is a transporter that moves glucose from outside the cell to inside the cell. Increased transcription of GLUT2 would suggest the need for more glucose to fuel growth and proliferation, eliminating choice D. Cytochrome c is a component of the electron transport chain that ultimately reduces molecular oxygen to water. If cytochrome c exited the mitochondria, the electron transport chain would become non-functional, leading to a significant decrease in the amount of oxygen consumed by cancer cells. Choice B is the best answer choice.

26. **D is the best answer.** Mutations that affect the codon of a single amino acid can be categorized as silent, missense, or nonsense. Silent mutations mean that the DNA sequence changed, but the identity of the amino acid was retained. A missense mutation is a change in the DNA sequence that induces a change in the amino acid as well. A nonsense mutation is a change in the DNA sequence that creates a stop codon, truncating a protein. Because the amino acid changes in all of the four answer choices, the scientists made a missense mutation. In order to prevent the activation of the intracellular cascade, the scientists likely changed an amino acid from one type to another to prevent it from catalyzing similar chemistry. Amino acids are grouped into nonpolar, polar, acidic, or basic. Isoleucine, I, is changed to leucine, L, in choice A. These are both nonpolar amino acids and would stabilize similar functional groups in other proteins. Choice A is less likely to be the best answer because the two nonpolar amino acids may mediate similar chemistry that could trigger the intracellular cascade. Valine, V, is a nonpolar amino acid, as is glycine G. Choice B can be eliminated. Serine, S, and threonine, T, are both polar amino acids with hydroxyl groups. They could help catalyze similar chemistry due to the same functional group, making choice C less likely to be the best answer. Alanine, A, changed to arginine, R, in choice D which represents the change from a nonpolar amino acid to a basic amino acid. These amino acids are likely to interact with different functional groups on target proteins, meaning that this change could prevent the initiation of the apoptosis cascade. Choice D is the best answer choice.

Stand-alones (Questions 27-30)

27. **D is the best answer.** This question includes a lot of intimidating jargon, but understanding the basic science principles that underlie DNA replication can lead to the best answer. Generally DNA is synthesized by an enzyme that strings together base pairs using the base pairs on the opposite strand as a template. According to the question stem, telomerase is different. First, it is not using another strand as a template because it is extending single strands. If it is not using the chromosome's own DNA template, telomerase must have an on-board template of its own. The only answer choice that reflects a subunit with its own nucleic acid template is choice D. There is not a double-stranded helix at the chromosome end for telomerase to straighten or unwind, so choices A and B can be eliminated. Since telomerase functions at the end of the chromosomes, there is no reason telomerase would need to cut the DNA to extend it, so choice C can be eliminated.

28. **A is the best answer.** As described by the question stem, NHEJ is one mechanism of repairing double strand breaks when they occur during G_1 of the cell cycle when no second copy of DNA is present. A kinase would likely be recruited first in NHEJ, as kinases serve to phosphorylate targets to set off signaling cascades. The signaling cascade would be important to prevent the continuation of the cell cycle and to recruit other DNA damage proteins, eliminating choice B. An endonuclease would likely be recruited next in order to trim DNA ends that could not be put together, eliminating choice C. A polymerase may also come in to fill in missing bases on one strand if the endonuclease had not hydrolyzed the ssDNA that resulted from the break. Choice D can be eliminated. After the DNA was repaired, the closure of the phosphodiester backbone would be last step. This is mediated by a ligase, making choice A the best answer choice.

29. **A is the best answer.** Gene inversion is a chromosome-level change that occurs when a portion of a chromosome arm is flipped around, reversing the 5′ and 3′ ends of the DNA. This change would not mutate a single codon but is likely to mutate all codons, as the orientation of the DNA has changed. Choice B can be eliminated. Transposons are segments of DNA that can excise from one genomic location and move to a different location. The movement of transposons is generally random, meaning that mutation of one particular codon would be highly unlikely. Even if this were to occur, codon 532 would be removed from the protein rather than changed to a different codon. Choice C can be eliminated. Gene duplication would serve to duplicate the codon but not change the identity of the codon itself, eliminating choice D. Homologous recombination occurs during mitosis and is a way to generate genetic diversity. Scientists could inject artificial DNA containing the exact mutation of choice in a particular codon into a cell and allow homologous recombination to occur between the nuclear DNA and the DNA of a plasmid. The change in the genomic DNA would only be that of one particular codon that was contained in the transfected plasmid. Choice A is the best answer.

30. **C is the best answer.** DNA serves as the informational content, or genetic material, of the cell that is replicated and passed along to daughter cells during mitosis and meiosis. Tumors undergo mitosis at a high rate to generate daughter cells that allow the tumor to grow in size. If the parent cell contains a mutation, it is highly likely that the mutation will be passed along to its daughter cells, eliminating choice A. However, each of the clones is likely to gain some additional mutations by chance as it makes mistakes during DNA replication. Each clone likely contains the mutations that allow it to proliferate and survive as well as some non-shared mutations that result in passenger genes being mutated. Tumor suppressor genes help drive cancer formation and are likely key genes that mediate survival. These mutations that inactivate tumor suppressors would likely be passed along to daughter cells, eliminating choice B. As the clones grow out and accumulate different mutations on their own, it is unlikely that they will share all mutations, eliminating choice D. Subclones are likely to maintain the same mutations that provide survival and proliferation advantages in tumor suppressor genes and oncogenes but also have some mutations that are not shared, making choice C the best answer.

Passage 6 (Questions 31-34)

31. **C is the best answer.** According to paragraph two, metformin decreases the concentration of ATP in the cell. Option I describes the formation of the cytoskeleton, which consists of actin, microtubules, and intermediate filaments. Actin is a polymer made of many individual actin proteins, which require energy, in the form of ATP, to link together. If the energy currency of the cell, ATP, was decreased by metformin, it would be harder to form the polymers of actin, making option I a component of the best answer. The oxidation of glucose occurs through two main pathways, glycolysis and the citric acid cycle. During these two processes, glucose is broken down to give ATP and molecules like NADH and $FADH_2$, which feed into the citric acid cycle to generate more ATP. Because metformin reduces ATP production in the cell, it is reasonable to assume that it may inhibit glucose oxidation. Option II is a component of the best answer. The passage does not talk about the role of metformin in the exact phases of mitosis, like prophase where the nuclear membrane would be broken down. Because there is no information in the passage that would suggest that ATP is directly involved in nuclear membrane breakdown, option III is unlikely to be in the best answer choice. Choice A can be eliminated because metformin may also inhibit glycolysis. Choice B can be eliminated because ATP helps to alter the cytoskeleton. Choice D can be eliminated because there is no evidence that metformin alters the nuclear membrane in the passage. Choice C is the best answer choice, as metformin has the potential to alter ATP concentrations, which affects the cytoskeleton and metabolism.

32. **A is the best answer.** According to Figure 2, cells treated with ionizing radiation are more likely to be arrested in G_2/M than cells that are not treated with ionizing radiation. Being arrested in G_2/M means that the cells are stuck at some point in either G_2 or early mitosis, before the chromosomes separate in anaphase. Metaphase is the phase of mitosis where chromosomes are aligned at the metaphase plate, eliminating choice B. A partially broken down nuclear membrane occurs in prophase of mitosis, eliminating choice C. Centrioles are duplicated in S phase, meaning that two centrioles would be found in G_2/M, eliminating choice D. One copy of DNA is only found in G_0/G_1, which is not where most cells would be after being treated with ionizing radiation, making choice A the best answer.

33. **A is the best answer.** According to the question stem, a western blot was used to measure protein levels to determine whether cells were arrested in G_2/M. DNA polymerase would be expressed during S phase, as this is the phase of the cell cycle where DNA is duplicated, eliminating choice B. RNA polymerase would be expressed during all phases of the cell cycle in order to produce the necessary proteins during that phase, eliminating choice C. Actin would also be expressed during all phases of the cell cycle in order to mediate the cytoskeletal architecture, eliminating choice D. Cyclin proteins bind cyclin dependent kinases to drive cell cycle progression and the cyclin specific to G_2/M could be the target of a western blot to determine whether cells are arrested in this phase. Choice A is the best answer choice.

34. **A is the best answer.** Aneuploidy is caused by the failed segregation of chromosomes during anaphase. Chromosomes separate into the daughter cells based on the catastrophe of microtubules that pulls the two chromosomes apart. ADP kinase would add an additional phosphate to ADP to create ATP. ATP is necessary for actin polymerization according to answer choice B. Because GDP kinase, not ATP kinase, affects microtubule polymerization, choice B can be eliminated. RNA polymerase is likely to cause defects in mRNA production, not inhibit the catastrophe or polymerization of microtubules, eliminating choice C. Similarly inhibition of the ribosome would cause defects in protein production, not inhibition of microtubule catastrophe or production, eliminating choice D. GDP kinase would add a phosphate to GDP to create GTP. GTP is the molecule necessary to allow microtubules to polymerize, according to answer choice A. If GDP kinase was inhibited, less GTP would be produced, preventing microtubules from polymerizing from the microtubule organizing center to the centrosome of the chromosomes. If microtubules cannot polymerize, the chromosomes may not separate correctly, causing aneuploidy or failed separation of chromosomes, making choice A the best answer choice.

Passage 7 (Questions 35-39)

35. **D is the best answer.** The question asks about the role of the confidence intervals (CI) in statistical significance. Confidence intervals, also known as standard deviation, provide a range of values that the mean will fall in 95% of the time. Another way of thinking about standard deviation and confidence intervals is that 5% of the time, purely by chance, the real mean of a measurement will fall outside of the listed range. According to the last paragraph, the average number of short IRs in DSB regions in malignant melanoma was 28.5 ± 4.7 (mean ± SD) in malignant melanoma cells and 21.4 ± 5.0 (mean ± SD) in normal human melanocytes. The mean of melanoma is higher than that of normal melanocytes, eliminating choice B. Choice C refers to the size of the confidence interval of the quantification of short IRs – ± 4.7 for melanoma and ± 5.0 for melanocytes. The confidence interval is wider for melanocytes, eliminating choice C. The difference between choices A and D revolves around comparison of the mean and comparison of the mean ± the confidence interval. Two measurements are only statistically significant when their confidence intervals do not overlap. Accounting for the 95% confidence interval, the number of short IRs in melanoma could be 33.2 to 23.8, while the number of short IRs in melanocytes could be 26.4 – 16.4. Because the confidence intervals overlap, the values are not significantly different and no robust conclusions can be drawn between the two results.

36. **C is the answer.** Okazaki fragments are 100-200 nucleotide sequences found on the lagging strand of DNA during DNA replication. In contrast to replication of the leading strand, lagging strand synthesis occurs in a disjointed fashion by synthesizing Okazaki fragments. The question stem informs us that Okazaki fragments contain many short IRs and information from paragraph two links short IRs with cruciform DNA formation and cancer. The best answer choice should contain both cancer cells and difficulty replicating Okazaki fragments, as the polymerase would get stalled at these by the cruciform DNA, making choice C the best answer. Choices A and B can be eliminated because the question is concerned with the replication of Okazaki fragments, which are on the lagging, not the leading, strand of DNA. Choice D can be eliminated because the melanoma cells should contain the large genomic fraction of short IRs, not the normal melanocytes.

37. **D is the best answer.** DNA polymerase associates with numerous proteins at the origin of replication (ORI) to initiate DNA replication in the S phase of the cell cycle. The other proteins that the polymerase binds are responsible to identifying where in the genome DNA replication beings. Choice A can be eliminated because DNA polymerase uses an RNA, not a DNA, primer to initiate DNA replication. Choices B and C describe the process of transcription from DNA to RNA by RNA polymerase, not the process of DNA to an identical DNA copy by DNA polymerase.

38. **A is the best answer.** After DNA helicase unwinds the two strands of the double stranded DNA molecule, the DNA polymerase reads the parent strand from the 3′ end towards the 5′ end. Synthesis occurs in the opposite direction on the complementary strand, in the 5′ to 3′ direction, making choice A the best answer. Choice B can be eliminated because synthesis occurs in the 5′ to 3′ direction. Choice C can be eliminated because the parent DNA molecule is read in the 3′ to 5′ direction. Choice D can be eliminated because the parent DNA strand is read in the 3′ to 5′ direction and synthesis occurs in the 5′ to 3′ direction.

39. **C is the best answer.** The passage notes that cruciform DNA is formed by short IRs that stall DNA polymerases at replication forks. DNA replication occurs during DNA Synthesis Phase or S phase, making choice C the best answer. The Mitosis Phase or M phase occurs after DNA replication when the cell is preparing for duplication and cytokinesis, eliminating choice A. Choices B and D can be eliminated because the two phases of cellular growth, G_1 and G_2, are primarily characterized by carrying out normal cellular functions, producing proteins, and synthesizing amino acids and lipids, not DNA replication.

Passage 8 (Questions 40-43)

40. **B is the best answer.** The question provides information from a separate experiment, requiring incorporation of passage understanding and knowledge of proper base pairing. Remember that A pairs with T and C pairs with G in a DNA double helix. The question stem notes that BRCA1 can only recognize one single nucleotide mismatch and must have correctly incorporated sequences surrounding it. Choice B is the best answer because the C-C mispairing is surrounded by correctly matched nucleotide pairs of greater than 3 on each side. Choice A does not display proper base pairing. Choice C can be eliminated because it contains two mismatches directly next to each other at the 5′ end of the sense strand. Choice D can be eliminated because all of the nucleotides are correctly paired.

41. **C is the best answer.** The first paragraph of the passage informs the reader that TNBC has the poorest clinical outcomes due to a lack of targetable oncoproteins. ER+/PR+ breast cancer, by contrast, should contain two targetable proteins that TNBC does not, leading to an increase in RFS and OS, presumably by better response to available treatment. Choice A can be eliminated because the presence of two targetable proteins will increase survival, as paragraph one notes that TNBC has the lowest overall survival and time to recurrence. Choice B is the opposite of what should be observed. Choice D can be eliminated because RFS will increase in ER+/PR+ breast cancer as compared to TNBC.

42. **C is the best answer.** mRNA contains the nucleotide coding information necessary for translation of RNA to proteins. mRNA is initially copied directly from DNA and contains introns and exons. The introns are spliced out during the maturation process of a newly synthesized RNA to mature mRNA. Gene promoters are never transcribed into RNA and could not be part of cDNA. Choice C is the best answer. Exons are gene encoding sequences and are always part of mRNA, eliminating choices B and D. Choice A can be eliminated because gene promoters are not transcribed as well.

43. **A is the best answer.** In Figure 1, the solid line represents simultaneous BRCA1 and p53 mutation, the dotted line represents p53 mutation, and the dashed line represents BRCA1 mutation. Notice that each of the lines decreases with time, indicating that overall survival diminishes for all three mutation statuses, eliminating choices C and D. Choice B can be eliminated because the solid line, the BRCA1 and p53 mutations, indicates the lowest overall survival of all three groups.

Stand-alones (Questions 44-47)

44. **C is the best answer.** Radical oxygen species (ROS) can react with nearly every molecule in a cell to cause oxidative damage. The question stem implies that ROS can break the backbone of DNA, which would generate a double strand break. Missense mutations change the identity of the amino acid and are likely to occur when one base gets substituted for another in an error in DNA replication or mispairing of bases. DNA double strand breaks are most likely to result in error-prone rejoining of the two strands, which is usually done by trimming bases then ligating the backbone. Choice A can be eliminated because it is unlikely that no bases are removed. Choice B can be eliminated by the same logic, as sense mutations are nucleotide substitutions that maintain the identity of the amino acid. Insertions require that additional nucleotides be polymerized at the end of the broken DNA prior to ligation. Unless the break occurs during replication, it is unlikely that a DNA polymerase would be around to add in these extra bases, making choice D less likely to be the best answer. The ends of the damaged DNA are trimmed in order to ligate the two backbones back together. This would result in a deletion mutant, making choice C the best answer choice.

45. **A is the best answer.** During prophase I of meiosis, homologous pairs come together to form a tetrad, which consists of four chromatids. Synaptonemal complexes form and allow for crossing over. Under the light microscope this is observed as chiasma. Pieces of DNA are exchanged between the four chromatids to produce genetic recombination. If a child has paternal chromosomes that are identical to the grandfather's chromosomes, then it is likely that no crossing over occurred during gametogenesis of the parents. Choice A is the best answer because the failure of tetrad formation would prevent crossing over from occurring. Although the child does receive the grandfather's genetic information via the sperm and egg, crossing over should have occurred during gametogenesis, and in a normal circumstance the DNA sequences would not be identical. This eliminates choice B. Choice C suggests that the genome is altered after the formation of the zygote. Remember that the DNA the child receives is determined by meiosis, which forms the parents' gametes. This eliminate choice C. Choice D is possible but unlikely. Crossing over is an integral part of meiosis, and there is a very low probability that no crossing over or double crossing over occurred in every tetrad during gametogenesis.

46. **C is the best answer.** Synaptonemal complexes form between homologous chromosomes during crossing over in prophase I of meiosis. Crossing over works to increase genetic diversity. Without crossing over, it would be possible for a child to be related to only one of her paternal grandparents, and completely unrelated to the other. It is not necessary to know what a coefficient of relatedness is to answer this question: only to understand the principles that crossing over increases genetic diversity during meiosis, and inhibiting it would interfere with genetic diversity. There is no indication that a lack of crossing over would inhibit mitosis, eliminating choice A. Environmental toxins can be associated with cancer, and prevention of crossing over would likely increase the risk of cancer, if any effect at all. Choice B can be eliminated. Crossing over occurs during prophase I, so assuming that the cell survives prophase I, there is no reason to think that it would arrest as late as prophase II as a result of this toxin, eliminating choice D. By process of elimination, choice C is the best answer. If no crossing over occurred, siblings could potentially either inherit the same set of chromosomes or none of the same genetic material from their parents, increasing or decreasing their relatedness, respectively.

47. **B is the best answer.** A postzygotic barrier to replication is one that occurs after the sperm and egg have fused into a zygote. These barriers limit the proliferation of the zygote through mitosis. A mutation that prevented ATP production would leave the sperm unable to migrate towards the egg due to lack of ATP to power the tail. This would be a prezygotic barrier, eliminating choice A. Similarly, choice C would be a prezygotic barrier that would destroy the sperm, preventing fertilization, eliminating it as a possible answer. Choice D would be a mutation that occurred after the individual would have been fertile. Additionally, an oncogene would likely be a somatic, not germline mutation, meaning that it would not be passed along to offspring. A sperm and egg with different numbers of chromosomes would be able to fuse to form a zygote but would be unable to undergo mitosis because the chromosomes would not be able to perfectly pair, as one chromosome does not have a partner to pair with. This would be a postzygotic barrier, making choice B the best answer choice.

Passage 9 (Questions 48-51)

48. **C is the best answer.** According to paragraph three, C deaminates to 5mC then finally to U before the next round of DNA replication can begin. This means that C turns into a U, which is normally found in RNA. Uracil, while typically found in RNA, is able to pair with A in DNA, creating a C > T change in the DNA sequence during the following round of replication. The best answer will be the graph that shows the greatest percentage of total changes that are C to T. Choice C shows that around 90% of the total changes are C > T making it the best answer. Choices A, B, and D are less likely to be the best answer because the C > T change does not predominate over other changes.

49. **A is the best answer.** According to the passage, patients that develop cancer early, such as the 29-year-old woman, may contain a genetic predisposition to developing cancer. In this example, the *BRCA1* gene is mutated in a heterozygous manner. This means that of the two gene copies, one is nonfunctional and one is functional. Because this patient already has one nonfunctional copy of the gene, mutation of the other copy would result in loss of function of the BRCA1 protein genome wide. An oncogene gains a function, not loses one, with a mutation. Typically an oncogene will only require one allele to cause cancer because that allele has a gain of function. If *BRCA1* was an oncogene, inheriting the mutated allele should cause cancer soon after birth. The passage does not suggest that the cancer occurs this quickly so choice B is not the best answer. A promoter is a sequence of DNA that determines where the start of transcription is for a gene. There is no indication in the passage that *BRCA1* is a promotor, eliminating choice C. A ribozyme is an enzyme composed of RNA that mediates chemistry between two molecules. The passage does not suggest that *BRCA1* is made up of RNA, making choice D less likely to be the best answer. Mutation of one copy of *BRCA1* predisposes the patient is the passage to developing breast cancer. This means that the gene is likely acting as a tumor suppressor, making choice A the best answer choice.

50. **B is the best answer.** Almost all methylation of C nucleotides occurs in the context of C next to G, the CpG nucleotide motif. The p in CpG represents the phosphodiester linkage between the C and G nucleosides. Methylation helps "mute" genes that are associated, preventing their expression. Expression of a gene creates an RNA transcript that is later translated into protein. Decreases in CpG would decrease methylation and allow for more expression of genes, which would create more protein product, eliminating choice A. Methylation causes DNA to be more tightly bound to histones. Decreased methylation should allow more DNA to be free from the histone, eliminating choice C. Nucleosomes are the complex of DNA and histone proteins. This concentration should either not change or should increase with decreasing CpG content, as methylation allows the histone to associate more tightly with the DNA. This eliminates choice D. Decreased CpG content would decrease methylation, which serves to bind DNA more tightly to the histone proteins. This would increase the transcription of the *BRCA1* gene, making choice B the best answer.

51. **C is the best answer.** The last paragraph of the passage states that the number of mutations in CpG sites is proportional to the number of cells divisions that a cell has undergone. Knowledge of how many rounds of replication a particular cell has undergone is not necessary to answer this question. Stem cells are a type of undifferentiated cell that continue to divide to produce a multitude of cell types but always maintain their undifferentiated state. Epithelial cells in the skin are unable to divide, eliminating choice A. Similarly, endothelial and gastric mucosal cells have arisen from stem cells and are less likely to accumulate as many mutations as stem cells over time. Hematopoietic stem cells are the precursors for the cells in the blood and can be found in the bone marrow. Stem cells have the ability to divide continually to produce new daughter cells that can form nearly all cells of the body. Because they have the greatest number of divisions over the lifetime of a person, they would be expected to accumulate the greatest number of mutations, so choice C is the best answer.

Passage 10 (Questions 52-56)

52. **D is the best answer.** The goal of the imaging experiment is to compare microtubule to chromosomal attachment in control and mutant oocytes. The researchers would want to preserve the structures before imaging them so that the images closely represent how the oocytes look at a specified point in time. Choice D is the best answer because lowering the temperature of the oocytes would slow all reactions in the cell, as the rate of reactions would decrease as temperature decreases. The activation energy of a reaction only changes in the presence of a catalyst, eliminating choices B and C. Choice A is unlikely since the samples were already contained in a different medium for 8.5 hours not at 4°C, so if the logic in choice A is followed, then contamination would already not have been prevented.

53. **C is the best answer.** Oocytes missing the ERK3 gene have decreased rates of microtubule attachment to the chromosomes. During meiosis, the microtubule-containing spindle apparatus forms during anaphase I to separate homologous chromosomes and anaphase II to separate sister chromatids. If the chromosomes are unevenly divided among gametes, gametes would have extra or fewer chromosomes, resulting in aneuploidy, making options I and II likely. Although failure of the mitotic spindle could result in an abnormal number of chromosomes, it would not cause more than two identical chromosomes to enter the cell. DNA replication occurs during the S phase of the cell cycle, before mitosis or meiosis begins. No information in the passage suggests that ERK3 influences DNA replication, eliminating option III and making choice C the best answer.

54. **A is the best answer.** Spindles begin forming during prophase, but do not attach to chromosomes until metaphase, making choice A the best answer. Homologous chromosome pairs are arranged in the middle of the cell during metaphase I of meiosis, and sister chromatids are arranged in the middle of the cell during metaphase II, eliminating choices B and C. Microtubules pull homologous chromosome pairs apart during anaphase I and must be attached to the chromosomes to do this, eliminating choice D.

55. **B is the best answer.** Crossing over occurs during prophase I of meiosis and requires the DNA of two homologous chromosomes to be exchanged. This process requires cutting the phosphodiester bonds of DNA and rejoining the cut strands with DNA from the homologue. Endonucleases are enzymes that cut phosphodiester bonds, and DNA ligases join severed DNA strands, corresponding to options I and III, respectively. Choice B is the best answer.

56. **C is the best answer.** Nondisjunction is a term that describes sister chromatids or homologous chromosomes that have not properly separated. Passage evidence suggests that ERK3 is necessary for microtubule attachment to chromosomes, making ERK3 deficient oocytes more likely to experience nondisjunction, making choice C the best answer. Cell cycle arrest must occur at a cell cycle check point before mitosis or meiosis begins, eliminating choice A. The passage does not indicate how ERK would alter genetic recombination, eliminating choice B. Frameshift mutations would occur during DNA replication during S phase, not mitosis or meiosis, eliminating choice D.

Stand-alones (Questions 57-59)

57. **B is the best answer.** In humans, sex is determined by the presence of a Y chromosome that contains the SRY gene that produced the testes determining factor protein, which increases the transcription of male-specific transcription factors by binding DNA. Mullerian inhibiting substance is one of the targets of the TDF protein but does not control sex differentiation itself, eliminating choice A. Both FSH and LH are hormones produced by both males and females that help regulate reproduction. They are not specific to one gender and do not function to determine sex, eliminating choices C and D. The presence of the Y chromosome allows TDF to be expressed, which serves as a transcription factor to transcribe male-specific genes, making choice B the best answer.

58. **D is the best answer.** According to the question stem, myelin genes evolved as the genes recombined. Exons are the coding portions of genes that produce protein products. In eukaryotes the exons are significantly smaller than introns and other noncoding portions of the DNA. Failed crossing over in exons is likely to have a significant negative effect on the organisms and would be evolutionarily disadvantageous, eliminating choice A. Promoter regions bind the transcriptional machinery to encourage gene expression. Like exons, failed crossing over in this region would prevent gene expression and be deadly to the organism, eliminating choice B. Enhancers are DNA sequences that increase the transcription of a gene. Similar to promoter regions, failed crossing over in enhancer regions would prevent myelin gene expression that would insulate neurons, eliminating choice C. Introns are long stretches of noncoding DNA that serve as regions that facilitate homologous recombination that occurs during crossing over events. This crossing over is a source of genetic diversity and could help organisms acquire more copies of advantageous genes that would help produce myelin in a more efficient manner, making choice D the best answer choice.

59. **C is the best answer.** While blood-typing follows classical Mendelian inheritance, its expression is different. It does not follow complete dominance because while i^Ai and i^Bi might show type A and type B, respectively, i^Ai^B would be type AB, without one completely dominant. Choice A can be eliminated. Incomplete dominance refers to a phenotype that is an intermediate between the homozygous counterparts. For example, a red flower with a white flower would produce a pink flower. In blood-typing, there are no intermediate blood forms so choice B can be eliminated. Penetrance refers to the probability of a phenotype being expressed if the genotype is present. A person with a genotype of i^Ai^B would express both A and B antigens on their blood and would show complete expression of both alleles. This is complete penetrance, so choice D can be eliminated. Only co-dominance best describes how type AB blood works and is the best answer.

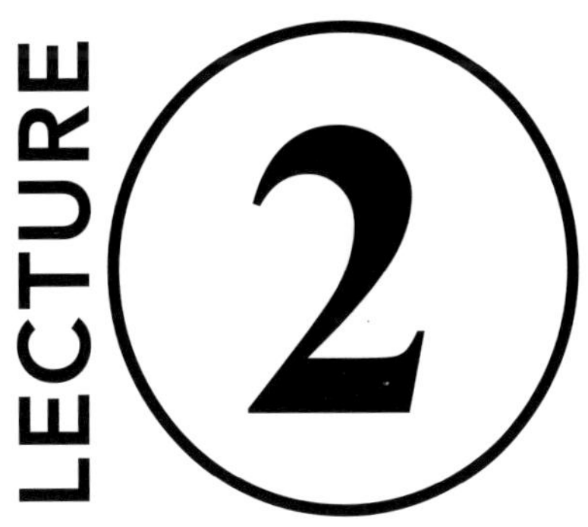

Genetics

TEST 2C

ANSWERS & EXPLANATIONS

Questions 1–31

TEST 2C A&E

Passage 1 (Questions 1-4)

1. **A is the best answer.** For this question, it is helpful to remember what is going on at this particular stage of meiosis. In meiosis I, chromosomes line up in homologous pairs as tetrads, and there is crossing over of similar genetic units. After the completion of meiosis I, only one of each pair is segregated to a daughter cell. This results in two haploid cells, which each contain only a single set of chromosomes as opposed to diploid cells that carry duplicates of each chromosome. Each of these cells consists of chromosomes made up of sister chromatids. There is no longer any crossing over as there are no homologous chromosomes. Choice A is the best answer as this is a true statement. Choices B and C refer instead to meiosis I and not meiosis II. Choice D can be eliminated because chromosomes are maximally condensed and are also organized along a midline. During this step chromosomes are detectable by light microscopy.

2. **C is the best answer.** During oogenesis, only one egg is formed by the end with the remaining cells becoming polar bodies. This is in contrast to spermatogenesis where four equal and viable spermatozoa are formed. Polar bodies contain the same number of chromosomes but are much smaller than oocytes and contain much less cytoplasm. This allows for the mature egg to contain abundant mitochondria as well as other organelles to be used by the future zygote. The sperm donate their genetic material but little else to what becomes the future zygote. As such, the unequal division of cytoplasm in oogenesis is crucial to sustaining life in the initial zygote. Choice A can be eliminated as there is an unequal and not an equal division of cytoplasm. Choice B can be eliminated as there is an equal division of chromosomes. Choice C is the best answer because it accurately describes both the pattern of division and the purpose of it. Choice D is misleading as there is an unequal division of all organelles, not solely mitochondria.

3. **D is the best answer.** The key to answering this question is not in the figures but in the text at the end of the first paragraph. It explains that aneuploidy is associated with other issues including chromosomal breakage. The cause of abnormal chromosome number like also causes chromosomal instability in general. The proposition in the question stem would solve the issue of incorrect chromosome number, but it does not account for the underlying chromosomal instability that can cause other mutations. Because of this, choices A and B can be eliminated. Choice C is misleading because while it is true, it does not address the consequence that would make the procedure unfavorable. Choice D is the better answer as it identifies the potential negative consequences of inheriting both sex chromosomes from a single parent.

4. **D is the best answer.** The passage indicates that only aneuploidies in autosomal chromosomes 13, 18 and 21 are compatible with life. In all other cases, there would be spontaneous abortions or stillbirths. The researchers are interested in the effects of time on spermatozoa and the association that it carries with aneuploidy. In cases where some spermatozoa used for fertilization are deficient or have an extra copy of chromosome 1, there would be no viable embryo or fetus. The researchers are interested in aneuploidy in cases that are compatible with life, resulting in children with abnormalities. Choice A is true but does not explain why the researchers are not interested in chromosome 1 aneuploidy. Choice D is the best answer, since it identifies the likely reason for the exclusion. Such an abnormality is incompatible with life and is not of interest to the researchers in this experiment. Choice C states that the researchers should have tested for aneuploidy of chromosome 1. This is contrary to what was performed, and can be eliminated as an answer choice. Choice B can be eliminated since the passage does not state that other aneuploidies do not occur. While aneuploidy of 13, 18, 21, and the sex chromosomes are the only cases where that produce viable offspring, there is no reason to assume that other aneuploidies do not occur.

Passage 2 (Questions 5-9)

5. **A is the best answer.** This question asks about the principles behind gel electrophoresis, namely the separation of molecules by size and charge. Molecules must either be charged natively or given a uniform charge to migrate in the applied electrical field and will travel through a matrix, with the shortest sequences traveling the furthest down the gel. While it is true that DNA does not contain uracil bases, the identity of the uncharged base does not affect how a specific DNA sequence will in an electric field, eliminating choice B. Proteins, not DNA, are held together in 3D structures by cysteine bonds, making choice C unlikely to be the best answer. Electrophoresis utilizes an applied electric, not magnetic, field to move molecules through the length of the gel. Choice D can be eliminated. Choice A is the best answer choice because the DNA backbone is comprised of phosphate molecules that carry a negative charge. The negative charge allows the molecules to move in an electric field, separating the various sizes by the speed in which they can migrate through a gel.

6. **B is the best answer.** This question references the Hardy-Weinberg principle to determine the frequency of the carriers in the population, namely those that are not affected with CPC but carry the deleterious allele. Those that carry the deleterious allele are heterozygous for the mutation. The frequency of the mutant allele is 10% or 0.1. This value represents q in the Hardy-Weinberg formulas. Because $p + q = 1$, the p value, or the frequency of the wild-type allele, is 0.9 or 90%. The frequency of the carrier is found by $p^2 + 2pq + q^2 = 1$, solving for the value of 2pq. Using $2 \cdot 0.1 \cdot 0.9$, the frequency of the carrier is 0.18 or 18%. Choice A can be eliminated because it is the frequency of the mutant allele, while choice D is also unlikely because it represents the frequency of the wild-type allele. 0.28 or 28% is not a mathematical combination of the Hardy-Weinberg formula and can be eliminated. Because $2 \cdot 0.1 \cdot 0.9$ equals 0.18 or 18%, choice B is the best answer choice.

7. **B is the best answer.** Figure 1 provides the best information to answer this question. The first step to choosing the best answer is to determine whether the disease is segregating in an autosomal or sex-linked manner. Autosomal diseases tend to occur with equal frequency in both men and women, while sex-linked diseases tend to be seen in males only. In Figure 1, the disease occurs in 3 females and 1 male, making it more likely to be autosomal. Choices C and D can be eliminated. The next step is to determine if the disease is dominant or recessive. A dominant disease is found in each generation because it only requires one allele to cause a disease, while a recessive disease skips generations due to the probability of inheriting two recessive alleles. In Figure 1, the disease skips the offspring of the first generation, since both sons lack the disease. The offspring of the second generation on the left has the disease while both parents lack it. This means the parents were heterozygous carriers of the recessive allele. This most strongly indicates an autosomal recessive inheritance pattern, making choice B the best answer.

8. **A is the best answer.** The inheritance pattern shown above can be narrowed down to X-linked recessive or a mitochondrial inheritance pattern. Mitochondrial inheritance patterns pass from mother to all children, and do not pass from father to any offspring. This is seen in the above pedigree. X-linked recessive affect males more than females, since they only have one copy of the X chromosome. A single copy of the recessive mutation will cause the phenotype in males while females need two recessive copies to display the phenotype. X-linked recessive transmission cannot be ruled out from this pedigree. Autosomal recessive can be ruled out since the F1 male is not a carrier, but both offspring show the mutation. Choice C can be eliminated. Autosomal dominant can be ruled out since it is very unlikely that none of the third generation would have the mutation given that one of the parents does. In a normal autosomal dominant inheritance, it would be expected that 50% of the offspring of a heterozygous parent would show the phenotype. Since it can be deduced that the mutation is either on the mitochondrial DNA or in the sex chromosomes, choice B can be eliminated. If the inheritance were X-linked dominant, then all of the daughters in the third generation would show the mutation. Choice D can be eliminated. Choice A is the best answer because if the inheritance pattern can be narrowed down to either mitochondrial DNA or sex chromosomes, then the mutation is not on chromosome 17.

9. **C is the best answer.** The passage states that the R337H mutation is a point mutation. Inversions and duplications are chromosomal mutations that affect more than a single base. Choices B and D can be eliminated. A sense mutation, also called a synonymous mutation, does not change the amino acid identity. Since there is no change with a sense mutation, choice A can be eliminated. A missense mutation is a point mutation that changes the identity of the base. A conservative missense mutation changes the identity of the base to a base of similar type (for instance a hydrophobic base with another hydrophobic base). Choice C is the best answer since it alters the identity of the protein and is a point mutation.

Passage 3 (Questions 10-14)

10. **C is the best answer.** The gene pool is the set of all genes that are in an organism. Genes create protein products that function in groups and networks to regulate intracellular signaling, movement, metabolism, and many other roles. Aurora A and B are two genes in the gene pool of the humans. PCR specific for the Aurora A and B loci could be used to amplify the promoter, as well as coding regions, of Aurora A, eliminating choice A. *cis* sequences are found on the same chromosome as a gene, and if the enhancers were close to the Aurora B loci, could also be amplified by PCR, eliminating choice B. Introns are one component of a gene and would be amplified by PCR specific for the Aurora B gene, eliminating choice D. *Trans* genes are other genes in the gene pool that are located on different chromosomes. Because they are not in the same loci as Aurora A and are on different chromosomes, it is unlikely that they would be amplified out and later sequenced. Scientists would incorrectly interpret how evolutionary changes in these other genes affected Aurora A, making choice C the best answer choice.

11. **A is the best answer.** According to the question stem, the Aurora A I57V mutation is highly penetrant in cancer and information from paragraph one points to the role of Aurora A in mitosis. Cancer cells are able to outcompete their neighboring cells due to dysregulation of their genome. Aurora A provides an advantageous mutation to cancer cells to allow them to outcompete their normal cellular counterparts. Decreased cell survival would be a deleterious mutation, which would be driven out of the population due to increased cell death. A deleterious mutation would be found at very rare frequencies in a population, not at 90%. Choice B can be eliminated. An increased number of cells in G_2 or G_1 phase implies that progress through the cell cycle is somehow inhibited. This would be the normal cellular response to cancer. Aurora A provides a way for the cancer cell to escape this inhibition, which would likely decrease the number of cells stuck in growth phases, though it may increase the number in mitosis. Choices C and D can be eliminated for this reason. The I57V mutation provides a proliferation advantage to cancer cells and is found in nearly all cells of the tumor, making choice A the best answer choice.

TEST 2C A&E

12. **A is the best answer.** According to the question stem, nitrosamines are compounds in smoke that add chemical groups like alkyl groups to DNA bases. Cigarette smoke, along with many other compounds, is a carcinogen, meaning that it causes cancer. Most carcinogens create mutations in DNA that lead to cancer formation. A mutated DNA base is likely to mispair with a base on the other DNA strand. When the cell replicates, that mispaired base now creates a mutation in a gene that could result in a change in the amino acid sequence of a protein. A nonsense mutation is one that creates a stop codon. There are 64 different codons and 3 of them code for stop codons. A change in the codon sequence would be more likely to change to any of the other 60 remaining codons than one of the three codons by chance, making choice B unlikely to be the best answer. Insertions and deletions may result in frameshift mutations that destroy the reading frame of a protein, making it nonfunctional. Insertions and deletions usually occur during repair of double stranded DNA breaks, not single base changes, eliminating choices C and D. Missense mutations occur when the amino acid changes due to a change in the codon. A mispairing could change the codon to any one of the other 63 codons, most likely causing a missense mutation. Choice A is the best answer choice.

13. **B is the best answer.** When the mutation was first detected, the allele frequency was 10%, while at a later time point, the allele frequency was 6%. This means that as the tumor grew, the allele frequency dropped by 4%. Positive selection occurs when a mutation is advantageous. The percentage of cells with the mutated allele would be expected to be greater than 10% if it was undergoing positive selection, eliminating choice A. A heterozygous advantage implies that one copy of a gene is wild type and the second copy has a mutation that increases fitness in some aspect over that of either the homozygous wild type or the homozygous recessive. The question does not imply that the gene only contains one copy of the mutated allele, making choice C less likely to be the best answer. Incomplete dominance describes a phenotypic, not genotypic, phenomenon where one allele is not completely dominant over a second. No information is provided about phenotype in the question, making choice D less likely to be the best answer. Genetic drift is the process where the allele frequency changes due to random sampling of a population, usually over time. Some cells may proliferate more than others either because they contain an advantage or just by chance. This would change the allele frequency at a later time point, making choice B the best answer.

14. **C is the best answer.** A tumor is a population of cancer cells that grows over time due to increased proliferation and survival, not increased cell death, eliminating choice A. DNA replication is not perfect and some mutations are introduced due to errors made by DNA polymerase. This would increase, not decrease, the genetic diversity, eliminating choice B. DNA damage repair would cause a decrease in the number of mutations, which would lower the mutational diversity, eliminating choice D. Synapsis, or crossing-over, is one way for genetic diversity to be increased. Cancer cells that remain stuck at the metaphase plate due to delayed separation would have a greater chance to undergo synapsis. This could lead to additional mutations, increasing the genetic diversity of the cancer cell population. Choice C is the best answer.

Stand-alones (Questions 15-18)

15. **B is the best answer.** A test cross is used to determine the genotype of a specimen by breeding them with a known organism recessive for all traits of interest and observing the phenotypes of the offspring. Since all dominant genes would come from the unknown organism, the ratio of the phenotypes will allow for identification of the genotype of the unknown organism. If the organism is homozygous dominant, then all offspring will have the dominant phenotype. If the organism is heterozygous dominant, then half the offspring will have the dominant phenotype and half will have the recessive phenotype. Choice A, the chi-square test, evaluates the fit between statistically expected values and those observed in a sample. This is used in determination of whether genes are linked, but would not be appropriate to this situation, so choice A can be eliminated. Choice C is used to determine the location of genes on a chromosome by the rate of crossovers, rather than determining whether the organism is heterozygous or homozygous. Choice D, Hardy Weinberg analysis, is generally used in the context of populations, rather than individuals. Choice B is the best answer.

16. **C is the best answer.** Dominance can be complete, incomplete, or co-dominant. If an allele is completely dominant, either the recessive or the dominant phenotype will be expressed, depending on the genotype. If alleles display incomplete dominance, then an intermediate phenotype will be expressed in a heterozygote. If alleles are co-dominant, then both phenotypes will be expressed in a heterozygote. The trait for hairline in the child is a straight hairline, which means that the allele is completely dominant over a widow's peak. Option I can be eliminated. The trait for freckles is not displayed in the child, which means no freckles is completely dominant, eliminating option II. The trait for hair texture is an intermediate between the parental phenotypes, which is incomplete dominance. Choice C, option III only, is the best answer.

17. **A is the best answer.** A completely dominant mutation means that every individual that has that particular genotype will show a certain phenotype, which in this question is brain cancer. A completely dominant allele is 100% penetrant, so all 10 patients would be expected to develop brain cancer, eliminating choice B. The mutation always gives a stage IV brain cancer, meaning there is no variability in the severity of the disease. Expressivity reflects the variability in the disease and would be fully expressive because all individuals get the same severity of disease, eliminating choice C. No information is provided about whether the mutation is heterozygous or homozygous, eliminating choice D. Only 70% of the individuals with the mutation develop brain cancer, meaning that it is not fully penetrant, making choice A the best answer choice.

18. **B is the best answer.** The pattern described is an X-linked recessive condition. This is inferred from the fact that only males are affected. The mother has a normal phenotype, and so can be assumed to be a heterozygous carrier. The father cannot be a carrier, since he has a single X chromosome and is not affected. This means that her daughters will either be carriers or completely unaffected, and her sons will either be affected or normal. Since there sex of the child is not given, there is a 50% chance that the child will be a boy, and a 50% chance that the boy will be affected. $0.50 \cdot 0.50 = 0.25$ or 25%. This makes choice B the best answer. Choice A would be the answer if the child was known to be the female. Choice C would be the answer if the child was known to be a male. Choice D does not follow a sex-linked pattern.

TEST 2C A&E

Passage 4 (Questions 19-22)

19. **B is the best answer.** Figure 1 shows the pedigree of the family whom has premature atherosclerosis. As with all pedigrees, the squares represent males and the circles represent females. The filled in shapes are people that are affected by the disease. Notice that the disease is found in each generation. An autosomal recessive disease would be found in both men and women but would likely skip generations, eliminating choice A. An X-linked recessive disease would be expected to be seen primarily in men and also skip generations. As the disease is seen nearly equally in both men and women and occurs in each generation, choice C can be eliminated. A Y-linked disease would be rare, as there are very few genes on the Y-chromosome. Additionally, women could not be affected by a Y-linked disease and because there are affected females, choice D can be eliminated. An autosomal dominant disease segregates in each generation of a family and affects both men and women. This is reflected in the pedigree, making choice B the best answer choice.

20. **A is the best answer.** A completely dominant mutation means that every individual that has that particular genotype will show a certain phenotype, which in this passage is hyperlipidemia. A completely dominant allele is 100% penetrant, so all 12 patients would be expected to develop hyperlipidemia, eliminating choice B. The mutation always causes hyperlipidemia, meaning there is no variability in the severity of the disease. Expressivity reflects the variability in the disease and would be fully expressive because all individuals get the same severity of disease, eliminating choice C. No information is provided about whether the mutation is heterozygous or homozygous, making choice D less likely to be the best answer. Only 50% of the individuals with the mutation develop hyperlipidemia, meaning that it is not fully penetrant, making choice A the best answer choice.

21. **A is the best answer.** The wild type allele is the allele that is found in the majority of the population, while the mutant allele is found in the minority of the population. A mutation is by definition a change in sequence relative to the wild type sequence. The serine to cysteine mutation means that the UGU codon produces the mutation. UCA produces serine, which is found in the majority of people that do not have the disease, meaning that it is the wild type allele, not the mutant allele. Choices B and D can both be eliminated. UGU that produces cysteine cannot be the wild type allele because it is found in only the few individuals that have the disease. Choice C can be eliminated, and choice A is the best answer choice.

22. **B is the best answer.** The child of the two parents is a recombinant, meaning that it does not have the genome of either one of the parents but instead represents a recombination event. If no recombination occurred, the affected child would have the genotype of one of the two parents, eliminating choice A. A double crossover between the two genes could restore the genotype at those two genes back to the parental genotype, while some portions of the DNA between the genes would be exchanged. Because the child has a recombinant, not parental, genotype, choice C can be eliminated. Similar to choice C, a quadruple crossover, while exceedingly rare, would also restore the parental genotype. Any multiple of 2 has the potential to restore the parental genotype, depending on where the recombination events occurred and how closely the *KERA* and *APOB* genes were linked. A single crossover would give the recombinant genotype seen in the child, making choice B the best answer.

Passage 5 (Questions 23-27)

23. **A is the best answer.** According to the question stem, unlike patients that do carry mutations in VWF that have varying penetrance, mutations in other genes that result in type 1 VWD have high penetrance. This means that every time a person inherits a particular nucleotide sequence, he or she is almost 100% certain to be affected by the disease. A gene is a heritable nucleotide sequence that codes for a set of products, like proteins, depending on alternative splicing and other modifications. An environmental toxin is unlikely to be shared by all persons whom inherit VWD, making choice B less likely to be the best answer. Choice C describes a complex disease, where many genes mediate a phenotypic trait. Because nearly 100% of persons inherit VWD, is it more likely that the disease is Mendelian, indicating that one gene controls disease risk. Choice C can be eliminated. Similar to choice B, it is unlikely that all persons whom inherit VWD share a common environment, eliminating choice D. A gene is a particular nucleotide sequence that is inherited within families, making choice A the best answer choice.

24. **A is the best answer.** An allele is an alternate version of a gene created by a mutation that resides at the same locus, or position, on a chromosome. One allele differs from another allele of the same gene by having a different nucleotide sequence. According to Table 1 and the question stem, the C at position 1029 in the *F2RL3* gene is changed to a G in a synonymous mutation. A truncated protein results from a nonsense mutation, which changes the nucleic acid sequence to generate a stop codon. A synonymous mutation is one that changes the nucleotide sequence but does not change the amino acid sequence. Choice B can be eliminated. A single amino acid change would likely be created by a missense mutation, which is a type of nonsynonymous, not synonymous, mutation. Choice C can be eliminated. Multiple amino acid changes likely result from a frameshift mutation, which changes the reading frame of a gene. This is also nonsynonymous, eliminating choice D. A new allele is created when the nucleotide sequence of a gene changes but not the location on the chromosome itself. This would be the case with the change from C to G, making choice A the best answer choice.

25. **A is the best answer.** Notice that the parents carry different alleles in both the *F2R* and *F2RL3* genes. The father is GC-GC and the mother is CA-CA. Because each parent passes along one allele to the children, the children will be GC-CA. The question stem asks about the probability of getting a GA genotype in the germ cells of the children. The GA allele is a combination of the two parental alleles, meaning a recombination event must have occurred. The centimorgan distance represents the crossover frequency and is a way of mapping the distance between genes. A 25 cM distance means that there is a 25% chance that a recombination event will occur between two loci. This means that 75% of the germ cells will be GC or CA, and 25% of the time they will be GA or CC. Since there is equal probability to get the nonparental GA or CC genotype, there is a 12.5% chance, or 1/8, of getting GA. Choice A is the best answer. If the distance was 50 cM, the probability of recombination to give GA or CC would be 50%, meaning a 25% chance to get GA. Because the distance is 25 cM, choice B can be eliminated. The recombination frequency cannot exceed 50% or 50 cM. It is not possible that the probability can exceed 25%, eliminating choices C and D.

26. **A is the best answer.** According to the passage, *F2RL3* is a gene that may be responsible for causing type 1 VWD in patients that do not have mutations in VWF itself. Because the passage does not suggest that the disease segregates predominantly in men, whom only have one X chromosome, there is no evidence to suggest that it occurs on the X chromosome. Choice B is possible. Choices C and D are both autosomes that would be expected to give relatively equal frequencies of disease in men and women. However, the passage does not provide any information that would help distinguish between these two chromosomes, making both choices C and D less likely to be the best answer. The Y chromosome is only in men and the passage does not suggest that the disease occurs only in males. Additionally, the Y chromosome contains very few genes and predominantly helps determine the male gender during development. Choice A is a better answer than choice B, and is the best answer.

27. **C is the best answer.** The Law of Independent Assortment says that for unlinked genes either far away from each other on the same chromosome or on different chromosomes entirely, each allele has a 50% likelihood of migrating to one of two daughter cells. Chromosomal nondisjunction implies that chromosomes or chromatids do not uncouple and segregate properly during anaphase. Because the alleles are found to segregate without issues to daughter cells, choice A is unlikely to be the best answer. Incomplete dominance does not describe segregation of alleles but rather whether one genotype is able to completely determine the phenotype. Choice B can be eliminated. Linkage disequilibrium occurs when two genes are close together on the same chromosome and have a decreased chance of segregating independently. The question stem states that the two genes are on different chromosomes, meaning they cannot be linked, eliminating choice C. The law of independent assortment states that each chromosome, which in this case contains the allele for one gene, has a 50% chance of segregating to one of two daughter cells, making choice C is the best answer choice.

Stand-alones (Questions 28-31)

28. **C is the best answer.** Since Marcus does not have the disease, he has no chance of being a double recessive. Because Marcus' brother had the disease, it is known that both parents were heterozygotes. The Punnett square would normally have 4 choices, but since Marcus' cannot be double recessive, the fourth option is eliminated. Marcus' chance of being heterozygous, is 2/3. Choice C is the best answer. Choice A is the chance of Marcus being homozygous dominant, and can be eliminated. Choice B would be the case if it were unknown if Marcus had the disease. Choice D is a probability that is appropriate in a dihybrid cross, which this question does not ask. Choice C is the best answer.

29. **A is the best answer.** A dihybrid cross for two genes that segregate independently will always produce a genotype of 9:3:3:1 in the F_2 generation. Other ratios commonly seen after a dihybrid cross refer to the ratios of F_2 phenotypes. If the two genes do not interact, then the phenotypic ratio will also be 9:3:3:1. If the genes interact, for example as in dominant epistasis, the phenotypic ratios will be altered. Choice B represents the F_2 phenotype in the case of dominant epistasis, while choice C represents the F_2 phenotype of recessive epistasis. Choices B and C can be eliminated. Choice D represents the F_2 phenotype of co-dominance or incomplete dominance of a single gene after a $F_1 \times F_1$ cross. Choice D can be eliminated, and choice A is the best answer.

30. **A is the best answer.** According to the question stem, the father has one allele that is mutated and one allele that is normal. He has a 50% chance of passing along the mutated allele to his child. The mother has two normal alleles that do not increase the risk of getting Alzheimer's disease. She has a 0% change of passing along an allele that increases risk. A risk of 50% multiplied by a risk of 0% gives no increased risk of developing early onset Alzheimer's disease. A 25% increase in risk would occur if the mother had one allele that was mutated. As she does not, choice B can be eliminated. A 50% increase in risk would occur if the mother had two mutated alleles. As she has no mutated alleles, choice C can be eliminated. A 75% increase in risk could not be found in any combination of alleles from the parents, eliminating choice D. Because the mother passes along no mutated alleles, the chance of developing early onset Alzheimer's disease is close to 0%, making choice A the best answer.

31. **A is the best answer.** According to the question stem, one germline mutation, meaning a mutation in one of the alleles from the father or mother, predisposes those with the mutation to developing breast cancer. Some of the patients who carry the mutation may not develop breast cancer, as long as the allele inherited from the other parent does not become mutated. A dominant mutation would not require the mutation of the other allele to cause disease. Germline mutations are often covered up by the wild type allele inherited from the other parent but may cause disease when the other allele mutates, eliminating choice B. Because only one of the two alleles is mutated initially, the patients do not have homozygous mutations, eliminating choices C and D. A recessive mutation is not expressed until the wild type allele becomes inactivated. When this happens, the mutated allele can begin to show its phenotype, causing breast cancer. Choice A is the best answer choice.

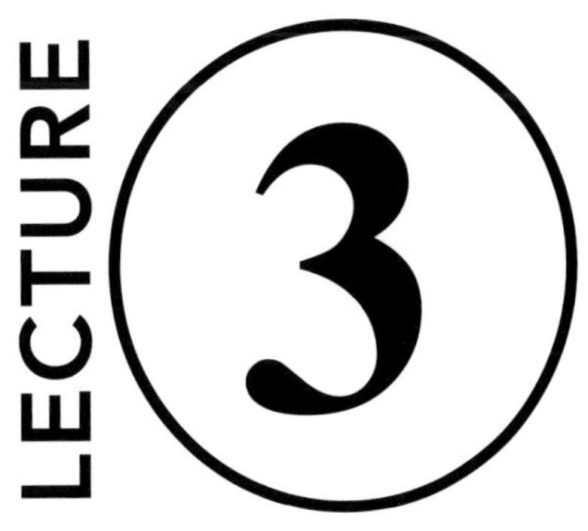

Metabolism

TEST 3A

ANSWERS & EXPLANATIONS

Questions 1–59

LECTURE 3 ANSWER KEY

TEST 3A		TEST 3B		TEST 3C	
1. D	31. B	1. C	31. B	1. D	16. C
2. B	32. C	2. D	32. A	2. A	17. D
3. B	33. C	3. B	33. D	3. B	18. B
4. A	34. A	4. B	34. B	4. C	19. A
5. A	35. D	5. D	35. C	5. C	20. A
6. C	36. B	6. C	36. A	6. A	21. D
7. D	37. B	7. B	37. A	7. C	22. C
8. A	38. C	8. A	38. C	8. A	23. A
9. B	39. A	9. B	39. C	9. C	24. D
10. A	40. A	10. B	40. B	10. C	25. C
11. A	41. B	11. D	41. A	11. C	26. A
12. B	42. A	12. B	42. A	12. B	27. B
13. D	43. C	13. C	43. B	13. C	28. B
14. C	44. A	14. B	44. C	14. A	29. A
15. D	45. C	15. C	45. C	15. B	30. C
16. C	46. B	16. D	46. D		31. A
17. C	47. A	17. A	47. A		
18. C	48. A	18. A	48. A		
19. A	49. B	19. A	49. B		
20. B	50. A	20. A	50. D		
21. B	51. D	21. C	51. B		
22. C	52. A	22. B	52. A		
23. D	53. C	23. B	53. C		
24. C	54. A	24. D	54. B		
25. D	55. C	25. C	55. D		
26. B	56. B	26. D	56. A		
27. A	57. A	27. A	57. B		
28. D	58. B	28. A	58. A		
29. C	59. A	29. C	59. A		
30. D		30. C			

EXPLANATIONS FOR LECTURE 3

Passage 1 (Questions 1-5)

1. **D is the best answer.** The passage states that cancer cells have higher levels of reactive oxygen species, which are generated by partial reduction of oxygen. In addition, mutations are known to generally decrease the binding affinity of reactants and/or products to an enzyme. In this case, one of the products is partially reduced oxygen. The best answer will be the complex that is responsible for reducing oxygen to water via electron transfer. Complex IV is responsible for this reaction, making choice D the best answer choice. Complexes I and III pass electrons and move protons to generate the proton gradient, while complex II receives electrons from $FADH_2$ and transfers them to complex III in order to move protons. Complexes I, II, and III do not utilize oxygen in their reactions, making choices A, B, and C less likely than choice D.

2. **B is the best answer.** The question stem notes that cyanide is an inhibitor of complex IV, the electron transport chain complex that transfers electrons to oxygen to produce water. If cyanide inhibits complex IV, electrons cannot be passed to oxygen, resulting a stalled electron transport chain. Because electron transfer is required for establishing and maintaining the electrochemical gradient, it would collapse, making choice B the best answer choice. Cyanide would decrease, not increase, the electrochemical gradient, making choice A unlikely. The passage does not provide information about cytochrome C. Because choice C is out of the scope of the passage, it is less likely than choice B to be correct. As the question stem notes that cyanide inhibits complex IV, it is unlikely that it also directly inhibits complex V, also known as the ATP synthase. Thus, choice D can be eliminated . A second method of reasoning through this question is based on the question stem indicating that cyanide inhibits the electron transport chain. The main purpose of the electron transport chain is to create an electrochemical proton gradient that drives ATP production. Inhibition of the ETC would thus halt the gradient, preventing ATP production.

3. **B is the best answer.** Controls for experiments are chosen in order to account for differences between the normal and experimental conditions that are not directly being tested. This passage explores the difference in ROS between pancreatic cancer cells and normal cells. Thus, a pancreatic non-cancer cell line should be chosen as the control because background expression of genes is likely to be similar between the cell lines, with differences resulting from the normal cell transforming into a cancer cell. Other cell types, such as skin or muscle, may have different transcriptional and translational programs than pancreatic cells, preventing the researchers from attributing differences in ROS formation to a cell being cancerous. It would be equally reasonable to assume that the differences in ROS formation could be due to differences between the cell types themselves. Thus, the best answer will be the normal cell line that most closely matches the cancerous cell line. The passage notes that pancreatic epithelial cancer is being characterized, meaning that a pancreatic epithelial cell line would be the best control. Choice B is therefore the best answer choice. Beta cells of the pancreas are endocrine cells, not epithelial cells, eliminating choice A. Choices C and D are unlikely because they are not pancreatic cell lines.

4. **A is the best answer.** The passage states that cancer cells have increased growth and proliferation due to ROS generation. However, cancer cells must carefully control these high levels of ROS in order not to reach a level of oxidative stress that results in cell death. Capsaicin is able to selectively kill cancer cells by increasing the levels of ROS above that threshold. Scientists most likely used both catalase and EUK to confirm that the levels of ROS had exceeded the threshold, resulting in significant oxidative stress. Figure 1 provides additional information that helps answer the question. Addition of capsaicin reduced ATP levels significantly, while addition of either catalase or EUK restored the ATP levels nearly to that of the control. Because EUK neutralizes ROS, it can be used as a validation for the function of catalase, making choice A the best answer choice. The passage does not refer to catalase as a potential treatment option, eliminating choice B. Addition of EUK caused a small decrease in ATP levels compared to control in Figure 1, not an increase. Thus, choice C can be eliminated. In addition, the passage does not provide information as to whether or not capsaicin would directly interact with catalase or EUK. Because choice D is not addressed in the passage, it is unlikely to be the correct answer.

5. **A is the best answer.** The passage states that cancer cells rely on higher than normal levels of ROS to increase growth and proliferation. In addition, the passage notes that reactive oxygen species are formed during incomplete reduction of oxygen in the electron transport chain. The best answer will be the molecule that, when its intracellular concentration is low, results in decreased flux through the electron transport chain. NADH delivers the most reducing equivalents to the electron transport chain. A reduction in NADH, possibly as a result of a decrease in the activity of the citric acid cycle, would most likely reduce flow of electrons in the mitochondrial membrane. Thus, choice A is the best answer choice. $FADH_2$ delivers fewer reducing equivalents later in the chain, making choice B unlikely to be the best answer choice. AMP and pyruvate do not contribute to directly transferring electrons to the electron transport chain, eliminating choices C and D as the best answer.

Passage 2 (Questions 6-10)

6. **C is the best answer.** Lipids are hydrophobic and as such need to be transported in lipoprotein particles, which have a hydrophobic core. Choice A leaves out any mention of a hydrophobic carrier, so it can be eliminated. Choice B misidentifies the carrier as the HDL particle. The passage indicates that HDL surveys the blood to pick up excess lipids, and HDL particles are not the primary method of transport from the gut to other tissues. Choice C is the best answer because it correctly identifies the specific lipoprotein used to transport the lipids from the gut after a meal as the chylomicron. Choice D is not accurate because while intestinal epithelial cells may keep some lipids, the majority are sent out to be used by other tissues.

7. **D is the best answer.** This question refers to the relationship between EL and HDL discussed in the first paragraph of the passage. EL hydrolyzes HDL, and the following sentence also indicates that it metabolizes HDL. There is an inverse relationship between the endothelial lipase level and the amount of HDL such that when the former is high, the latter would be low. The graph indicates that a high endothelial lipase level is associated with the greatest degree of artery calcification. The answers are written in two-part form as a way to confuse the reader. It is easiest in such situations to think of the correct answers first and to then find answer choice which matches it. Choice A can be eliminated, since it mentions a high level of HDL when the opposite is true. Choices B and C can be eliminated, since they both mention a low level of EL when the opposite is true. Only Choice D accurately conveys that there should be a high endothelial lipase level and a low level of HDL in those with the greatest degree of atherosclerosis. So, choice D is the best answer.

TEST 3A A&E

8. **A is the best answer.** Both liver and muscle convert to using fatty acids and ketone bodies for energy in the fasting state in order to preserve glucose for the brain and red blood cells. The brain uses ketone bodies for some of its energy in the fasting state, but it also requires glucose, so choice A is the best answer. It is true that red blood cells continue to use glucose in the fasting state, but they are not capable of using ketone bodies because they lack mitochondria, so choice B can be eliminated. Ketone bodies are converted to acetyl-CoA and enter the citric acid cycle in mitochondria. Choices C and D are inaccurate because the liver and skeletal muscle use fatty acids and ketone bodies in the fasting state and do not use glucose.

9. **B is the best answer.** This question is a research-based question that involves some critical thinking based on the discussion of heparin in the third paragraph. Since heparin binds EL, heparin will release it from its regular place attached to the endothelial surface and draw it into the blood. This causes the EL level post-heparin to be higher than it is normally in the plasma. Choice A may seem true based on the better correlation values in the table, but it is not the best answer because it fails to explain why heparin should be discontinued in the future experiment. Choice B more correctly identifies the rationale for the decision and may explain why the results are better in the pre-heparin samples . Choice C is misleading because while the EL levels will be higher with heparin treatment, they do not give better correlation data. Choice D is inaccurate because heparin artificially inflates the EL level in circulation .

10. **A is the best answer.** The LDL receptor, as its name implies, binds LDL in the blood, and thereby takes it out of the circulation. If PCSK9 causes the loss of the receptor, loss of PCSK9 then means that the cell will have a greater than average number of LDL receptors to pull LDL particles out of blood. There is no implied correlation between HDL or EL and LDL. HDL and EL should be unaffected, making options II and III inaccurate. This eliminates choices B and C. Atherosclerosis is caused by excess lipid in the blood, as implied in the passage, and therefore, the loss of LDL in the blood should lead to a reduced risk of atherosclerosis. This eliminates option IV, thereby eliminating choice D. As a result, only option I and choice A are left. People with a PCSK9 mutation are expected to have a very low serum LDL and, consequently, a reduced risk of atherosclerosis.

Passage 3 (Questions 11-14)

11. **A is the best answer.** Usually, phosphatases are enzymes that remove a phosphate group from their substrate, while kinases are enzymes that add a phosphate group to their substrate. In the mitochondria, the kinases and phosphatases are working in balanced opposition to facilitate smooth energy flow without inducing oxidative stress. As stated in the passage mutated PINK1 does not effectively phosphorylate TRAP1. This leaves the cell vulnerable to oxidative stress. One way to intervene would be to maintain TRAP1 in the phosphorylated form. This can be achieved using choice A. Choice B, PINK1 inhibitors, would only promote the pathogenesis of PD by further blocking the ability of PINK1 to phosphorylate TRAP1. Similarly, choice C, complex I inhibitors, would lead to increased ROS, which create oxidative stress that mutated PINK1 cannot compensate for. As shown in Figure 1, failure of PINK1 to phosphorylate TRAP1 would cause the release of cytochrome c (cyt c). Cyt c leads to cell apoptosis and would not prevent PD. Choice D would not act as a therapeutic agent.

12. **B is the best answer.** Flavoproteins are an enzyme family that use flavin as a cofactor. A cofactor is a non-protein component required for the enzyme to function properly. Oxidative stress is caused by free radicals. Choice A would be attempting to control the enzyme's activity by controlling the substrate concentration. While this could work, it is a less direct method of controlling the enzyme than using a cofactor . For example, the experimenter would have to consider the kinetics of the enzyme and how it would equilibrate with the substrate concentration. Because flavin is needed for the flavoprotein to function properly, controlling the concentration of flavin would be an effective method to control the enzyme. An experimenter could add flavin to increase the activity of the flavoprotein or sequester flavin to decrease its activity. Choice C and choice D would alter the activity of the enzyme because each enzyme has an optimal pH and temperature at which it works. However it would be more difficult to control the enzyme using these parameters because it can function outside the optimal temperature or pH. Moreover there is a danger that the enzyme could denature and not reform if too extreme of a pH or temperature was used to turn it off . Potential damage to the protein would make these parameters undesirable to use to control enzyme activity. Each answer choice is a way to manipulate enzyme activity, but choice B is the best answer.

13. **D is the best answer.** Recall that ATP is generated by oxidative phosphorylation in the mitochondria. Complex I is one of the proteins in the inner mitochondrial membrane that facilitates the electron transport chain. Based on the information in the passage, Cyt c and caspase activators, choice A and choice B respectively, are both released once MMP has already been activated. They are not processes that would initiate cell death but rather carry it out. It is also important to be wary of answer choices that uses terms that are unfamiliar. If the term is not defined and explained in the passage, it is most likely a distractor attempting to create uncertainty about the material. Choice C is the opposite of what occurs according to the passage: increased ROS species lead to further complex I inhibition. Inhibition of complex I would prevent the electron transport chain from generating the proton gradient needed to power ATP synthase. Thus, choice D, ATP depletion, would ultimately lead to cell death and is the best answer choice.

TEST 3A A&E

14. **C is the best answer.** It is important to remember that biological systems function in terms of balance and equilibrium. If a person has a PINK1 enzyme that can phosphorylate TRAP1 but not at full capacity, the person's susceptibility to PD is a matter of how much oxidative stress their cells experience and if the mutated PINK1 can keep up. To visualize it, imagine that as oxidative stress is applied to the system, PINK1 must be able to shift this equilibrium, TRAP1 $\leftrightarrow$ TRAP1-P, to the right a sufficient amount to prevent MMP. Choice C describes a scenario that fits with this biological principle of balance and is the best choice. The function of antioxidants can be determined from their name: "anti" (against) –"oxidants" (molecules that oxidate other molecules). They neutralize ROS by donating a pair of electrons to them. Choice A, choice B and choice C describe properties that antioxidants do not have, namely kinase activity, enzyme inhibitor function and cofactor function.

Stand Alones (Questions 15-18)

15. **D is the best answer.** Acetone is an intermediate between beta-hydroxybutyrate and acetoacetic acid, which are all referred to as ketone bodies. They build up in the fasting state due to ketogenesis, or the production of ketone bodies by the liver. While the pairings in Choices A, B and C are independently accurate, the acetone in the stem indicates an overproduction of ketone bodies, making Choice D the best answer.

16. **C is the best answer.** Unlike most ATP that is generated by the electron transport chain in the inner mitochondrial matrix, ATP that is generated in glycolysis occurs by substrate level phosphorylation. Inorganic phosphate is reacted with an ADP molecule during the "payoff phase" of glycolysis in the reaction converting 1,3-bisphosphoglycerate into 3-phosphoglycerate, making choice C the most likely answer choice. Oxidative phosphorylation that occurs in the inner mitochondrial matrix is defined by the transferring of electrons between redox centers, making choice A less likely to be the best answer. The phosphates used to make ATP are not added to proteins, eliminating choice B. Additionally, ATP is not imported into the cell but is instead synthesized from its precursors, making choice D unlikely.

17. **C is the best answer.** The question states than the scientists were interested in electron carriers in the electron transport chain, meaning that the best answer will be one of the two carriers that function to transfer reducing equivalents in the electron transport chain. Ubiquinone, which moves electrons from complex II to complex III, and cytochrome c, which moves electrons from complex III to complex IV, are the two options. Thus, choices A and D can be eliminated because they do not carry electrons. Cytochrome c is also known to induce apoptosis upon release from the mitochondria, making choice C the best answer choice. Ubiquinone has not been shown to trigger apoptosis, which makes choice C a stronger answer than choice B.

18. **C is the best answer.** Fatty acids undergo beta oxidation which sequentially removes two-carbon acetyl-CoA molecules from the fatty chain. Even-chain fatty acids can therefore be fully metabolized to acetyl-CoA units that enter the Kreb's cycle. Intermediates in the Kreb's cycle such as oxaloacetate can be used for gluconeogenesis. But, this removes oxaloacetate from the Kreb's cycle so it cannot continue to run. Although acetyl CoA can theoretically be used to make glucose, it is very inefficient. So, choices A and B are not strong answers. Odd chain fatty acids are broken down to many acetyl-CoA molecules and one 3-carbon molecule. The 3-carbon fat can be directly used for gluconeogenesis. So, choice C is the best answer.

Passage 4 (Questions 19-22)

19. **A is the best answer.** According to paragraph one, cancer cells show increased lipogenesis, meaning synthesis of new fatty acids, as well as increased beta-oxidation, or catabolism of fatty acids. Lipogenesis occurs in the cytosol and smooth ER, while beta-oxidation occurs in the mitochondria. A cancer cell that has increased rates of beta-oxidation could have more mitochondria than a normal cell, making option II and, thus, choice A the best answer. The nucleolus is the site of ribosome synthesis and assembly. The passage does not supply additional information that indicates more ribosomes in cancer cells, making option I unlikely, thus eliminating choices B and D . Additionally, human cells typically have only one nucleolus. Lysosomes break down intracellular proteins and extracellular molecules taken up by endocytosis. As with option I, the passage does not supply additional information indicating that increased intracellular protein turnover is occurring in cancer cells, making choice C unlikely to be the best answer choice. The rough endoplasmic reticulum is involved in protein synthesis. Smooth ER does perform some fatty acid synthesis but rough ER does not. Thus, option IV is unlikely to be contained in the best answer.

20. **B is the best answer.** According to paragraph one, cancer cells have increased lipogenesis, or synthesis of fatty acids. These fatty acids can become triglycerides, membrane lipids (including cholesterol and phospholipids), and signaling molecules. Because a cancer cells has increased lipogenesis, the passage implies that cancer cells would have higher levels of all three of these molecules. Both cholesterol and phospholipids are components of the plasma membrane. Cholesterol makes the membrane more fluid because it interferes the intermolecular forces between the otherwise tightly stacked phospholipids. Intermolecular forces make the membrane more solid so disruption of these forces makes the membrane fluid. Because cancer cells would have higher levels of cholesterol, their plasma membranes are likely to be more fluid, making choice B the best answer choice. Choice A is unlikely to be correct because it is the opposite of what should be observed in cells with more cholesterol. The passage indicates that cancer cells have increased triglycerides, which is the opposite of the state indicated in choice C. Thus, choice C can be eliminated. Some types of signaling molecules can cause inflammation, specifically prostaglandins. A cancer cell produces more signaling molecules and could likely cause more inflammation, eliminating choice D as the best answer choice.

21. **B is the best answer.** Figure 1 displays the amount of ^{14}C incorporated via lipogenesis into total lipids in four cell lines treated with orlistat. According to paragraph one, cancer cells that display increased lipogenesis incorporate the newly synthesized lipids into the plasma membrane via cholesterol and phospholipids. Thus, the correct answer will have the lowest incorporation of ^{14}C into the plasma membrane. The U-266B1 cell line has the lowest incorporation of ^{14}C into total lipids of the cell lines treated with orlistat, indicating that it would have the lowest amount of ^{14}C present in its plasma membrane. Thus, choice B is the best answer. The three other cell lines have higher levels of ^{14}C lipids and would likely have more radiolabeled carbon in the plasma membrane, eliminating choices A, C, and D.

22. **C is the best answer.** Figure 2 provides the most useful information to answer this question. Orlistat acts as an inhibitor of lipid synthesis and is plotted with increasing doses in Figure 2 against overall cell viability. As the dose of orlistat increases, meaning lipogenesis is more inhibited, the cell viability decreases. Notice that the cell viability for RPMI-8226 is the lowest at all concentrations of orlistat, indicating that it is most sensitive to orlistat treatment. Because orlistat serves to inhibit lipogenesis, it is reasonable to conclude that RPMI-8226 is most dependent upon lipogenesis for survival because inhibition of lipogenesis decreases survival the most in this cell line. Thus, choice C is the best answer choice. Choices A and B can be eliminated because they have higher survival than RPMI-8226, regardless of the level of lipogenesis inhibition. Because a conclusion can be drawn from Figure 2, choice D is unlikely to be the correct answer.

Passage 5 (Questions 23-26)

23. **D is the best answer.** Substrate-level phosphorylation occurs when the phosphorylation of ADP to ATP is not directly connected to oxidation and instead is carried out by metabolic enzymes. This is different from oxidative phosphorylation where the energy released from oxidation reactions is used to produce ATP. Substrate-level phosphorylation occurs in glycolysis and the Kreb's cycle. Option I involves the use of ATP and not the generation of ATP, since the product in this case has an additional phosphate group. Options II and V are descriptions of oxidative phosphorylation and not substrate-level phosphorylation. Option III describes what happens in the Kreb's cycle when acetyl-CoA is converted to carbon dioxide. Option VI is also a description of the Kreb's cycle where citrate is converted to oxaloacetate, which is then combined with acetyl-CoA to form citrate once again. These are cases where ATP is generated from ADP as a substrate of the enzymes involved in the Kreb's cycle. Option IV describes the large majority of glycolysis from the second step to the final step, and ATP is made in this process as well. Choices A, B and C all contain Option II and can be eliminated. Only Choice D identifies all of the true options.

24. **C is the best answer.** The second paragraph of the passage states that cells from Sample A express high levels of the insulin receptor. These cells correspond to white adipocytes based on the hollow appearance as noted in the table. While brown adipocytes also express the insulin receptor, the effect of insulin on those cells is unique and is beyond the scope of the question. Insulin is anabolic, which means it will generally stimulate processes that build macromolecules and not ones that break down macromolecules. Insulin stimulates the storage of fatty acids as triglycerides and will have a great effect on white adipocytes through its high expression of the receptor. Choice C correctly matches the effect of storage with the subtype of white adipocytes. Choice B misidentifies the effect of insulin as causing the storage of ketone bodies, whereas insulin prevents ketogenesis, or the formation of ketone bodies, in the first place. Choices A and D are not the best answers because insulin will inhibit the breakdown of lipids to free fatty acids and will not stimulate this.

25. **D is the best answer.** The passage indicates that white adipocytes produce leptin, a hormone that signals satiety and should signal to a person to stop eating. Increasing numbers of these adipocytes should in theory mean more leptin and more satiety leading to less eating, though that is not the case in those who are obese. Choice A incorrectly matches increased leptin with an increased appetite. Choice B is not accurate because there is no evidence suggesting less leptin is made, and there is no explanation given for why that would occur. Choice C is tempting because it gives a seemingly plausible rationale for an underproduction of leptin that would then cause hunger. Still, those who are obese tend to expand outwards in cases of adding fat, and there is no evidence for crowding of the cells, if such a phenomenon would even cause such an effect. Choice D is the best answer because it gives a logical reason for the effect in that as expected, there is increased leptin, but there is a diminished effect . It is important to remember that whenever there is a diminished effect as a result of a signal, either the signal is weak or the receptor for the signal is deficient. If the former is not the case here, it is likely that there is leptin resistance based on a receptor or signal cascade issue.

26. **B is the best answer.** The researchers first visualize the tissue under a microscope, so they should be able to differentiate between white and other adipose tissue without a protein expression assay. Still, perhaps the tissue is not adipose tissue but rather something that resembles it. Choice B is the best answer because the expression of adiponectin would classify the tissue as adipose tissue, and the *HOXC9* would help to differentiate between brown and beige adipose tissue. Choice A is lacking because if the expression test is negative, they could conclude that the tissue is brown fat when it may be another type of tissue altogether. Choice C is inaccurate because numerous types of cells express insulin receptors, so this would not help to classify the tissue as adipose tissue. Choice D is inaccurate because both beige and brown adipocytes should have a similar number of mitochondria based on their similar structure and function in thermogenesis, which requires numerous mitochondria.

Stand Alones (Questions 27-30)

27. **A is the best answer.** The process of beta-oxidation, or oxidation of free fatty acids, occurs by sequentially removing 2-carbon units of acetyl-CoA from the fatty acid. Each acetyl-CoA can then enter into the Citric Acid Cycle to generate NADH and $FADH_2$ that feed into the electron transport chain. Thus, a carbon chain that is longer will be able to produce more acetyl-CoA than shorter chains and, therefore, more ATP. Crotonic acid and myristoleic acid have fewer carbons than palmitic acid and palmitoleic acid, making them less likely to generate the most ATP because the chains are shorter. Choices C and D can be eliminated. The difference between the two remaining choices is the presence of a double bond (making the chain unsaturated) in palmitoleic acid versus palmitic acid. Because unsaturated fats have two fewer hydrogens per double bond as compared to saturated fats, their reducing potential is decreased. The best answer will be the fatty acid with the longest carbon chain and the fewest number of double bonds, making palmitic acid (16 carbons and no double bonds) the best answer choice. Thus, choice A is a better answer choice than choice B.

28. **D is the best answer.** Glycogen is stored in the liver and is broken down to glucose which is released into the blood stream when blood glucose levels are low. In order to release the glucose, glycogen is broken down through the process of glycogenolysis. If glycogenolysis is defective, then glycogen will accumulate in the liver and blood glucose levels will be decreased. Choices A, B, and C have no direct impact on glycogen storage and would not cause the described symptoms.

29. **C is the best answer.** A number of enzymes including trypsin, chymotrypsin, and carboxypeptidase are used in the human body to break down the protein content of food into small, absorbable, units. From a test taking perspective, a good way to remember these (with the exception of carboxypeptidase which advertises it's function in it's name) is that it takes a 'syn' to break a protein, this also works for the stomach enzyme pepsin. These break the peptide bonds that form the backbone of proteins, eventually resulting in the components of the smaller peptide polymers. While the answer to this question concerns dipeptides, mono, di, and tripeptides can all be absorbed by the cells of the brush border. Choice A is incorrect, but describes the synthesis of vitamin D using UV, specifically UVB, radiation. This is a major component in the skeleton, but is not related to amino acid acquisition. Choice B is also incorrect, mentioning disulfide bonds, the bonds that help for form tertiary protein structures by bonding the thiol groups of adjacent cysteines. Choice D is a biochemical synthesis series that can be used to create glycine. It is worth noting that this is a laboratory mechanism, not one used biologically.

30. **D is the best answer.** Regulation of oxidative phosphorylation is directly controlled by the amount of reactants available to generate ATP via this pathway. Oxygen acts as the final electron acceptor of the electron transport chain. If the cell is depleted of oxygen, the electron transport chain will cease to function and the proton gradient will not be maintained. While it is true that the muscle cell in this situation would need ATP and the rate of oxidative phosphorylation would be expected increase, if there is no oxygen available for the process to utilize, the rate will decrease. Choice A can be eliminated. If the amount of ADP increases, then the rate of oxidative phosphorylation will increase in an attempt to regenerate the necessary stores of ATP, so choice B can be eliminated. Ingesting a meal of carbohydrates will increase the amount of glucose in the body. Since the answer choice says that the individual is fasting, it can be assumed that this glucose undergoes glycolysis and eventually enters the TCA cycle. An increase in the flux through the TCA cycle will generate more high energy electrons for the electron transport chain. This will most likely result in an increased rate of oxidative phosphorylation, which eliminates choice C. Another important reactant for this process is NADH, which donates electrons to the electron transport chain. If the ratio of NADH to NAD^+ decreases, as seen when the rate of the citric acid cycle decreases, then the electron transport chain will not work as quickly, and the rate of oxidative phosphorylation will decrease. This makes choice D the best answer.

Passage 6 (Questions 31-34)

TEST 3A A&E

31. **B is the best answer.** According to paragraph three, bacteria that do not have a complete TCA cycle are still able to generate TCA cycle intermediates. These bacteria are also able to avoid losing carbon through the release of carbon dioxide, which is characteristic of the TCA cycle. By bypassing these carbon dioxide releasing steps, bacteria have two additional carbons to use in biosynthetic pathways and can provide additional starting materials for anabolic processes, making choice B the best answer choice. While choices A, C, and D could potentially be a reason that the glyoxylate shunt is beneficial, no supporting information or data are presented in the passage that would suggest a link between the choices and a potential evolutionary benefit. Thus, choices A, C, and D can be eliminated.

32. **C is the best answer.** According to paragraph three, bacteria that have an incomplete TCA cycle use the glyoxylate shunt to bypass steps that release carbon dioxide in the TCA cycle. Remember that one NADH molecule is generated during each of these decarboxylation steps and that two steps of the TCA cycle have carbon dioxide elimination. Thus, bacteria with incomplete TCA cycles create two fewer NADH molecules per turn, which is roughly equivalent to 6 ATP (one NADH generates 2-3 ATP, while one $FADH_2$ generates 1-2 ATP). 36-38 ATP are produced via glycolysis and the TCA cycle, so subtracting 6 ATP would give an estimated 30 ATP per unit glucose.

33. **C is the best answer.** The TCA cycle in both bacteria and humans serves to provide the primary source of reducing equivalents NADH and $FADH_2$ that are used to generate ATP. According to the last paragraph, the glyoxylate shunt, not the TCA cycle, is used to generate metabolic intermediates for synthesis of amino acids and heme through 2-ketogluterate and succinyl-CoA, respectively. Thus, choices A and B can be eliminated. Choice C is the better of the two remaining options because the TCA cycle produces 3 NADH per turn and 1 $FADH_2$. Additionally, NADH generates 3 ATP, while $FADH_2$ generates 2 ATP, making NADH more effective at providing the bacterium with ATP to power energetic processes.

34. **A is the best answer.** The third paragraph notes that the glyoxylate pathway is active when the bacteria are surviving on 2 carbon compounds, namely acetyl-CoA, due to a lack of glucose in the environment, eliminating choice C. Fatty acid oxidation, also known as beta-oxidation, breaks down fatty acids into acetyl-CoA, making choice A the most likely answer choice. Amino acids typically enter glycolysis, although some can enter the Citric Acid Cycle as a four carbon intermediate that would be conserved for biosynthesis. In addition, fats would provide the greatest number of acetyl-CoA molecules per starting molecule (i.e. 8 acetyl-CoA from one 16-carbon fatty acid versus 2 acetyl-CoA from an amino acid). Amino acids that enter as glycolytic intermediates would be conserved for biosynthesis and not provide ATP, making choice B a less attractive answer choice. Because the passage does not provide information that indicates the bacteria are in an anaerobic environment, choice D can be eliminated, as lactate would be the result of anaerobic glycolysis.

Passage 7 (Questions 35-39)

35. **D is the best answer.** Figure 1 shows glucose accumulation in nanomoles on the y-axis for each of 32 segments of intestine shown on the x-axis. Overall, the white boxes, representing the wild-type (Sglt1$^{+/+}$) measurements, are higher throughout, though the glucose accumulation trails off dramatically at the far end. It is best to avoid the trap of picking the choice with the knock-out background without first looking at the graph. The black boxes for the knock-out (Sglt1$^{-/-}$) measurements are generally lower, but there is nevertheless a peak at segment 6 that is higher than the measurements towards the very end of the intestine for the wild-type mice. Insulin is released in the pancreas when blood glucose levels rise, so a low insulin release is connected to a low blood glucose, meaning a poor accumulation in that segment. Choice A can be eliminated because that segment has nearly the highest glucose accumulation overall. Choice B can be eliminated because that segment has a higher accumulation of close to 200 nmol/cm than does choice D with 100 nmol/cm. Choice C can be eliminated, since it too has a much higher glucose accumulation than does choice D. Choice D is the best answer because in segment 30 for the wild-type mice, the glucose accumulation is the lowest of all the answer choices, and insulin release will be the lowest as a result.

36. **B is the best answer.** The first paragraph explains that while SGLT1 acts to transport glucose into intestinal cells, GLUT2 is responsible for efflux, or transport out to the blood. For this reason, with a GLUT2 deficiency, it is expected that glucose can be transported into the intestinal cells by SGLT1, but it would not be transported out. Choice A is inaccurate because one would expect there to be less glucose in the blood, since less glucose is being transported to the blood. Choice B is the best answer because it identifies the resulting scenario as an increase in glucose within the cells. Choice C is possible if there is a buildup in the cell causing SGLT1 to be inhibited by a glucose saturation in the cell. Glucose would then be passed out to the stool with other items that are not absorbed. Still, this would not be the best answer because this is only a possible outcome that would be secondary to a high glucose within the cell as in choice B. Choice D is inaccurate, since glucose will be in short supply, and in such cases, the liver will break down glycogen for glucose rather than storing more glucose as glycogen.

37. **B is the best answer.** This question refers to the third paragraph that discusses the relationship between SGLT1 and GLP-1 and insulin. The text explains that SGLT1 serves as a glucose sensor for the release of GLP-1. GLP-1 in turn increases insulin secretion. Insulin in the nonfasting state increases glucose uptake in muscle and fat cells and thereby lowers blood glucose. Red blood cell glucose uptake is not under hormonal control since red blood cells always requires glucose for function, even in the fasting state. When everything operates properly in wild-type mice, one expects there to be normal insulin release, a low blood glucose and increased glucose uptake in fat and muscle cells. By contrast, with an SGLT1 deficiency, one would expect less insulin release, a high blood glucose and decreased glucose uptake in fat and muscle. Choice B is the best answer because it identifies that wild-type mice would be expected to have lower blood glucose levels than would the SGLT1 deficient mice. Choice C is inaccurate because red blood cell glucose uptake should not change. Choices A and D are the opposite of what is expected, namely one would expect more glucose uptake to muscle and more insulin release in the wild-type mice and not less.

38. **C is the best answer.** This is a tricky research question because it requires thought and an understanding of the way MCAT® questions are structured. In general, the most specific and most accurate answer will always be considered correct since it is deemed the most correct. If there are other answers that are more general in nature, they lack that designation as being the most correct. The question is asking why the researchers chose to design the experiment with knock-out mice instead of perhaps the easier choice of a drug that does the same thing. The choice to go in the former direction presupposes that the drug carries with it some issue. The stem also contains a hint by discussing the inhibitor as an SGLT inhibitor and not an SGLT1-specific inhibitor. Indeed, the inhibitor could block other transporters in the body, and if so, the results could be drastically skewed by confounding variables. Choice A may be true but it is not the best answer. If the inhibitor is indeed potent, one would likely still get statistically significant results and have an easier design setup. Choices B and D are both true, but they are also too general. The difference with choice C is that it actually explains what the undesired consequence or other variables could be, so choice C is the best answer.

39. **A is the best answer.** This question asks for the connection between fructose and insulin secretion disorders based on the passages. The first paragraph indicates that mice deficient in SGLT1 can only live on a glucose and galactose-free diet, indicating that the mice can tolerate fructose. Fructose is transported by GLUT5 and not by SGLT1. This fact does not need to be known to answer the question, since it can be reasoned out by process of elimination. Choice A is the best answer because it is accurate and fits best with the information in the passage. The lack of SGLT1 activity would result in less GLP-1 release and less insulin secretion. Insulin is critical to maintain blood glucose, and many with diabetes have impaired insulin secretion. Choice B is the opposite of what is expected. SGLT1 activity is tied to more GLP-1 and insulin secretion as shown in Figures 2 and 3 with the wild-type mice showing strong increases in both following glucose administration. Choices C and D may be true, but they have no basis in the passage.

Passage 8 (Questions 40-43)

40. **A is the best answer.** In addition to supplying ATP, glycolysis also provides intermediates for other biosynthetic pathways, including nucleic acid synthesis from the Pentose Phosphate Pathway. Cancer cells undergoing rapid growth and division would need additional macromolecules to support their proliferation, making choice A the best answer choice. Decreasing oxidative phosphorylation would decrease the net movement through the electron transport chain and thus reduce the number of oxygen free radicals generated in Complex IV. Choice B states that there would be an increase in free radicals. This would not be beneficial to the cell and would not be expected if the cell is undergoing anaerobic respiration so choice B can be eliminated. Increased glycolysis would increase, not reduce, the amount of glucose used for ATP production, making choice C less likely to be the correct answer. Anaerobic glycolysis serves to regenerate NAD^+, not NADH. Additionally, NADPH is used for anabolic, or biosynthesis pathways, whereas NADH is generated in catabolic pathways. Thus, choice D is not the best answer.

41. **B is the best answer.** According to paragraph one, mice infected with HBV switch from a glycogen-storage state to a glycogen-depleted state, indicating that the metabolic alteration reduces glycogen levels. The best answer choice will be the enzyme that catalyzes glycogen breakdown, making the glycogen phosphorylase gene the most likely gene to be overexpressed. Thus, choice B is the best answer choice. Glycogen storage, mediated by the glycogen synthase gene, is the opposite of the metabolic alteration described in the passage, making choice A less likely than choice B to be the correct answer. Pyruvate dehydrogenase is used to convert pyruvate to acetyl CoA. The passage states that cancer cells use anaerobic metabolism so pyruvate is converted to lactate, not acetyl CoA. Additionally, choice C does not pertain to glycogen synthesis or breakdown and may be eliminated. Glucose-6 phosphatase mediates the conversion of glucose-6 phosphate to free glucose in the liver in order to raise blood glucose. The passage indicates that transformed cancer cells show abnormally high levels of glycolysis, so it is likely the HCC cells are using glucose-6 phosphate for glycolysis instead of converting it to free glucose to be released in the blood, eliminating choice D.

42. **A is the best answer.** According to paragraph one, hepatocellular carcinoma is characterized by an increase in anaerobic glycolysis and decrease in glycogen levels. Thus, the best answer choice, meaning the least likely to describe the metabolic state of HCC, would suggest a decrease in glycolysis and an increase in glycogen storage. Glycogen synthase is responsible for synthesizing glycogen and would be expected to have reduced activity in HCC, making choice A the best answer choice. An increase in glucokinase would be expected in HCC, as glycolysis is occurring at a higher rate, making choice B less likely than choice A to be the correct answer. The breakdown of glycogen, catalyzed by glycogen phosphorylase, would be expected to be high, eliminating choice C. Choice D can be eliminated because succinate dehydrogenase is a component of the Citric Acid Cycle and the passage informs that HCC has reduced oxidative phosphorylation, indicating that the Citric Acid Cycle is likely not running at maximum efficiency.

43. **C is the best answer.** Figure 1 helps to best answer this question because it correlates stored glucose, also known as glycogen, with the identity of various mice. Based on the graph, the mice with mutated pre-S2 have higher glycogen levels than their non-tumorous control mice, meaning that they store more glucose in the form of glycogen. Thus, choice C is the best answer choice. As the wild-type mice have lower stores of glycogen, choice D can be eliminated because it is the opposite of the information presented in Figure 1. Additionally, while YY1 and mTOR were presented in the passage as proteins that could help mediate metabolism in HHC mice, no additional information is presented correlating mTOR or YY1 levels with glycogen levels, making choices A and B less likely than choice C to be the correct answer.

Stand Alones (Questions 44-47)

44. **A is the best answer.** The question references a specific disease, type 2 diabetes, but knowledge of this disease is not needed to answer the question. The question states that in patients with type 2 diabetes, glucose is not efficiently absorbed into peripheral tissues. In order to compensate for the lack of metabolic fuel, fatty acids need to be broken down into acetyl-CoA through the process of beta oxidation, which is choice A. Choice B and D can be eliminated because internalization and transport of insulin receptors is a process that would require an extended response time and the question stem specifically states about the immediate response. Choice C can be eliminated because cells have mechanisms to compensate for situations where glucose levels are low.

45. **C is the best answer.** Tyrosine is a hydrophobic amino acid that can be used to make proteins and hormones. Tyrosine is the amino acid used to produce neurotransmitters like epinephrine and norepinephrine, so choice A is not the best answer. Tyrosine also serves as the basis for thyroid hormones T_3 and T_4 that regulate basal metabolic rate, so choice B is not the best answer. Since tyrosine can be used to make proteins, it is likely present in hemoglobin which carries oxygen in the blood, so choice D is not the best answer. The fluidity of the plasma membrane is primarily controlled by cholesterol levels in lipid bilayer. Cholesterol is synthesized from acetyl-Coa, not amino acids like tyrosine. Thus, choice C is the best answer choice. Choices A, B, and D, as explained above, are all ultimately formed from amino acids and can be eliminated.

58. B is the best answer. To identify the best answer choice, the cytosolic process that provides molecules important in cholesterol synthesis needs to be identified. The first key is that the question asks about an anabolic (synthesis) not a catabolic (break down) pathway. Choice B is the only synthetic pathway , leading to the formation of NADPH and 5 carbon sugars such as ribose that are important in nucleotide synthesis. The Pentose Phosphate Pathway generates NADPH which provides additional hydrogen atoms to cholesterol as it is being synthesized, making choice B the best answer choice. Glycogenolysis is the breakdown on glycogen and is thus catabolic, making choice A unlikely to be the best answer choice. Glycolysis is also catabolic in that it breaks down glucose into pyruvate, making choice C less likely than choice B to be the correct answer. The Citric Acid Cycle breaks down acetyl-CoA into carbon dioxide and reducing equivalents that are transported to the electron transport chain. Thus, choice D is unlikely to be the correct answer, as it is also catabolic.

59. A is the best answer. The first step of answering this question is to determine what type of molecule the electron transport chain complexes require in order to receive reducing equivalents. Delivering more reducing equivalents would increase the number of electrons that moved through the chain over time. Flavoproteins, proteins that include derivatives of nucleic acids like flavin adenine dinucleotide (FAD), flavin mononucleotide (FMN), and nicotamide adenine nucleotide (NAD), all transport electrons to the electron transport chain. Riboflavin is the key co-factor in these molecules. Thus, supplementation of the diet with riboflavin would likely support the synthesis of these proteins, making choice A the best answer choice. While iron and zinc are components of Electron Transport Chain complexes, increasing their concentrations would likely not change the concentration of the co-factor in Complexes I-IV and would be unlikely to increase the number of electrons that pass through the chain over time, eliminating choices B and C. Vitamin C is not a co-factor involved in the electron transport chain, eliminating it as a potential answer choice.

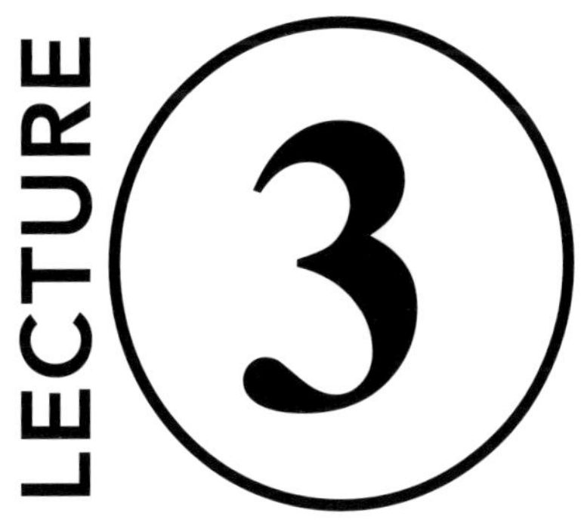

Metabolism

TEST 3B

ANSWERS & EXPLANATIONS

Questions 1–59

Passage 1 (Questions 1-5)

1. **C is the best answer.** The question is asking for the cause of the abnormal metabolic state of the experimental mice. The passage states that they are prone to lipid deposition in the arteries, indicating that there is an excess of lipids in the bloodstream. The passage also indicates that ApoE is a major constituent of chylomicrons, which function to carry lipids from the intestines to the liver. Choice A is somewhat misleading because the defect in this case is not the inability to break down the lipids but is rather the inability to t ransport the lipids. The chylomicrons carry lipids to the liver, so they help to clear the lipids from the blood. Because the ApoE of chylomicrons is associated with the transport of lipids and not the absorption of lipids into the intestinal cells, choice B is not the best answer. Choice C is the best answer because it identifies that the issue here is one of transport, and as such, the lipid particles build up in the bloodstream to abnormal levels. Choice D is misleading because while it is true that the brain requires glucose for some of its energy even in the fasting state, humans cannot convert most lipids to glucose, with the exception of some odd-chain fatty acid remnants.

2. **D is the best answer.** The graph in Figure 1 gives data on aconitase activity, though the numerical values are not explained. The question is asking what could have been the basis of these values to assess aconitase activity from the samples. This question can be answered without specific knowledge of the enzymes involved in the TCA cycle by some reasoning. Choice A is misleading. While isocitrate does lose carbon dioxide, this step occurs following the aconitase-mediated step. Also, this choice can be eliminated, since other steps also produce carbon dioxide, and this marker would not be a specific test for the enzyme. Choice B is tricky, since this reflects the reaction carried out by aconitase. However, the measurement for the graph cannot be a loss of citrate, since the graph indicates that with a higher value, there is greater aconitase activity. Choice C represents a very general measure of the activity of the TCA cycle, but it would not give any specific data on the function of aconitase on its own, since ATP is made at many steps. Choice D is the best answer, since this is ultimately a specific test for aconitase, which carries out this reaction. The additional phrase that seems irrelevant to the question only serves to obscure the answer.

3. **B is the best answer.** In the passage, the use of apoE deficient mice is deliberate, as these mice are already prone to develop plaque in the arteries. This allows a relatively minor risk such as second-hand smoke to result in an increase in disease progression. In order to replicate the results, the experimental mice would have to be compromised or else the minor risk of SHS would be unlikely to show a significant effect. Choice A is a case where the LDL receptor is incapable or less capable of absorbing the lipid particles, leading to an excess of lipids in the blood. These mice would be prone to atherosclerosis and are similar to the apoE deficient mice. An intestinal lipase inhibitor would have the effect of decreasing the amount of lipid absorbed by the gut. This would lead to mice having very low levels of lipids in the blood, and these mice would be very unlikely to develop atherosclerosis, which is caused by lipid deposition in the arteries. So, choice B is a strong answer. Choice C is a case where the mice would have decreased HDL, which serves to pick up excess lipids from peripheral cells and is beneficial for heart health. The low HDL level is therefore deleterious and would compromise the mice. Choice D is a case where the mice would not be compromised, but it is still not as good of a choice as choice B where the mice have a decreased risk of atherosclerosis.

4. **B is the best answer.** The passage indicates that the mice were studied in different ways to look at the effects of second-hand smoke. The mice were not examined for atherosclerosis and other effects until 12 weeks, which represents adulthood for the mice. This gives some indication that many of the effects of SHS are long-term effects. However, the decreased aconitase activity through superoxide and peroxynitrite inhibition represents a more immediate change and is not caused by a slow buildup over time. While choice A is mild with the point about some arteries, it is still too extreme, as atherosclerosis is a long-term process in any event. Choice B is the best answer, since the reactive oxygen compounds will impair aconitase activity, leading to an excess of acetyl-CoA in the cell. During starvation when insulin is low, the acetyl-CoA is used for ketone body production instead of the TCA cycle. Choice C is inaccurate, since the high triglycerides are a function of the apoE deficiency and are unrelated to the smoke. Choice D describes a long-term effect, since while it is true that cigarette smoke is a risk factor for lung cancer, the development of lung cancer can take a significant amount of time.

5. **D is the best answer.** The transition from pyruvate to the TCA cycle involves the transport of pyruvate and other necessary factors from the cytoplasm to the mitochondrial matrix where the TCA cycle is carried out. Pyruvate is converted to acetyl-CoA through pyruvate dehydrogenase. Choice A is inaccurate, since pyruvate must be transported by facilitated diffusion to the matrix, since it is polar. The outer membrane has protein channels for pyruvate and NADH. Choice B is also inaccurate, since the inner membrane is even less permeable, and this transporter is required. Choice C is tempting, since while NADH is generated in this step, one might assume that the transport into the matrix of NADH would be unrelated. However, NADH must reach the matrix to be oxidized to NAD^+ by the electron transport chain in order to be recycled for future use. Choice D is the best answer because pyruvate dehydrogenase is the necessary enzyme in this step. Pyruvate carboxylase is involved in gluconeogenesis to convert pyruvate to oxaloacetate.

Passage 2 (Questions 6-9)

6. **C is the best answer.** Paragraph 4 of the passage provides the qualitative results of the first experiment by the scientists, where they knock down the protein levels of HSP40 and measure the change in glucose consumption, lactate production, and oxidative phosphorylation. The question asks specifically about oxidative phosphorylation, so the best answer will be the most specific to oxidative phosphorylation. Oxidative phosphorylation occurs in the inner mitochondrial matrix and uses the reducing power of NADH and $FADH_2$ to create a proton gradient that drives the ATP synthase. In order for the proton gradient to be established, electrons must flow through the electron transport chain complexes to Complex IV, where they are finally transferred to oxygen. Thus, oxygen is the molecule required for the electron transport chain to function. Measuring oxygen levels would allow researchers to see how HSP40 affected oxidative phosphorylation, making choice C the best answer choice. Glucose and glycogen (a polymer of glucose) serve as the starting point for glycolysis, meaning measuring these levels would inform the researchers about glycolysis, not oxidative phosphorylation. Choices A and B can be eliminated. ATP is also produced in glycolysis, meaning it is not a specific measure of oxidative phosphorylation. Thus, choice D is a less strong answer compared to choice C.

7. **B is the best answer.** Based on Figure 2, knockdown of HSP40 using anti-sense oligonucleotides results in an increase in the activity of pyruvate kinase (PK). The increased activity of PK would allow it to convert more PEP into pyruvate, thus decreasing the concentration of PEP and increasing the concentration of pyruvate, making choice B the best answer. As the concentration of PEP would decrease, not increase, choice A can be eliminated. The question stem implies that the cells in which glycolysis is occurring are in an oxygen rich environment and undergoing aerobic metabolism. Lactate is not produced in aerobic metabolism. Thus, the concentrations of lactate are unlikely to change, as lactate is not a component of aerobic glycolysis, making choices C and D less likely than choice B.

8. **A is the best answer.** The question stem indicates anaerobic glycolysis is now occurring, because the cells are demonstrating the Warburg Effect. According to the passage and Figure 1, PKM2 activates pyruvate kinase, which is responsible for converting PEP to pyruvate. Figure 2 displays the results of the experiments that reduce HSP40 expression to determine its effect on glycolysis and gene transcription. To confirm the results of a downregulation experiment, the scientists would most likely wish to overexpress the HSP40 protein and observe whether or not an opposite effect of that seen in Figure 2 emerges, making choice A the best answer choice. Knockdown of HSP40 is already presented in the passage in Figure 2. Additional knockdown experiments would not add new information, making choice B unlikely. Given that the scientists wished to determine the role of HSP40, not PKM2, the scientists would want to observe the effect of modifying HSP40 levels, not PKM2 levels.

9. **B is the best answer.** According to paragraph one, the Warburg Effect is characterized by anaerobic glycolysis, even though oxygen is present in the environment. During anaerobic glycolysis, pyruvate is converted into lactic acid (lactate) in order to regenerate NAD^+ that is necessary as a co-factor in glycolysis. Thus, in cancer cells undergoing anaerobic glycolysis, the levels of lactate should increase, making choice B the best answer. The lactate levels are unlikely to decrease during anaerobic glycolysis because pyruvate is being converted to lactic acid to regenerate NAD^+, making choice A less likely than choice B. As lactate would continually accumulate, the levels are not likely to remain constant or decrease over time, making choices C and D less likely than choice B as well.

Passage 3 (Questions 10-13)

10. **B is the best answer.** As drawn in Figure 1, sphingomyelin has only one charge. A zwitterion has a positive and negative charge but sphingomyelin has only a positive charge so choice A is not a strong answer. Amphipathic means parts of a molecule are hydrophobic and other parts are hydrophilic. Sphingomyelin has a charged phosphocholine head and a long fatty tail so it is amphipathic and choice B is a strong answer. A phosphoglyceride has a similar structure to sphingomyelin in that it has a charged head and a fatty tail but by definition, it must have a glycerol molecule on the charged head. It is not necessary to know the structure of glycerol to answer this question. Figure 1 shows that the sphingomyelin includes a phosphocholine head and ceramide tail. The ceramide has a secondary amine group that cannot be found on glycerol, which is a three carbon carbohydrate. Figure 1 indicates that the sphingomyelin does not have a glycerol molecule so choice C can be ruled out. Waxes are lipids with an ester linkage between a fatty alcohol and fatty acid. From Figure 1, sphingomyelin is composed of ceramide which may be a wax since it appears to have a long chain fatty alcohol and a long chain fatty acid (the NH has replaced the OH of the fatty acid). Choice D is a possible answer but is too simple since it does not describe sphingomyelin as a whole. Between choices B and D, choice B is the best answer.

11. **D is the best answer.** Substrate level phosphorylations are used in glycolysis to directly make ATP. Ceramide is primarily a lipid. Lipid metabolism does not utilize substrate level phosphorylation so choice A can be eliminated. Ceramide is a fat. It cannot be metabolized by the enzymes in glycolysis, which are specific for glucose. It also does not function as a cofactor so there is no evidence to support choice B and it can be eliminated. Ceramide is a long fat but humans are capable of metabolizing fats that are much larger than ceramide. The mitochondria is able to metabolize fats up to 22 carbons long through β-oxidation. The peroxisome can metabolize chains longer than 22 carbons. Ceramide is composed of two chains of fatty acids, both less than 22 carbons, so choice C can be eliminated. Fats are metabolized through β-oxidation which produces acetyl-CoA that enters the citric acid cycle to produce NADH. NADH is then used to generate ATP through oxidative phosphorylation. Choice D is the best answer.

12. **B is the best answer.** First, determine what type of metabolism is used by *Npc1*$^{-/-}$ mice. Figure 2 shows elevated lactate in *Npc1*$^{-/-}$ mice. Lactate is a produce of anaerobic respiration so choices A and C can be eliminated. Between Choice B and D, the decision is more difficult but can be addressed two ways. Anaerobic respiration does not require oxygen so breathing should not be affected by use of anaerobic respiration. The opposite may be true, difficulty breathing may cause the overuse of anaerobic respiration, but that is not what choice D says. Additionally, Figure 2 shows that the metabolites are measured in the cerebellum. The cerebellum is responsible for coordination so mice may have trouble walking if the cerebellum is damaged. For these reasons, choice B is better than choice D.

13. **C is the best answer.** Glutamate serves many functions, especially in the nervous system. Glutamate is an excitatory neurotransmitter. Damage to inhibitory neurons may cause release of inhibitory neurotransmitters but not excitatory ones so choice A can be eliminated. Glutamate is also an amino acid that is used to make proteins. Synthesis of proteins would decreased levels of glutamate, so choice B can be eliminated. Glutamate can also serve as a source of energy by entering the citric acid cycle as α-ketoglutarate. If the citric acid cycle is slowed, glutamate levels may rise because it is not being metabolized. The citric acid cycle often slows during anaerobic respiration, which is indicated by the elevated level of lactate if Figure 2. Choice C is a strong answer. Figure 2 shows that, at 3 weeks, glutamate levels in *Npc1*$^{-/-}$ mice are elevated compared to controls, so choice D is inaccurate and can be eliminated.

Stand Alones 5 (Questions 14-16)

14. **B is best answer.** The mitochondria are responsible for generating ATP from NADH and $FADH_2$, regenerating NAD^+ and FAD. This is achieved through a proton gradient in the intermembrane space. If this gradient is lost, the mitochondrion is likely damaged and may be destroyed. Option I is likely a component of the correct answer. Destruction of mitochondria would lead to a buildup of NADH and $FADH_2$, not NAD^+ and FAD so option II is not accurate and choices A, C and D can be ruled out. cAMP is made when concentrations of ATP are low which would be expected when mitochondria are damaged. This isn't knowledge explicitly required by the MCAT® but it is logical. The cell only has so much adenosine, which can exist as ATP, ADP, AMP, or cAMP. When ATP is low, ATP has not be destroyed, just converted to a lower energy form. If ATP is low, ADP, AMP, and or cAMP must be high. Option III is likely a component of the correct answer which makes choice B the best answer.

15. **C is the best answer.** Unsaturated fat differs from saturated fat in terms of the number of bonds between carbon and hydrogen. Saturated fat is considered fully saturated with hydrogen bonds, whereas unsaturated fat has carbon-carbon double bonds. Unsaturated fat stores fewer calories per unit they have less electrons and therefore less reducing potential. Less reducing potential means less ATP formed and fewer calories. Choice A is incorrect as this states the opposite. Choice C is correct because it correctly identifies the relationship between unsaturated fat and storing fewer calories. This would account for why it is more healthy, since more of it can be eaten and burned to produce the same amount of energy as would be produced from less saturated fat. Choice B is not accurate as both types of fat can be broken down or stored depending on the need. Choice D is also inaccurate as neither is typically converted to glucose with the exception of odd-chain fatty acids and glycerol.

16. **D is the best answer.** Blood sugar levels are controlled by glucagon and insulin, making choices A and B less likely than choices C and D. Glucagon leads to an increase of glucose in the bloodstream while insulin causes a decrease in blood sugar, like the change in the question. Choice D is the best answer.

Passage 4 (Questions 17-20)

17. **A is the best answer.** Similar to carbohydrates and fats, proteins can be used as a source of energy to create ATP. Protein breakdown, called catabolism, occurs primarily in the fasting state. Protein formation, or anabolism, occurs primarily in the fed state. This means that increased breakdown of PrP should occur in the fasting state. Gluconeogenesis, the synthesis of glucose from oxaloacetate, occurs in the fasting state as well, eliminating choice B. Oxidation of fatty acids to create acetyl-CoA to power the citric acid cycle also occurs in the fasting state, eliminating choice C. Ketone body synthesis is the end stage of fasting and works to create ketone bodies that can be used by the brain as an energy source. This eliminates choice D. Glycolysis is the oxidation of glucose to pyruvate, which occurs in the fed, not fasting state. Because this is the opposite scenario that would co-occur with protein catabolism, choice A is the best answer.

18. **A is the best answer.** The lysosome is an acidic organelle in the cell that is responsible for breaking down peptides. According to information contained in the passage, the lysosomes of CJD patients are defective and unable to break down PrP^{Sc} peptides. The reaction that breaks down peptide bonds into amino acids is called a hydrolysis reaction and occurs when water attacks the electrophilic carbon of the carbonyl. A peptide of n amino acids reacting with one water molecule would produce a peptide of n-1 amino acids and one free amino acid. Because the reaction is in an acidic environment in the lysosome, not a basic environment, choice B can be eliminated. Carboxypeptidase is an enzyme that breaks down peptide bonds in the small intestine, not the lysosome, eliminating choice C. One water molecule frees one amino acid, not three amino acids, eliminating choice D. Choice A is the best answer choice because it depicts an acid-catalyzed hydrolysis of a peptide to free one amino acid.

19. **A is the best answer.** According to the passage, PrP^{Sc} aggregates when it cannot be degraded effectively by the lysosome. In the hydrophilic cytosol, proteins that are hydrophobic, or contain a stretch of nonpolar amino acids, have a tendency to aggregate to avoid associating with water. Arginine, R, lysine, K, aspartate, D, and glutamate, E, are all polar amino acids that are charged. Because they are relatively evenly dispersed in sequence B, it does not have a long stretch of nonpolar amino acids. This eliminates choice B. Threonine, T, tyrosine, Y, and serine, S, are polar amino acids that are also hydrophilic, not hydrophobic, eliminating choice C. Cysteine, C, serine, S, and histidine, H, are also polar amino acids that are hydrophilic, eliminating choice D. Only choice A contains an unbroken stretch of nonpolar amino acids including alanine, A, valine, V, leucine, L, isoleucine, I, proline, P, and methionine, M. These nonpolar amino acids could aggregate together in the hydrophilic environment of the cytosol, making choice A the best answer.

20. **A is the best answer.** The lysosome is one of the organelles that is responsible for breaking down proteins, primarily by spitting the protein bonds with high levels of acid. Lysosomes are more acidic than other organelles of the cell. Additionally, the passage describes that CJD patients have defective lysosomes compared to normal individuals. The lysosome would fail to break down proteins if it were not acidic enough. The lysosome, not the cytoplasm, would have a lower pH needed to break down proteins, eliminating choice B. The lysosome in normal patients would have an acidic pH, eliminating choice C. The cytoplasm in normal patients should be around a pH of 7, not an acidic pH, eliminating choice D. Choice A is the best answer because it depicts a normal cytoplasmic pH for both patients and a less acidic lysosome in CJD patients versus normal individuals. The increased pH would prevent PrP^{Sc} proteins from being broken down as effectively, contributing to the pathogenesis of the disease.

Passage 5 (Questions 21-25)

21. **C is the best answer.** The graph shows that BBR reduces the amount of mRNA that hepatic cells produce. Reduced mRNA will cause a decrease in the amount of G6Pase and PEPCK present in the cell. These two enzymes are essential for gluconeogenesis. By administering BBR, the amount of these essential gluconeogenic enzymes decreases which will cause the rate of gluconeogenesis in the hepatic cell to decrease as well. When the rate of gluconeogenesis decreases, the concentration of blood glucose will also decrease. Choice A and B can be eliminated because they state an inverse relationship between gluconeogenesis and blood glucose concentration, but they actually have a direct relationship. Gluconeogenesis produces glucose and raises the concentration of glucose in the blood. If gluconeogenesis decreases, blood glucose concentration will decrease as well. Choice D can be eliminated because the graph shows that the level of mRNA for essential enzymes changes. The change in the level of mRNA will affect the amount of enzyme present which will change both the rate of gluconeogenesis and blood glucose concentration.

22. **B is the best answer.** This question has two parts. The first part is to identify in which state these transcription factors will be the most active. The transcription factors lead to an increase in essential gluconeogenic enzymes. During the fasting state, glucagon is released. The liver is an altruistic tissue and will respond by producing glucose through gluconeogenesis. The increase in gluconeogenesis is due to an increase in the level of enzymes as a result of activation of these transcription factors. The second part of the question is asking about the level of ATP in the liver cells. This piece of information can be found from Figure 1. Berberine inhibits the mitochondria which decreases the level of ATP in the cell. This then decreases the activity of the transcription factors. In an opposite condition without Berberine, the mitochondria produce ATP and this activates the transcription factors. A hepatic cell cannot carry out gluconeogenesis if it does not have the means to first produce energy for itself. Choice A and C can be eliminated because in a fed state gluconeogenesis is not active and the transcription factors that activate gluconeogenic enzymes will have low activity. Choice B is better than choice D because in a condition with low ATP, the liver will need to produce energy to feed itself rather than the rest of the body.

23. **B is the best answer.** This question does not require the passage. Glucose-6-phosphatase is the final enzyme of gluconeogenesis and converts glucose-6-phosphate to glucose. The reverse of this step takes place during glycolysis. Glycolysis takes place within the cytosol and most of gluconeogenesis takes place here as well. Additionally, gluconeogenesis only takes place in the liver and the kidney. Choice B is correct because it matches the correct location within the cell as well as the cell type. Choice A and D can be eliminated because the final stages of gluconeogenesis do not take place in the mitochondria. Choice C can be eliminated because only the liver and the kidney are able to carry out gluconeogenesis .

24. **D is the best answer.** This question is asking why mRNA was examined rather than enzyme activity. To answer this question, it is important to understand the mode of regulation that is discussed in this passage. The passage specifically discusses the transcription factors which leads to mRNA transcription. Nothing in the passage specifically talks about the activity level of the gluconeogenic enzymes. The correct answer needs to focus on the transcription factors. While correct, choice A can be eliminated because the mode of regulation discussed in the passage is at the transcription level. The scientists were not concerned with allosteric regulators. It is important that the correct answer matches both the question as well as the passage. Choice B can be eliminated because it is worded too definitively and is not always correct. Hormones can act through other means rather than transcriptional control. Choice C can be eliminated because there are methods of measuring enzyme activity.

25. **C is the best answer.** Berberine is an inhibitor of gluconeogenesis. FoxO1 is a transcription factor that promotes gluconeogenesis. Inhibition of FoxO1 will cause the rate of gluconeogenesis to decrease. The brain is a tissue that heavily relies on blood glucose as its source of energy. During periods of low blood glucose, gluconeogenesis becomes essential in order to maintain sufficient levels of glucose for the brain to use for metabolism. Choice A is can be eliminated because during periods of high blood glucose, gluconeogenesis is not needed to maintain glucose levels. Choice B is can be eliminated because fatty acid metabolism is sufficient to provide energy to all tissues that are able to carry out this process. Fatty acid metabolism is not a direct indicator of low blood glucose and is not the best answer choice. Choice D can be eliminated because the muscles have glycogen stores available to them as well as the ability to carry out fatty acid metabolism.

Stand Alones (Questions 26-29)

26. **D is the best answer.** Glucokinase in an enzyme involved in glycolysis. Metabolic enzymes are composed of amino acids. The breakdown of amino acids to get rid of nitrogen and recover the carbon backbone for processes like gluconeogenesis begins by removing the nitrogen group, producing ammonia and a carbon chain. The ammonia is fed into the urea cycle to become urea, which is a water-soluble molecule that is later eliminated in the urine. While most of the process occurs in the cytosol, the urea cycle also takes place in the mitochondria. Choices A and B can be eliminated because the nitrogen contained in the urea molecule is water-soluble, not fat-soluble, so it will be eliminated in the kidney and not in the bile. Because the urea cycle takes place in the mitochondria and cytosol, not the nucleus and peroxisome, choice C can be eliminated to make choice D the best answer choice.

27. **A is the best answer.** The question is asking for an effective means of evaluating the basis of the high lactate for a collection of cells with a flavoprotein deficiency. Despite the presence of unfamiliar names in the passage, the answer can be determined without memorization. FAD, or flavin adenine dinucleotide, is an important cofactor for pyruvate dehydrogenase as well as other enzymes. The actual supplementation is not significant, since riboflavin is necessary to make FAD and is converted to it. If the experiment is carried out correctly, the specific inhibition should mimic the effects of the flavoprotein deficiency. Choice A is the best answer, since the lack of activity of pyruvate dehydrogenase to convert pyruvate to acetyl-CoA can result in increased lactate production from pyruvate. Choice B is inaccurate, since this enzyme is involved in gluconeogenesis. A failure to carry out gluconeogenesis should not lead to increased lactate production, since the pyruvate can be made to acetyl-CoA and can be made to ketone bodies, can be made to fatty acids or can be broken down further. One can notice from the name that the enzyme attaches a carboxylic acid to pyruvate, and this represent increasing the number of carbons. Choice C is a case where an important enzyme of glycolysis is inhibited. Such an inhibition could not cause an excess of lactate, since pyruvate cannot be made where glycolysis is inhibited. The name implies that the enzyme adds a phosphate group to a fructose that has a phosphate group already. This is the step in glycolysis of converting fructose-6-phosphate to fructose-1,6-bisphosphate. Choice D involves glycogen synthesis, and the hint is that the enzyme converts a glucose-1-phosphate, which is a building block of glycogen. The glycogen pathway should have no effect on lactate.

28. **A is the best answer.** This question is somewhat ambiguous as it asks about the different effects on glycogen synthesis that can be seen and measured as a result of insulin. Though there are many specific details in the question and the answer choices, there is no need to memorize information about glycogen synthesis to answer the question correctly. Insulin exerts its effect on metabolic pathways through the increased expression of enzymes, altered phosphorylation sites, and changes in external factors. Insulin itself is a polypeptide hormone that is polar and binds to a receptor on the cell surface to trigger a cascade of effects inside the cell. Choice A is an appropriate measurement, since insulin could conceivably alter the gene expression of glycogen synthase to increase its expression such that more glycogen can be made. Choice B is inaccurate, since insulin will not bind to the enzyme directly, since it signals from outside the cell by a signal cascade. Choice C is tricky, since the stem only mentions glucose-1-phosphate, though one should recognize that insulin has many effects on metabolism and increases or decreases in glucose-6-phosphate can result in effects on glycogen synthase by allosteric regulation. Choice D is an appropriate measurement, since insulin may result in an increase in kinases or phosphatases that have effects on enzyme function by phosphorylating or dephosphorylating glycogen synthase.

29. **C is the best answer.** The best fit line on the scatter plot shows a inverse relationship between the concentrations of molecule A and molecule B. An example of this would be a compound that is consumed in order to produce a second compound. Choice A is not likely to be the best answer choice because NADPH and NADH are both produced as a product of glucose entering in the cell, with NADPH through the Pentose Phosphate Pathway and NADH through glycolysis and the Citric Acid Cycle. Choice B can be eliminated because $FADH_2$ and GTP are both produced in the Citric Acid Cycle, so would have a positive linear relationship. 5-ribulose, a 5-carbon sugar, and NADPH are both produced from the pentose phosphate pathway beginning with glucose-6-phosphate. The concentrations of both 5-ribulose and NADPH should increase when the pentose phosphate pathway is running. When the pyruvate concentration is high, it is because one glucose molecule has been used to create two pyruvate molecules. Thus, molecule A would be represented by pyruvate, while molecule B would be represented by glucose. This inverse relationship is depicted in the figure and makes choice C the best answer choice. Choices A, B, and D all show positive direct relationships.

Passage 6 (Questions 30-33)

30. **C is the best answer.** The passage states that celiac disease is caused by a cell mediated response to the polypeptide gluten. Gluten is therefore a protein and avoiding glucose-containing foods would not be helpful so choice A can be ruled out. White blood cells are responsible for the symptoms of celiac disease but destruction of white blood cells would put a person at risk for serious infection so choice B can be ruled out. Giving a protease with a gluten containing meal may be helpful. The protease could destroy the gluten so choice C is a strong answer. Choice D is a vague answer that would not clearly have any effect on celiac disease.

31. **B is the best answer.** Isotretinoin is similar in structure to vitamin A which is a fatty vitamin along with vitamins D, E and K. Fats are metabolized mostly in the mitochondria so choice B is the best answer. The cytosol is the site of glucose metabolism. The smooth ER is the site of fat synthesis but not catabolism so choice C can be ruled out. Very little metabolism occurs outside of cells so choice D can be ruled out.

32. **A is best answer.** The passage states that the authors measured celiac disease in those with and without prior isotretinoin exposure. Ensuring that isotretinoin was used prior is a way to control for temporality. Choices C and D can be eliminated. Table 1 indicates that 1.8% of those exposed to isotretinoin developed celiac disease and 1.4% of those not exposed to isotretinoin developed celiac disease. This is associated with a p value of 0.474 which is well above the level of 0.05 which is used to indicate statistical significance. From these findings, there is no relationship between isotretinoin and celiac disease so choice A is the best answer.

33. **D is the best answer.** The passage states that isotretinoin can bind nuclear receptors. Steroid hormones also do this so choice A is true and thus not the best answer. Isotretinoin is a modified form of vitamin A which is a fatty vitamin. Dietary fats are absorbed in the gut and transported in lipoproteins called chylomicrons. Choice B is true and thus not the best answer. Fats can be metabolized to ketone bodies so choice C is true and thus not the best answer. Lipase is the enzyme responsible for the production of free fatty acids from triacylglycerides. Isotretinoin is not a triacylglyceride so choice D is not accurate and thus the best answer.

Passage 7 (Questions 34-38)

34. **B is the best answer.** Choice A can be eliminated because during ischemia (low O_2), oxidative phosphorylation is not occurring and the ATP synthase is not active. PCr is used in cells because during times of low oxygen concentration, it can be coupled to the production of high energy molecules such as ATP through substrate-level phosphorylation, not through oxidative phosphorylation (ATP synthase). The recovery rate of PCr is an indicator of the rate at which ATP is being produced through oxidative phosphorylation. If PCr concentration is increasing, it means that oxidative phosphorylation has taken over the production of ATP in the cell. Additionally, oxidative phosphorylation produces ATP much faster than substrate-level phosphorylation and it determines ATP_{max}. Choice B is the best answer. Substrate-phosphorylation always requires the coupling of chemical reactions in order to provide the energy for ATP formation; however, there are numerous high energy compounds that can be coupled to this process. Choice C can be eliminated because its wording is too definite. While choice D is partly true, it is not the best answer. PCr is a marker of cellular energy but it is not a direct marker of a functioning electron transport chain. PCr only serves as a marker of ATP concentration in the cell and cannot be used to determine the function of the electron transport chain.

35. **C is the best answer.** The question is asking in which area of the mitochondria does a proton gradient build up. The question stem is confusing because it asks where protons are pumped after the recovery of PCr. The recovery of PCr is an indicator of oxidative phosphorylation; however, to answer this question it is only important to know where protons are pumped prior to passing through the ATP synthase. The electron transport chain pumps protons out of the mitochondrial matrix and into the mitochondrial intermembrane space. This causes a buildup of protons which can then pass through the ATP synthase and generate ATP . Choice A can be eliminated because it indicates where the protons are pumped out of rather than where they go. Choice B can be eliminated because protons do not pass into the cytosol. The ATP synthase is within the mitochondria so the answer choice will at least contain a place associated with it. Choice C is the best answer because protons are pumped into the intermembrane space. Choice D can be eliminated because ATP synthase is not associated with the extracellular space.

TEST 3B A&E

36. **A is the best answer.** P/O is the production of ATP relative to O_2 consumed. A reduction in P/O means greater amounts of O_2 are needed to maintain ATP_{max}. O_2 is consumed in the mitochondria during the oxidation of NADH to NAD^+. The increased rate of oxygen consumption seen in cells treated with PQ can be explained by more NADH passing electrons through the electron transport chain. Additionally, the large amount of NADH will also result in maintaining the maximum amount of ATP production. Choice A is a strong answer because it provides evidence that P/O can be reduced and ATP_{max} can be maintained. Choice B can be eliminated because changing the amount of ATP synthase proteins would alter the ATP_{max}. The ATP synthase is responsible for producing ATP and by increasing the amount of this protein, the amount of ATP would also be increased. Choice C can be eliminated because it suggests that oxidative phosphorylation is not occurring and this is not true. Pyruvate only converts to lactic acid when oxygen is not available and oxidative phosphorylation has stopped. The passage indicates that mitochondrial ATP production is occurring which means that pyruvate will be fed into the Kreb Cycle rather than be converted to lactic acid. Choice D can be eliminated because increasing the amount of glucose transporters would not alter the metabolism of the cell. Storage mechanisms would remove excess glucose and metabolism would remain the same.

37. **A is the best answer.** A partial uncoupling of the proton gradient from the electron transport chain can be overcome by an increase in the amount of electrons that are passed through. The maintenance of ATP_{max} along with the increased level of oxygen consumption suggests that this is the case. By passing more electrons through the electron transport chain, more oxygen is consumed because it is the final electron receptor. ATP_{max} is maintained because additional protons are pumped in order to make up for the loss of some. Choice A is the best answer. Choice B can be eliminated because the P/O alone is not sufficient evidence. It would be possible that the amount of ATP produced decreased and that was responsible for the decrease P/O, but this is not what is described in the passage. Choice C can be eliminated because the disrupted proton gradient can be overcome by a large amount of protons being pumped. Additional protons being pumped can make up for the loss of some of the protons. Choice D can be eliminated because it is stated in the passage that there is an increased rate of oxygen consumption. The increased rate of oxygen consumption is evidence that the electron transport chain is still functioning properly.

38. **C is the best answer.** The question is asking how the amount of electron carriers effects the oxygen consumption of the cell. A soluble electron carrier such as NADH or $FADH_2$ serves to pass electrons to the electron transport chain. If twice as many electrons are passing through the electron transport chain, it must mean that there is twice the amount of oxygen being consumed. The equation for P/O can be found on the y-axis label of Figure 1. Choice A can be eliminated because it is the inverse of the correct answer. Oxygen consumption is in the denominator of the P/O ratio, so doubling oxygen consumption would not double the ratio. Choice B can be eliminated because it shows that there is no change to the P/O ratio. The question stem states that ATP production remains the same but the oxygen consumption will change. The P/O ratio must be changing as well since only one of the variables is being effected. Choice C is the best answer. By doubling the oxygen consumption, the P/O ratio is cut in half because oxygen consumption is in the denominator. Choice D can be eliminated because it is half of the correct answer. This is a trap answer and uses the formula for P/O incorrectly. The P/O ratio already includes the 2 in the denominator so it does not need to be included when determining how the P/O ratio changes.

Passage 8 (Questions 39-42)

39. **C is the best answer.** The pentose phosphate pathway uses glucose to create reducing equivalents for reactions that build macromolecules, also known as anabolic reactions. NADH is formed in catabolic reactions, like glycolysis and the citric acid cycle, and is used to generate ATP in the mitochondrial electron transport chain. The PPP does not produce NADH, eliminating choice A. NAD^+ is an important co-factor in glycolysis but is not created during the PPP, eliminating choice B. $NADP^+$ is a reactant co-factor in the pentose phosphate pathway that is reduced to form NADPH. Because $NADP^+$ is used, not made, choice D is less likely to be the best answer. The two main roles of the pentose phosphate pathway are to create NADPH, which can be used to help build macromolecules, and to create 5-carbon molecules that serve as the building blocks for nucleotides. This makes choice C the best answer choice.

40. **B is the best answer.** The data in Figure 2 show that tumor volume of KRAS wild type but not KRAS G13D mutant tumors decreases upon ixazomib treatment. This is presumably due to reduced growth and proliferation in the KRAS wild type cancer cells relative to KRAS G13D cells. Nucleotides, such as CTP, are important building blocks of DNA in cells. After treatment with ixazomib, KRAS G13D mutant tumors would still be proliferating at a high rate, meaning that they would need a constant supply of CTP to help synthesize new DNA. This makes option I a component of the best answer. Similarly, cholesterol uptake would be greater in the KRAS G13D mutant tumors, as cholesterol is an important building block of the plasma membrane of cells. This makes option II a component of the best answer. NADPH is a molecule produced in the pentose phosphate pathway that is used to help build macromolecules that a cell needs to survive and proliferate. The untreated tumors show relatively even growth over the 20 days plotted in the two figures. It is more likely that they would have relatively equal concentrations of NADPH, which could be used to help build the macromolecules needed for cell proliferation and division, making option III less likely to be part of the best answer. Choice A can be eliminated because increased cholesterol uptake would likely be seen in treated KRAS G13D tumors. Choice C can be eliminated because NAPDH levels should be comparable in the untreated tumors. Choice D can be eliminated for the same reason. Choice B is the best answer because treated KRAS G13D tumors do not show a decrease in growth compared to the KRAS WT tumors and would require more building blocks for new cells.

41. **A is the best answer.** According to the last paragraph, ixazomib treatment results in increased breakdown of glycogen and increased movement and breakdown of fatty acids. Insulin is the hormone that is released from the pancreas when circulating levels of glucose are high. It induces storage of glucose as glycogen and the synthesis of fatty acids. Because the effect of insulin is opposite that of ixazomib, choice B can be eliminated. PTH is the parathyroid hormone that breaks down bone to release calcium into the blood stream. The passage does not imply that ixazomib treatment changes circulating calcium levels, eliminating choice C. LH is the hormone that induces ovulation and helps with sperm maturation in females and males, respectively. Ixazomib is not described to play a role in sexual development, making choice D unlikely to be the best answer. Glucagon is the hormone that acts opposite to insulin and is released from the pancreas in times of low glucose. It stimulates the breakdown of glycogen and increases β-oxidation, meaning it mimics some of the effects observed with ixazomib treatment. This makes choice A the best answer choice.

42. **A is the best answer.** According to the question stem, the G13D mutation that changes glycine to aspartic acid in KRAS renders the enzyme constitutively active. Normally enzymes can be turned on or off through multiple levels of regulation, including the presence or absence of a phosphate. The mutation removes the need for this phosphate to turn on KRAS, making it always active. Compared to the wild type tumors, KRAS G13D mutant tumors are resistant to treatment and can grow regardless of proteasome function. Tumor suppressor genes help prevent cancer formation, which is the opposite of the action of KRAS, eliminating choice B. A phosphatase is an enzyme that removes a phosphate group from target proteins. The passage and the question stem do not suggest that KRAS acts to change phosphorylation status of other proteins, only that the mutation removes that level of regulation of the KRAS enzyme itself. Choice C can be eliminated. The passage also does not imply that KRAS binds DNA to increase the transcription of other genes. This makes it less likely to be a transcription factor, eliminating choice D. An oncogene drives cancer growth and formation. Upon mutation, cells that harbor KRAS G13D become more cancerous and resistant to treatment, making choice A the best answer choice.

Stand Alones (Questions 43-46)

43. **B is the best answer.** Riboflavin is a B vitamin that is used as a coenzyme in many metabolic reactions. A key function of riboflavin is production of flavins like FAD and FMN that can be used in flavoproteins in the electron transport chain. Choice A is true and can be ruled out. Metalloproteins are proteins that include a metal . Cytochromes in the electron transport chain include iron and are therefore metalloproteins. Metalloproteins may or may not also utilize flavins. The two are closely related but not synonymous so choice B is a strong answer. Riboflavin can be modified to make FAD and FMN which can be reduced to $FADH_2$ and $FMNH_2$. So, riboflavin can be used to make a reducing agent or an oxidizing agent. Choices C and D are true and thus not the best answers.

TEST 3B A&E

44. **C is the best answer.** This question is asking why electrons pass successively to each electron carrier. Choice A can be eliminated because oxidative potential is the ability of a molecule to donate electrons. Successive electron receptors receive electrons, so increased oxidative potential is the opposite of the correct answer. Choice B can be eliminated because it is favorable for electrons to pass down the electron transport chain. A high (positive) Gibbs free energy would indicate that it is less favorable and the electron transport chain would not function properly. Choice C is the best answer because it correctly describes the property of successive electron receptors. The reduction potential is how likely a molecule is to accept electrons. Electrons flow down the electron transport chain because successive electron receptors have a greater reduction potential and are able to strip the electrons from the previous electron receptors. Choice D can be eliminated because this property does not influence why electrons are passed down the electron transport chain. Electronegativity pertains to the polarity of molecules and not as much to the electron transport chain.

45. **C is the best answer.** Acetyl-CoA is the secondary product of glycolysis and the primary product of β-oxidation. Excess acetyl-CoA would be stored either as fats or be shunted into ketogenesis, which is the process of making ketones. Ketones, namely acetone and β-hydroxybutyrate, serve as reserve fuels for red blood cells and the brain during period of starvation, eliminating choice A. Excess acetyl-CoA would also be converted into a three carbon malonyl-CoA, which is the starting molecule for fatty acid synthesis. High concentrations of acetyl-CoA would drive storage of excess energy as fat, eliminating choice B. Acetyl-CoA feeds into the citric acid cycle, which makes the reducing equivalents that feed into oxidative phosphorylation to make ATP. Excess acetyl-CoA would increase the formation of ATP by phosphorylating ADP, eliminating choice D. LDL particles are a type of lipoprotein that contains fats and cholesterol. Cells with high concentrations of fats would be unlikely to absorb more fats by increasing their uptake of LDL particles, making choice C the best answer.

46. **D is the best answer.** Amino acids are able to be used for gluconeogenesis as well as ketogenesis, harnessing these molecules for ATP production. Thus, options I and II are in the correct answer. Next, there are both protein and amino-acid derived hormones in the body, so option III is also correct and choice D is the best answer.

Passage 9 (Questions 47-50)

47. **A is the best answer.** The two figures show acidification rate and presence of lactate in the extracellular space. When discussing metabolism, lactate is always linked to fermentation, which generates lactic acid. As with all acids, lactic acid can dissociate into a proton and its conjugate base, lactate. This process increases acidity due to the released proton. This closely matches choice A, which correctly states how they dissociate and. This also rules out choices B because lactate does not dissociate into lactic acid and a proton. Choice C correctly states the dissociation, but is a poor answer because the results actually support each other. Carnosine decreases ECAR and lactate levels. Choice D is unlikely for the same reason as choice B, which is that it incorrectly states the dissociation reaction. The latter indicates that carnosine decreases lactic acid production, which in turn would decrease acid. This means that the results support each other, making choice A the best answer.

48. **A is the best answer.** The aerobic metabolic processes like the electron transport chain depend on reduced electron carriers getting into the mitochondria. Choice A is a good answer because reduced electron carriers in the cytoplasm can be moved into the mitochondria, leading to ATP production. Choices B and C are not as likely as choice A because pyruvate and glucose are slightly farther in sequence from the electron transport chain and generating ATP using aerobic processes. Glucose is the first compound going into glycolysis, and pyruvate is the end product of glycolysis. Lastly, administration of protons to the cytoplasm would not impact the proton gradient within the mitochondria required to generate ATP. Choice D is not likely, and choice A is the best answer.

49. **B is the best answer.** The Warburg effect is characterized by massively increased glycolysis with lowered levels of oxidative phosphorylation. These processes occur in the cytoplasm and mitochondria, respectively. No major ATP production occurs in the nucleus, making choices A unlikely. Next, if glycolysis is dramatically increased, then choice B is the best answer. Choice C is unlikely since oxidative phosphorylation is decreased in these cells. Choice D is unlikely for the same reason as choice A, as no major ATP production occurs in the vacuoles.

50. **D is the best answer.** Carnosine reduces fermentation based on the reduction in ECAR and lactate levels . When these are reduced, it can be inferred that fermentation is reduced. Fermentation is required for cancer cells to continue glycolysis because it regenerates NAD+, a key reactant in glycolysis. Choice A is unlikely because glycolysis is reduced by carnosine. Glycolysis is key to cell growth due to its generation of carbon molecules and ATP. Choice B is unlikely since increased growth will not occur if glycolysis is inhibited. Choice C is unlikely for the same reason as choice A. This makes choice D the best answer. Carnosine reduces glycolysis through reduction of fermentation, leading to a reduced growth rate.

Passage 10 (Questions 51-55)

51. **B is the best answer.** Enzymes are typically named after their substrate although rarely they are named by their product. So, glucose-6-phosphate is likely the substrate for G6PD. Dehydrogenases remove hydrogen atoms (a proton and an electron) and thus perform oxidations on the substrate. So, the correct product should sound like an oxidized from of glucose-6-phosphate. Choice A is glucose. Glucose would be a dephosphorylated glucose-6-phosphate with no change in oxidation state, so choice A is unlikely. Choice B is called 6-phosphogluconolactone. Notice that it has a ketone present. Ketones are made from oxidization of the hydroxyl groups on glucose, so choice B is a likely answer. Choice C is ribose. Ribose is a 5-carbon sugar that is made by the pentose phosphate pathway but not by G6PD, so choice C is not a strong answer. Choice D is fructose 1,6 bisphosphate. Fructose 1,6 bisphosphate is an intermediate in glycolysis. It can be made by adding another phosphate to fructose-6-phosphate which can be made from glucose-6-phosphate. Neither of those reactions are oxidations, so choice D is not a strong answer. This leaves choice B as the best answer.

52. **A is the best answer.** Research ethics are very important to scientific design and are sometimes tested on the MCAT®. A common reason to perform experiments on cells is that it is unethical to infect people with diseases. Both choice A and B mention this so these are strong answers. Choice C and D are not relevant to ethics, so they are not as likely. Between choices A and B, it is necessary to determine what cells were used. The passage states monocytes were used for the experiment. Monocytes are the macrophages of the blood and are phagocytes, so choice A is the best answer. The granulocytes include neutrophils, basophils, and eosinophils.

53. **C is best answer.** Figure 3 shows that cells with G6PD deficiency and dengue virus have the highest amount of oxidative stress, followed by dengue virus without G6PD deficiency, followed by G6PD deficiency alone. Patients with dengue virus are at risk for destruction of red blood cells and white blood cells and this may be due to the oxidative stress on the cells. The purpose of the experiment was to determine differences between normal and G6PD patients, not uninfected and infected individuals. Although choice A is a true statement, it is probably not the best answer. Choice B is disproven by the data in Figure 2, G6PD deficiency puts patients at greater risk for dengue virus so this is not the best answer. G6PD deficiency does result in decreased levels of the antioxidant GSH which may be why there is excessive oxidative stress in these patients. Choice C is a strong answer. According to Figure 3, dengue virus and G6PD deficiency are both associated with oxidative stress but we cannot determine if they cause oxidative stress. Causal claims are very difficult to make and this experiment does not control for enough confounding variables or control for temporality so choice D is not the best answer.

54. **B is the best answer.** The pentose phosphate pathway is essential for production of ribose, which is used to make DNA and RNA, so choice A is a false statement. Choice B is true and is an important general concept. Inborn errors in metabolism are usually fatal if there is a complete loss of an enzyme. In general the errors that are found in adults are only partial decreases in enzymatic function. Choice C is possible but very uncommon. For some cells to have normal enzyme, those cells must have a different gene. This is only possible when a person is a chimera where he or she has some cells with one gene and some cells with another gene. It is very uncommon, so choice C is not as good as choice B. Determining if the mutation is autosomal dominant or recessive is not relevant to disease severity. For example, cystic fibrosis is autosomal recessive and is fatal. Huntington disease is autosomal dominant and is also fatal. As it turns out, G6PD deficiency is X-linked recessive, but that knowledge is not required or helpful in answering this question.

55. **D is the best answer.** The questions is asking which enzyme is in the same class as G6PD and can be found in glycolysis. So, the answer choice should be a dehydrogenase. Choices A and B are not dehydrogenases, but they do act on six carbon sugars. In that way, they are similar to G6PD but the mechanism is likely very different, because they are not dehydrogenases. Pyruvate dehydrogenase is not an enzyme found in glycolysis. Pyruvate is the final product of glycolysis and is oxidized by pyruvate dehydrogenase after glycolysis. Enzymes are typically named for their substrates, so knowing that pyruvate is the final product in glycolysis is sufficient knowledge to assume that pyruvate dehydrogenase is not found in glycolysis. Glyceraldehyde-3-phosphate dehydrogenase oxidizes GAP (glyceraldehyde-3-phosphate) to DHAP (dihydroxyacetone phosphate). This is a step in glycolysis and is a dehydrogenation, so choice D is the best answer.

Stand Alones (Questions 56-59)

56. **A is the best answer.** This question can be answered with reasoning or with pure memorization. The role of the oxidative phase of the pentose phosphate pathway is NADPH production. NADPH is a reducing agent is used mostly to regenerate GSH which is an antioxidant, meaning it is sacrificed and oxidized instead of other molecules. The non-oxidative phase is used to produce ribose, a 5-carbon sugar (pentose), which is used to make nucleotides found in DNA and RNA. This is exactly what is mentioned in choice A, so choice A is the best answer. Reasoning can also be used to rule out the other answer choices. NAD^+ is the oxidized from of NADH. The oxidative arm of the pentose phosphate pathway refers to oxidation of the sugar substrate which must be coupled to reduction of a cofactor. Since NAD^+ is oxidized it cannot be formed when a sugar is also being oxidized, so choice B can be ruled out. NADPH is made in the oxidative phase of the pentose phosphate pathway because it is a reducing agent. This rules out choice C. The only pathways that generate glucose are glycogenolysis and gluconeogenesis, so choice D can also be ruled out.

57. **B is the best answer.** cAMP is the cyclic form of AMP, which has only one adjoining phosphate group. To form AMP, two phosphate groups must be cleaved from ATP. This cleavage necessarily occurs between the first and second phosphate groups from the 5' position on the ribose derivative. Cleavage at the α-position would result in loss of all three phosphate groups, so choice A can be eliminated. Cleavage at the β-position appropriately characterizes the conversion from ATP to AMP, so choice B is a strong answer. Choice C, cleavage at the γ-position, would describe the conversion from ATP to ADP, so it is a weak choice. Because δ-position exists on this molecule, Choice D is a distractor and can be eliminated.

TEST 3B A&E

58. **A is the best answer.** If carboxin blocks the action of Complex II, one part of the electron transport chain will be inhibited. Notice that the question stem also informs the test taker that this complex has an enzymatic function for an intermediate in the citric acid cycle. That will be important information as each answer choice is considered. If the enzymatic function of this complex is inhibited, the citric acid cycle will not be able to produce fumarate and regenerate the malate intermediate needed to continue the cycle. The citric acid cycle will cease without the ability to complete this step, so choice A is a strong answer. Choice B exaggerates the importance of Complex II as a major regulatory enzyme. It also makes the erroneous claim that the citric acid cycle is reversible. For those reasons, choice B is a weak answer. Although the halting of the citric acid cycle will eventually impair the electron transport chain by halting production of NADH and $FADH_2$, this will not be an immediate effect because electron carriers are already present when carboxin inhibits Complex II. Choice C also mistakenly attributes the ability to reduce oxygen to Complex II when in fact Complex IV is responsible for that process. Choice C can be eliminated. The introduction of carboxin would eventually relieve the proton gradient across the membrane because of the halting of the citric acid cycle, but notice that the situation in choice A proceeds this effect. Also recall that Complex II does not pump protons across the membrane and therefore does not itself contribute to the proton gradient. Choice A states the most immediate effect of this compound and is the best answer.

59. **A is the best answer.** Reactions with a positive ΔG value do not proceed spontaneously. The best answer choice will not proceed without an input of energy or catalysis. Notice that all of the answer choices refer to the absence of some substrate. If the concentration of reagents or products changes such that the reaction quotient Q is no longer equivalent to K_{eq}, the reaction will shift according to Le Châtelier's principle to re-establish equilibrium. When the concentration of products and reagents changes, forward or reverse reactions may become more favorable, which temporarily affects ΔG. While evaluating the answer choices, determine whether each will proceed according to Le Châtelier's principle. If it does not, ΔG will be positive. When ATP is scarce, the cell will face a deficit in its primary energy source. It will need new glucose to produce more ATP, so gluconeogenesis will proceed. Choice A is a strong choice. If cellular glucose and ATP are absent, the cell requires energy but does not have its preferred substrate for ATP synthesis. Under these conditions, fatty acids will undergo beta-oxidation to meet the cell's energetic requirements. Choice B can be eliminated. If levels of acetyl CoA are low, the cell will oxidize pyruvate to replenish the first reagent in the citric acid cycle, so choice C is a weak answer. If the cell lacks ribose, it will be unable to synthesize DNA and undergo cell division. The pentose phosphate pathway will proceed, so choice D can be eliminated. Note that the pentose phosphate pathway can be inhibited by an abundance of NADPH, but it constantly runs within the cell since it serves many different functions. Choice A is the only pathway that will not proceed among those presented.

Metabolism

TEST 3C

ANSWERS & EXPLANATIONS

Questions 1–31

Passage 1 (Questions 1-5)

1. **D is the best answer.** The experiment described in the question and the results presented in the graph show the amount of oxygen consumed in the presence of none, one, or two agonists. CO_2 is produced in the Citric Acid Cycle by decarboxylating isocitrate and α-ketoglutarate, producing an NADH in each step. These NADH molecules are fed into the electron transport chain, generating a proton gradient that consumes oxygen during the process of making ATP. Thus, high levels of NADH production should lead to more flux through the electron transport chain and more consumption of oxygen. The greatest amount of CO_2 produced should correspond to the most oxygen consumed per minute. PPARδ agonism increases the consumption of oxygen and it appears that the confidence interval (CI) does not overlap with the no agonism condition, meaning the difference is statistically significant. However, the PPARδ agonism CI overlaps with that of dual agonism, meaning these two conditions cannot be distinguished. Thus, choice A cannot be correct because it cannot be differentiated from the dual agonism of choice C. AMPK agonism does not significantly increase the amount of oxygen consumed compared to the no agonism control because the confidence intervals overlap. Choice B can be eliminated. Dual agonism cannot be differentiated from single PPARδ agonism, as described above. Choice C can be eliminated. Choice D is the best answer because the confidence intervals of PPARδ agonism and dual PPARδ and AMPK agonism overlap, meaning the consumption of oxygen is not statistically different between the two conditions.

2. **A is the best answer.** The question asks for a plausible reason that the rate of FAO does not increase, despite a corresponding increase in the concentration of enzymes involved in the FAO process. The key point is that, under Michaelis-Menten kinetics, an increase in enzyme concentration will increase the velocity of a reaction. However, if the enzymes are inhibited, the enzyme concentration is irrelevant. High levels of ATP serve as a marker that sufficient energy is being provided to a cell through other substrates, such as glucose. If the glucose concentration is high, flux through glycolysis will be great enough to provide the necessary ATP for cellular functions. High levels of ATP could inhibit the enzymes involved in FAO, making the concentration of FAO-related enzymes irrelevant. This eliminates choice B, which would decrease the protein level of PDK4, but this decrease would not matter for the reaction rate. The relationship between AMPK and PDK4 would also be irrelevant if ATP served to inhibit both enzymes, eliminating choice C. As described, the rate of reaction is dependent upon the concentration of an enzyme but this property becomes irrelevant if the enzymes are inhibited by high ATP levels, eliminating choice D. If FAO were determined by additional conditions, such as ATP demand, the levels of proteins could change but the amount of overall FAO could not. This would be especially true if ATP served as an allosteric inhibitor of the various enzymes. If ATP levels are high, FAO would most likely not be occurring, making choice A the best answer choice.

3. **B is the best answer.** Pyruvate dehydrogenase (PDH) is responsible for taking pyruvate derived from glycolysis and converting it into acetyl-CoA, which is fed into the Citric Acid Cycle. One of the Citric Acid Cycle intermediates, oxaloacetate, is the four-carbon source for gluconeogenesis, or the synthesis of glucose. Oxaloacetate is converted into phosphoenolpyruvate (PEP) and runs through gluconeogenesis, which is essentially glycolysis in reverse, to make glucose. Overexpression of PDK4 would lead to increased inactivation of PDH, causing fewer acetyl-CoA molecules to be produced, decreasing the amount of oxaloacetate. Choice A is unlikely to be the best answer because PDK4 overexpression would decrease, not increase, oxaloacetate levels. Choice A is true of pyruvate and the other intermediates in gluconeogenesis, but none of these are four-carbon molecules. Choice C can be eliminated because overexpression would decrease the flux through the Citric Acid cycle, lowering the amount of oxaloacetate. Choice D is reserved for when the question stem does not relate to a particular pathway or no link between pathways can be established. Because PDH creates the raw starting materials for the Citric Acid Cycle, choice D can be eliminated. Choice B is the best answer choice because PDK4 overexpression, leading to decreased acetyl-CoA production, would decrease oxaloacetate concentrations.

4. **C is the best answer.** In Figure 1 shows that both PPARδ and AMPK agonism increase PDK4 mRNA, thought PPARδ increased mRNA levels to a much greater extent than does AMPK agonism. In contrast, Figure 2 shows that both agonists increase PDK4 protein levels but AMPK4 agonism increases protein levels significantly more than PPARδ agonism. The best answer will explain a lower mRNA level could still correspond to a greater increase in protein level. Choice A is unlikely to be the best answer because an increase in ribosome synthesis would lead to more ribosomes that would increase in protein levels in PPARδ versus AMPK agonism. Because this is not the trend seen in Figure 2, choice A can be eliminated. Destabilization of nascent RNA transcripts that are not spliced and are still in the nucleus would decrease both mRNA and protein levels in the AMPK agonist condition relative to the PPARδ agonist. Because protein levels are increased in AMPK agonism over PPARδ agonism, choice B can be eliminated. Choice D is unlikely to be the best answer because ribosome proteolysis would decrease protein levels for the dual agonist condition. Figure 2 shows that dual agonism creates the most protein, not the least. Thus, choice D can be eliminated. If mRNA was rapidly degraded after translation, mRNA levels could be low, while the protein levels could be high. Thus, choice C is the best answer choice.

5. **C is the best answer.** This question asks about the most appropriate control for an experiment that measures RNA levels in a cell. When comparing relative levels of mRNA between different cells, in this experiment, between no agonism, PPARδ agonism, and AMPK agonism, the amount of RNA put into an experiment must be the same. Otherwise, differences in RNA levels could be the result of actual differences in gene expression or an error in how much DNA was put into an experiment. The expression of the control gene should not be affected between different cell populations. Option II can be eliminated because macrophages are eukaryotic cells, not prokaryotic bacterial cells, which have a 30S ribosome. Thus, an RNA in prokaryotes would not be an appropriate control because no information is provided about whether or not it is found in eukaryotic cells also. The passage notes that the two agonists impact FAO-associated genes. Thus, it can be assumed that GAPDH, a glycolytic enzyme, and actin, a structural protein, are not impacted by agonist treatment. Choice A can be eliminated because it does not contain option III. Choices B and D can be eliminated because they contain option II that is found in prokaryotes. Choice C is the best answer choice because it contains both options I and III, which are genes whose transcript levels should not be affected by agonist treatment according to the passage.

Passage 2 (Questions 6-10)

6. **A is the best answer.** The passage states that Glut1 deletion had a larger impact on CD4 T_h cells than CD8 cells. This indicates a greater dependence on glycolysis for CD4 T_h cells, because Glut1 moves glucose into the cell. This statement corresponds to choice A, and is the opposite of choice B. No conclusion can be drawn about higher overall glycolysis levels, because CD8 cells could have higher levels of glycolysis, while also having disproportionately higher levels of other metabolic processes, lessening their dependence on glycolysis.

7. **C is the best answer.** OCR is oxygen consumption rate, which directly suggests that it indicates the level of aerobic metabolism. Next, ECAR is acidification rate. The primary process that produces acid is fermentation, which occurs when there is not enough oxygen, in anaerobic conditions. This involves glycolysis and fermentation, which regenerates starting molecules required for glycolysis. This makes choice C the best answer. Choice D is the direct opposite of this ratio and would describe ECAR/OCR . Choices A and B are unlikely because neither oxygen consumption nor acidification describe gluconeogenesis or glycogenolysis – OCR/ECAR would be, at best, a very indirect way of monitoring either of these processes.

8. **A is the best answer.** OCR and ECAR are representative of aerobic and anaerobic metabolism, respectively. CD8 cells have higher OCR and ECAR based on the data in the passage, ruling out choices B and D. Next, higher ATP production and generation of carbon metabolites through these processes should be corresponded with higher growth, making choice A the best answer.

9. **C is the best answer.** CD4 has higher OCR/ECAR, meaning a greater ratio of aerobic to anaerobic processes. This contradicts choices B and D. Next CD8 cells have an overall higher level of both OCR and ECAR, indicating greater metabolism. These two conclusions match with choice C

10. **C is the best answer.** Lipase hydrolyzes triglycerides and releases fatty acids into the bloodstream. This is a potential answer, as fatty acids can be used for energy in the CD8 cells. Trypsin is a digestive enzyme that breaks apart proteins into smaller peptides. This is more related to digestion than energy distribution, so choice B is unlikely. To answer this question, consider the role of each hormone listed. Glucagon increases blood sugar levels, fatty acid release, and increases energy production in general. These effects correspond closely to the requirements of CD8 cells during expansion, so choice C is very likely. Finally, choice D is also a decent answer, but not as good as choice C. Cortisol increases gluconeogenesis, increasing glucose available to growing cells. However, it does not have the widespread impact that glucagon does on metabolism.

Passage 3 (Questions 11-14)

11. **C is the best answer.** Compared to SUM1315 cells, SUM1315ΔBRCA1 cells have lower lactate production and use less glucose. The conversion of pyruvate to lactose generates NAD^+ from NADH, while the conversion of glucose to pyruvate generates NADH from NAD^+. SUM1315ΔBRCA1 cells have about 25% less lactate conversion than SUM1315 cells, meaning they convert 25% less NADH to NAD^+. SUM1315ΔBRCA1 cells, however, use about 50% less glucose compared to SUM1315 cells, meaning they generate 50% less cytosolic NADH. Because Figure 1 only concerns lactate and glycolysis, the other cytosolic processes do not need to be considered. Considering the two processes, SUM1315ΔBRCA1 have about 25% less NADH than SUM1315 cells, because, although they lose less NADH to the pyruvate to lactate conversion, they also produce less NADH from glycolysis. This 25% decrease in NADH corresponds to choice C. A 1:1 ratio would result if there was no difference in lactate production or glucose utilization. Because Figure 1 shows differences, choice A can be eliminated. Choice B suggest that SUM1315ΔBRCA1 cells have higher NADH due to glycolysis and decrease conversion of lactate to pyruvate. This choice can be eliminated by comparing the relative increases and decreases in pyruvate to lactate conversion and glycolysis. Choice D can be eliminated because the graphs show that the ratio is closer than a 10:1 ratio.

12. **B is the best answer.** An inactivating mutation in *BRCA1* would resemble a deletion of the gene, preventing enough functional product from being produced. This means that an inactivating mutation would resemble SUM1315ΔBRCA1 cells and, according to Figure 1, would produce less lactate than wild type cells. Lactate is lactic acid, which would result in a lower pH. Remember that higher acid means lower pH and pH is the negative log of the acid concentration. SUM1315ΔBRCA1 cells have about a 25% decrease in lactate compared to wild type cells. Because pH is on a log scale, a 10-fold decrease would result in a pH change of one. Because this is less than a concentration change of 10, the change in pH unit must be less than 1, eliminating choices A and C. A synonymous mutation does not change the amino acid sequence and would not result in an inactivating mutation, helping to eliminate choice D. Because the lactate concentration is less than 10 times less in the SUM1315ΔBRCA1 cells versus the wild type cells, the pH change will be higher and less than 1 pH unit higher, making choice B the best answer.

13. **C is the best answer.** An increase in ATP levels can come from two places – an increase in substrate-level phosphorylation from glycolysis and an increase in ATP synthesis from the TCA cycle and oxidative phosphorylation. Cells with *BRCA1* deleted show decreased glycolysis compared to wild type cells, meaning glycogenolysis, the process of breaking down glycogen into glucose for use in glycolysis, would not provide the excess ATP. This eliminates choice A. Gluconeogenesis is the production, not breakdown, of glucose. Gluconeogenesis uses ATP instead of generating it, eliminating choice B. Fatty acid synthesis uses acetyl-CoA to build up larger fat molecules, instead of breaking down fats into the two carbon molecule that can enter the TCA cycle to produce reducing equivalents for oxidative phosphorylation. This eliminates choice D. Increased β-oxidation provides acetyl-CoA molecules that eventually produce NADH, $FADH_2$, and GTP. NADH and $FADH_2$ provide reducing equivalents to the electron transport chain that pumps hydrogen to build up a gradient that can drive ATP synthase to produce ATP. This makes choice C the best answer.

TEST 3C A&E

14. **A is the best answer.** Allosteric regulation of an enzyme involves a distinct compound associating with an enzyme to increase or decrease its activity. In the case of this question, the allosteric molecule increases the rate of glycolysis. High acetyl-CoA, which is the end product of fatty acid oxidation and glycolysis, by way of pyruvate dehydrogenase, would signal high energy stores and most likely decrease flux through glycolysis, eliminating choice B. Malate is a component of the citric acid cycle. If the citric acid cycle was running at an increased rate, more malate would be present, signifying an excess of energy, helping to eliminating choice C. Similarly, high levels of NADH would come from increased glycolysis and the citric acid cycle, meaning energy stores were abundant. This eliminates choice D. High ADP would represent a proportional decrease in ATP concentration, which would signal the cell that it needs to make more ATP by oxidizing glucose. This makes choice A the best answer.

Stand Alones (Questions 15-18)

15. **B is the best answer.** ATP can undergo hydrolysis to ADP in a process that releases energy. This energy is used in many cell processes such as protein synthesis and muscle contraction to drive otherwise unfavorable processes forward. A negative change in free energy indicates a release of energy, and the type of reaction that releases energy is an exergonic reaction. This is also known as a spontaneous reaction, since it is energetically favorable and does not require a large input of energy. This is in contrast to an endergonic reaction that requires the input of energy to proceed in the forward direction. Because the change in free energy for the hydrolysis of ATP is well below zero, the process can be coupled to an unfavorable process with a positive change in free energy to create a favorable reaction with an overall negative change in free energy. Choice A is inaccurate, since the hydrolysis of ATP is an exergonic reaction and would be coupled with an endergonic process. Choice B is the best answer, since it combines the hydrolysis of ATP with an endergonic process. It also explains that the result is a process that is favorable with a negative change in free energy. This eliminates choices C and D, which both state that the overall result is a positive change in free energy.

16. **C is the best answer.** This question may be somewhat tricky given the level of detail. The best way to approach it is by understanding that processes involving the transfer of electrons are most at risk, since these are redox reactions. Unstable electron groups tend to react with electron acceptors and can thereby reduce them. These electron carriers are then no longer able to accept electrons as part of their normal function. Choice A is a process in glycolysis where the two compounds are isomers. The conversion of one to the other does not involve a transfer of electrons to an electron acceptor, so choice A can be eliminated. The hint is that the enzyme involved is an isomerase, so it is not expected to catalyze a redox reaction, since that involves changes in bonding to additional hydrogen or oxygen atoms. This is also the case with choice B. Choice C is the best answer, since while the conversion of ADP to ATP does not involve the exchange of electrons, the reaction is the final process in the electron transport chain, which involves multiple redox steps. Impairment of oxidative phosphorylation affects the synthesis of ATP, which is made possible through the electron transport chain. Choice D is an example of a reaction where two smaller compounds form a larger compound. Since it does not involve a transfer of electrons, it is not the best answer.

17. **D is the best answer.** Read each answer choice to find the one that is false. The mitochondrion can insert transporters in the inner membrane that allow protons to flow back into the inner compartment of the organelle. This passive transport relieves the gradient and dissipates heat in the process, and it is useful when the body requires additional heat to be generated. Choice A is a true statement, so it can be eliminated. Chemiosmotic synthesis occurs when ATP synthase combines an inorganic phosphate group with a molecule of ADP. Oxidative phosphorylation is another name for this process, so choice B can be eliminated. The "end" of the electron transport chain is often described as the reduction of oxygen to form water, but remember that all reductions must be coupled with an oxidation. In this process, cytochrome C gets oxidized when it passes its electrons to oxygen, so choice C is true and can be eliminated. Choice D is worded strangely because normally redox reactions are described in terms of reduction potentials, which are inversely related to oxidation potentials. For electrons to be passed along the electron transport chain, each complex must be more willing to accept electrons than the previous one. That means that each one must have a higher reduction potential than the complex preceding it. If a subsequent complex had a lower reduction potential, it would be energetically favorable for the electrons to stay put. In other words, it wouldn't make sense for them to transfer along the chain in that case. Because reduction and oxidation potentials are inversely related, it follows that those complexes have increasingly lower oxidation potentials, so choice D is not true and is the best answer.

18. **B is the best answer.** Cytochrome C transfers electrons in the intemembrane space, which contains hydrophilic molecules, and NADH is found the cytoplasm and mitochondrial matrix, both hydrophilic environments. Ubiquinone is transferred between membrane bound proteins of the electron transport chain within the plasma membrane, and is lipid soluble. Option II is correct, while option I and II are not. Choice B is the best answer.

Passage 4 (Questions 19-22)

19. **A is the best answer.** One of the main actions of insulin is to increase the intracellular concentration of glucose by inserting glucose channels on the plasma membrane. This would raise the intracellular concentration of glucose, leading to greater entry into numerous metabolic pathways, including glycogenesis. Glucagon is released from pancreatic alpha cells. However, the levels of insulin and glucagon balance each other. When insulin is high, glucagon is low, eliminating choice B as the best answer. The passage does not comment on bone mineralization in patients with or without diabetes. In general, insulin regulates blood glucose, not blood mineral content. Additionally, because the passage does not provide information on this topic, choice C is less likely to be the best answer. Using Figure 1 as a guide, the number of unsaturated fatty acids increases in the high insulin environment. It is reasonable to assume that the number of *cis* fatty acids would also increase, eliminating choice D. Increased glucose in skeletal muscle cells gets stored as glycogen to be used in times of reduced energy availability. Some of the extra glucose taken up by the cell would be incorporated into glycogen, making choice A the best answer choice.

20. **A is the best answer.** One of the first keys to reasoning through this question is to determine the difference between the two molecules mentioned. The question stem notes that palmitate is a saturated fatty acid, meaning that it only contains single bonds. Unsaturated fatty acids contain –ole- in their names, indicating that they contain one or more double bonds. By definition, all fatty acids contain a carbonyl group, typically in the form on an ester that links the long hydrophobic chain to other molecules or a carboxylic acid functional group, eliminating choice B. Both palmitate and palmitoleic acid contain the same number of carbons but different numbers of double bonds, eliminating choice C. Additionally, amylases break down starches, not fats, also helping to eliminate choice C. Glycogen, not fatty acids, are stored as linked, branched molecules in the cell, eliminating choice D. Saturated fatty acids contain more reducing equivalents, in the form of two additional hydrogens per single bond that is converted to a double bond in an unsaturated fatty acid. Thus, reducing the content of saturated fatty acids in the diet would help lower the energy derived exclusively from fat, making choice A the best answer choice.

21. **D is the best answer.** Cellular membrane fluidity is primarily determined by cholesterol content. Cholesterol allows a membrane to remain fluid at lower temperatures and hold the membrane together at higher than normal temperatures. One way to find the best answer to this question is to determine which molecule has the highest concentration of cholesterol and fatty acids. The molecules are named by the concentration of protein they contain, which makes them more dense. High density lipoprotein, HDL, contains the lowest levels of fatty acids and cholesterol, eliminating choice A. IDL, or intermediate density lipoprotein, contains an intermediate level of cholesterol and fatty acids compared with HDL and low density lipoprotein, LDL, eliminating choice B. VLDL contains the highest concentration of cholesterol and fatty acids in circulation and is tasked with delivering these to cells. Delivering more cholesterol to a cell could have the greatest impact on membrane fluidity, making choice D the best answer choice.

22. **C is the best answer.** Triacylglycerols (TAGs) are composed of three fatty acids that have been esterified to a glycerol molecule. A TAG can contain any type of fatty acid, as long as it can contains a carboxylic acid group at its end that can react with the hydroxyl on the glycerol molecule, eliminating choice A. While the type of TAG is determined by the groups attached, choice B does not help answer the question if only moderate changes were seen in TAG levels but significant changes were seen in PUFA levels, making choice B less likely to be the best answer. If increased chylomicron concentrations were noted in the blood of diabetic patients, these chylomicrons would likely contain high levels of all types of fatty acids and TAGs that were reflective of diet, not necessarily insulin levels. Additionally, chylomicrons have not been processed by the liver into VLDL particles, so they should reflect dietary lipids, not the effect of systemic hormones, eliminating choice D. A PUFA has a double bond in place of a single bond. This reaction would be mediated by a dehydrogenase that removed hydrogens to place the double bond. If the fatty acids did not have to be free in order to undergo reactions, this could explain why the PUFA levels increased but not the TAG levels, making choice C the best answer choice.

Passage 5 (Questions 23-27)

23. **A is the best answer.** Glycogen is composed of α-1,4 and α-1,6 glycosidic bonds. Glycogen does not contain α-1,5 or β-1,4 glycosidic bonds so choices B and D are incorrect. Between choices A and C, it is necessary to choose the *best* answer. Glycogen is primarily α-1,4 bonds with some α-1,6 branch points. Since there are mostly α-1,4 bonds, choice A is the best answer.

24. **D is the best answer.** Glucagon is released in response to low blood glucose. The genotype with the lowest blood glucose likely has the highest muscle concentration of glycogen because the disease is characterized by an inability to make glucose from glycogen. The genotype with the highest level of glycogen is consistently $GAA^{-/-} \times S6K1^{-/-}$ so choice D is the best answer.

25. **C is the best answer.** Pompe disease represents an inborn error in metabolism. The disease is caused by a mutation in an enzyme so the correct answer should also be caused by a mutation in an enzyme. Choice A refers to a mutation in a protein. Although hemoglobin is sometimes considered an enzyme because it binds O_2, no chemical change occurs to the substrate so choice A is not a strong answer. Choice B refers to a change in an ion-transport protein. As with choice A, choice B does not describe a protein that chemically changes a substrate so choice B is not a strong answer. Choice C refers to an enzyme mutation because the disease prevents metabolism of phenylalanine, so choice C is a possible answer . Choice D refers to diabetes which although it plays a role in glucose metabolism, it is not an inherited enzyme defect so choice D is not the best answer . This makes choice C the best answer.

26. **A is the best answer.** $GAA^{-/-}$ mice have greater concentration of glycogen in the muscle than do $S6K^{-/-}$ mice. When a concentration of a reactant is high, the equilibrium of the reaction favors the products, according to Le Chatelier's principle. In the reaction of glycogen → glucose, high concentration of glycogen will favor spontaneous hydrolysis of glycogen. So, choice A is a possible answer and choice B is not a possible answer. Activation energy for glycogen hydrolysis is lowered by the GAA enzyme so $GAA^{-/-}$ mice are unlikely to have a lesser activation energy than $S6K2^{-/-}$ mice and choice C is not a strong answer. ΔG for glycogen hydrolysis is dependent on the K_{eq} of the reaction where K_{eq} = [products]/[reactants]. Mice with high concentration of glycogen will have a large K_{eq}. The formula for ΔG is $\Delta G = -RT\ln K_{eq}$. A large K_{eq} corresponds to a large negative ΔG. $GAA^{-/-}$ mice have the most glycogen and thus would have a more negative ΔG. So, choice D is not the best answer.

27. **B is the best answer.** People with Pompe disease are unable to obtain glucose from glycogen because of a nonfunctional enzyme in glycogen catabolism. When fasting, they need to obtain energy from other metabolic pathways. Choice A is not a strong answer because it states people with Pompe disease can perform glycogenolysis, which they cannot. Choice B is a strong answer because both gluconeogenesis and ketogenesis are sources of energy when fasting. Choice C is a possible answer because people with Pompe disease are able to perform ketogenesis and the pentose phosphate pathway. However, the PPP is primarily anabolic, not catabolic. So, choice C is not as strong as choice B. Choice D is incorrect for the same reason as choice A so choice B is the best answer.

Stand Alones (Questions 28-31)

28. **B is the best answer.** Spontaneity of a reaction is synonymous with a large negative ΔG for a reaction. Normally these reactions involve transfer of phosphate to or from ATP or transfer of electrons (redox). Of the reactions listed, only choice B involves transfer of phosphate to or from ATP. None of the reactions represent oxidations or reductions. So, choice B is the best answer. Usually high energy (large, negative ΔG) reactions are highly regulated. So , in glycolysis, reactions 1, 3, and 10 have the largest negative ΔG. This is why those reactions are considered irreversible.

29. **A is the best answer.** The table provided shows a collapse in the transmembrane potential and a decrease in the concentration of ATP when compound A is added to cells. If compound A hydrolyzed ADP to AMP, a decrease in the ADP concentration would be seen. The provided table does not display concentrations of ADP or AMP, so the effect of the compound cannot be fully interpreted with the provided data. Choice B is thus unlikely to be the best answer. A decrease in a transmembrane potential would be seen if compound A inhibited the Na^+/K^+ pump but no change would be expected in the [ATP]. Thus, choice C can be eliminated. In contrast, a decrease in the [ATP] would be seen with inhibition of ATP synthase but the transmembrane potential would be expected to become more negative as H^+ ions built up in the mitochondrial matrix. Thus, choice D can be eliminated. Choice A is the best answer choice because an ion pore in the inner mitochondrial membrane would collapse the gradient by allowing H^+ to run down its concentration gradient without synthesizing ATP. ATP would still be used in cellular processes, however, so its concentration would be expected to decrease. Thus, choice A is the most likely answer choice.

30. **C is the best answer.** This is a typical case of blocking a multistep process where the substrates before build up while the products following that step will be diminished. Cytochrome c oxidase is an important part of the electron transport chain, and without the ability to carry out the process, aerobic respiration will not be possible. Choice A is incorrect because pyruvate is not a viable end product for the cell, since there will be an attempt to recycle NADH by making lactate so as to allow glycolysis to continue in the cell. Choice C is the better answer as NAD^+ is the coenzyme needed for glycolysis, and the production of lactate, an organic acid, allows NADH to be converted back to NAD^+. Choice B is incorrect, since ADP will be high due to the inability to make significant amounts of ATP by oxidative phosphorylation. Choice D is tempting, though there is no evidence for such an effect. Also, were this to occur, there would be no concept of cyanide poisoning, since the cytochrome would thereby have a way to resume function on its own.

31. **A is the best answer.** A meal is a huge intake of metabolic resources. This causes the body to release signals that lead to energy storage and enter an anabolic state, where smaller molecules tend to be incorporated into larger ones. The large storage forms of lipids and carbohydrates are triglycerides and glycogen, respectively. Thus, the best answer is choice A, describing fatty acids being converted into triglycerides and glucose being converted into glycogen. Choices B, C, and D all contain at least one reference to the storage forms being catabolically broken down.

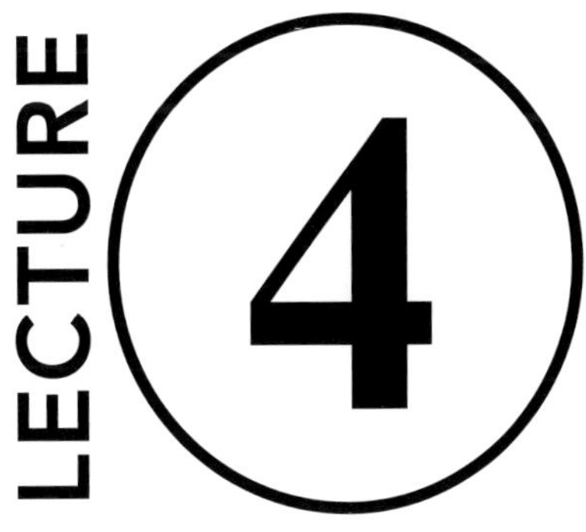

Laboratory Techniques

TEST 4A

ANSWERS & EXPLANATIONS

Questions 1–59

LECTURE 4 ANSWER KEY

TEST 4A		TEST 4B		TEST 4C	
1. B	31. B	1. B	31. B	1. A	17. C
2. C	32. A	2. B	32. B	2. A	18. B
3. D	33. C	3. A	33. D	3. A	19. C
4. A	34. B	4. D	34. D	4. D	20. B
5. D	35. C	5. C	35. C	5. D	21. C
6. B	36. C	6. C	36. B	6. A	22. A
7. A	37. D	7. B	37. C	7. C	23. C
8. C	38. A	8. C	38. B	8. A	24. C
9. A	39. D	9. A	39. C	9. B	25. B
10. C	40. C	10. D	40. D	10. A	26. B
11. A	41. A	11. B	41. C	11. D	27. D
12. B	42. A	12. A	42. D	12. B	28. A
13. B	43. B	13. C	43. C	13. A	29. D
14. A	44. B	14. D	44. C	14. A	30. A
15. C	45. C	15. D	45. D	15. D	31. D
16. B	46. B	16. A	46. C	16. C	
17. B	47. C	17. A	47. D		
18. B	48. A	18. D	48. D		
19. C	49. A	19. B	49. A		
20. A	50. B	20. A	50. A		
21. A	51. A	21. D	51. A		
22. A	52. A	22. B	52. B		
23. C	53. B	23. B	53. B		
24. A	54. A	24. A	54. A		
25. C	55. B	25. C	55. A		
26. A	56. A	26. C	56. B		
27. A	57. A	27. A	57. B		
28. C	58. A	28. A	58. C		
29. B	59. D	29. A	59. A		
30. A		30. A			

EXPLANATIONS FOR LECTURE 4

Passage 1 (Questions 1-5)

1. **B is the best answer.** HPLC uses high pressure to drive a solution down through a column. Polar compounds travel more slowly during HPLC because they interact more strongly with the polar column and resist the pressure to travel downwards. Polar molecules travel more slowly during HPLC, so choices A and C can be eliminated. Next, examine compound polarity. The major difference between compounds 1 and 2 is an extra aldehyde in compound 1. Aldehydes are polar due to the electronegativity difference between carbon and oxygen. This means compound 1 is more polar than compound 2. Choice B is the best answer.

2. **C is the best answer.** The major functional groups to memorize for IR absorbance are carbonyl at 1700, hydroxyl at 2500-3500, and amine at 3300. Carbonyls consist of a carbon double bonded to an oxygen. Hydroxyls consist of an –OH group bonded to a carbon, and an amine consists of a nitrogen bonded exclusively to carbons and/or hydrogens. There are several carbonyls in compound 1, as well as two hydroxyls, one of which is part of a carboxylic acid group. Because there are no nitrogens, there are no amines in the molecule, and a 3300 band would not be expected. The best answer is choice C, options I and II.

3. **D is the best answer.** UV spectroscopy is used to detect and characterize molecules with conjugated systems and delocalized electrons, including aromatic molecules. Aromatic compounds are planar rings with specific numbers of π electrons. This number must obey Hückel's rule, which says it must equal 4n+2, where n is 0 or any positive integer. The ring in compound 1 has 3 π bonds, meaning it has 6 electrons. Thus, this ring is aromatic and compound 1 will show absorbance. Choices A and C can be ruled out. Compound 2 also has an aromatic ring, leading to UV absorbance and ruling out choice B. Choice D is the best answer because both compounds show absorbance.

4. **A is the best answer.** Both compounds 1 and 2 are polar based on their carbonyls and hydroxyl groups. Neither compound has symmetrical structure, so the polarity of these functional groups does not cancel out. This rules out choices C and D. Ethyl acetate is an ester and a polar molecule primarily due to the presence of the carbonyl. "Like dissolves like" in terms of polarity, so ethyl acetate will dissolve compounds 1 and 2. This makes choice A the best answer.

5. **D is the best answer.** Western blots use the specificity of antibodies to quantify the amount of protein in a sample. Southern blots and northern blots use the complementarity of DNA and RNA in order to quantify nucleic acid sequences within a sample. None of these techniques is targeted towards aromatic compounds or is capable of characterizing and distinguishing them. The best answer is choice D, none of the above. Potential techniques that could be used to distinguish between aromatic compounds include UV spectroscopy and certain types of chromatography, depending on the polarity differences of the compounds.

Passage 2 (Questions 6-9)

6. **B is the best answer.** NMR allows for the characterization and determination of functional groups of a molecule. Each peak on an NMR graph corresponds to a chemically different carbon. The question notes that the NMR presented is for D-arabinose, but the question asks about L-arabinose. L-arabinose and D-arabinose are diastereomers of one another that differ in the chiral configuration of their alpha carbons, making them epimers. While the peaks may be shifted due to differences in shielding that would occur by moving the hydroxyl group on the alpha carbon from one orientation to another, the number of peaks would remain the same because the number of carbons did not change. Four chemically distinct carbons are present in the molecule, as four peaks can be seen on the NMR. The four peaks seen in the NMR correspond to four chemically distinct carbons, making choice B the best answer.

7. **A is the best answer.** When interpreting the results of mass spectrometry, the molecular ion is the largest ion. The molecular ion is the size of the original molecule but contains one less electron. If D-arabinose were the sample, the molecular ion would be D-arabinose$^+$. The molecular ion is always the one with the highest peak in a mass spectrogram, due to the greatest abundance. An m/z of 110 represents the second tallest peak, eliminating choice B. An m/z of 95 represents the third tallest peak, eliminating choice C. An m/z of 80 represents the smallest peak, eliminating choice D. The tallest peak is the one with an m/z of 150, likely indicating that this is the molecular ion, D-arabinose$^+$. Choice A is the best answer.

8. **C is the best answer.** According to paragraph three, a hydrophobic interaction column was used to separate the epimers of arabinose used in the study. Hydrophobic forces occur between nonpolar regions of molecules. Covalent bonding would be unlikely to separate the epimers, as the molecules would become permanently attached to the column and would not elute. Choice A can be eliminated. Electrostatic forces are not hydrophobic but rather hydrophilic, eliminating choice B. Hydrogen bonding occurs between atoms of F, O, and N and the hydrogens attached to those atoms. Because hydrogen bonding is the strongest type of intermolecular bonds, it is unlikely to be used for separation of epimers. Van der Waals forces occur between hydrophobic molecules and were most likely the forces at work in separating epimers of arabinose in the hydrophobic interaction column. Choice C the best answer.

9. **A is the best answer.** According to paragraph two, LAM has an average molecular weight of 17.9 kDa but is distributed over a range of molecular weights due to different glycosylation patterns by mannose residues. This means that some mannose-tagged LAM molecules are smaller than 17.9 kDa, while some are larger. Mass spectrometry would allow for the detection of LAM with various numbers of mannose residues, but would be unable to separate them, eliminating choice B. Proton NMR (^1H NMR) would also be unable to separate the molecules, but would allow for them to be detected, eliminating choice C. Gel electrophoresis is used to separate nucleic acids and proteins, but is not used to separate sugar-modified lipids, eliminating choice D. Size-exclusion chromatography would allow for separation of the different molecular weights of LAM depending on how long it took them to move through the column. Choice A is the best answer.

Passage 3 (Questions 10-13)

10. **C is the best answer.** The purpose of a deadenylase assay is to describe the activity of an enzyme. This question is difficult because the passage does not explicitly describe how the results of the SEC shown in Figure 1 would be used to determine enzymatic activity. The way to look at any reaction is to consider at the substrates and the products. Ideally, the SEC would clearly separate the substrate and the product. Choice D can be eliminated because the question asks for the least suitable substrate, and AMP is the product of the reaction rather than a substrate. To choose between the remaining options, determine the substrate that has an elution volume closest to the elution volume of AMP. Choice C, A6, is the best answer because the peaks may partially overlap during an assay, making an analysis more difficult. Choice A, A2, and choice B, A20, peak further away from AMP and are better candidates for the deadenylase assay.

11. **A is the best answer.** Based on the passage, AMP is one product of the reaction catalyzed by deadenylase. The presence of AMP in the SEC indicates that the reaction is occurring, so AMP is an indicator of enzymatic activity. Choice A is the best answer. To assess choice B, the speed of the reaction, Figure 1 would need to include information about time. To evaluate choice C, specificity of the reaction, Figure 1 would need to provide information on the interaction between the substrate and the enzyme. Both choice B and choice C can be eliminated because the data does not provide a way to deduce these parameters. AMP cannot act as a control variable because it is the product of the reaction. Choice D can be eliminated.

12. **B is the best answer.** First examine Figure 1. The elution volumes of A20, A6, A2, and AMP are approximately 18 mL, 19 mL, 22 mL, and 20 mL, respectively. The relationship between the molecular weights of the four RNA fragments is A20 > A6 > A2 > AMP. With the exception of A2, the general trend is that the higher the molecular weight, the lower the elution volume. Size exclusion chromatography works via gel filtration. Larger molecules are less likely to be trapped by the gel and elute faster than smaller molecules. The larger the molecular weight, the shorter the elution time. Since both elution time and elution volume are inversely related to molecular weight, they are directly related to one another. This makes choice B the best fit for the data shown in Figure 1 when combined with the principles of size exclusion chromatography. Choice A is the opposite of the relationship described. It cannot be determined whether choice D is true because Figure 1 does not give information on the exact elution times.

13. **B is the best answer.** As stated in the passage, when deadenylase cleaves the poly-A tail, an AMP product is always produced. Choice C can be eliminated. According to the passage, the 5′ phosphate group was removed from A2, A6, and A20. This means that A2, a 2-mer oligoA, is an AMP bonded to an adenosine. When the deadenylase cleaves an AMP, the adenosine remains. The final products of the reaction are AMP and adenosine. This leaves choices B and D. Deadenylase is the catalyst of the reaction and is not considered either a substrate or a product. Choice D can be eliminated and choice B is the best answer.

Stand-alones (Questions 14-17)

14. **A is the best answer.** Consider the characteristics of each technique. Western blots are used to detect and particular proteins from a mixture of proteins using antibodies. Microarrays compare the levels of mRNA between two cells or conditions, and may contain probes for hundreds or thousands of genes. This means DNA microarrays are used more to analyze gene expression at the mRNA level on a genome-wide scale. Because DNA microarrays do not directly measure protein levels, choices B and D can be eliminated. Western blots probe for proteins, so they do not directly measure RNA levels. Choice C can be ruled out. The best pair of statements is that Western blots directly measure protein levels, and microarrays measure gene expression on a larger scale. Choice A is the best answer.

15. **C is the best answer.** When a compound absorbs a certain color of light, the color of that compound will appear to be the complement of the color absorbed. This question can be answered by quickly drawing a color wheel. Draw a circle and then divide it into six equal parts. Use the order of the rainbow to label the wedges of the circle red, orange, yellow, green, blue, and purple. The complementary color is the color that is found on the opposite side of the circle. The complementary color of blue-green is red-orange because it is located directly opposite blue-green on the color wheel. Choices A, B, and D can be eliminated because they are not the complement of blue-green light. This leaves choice C as the best answer.

16. **B is the best answer.** ^1H NMR measures the electronic environment surrounding protons in a compound. ^1H NMR may be helpful in differentiating which proton is adjacent to carbonyl relative to another functional group, but it does not detect carbonyls directly. Choice A is unlikely to be the best answer. IR spectroscopy is useful for detecting functional groups. Carbonyls have a distinct peak on IR spectra at 1700 cm^{-1}. Choice B is a strong answer. Ultraviolet spectroscopy is best used for identifying conjugated systems, so choice C would not be an efficient way to identify a carbonyl. Mass spectrometry is used to identify a compound's molecular weight and, in some cases, molecular formula. It would not be an efficient method of detecting a carbonyl, so choice D can be eliminated. Choice B is the best answer.

17. **B is the best answer.** High temperatures provide significant kinetic energy to molecules, which would prevent them from interacting with one another enough to form a crystal structure that could precipitate out of solution. The high kinetic energy conveyed by high temperatures helps to eliminate choice A. Low temperatures would allow proteins or other molecules to overcome repulsive forces and aggregate together to create crystals. This makes choice B the best answer. Because of the differences in kinetic energy, high and low temperatures are not equivalent in terms of allowing molecules to associate and form a crystal. Choice C can be eliminated. Because increased temperature increases the kinetic energy of molecules in solution, preventing them from associating enough to precipitate, temperature does affect crystal formation. This effect eliminates choice D.

Passage 4 (Questions 18-21)

18. **B is the best answer.** An antibody is a protein that recognizes an epitope on its target protein by interactions between amino acids. These interactions are intermolecular forces and consist of hydrogen bonds, van der Waals interactions, dipole-dipole interactions, and electrostatic interactions. Disulfide bonds, by contrast, are covalent bonds between two cysteine amino acids and are typically intramolecular bonds. Hydrogen bonds occur between amino acids that have F, O, and N that can accept a hydrogen bond and amino acids that have hydrogens attached to these elements which can donate a hydrogen bond. Van der Waals interactions occur between non-polar amino acids. The best answer choice will contain options I and III, omitting option II, as it is typically intramolecular. Choice A can be eliminated because it does not contain option III, while choice C can be eliminated because it does not contain option I. Choice D is unlikely to be the best answer because it also includes option II. By process of elimination, choice B is the best answer.

19. **C is the best answer.** The first key to answering this question is to realize that immunohistochemical analysis sounds similar in theory to a western blot. An antibody specific to a protein is incubated with a tissue sample, followed by a secondary antibody that allows for visualization of the binding of the primary antibody. The best answer will be the one that is least likely to explain the lack of staining in the tissue sample. If pStat3 were denatured during the tissue preparation process, the antibody would no longer be able to recognize the epitope of amino acids on pStat3, thus accounting for the lack of staining. Choice A can be eliminated. The second paragraph states that the staining was for highly malignant tumors only. Thus, if low grade tumors with presumably low levels of pStat3 were stained instead, this could account for the lack of staining by immunohistochemistry. Choice B can be eliminated. A secondary antibody-enzyme conjugate is used to visualize a primary antibody. If no secondary were used, the primary could not be visualized, even if bound to pStat3. Choice D can be eliminated because it could explain the difference. If the antibody to pStat3 also recognized pStat5, the staining pattern on immunohistochemistry would likely be stronger than that seen in the western blot. This is the opposite of what was observed, making choice D the best answer.

20. **A is the best answer.** The isoelectric point (pI) of a protein is the pH at which the amino acid, or string of amino acids, carries no charge. This means that the R groups of an amino acid chain have a net charge of zero. For basic amino acids, the pI is basic, while for acidic amino acids, the pI is acidic. Neutral amino acids have pI close to a pH of 7. The question stem notes that the pI of the epitope is 10.25, meaning that the pH at which the epitope is neutrally charged is 10.25. Choice B contains a string of neutral amino acids that would become negatively charged at such a basic pH, eliminating choice B. Choices C and D contain the acidic amino acids aspartate and glutamate, respectively, and would be negatively charged at a basic pH. Choices C and D can be eliminated. Choice A contains the basic amino acids lysine and arginine that would be neutrally charged at a pH of around 10. This high pH ensures that the nitrogens on the R groups are not additionally protonated to yield a positive charge. Choice A is the best answer.

21. **A is the best answer.** Both Figure 1 and the final paragraph of the passage provide information to help answer this question. According to Figure 1, when levels of pStat3 are high, bands corresponding to ATX appear by western blot, indicating that pStat3, the activated version of Stat3, is upregulating ATX levels. The final paragraph indicates that pStat3 correlates with increased breast cancer invasiveness. Choice B can be eliminated because activated Stat3 (pStat3) activates ATX, not the inactive Stat3 form. Stat3 is activated by phosphorylation before it can activate ATX transcription. Tubulin is used as a loading control in Figure 1 and does not activate Stat3, as seen by the uniform levels of tubulin regardless of the intensity of the pStat3 band. Choice C can be eliminated. ATX is activated by but does not activate Stat3 because the bands for ATX only appear by western blot when the pStat3 levels are high, eliminating choice D. Choice A is the best answer because the high levels of pStat3 seen on western blot lead to the appearance of ATX bands and high levels of pStat3 are correlated with increased invasiveness.

Passage 5 (Questions 22-25)

22. **A is the best answer.** The passage states that Cry j 1 is 45kD whereas Cry j 2 is 32 kD. The difference in the size of these proteins is more than 20%, which is a significant difference. Size-exclusion chromatography separates proteins of varying sizes. Choice A is plausible because size-exclusion chromatography could effectively separate allergens which varied in size by more than 20%. DNA sequencing cannot separate the allergens because it does not interact with proteins. Only techniques that apply to proteins would be effective here, so choice B can be eliminated. NMR structural analysis can predict the structure of a protein based on the configuration of protons in the molecule. However, NMR structural analysis is an identification technique and is not a useful isolation method. NMR would not be able to separate the different allergens. Choice A is better than choice C because size-exclusion chromatography can separate proteins. Western blotting uses antibodies to identify proteins, but is not used to separate proteins. Choice D can be eliminated because the question stem indicates that the allergens need to be separated, not just identified. Choice A is the best answer.

23. **C is the best answer.** Researchers can incorporate different types of tags in order to make it easier to identify and isolate proteins of interest. A histidine tag is particularly useful because histidine residues can become positively or negatively charged depending on their environment. The egg white has a pH of 9 so histidine will be negatively charged, giving up a proton. Ion-exchange chromatography works by forming ion pairs between oppositely charged species. A negatively charged ion-exchanger would not attract the negatively charged histidine tag, so choice A can be eliminated. Gel-electrophoresis separates proteins based on size. Adding a histidine tag to cLys-7crp would increase its size, but it would not make it easier for gel-electrophoresis to isolate the protein. Gel-electrophoresis would be equally capable of isolating cLys-7crp without the tag, so choice B is not the best answer. A negatively charged histidine tag would be attracted to a positively charged ion-exchanger. An ion-pair would form between the tag and the ion-exchanger, and the cLys-7crp protein could be isolated. Choice C is a plausible explanation for the inclusion of the poly-histidine tag. Choice D can be eliminated because size-exclusion chromatography would be able to isolate the cLys-7crp protein without the histidine tag. As long as there is a difference between the size of the desired protein and the contaminants, size-exclusion chromatography is capable of separating the particles. Choice C is the best answer because it matches an appropriate technique with a reasonable explanation.

24. **A is the best answer.** This question asks about the stage of PCR at which the primers are added to the reaction. Primers are used to bind to single strands of DNA and provide a starting point for DNA polymerase to expand the growing strand. Denaturing DNA means that the two strands are separated from one another. After the original DNA strands have been denatured, primers need to be added to the reaction so that single stranded DNA sequences can form double stranded DNA. Choice A is a plausible answer. Hybridization refers to the binding of a piece of DNA or RNA to a single strand of DNA. After hybridization occurs, no more DNA can bind to the original single strand because base pairing has already taken place. Choice B can be eliminated. Only one set of primers is needed in a PCR setup. If complementary cLys primers were added to the reaction, the retroviral vector primers would not be needed. Choice C can be eliminated because two sets of primers cannot be used in PCR. Reannealing is the rejoining of two DNA strands. Once this occurs, the primer could not bind to the DNA because base pairing has already occurred. Choice D can be eliminated. Choice A is the best answer.

25. **C is the best answer.** EGFP is a protein with a barrel structure that contains a highly conjugated chromophore at its center. This protein is often used in experiments due to the ability of conjugated structures to fluoresce under ultraviolet light. The environment of the protein is not the main factor that causes fluorescence to occur, so being under acidic conditions is not a determinant of fluorescence. Choice A can be eliminated. The only two regions of the electromagnetic spectrum that typically cause fluorescence are visible light and ultraviolet light. IR light has too little energy to be absorbed and cause fluorescence of the EGFP chromophore, so choice B can be eliminated. Conjugated molecules can fluoresce under ultraviolet light. EGFP is often used in experiments because it can easily be visualized in the presence of ultraviolet light due to the conjugation of its chromophore. Choice C is a plausible explanation for why EGFP can serve as an indicator of cLys-7crp expression. Proteins themselves are not able to absorb and fluoresce light. In order for a protein to emit light, it must contain a chromophore or another type of conjugated molecule. Choice D can be eliminated because it does not properly describe how EGFP functions. Choice C is the best answer because it identifies a valid explanation for the function of EGFP.

Stand-alones (Questions 26-29)

26. **A is the best answer.** The isoelectric point, or pI, is the pH at which the charges on amino acids are neutralized and the overall protein no longer has a net charge. If the number of acidic residues is greater than the number of basic residues, the pI will be more acidic. The opposite is true if the protein has a greater number of basic amino acids. Assessing the pI would suggest the relative ratio of acidic to basic amino acids, making choice A the best answer. The pH describes the concentration of protons in solution, not the specific number of amino acids that can accept or donate a proton, eliminating choice B. The number of secondary structures like alpha helices or beta-pleated sheets does not suggest whether acidic or basic residues are most common. Many acidic and basic residues fall in regions between these secondary structures in order to remain in a hydrophilic environment. This helps to eliminate choices C and D. Choice A is the best answer.

27. **A is the best answer.** Column chromatography is a method used to separate compounds that have differences in polarity. Enantiomers, such as D- and L-arabinose, can only be separated by other chiral compounds, often tartaric acid. Enantiomers share most of the same physical properties, with the exception of the rotation of plane polarized light. Because the polarity of D- and L-arabinose would be identical, column chromatography would be unable to separate these two compounds. Glucose and mannose are structurally distinct compounds that would have different polarities. Column chromatography would likely be able to separate these two molecules, eliminating choice B. Fructose and glucose, as well as lactose and arabinose, are also unique molecules that may be able to be separated on the basis of polarity. This makes choices C and D less likely than choice A.

28. **C is the best answer.** Reverse transcriptase is responsible for taking RNA and turning it into cDNA that can be integrated into the genome of the host cell to permanently overexpress a gene. Reverse transcriptase is an enzyme, and would be unlikely to serve as an allosteric activator of ribosomes. Choice A can be eliminated. Reverse transcriptase does not replicate RNA to create more RNA but instead creates cDNA, eliminating choice B. Permanent integration of an anti-viral gene into the host genome would provide an additional defense mechanism against invasion upon challenge with a virus, making choice D unlikely. Reverse transcriptase creates the cDNA equivalent of the RNA of the anti-viral gene, which could integrate into the host genome. Choice C is the best answer.

29. **B is the best answer.** Southern blot is a technique that uses radioactive or fluorescent nucleotides that hybridize to target DNA sequences. A Southern blot allows for identification of DNA fragments. RNA is detected in a similar manner by a northern blot rather than a Southern blot, eliminating choices C and D. In order for the DNA sequences to be separated so they can hybridize to a probe, they are subjected to gel electrophoresis, which exposes them to an electric voltage that separates them based on size. Choice A can be eliminated, and choice B is the best answer.

Passage 6 (Questions 30-33)

30. **A is the best answer.** The third paragraph notes the key differences between metabolites measured in ALS and non-ALS patients and provides clues to help answer this question. At the end of the second paragraph, ascorbate is classified as an antioxidant molecule. The question stem also notes that ascorbate scavenges two free radicals that cause oxidative damage in cells. The third paragraph says that ALS patients have higher levels of ascorbate than in non-ALS patients. Thus, oxidative states are likely reduced by the higher levels of ascorbate, leading to a lower oxidation-reduction state in ALS patients than in non-ALS patients. Choice A is the best answer. Choice B can be eliminated because it makes the opposite claim. Because of the differences in ascorbate levels, a noted antioxidant, it is unlikely that the oxidative stress levels are similar, making choice C less likely than choice A. Enough information is provided in the passage to answer the question, eliminating choice D.

TEST 4A A&E

31. **B is the best answer.** The key to answering this question is understanding that p-values which are less than or equal to 0.05 are considered statistically significant. According to the chart above, acetate, pyruvate, and ascorbate levels are significantly different between ALS patients and non-ALS patients. Pyruvate is significantly lower in non-ALS patients, making choice B the best answer. The amino acids alanine, glutamine, and tyrosine have $p > 0.05$, so they are not significantly different, eliminating choice A. Carbohydrate levels, including glucose and fructose, are not significantly different, eliminating choice C. Citrate is a citric acid cycle intermediate and also has a $p > 0.05$, making choice D less likely than choice B.

32. **A is the best answer.** Peaks that are shifted downfield (to the left on an NMR spectrum, corresponding to higher ppm values) are those closer to electron-withdrawing groups, as these electron-withdrawing groups lower shielding and decrease the magnetic field at which resonance occurs. The best answer will be the one that is electron-withdrawing. Carboxylic acid, choice A, has two oxygen atoms that withdraw electrons, making it the best answer choice. The methyl and methine groups, choices B and C, respectively, do not contain electron withdrawing groups and most likely donate electrons, which would lead to a shift upfield instead. Choices B and C can be eliminated. Choice D also contains an oxygen, but would be balanced out by the electron donating effects of methyl groups also attached, making choice D less likely.

33. **C is the best answer.** The researchers measured the concentration of metabolites in the CSF as a proxy for the metabolite concentrations in neurons. However, the concentrations in the CSF may not be a direct consequence of metabolism in neurons due to other independent factors, such as the blood-brain barrier and release of metabolites from endothelial cells that line the spinal column. If the NMR spectrum did not represent the metabolism occurring in neurons, the conclusions drawn by the authors that suggest specific differences in metabolites in ALS versus non-ALS patients would be weakened. If the pyruvate peak, shown at 2.4 ppm, is not found in an isolated neuron but is found in the CSF, the pyruvate most likely came from a location other than a neuron. If one of the three significant molecules identified between ALS and non-ALS patients was found to come from a secondary location, it would call into question the validity of ascorbate as a real difference. Choice C is the best answer. Choices A, B, and D all note that peaks found in the CSF are also found in various cells of the brain, including neurons, astrocytes, and oligodendrocytes. Thus, there could be differences in the metabolism of these cells in ALS patients versus non-ALS patient, supporting the author's conclusions. Because these choices would support the study, they are less likely to be the best answer.

Passage 7 (Questions 34-39)

34. **B is the best answer.** This is a research question that asks one to evaluate the purpose of the various techniques carried out in this experiment. The stem of the question hints that the most conclusive test uses external means to confirm the results such that it limits the amount of human error that could affect the results. Mass spectrometry is used on the fractions, and the passage indicates in the final paragraph that the results are compared to the ProteinPilot database. Choice A is misleading because the figure in the passage would seem to indicate a strong indication that there are ribosomal proteins in the second elution by comparing the bands from the gel. Still, there is no external confirmation, and one could argue that the samples were loaded incorrectly on the gel. Choice B is a better answer because it strongly limits the possibility of human error where the results are compared to an external database using data from thousands of experiments. Choice C is inaccurate because it is too harsh, and these answer choices should generally be avoided. There is a level of certainty that comes with the techniques that is sufficient to make this determination. This is what is required for the paper the passage is based on to be published in the first place. Choice D is confusing since it uses words from the passage, though this technique as discussed in the first paragraph is used for the initial separation and not for identification.

35. **C is the best answer.** This question is asking for a proper replacement to the NaCl solution that could be used in the chromatography experiment to yield the same results. The best answer is one that is most similar to NaCl and takes advantage of the type of chromatography used in the experiment. The passage indicates that ion exchange chromatography is the basis of the separation where the rRNA of the ribosomes have many negative sites that would presumably allow for binding to the column stationary phase. The use of the NaCl salt solution provides competing anions for binding to the column to free the rRNA into the mobile phase in order to elute. Choice A is inaccurate because while a polar solution is used currently, it is not the polarity that drives the separation in this case. It is the ion exchange through the salt solution that is the basis of the separation. Choice B is also inaccurate for this reason. Choice C is the best answer as it takes into account the basis of the current method and provides a comparable replacement with another salt solution. Choice D is misleading as this is the basis of high pressure liquid chromatography, though the passage indicates that high pressures are not needed in this experiment.

36. **C is the best answer.** Gel electrophoresis separates proteins based on size where proteins are first denatured and coated in negatively-charged SDS particles. The peptides then travel through the gel on the basis of an applied external electric field. The voltage is a measure of the strength of the field, and a higher voltage means a stronger pull on the peptides to more quickly drag them through the gel. The control ladder is a collection of nucleic acids and peptides of known size used to mark the size for bands in the sample mixture. The compounds of the control ladder would move faster but so would those of the sample mixture, so choices A and B can be eliminated. The point of the control ladder is that the compounds of a similar size to those of the sample mixture travel the same distance. Choice C is the best answer as it correctly identifies the relationship between field strength and the movement of the compounds through the gel. Choice D is inaccurate, since the compounds would move faster and not slower. It is best not to be confused by verbose or two-part answer choices. Try to figure out the best answer and then look for the matching answer choice. The other answer choices misidentify one or both parts of the relationship.

37. **D is the best answer.** This question asks about the factors that affect the time it takes a compound to elute from an HPLC column. These measures do not need to be memorized but can be figured out intuitively. A compound will attach to the stationary phase and will be subsequently eluted based on differences in polarity between the mobile and stationary phases. The amount of pressure added can greatly affect retention time because it will control the speed of the mobile phase, so choice A is an example of something that affects retention time. The ability to dissolve in the mobile phase is also important, and temperature is a major factor that affects solubility, so choice B is another example of a factor that is important to retention time. Particle size will affect the ability of the compounds to bind to the column, so choice C can be eliminated. With smaller beads, there is more surface area and a greater chance for the compound to bind. Choice D or the amount of sample mixture is a case where the factor is not relevant to the retention time. Think of the retention time as an intrinsic property of the compound similar to its density. The amount of the compound has no effect on its ability to bind to the column or mobile phase. If there is more of a compound, more of it will be eluted at the time when it is expected to elute. Choice D is the best answer.

38. **A is the best answer.** This question is asking how one could have eluted the ribosomal proteins earlier than expected. This means there is either less binding to the stationary phase or increased solubility in the mobile phase. The passage indicates that an NaCl gradient is used, implying that the concentration of the NaCl is changed over time. Because ion exchange chromatography is used for the experiment, the NaCl serves as the basis for the exchange, and a higher concentration of NaCl means more competition for binding to the stationary phase. This leads to the negatively-charged rRNA being freed into the mobile phase. Choice A is the best answer because it addresses this relationship directly. Choice B is the opposite because with a low NaCl concentration, the ribosomal proteins would be slow to elute. Choice C is misleading because this experiment does not use high pressure as in HPLC for the elution, as stated in the second paragraph. Choice D is tricky as this could conceivably be true. Still, it is not the best answer, since the proteins were still eluted but were eluted too early. The presence of beads would be expected to severely slow the experiment due to the high back pressure, as mentioned in the passage, and it is unlikely the proteins would elute under normal pressures.

39. **D is the best answer.** The question is asking the reader to identify a fault in a new setup based on the current experiment. The passage establishes that the ribosomal proteins are eluted in the second fraction, but there are other proteins as well in that fraction as evidenced by the mass spectrometry data. Chromatography provides a means of separating compounds, but it is not always able to fully isolate a compound from other similar ones. The researchers are doing an experiment to see which antibiotics may be able to bind to the bacterial ribosome proteins, but the experiment has a flaw in that they are assuming the sample mixture to be purified ribosomal proteins when there are other proteins in the mixture. Choice A is inaccurate, since there is no evidence of anything that would cause the proteins to be denatured. The passage makes no mention of temperature extremes or the addition of any acid. Choice B is inaccurate as NaCl is prevalent in all cells, and even in high concentrations would not be expected to affect protein structure. Choice C is true as it identifies that other separations would be needed, but it is not the best answer. The question asks for the specific fault, and this is more directly addressed in choice D in light of the above explanation.

Passage 8 (Questions 40-43)

40. **C is the best answer.** This question is asking how one would interpret a ^{1}H NMR spectrum to determine the relative quantity of a compound. The chemical shift is a measure of the degree of electron shielding for the hydrogens in the compound, but it does not indicate anything about quantity. The area under the peak is a measure of the relative number of identical hydrogens with a certain shift. In the case of Figure 1, the various peaks are labeled to indicate the compounds they correspond to. Chemical shifts have nothing to do with quantity, so choice A can be eliminated. Choice B represents a common mistake—the height of a peak is not an accurate measure of the quantity of a compound. Choice C is the best answer because it accurately identifies the area under the curve as the measure of the relative quantity of identical hydrogens and, by extension, the relative quantity of lactate compared to other molecules in the serum. Choice D is a common distractor that would suggest that the evidence is lacking in this case, though the area under the curve would lend evidence to the given conclusion.

41. **A is the best answer.** This question tests the relationship between chemical shift and electron shielding for ^{1}H NMR spectroscopy. For hydrogens that are well shielded by electrons from the external magnetic field, the magnetic field strength required for resonance is increased, and the shift will be upfield closer to 0.0 ppm. By contrast, hydrogens that are adjacent to electron-withdrawing groups such as aldehydes will be more fully exposed to the external magnetic field and will require less magnetic field strength for resonance. The shift in such a case would be in the downfield direction towards 10.0 or more ppm. Aldehyde is more electron-withdrawing than a methyl group, so this substitution would yield a leftward or downfield shift in the direction of 10.0 ppm. It is helpful to remember that aldehyde has a distinct peak at 9.5 ppm. Choice A is the best answer. Choice B is the opposite of the best answer. Because aldehydes are more electron-withdrawing than methyl groups, the peak would shift, so choice C can be eliminated. Choice D is untrue because the value for the chemical shift will increase, not decrease.

42. **A is the best answer.** Splitting occurs when the peak for a hydrogen or a group of chemically identical hydrogens is split into two or more peaks resulting from the number of nonequivalent hydrogens on adjacent carbons. The number of resulting peaks is given as n+1, where n is the number of neighboring hydrogens. In this case, the question indicates that there is a peak split into two peaks. This means there is one neighboring, nonequivalent hydrogen that is splitting the peak of a hydrogen or a group of equivalent hydrogens. Choice A is the best answer because it makes no assumption about the number of hydrogens composing the peak, which in this case is three, and accurately identifies the number of neighboring hydrogens. Two hydrogens on an adjacent carbon would result in a split of the peak into three peaks, so choice B can be eliminated. A split is not caused by hydrogens on the same carbon, as those hydrogens would have an identical electronic environment. Choice C is not the best answer. Choice D is misleading because a double peak does not imply only two hydrogens, but could also result from three identical methyl hydrogens and a single nonequivalent hydrogen on the neighboring carbon.

43. **B is the best answer.** This question asks the reader to combine information from the passage about the treatment of WD with the data from Figure 2 to make a useful conclusion about other effective treatments. The second paragraph indicates that penicillamine is a copper-binding agent that helps with the excretion of copper in urine. Urine is mostly composed of water, so the ability to excrete copper in urine would be enhanced by a compound that binds copper and is water-soluble such that more of it will be dissolved in urine. Figure 2 indicates that the affected rats treated with penicillamine had greatly enhanced urine excretion of copper. A compound that is soluble in water is unlikely to be soluble in oil, so choice A can be eliminated. Choice B is the best answer, as it points out that the major factor indicated in both the passage and Figure 2 regarding the treatment of WD pertains to the solubility of penicillamine in water. The ability to bind copper is a major factor in the success of the drug, but there is nothing in Figure 2 that addresses this relationship directly. Choice C is not the best answer because it does not answer the question. Choice D makes no mention of the treatment, so it is not the best answer.

Stand-alones (Questions 44-47)

44. **B is the best answer.** α-amino acids can be synthesized in one of two ways: via the Gabriel synthesis or via Strecker synthesis methods. The method described in the answer choices represents the Strecker synthesis, which begins with an aldehyde that carries the future side chain of the amino acid reacting with a cyanide anion that acts as a nucleophile. Remember that amino acids have one H on the alpha carbon, meaning that the initial reactant must be an aldehyde, not a ketone. Because a ketone would have an R group instead of the H, choices C and D can be eliminated. The negative charge on cyanide makes it a strong nucleophile, eliminating choice A and making choice B the best answer.

45. **C is the best answer.** A probe is a nucleic acid with an attached fluorophore that binds its complementary sequence. When the DNA polymerase processes by the bound fragment, the fluorescent probe is kicked off, giving a signal that is read by the PCR machine. A and T pair by two, not three hydrogen bonds, and G and C pair by three, not two hydrogen bonds. Choice A can be eliminated. The DNA polymerase, not the RNA polymerase is responsible for mediating PCR DNA replication, eliminating choice B. The nucleic acid sequence of the probe itself, not the fluorescent molecule, provides the specificity of binding, eliminating choice D. Hydrogen bonds are intermolecular bonds that form between A and T and G and C to allow nucleic acids to pair. Choice C is the best answer.

46. **B is the best answer.** After DNA strands have been denatured, they will reanneal by themselves as long as the temperature is sufficiently low. If the temperature were raised, the DNA strands would not come back together because the high temperature does not allow hydrogen bonds to form between complementary nucleotides. Choice A can be eliminated. Lowering the temperature will allow the hydrogen bonds to reform, so choice B is the best answer. DNA ligase is often used to form recombinant DNA because it can create phosphodiester bonds between nucleotides. No phosphodiester bonds need to form during reannealing, so choice C can be eliminated. DNA primers are used extensively in PCR by acting as a template for newly forming DNA strands. They are not required for DNA strands to reanneal, so choice D can be eliminated.

47. **C is the best answer.** Addition of halogen atoms to phospholipids would make these lipids more soluble due to their increased polarity. In chromatography, the "like dissolves like" concept applies. If the sample is polar, it should be dissolved in a polar mobile phase, while the stationary phase is a more nonpolar molecule. In molecules with carbon chains, the longer the carbon chain, the more nonpolar a compound becomes. The lack of functional groups on the four carbon butane renders it nonpolar in the aqueous solution, eliminating choice A. The addition of a nitrogen atom makes choice B slightly more attractive than choice A, but the number of carbons has increased, making this a relatively nonpolar molecule as well. Choice D is a completely nonpolar compound due to the symmetry of its structure, as each dipole created by the chlorine is canceled out by the other carbon-chlorine bonds. Choice D can be eliminated. The hydroxyl group and short carbon chain of choice C make it the most polar of the options listed, making choice C the best answer.

Passage 9 (Questions 48-51)

48. **A is the best answer.** The non-mutated p53 protein is fully functioning and should have the greatest rate of ATPase activity. The saline solution will have no ATPase activity because there is no p53 protein present. The rate of ATPase activity can be determined by examining which line in Figure 2 has the steepest slope. The line with the steepest slope will have the greatest ATPase activity. As stated in the passage, the absorption spectrum is measuring the concentration of NADH, which is inversely proportional to the rate of ATPase activity. This problem can be most efficiently solved by isolating the answer choices with the steepest and the flattest absorption spectra. The non-mutated p53 protein will have the greatest ATPase activity and will have the steepest line, whereas the saline solution will have no ATPase activity and the flattest line. Choice A is the best answer because it matches the steepest line with the non-mutated p53 protein and the flattest line with the saline solution. Choice B can be eliminated because line F is not the steepest line and therefore does not represent the non-mutated p53 protein. Choice C can be eliminated because it reverses the order of the non-mutated p53 protein and the saline solution. Choice D can be eliminated because line C is neither the steepest nor the flattest line, so it cannot represent either the non-mutated p53 or the saline solution.

49. **A is the best answer.** One of the benefits of DNA sequencing is that genes can be compared to other genes with known functions, which can provide evidence about the unknown gene. DNA sequencing would provide the strongest evidence that the p53 protein is able to carry out ATP hydrolysis. Choice A is the best answer. While NMR could be used to examine the structure of p53, ATP binding does not necessarily mean that ATPase activity is occurring. There are many instances where ATP binds to proteins as an allosteric modulator but is not hydrolyzed to ADP. Choice B can be eliminated. Choice C implies that the conditions of the experimental setup take place in the cell, which is untrue. Choice C can be eliminated. NADH concentration does not necessarily correspond to p53's ATPase activity in the cell. Choice D can be eliminated because defective p53 and high levels of ATP in the cell may not have a causal relationship due to the complex nature of cellular functions. While p53 has ATPase activity and can convert ATP to ADP, it is not the only protein in the cell that carries out this reaction. No causal conclusion can be drawn from defective p53 and high levels of ATP. Choice A is the best answer.

50. B is the best answer. This question is asking which variables are necessary for the calculation of absorbance using Beer's Law. Beer's Law states that the absorbance of a solution is equal to the length of the light path multiplied by the concentration and the molar absorptivity, which is a constant. Option I is present in all of the answer choices, so it must be necessary for the calculation of absorbance. Length of light path and molar absorptivity are also variables needed to calculate absorbance according to Beer's law, so options II and IV will be included in the best answer. Option III, frequency of light, is not a variable in the Beer's law equation, so it is not needed to calculate absorbance. Choice B is the best answer.

51. A is the best answer. Electrophoresis separates proteins based on length and charge. The primary structure of a protein contains all of the amino acids that make up the total structure and it is the determinant of protein length. Choice A is the best answer. The secondary structure of the protein is composed of alpha-helices and beta-sheets. These are not significant for determining the size or charge of the protein, so choice B is a weaker answer than choice A. The tertiary and quaternary structures are the final folded structures of proteins with a single chain or multiple subunits. These structures do not affect how far a protein travels via electrophoresis. Choices C and D are not the best answer.

Passage 10 (Questions 52-56)

52. A is the best answer. The question stem notes that the functional group contains conjugated double bonds but is not detectable by UV spectroscopy. As a reference, UV spectroscopy is able to identify compounds with 7 conjugated bonds or fewer, while visible light spectroscopy identifies molecules with 8 or more conjugated bonds. The colors of light absorbed by a particular compound typically correlate with the number and arrangement of conjugated double bonds. The orange color of carotene is due to the presence of 12 conjugated double bonds, for example. The scientists are most likely to try shifting the wavelength of light used in the spectroscopy to identify a functional group with more conjugated double bonds, making choice A the best answer. The scientists may use proton NMR and IR spectroscopy to additionally characterize the functional group, but the indication of conjugated double bonds in the question stem points toward visible light spectroscopy over these tests. Choices B and D are less likely than choice A. Because the passage and question do not indicate that the scientists performed the UV spectroscopy incorrectly, choice C is not a strong answer as the second sample would likely provide the same results as the first.

53. B is the best answer. The final paragraph of the passage details absorption in the IR spectrum around 1700 cm-1 and 3200-3600 cm^{-1}, corresponding to the C=O carbonyl stretch and the –OH alcohol stretch. The best answer choice will be the one that contains both a carbonyl and an alcohol, making a carboxylic acid, choice B, the best answer. Aldehydes and ketones contain a carbonyl but no hydroxyl group, making choices A and C less likely than choice B. An alcohol contains an –OH stretch but does not contain a carbonyl stretch, eliminating choice D.

54. A is the best answer. The key to correctly answering this question is recognizing that the 200 – 1000 cm^{-1} range is known as the fingerprint region. The complex intramolecular vibrations between carbon-carbon single, double, and triple bonds are found here and are unique to a particular molecule. Choice A is the best answer. An alcohol functional group is found as a broad dip around 3300 cm^{-1}, which is far from the region described. Choice B can be eliminated. In order for an IR spectrum to be produced, a bond must be polarized, meaning that the two atoms of a bond have a difference in electronegativity. Br_2 would have no difference in electronegativity because both atoms are Br. Br_2 contamination would be unlikely to appear on an IR spectrogram, making choice C a weaker answer than choice A. An amine functional group appears around 3300 cm^{-1} but is not as broad or deep as an alcohol dip. Choice D is also unlikely to be the best answer.

55. B is the best answer. Control samples in this experiment allowed for the background of non-tumor tissue to be established. In the third paragraph, the researchers note that they are able to detect specific proteins at a given m/z ratio. Pure protein corresponding to cyclin D, p53, and actin would have been used to specify the peaks that corresponded to the proteins that are potentially part of a sample, making option I a necessary component of the best answer. Given that the purpose of the experiment was to determine whether or not a tumor was part of a clinical sample, the background of the normal tissue type must be known in order to compare the experimental mass spectra to it to detect cancer cells. Option II should also be included in the best answer. Cyclin A was not mentioned in the passage as an identified protein, though cyclin D was. Option III most likely did not serve as a necessary control. The best answer will be the one that corresponds to options I and II, making choice B the best answer. Choice A is partially correct but does not include the control for the tissue, making it less likely than choice B. As cyclin A was not identified in the paper, choices C and D can be eliminated.

56. A is the best answer. The question asks the student to identify a peak that could correspond to the most abundant protein in a metastatic cancer cell. Figure 1 provides the most help in answering this question. In MS the relative abundance of a particular peak is plotted against an m/z ratio. The peak with the highest intensity most likely corresponds to the most abundant protein because more ions would arrive at a detector if more of the original protein were in the sample. The metastatic bars are in grey in Figure 2 and the peak with the highest intensity is one around 15000, making choice A the most likely answer. The peaks around 7000, 4250, and 2000 have peak intensities lower than that of the 15000 peak, meaning that the ions corresponding to those peaks are in lower abundance in the original sample. Choices B, C, and D are less likely than choice A.

Stand-alones (Questions 57-59)

57. **A is the best answer.** Nonsynonymous mutations in RNA polymerase could lower levels of all RNA transcripts. Nonsynonymous mutations change the identity of the amino acid, which has the potential to change the activity of the enzyme. Choice A is a strong answer choice. Hypomethylation of the *Rb* gene would lead to higher levels of transcription, not lower levels. Methylated DNA is "muted" from transcription and would be the opposite finding that the scientists saw, eliminating choice B. DNA is negatively charged and a higher level of glutamate, which is also negatively charged, would lead to less DNA being bound to the histone. An increased amount of unbound DNA would lead to more DNA being open for transcription, which would likely lead to increased levels of *Rb* RNA. Choice C can be eliminated. A synonymous mutation is also known as a silent mutation and does not affect the sequence amino acids or the function of the protein. Choice D would not explain a difference in RNA levels, making it unlikely to be the best answer. Choice A provides the most likely explanation for reduced *Rb* RNA levels.

58. **A is the best answer.** This question requires an understanding of how TLC works and the various measurements that are taken to quantify the results. In TLC the R_f value reports the distance the compound traveled up the plate divided by the distance the solvent traveled up the plate. A larger R_f value would imply that the given compound moved further. In TLC, the solvent is typically a nonpolar substance, meaning that nonpolar compounds tend to move faster and further up the plate. With this in mind, choice A is the best answer because the nonpolar hydrocarbon would have a larger R_f value than the polar phenol. Choice B can be eliminated because the polar phenol would actually travel a shorter distance than the hydrocarbon. Choice C can also be eliminated because it says the same thing as choice B, but uses R_f values rather than absolute distance. Choices B and C are the opposite of the best answer, and both reverse the roles of the stationary and mobile phases. Although phenol does have a characteristic scent, smell is not considered to be a reliable lab identification technique. Choice D is not the best answer.

59. **D is the best answer.** The R_f factor is the ratio of the distance traveled by a solute over the distance traveled by the solvent from the same starting point. The compound can never travel farther than the solvent that carries it, so choice B is inaccurate, as the ratio should always be below or equal to 1. R_f value is a relative measure of polarity and would not be an effective modality for identification in the way elution time for HPLC would. Choice A is overreaching in that regard. Choice C is also too extreme—the R_f factor is a relative rather than an absolute measure of polarity. Choice D is the best answer because the denominator is equal to the distance traveled by the solvent, which is calculated by the distance from the starting point to the solvent line.

TEST 4A A&E

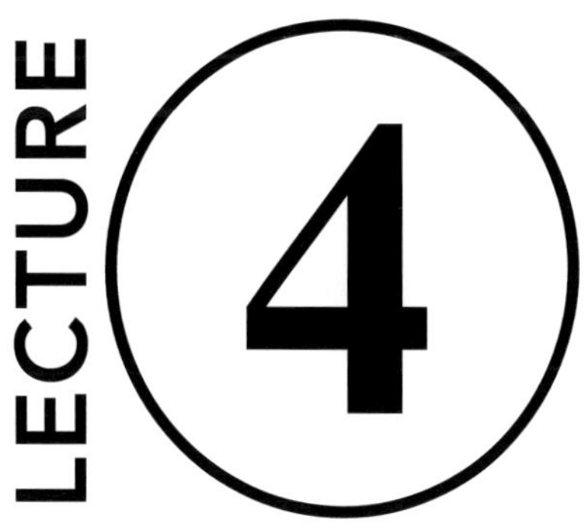

Laboratory Techniques

TEST 4B

ANSWERS & EXPLANATIONS

Questions 1–59

Passage 1 (Questions 1-5)

1. **B is the best answer.** In Experiment 2 the scientists are comparing different levels of trisomy 21 DNA in a sample. A key part of answering the question correctly comes from understanding that a trisomic sample is aneuploid, meaning that it does not contain the normal two copies of each chromosome. A trisomic sample has three copies of one chromosome, meaning it should have higher than normal levels of a specific gene when sequenced. The best test will differentiate between normal and high levels and will allow a comparison between two non-normal samples simultaneously. A t-test compares the mean values of a continuous variable between two categories or groups. The primary difference between a one-tailed and a two-tailed t-test is that a two-tailed test explores the possibility of differences in both directions. In this passage, the two directions are either underrepresentation or overrepresentation of trisomy 21 DNA in the sequenced sample. A one-tailed t-test only looks for either underrepresentation or overrepresentation. The authors of the study were most likely interested in determining whether the sequencing was able to accurately represent the fraction of trisomic DNA and were thus interested in exploring both directions, making choice B the best answer. A one-tailed t-test would only show whether a fraction was overrepresented or underrepresented, making choice A less likely than choice B. Linear regression was used in the first experiment and provides r values, not p values, eliminating choice C. ANOVA is commonly used in large data sets where variance between groups must be accounted for statistically. ANOVA is usually used when three or more variables are tested, eliminating choice D.

2. **B is the best answer.** Sequencing of nucleic acids, including DNA and RNA, provides information about the order of nucleotides contained in a given sample and can be compared to a reference human genome to find mutations, including missense, nonsense, and silent (sense) mutations, eliminating choices A and D. Missense mutations are those that confer a change in amino acid, while nonsense mutations create a stop codon, resulting in a truncated protein. Silent mutations are those that do not change the amino acid identity, even though the nucleotide sequence changed. By determining the sequence of RNA samples, splice variants of a particular gene can be mapped, making choice C unlikely. Protein levels are primarily determined by a western blot, not nucleic acid sequencing, making choice B the best answer.

3. **A is the best answer.** The question stem notes that a scientist believes that the sequencing protocol described in the passage would also be able to tell whether a gene had copy number alterations. A gene that has been deleted from the chromosome would show decreased detection by DNA sequencing, while a gene that has been amplified would show increased amplification by DNA sequencing. This is because PCR is first used to generate the regions of DNA that will be sequenced. If more starting templates exist during PCR, amplification will occur on more templates, generating more identical regions for sequencing. The best answer will support the concept that FAST-SeqS can differentiate between two different percentages of DNA in a sample, as this would model copy number changes. The best evidence comes from the third paragraph, where increasing the amount of trisomy 21 DNA corresponds with an increase in the detection of trisomy 21 DNA by FAST-SeqS, making choice A the best answer. Choice B provides no experimental evidence to support the scientist's claim, eliminating it as a possible choice. While Digital Karyotyping is unable to identify all genes due to experimental limitations, choice C does not provide any evidence for why FAST-SeqS would be useful, only why Digital Karyotyping would not be useful. Choice C can be eliminated. The repeated regions referenced in choice D are those from retroviral insertion, not gene amplifications. Choice D does not pertain to copies of genes, so it is not the best answer.

4. **D is the best answer.** The use of DNA technology has raised issues surrounding the ethics and safety of detecting and manipulating DNA sequences. Testing of circulating DNA for trisomy 21 may inform parents about the risk of their child being affected with a disease. If the false positive rate of a test is high, such as 5% in this question, a significant number of genetically normal children will be incorrectly diagnosed *in utero* with trisomy 21. Because parents may consider making different medical choices using this information, a high false positive rate raises the ethical discussion of how FAST-SeqS should be used in a clinical setting, making choice D the best answer. Choice A is unlikely to be the best answer because even if the test is not 100% accurate, other mechanisms of testing could be used to supplement pre-natal diagnoses. Choices B and C provide information about the utility of FAST-SeqS, but additional information about gene copy number or the use of the algorithm on all chromosomes does not necessarily a considerable ethical discussion, making them weaker than choice D.

5. **C is the best answer.** The question stem indicates that the scientists are interested in measuring the expression of multiple genes simultaneously. The best answer choice will be the one that measures RNA levels of multiple genes at a time. A DNA microarray contains probes that hybridize to hundreds or thousands of genes or RNA transcripts, making choice C the best answer. A Southern blot hybridizes to DNA rather than RNA, and would not provide information about gene expression. Choice A can be eliminated. A western blot measures protein levels, not RNA levels, eliminating choice B. While a northern blot measures RNA, it can only be used for one gene at a time, not multiple genes simultaneously, making choice D less likely than choice C.

Passage 2 (Questions 6-10)

6. **C is the best answer.** According to the question stem, decreased proliferation of Paneth cells prevents the maintenance of microvilli in the colon and rectum, which are both parts of the large intestine. Glucose is primarily absorbed in the jejunum and ileum of the small intestine and its absorption would be largely unaffected by changes in the large intestine. Since the question asks for the substances *least* likely to be affected, option I should be included in the best answer. Amino acids are also absorbed in the small intestine rather than the large intestine, so option II should also be included in the best answer. Water is one of the main molecules absorbed in the large intestine. The microvilli increase the surface area available for absorption and a decrease in the number of microvilli would greatly decrease the amount of water that could be absorbed, likely resulting in diarrhea. Water absorption would be affected, so option III can be eliminated. The choice that includes options I and II but leaves out option III will be the best answer. Choice C is the best answer because loss of surface area in the large intestine would lead to a decrease in the amount of water that can be absorbed, but would not have a significant effect on glucose or amino acid absorption.

7. **B is the best answer.** The question stem notes that unmethylated C will be changed to uracil, which would pair with A during DNA replication. This means that unmethylated C will be converted to T in the genome. Because there are three bonds between C and G, it takes more energy in the form of heat to split apart DNA sequences that are GC rich. Once the DNA has been converted, most of the Cs in the genome will be converted to T, meaning that a vast portion of the genome is only made up of A and T, which are paired by only two hydrogen bonds and would require less heat to denature the strands. This means that lower temperatures, not higher temperatures, could be used to denature DNA, eliminating choice A. Choice C can be eliminated because lower extension temperatures would likely be required in order to prevent the AT-rich DNA from denaturing during extension. There is no evidence that this substitution would decrease the number of PCR cycles required. If anything, with fewer hydrogen bonds between A and T, the primers used for PCR are likely to bind less efficiently, requiring more PCR cycles to generate the same amount of PCR product since primers that do not bind cannot create a PCR product. Because a higher, not lower, number of PCR cycles is more likely to be required, choice D can be eliminated. A lower annealing temperature would be required in order to allow the AT-rich primers to bind the converted DNA. If the annealing temperature was too high, the primers would not bind. Choice B is the best answer.

8. **C is the best answer.** Panel B in Figure 2, the western blot, shows that the use of lgr5 siRNA decreases the lgr5 protein level. Panel A shows that lgr5 mRNA levels also decrease, which probably causes the decrease in lgr5 protein levels. The peptidyltransferase reaction in the ribosome adds an amino acid from a tRNA to the growing peptide chain. If the peptidyltransferase reaction were inhibited, the protein concentration would be expected to decrease, but the mRNA levels would be expected remain constant. Because mRNA levels also fall, choice A is not the best answer. A DNA polymerase is responsible for copying DNA during the S phase, not for creating mRNA from DNA, eliminating choice B. Ubiquitin is a protein modification that targets a particular protein target for degradation by the proteasome. Increasing the ubiquitination of the lgr5 protein would decrease its protein levels but would not impact its RNA levels, eliminating choice D. Addition of siRNA results in a decrease in mRNA levels, as shown in panel A of Figure 2. siRNA works by hybridizing to the single stranded mRNA, increasing its degradation by cytosolic proteins, making choice C the best answer.

9. **A is the best answer.** According to the last paragraph, there is a negative correlation between the methylation levels of lgr5 and larger tumor size. This means that lower levels of methylation lead to larger tumors. Lower levels of DNA methylation would lead to greater expression of the lgr5 gene. The scientists determined that siRNA against lgr5 was effective at reducing the mRNA and protein levels of lgr5. The most likely follow-up experiment would be to test whether decreasing lgr5 expression in animals would lead to smaller tumors. An agonist activates a receptor and would likely lead to larger tumor growth, not smaller tumors, eliminating choice B. The western blot shown in panel B of Figure 2 uses α-tubulin as a loading control, meaning that it should stain at the same density in all experimental conditions, assuming the same amount of protein was loaded in the western blot gel. Because α-tubulin levels are the same in the control and experimental conditions, it is unlikely that scientists would choose to knock down the levels of α-tubulin mRNA, eliminating choice C. DNA sequencing of Paneth cells could identify other GPCRs that the cells have. However, it would not be used to predict relative protein levels of the GPCRs and would be unlikely to identify new receptors that are differentially expressed between cancer and normal cells, making choice D unlikely. Because scientists were able to show that siRNA decreased lgr5 mRNA and protein levels in cells, they would be most likely to try and test this in animals, making choice A the best answer. If the experimental therapy worked in animals, they might consider designing a treatment for humans as a follow up to those studies.

34. **D is the best answer.** Chromatography uses differences in polarity to separate compounds. Using the principle of "like dissolves like," the more nonpolar a compound is, the longer it will remain bound to a nonpolar stationary phase. The opposite is true for a polar compound and a nonpolar stationary phase. According to the passage, resveratrol is highly nonpolar and associates with the lipids in the HDL molecule as a means of being transported to target cells. HDL particles are a mix of proteins, which are polar, and lipids, which are nonpolar. Adding resveratrol to an HDL molecule would increase the relative proportions of the molecule that were nonpolar versus polar. HDL/res should therefore be more nonpolar than HDL alone. In general, chromatography uses a mobile phase that can partially but not fully solvate the particles being separated and a stationary phase that is of similar polarity type to the particles, allowing them to associate over the length of the column. In this case, the particles are nonpolar, meaning a partially polar mobile phase should be paired with a nonpolar stationary phase. If HDL/res were more nonpolar than HDL, it should elute later than HDL with a nonpolar stationary phase and a partially polar mobile phase. Because HDL/res elutes first, choice A can be eliminated. Choices B and C pair two nonpolar compounds as the stationary and mobile phase. Since chromatography uses differences in polarity to separate compounds, choices B and C can both be eliminated. A partially polar heptanol stationary phase should associate with the more polar HDL, keeping it on the column longer. Elution with CCl_4 would help carry the nonpolar particles through the column, allowing HDL/res to elute before HDL, making choice D the best answer.

35. **C is the best answer.** A western blot uses antibodies against a particular string of amino acids on a protein called an epitope. $CD4^+$ T helper cells help activate B cells directly to start producing antibodies but do not produce antibodies themselves. Choice A can be eliminated. $CD8^+$ T cells are responsible for cytotoxic activity but do not produce antibodies, eliminating choice B. Natural killer cells are part of the innate immune system and are responsible for surveying the tissues for pathogens. They do not produce antibodies, eliminating choice D. Plasma cells are specialized B cells that robustly produce antibodies against specific epitopes, making choice C the best answer.

Passage 7 (Questions 36-39)

36. **B is the best answer.** The second paragraph describes HILIC, noting that it uses a highly nonpolar carbon chain as the stationary phase in order to mediate separation of compounds. The best answer will contain the molecule that is the most nonpolar. A lack of electronegative functional groups and an extended carbon chain both serve to make a molecule more nonpolar. While choice A is tempting because it contains a long carbon chain, it also contains a carboxylic acid group, which is polar and therefore unlikely to be in the stationary phase of an HILIC. Choice B contains no electron-withdrawing groups and has a chain of 19 CH_2 groups, making it a strong answer. Choice C contains a polar F atom, making it less likely than choice B. Choice D contains no electronegative groups, but its CH_2 chain has fewer groups than choice B, so it is not as strong of an answer. Choice B is the best answer.

37. **C is the best answer.** This question is really asking for the main difference between liquid chromatography and gas chromatography. Liquid chromatography is able to separate polar and nonpolar compounds that are miscible in the liquid solvent. Gas chromatography vaporizes particles into a heated, inert carrier phase and then separates them over a liquid stationary phase, allowing the compounds to partition based on polarity. If compounds cannot be vaporized, they cannot be separated or run through the column, making choice C the best answer. Krypton and argon are both inert gases, as they are noble gases, so the substitution of krypton for argon would not change the results. Choice A can be eliminated. The scientists used a similar number of samples to the experiment presented in the passage, making choice B unlikely. Gas chromatography is able to separate polar and nonpolar compounds, eliminating choice D. Choice C is the best answer.

38. **B is the best answer.** This question references how the scientists might isolate a weak base using an extraction technique. A strong acid removes weak bases by protonating functional groups that have high pK_a values, thus moving them to the aqueous layer. Urea is a weak base, so choice B is the best answer. Weak acids are able to protonate and remove strong bases by making them soluble in the aqueous layer. Urea is not a strong base, so choice A is not the best answer. A weak base, choice C, eliminates strong acids by being the recipient of a proton given off from the strong acid, moving it to the aqueous layer, making choice C unlikely. Sodium hydroxide is a strong base and is used to remove weak acids by deprotonating functional groups that have high pK_a values, moving them to the aqueous later, eliminating choice D. In general for extraction, the acid or base that is added is used to donate or accept a proton, respectively, from compounds in the mixture. Compounds being extracted that donate or receive a proton become charged, and can therefore be dissolved in and drained out of the aqueous layer.

39. **C is the best answer.** Table 1 provides the information needed to answer this question. The stationary phase of the HILIC column described in the passage is nonpolar, meaning that nonpolar molecules will interact with the column longer, lengthening their retention times. The most nonpolar molecules will have the longest retention times, while the most polar molecules will have the shortest retention times. 2-oxoglutarate has a retention time of 15.52 seconds, indolylacryloglycine has a retention time of 6.74 seconds, and acetylvanilalinine has a retention time of 5.01 seconds. Option III, 2-oxoglutarate, is the most nonpolar, eliminating choices A and B. Indolylacryloglycine, option II, has the next longest retention time and would be more non-polar than acetylvanilalinine, option I, making choice C a better answer than choice D.

Passage 8 (Questions 40-43)

40. **D is the best answer.** Each cycle of PCR doubles the amount of DNA. The mass of DNA is increased 128 fold from 10 μg to 1,280 μg. A 128 fold increase equates to an increase of 27, so increasing the size of the sample from 10 μg to 1280 μg is the result of 7 PCR cycles. Choice D is the best answer.

41. **C is the best answer.** Consider each option and determine its purpose. The antibody-antigen interaction is the source of specificity. Antibodies bind to specific molecules, in this case, a *Y. pestis* protein. Choice A accounts for the specificity of the iPCR, but not for its ability to work with a smaller sample. The isolation of the dental pulp is the step that produces the initial sample of ancient *Y. pestis*. Choice B also does not account for iPCR's lower need for a large sample. PCR amplifies the DNA tag attached to the antibody, resulting in an amplification of signal. This decreases the initial requirement of sample, so choice C is the best answer. ELISA is not a step in iPCR, so choice D is a distractor.

42. **D is the best answer.** A control sample attempts to be as similar to the experimental samples as possible, with the exception of the independent variable: presence of *Y. pestis*. Ancient samples would thus make better controls than modern samples as they have undergone the same degradation as other ancient samples. Choices A and B can be eliminated. When controlling for false positives, a negative control is required. A negative control group is one in which no result or change is expected. Negative controls would have no *Y. pestis* present, so choice D is the best answer.

43. **C is the best answer.** Primers bind to both DNA and RNA based on complementary sequences. There should be no significant difference in binding, so choices A and B can be eliminated. DNA is much more resistant to change than RNA. Consider the function of DNA and RNA in the cell. DNA is meant to carry on information through generations of cells, while RNA is used temporarily to produce proteins. DNA must therefore be more stable and resilient than RNA to carry out its cellular purpose. When ancient samples are tested, DNA is the better choice due to the length of time that has elapsed. Choice C is the best answer.

Stand-alones (Questions 44-47)

44. **C is the best answer.** The first role of detergents is to make all proteins in a sample have a consistent straight chain shape. This is done by removing secondary structures and other interactions between amino acids. Denaturing the protein is important to having all proteins run through the gel at speeds proportional to their size. Next, the detergent coats a protein with negative charge proportional to the length of the protein. Option II is also likely to be included in the answer. Detergents do not cleave proteins, ruling out option III and making choice C the best answer.

45. **D is the best answer.** Recall that enantiomers are mirror image molecules, and a racemic mixture is composed of an equal mix of both enantiomers. Enantiomers can be separated in several ways. One way is by visualization of the crystallized enantiomers. Choice A can be eliminated. Choice B could separate the enantiomers because a stereospecific enzyme would only work on only one of the enantiomers. Once the product of the enzymatic reaction is separated, the reaction can be reversed to collect the pure enantiomer. Choice C would also work to separate enantiomers because diastereomers have distinct physical and chemical properties. Choice D is the best answer because enantiomers have almost exactly the same physical and chemical properties. Size exclusion chromatography works based off of differences in size and would not be able to separate two enantiomers.

46. **C is the best answer.** The question stem refers to the *de novo* synthesis of an amino acid, followed by the addition of a radioactive isotope that could be used for cancer therapy. The synthesis described in the answer choices reflects the process of Gabriel synthesis. This question can be answered by either chemical reasoning or by understanding the process of Gabriel synthesis. Because carbocations are positively charged and are not nucleophiles, they will not "attack" as nucleophiles. This eliminates choices B and D. Tyrosine has a benzyl ring and could be formed by the reaction in choice C, making choice C a better answer than choice A. To answer the question by understanding Gabriel synthesis requires remembering that a nitrogen is protected by a phthalimide that substitutes a bromide on diethyl-bromomalonate. After the hydrogen leaves the middle carbon of diethyl-bromomalonate, the compound becomes a carbanion with a negative charge that is highly nucleophilic. Because a carbanion is formed, choices B and D that describe carbocations can be eliminated. The carbanion then attacks a new alkyl halide, adding the future side chain of the amino acid. The nitrogen is then hydrolyzed from the phthalimide to form the free amino acid. Discriminating between choices A and C requires knowledge of the R chain of tyrosine, which contains an aromatic ring with one hydroxyl group. The sidechain of alanine is described in choice A, as it contains an $-CH_3$ group. Because this is not the tyrosine amino acid, choice A can be eliminated, making choice C the best answer.

47. **D is the best answer.** There are two major factors within specificity. Specificity of the tissue, and specificity of time. A total knockout would constantly stop gene expression in all tissues. A conditional knockout will occur in a certain tissue, but would also be in effect at all times. Choices A and B can be eliminated. A DNA polymerase inhibitor would stop replication, causing major issues for the organism. This would not be a viable technique for gene expression control. Choice C can be eliminated. Choice D is the best answer because RNAi can be applied at a specific time, to a specific tissue, to act against expression of a specific gene. This is the best technique for specific gene expression control.

Passage 9 (Questions 48-52)

48. **D is the best answer.** Compound 11 closely resembles the structures of hormone molecules, which generally contain multiple rings and are mostly hydrophobic. Their hydrophobic nature allows hormones to diffuse through the lipid plasma membrane to bind cytosolic receptors, which then translocate to the nucleus to bind Hormone Receptor Elements (HRE) on target DNA to affect the transcription of target genes. As hormones do regulate the transcription of target genes, including ribosomal genes, choice A can be eliminated. Cytosolic receptor concentration would decrease due to their translocation to the nucleus, eliminating choice B. Choice C can be eliminated because hormone receptors are cytosolic proteins that translocate to the nucleus to bind HRE upon binding their target hormones. Lipophilic hormones do not bind cell surface receptors, but instead bind cytosolic receptors. Thus, compounds structurally resembling compound 11 are least likely to bind cell surface receptors, making choice D the best answer.

49. **A is the best answer.** According to the question, a tryptophan ring is exposed upon binding of the acarbose sugar molecule to the enzyme. Tryptophan is a nonpolar amino acid that contains conjugated rings. Prior to binding, the tryptophan would be unavailable for spectroscopy, as it would be hidden in the interior of the protein. Upon binding, however, the amino acid would flip out and be able to absorb light. UV spectroscopy is useful for molecules that contain conjugated double bonds, such as those contained in the aromatic rings of the tryptophan amino acid. Since tryptophan becomes available for absorbing UV light once it flipped out of the hydrophobic interior upon acarbose binding, UV spectroscopy would serve as the best way to assay for binding of the molecule. Choice A is the best answer. Mass spectrometry measures the molecular weight of compounds, including amino acids. If the acarbose molecule bound tightly in the active site, mass spectrometry may be a way of measuring binding. However, this would be laborious and may not work if the acarbose dissociates from the enzyme during ionization, making choice B less likely than choice A. A Bradford assay measures the concentrations of proteins in a solution by a dye that binds multiple amino acids. The Bradford assay would not be specific to the binding of the sugar to the enzyme, eliminating choice C. Molecular docking studies are done *in silico* and could model how tightly an acarbose may bind, but not predict *in vitro* when the binding occurs, making choice D less likely than choice A.

50. **A is the best answer.** Chromatography is able to separate compounds based on polarity. The question stem notes that compound 1 is substituted with unique functional groups on carbon 3 in Figure 1. Each molecule would thus have a distinct polarity, determined by the identity of the substituted functional group. In column chromatography, the "like dissolves like" rule applies to the mobile phase, and the stationary phase is usually the opposite polarity of the mobile phase. Because the substituted compounds are polar, the mobile phase will also be polar to dissolve the compounds. The stationary phase, *n*-decane, is a nonpolar carbon chain. Cyclohexane is a cyclic nonpolar compound that would not dissolve polar compounds. It would likely associate with the nonpolar phase instead, eliminating choice B as the best answer. *N*-nonane closely resembles the stationary phase and is a hydrophobic carbon chain that would not dissolve polar compounds, eliminating choice C. CCl_4 contains polar chlorine-carbon bonds. However, the dipoles of the bonds cancel out, creating a nonpolar molecule overall. Because CCl_4 is also nonpolar, it would be unlikely to solvate polar compounds, eliminating choice D. Methanol contains an alcohol functional group, which makes the molecule polar. It would likely be able to solvate the polar substituted compounds and serve as the mobile phase for column chromatography, making choice A the best answer.

51. **A is the best answer.** Unlike hydrogen NMR, carbon NMR does not have splitting. However, the area under each peak curve is still proportional to the number of carbons giving rise to that peak. Notice that the peak at 78 ppm is the highest, meaning that the carbon giving rise to that peak should be the one that is found the most often in compound 11. Identifying the contexts of the carbons in compound 11 allows for them to be counted and for the carbon giving rise to the highest peak to be identified. Nine – CH_2 – (methane) carbons exist in the rings of the molecule. While six – CH_3 (methyl groups) exist in compound 11, this number is lower than the nine methine carbons, eliminating choice B. Five – CH(R) – exist, which is also lower than the nine methine carbons, eliminating choice C. No – CH_3(R) exist, as carbon can only have four bonds and – CH_3(R) has five, eliminating choice D. The carbon type with the greatest abundance is – CH_2 –, which will thus correspond to the highest peak in the carbon NMR. Choice A is the best answer.

52. **B is the best answer.** Mass spectrometry ionizes compounds into fragments and then accelerates them to the same kinetic energy in an electric field. Though each compound contains the same kinetic energy, the differences in mass provide differences in velocity, as $KE = \frac{1}{2} mv^2$. The mass of the compounds can be inferred by the timing of the fragment hitting the detector. Particles of lower mass arrive first, as they have the highest velocity, while particles that of higher mass arrive later. Choice B, size and charge, represents the parameters used in mass spectrometry, and is the best answer. Size-exclusion chromatography is the method that separates compounds by size. Choice A can be eliminated. Column and gas chromatography separate compounds by differences in polarity. Choice C is not the best answer. Fractional distillation separates compounds by boiling point, eliminating choice D.

Passage 10 (Questions 53-56)

53. **B is the best answer.** Use the structure in Figure 2 to answer this question. Hydrogen NMR follows the splitting rule of n+1, where n is equal to the number of hydrogens on the neighboring carbon atoms. Three carbons are bonded to carbon 12 – carbon 7, carbon 11, and carbon 13. Carbon 11 has two hydrogens, carbon 7 has one, and carbon 13 has one. Notice that the double bond on carbon 13 takes away one of the hydrogens that would be present if the double bond were a single bond instead. The hydrogen on carbon 12 would be split into two peaks if there were only one neighboring hydrogen. Choice A can be eliminated. If carbon 13 were in a single bond instead of a double bond to carbon 14, the hydrogen on carbon 12 would be split into six peaks. Choice C can be eliminated because it of the double bond on carbon 13. As neighboring carbons are bonded to hydrogen atoms, the peak will be split, eliminating choice D. Choice B is the best answer because the four hydrogens on the neighboring carbons to carbon 12 give 5 peaks by the n+1 rule.

54. **A is the best answer.** Figure 1 provides the structure of TZA-A. Notice that TZA-A contains an aromatic ring and conjugated double bonds on the aliphatic chain. UV spectroscopy can detect molecules with conjugated bonds and can determine concentration of a compound in an aqueous solution. Because choice A is specific to conjugated double bonds, it would be the most effective method of determining TZA-A concentration, making it the best answer. IR spectroscopy allows for the detection of different functional groups but does not estimate the concentration of a molecule in a solution, making choice B an unlikely answer. Carbon NMR can help determine the structure of a molecule, but not its concentration in a sample. Choice C can be eliminated. Mass spectrometry requires molecules to be ionized and accelerated through a magnetic field. It is possible but challenging to use mass spectrometry to determine concentration. UV spectroscopy is more straightforward than mass spectrometry, helping to eliminate choice D.

55. **A is the best answer.** Notice that compounds TZA-A, TZA-B, and TZA-E are highly similar but contain small variations that increase or decrease their efficacy in preventing bacterial conjugation. Compared to compounds TZA-A and TZA-B, TZA-E has a hydroxyl group located at carbon 10 that would be able to undergo hydrogen bonding with other polar functional groups. If the TZA molecules were designed to prevent conjugation, they are likely hydrophobic, so they can insert into the membrane to prevent assembly of the plasma membrane into the conjugation tube. Addition of the hydroxyl at carbon 10 prevents the ability of TZA-E to inhibit conjugation, as shown in Figure 1. Electrostatic and dipole-dipole interactions all occur between polar or charged molecules and would prevent compound TZA-B from inserting into lipid membranes, eliminating choices B and C. The passage does not suggest that TZA chemically reacts and bonds with the membrane lipids, so choice D is unlikely to be the best answer. Van der Waals forces are important for hydrophobic interactions. Addition of a hydroxyl would prevent the region of the molecule that carbon 12 resides in from participating in hydrophobic interactions. Because TZA-B does not contain a hydroxyl group here, hydrophobic interactions are likely crucial for drug efficacy. Choice A is the best answer.

56. **B is the best answer.** The first step to this problem is to determine what types of bonds are being characterized in the table. The bond between carbons 7 and 12 is a single bond in TZA-B and a double bond in TZA-A. The bond between carbons 8 and 9 is a single bond in both drugs. Stretch frequency, which is measured by IR spectroscopy, increases significantly with stiffer bonds like double and triple bonds. Because the bond between carbons 8 to 9 does not change in type, it is unlikely that the IR spectroscopy would shift appreciably for this bond, eliminating choices A and D. The wavenumber for double bonds increases compared to a single bond. The best answer will be the one that has a higher wavenumber for the bond between carbons 7 and 12. Because choice C has a decreased wavenumber, it can be eliminated. Choice B is the best answer because it shows an increase in the frequency corresponding to the double bond and maintains the relative frequency of the single bond between carbons 8 and 9.

Stand-alones (Questions 57-59)

57. **B is the best answer.** A restriction enzyme makes a cut at each restriction site, cleaving the DNA into fragments. Consider a length of rope cut at 5 points. There will be 6 pieces of rope, so choice B, 6 strands of DNA, is the best answer.

58. **C is the best answer.** Mass spectrometry uses measurement of the mass to charge ratio of various pieces of a parent molecule in order to determine characteristics such as molecular mass. A molecule is bombarded with electrons, causing it to ionize and break apart. These ions are then accelerated through a magnetic field and their subsequent curved path can be measured and correlated to a mass to charge ratio. Option I is likely as the mass/charge ratio is measured. Option II is untrue as the sample is bombarded by electrons rather than neutrons, which would not cause ionization of the molecular fragments. Option III is true as molecular mass is a potential application of mass spectrometry. Choice C is the best answer since it contains both true options and excludes option III.

59. **A is the best answer.** Boiling of water occurs at 100ºC. The denaturing of DNA in PCR occurs after the sample has been heated to 95°C. Choice A occurs at a higher temperature than choice B, so choice B can be eliminated. Primer annealing and activation of DNA polymerase are stages of PCR that occur at 60°C and 72°C, respectively. Without remembering these exact temperatures, recognize that the temperature for PCR reaches a maximum during the denaturation step, so choice C and D can be eliminated. Choice A is the best answer because it occurs at the highest temperature.

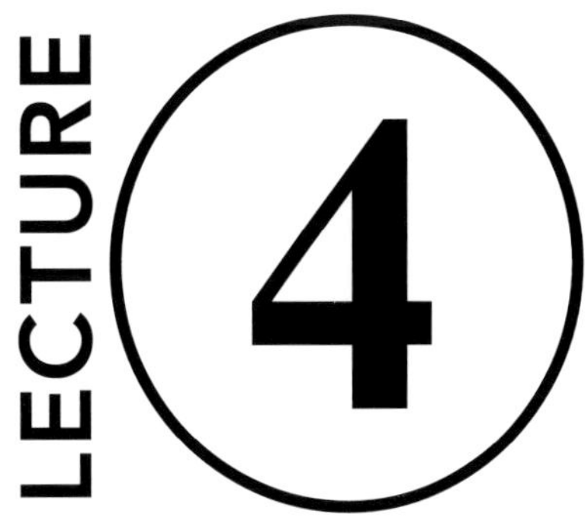

Laboratory Techniques

TEST 4C

ANSWERS & EXPLANATIONS

Questions 1–31

Passage 1 (Questions 1-5)

1. **A is the best answer.** Bacteria use DNA methylation, adding a $-CH_3$ group to DNA, to protect genomic DNA from digestion by endogenous restriction enzymes. Restriction enzymes cleave double stranded DNA at specific recognition sequences and likely evolved as a mechanism of defending bacteria against viral infection. The question stem and passage do not provide information that would suggest a DNA demethylating agent would inhibit enzymes, eliminating choices B and D. Similar to the now demethylated bacterial genomic DNA, exogenous DNA to be ligated into the vector would also be cleaved, eliminating choice C. In demethylating DNA in the bacterium, the bacterial genomic DNA would become susceptible to cleavage by restriction enzymes, making choice A the best answer.

2. **A is the best answer.** Paragraph two states that Body Doubles do not create palindromic ends, eliminating choice B. It is DNA ligase, not a restriction enzyme, which repairs the phosphodiester backbones of DNA. Choice C can be eliminated. Because bacterial genomic DNA is methylated, it is generally protected against cleavage by restriction enzymes, eliminating choice D. According to Figure 1, digestion of a plasmid with a Body Double, in this case BsmBI, removes the BsmBI cleavage site, replacing it with an NcoI cleavage site. In addition to being able to create sticky ends (the single stranded ends of DNA created when a restriction enzyme cleaves the two strands asymmetrically), the Body Double can be used to remove other restriction enzyme sites. Choice A is the best answer.

3. **A is the best answer.** In order to confirm that successful ligation of a particular DNA fragment occurred, scientists would be interested in ensuring that the distance between the recognition and cutting sites of a endonuclease were not too long, therefore accommodating a PCR primer. If the distance between sites was greater than the length of the PCR primer, scientists would not be able to amplify a region that corresponded to both the cleavage site and the ligated DNA. Thus, a distance shorter than the length of a primer, in this question 18 bp, would ensure that both the cutting site and ligated DNA would be included in the PCR amplification product, making choice A the best answer choice. Choices B, C, and D can be eliminated because the amplification would not be specific for vectors that contained ligated DNA. Instead all vectors, regardless of whether or not patient DNA had been ligated in, would show amplification on PCR because all vectors would contain recognition sites.

4. **D is the best answer.** According to information contained in paragraph three, Type IIP enzymes could not be used in ligating the *APP* gene from the patient's DNA because it contains NcoI recognition sites. The passage does not indicate whether Type IIP enzymes cleave bacterial DNA, eliminating choice A as an option. Type IIP, but not Type IIS, endonucleases create palindromic sticky ends, eliminating choice B. According to Figure 1, NcoI, a Type IIP ENase, is able to cleave the acceptor sequencing vector, eliminating choice C. If the inserted DNA contained recognition sites, it would also be cleaved by NcoI, preventing the gene fragment of interest from being successfully inserted into the sequencing vector. Choice D is the best answer.

5. **D is the best answer.** In order for a Type IIS ENase to be useful in generating the DNA sequencing library presented in the passage, the cleaving would have to be reproducible, specific, and able to be religated to the inserted DNA. Option I must be fulfilled because the ENase would need to cut at a specific sequence, allowing for cutting sites to be determined in a predictable manner. Additionally, the distance between the recognition site and cutting site should be fixed, so the sequences generated by the restriction enzyme can be determined, making option II a requirement. In order for the fragment to be inserted and sequenced, the vector that now has a ligated fragment must be religated, making option III necessary. In order to have successful religation, the ends must be of the same length and be complementary sequences, making option IV a criterion. The best answer will contain all four options, making choice D the best answer.

Passage 2 (Questions 6-9)

6. **A is the best answer.** According to the question stem, ESI mass spectrometry donates a proton to a compound during ionization. The tallest peak of a mass spectrogram represents the most prevalent molecule and is the parent molecule that has gained a proton or lost an electron, depending on the type of mass spectrometry. The tallest peak in the spectrogram presented is at 393 m/z and represents the parent compound. No math is required to find the m/z ratio, because this can be found in the mass spectrogram as the tallest peak. Choices B and D can be eliminated. Because the question stem indicates that ESI mass spectrometry adds only one proton, the parent compound would become monoprotonated, making choice A the best answer.

7. **C is the best answer.** The column chromatography in the passage involves a hydrophobic, or nonpolar, column and a polar mobile phase that is made up of water and acetonitrile. By the "like dissolves like" principle, non-polar compounds will remain on the column the longest and will be eluted at a longer time. The order of polarity from most polar to least polar is CPT-11 < APC < SN-38 < SN-38G, based on the retention times on the column. Because SN-38 interacts with the column the most, it is the least polar. This makes choice C the best answer.

8. **A is the best answer.** According to the passage, irinotecan (CPT-11) is a topoisomerase inhibitor. Topoisomerases are responsible for unwinding supercoiled DNA. DNA replication occurs when the two strands of DNA are copied to create new daughter strands. Copying of the DNA strands would create coiled DNA in front of the DNA polymerase that would be released by a topoisomerase. Inhibition of the topoisomerase would prevent the polymerase from moving forward, making choice A the best answer. Translation is the process that occurs when an mRNA is translated to a protein. Choice B can be eliminated. mRNA is single-stranded and does not experience supercoiling, and would therefore not require topoisomerase. This eliminates choice C. Similarly, alternative splicing would not be inhibited because mRNA is single-stranded. Choice D can also be eliminated.

9. **B is the best answer.** The R group that defines SN-38G can be found in Figure 1 and is a cyclic molecule that contains hydroxyl groups and a carboxyl group. Notice that the question is asking specifically about the R group, not the SN-38G compound as a whole. Cyclic AMP (cAMP) is derived from a nucleic acid, and therefore contains nitrogen. As the R group does not contain nitrogen, choice A can be eliminated. Glucose exists as a cyclic 6-carbon molecule that contains hydroxyl and carboxyl substituents. SN-38G contains a similar six-membered ring that has hydroxyl and carboxyl substituents, making choice B a likely answer. Fructose, similar to glucose, is also a 6-carbon cyclic molecule containing hydroxyl and carboxyl substituents. Fructose, however, is a furanose rather than a pyranose, meaning that it forms a five-membered ring instead of a six-membered ring. Choice C is less likely than choice B. Cholesterol is a polycyclic compound that contains four linked rings. SN-38G contains linked rings but the R group does not. Because the question is asking only about the R group, choice D can be eliminated. Choice B is the best answer.

Passage 3 (Questions 10-14)

10. **A is the best answer.** According to the passage, crystallization occurs when the urate oxidase enzyme forms polymers and precipitates out of solution. Figure 1 provides two conditions that were tested in order to improve the crystallization technique. A lower concentration in solution would suggest that the enzyme had precipitated out of solution into a crystal. The lowest concentration in each condition thus provides the optimal conditions. From part A of Figure 1, the lowest concentration of UOx occurs around a pH of 8.5, which would be considered slightly basic relative to a neutral pH of 7. The lowest temperature also has the lowest concentration of UOx in solution, meaning more has crystallized out of solution. Choice A is the best answer because it notes that conditions of slight basicity and low temperature have the lowest concentration of UOx. Choice B can be eliminated because high temperatures would dissolve more UOx and prevent it from precipitating out of solution. Choice C can be eliminated for the same reason. Acidic pH values fall below 7. Because the lowest concentration is around a pH of 8.5, choice D can be eliminated.

11. **D is the best answer.** Proteins are held in tertiary structure in part by the electrostatic attraction of charged amino acids. Disruption of these charges allows a protein to denature. The pI, also known as the isoelectric point, of a protein is the pH at which the net charge on the protein is neutral and it no longer migrates in an electric field. According to the question stem, the protein contains more glutamate (E) and aspartate (D) residues than arginine (R) and lysine (K) residues, meaning that it is more acidic and negatively charged than positively charged. Once the pH becomes too basic, acidic amino acids like E and D will become protonated and lose their negative charge. Notice that choices A, B, and C are all acidic pH values because they fall below 7. Choice D is the outlier because it is above 7, meaning it is basic. Because the protein contains more acidic than basic amino acids, a switch to a basic pH is more likely to impact the structure of the crystalized enzyme. Choice D is the best answer.

12. **B is the best answer.** Figure 2 shows a UV spectrogram of compounds eluted at various times from the size exclusion column. UV light is absorbed by conjugated double bounds, which in this case would be found in the side chains of amino acids. Tryptophan contains two aromatic rings that contain conjugated bonds, eliminating choice A. Valine is a nonpolar amino acid with a hydrocarbon side chain that contains no double bonds. This means valine is unlikely to contribute to the absorbance of UV light, making choice B the best answer. Phenylalanine contains an aromatic ring, allowing it to absorb UV light. Choice C can be eliminated. Tyrosine also contains an aromatic ring with conjugated double bonds. This eliminates choice D, as tyrosine can absorb UV light.

13. **A is the best answer.** Figure 2 is needed to answer this question. The exact purity percentages given are irrelevant for this question. What is important is the relative purity between pool 2 and pool 4. Notice that pool 2 has two peaks and pool 4 has one peak after size exclusion chromatography. Chromatography is designed to separate molecules from one another based on differences in polarity, size, charge, or other characteristics. When a population has only one peak, it most likely represents a single molecule. Multiple peaks indicate multiple compounds. Choice A is the best answer because a lower purity would indicate more than one compound. Pool 2 has two peaks, meaning its purity should be less than that of pool 4, which has only one peak. Choice B can be eliminated because a purity of 99% should be nearly pure and would be unlikely to contain a large contaminating fraction that gives rise to the peak around 11 min in pool 2. A purity of 60% for pool 4 would suggest it was not pure and the chromatograph would likely show multiple peaks rather than just one. This eliminates choice C. Both choices B and C suggest that pools 2 and 4 have equivalent purity, which is unlikely given their unequal number of peaks. Choice D is the opposite of the best answer, because the purity of pool 4 is likely higher than that of pool 2 because it contains fewer peaks eluted off the column.

14. **A is the best answer.** The second paragraph indicates that the tetramer has a molecular weight of 135 kDa and the monomer has a molecular weight of 34 kDa. These two molecular weight proteins or protein complexes could be bound by the same antibody, which would provide information as to whether the crystals are tetramers or monomers. The binding of a protein with an antibody is used in a western blot, which is described by choice A and is the best answer. Because the UOx gene would code only for one of the monomer products, regardless of whether that product was isolated as a tetramer or monomer, choice B can be eliminated. Also remember that antibodies are used to target proteins, not genes. Oligonucleotides bind other nucleic acids, not proteins, eliminating choice C. Because the scientist is interested in the quaternary structure of the protein, not whether the individual monomers are transcribed at all, choice D is a less likely answer than choice A.

Stand-alones (Questions 15-18)

15. **D is the best answer.** UV photons can be absorbed by conjugated systems, meaning those that have a double bond separated by a single bond. In conjugated systems, electrons can absorb photons from UV radiation and move from a $\pi \rightarrow \pi^*$ state, meaning that they move to a vacant orbital close to their highest occupied molecular orbital. In other words, the electron moves from the ground state to the lowest unoccupied molecular orbital, also known as the LUMO, making choice D the best answer. A single bond does not contain π electrons and would be unlikely to absorb UV radiation, eliminating choices A and C. Choice B can be eliminated because the highest occupied molecular orbital is not vacant to receive an energized electron.

TEST 4C A&E

16. **C is the best answer.** Sequencing is generally done with double stranded DNA by allowing fluorescently tagged nucleotides to base pair with their complementary bases. In order to prepare a sequencing library using clones of bacteria, DNA would be digested with a restriction enzyme that cuts double stranded DNA at specific base pair sequences. These recognition sites are not always evenly spaced in the human genome, giving DNA fragments of varying sizes that will be ligated into a vector, making choice C a better answer than choice A. A sequencing library will contain many DNA sequences, as it is derived from a genome that is made up of genes with different arrangements of base sequences, eliminating choice B. Whole genome sequencing is not done with RNA, but instead with DNA, eliminating choice D.

17. **C is the best answer.** Affinity chromatography uses highly specific associations to separate compounds, such as using antibodies to separate antigens. The distractor choices for this question misrepresent different aspects of the question or chromatographic method. Choice A describes a case of attaching antigens to a plate, but implies nothing about separation. Choice A is not the best answer. Choice B is misleading in its use of the word "affinity," though it more accurately describes column chromatography rather than affinity chromatography. Choice D describes the basis of ion exchange chromatography, in which ions are attracted to the stationary phase and are eluted by the addition of competing ions. Choice C is the best answer as it depicts an isolation, or separation, and also characterizes a receptor-ligand relationship.

18. **B is the best answer.** Size-exclusion chromatography separates proteins based on overall shape of a protein. The total length of the protein as well as the fold is important for separation to occur. Choice A can be eliminated because the charge of a protein does not affect the separation of proteins in size-exclusion chromatography. All proteins pass through the matrix regardless of charge, so this is unlikely to explain the distinct elution times. Choice B is the best answer because the fold of a protein is just as important as the length in determining its final size. Globular proteins are much larger than fibrous proteins with the same number of residues. The difference in the time the proteins spent in the column can be explained by a difference in tertiary structure. Choice C can be eliminated because the hydrophobicities of the proteins will not affect how they get separated by a size-exclusion chromatography column. Choice D can be eliminated because proteins of the same length can be eluted differently depending on their fold and structural size. This is not a defect in the chromatography setup .

Passage 4 (Questions 19-22)

19. **C is the best answer.** qPCR, according to the passage, measures the relative quantity of the mRNA of one gene as compared to another. A Southern blot measures DNA levels, not RNA, eliminating choice A. A protein microarray would be able to determine the relative expression of the MTUS1 protein, but not the mRNA directly, making choice B unlikely to be the best answer. UV spectroscopy can measure the concentration of molecules with conjugated double bonds in a solution. Measurements would not be specific to MTUS1 mRNA, eliminating choice D. A northern blot uses a fluorescently or radioactively labeled probe to detect a particular nucleotide sequence and could detect the presence of a particular sequence of mRNA, making choice C the best answer.

20. **B is the best answer.** According to paragraph one, ATIP has three splice variants that result from alternative splicing of the *ATIP* gene. ATIP1 splices out exon 2, while ATIP2 splices out exons 4 and 5 and ATIP3 splices out exons 3, 4, and 7. Reverse transcription takes cDNA and makes DNA, which could them be amplified and run on a gel. Because ATIP1 splices out the fewest exons, it should have the longest mRNA. ATIP2 should have the second longest because it splices out two exons, and ATIP3 the shortest because it splices out three exons. Two bands should not be seen for any of the products, eliminating choices A and C. Choice B is a better answer than choice D because ATIP3 has a shorter amplicon than ATIP2.

21. **C is the best answer.** According to the passage, one of the main reasons *MTUS1* shows reduced expression in head and neck cancer is deletion of a portion of chromosome 8. The patient described in the question does not have a deletion but still shows decreased expression of the gene. A tumor with a heterozygous deletion of the gene encoding the catalytic unit of DNA polymerase would be unlikely to be able to replicate its genome. Additionally, DNA polymerase is not responsible for transcription, eliminating choice A. A deletion that occurs in a repressor region would prevent the repressor sequence from decreasing transcription of the *MTUS1* locus, resulting in increased expression of the gene. This is the opposite of the expression in the tumor of patient 3, eliminating choice B. Increased expression of a ubiquitin ligase could increase destruction of the *MTUS1* protein but would not affect mRNA levels, eliminating choice D. Methylation of the promoter for the *MTUS1* gene would more tightly associate the DNA to the chromatin structure, reducing the ability of RNA polymerase to access the promoter. This would decrease transcription and subsequent levels of *MTUS1* RNA. This makes choice C the best answer.

22. **A is the best answer.** Loss of a chromosomal arm that contains a key tumor suppressor gene is one of the main drivers of cancer. If primers are designed for the *TP53* locus, a failure to amplify by PCR could occur for two reasons. The first is that the locus has been deleted, so the gene does not exist in the cell to amplify. Alternatively, if the DNA is too fragmented, the complementary sequence for the primer to bind to in DNA may not exist, also preventing amplification. qPCR on fragmented DNA would be unable to distinguish between these two scenarios, eliminating choice B. DNA sequencing of normal cells would not address the loss of a gene in cancer cells, eliminating choice C. Sequencing RNA would not allow for the scientists to distinguish between absent transcription of the *TP53* locus and loss of the chromosome arm. This eliminates choice D. Fluorescently labeled oligonucleotides that are able to bind to a complementary sequence of DNA could show that a gene is deleted because hybridization would not occur. It is important that the DNA is not fragmented, as fragmented DNA could still contain the gene but disrupt the binding sequence of the probe. This makes choice A the best answer.

Passage 5 (Questions 23-27)

23. **C is the best answer.** TLC uses a polar immobile phase of silica, and a nonpolar mobile phase. What this means is that the nonpolar molecules elute fastest and farthest, while polar molecules interact more strongly with the immobile phase. With similar hydrocarbons, polarity can be determined by the length of the carbon chain. A longer carbon chain means a longer area of nonpolarity and hydrophobicity. Because C32 is longer than C29 and C30, choice C is a better answer than choices A or B. The answer can be determined based on carbon chain length, ruling out choice D.

24. **C is the best answer.** The hydrogen NMR is based on the electronic environment of each hydrogen. The three molecules listed as answer choices are identical other than the length of their carbon chains. Each successive carbon is slightly farther from the polar group at the head of the lipid, so the hydrogens all have a different electric environment in terms of distance from the polar group. This means that C32 has the greatest number of unique hydrogens, as it has the longest carbon chain. Choice C is the best answer.

25. **B is the best answer.** According to the passage and their structures, the compounds being investigated are lipids. Enzymes are typically named by their substrate, so it follows that lipases works on lipids. Choice B is the strongest answer. Pepsin is an enzyme that catalyzes digestion of proteins, so it is unlikely. Choice A can be eliminated. Choices C and D are unlikely because amylases digest sugars rather than lipids.

26. **B is the best answer.** Affinity chromatography works by selective binding to single molecules within a sample in order to isolate them. All three molecules are esters, with the only difference being the length of the carbon chain. A molecule that binds to esters would bind to all three, meaning no separation occurs and option I is true. Option II would result in no binding, as none of the three molecules are carboxylic acids. Options I and II are likely to be in the best answer. Next, there are no hydroxyl groups, so none of the compounds would be bound in option III, making it false. Choice B, options I and II, is the best answer.

27. **D is the best answer.** As the sample is cooled, the compounds go from the gaseous phase to the liquid phase. Phase changes are dictated by the strength of intermolecular forces. The molecule with the strongest intermolecular forces will stay as a gas until a lower temperature is reached. This molecule is C32, which has the longest hydrocarbon chain. Choices A and B can be eliminated. When judging intermolecular forces of lipids, the length of the hydrocarbon chain is key. The chain length determines the ability of the molecule to undergo stacking and strong van der Waals' interactions. Choice D is a better answer than choice C.

Stand-alones (Questions 28-31)

28. **A is the best answer.** The purpose of a western blot is to detect a particular protein in a mixture of proteins. Choice A would therefore not explain why the western blot failed to detect the protein of interest. The process of protein identification by western blot typically begins with the separation of proteins using gel electrophoresis. The resolved protein mixture is then transferred from the gel onto a separate membrane. If this step does not occur successfully, visualization of the protein of interest will be disrupted, so choice D is true and can be eliminated. Once on this membrane, the primary antibody is applied, which this binds to the protein of interest. The secondary antibody is then applied and will provide some type of visualization, usually fluorescence or radiolabeling, when bound to the primary antibody. Insufficient secondary antibody could prevent a successful visualization of protein because without enough secondary antibody, there would not be sufficient visualization signal to be detected. Choice B is possible and can be eliminated. Contamination of the primary antibody may also prevent adequate visualization. Contamination of primary antibody could prevent proper binding to the protein of interest, which would indirectly inhibit fluorescence by preventing adequate secondary antibody binding. Choice C is also true and can be eliminated, leaving choice A as the best answer.

29. **D is the best answer.** A Southern blot represents DNA that has been hybridized to a nucleic acid probe specific to a particular gene. Patient A has two bands, corresponding to a 400 bp and a 100 bp fragment that both hybridize the specific probe, while patient B has three bands, corresponding to a 500 bp fragment, a 400 bp fragment, and a 100 bp fragment. Patient A could be homozygous for the *APP* gene if that gene produces a 400 bp fragment and a 100 bp fragment that anneal to the probe, eliminating choice A. Alternatively, if the patient were heterozygous, the banding pattern in patient B could appear, where the 500 bp fragment represents one allele and the 400 bp + 100 bp pattern represents the other allele. Choice B can be eliminated. If the 500 bp fragment were alternatively spliced from a pre-mRNA of 500 bp to one that is 400 bp and one that is 100 bp, the banding pattern of patient B could be observed, eliminating choice C. Notice that there is no 800 bp fragment in either patient, and not any combination of cleaved fragments that could add up to an 800 bp fragment. Choice D is the best answer.

30. **A is the best answer.** The question stem describes a specific base change in a PCR product that would create a new restriction site that could be cut by a restriction enzyme. After the PCR product was cut by a restriction enzyme, the products could be detected by Southern blotting with oligonucleotides that would anneal to regions of the *SMAD4* gene. PCR replicates DNA strands to create millions of copies of the same sequence, specified by the specific selection of primers. A northern blot describes the detection of RNA rather than DNA, eliminating choice B. Agarose gel electrophoresis can only separate products by size, and cannot provide any information about a particular sequence. Thus, a G to C transversion would not be detected, eliminating choice C. A Western blot detects proteins rather than nucleic acid sequences, eliminating choice D. A DNA probe specific to the mutated *SMAD4* gene could be used in a Southern blot to detect a sequence variation. Thus, choice A is the best answer.

31. **D is the best answer.** DNA sequencing is an experimental technique that allows scientists and doctors to determine a patient's DNA down to the single base level. A significant number of diseases have a genetic component and alleles that are associated with an increased or decreased risk of contracting a disease. Because DNA is heritable material, it is passed down through families. Even though the patient may give informed consent to have sequencing done, the DNA sequence of that patient is also shared by other family members that have not given consent, making option I an ethical concern. Some diseases, like Huntington's disease, a devastating neurological disease, have no known treatments. Patients that have an allele that increases risk for diseases like Huntington's are likely to experience psychological stress as a result of the DNA sequencing. A significant ethical concern is whether or not a test should be given if there is no treatment or intervention that can be offered based on the outcome of the test, making option II true. While recent legislation has made it illegal to discriminate against patients on the basis of their DNA sequencing, this still remains a concern for many patients and doctors when weighing the benefits and risks of genetic testing, making option III a component of the best answer. Because options I, II, and III describe various ethical considerations of genetic sequencing, choice D is the best answer.